M. *Orcinus orca*
N. *Megaptera novaeangliae*
O. *Kogia breviceps*
P. *Balaenoptera borealis*

Q. *Globicephala melaena*
R. *Delphinapterus leucas*
S. *Balaenoptera musculus*
T. *Balaenoptera edeni*

U. *Globicephala macrorhynchus*
V. *Hyperoodon ampullatus*
W. *Eschrichtius robustus*

SEA GUIDE TO
WHALES OF THE WORLD

LYALL WATSON

SEA GUIDE TO

WHALES OF THE WORLD

ILLUSTRATED BY TOM RITCHIE

E. P. DUTTON
New York

First published in the United States in 1981 by Elsevier-Dutton
Publishing Co Inc, 2 Park Avenue, New York,
NY 10016

Designed and produced by
Bellew & Higton Publishers Ltd
17–21 Conway Street, London W1P 5HL

Computerset by MFK Graphic Systems
(Typesetting) Ltd, Saffron Walden, Essex, England
Colour separations by Fotographics Ltd
Printed and bound in Hong Kong by Lee Fung Asco

Library of Congress Catalog Card Number: 81-66869

ISBN 0-525-93202-X

10 9 8 7 6 5 4 3 2 1

CONTENTS

The MS *Lindblad Explorer* is a very special little expedition ship. With an ice-breaking bow, shallow draft, long range and special landing craft, she is equipped to go anywhere in the ocean.

For the last ten years she has done just that, going as far north and south as it is possible for any vessel to go, easing into atolls where no other ship of her size has ever been, penetrating great distances up the world's major rivers – and we have had the good fortune to travel there with her as resident naturalists.

We dedicate this book with gratitude to our ship and to her officers and crew, who have made it possible for us to get close to most of the world's living whales, dolphins and porpoises in their natural habitats.

LYALL WATSON
TOM RITCHIE

Preface

This is more than just a book about whales. It is a new kind of book about whales. It is not a paraphrase of the same old information nor yet another polemic against whaling. We happen to find commercial whaling in any guise distressing and anachronistic, but that argument has no place here.

This is a celebration of cetaceans themselves, the first complete survey of all the world's living whales, dolphins and porpoises. We deal here with the whole animals, alive and alluring, and touch on internal structures only in so far as these affect behaviour or offer assistance in identification.

Our account of each species includes a summary of all known information on its appearance, distribution and habits in the wild. Much of this is published here for the first time, because we have been able to see most of these animals for ourselves. The illustration of the Gulf Porpoise (*Phocoena sinus 46*), for instance, is taken from life and is the first ever printed which shows what the animal looks like. Wherever relevant, we offer our own field observations in the hope that these may prove useful to others faced with the problem of identifying a dolphin by the flash of its fin, or a whale from nothing more than the after-image of its last lungful of air.

We share, with all others who have made direct contact with whales in the wild, a sense of privilege, a strange synthesis of honour and awe, in their company. We believe that cetaceans are extraordinary, but that is also an argument which has no place here. Whatever the truth about their intelligence, we can only report that we feel different when they are around, and we hope that some sense of this respect comes through in our account, without intruding too much on essential objectivity.

In an attempt to look at cetaceans as a whole in a new and creative way, we include a linking key to classification which makes it possible for any novice, using a few simple characteristics, to identify an animal at sea or cast up on the shore. We hope that this will prove useful to sailors, merchant mariners, cruise passengers, coastguards, beachcombers, and even armchair enthusiasts, who come into fleeting contact with whales or dolphins and want to know more about them. We offer also some general notes, concentrating still on visible features and observable patterns of behaviour, which shed light on the origin and evolution of these fascinating mammals that chose to go back to their source in the sea.

It has taken us some time to put all this together, and the freedom to do so has been purchased entirely with generous support from *The Threshold Foundation*, which specializes in seeding projects that promise to enhance ecological awareness.

We also owe thanks to Martin Sheldrick of the British Museum (Natural History) in London, and to James Mead of the National Museum of Natural History in Washington, for their valuable time and for access to the collections in their charge.

This book comes in gratitude for what we have been allowed to see and in hope that many more may share the privilege.

Species List

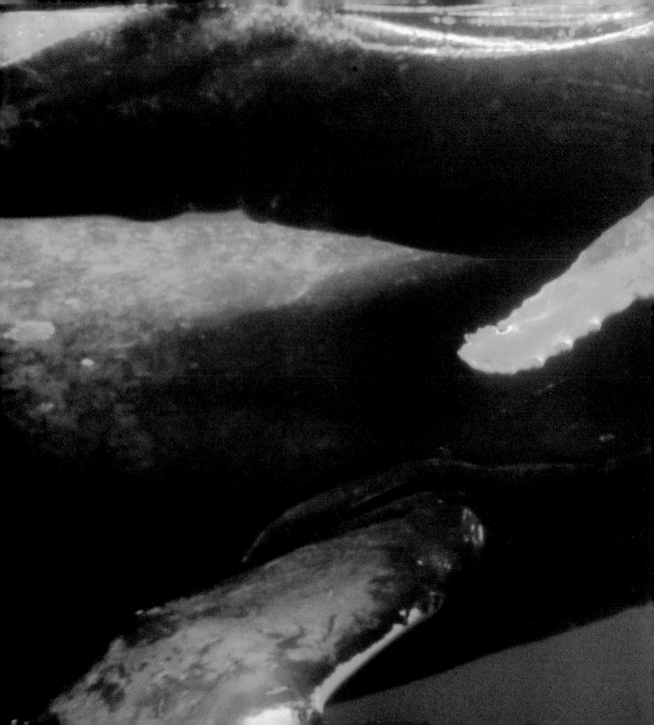

1

Cetology and Cetologists

Cetology, the scientific study of whales, began in the fourth century BC, but in 2,300 years has progressed remarkably little.

The Greek philosopher Aristotle, whose lectures were collected into a one-man encyclopedia, was a careful and meticulous observer, fascinated by natural history. In *Historia Animalium* he dealt with over five hundred different kinds of animals, having dissected many of them to find out how they really worked. He was particularly interested in sea life, and wrote of the Common Dolphin:

'The dolphin is provided with a blowhole and lungs ... and has been seen asleep with his nose above the water, and when asleep he snores. No one is ever seen to be supplied with eggs, but directly with an embryo, just as in the case of mankind. Its period of gestation is ten months, and it brings forth its young in the summer. The dolphin is provided with milk, and suckles its young ... which accompany it for a considerable period. In fact, the creature is remarkable for the strength of its parental affection. The young grow rapidly, being full grown at ten years of age. It lives for many years; some are known to have lived for more than twenty-five, and some for thirty years; the fact is fishermen nick their tails sometimes and set them adrift again, and by this expedient their ages are ascertained.'

This is an astonishing piece of natural history, filled with accurate observations which directly refute those whose superficial reading of Aristotle leads them to dismiss or ridicule him for classifying dolphins as fish. His information was acquired as a direct result of observation and experiment with live animals in the field and his account of the Common Dolphin (*Delphinus delphis 75*) is so good that there is little we can add to it even now.

Following Aristotle, Gaius Plinius Secundus (Pliny the Elder) compiled a 37-volume *Historia Naturalis* which was published in Rome in AD 77 and included a whole book on dolphins and whales. His works are invaluable compendia but contain little or no original observation, drawing on and digesting two thousand other ancient books by almost five hundred writers. Pliny was certainly thorough, but he was also completely credulous and undiscriminating. It is nevertheless to him that we have to turn for the earliest surviving account of great whales, in which a distinction is drawn between the right whale (*balaena*) and the sperm whale (*physeter*), using terms which are still the accepted generic names for these cetaceans.

As far as cetology is concerned, nothing was added to Aristotle's contribution until the Renaissance, when original research was re-born. The impetus for this was provided largely by a rapid increase in exploration and by a flush of published reports on various 'Navigations, Voyages, Traffiques and Discoveries'. The earliest and best of these was *Speculum Regale (The Mirror of Royalty)*, an account of Iceland in the thirteenth century which concluded that few things in that country were worth talking about except whales. The author discusses whales in detail from direct observation and, amongst other things, describes the difference between the Great Right Whale (*Balaena glacialis 1*) and the Bowhead Whale (*Balaena mysticetus 2*), a distinction that continued to elude most zoologists for a further five hundred years.

Attempts to discover a northern passage to the Indies in the sixteenth century took explorers into the Arctic and revealed for the first time the rich feeding grounds in those high latitudes with their vast whale populations. In 1596 the Dutch navigator Willem Barents discovered Spitzbergen and, early in the seventeenth century, commercial whalers were sent there by Dutch and English companies.

These expeditions were concerned mainly with whale products and added little to knowledge of the living animals, but they also spawned a number of publications which at least produced reasonably accurate descriptions of the external appearance of the most common kinds of whale. The best of these were *Spitzbergische oder Gröenlandische Reise-Beschreibung* by Frederick Martens in 1675 and *Bloeyende Opkomst der Oloude en Hedendaagsche Groenlandsche Visschery* by C. G. Zorgdrager in 1720, both of which contained engravings which continued to be copied from book to book until the early nineteenth century.

In the eighteenth century, a young Swedish botanist Linné, better known as Linnaeus, changed the face of biology by making it truly systematic. His system of classification, published for the first time in 1735 and refined in the tenth edition of *Systema Naturae* in 1758, not only imposed a new order on natural history, but exerted a profound effect on the way we still see and think about the world around us.

The sheer physical difficulty of working with animals that live in the open ocean has meant that cetology has had to rely almost entirely on the whaling industry. As a result most of the last two hundred years has been devoted to little more than imposing taxonomic order, from a distance. This endeavour began with a small group of European museum men, who systematized the existing knowledge of cetaceans. Their material came from all over the world and found its way into a handful of institutions in France, England and the United States. The centre of the French web was the Musée Nationale d'Histoire Naturelle in Paris; in London it was the Royal College of Surgeons and later the British Museum (Natural History); and in the United States it was either the American Museum of Natural History in New York or the United States National Museum at the Smithsonian Institution in Washington.

In France the process began with Georges Louis Leclerc (later Comte de Buffon), a naturalist with legal training, who became Keeper of the Jardin du Roi in 1739 and was charged by King Louis XV with the task of cataloguing the collection in the royal museum. He turned this relatively simple task into an account of the whole of nature, which became his life's work. Buffon wrote clearly and simply but thought nothing of doing violence to factual details when it suited his purpose. The first part of *Histoire Naturelle – Générale et Particulière* was published in 1749, but the last of the forty-four beautifully illustrated volumes did not appear until sixteen years after his death in 1788. While Buffon was alive he was assisted by Louis Daubenton, a meticulous naturalist-physician, who performed and illustrated most of the dissections. The last eight volumes, including the one on cetaceans, were completed by Bernard La Cépède (later Comte de Lacépède).

Lacépède was a naturalist (and a musician) who did a thorough job of completing his master's work, but like Buffon he relied largely on compilation from other sources and most of the illustrations in his volume on whales (later published separately as *Histoire Naturelle des Cetacées*) were copied from previous publications. Lacépède acknowledged that, not having seen whales, he had taken everything from research.

Daubenton went on to become Professor of Natural History at the Collège de France. His assistant, and eventual successor, was the legendary Georges Leopold Dagobert, later Baron Cuvier. Cuvier added a new dimension to the study of taxonomy by taking internal as well as external characteristics into account. He obtained a post at the Musée Nationale in Paris and went on to build up the natural history collection into the largest of its kind anywhere in the world. He not only founded the science of comparative anatomy, but extended it to include the comparable study and classification of fossils, thereby giving birth also to the science of palaeontology. In cetology he made several fundamental advances. His *La Regne Animal* and *Recherches sur les Ossements Fossiles* are basic texts much in use today. They contain the original, and still the best, descriptions and illustrations of the three species of cetacean which now bear his name.

The Paris museum was kept supplied during this period by a constant stream of material from travelling naturalists such as Baron Louis Bougainville, Antoine Delalande, the Verreaux brothers and Jean Dussumier.

In Britain the pioneer of cetology was a Scot called John Hunter who studied medicine in London and served as a surgeon at St George's Hospital. He was particularly interested in cetaceans, and not only described all those stranded locally, but even went to the expense of sending someone on a whaling expedition to the Arctic to collect further material for him. After his death in 1793 his vast collection of comparative material was purchased by the government and housed in the Royal College of Surgeons.

Hunter's secretary, William Clift, became the first Curator of the Hunterian collections at the Royal College, where his assistant, who eventually became both Hunterian Professor at the College and his son-in-law, was Sir Richard Owen. During the first half of the nineteenth century, cetacean studies in England were dominated by Owen at the Royal College and by John Edward Gray at the British Museum. No two men could have been less alike.

Gray started working at sixteen as a casual assistant at the British Museum helping to arrange the collections. He was a dedicated, single-minded man who, in more than fifty years at the museum, never published less than thirty papers a year. Indeed, when partly paralysed by a stroke at the age of

sixty-nine, he learned to write with his left hand and increased his output to over sixty papers a year. The quality of his work was erratic. He had a tendency to rush into print, creating new species and genera on the basis of single skulls, or even the drawing of a skull, later altering these when new and contradictory evidence came to light, but he was nevertheless a first-class museum man. When he became Keeper of the Zoology Department in 1840, the British Museum was way behind those of Berlin, Leiden and Paris; but by the time he died, still hard at work in 1875, the collection held more than a million specimens and was the largest, best known and most meticulously catalogued in the world.

Owen, on the other hand, was a total extrovert, a brilliant lecturer and an outstanding public figure, often to be seen at Court. He began his career as an assistant to the Conservator of the Museum at the Royal College of Surgeons. He was a physician but became a brilliant zoologist, writing a large treatise on the comparative structure of teeth. He studied with Cuvier in Paris and returned to the Royal College to build up its anatomical collection and to serve as Hunterian Professor. He was autocratic and irascible, quick to take offence and slow to give credit to others; but he was highly ambitious and succeeded finally in winning the long-standing feud with Gray by being appointed, over Gray's head, as Superintendent of the entire British Museum (Natural History).

Gray's greatest contribution, and the strength of the British Museum during this period, was the string of contacts he built up with other museums and with amateur naturalists throughout the Empire who sent material back to London, secure in the knowledge that it was welcome and that it would be described in a way which gave due credit to the finder. Notable amongst these field naturalists were John Anderson and Sir Walter Elliot in India, Sir Julius von Haast and Sir James Hector in New Zealand, and Robert Swinhoe in China.

In Germany during the same period Carl Rudolphi founded and built up the Zoological Museum in Berlin; and in Holland Herman Schlegel became Director of the Rijksmuseum in Amsterdam. Both contributed pioneer studies on whales, but the main work on cetacean taxonomy continued in Paris and in London, where Gray and Owen were succeeded by Sir William Flower, one of the great pioneers of museum display, who published several influential papers on the marine mammal collections.

In America the foundations of New World natural history were being laid down by talented immigrants such as the Swiss naturalist Jean Louis Agassiz, who started the Museum of Comparative Zoology at Harvard, and the Norwegian Leonhard Stejneger, who became Curator of the United States National Museum. These institutions were well served by hardy young native American naturalists such as Edward Cope, who collected fossils amongst hostile Indians, spade in one hand and rifle in the other; Spencer Baird, who founded the Woods Hole Oceanographic Institute; William Dall, who sailed to the Arctic and Alaska; and Roy Chapman Andrews, who took the *Albatross* to the Far East and returned to become Director of the American Museum of Natural History.

With the arrival of the twentieth century, the ascendancy of the European collections was challenged by these new American institutions, and it was Gerrit Miller at the Smithsonian in Washington and Frederick True at the American Museum of Natural History in New York who did most during this period to bring the discipline of cetology to maturity.

Meanwhile the whaling industries of several countries were making their contribution to cetology. Only at sea are we still primaeval hunters and gatherers, involved in the old pursuit of wild creatures in their natural habitat, but with the assistance of new weapons. The success of our endeavours now depends not so much on our ability to locate and capture the prey, but on our willingness to control the harvest in ways which will ensure its continued productivity. The successful imposition of restraints depends on the acquisition of knowledge about the natural history of the species involved. Most maritime countries therefore have fisheries research projects and all the major whaling nations have, to a greater or lesser degree, sponsored cetacean investigations.

The literature on whaling is immense, most of it devoted to the history and technology of the hunt or to the economics of its product; but a few live whales do somehow manage to surface through the prevailing gore. That they do is largely thanks to enlightened whaling captains such as William Scoresby and Charles Scammon, who depended for their livelihood on knowing something of the ways of the prey, and who made their own observations in the field or collected those of their colleagues. Scoresby in 1820 published *An Account of the Arctic Regions*, which still constitutes most of what we know today about the northern form of the Great Right Whale. Scammon's book *The Marine Mammals of the North-western Coast of North America* was published in 1874 and has become a classic, particularly valued for its description of the natural history of the Grey Whale (*Eschrichtius robustus 4*) in California.

It was however the shore stations used in more modern whaling that provided the material for recent and more intensive research. That at St Johns in Newfoundland was a field site for Frederick True of the New York Museum, who worked there while compiling his 1904 monograph *The Whalebone Whales of the Western North Atlantic*. His associate, Roy Chapman Andrews, took similar advantage of the Californian stations to produce his valuable 1906 monograph on the Sei Whale (*Balaenoptera borealis 8*) in the Pacific.

The intensive study of southern whales was pioneered by Major Barrett-Hamilton at the British whaling station on South Georgia in 1913. This was extended by a series of *Discovery* expeditions on which two other British scientists, N. A. Mackintosh and J. F. G. Wheeler, examined 1,600 carcasses in order to produce their report on Blue (*Balaenoptera musculus 6*) and Fin (*Balaenoptera physalus 5*) whales in 1929. Leonard Harrison-Matthews continued with similar reports on the Humpback Whale (*Megaptera novaeangliae 10*), Sperm Whale (*Physeter macrocephalus 36*) and the southern form of the Great Right Whale (*Balaena glacialis 1*) in 1938.

The skill and experience of the old whalers have today been replaced by sonar, explosives and high-speed diesel engines.

Little knowledge of whales is now needed to kill them. Yet it has been this very facility, together with a mindless mass slaughter that threatens to destroy the industry itself, which has given rise to a good part of the current boom in cetacean studies. Those pioneer investigations in the Antarctic were made specifically in order to gather information on the basic biology of whales as a necessary prerequisite to framing protective legislation. They led to the formation, after the Second World War, of the International Whaling Commission which still encourages similar research.

As far as cetology is concerned, the existence of a profitable whaling industry has been invaluable. It has provided the motivation, the machinery and the money for a growing group of biologists to extend their studies into the field. We now know a fair amount about the gross anatomy and general physiology of whales and we have some information on their pregnancy, growth, maturation and longevity, but such knowledge is restricted to the few species of commercial interest and is biased towards those measurements that are likely to be useful in the construction of models that help predict population dynamics.

Only in the last decade has there been a change. It began with the aqualung, with a number of Bottlenose Dolphins in captivity and with the haunting recordings of Humpback Whales at sea. In 1967 Roger Payne of the Rockefeller University turned from a study of the ability of owls to hear and locate their prey in total darkness to the equally mysterious underwater vocalizations of Humpback Whales. Every spring until 1971 he and his wife Katherine floated in the waters of the whales' breeding ground near Bermuda, recording their long, repeating patterns of sound. These 'song cycles' are now believed to be the most elaborate single display known in any animal species, and their impact on scientists and laymen alike has been immense. The sheer range and evocative power of the songs have brought the world of the great whales into everyday consciousness, creating a new concern for their survival; and the Paynes' continuing analysis of the way in which the songs grow and change is providing science with a unique window on to the mysteries of whale social behaviour and mentality.

The Paynes have now extended their studies to the winter breeding ground of Pacific Humpbacks around the islands of Hawaii and added their weight to a growing community of researchers based on Lahaina in Maui, who monitor the whales there each January, February and March. Their information and recordings, and the magical deep-blue photographs now coming out of Hawaii, are at last putting us close enough to these giant animals to begin to appreciate what their lives must be like.

In Alaska Charles Jurasz and his family have been watching the eastern Pacific Humpback Whales at the other end of their annual migration and, apart from turning up fascinating new information about their feeding behaviour (see *Megaptera novaeangliae 10*), have proved after twelve years of observation that the whales which turn up each summer are the same ones which winter off Hawaii. On the other side of the continent, Stephen Katona and his associates at the College of the Atlantic are getting to know the individual whales which come to feed off Newfoundland and Maine and are forging similar links in the spring mating grounds off Bermuda.

Roger Payne has also made what may be the single most important contribution to cetology since Aristotle's. Until recently there has been no way of measuring the condition or requirements of whale herds without destroying some individuals. All the traditional scientific methods of assessing population size and breeding potential depend on measurements made on corpses provided by the whaling industry. Payne, in his study of the southern form of the Great Right Whale (*Balaena glacialis 1*), has shown that it is possible to identify all the whale individuals by their conspicuous markings, and that their fortunes can be followed from year to year. By aerial photography and new techniques of measuring live whales and recording their movements and feeding behaviour, Payne is already providing information on age, sex and growth without killing, touching, marking or molesting a single whale. For the first time we know something of the true nature of a whale herd, which may be spread out over hundreds of miles, and can begin to understand what really constitutes a whale population. The success of this study is now providing an important incentive for others working with whales in the wild.

Next to the Humpback and the Great Right Whale, the best-known large cetacean is certainly the Great Killer Whale (*Orcinus orca 51*). The existence of a number in captivity and the presence of a resident wild population in Puget Sound have stimulated tremendous enthusiasm amongst those who have seen them, and led to intensive studies based in Seattle and in British Columbia.

We believe that it is non-intrusive field studies such as these which will continue to provide the best insights into cetacean life histories, but we concede that a great deal has been learned from animals kept in captivity.

Thirty years ago there were very few cetaceans in captivity anywhere, but a series of photogenic Bottlenose Dolphins changed that. There was a demand for dolphin shows, which burgeoned until there were over 300 Bottlenose Dolphins in captivity in the United States alone. The vast majority of the dolphinaria were, and still are, devoted to simple repetitive public performances which do little either to stretch the dolphins' abilities or to increase our knowledge about them. The dolphinaria all, however, employ trainers who continue to be amazed by the speed at which dolphins learn. As the store of anecdotal material grows some trainers are turning to more methodical investigation and academics are being recruited to help pose the right questions. In 1959 John Lilly, an experimental neurologist, founded the Communication Research Institute at St Thomas in the Virgin Islands in order to explore the potential of the dolphin's big brain. During the following ten years, he and his small team demonstrated that dolphins could produce sounds in air which seemed to be direct and relevant imitations of human speech patterns, and a long experiment with Margaret Howe and a Bottlenose Dolphin called Peter showed that it was possible for a human and a dolphin to live together constantly for several months and learn a great deal from each other.

In 1968 Lilly closed his Institute, saying: 'I no longer want to run a concentration camp for my friends', but in 1978 he returned to cetology. He believes that humans and dolphins have the capacity to communicate with each other despite their physical differences, and he proposes to lower the barriers between the species by means of new techniques using modern sophisticated programming and minicomputer technology. His supporters and detractors alike wait with fascination to see what comes of the project Lilly is calling JANUS (for Joint Analog Numerical Understanding System).

Lilly's results are still the subject of debate, but there is little doubt that he has had a dramatic influence on a whole generation of students now starting work with cetaceans. There is amongst them a new determination to deal with whales and dolphins in an open-minded way, to concede that they have large and complex brains and to admit, when the evidence makes such a conclusion appropriate, that they could be conscious creatures.

Time chart of prominent cetologists

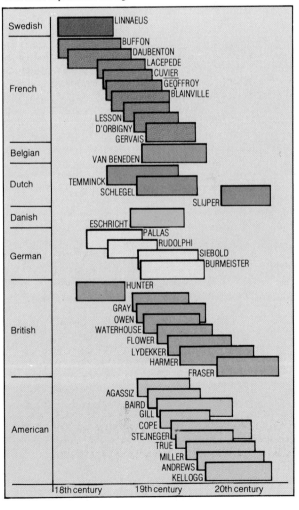

17

2
The Origin and Evolution of Whales

No direct ancestor of any modern whale has been discovered in the fossil record, and so the precise origin of both baleen and toothed whales remains a mystery.

The first animals recognizable as cetaceans occur in Middle Eocene strata. They are classified in a totally extinct order known as the Archaeoceti, the 'ancient whales', but although these creatures were primitive in comparison to modern whales and dolphins, they were well adapted to aquatic life and already so specialized that they cannot be considered as possible ancestors. The baleen, toothed and ancient whale groups seem to have been derived from even earlier animals that left the land during the Cretaceous period.

When living cetaceans are compared to other mammals it is obvious that their nearest relatives are the carnivores and ungulates. An analysis of the chemistry of their bodies shows that the greatest affinity exists between whales and the even-toed ungulates (the cattle, sheep and camel group), with whom they share at least 11 per cent of their proteins. It therefore seems likely that they had a common ancestor. From the little we know of the early mammals the most likely candidates seem to be a group of small terrestrial carnivores known as the Creodonta, who in turn seem to have been derived from a sort of primitive proto-ungulate stock.

We can imagine the earliest cetacean ancestors living on the fringes of slow-moving rivers in a tropical area. They were perhaps as aquatic as modern hippopotami, although considerably less bulky and specialized. They may have lived on molluscs and crustaceans grubbed out of the mud, along with some of the more sluggish species of fish. Selection favoured those who swam best and could hold their breath longest or those whose teeth were suited to holding on to slippery prey.

It seems almost certain that the ancestral cetaceans evolved to fill the niche left vacant in the ecology by the extinction of the great reptiles at the end of the Cretaceous. The fossils could be as sparse as they are precisely because their evolution was so rapid and so localized. The only thing we know for certain is that suddenly, around 50 million years ago at the height of the Eocene, there were lots of Archaeocetes. Some of them were long and serpentine but a few had already become torpedo-shaped like modern whales. Most had the primitive mammalian 44 teeth, differentiated into types both for biting and chewing, very much like those of some living crab-eating seals. They were clearly active and successful carnivores, reaching their peak somewhere in the Oligocene period, between 26 and 38 million years ago, but by the middle Miocene, 10 million years later, the last had disappeared.

The first baleen and toothed whales seem to have appeared about the middle Miocene, but no known forms bridge the gap between them and the Archaeocetes. The three major groups of cetacean seem to have totally independent origins. No fossils belonging to any of them could have been ancestral to either of the others. The similarities that exist can be accounted for as parallel adaptations to the same kind of pelagic life; and the differences between them are as great as those between any other orders of animals.

Archaeoceti

These were archaic cetaceans with teeth differentiated into incisors, canines and grinders. The nostrils were displaced a short distance from the tip of the jaw. The skulls were symmetrical. Four families are known: *Protocetidae*, the most primitive, 2–9 m (7–30 ft) long, with reduced hind limbs and long reptilian snouts; *Dorudontidae*, up to 6 m (20 ft) long, with typical whale shapes and little or no trace of hind limbs; *Basilosauridae*, 12–21 m (40–70 ft) long, with eel- or snake-like shapes; *Patriocetidae*, the most modern, medium-sized with nostrils which have already migrated a long way back.

An Ancestral Whale

In 1832 a column of 28 giant vertebrae was unearthed in Louisiana in the United States. It was identified as the remains of a dinosaur by the American geologist Harlan and named *Basilosaurus* or 'King Lizard', from the Greek *basileus*, a king, and *sauros*, a lizard. By 1839 a skull had been discovered and Sir Richard Owen at the Royal College of Surgeons realized that it was not a reptile at all but a mammal. He described the complex, multi-cusped grinding teeth in detail and decided to change the alleged dinosaur's name to *Zeuglodon*, from the Greek *zugotos*, yoked or joined, and *odous*, a tooth. During the next few years many similar fossils were discovered in the Eocene beds of Alabama and South Carolina. An American fossil-hunter called Albert Koch collected a number of these and strung the vertebrae from several individuals together to produce a monster 35 m (114 ft) long, which he identified as a 'sea serpent' and exhibited in New York in 1845.

Zeuglodon was a large cetacean averaging 15 m (50 ft) long, with a maximum of more than 21 m (70 ft) and a weight of some 5,000 kg (about 6 tons). The proportion of head to body was lower than in any living whale, with the skull representing only 7 per cent of the total length, giving it a very long, cylindrical body with a serpentine shape. The neck was short and compact, relatively immobile like that of most modern cetaceans, but still with 7 completely independent neck vertebrae. The rest of the spinal column was extraordinarily long and sinuous. The forelimbs were modified as short, broad paddles but, unlike those of any living whales, they were still hinged at the elbow. The pelvis was pronounced, with a distinct ball-and-socket joint holding a well-developed femur. In some cases these hind limbs could be large enough to show through the surface of the body, but they were nevertheless too small to be of much use. The vertebrae lacked the massive processes which in modern whales make the spine rigid and restrict locomotory movements to the tail; these ancient whales may have swum with lateral wriggles of the body, but it is equally likely that they had already begun to develop the horizontal tail flukes which characterize all living whales.

It seems likely that these relatively slow-moving animals did

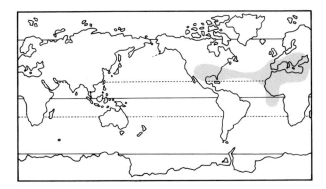

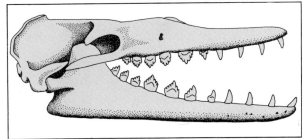

Skull of the Dorudont, fossil *Zygorhiza kochi* from the Southern United States

is even possible that the ancient whales used the hinged forelimbs to wriggle up on to sandy shores to rest or to get across mudbanks in the shallows.

The Evolution of Modern Cetaceans

Apart from obvious aquatic adaptations, such as streamlining and the loss of hair and hindlimbs, the main tendency of cetacean evolution has been towards a progressive development of the jaws at the expense of all other parts of the skull. This has been encouraged by the need for the blowhole to be in the most efficient position on the top of head, but it has taken place largely in response to the need for greater efficiency in feeding and in finding food. The net result has been the evolution of structures holding long rows of sharp uniform teeth, or large numbers of baleen plates, and providing support for a new, sophisticated sonar system.

The skulls of both toothed and baleen whales have been telescoped so that the brain case and the nasal apparatus of most species are squeezed into a compact mass behind a long rostrum composed entirely of enlarged maxillary and premaxillary bones. The heads of Archaeocetes were not telescoped in this way, with the possible exception of one of the most recent forms in which the nostrils became displaced a good distance back from the tip of the snout; this form, *Patriocetus*, lived about 25 million years ago and is in some ways intermediate between ancient and modern whales, but it could not have been ancestral to either of the living groups because both already existed at that time.

The earliest true toothed whales (Odontoceti) were a group known, because of their sharklike teeth, as the Squalodontidae. They were most abundant about 30 million years ago and seem to have branched into two quite distinct lines. One, apparently centred in the southern hemisphere, was relatively short-beaked and may have given rise to the modern killer whales of the family Globicephalidae. The other (rather long-snouted) group, which seems to be directly ancestral to the living beaked whales of the family Ziphiidae, had a more northerly centre. Both of these early groups were extinct by the Pliocene.

The baleen whales (Mysticeti) are obviously descended from some kind of toothed ancestor; most of the living forms still have teeth during the early stages of foetal development. However the fossils we know of, most of which have been

not have or need a dorsal fin. We know nothing of the nature of the skin in Archaeocetes, but it is likely that they had already lost most or all of their body hair. They were certainly streamlined.

The teeth of the ancient whales were differentiated into sharp incisors and canines for grasping wriggling prey such as fish, and complex grinding teeth well adapted for dealing with hard-bodied molluscs and crustaceans. This mixed diet means that they probably spent a great deal of their time foraging in warm, shallow, coastal waters. They were ill-adapted for fast swimming in deep water and must have been much more at home in the shallows along the 5-metre line where they could rest part of their great length on the bottom while reaching up for air. The nostrils lay at the top of the snout, a short distance back from the tip, making it possible for them to breathe without surfacing completely, but the centre of gravity was so far forward that the head and shoulders could easily be raised above the water to look around as many modern whales do. It

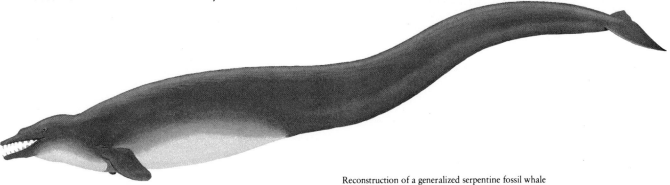

Reconstruction of a generalized serpentine fossil whale

classified in the family Cetotheridae, date back only to the beginning of the Miocene, perhaps 30 million years ago, and by then the adults had already lost their teeth.

It is far from clear whether or not the toothed and baleen whales ever had a common ancestor at all. The best that can be said is that the data reveal an ancient and basic separation between the three main lines, but do not prove that the two living groups had separate origins or provide evidence to the contrary.

(a) Order – Mysticeti

Amongst living great whales, the least specialized is the Grey Whale (*Eschrichtius robustus 4*), which gives us the best idea of what the first baleen whales must have been like. It seems to be a direct descendant of the Cetotheres, relatively little changed.

The other two surviving families have become specialized, each in its own way, for more effective filter feeding. The right and bowhead whales of the family Balaenidae continued along the path of greater baleen development, growing larger heads and more exaggerated jaw arches to house the ever-expanding filters.

The rorqual whales of the family Balaenopteridae took another direction. Rather than growing huge cumbersome plates of baleen, they improved the efficiency of their feeding by developing a way of passing more water over the same small filters. They produced a pattern of pleats in the throat which allow this to puff up like the pouch on a pelican and engulf whole shoals of fish or plankton at a single gulp. We now know, from underwater photographs of live rorquals, that when they are not feeding the pouch is contracted in a way that preserves the sleek hydrodynamic lines important to an aquatic creature.

(b) Order – Odontoceti

Evolution and differentiation amongst toothed whales seem to have been determined largely by developments of the ability to use sound to send and receive information about the environment. A number of specialized organs have been developed for this purpose. Perhaps the most extreme of these is the spermaceti case which gives the Great Sperm Whale (*Physeter macrocephalus 36*) its enormous square head which is involved in the control of buoyancy during deep dives but is primarily a sonar apparatus of enormous sensitivity. This development, together with the fact that the Sperm Whale's chromosomes differ markedly from those of all other toothed whales, suggests that the family Physeteridae have been developing in their own direction for a long time and probably diverged from the toothed whale stock at a very early stage.

All other toothed whales have sonar systems of varying sophistication, the most effective tending to be those of species with the most pronounced acoustic bumps or 'melons' on their heads, such as the Monodontidae and the pilot and killer whales of Globicephalidae.

Chart of the eleven families of living cetaceans to show their divergence from two basic stocks and their present relationships

On purely anatomical grounds the most primitive families are beaked whales of the Ziphiidae and the freshwater dolphins of Platanistidae. In several respects they are still very much like their fossil relatives, but both have now also become specialized in ways which put their long-term survival at risk. The beaked whales have taken to feeding almost exclusively on squid and have in many cases lost all but two of their teeth. The freshwater dolphins exist now only in relict

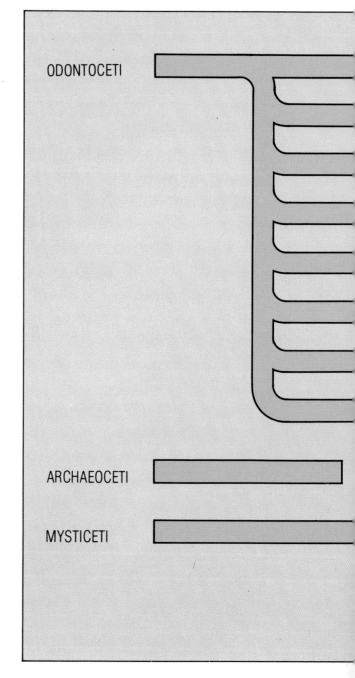

populations, each restricted to a single river system.

The coastal dolphins of the family Stenidae and the porpoise family Phocoenidae are both still reasonably widespread, but the most successful group is without a doubt the family Delphinidae. The classic dolphins have changed to the extent that many of them have a few extra teeth and a more complex air sinus system than their ancestors, but on the whole they are so successful because they are the least specialized. The best known species of all are those such as the Bottlenose Dolphin (*Tursiops truncatus* 76) which have remained free to adapt to changing circumstances.

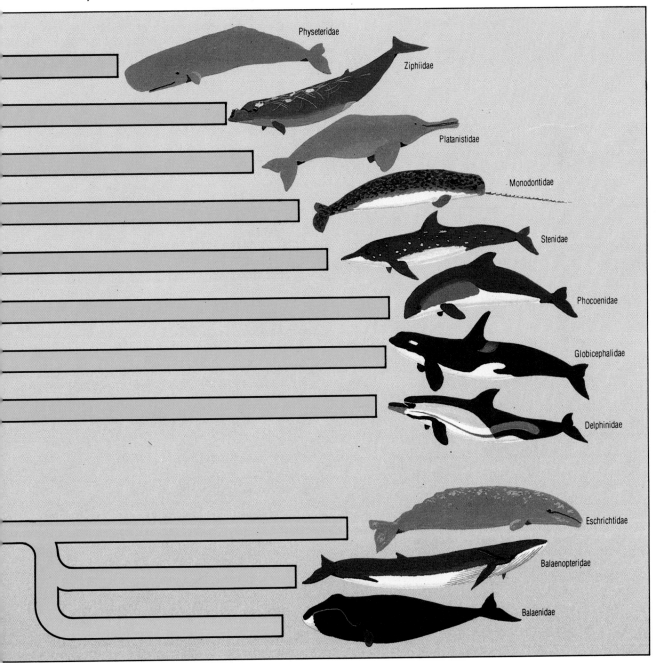

3
Description
Size

Cetaceans differ a great deal in their shape, length, weight, colour and marking. These differences are important not only for distinguishing between species but also for determining age, sex and local variation within any given species. Many old records of length which now seem exaggerated may be accounted for by the fact that they were made along the curve of the body instead of in a straight line parallel to the long axis of the body or appendage.

The precise weight of some small cetaceans in captivity is known, and the mass of a few large whales is fairly well known from the sum of the weights of their parts taken and used by the whaling industry. But field conditions and the sheer bulk of many animals preclude the possibility of making any really accurate measurements. There is no constant ratio between weight and length. A bulky Great Right Whale (*Balaena glacialis 1*) weighs three times as much, and a Sei Whale (*Balaenoptera borealis 8*) twice as much, as a Great Sperm Whale (*Physeter macrocephalus 36*) of the same length.

A large proportion of the total weight is blubber, lying outside the meat of the muscles. Water takes up body heat more than twenty times faster than air does, so the bigger and rounder the whale, and the thicker its layer of blubber, the more economical its system of thermoregulation. This is why animals found in the polar regions tend to be larger than their temperate relatives, and why 40 per cent of a Great Right Whale's weight consists of blubber, whereas the male Great Sperm Whale has just 30 per cent and the more temperate Sei Whale makes do with only 20 per cent fat.

A young cetacean must be able to swim, surface for air, follow its mother and keep itself warm from the moment it is born, so the weight of most whales and dolphins at birth represents a fairly high percentage of the mother's mass. The calves of some dolphins may be up to 45 per cent of their mothers' length and over 18 per cent of their weight.

Sex

Cetaceans commonly differ in size and shape between the sexes. For reasons which are not clear, most female baleen whales are larger than their mates, while male toothed whales are both longer and heavier than their females. In the interest of streamlining, all projections which might cause turbulence have been lost and the sex of most cetaceans is not immediately apparent. The testicles of males are no longer found in an external pouch and cannot be seen from the outside at all. They are white, smooth, shiny cylinders lodged behind the intestine on the body wall beside the kidneys. Although the penis of some great whales may be 3 m (10 ft) long, it is pulled back into the body by retractor muscles so that even the tip is concealed beneath the blubber. Relaxation of these muscles after death may result in its extrusion. The vulva of the female is also concealed beneath the blubber in a genital slit and alongside this are two smaller slits which provide similar cover and protection for the nipples of the mammary glands.

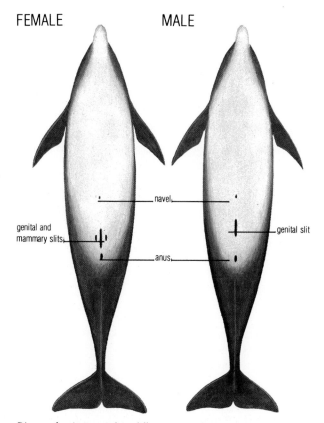

Diagram showing external sex differences in a schematic cetacean

Despite these hydrodynamic arrangements, it is still possible to sex a live animal, even a fully grown whale at sea. All that is needed is a glimpse of the belly. The genital slit of all females is relatively close to the anus, while that of males is placed roughly midway between the anus and the navel.

Pattern

How an animal looks to its predators and to its prey may make the difference between life and death. How it appears to members of its own species can decide whether or not its genes go on to be embodied in another individual.

Originally all animals were probably a single uniform colour, but under the influence of various selective pressures some became differentially marked. It may be assumed that those which retain the old solid colours are not subject to these pressures. The pure black Great Right Whale (*Balaena glacialis 1*), for instance, is too large to have to worry about hiding from predators; it feeds on plankton which do not have good enough eyes to see it coming and it is in such close vocal contact with others of its kind that it needs no visual signals.

The most widespread and basic pattern in all aquatic animals is a simple countershading. This means the whale has a dark topside and a lighter underside, which obliterates the deep ventral shadow that otherwise makes any animal in the top-lit areas of the ocean very conspicuous. All those species that show marked and simple countershading feed in the bright surface layers of the sea on free-swimming food such as fish and squid which have good eyesight. The Pygmy Killer Whale (*Feresa attenuata 53*), the Melonhead Whale (*Peponocephala electra 54*) and the Northern Rightwhale Dolphin (*Lissodelphis peronii 63*) are all excellent examples of species with simple countershaded patterns such as those in illustrations A and B.

The presence of a dark back and a white belly is the most generalized and primitive condition. The light ventral field follows the contours of the body precisely, confined to those areas in which the shadow would otherwise be deepest. The next evolutionary step seems to have been an expansion of this white belly area to include the throat, the area beneath the tailstock and that part of the flank above the flipper and in front of and below the fin, as shown in illustrations C, D and E. This slightly diminishes the strict obliterative effect of the countershading, but it has the advantage of breaking up and slimming the profile so that it looks less like that of a typical predatory cetacean. The Chilean Dolphin (*Cephalorhynchus eutropia 65*) and the Spectacled Porpoise (*Phocoena dioptrica 45*) show this stage well, but it reaches its most impressive development in the predatory Great Killer Whale (*Orcinus orca 51*) and in a smaller mimic, the Benguela Dolphin (*Cephalorhynchus heavisidii 66*).

A common consequence of the extension of the white belly up on to the forward flank is to leave a peninsula of dark pigment running from the still dark flipper to the eye or mouth. This persists and becomes a feature characteristic of many of the Stenella dolphins. It is rare for the flipper to lose colour as well, but this does happen in the Southern Rightwhale Dolphin (*Lissodelphis peronii 62*).

The bright white spot behind the eye of the Killer Whale and the further spread of pigment loss up on to the tailstock and the melon would appear to meet the need of gregarious species in fast-moving schools to identify each other easily. Probably all species with flash markings, such as bright lines or vivid patches, have developed these to act as signals for others of their species. Examples are the white dorsal fin markings of the Spray Porpoise (*Phocoenoides dalli 48*) and the bright white double flank patch on the Hourglass Dolphin (*Lagenorhynchus cruciger 59*).

The spread of white on to the back behind the fin (as a saddle) and across the shoulders behind the melon (like a cape) and the suppression of darker pigment in these areas seem to be under separate and independent genetic control. The Whitebeak Dolphin (*Lagenorhynchus albirostris 55*) shows the former, the Piebald Dolphin (*Cephalorhynchus commersonii 64*) the latter and the Spotted Dolphin (*Stenella plagiodon 74* and illustration *H*) a combination of the two. We suspect that the Spotted Dolphin may have been preceded in this series by an intermediate unspotted form with a vivid

A series of schematic diagrams to show the progressive evolution of complex pigmentation patterns from simple counter-shading in a typical dolphin

dark saddle (illustration *G*). Nobody has ever seen a dolphin with such markings but we would not be surprised if one turned up.

Different combinations of the separate units of pattern, the general dark dorsal field, the white belly, the light flank patch, the grey blanket across the top of the tailstock and the pale cape over the melon, with varying degrees of dominance, produce virtually every design found in porpoises and dolphins. When all the units are superimposed, they produce something remarkably like the Common Dolphin (*Delphinus delphis 75*), which has the most complex pigmentation of any cetacean.

Pale blazes and dark stripes produce disruptive coloration, disguising fins and flippers by cutting across the body and confusing the general shape. Lateral lines direct attention away from the business end of the animal, the mouth full of teeth, deceiving and diverting the prey for long enough to give the predator an advantage. Black rings or masks around the eyes conceal them and perhaps also protect the wearer against glare. Lip patches tend to destroy outlines of the mouth.

Superimposed on the basic design of several species of cetacean are additional spots that could act as cryptic coloration, helping cetaceans to blend into an environment frequently dappled by white-capped waves and the broken patterns of refracted sunlight. It is found in the Bridled Dolphin (*Stenella attenuata 73*), Bottlenose Dolphin (*Tursiops truncatus 76*), Unicorn Whale (*Monodon monoceros 34*), Sei Whale (*Balaenoptera borealis 8*) and Blue Whale (*Balaenoptera musculus 6*). The fact that nursing calves have uniform colours and acquire their spots only when they become old enough to forage for themselves suggests that spotting is predator camouflage rather than protective colouring against other predators. The fact that dorsal spots are light, while ventral ones are dark, so that both stand out against the basic countershading, indicates that spots are a recent refinement of the progressively complex pattern of cetacean pigmentation.

A more detailed discussion of the significance of adaptive coloration appears in an excellent paper by Edward Mitchell (1970).

Colour

The skin of most cetaceans has a smooth, thick epidermis with little or no hair, no glands and no horny keratin. Colour depends largely on the presence and density of granules of a pigment called melanin in the inner part of the epidermis. If these are plentiful and densely arranged, the skin looks black. If they are scarce and scattered, the skin looks white. Between these two extremes are the graded greys.

The basic colouring of all whales depends on neutral shades which, we suggest, should be arranged in a tonal scale of seven shades: white, black and five intermediates each containing double the amount of black pigment; these are named (after VILLALOBOS) as shown in the top row opposite.

Cetacean skin is well supplied with blood vessels, which are largely responsible for the flesh-coloured hues of many small whales. This is why an active living dolphin often seems to have a glowing pink belly and why no such colour can ever be seen in a dead animal. The blood drains from capillaries within seconds of death and the colour vanishes with it, leaving a cadaverous pale grey or white; this often undergoes further post-mortem changes and becomes uniformly dark.

Most of these evanescent tints are provided by blood in thin-walled venules parallel to the surface of the dermis. When seen through pure white, unpigmented flesh the effect is pink and when seen through a darker neutral shade, it can appear as a deep oxblood red or liver colour. We suggest that these blood colours be arranged in a further tonal scale of seven shades (as defined by KORNERUP & WANSCHER 1978) and named as shown in the second row opposite.

Many cetaceans have traces of eumelanin and phaeomelanin which in various concentrations can produce lightly tinted browns and yellows. These are particularly noticeable on the flank patches of the Common Dolphin (*Delphinus delphis 75*) and the Atlantic Whiteside Dolphin (*Lagenorhynchus acutus 56*). Many Delphinidae and Ziphiidae usually portrayed as black or deep grey are in fact often brown or yellow tinted. We include a graded series of yellow shades, arranged into a spectrum of yellows and named (KORNERUP & WANSCHER 1978) as shown in the third row opposite.

The filtering action of pale epidermal tissue and blubber, and the reflections from sky and sea produce greenish and bluish tints in many cetaceans. Sometimes these are illusory, depending only on environmental qualities, but often they are consistent enough to be regarded as valid field characteristics. These are described as tonal variants of a basic primary blue and a primary green (KORNERUP & WANSCHER 1978). Both colours may be modified by qualifying them as pale, light, medium, dark or deep shades of the primary colours in the fourth row opposite.

Tones not included above can be indicated by combination, e.g. ruddy sienna; by altering tone, e.g. pale cream; or by indicating texture, e.g. glossy black.

Descriptions in the text follow this system.

Age

Large animals generally live longer than small ones (seventy years for an elephant, compared with three for a mouse). In theory the great whales ought to live to a correspondingly great age. Cuvier wrote: 'The duration of their lives, judged by that of other animals, must be considerable.' Popular opinion has tended to support him, but until very recently there has been little evidence for it.

When modern whaling began in the twentieth century harpoons were marked with the year in which they were used and we learned, in due course, that Bowhead Whales (*Balaena mysticetus 2*) could live to at least forty, Fin Whales (*Balaenoptera physalus 5*) to thirty-seven and Sperm Whales (*Physeter macrocephalus 36*) to twenty-seven. Thus, the suspicion grew that the metabolic rate of large whales could be higher than that of elephants and that, despite their large size, they might not live to great ages.

Mammals in general become sexually mature at about 15 per cent of their maximum age, so that when it was learned

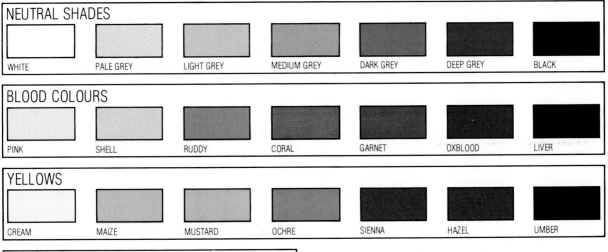

NEUTRAL SHADES

| WHITE | PALE GREY | LIGHT GREY | MEDIUM GREY | DARK GREY | DEEP GREY | BLACK |

BLOOD COLOURS

| PINK | SHELL | RUDDY | CORAL | GARNET | OXBLOOD | LIVER |

YELLOWS

| CREAM | MAIZE | MUSTARD | OCHRE | SIENNA | HAZEL | UMBER |

PRIMARIES

| BLUE | GREEN |

that most rorqual whales reach puberty between six and ten the suspicion was confirmed that their life spans were somewhere between forty and seventy years. The ovaries of all mammals contain a large number of germ cells which ripen in succession and burst, releasing an egg into the fallopian tube. Each time this happens a scar is left on the surface of the ovary and it is possible, by counting the scars, to determine how many times an animal has ovulated. Then, if the interval of ovulation (which tends to be the same as the time between calves) and the age at first pregnancy are known, the approximate age at death can be calculated. Estimates for most great whales confirm a life expectancy (in the presence of whaling) of roughly thirty years, but that is still only an approximation.

A longer and more satisfactory record was later discovered in the whale's ear. The external ear openings in most whales are so minute that they can hardly be seen. They are small enough to prevent water getting in, and are equally effective in preventing the wax, which forms in most mammalian ears, from getting out. As a result the waxy debris builds up until it forms a solid plug that fills the canal leading from the external ear hole to the ear drum. In adult whales this can be over a metre long and when it is sectioned it can be seen to be composed of alternate light and dark lines, the former corresponding to periods of rapid growth, the latter to slower development, each pair indicating one year in the whale's life. However the rate of lamination in the wax may vary with age and maturity and can be misleading.

Truly accurate measurements of maturity and longevity await studies of particular populations of whales in which individuals are recognized and observed throughout their lives. This is beginning to be done now, since Payne showed, with the southern Great Right Whales (*Balaena glacialis 1*), that it was possible.

Combining all methods we can to arrive at an approximation of the life history of most baleen whales. They seem to reach maturity at between five and ten years, to produce calves every two or three years after that and to live for an average of a little over thirty years. Extensive whaling has, however, altered these figures drastically. Few whales reach their potential maximum age, and the age and length at which they become mature falls as fast as their populations decline.

In toothed whales the dentine of their teeth is produced in layers, like the concentric rings in the trunk of a tree, and the teeth go on growing and providing this record throughout life. Even though the tooth tips wear down with age and use, the basal parts still retain their telltale rings which can be counted when the teeth are cut and polished. The cause of the rings is still unknown; they appear even in the teeth of captive dolphins which are fed and housed under the same conditions all year round. But they do seem to be annual rings and, from the study of those laid down in the teeth of captive animals of known age, may well provide an accurate estimate of age.

The best recent estimates for *average* longevity in a selection of cetacean species are: Great Right Whale (*Balaena glacialis 1*) forty; Grey Whale (*Eschrichtius robustus 4*) thirty; Fin Whale (*Balaenoptera physalus 5*) thirty; Humpback Whale (*Megaptera novaeangliae 10*) thirty; Northern Fourtooth Whale (*Berardius bairdii 12*) twenty; North Sea Beaked Whale (*Mesoplodon bidens 27*) twenty; Ganges River Dolphin (*Platanista gangetica 29*) twenty; Unicorn Whale (*Monodon monoceros 34*) twenty-five; Great Sperm Whale (*Physeter macrocephalus 36*) thirty-five; Common Porpoise (*Phocoena phocoena 43*) fifteen; Longfin Pilot Whale (*Globicephala melaena 49*) thirty-five; Great Killer Whale (*Orcinus orca 51*) twenty-five; Common Dolphin (*Delphinus delphis 75*) twenty; Bottlenose Dolphin (*Tursiops truncatus 76*) twenty years.

The maximum age for each species may be a great deal higher. The greatest age so far discovered by any method outlined here is that of a Sperm Whale killed in the Pacific, whose teeth contained seventy concentric rings.

4
Stranded Cetaceans

Despite their many impressive adaptations to an aquatic environment, all whales still breathe air. Apart from those killed by man, most die of drowning. Illness, weakness and old age may contribute, but the gravest danger faced by all cetaceans is an inability to breathe. There are numerous reports of whales of all sizes coming to each other's aid, assisting ill or injured group members to the surface where they can continue to respire. This supportive behaviour is clearly a well-established part of the repertoire of all social species. It may have its origin in the assistance given to newborn calves so that they can draw their first independent breaths, but it is a form of aid given to all foundering animals regardless of age or, often, even species. There are several records from captivity of succour across the species line, such as that offered by a False Killer Whale (*Pseudorca crassidens 52*) to a Bottlenose Dolphin (*Tursiops truncatus 76*) at Marineland of the Pacific in California (BROWN et al 1966). There is a large number of anecdotal reports of dolphins of various kinds coming to the assistance of drowning humans, holding them up and pushing them into shallow water.

A great many cetaceans are found each year stranded on beaches throughout the world. Strandings were amongst the first natural history events to be recorded. Stranded whales formed an important additional source of food and fuel for many coastal people, and they continue to provide cetology with its only source of information on some rare and elusive species.

On the coasts of Britain whales were stranded with sufficient frequency for large ones to be designated 'Fish Royal' with the choicest bits reserved for royal use. The British Museum (Natural History) now has the right to stranded whales and has kept a complete record of them since 1913. There have been 1,550 strandings involving over thirty species (FRASER 1974), including almost every kind of cetacean known to occur in or near British waters. Analysis of these shows that stranding happens to toothed and baleen whales, deep- and shallow-water species, young and old, male and female, solitary individuals or whole social groups, animals which are obviously injured as well as those which appear to be in perfect health. It is the most commonplace and at the same time the most mysterious aspect of cetacean behaviour.

In most cases the animals are still alive when they first become stranded, usually on gently shelving beaches. Postmortem operations often reveal an injury, infection or debility which must have caused discomfort and made it difficult for the whale to behave normally in deep water. Under these circumstances, faced with the risk of drowning, it would be natural for the cetacean to seek a place where it could continue to breathe while marshalling its strength to deal with other problems. We do not know how many whales rest in shallow water and return successfully to the sea without becoming permanently stranded.

In many parts of the world drives are organized to exploit this tendency. The Longfin Pilot Whale (*Globicephala melaena 49*) spends most of its life offshore, but since at least the sixteenth century whole schools have been captured in the Faroe Islands. When a suitable group is spotted somewhere near the coast in summer, the fishermen position themselves on the seaward side of the whales and set up a tremendous din, splashing, shouting and beating on metal pans and the sides of their boats, opposite traditional 'whale bays' which have sandy shorelines inclining evenly upward. The whales invariably respond by moving together into the shallows where they are despatched with knives and lances. In this way 117,456 were killed between 1584 and 1883 in the Faroes alone. Drives have also been organized in Iceland, Greenland, Newfoundland and Cape Cod, taking two thousand whales or more at a time. Similar methods are used now in Japan and the Solomon Islands.

Many mass strandings of course occur without human assistance. Pilot whales of both species, False Killer Whales (*Pseudorca crassidens 52*) and Great Sperm Whales (*Physeter macrocephalus 36*) seem to be particularly susceptible. These are all deep-water species and it has been suggested that they become disorientated and strand accidentally; but there is one clearly established fact which makes nonsense of this explanation. If stranded animals of any of these species are pulled back into deeper water, they immediately and unerringly return to the same piece of beach.

Most mass strandings occur on gently shelving, sandy or muddy beaches, from which it might be difficult to obtain a satisfactory echo. The activity of a large group of whales in a shallow-water area stirs up a great deal of sand and sediment, which could disturb underwater navigation. Swimming about on a level, shallow bottom may lead to disorientation and to an inability to find the way back out to the deeps. A hunting whale concentrating on the higher frequencies of short-range echoes from its prey could perhaps miss the low-frequency warning of shallows directly in its path. All of these are possible explanations for stranding, but they sound somewhat unlikely. They do not allow for the sensitivity of cetacean sonar systems, which are capable of operating in a range of frequencies and in several different directions at the same time and which function very efficiently in the muddy Amazon and Ganges where the density of particles in suspension reduces visibility almost to nil. Nor do they account for the fact that animals manhandled into clear, deep water have no difficulty in returning directly to their original stranding places in the shallows.

In 1971 a school of about forty Shortfin Pilot Whales (*Globicephala macrorhynchus 50*) went aground in Florida. Repeated attempts were made to refloat them, but each time they returned directly to the shore. Finally, the two largest whales were towed out to sea and restrained there 400 m (1,300 ft) from the beach. Only then could the rest of the school be persuaded to leave the shore and join them. Unfortunately, later that same day, a collector for a marine aquarium caught one of the lead whales, by tying a rope round its tail, and towed it slowly ashore, whereupon the rest of the school grouped tightly together and followed his boat on to another beach. Despite the fact that many of the whales were injured by sharp rocks, none of them could be induced to leave until the two biggest ones were once again forcibly held offshore. Eventually the herd were reunited and disappeared into a sudden storm, but that was not the end of the story. Five days later the same whales (including the two large ones, with rope burns round the tailstocks) stranded themselves again, this time fatally, on yet another beach 275 km (170 miles) away.

It is straining credibility to suggest that this school of Short-fin Pilot Whales became disorientated and accidentally stranded themselves on three separate beaches in seven days. There is clearly some other influence, which seems to be primarily social, at work.

In 1976 a group of thirty False Killer Whales (*Pseudorca crassidens 52*) went aground in Pine Island Sound in Florida. They relaunched themselves successfully with the next tide, but three days later the same school were stranded on the edge of a coral bank 260 km (160 miles) away in Dry Tortugas. One of these whales, a large male, was obviously hurt. He lay tilted to one side, bleeding from his right ear, and all the others formed a tight wedge-shaped configuration around him. Attempts were made to single out individual whales from the fringe of this group in the shallows and push them offshore, but the objects of these rescue operations always became highly agitated and no amount of human effort could prevent them from returning to the group. As soon as the whales touched each other they became docile again and, as long as they were all in contact, the entire group could be edged into deeper water.

Fortunately for this particular whale herd, tidal range in the Tortugas is only 60 cm (24 inches) and so none of the animals was left completely high and dry. Each had the option of leaving at any time, but despite the fact that many became severely sunburned in the process, they all remained in the shallows in support of the injured male until he died three days later. This sequence was watched by a group of whale enthusiasts who did everything possible to keep the whales wet and protect them from the sun. Without these people, and the low tidal flux, the entire group might have died during the ebb tide on the first day. Because of their presence the survival of the group was assured and we have learned several vital facts.

The first of these is that the whales were highly vocal, producing a constant chatter of chirps and squeaks that could be heard 15 m (50 ft) inland without the aid of a hydrophone. The second is that the injured male, who was furthest up the beach, continued to vocalize until he died and would have toppled over and drowned on the first day without the support of the whales nearest to him. The third is a fascinating report by James Porter, an oceanographer who took the opportunity to swim with the whales and discovered that whenever he used a snorkel – and was presumably making a noise like a whale with a waterlogged blowhole – he was promptly 'rescued'. One of the False Killers would detach itself from the group, slide underneath him, rise slowly so that he was lifted almost clear of the water, and carry him to the beach. Finally the observers were able to report that, following the death of the injured male during the third night, the group of whales slowly disintegrated and by morning on the fourth day all of them had gone.

This demonstrates that strandings in this species, at least, are not the result of panic or a blind self-destructive urge. They take place on soft sand and represent an attempt by an ailing individual to find a place where it is possible to rest from swimming and to try to recuperate.

The large male whale which died in the Tortugas was found, on post-mortem examination, to have a severe round-worm infection of the ear. This is probably what drove him to seek refuge in the shallows, but it is unlikely that the rest of the school were there for the same reason. Mass strandings clearly involve more complex social responses.

At 5.00 a.m. on 18 March 1970 an immature male Great Sperm Whale (*Physeter macrocephalus 36*) rushed at great speed on to the beach at Gisborne in New Zealand, skidding to a halt in about one metre of water. Offshore a large harem herd milled around just outside the breakers. They must have been in acoustic contact with the animal on the beach, because ten minutes later seven more whales came to join him. Two of these were young males and five were cows, one heavy with calf. Then the pattern was repeated, again and again, every few minutes, until after an hour and a half fifty-nine Sperm Whales were aground. The beaching of the first whale could, it seems, have had something to do with a severe electrical storm. The others were part of a chain reaction of concern.

Large societies require elaborate systems of social cohesion and communication, and it is these which lead to mass strandings. The initial cause of a single stranding may be illness (perhaps caused by parasites), injury, the birth of a calf too close to shore, evasive action under the threat of predation or simple accident. The more we learn about cetacean echolocation, the less likely it seems that mere errors in navigation are responsible, and if one fact emerges from the direct observation of actual strandings it is that panic is not normally involved. The process of beaching generally seems to be deliberate. In the final analysis neither illness nor injury can be considered as causes of, or explanations for, stranding; they are little more than contributory factors to situations which leave a cetacean in danger of drowning and lead it to take the most obvious evasive action, which is refuge in an archetypal habitat in the shallows.

Viewed in this light strandings seem not so much a lethal aberration, as natural behaviour with some survival value. We have no way of knowing how often it succeeds and allows the animal involved to recover and swim away again unscathed. The fact that individual action of this kind sometimes leads to mass mortality is unfortunate, but on balance it is probably a small and occasional price to pay for patterns of social cohesion and stability, which provide many biological dividends.

Lest it be thought that we have resolved all the mystery in stranding, it is worth pointing out that we do not even begin to understand why it is that so many mass strandings are connected with electrical storm activity, or why they tend to occur on the days directly before or after a full moon.

Parasites

Like all mammals, cetaceans are hosts to a number of internal parasites such as tapeworms, hookworms, roundworms and flukes. When the ancestors of modern whales left the land to take up a new life in the sea, they simply carried these lodgers with them, because their internal environments were largely unchanged. But life in the ocean was impossible for the external parasites to which cetacean ancestors were probably prone.

Initially, at least, the ancient whales were free of one source of irritation. The loss of body hair and the acquisition of smooth, streamlined skin made it difficult for passengers to get a secure foothold. Some of the sleek, fast-moving small cetaceans are still protected in this way, but, as every yachtsman knows, even the most polished hulls still accumulate hitch-hikers. The most numerous and striking of these are the barnacles, whose species differ mainly in the size and shape of their protective cases. The commonest are acorn barnacles of the genus *Coronula*. They are most often seen on the head, flippers and flukes of whales, particularly around the knobs of the Humpback Whale (*Megaptera novaeangliae 10*), on the callosities of the Great Right Whale (*Balaena glacialis 1*) (which is host to its own endemic species *Coronula balaenaris*) and on the head of the Grey Whale (*Eschrichtius robustus 4*), (to which the barnacle *Cryptolepas rachianecti* is peculiar). These whale species are chosen perhaps because they are large and slow. The riders seem to do the whales no

harm, although they do leave a permanent mark on the skin when detached. There are seasonal fluctuations in barnacle populations, which reach their peak density when the whales are in cold water, and tend to drop off in the tropics. At the end of a summer in polar waters, Humpback Whales may be carrying as much as 450 kg (1,000 lb) of barnacles.

Another group of barnacles have rubbery stalks that lift them up above the surface for greater efficiency in feeding. They are not nearly as well suited to finding purchase on smooth cetacean skin as the others, and only parasitize whales by settling on more sheltered spots, such as between the teeth or in a genital slit or throat groove, or by taking root on top of the tougher acorn barnacles. The most common of these stalked or ship barnacles are those of the genus *Conchoderma*. They are found on virtually every floating object in the sea, but *C. auritum* seems to specialize in whales.

A third group of barnacles has solved the problem of purchase by burrowing into the skin of cetaceans to various depths. The genus *Xenobalanus* still protrudes some distance; *X. globicipitis* and *X. strictus* occur on several species of Stenella dolphins. *Tubicinella* species are so deeply embedded that only their tips are exposed for feeding. None of these barnacles obtains any nourishment from its host, and although the parasites may appear to cause damage to the skin they do not seem to produce infection or inflammation.

A group of copepods or 'water fleas', which can be seen flitting around in plankton swarms with their oarlike antennules, have become parasites. One at least of these, *Penella*, is

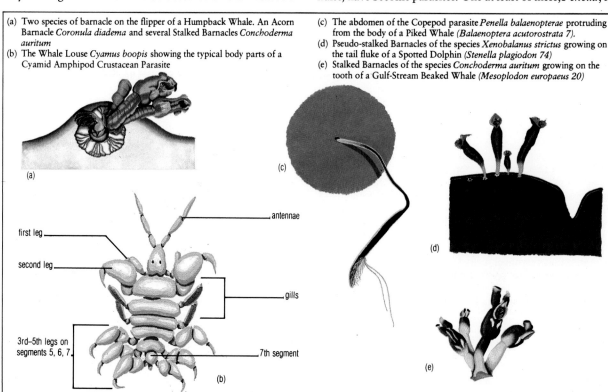

(a) Two species of barnacle on the flipper of a Humpback Whale. An Acorn Barnacle *Coronula diadema* and several Stalked Barnacles *Conchoderma auritum*

(b) The Whale Louse *Cyamus boopis* showing the typical body parts of a Cyamid Amphipod Crustacean Parasite

(c) The abdomen of the Copepod parasite *Penella balaenopterae* protruding from the body of a Piked Whale (*Balaenoptera acutorostrata 7*).

(d) Pseudo-stalked Barnacles of the species *Xenobalanus strictus* growing on the tail fluke of a Spotted Dolphin (*Stenella plagiodon 74*)

(e) Stalked Barnacles of the species *Conchoderma auritum* growing on the tooth of a Gulf-Stream Beaked Whale (*Mesoplodon europaeus 20*)

antennae

first leg

second leg

gills

3rd–5th legs on segments 5, 6, 7

7th segment

(a)

(b)

(c)

(d)

(e)

now totally specialized for life with whales. It is most often seen hanging from the flesh of several kinds of rorqual whale like a pink tassel about 1 cm (¹⁄₃ inch) in diameter. It is a lernaeid copepod whose larval stage is free living, but whose adult females settle on a convenient whale's skin and burrow into the blubber, where they metamorphose into wormlike creatures that send processes into the muscle tissue of the whale on which they feed. The body of this strange crustacean is composed almost entirely of ovaries, which pump eggs into a long abdomen that protrudes through the skin of the whale and hangs down in a limp frond or feathery structure, up to 30 cm (12 inches) long. On the end of this are two threadlike sacs from which eggs are expelled into the sea to re-start the cycle. Once the eggs have been released the parasite dies and drops off, and the wound heals over.

Another copepod crustacean, *Balaenophila*, is still nominally free living, but seems to live exclusively on the baleen plates of the large whales amongst the hairy fringes of baleen.

Among the barnacles, particularly around the acorn types which provide them with plenty of crevices for concealment, live a number of true parasites that feed on cetacean skin. These are the 'whale lice', which are amphipod crustaceans of the family Cyamidae.

Cyamids are pale, flat, spidery creatures, about 2.5 cm (1 inch) long, with strong claws at the ends of their ten legs, which enable them to cling on to the skin of their hosts. They are particularly successful on the bodies of large whales such as the Humpback (*Megaptera novaeangliae 10*) and the Great Right Whale (*Balaena glacialis 1*) which have callosities, crevices, wrinkles and knobs to which they can cling. On one occasion, more than 110,000 lice were taken from just two wounds on a single Grey Whale (*Eschrichtius robustus 4*). Lice are not normally the cause of disease, but will multiply to take advantage of new opportunities on an injured animal (LEUNG 1965).

All the great whales have cyamid parasites and in most cases provide such excellent habitats that the lice have become species-specific. The Grey Whale, for instance, harbours two species, *Cyamus kessleri* and *C. scammoni*, which infest its skin, blowhole, the crease at the angle of the jaw, the grooves on the throat, the anus, the eyelid and the genital slit, but occur nowhere else. On the exquisitely streamlined smaller cetaceans there are fewer places for cyamids to live and they are correspondingly rare. *Isocyamus delphini* has been recorded from False Killer Whales (*Pseudorca crassidens 52*), Great Killer Whales (*Orcinus orca 51*), Longfin Pilot Whales (*Globicephala melaena 49*), Grey Dolphins (*Grampus griseus 68*) and Common Dolphins (*Delphinus delphis 75*). The genus *Syncyamus* seems to be equally vagrant (LEUNG 1970).

If the same parasite is found on two different species of whale, the chances are they have been in contact at sea, because no cyamid has a free-living stage. Cross-infestations can only take place through bodily contact. *Cyamus monodontis*, for instance, is known only from the Unicorn Whale (*Monodon monoceros 34*) and the White Whale (*Delphinapterus leucas 35*), which are confined to the same Arctic areas. Similarly a difference in parasites within the same species of whale can offer evidence of disparate distribution. In South

African coastal waters, female and young Great Sperm Whales (*Physeter macrocephalus 36*) which spend their lives in warm water, are infested exclusively with *Neocyamus physeteris*, while males, which travel down to the cold Antarctic each summer, carry only the hardier *Cyamus catadontis* (BEST 1969).

Whale lice can therefore often be classified simply by identifying their hosts; but a point of greater relevance to a guide such as this is that in cases of doubt, a whale species (or even a small part of a whale) may be positively identified merely by its parasites, which are a great deal easier to carry back to the laboratory than is the cetacean itself.

We therefore offer the key overleaf to the classification and identification of all the sixteen species of cyamid currently recognized (LEUNG 1967).

Key to the Species

Neocyamus One known species, *N. physeteris*, most often found on the Great Sperm Whale (*Physeter macrocephalus 36*).

Platycyamus One species, *P. thompsoni*, is known from the Northern Bottlenose Whale (*Hyperoodon ampullatus 15*); but a second (still undescribed) species may exist on the Northern Fourtooth Whale (*Berardius bairdii 12*).

Isocyamus One widespread species, *I. delphini*.

Syncyamus One species, *S. pseudorcae*, is known from the False Killer Whale (*Pseudorca crassidens 52*), but others (which may be separate species) occur around the blowhole in several species of dolphin.

Some whales in Antarctic waters develop a bloom of unicellular algae on their skin, which gives them a greenish-yellow tinge. The Blue Whale (*Balaenoptera musculus 6*) shows this particularly well and so is sometimes known as 'sulphurbottom'. The alga is usually the diatom *Cocconeis ceticola*.

Individuals of all species of cetacean carry a number of scars. Some of these are parallel rakelike tracks which are clearly caused by members of their own species; the distance between the lines is exactly the same as the gap between the whales' teeth. In those species that feed on squid there are circular scars (particularly around the head area) which are obviously the result of contact with suckers on the tentacles of their prey. But on many whales and dolphins (most often on their bellies) there are round or oval lacerations with radiating groove patterns, whose origin is much more mysterious. They seem to be most common in animals which live on, or pass through, the tropics.

The most recent explanation suggests that the culprit may be a widespread small tropical shark called *Isistius brasiliensis* (JONES 1971). This and a related form in the genus *Istiophorus* are known as 'cookie-cutter' sharks from their habit of slicing clean little scoops out of their prey. They are only 60 cm (2 ft) long, but have unusual fleshy lips which act as suction cups by which they attach themselves to animals many times their size. It seems that they clamp on facing the tail of the host, sink

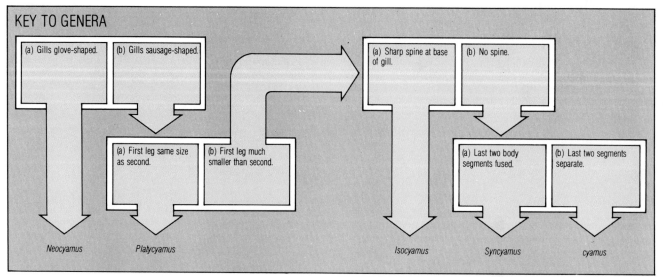

KEY TO GENERA

(a) Gills glove-shaped.

(b) Gills sausage-shaped.

(a) Sharp spine at base of gill.

(b) No spine.

(a) First leg same size as second.

(b) First leg much smaller than second.

(a) Last two body segments fused.

(b) Last two segments separate.

Neocyamus

Platycyamus

Isocyamus

Syncyamus

cyamus

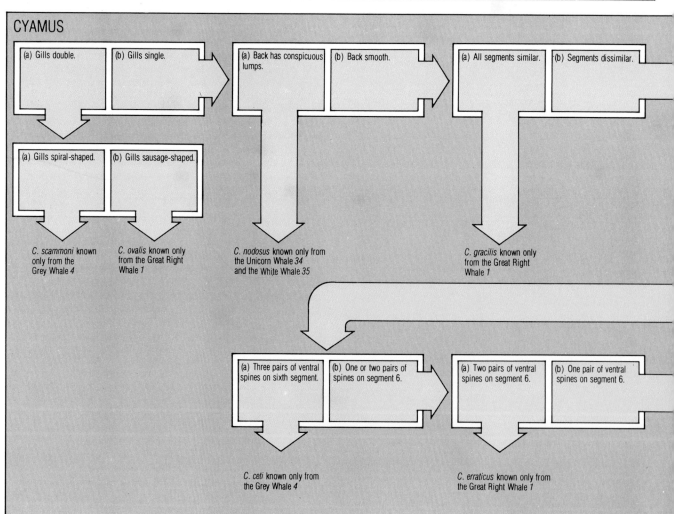

CYAMUS

(a) Gills double.

(b) Gills single.

(a) Back has conspicuous lumps.

(b) Back smooth.

(a) All segments similar.

(b) Segments dissimilar.

(a) Gills spiral-shaped.

(b) Gills sausage-shaped.

C. scammoni known only from the Grey Whale *4*

C. ovalis known only from the Great Right Whale *1*

C. nodosus known only from the Unicorn Whale *34* and the White Whale *35*

C. gracilis known only from the Great Right Whale *1*

(a) Three pairs of ventral spines on sixth segment.

(b) One or two pairs of spines on segment 6.

(a) Two pairs of ventral spines on segment 6.

(b) One pair of ventral spines on segment 6.

C. ceti known only from the Grey Whale *4*

C. erraticus known only from the Great Right Whale *1*

their sharp lower teeth into its flesh and then allow the slip-stream produced by the larger animal's motion through the water to swing them around, slicing out a perfect circle. This accounts for both the deep round scars and the incomplete, more superficial, semicircles.

Bones

Many cetaceans strand on remote beaches and by the time their bodies are discovered they have been reduced to skeletons. From these it is possible to make a positive identification of the species involved. In fact it is often necessary to reduce many dead cetaceans to this condition deliberately by means of controlled museum preparation in order to make such an identification.

The most simple systems of classification depend on characteristics of the baleen (see page 62) and the teeth (see page 62). More refined taxonomy deals largely with differences in the skull. The many species of Odontocete show variations in the arrangement of bones in the head, which depend on the extent to which the animals have become specialized for using sonar. These variations are apparent in the skull drawings which accompany each of the genera and many of the species in this guide. There are of course specific differences in other bones, but the post-cranial skeletons of all whales have much in common.

Cetaceans spend their entire lives in water and their skeletons are generally very much lighter than those of terrestrial animals of the same size would be. Bone forms only 17 per cent of the total body weight of even the largest Blue Whales (*Balaenoptera musculus 6*). Whale bones (not to be confused with 'whalebone', which is baleen) can be identified very easily by the fact that they consist of only a thin shell of compact outer material covering a spongy inner structure

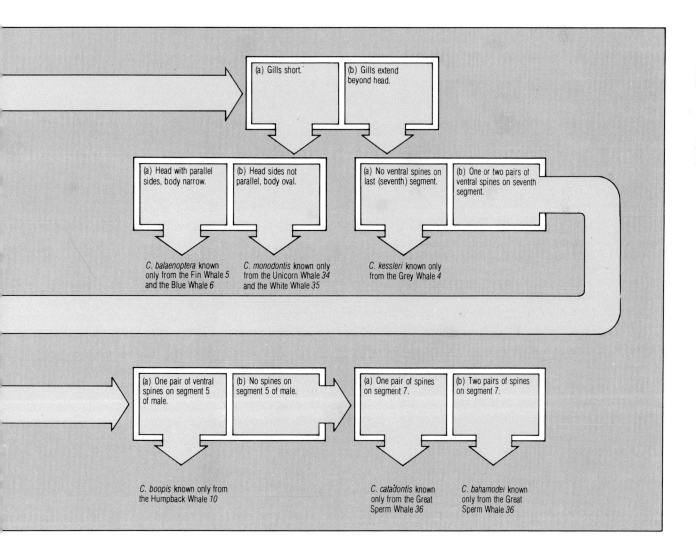

(a) Gills short.

(b) Gills extend beyond head.

(a) Head with parallel sides, body narrow.

(b) Head sides not parallel, body oval.

(a) No ventral spines on last (seventh) segment.

(b) One or two pairs of ventral spines on seventh segment.

C. balaenoptera known only from the Fin Whale *5* and the Blue Whale *6*

C. monodontis known only from the Unicorn Whale *34* and the White Whale *35*

C. kessleri known only from the Grey Whale *4*

(a) One pair of ventral spines on segment 5 of male.

(b) No spines on segment 5 of male.

(a) One pair of spines on segment 7.

(b) Two pairs of spines on segment 7.

C. boopis known only from the Humpback Whale *10*

C. catodontis known only from the Great Sperm Whale *36*

C. bahamodei known only from the Great Sperm Whale *36*

made up of delicate webs with large spaces between them. In life these spaces are filled with marrow which is unusually fatty in all cetaceans. A third of a whale's total oil yield comes from its bones, ensuring that even the densest parts of its body have a relatively low specific gravity. Whale bone often floats.

The long-necked giraffe and the no-necked whale both have seven vertebrae in their necks, but in whales the vertebrae have become compressed or even fused into a single rigid unit. There is a complete range of specialization amongst living whales:

All seven vertebrae free	Fin Whale (*Balaenoptera physalus 5*). Unicorn Whale (*Monodon monoceros 34*).
Two fused	Common Dolphin (*Delphinus delphis 75*).
Three fused	Pygmy Killer Whale (*Feresa attenuata 53*).
Four fused	Great Killer Whale (*Orcinus orca 51*).
Five fused	Finless Porpoise (*Neophocaena phocaenoides 47*).
Six fused	Longfin Pilot Whale (*Globicephala melaena 49*).
All seven vertebrae fused	Dwarf Sperm Whale (*Kogia simus 38*). Great Right Whale (*Balaena glacialis 1*).

Those whales with the greatest number of free neck vertebrae obviously have the most mobile necks. Common Dolphins and the river dolphins can move their heads to an angle of up to 45 degrees away from their trunks, but the large heavy heads of pilot and sperm whales are almost immobile. Even those species that can move their necks are restricted to an up-and-down motion, because no cetaceans have a joint between the atlas (first cervical) and the axis (second cervical) vertebrae. The reason for this rigidity lies in the demands of underwater locomotion: a short neck not only adds to the streamlining of the body, but in a dense medium avoids dislocation of the neck during rapid swimming. All propulsion is provided by a whale's tail, and without such rigidity the head, particularly if it were large, would be likely to flop around and slow progress through the water.

This rigidity extends to the thorax and abdomen. Most cetaceans lack joints or articulating surfaces between their thoracic and lumbar vertebrae, and many have processes which interlock with the bones in front of and behind them. In addition, running along the length of the body directly beneath the vertebral column, is a powerful ligament specifically designed to prevent the spine from sagging.

The most obvious departure from the normal terrestrial mammal pattern is that the lumbar (waist) region is greatly enlarged; here the powerful tail muscles are attached. The area available for muscle attachment has been increased by enlarging the vertebrae and their processes and by adding a few extra bones to the column. The Unicorn Whale (*Monodon monoceros 34*) is relatively unspecialized in having less than ten lumbar vertebrae (humans have just five), but the fast-swimming Northern Rightwhale Dolphin (*Lissodelphis borealis 63*) may have as many as thirty.

The caudal (tail) vertebrae of cetaceans are also better developed than those in many mammals. They are usually flat and disc-shaped and can be distinguished from the lumbar bones by the presence of special V-shaped bones lying directly beneath the vertebrae, shielding blood vessels and providing additional areas for muscle attachment. The muscles which raise a whale's tail (and provide most of its propulsion) are attached to the tall, broad, vertical spines on the dorsal surface of the caudal vertebrae. Many terrestrial mammals have similar (though smaller) fittings and need nothing more, because once the tail has been raised to defecate or swat a fly it falls down again under the influence of gravity. In the water, however, whales need an antagonistic set of muscles to pull the tail down in preparation for the next propulsive up-stroke.

Caudal vertebrae which extend to the flukes of the tail have no processes or chevrons. The flukes are supported entirely by ligament and fibrous tissue. None of the caudal vertebrae is as rigid as those in the rest of the spinal column. The great mass of muscle which moves the tail also controls the shape and position of the flukes. A complex net of long and powerful tendons fans out from the lumbar region to keep tension and rigidity in the fibres of the flukes and makes it possible for them to twist at an angle to the rest of the tail, rotating the caudal vertebrae about their longitudinal axes.

The Piked Whale (*Balaenoptera acutorostrata 7*) has transverse and dorsal processes on its lumbar vertebrae which are of approximately equal length; the Northern Bottlenose Whale (*Hyperoodon ampullatus 15*) has a very long dorsal process and short transverse ones; while the Southern Rightwhale Dolphin (*Lissodelphis peronii 62*) has wide transverse processes and a very low dorsal one. From the front these dorsal processes have the following shapes:

(a) Piked Whale (b) Northern Bottlenose Whale (c) Southern Right Whale Dolphin

Most whales have twelve or thirteen pairs of ribs, but a few species have several more. For some unknown reason, the Pygmy Right Whale (*Caperea marginata 3*) has seventeen pairs of very broad ribs. Some ribs articulate with the transverse processes of the thoracic vertebrae with single simple heads that give them great freedom of movement, but in many species of toothed whales a number of rib pairs (usually those nearest the neck) still have the more primitive and complex double heads. These numbers are consistent and can be used as an additional aid to identification.

In most mammals the lower ends of at least some of the ribs are connected to a sternum (breastbone). Amongst baleen whales the sternum is small and consists of a single bone which articulates only the first pair of ribs. In toothed whales the sternum consists of three or more separate bony elements and is connected to at least three pairs of ribs by additional struts known as sternal ribs. In the beaked whale (Ziphiidae) and sperm whale (Physeteridae) families these ribs are cartilaginous, but in almost all other toothed whales they are bony. The species which dive deepest need to have the greatest freedom, allowing their thoracic cages to collapse completely under pressure, thus preventing narcosis and the 'bends'.

The scapulae (shoulder blades) which form the rest of the pectoral girdle are typical broad, flattened, fan-shaped structures in all cetaceans. The flippers of cetaceans have the same basic structure as the forelimbs of most other mammals. They consist of humerus, radius and ulna bones, but these have become so short and squat that the elbow now lies flush with the surfaces of the body. The upper arm (humerus) is attached to the scapula in the normal way, but is buried in the blubber.

Ancient whales all had five digits and many of the modern ones still retain this basic number in the common integument of their paddle-shaped flippers, but some have now lost their thumbs. All the rorqual whales and a few toothed whales have only four fingers. In most mammals (including ourselves) every finger has three phalanges and the thumb has two. In many cetaceans, however, the central digits have a large number of bones. This is most pronounced in the Longfin Pilot Whale (*Globicephala melaena 49*) whose second and third fingers have fourteen and eleven phalanges respectively.

Generally speaking cetaceans have lost their hindlimbs and pelvic girdles altogether, but some of the baleen whales retain rudiments of both. These are not connected with any other part of the skeleton, but simply float freely in the flesh just in front of the anus. Blue Whales (*Balaenoptera musculus 6*) often have a vestigial pelvis with a tiny rudimentary piece of the old femur still attached to it. In the Bowhead Whale (*Balaena mysticetus 2*) there may also be a tiny tibia. In a few toothed whales, such as the North Sea Beaked Whale (*Mesoplodon bidens 27*), the vestige of a pelvis is present only in males, who seem to use it now to anchor muscles attached to the penis.

MYSTICETE

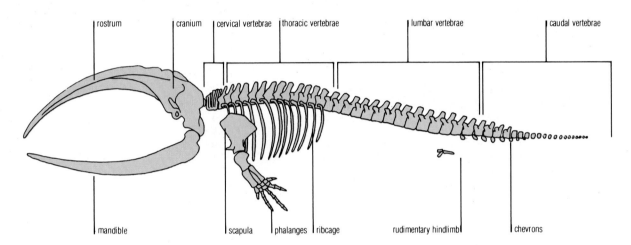

ODONTOCETE

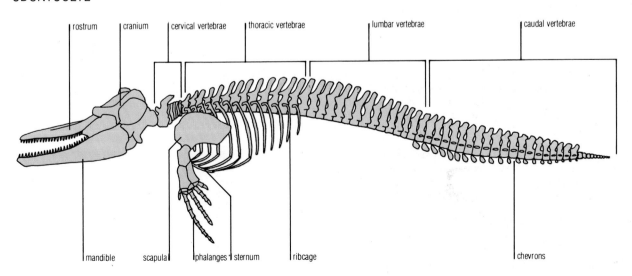

CHART OF VERTEBRAL FORMULAE
Average number of vertebrae

No.	SPECIES	CERVICAL	THORACIC	LUMBAR	CAUDAL	TOTAL
1	Great Right Whale (Balaena glacialis)	7	14	12	24	57
2	Bowhead Whale (Balaena mysticetus)	7	13	12	23	55
3	Pygmy Right Whale (Caperea marginata)	7	17	2	15	41
4	Grey Whale (Eschrichtius robustus)	7	14	12	23	56
5	Fin Whale (Balaenoptera physalus)	7	15	15	27	64
6	Blue Whale (Balaenoptera musculus)	7	15	15	27	64
7	Piked Whale (Balaenoptera acutorostrata)	7	11	12	18	48
8	Sei Whale (Balaenoptera borealis)	7	14	13	23	57
9	Tropical Whale (Balaenoptera edeni)	7	13	13	21	54
10	Humpback Whale (Megaptera novaeangliae)	7	14	10	22	53
11	Tasman Whale (Tasmacetus shepherdi)	7	11	14	17	49
12	Northern Fourtooth Whale (Berardius bairdii)	7	11	12	19	49
13	Southern Fourtooth Whale (Berardius arnuxii)	7	11	12	18	48
14	Goosebeak Whale (Ziphius cavirostris)	7	9	11	20	47
15	Northern Bottlenose Whale (Hyperoodon ampullatus)	7	9	12	18	46
16	Southern Bottlenose Whale (Hyperoodon planifrons)	7	9	12	18	46
17	Indopacific Beaked Whale (Indopacetus pacificus)	—	—	—	—	—
18	Skew Beaked Whale (Mesoplodon hectori)	—	—	—	—	—
19	Wonderful Beaked Whale (Mesoplodon mirus)	7	10	11	18	46
20	Gulf Stream Beaked Whale (Mesoplodon europaeus)	7	10	11	20	47
21	Arch Beaked Whale (Mesoplodon carlhubbsi)	7	11	9	19	46
22	Japanese Beaked Whale (Mesoplodon ginkgodens)	7	10	10	21	48
23	Scamperdown Beaked Whale (Mesoplodon grayi)	7	10	11	20	48
24	Bering Sea Beaked Whale (Mesoplodon stejnegeri)	7	10	10	19	46
25	Splaytooth Beaked Whale (Mesoplodon bowdoini)	7	10	10	20	47
26	Dense Beaked Whale (Mesoplodon densirostris)	7	11	9	20	47
27	North Sea Beaked Whale (Mesoplodon bidens)	7	10	9	20	46
28	Straptooth Beaked Whale (Mesoplodon layardi)	7	10	10	19	46
29	Ganges River Dolphin (Platanista gangetica)	7	11	8	25	51
30	Indus River Dolphin (Platanista minor)	7	11	8	25	51
31	Yangtze River Dolphin (Lipotes vexillifer)	7	11	8	19	45
32	Amazon River Dolphin (Inia geoffrensis)	7	13	5	17	42
33	La Plata River Dolphin (Pontoporia blainvillei)	7	10	7	16	40
34	Unicorn Whale (Monodon monoceros)	7	12	8	27	54
35	White Whale (Delphinapterus leucas)	7	12	8	26	53
36	Great Sperm Whale (Physeter macrocephalus)	7	11	8	24	50
37	Pygmy Sperm Whale (Kogia breviceps)	7	13	9	27	56
38	Dwarf Sperm Whale (Kogia sinus)	7	13	9	27	56

No.	SPECIES	CERVICAL	THORACIC	LUMBAR	CAUDAL	TOTAL
39	Roughtooth Dolphin (Steno bredanensis)	7	13	16	31	67
40	Indopacific Humpback Dolphin (Sousa chinensis)	7	12	10	22	51
41	Atlantic Humpback Dolphin (Sousa teuszii)	7	12	10	24	53
42	Estuarine Dolphin (Sotalia fluviatilis)	7	12	11	26	56
43	Common Porpoise (Phocoena phocoena)	7	14	13	30	64
44	Black Porpoise (Phocoena spinipinnis)	7	13	16	32	68
45	Spectacled Porpoise (Phocoena dioptrica)	7	13	16	32	68
46	Gulf Porpoise (Phocoena sinus)	7	12	11	32	62
47	Finless Porpoise (Neophocaena phocaenoides)	7	14	13	30	64
48	Spray Porpoise (Phocoenoides dalli)	7	16	26	48	97
49	Longfin Pilot Whale (Globicephala melaena)	7	11	13	28	59
50	Shortfin Pilot Whale (Globicephala macrorhynchus)	7	11	12	27	57
51	Great Killer Whale (Orcinus orca)	7	12	10	23	52
52	False Killer Whale (Pseudorca crassida)	7	10	10	23	50
53	Pygmy Killer Whale (Feresa attenuata)	7	12	16	33	68
54	Melonhead Whale (Peponocephala electra)	7	14	17	44	82
55	Whitebeak Dolphin (Lagenorhynchus albirostris)	7	15	26	44	92
56	Atlantic Whiteside Dolphin (Lagenorhynchus acutus)	7	15	20	40	82
57	Pacific Whiteside Dolphin (Lagenorhynchus obliquidens)	7	14	24	34	79
58	Dusky Dolphin (Lagenorhynchus obscurus)	7	15	23	36	81
59	Hourglass Dolphin (Lagenorhynchus cruciger)	7	15	22	34	78
60	Blackchin Dolphin (Lagenorhynchus australis)	7	15	24	35	81
61	Shortsnout Dolphin (Lagenodelphis hosei)	7	14	21	39	81
62	Southern Rightwhale Dolphin (Lissodelphis peronii)	7	14	29	38	88
63	Northern Rightwhale Dolphin (Lissodelphis borealis)	7	14	29	38	88
64	Piebald Dolphin (Cephalorhynchus commersonii)	7	12	24	20	63
65	Chilean Dolphin (Cephalorhynchus eutroupia)	7	12	24	20	63
66	Benguela Dolphin (Cephalorhynchus heavisidii)	7	12	23	22	64
67	New Zealand Dolphin (Cephalorhynchus hectori)	7	12	23	23	65
68	Grey Dolphin (Grampus griseus)	7	12	18	31	68
69	Snubfin Dolphin (Orcaella brevirostris)	7	14	14	28	63
70	Spinner Dolphin (Stenella longirostris)	7	15	20	36	78
71	Helmet Dolphin (Stenella clymene)	—	—	—	—	—
72	Striped Dolphin (Stenella coeruleoalba)	7	15	22	35	79
73	Bridled Dolphin (Stenella attenuata)	7	15	19	37	78
74	Spotted Dolphin (Stenella plagiodon)	7	15	19	36	77
75	Common Dolphin (Delphinus delphi)	7	14	21	32	74
76	Bottlenose Dolphin (Tursiops truncatus)	7	14	15	29	65

5
Natural History
Swimming

Most cetaceans swimming at the surface leave a slick of smooth water. This may be partly caused by oils in the animal's skin or nasal passages, but it is most often produced by vortices set up by motion. When following a whale or dolphin that has dived and is swimming out of sight not too far below the surface, it is often possible to track it. Each time it beats its tail, a volume of water spills up and produces a distinct localized calm patch.

Unlike seals and walrus, cetaceans are powered completely by their tails. The flippers are involved only in steering and balance, and in some species are actually folded away into 'flipper pockets' or depressions in the body wall while swimming. The main locomotor muscles lie along the upper side of the spinal column, pulling the broad tail flukes up against water resistance in the power stroke. Another smaller set of muscles beneath the tailstock returns the flukes in a passive downstroke. At slow speeds the flukes sweep up and down in broad measured strokes, but at high speeds the amplitude of their movement is small. Common Dolphins (*Delphinus delphis* 75) travelling at 38 kph (20 knots), and Fin Whales (*Balaenoptera physalus* 5) at 19 kph (10 knots) both beat their tails about twice a second.

When swimming fast, many cetaceans jump clear out of the water while breathing. There are sound hydrodynamic reasons for this. If a whale exposes part of its body in bringing the blowhole to the surface, it meets maximum turbulence and drag. By jumping clear out of the water it can maintain speed without expending too much energy.

The speed of a body in water depends on the relationship between its energy output and the resistance it has to overcome. Large bodies encounter more resistance than small ones of the same shape, but not in direct proportion to the increase in size. The bigger animals also have proportionately greater volume and therefore greater resources of energy to draw on. At slow speeds the effort required is no real problem but resistance increases dramatically with acceleration. In a large whale there is enough muscle to drive the body at speeds in excess of 30 kph (16 knots). In theory the smaller dolphin does not have sufficient meat on it to do so; GRAY (1936) calculated that it needs seven times as much muscle as it possesses; yet dolphins still persist in travelling at speeds greater than 45 kph (24 knots).

The resolution of the paradox is simple. It is based on the fallacious assumption that the power needed to move a dolphin is the same as that needed to move a rigid body of the same size and shape. A living dolphin may have a relatively rigid spinal column, but its surface is far from stiff. It has properties which add to the efficiency of its streamlining in ways we still poorly understand.

When a fluid flows past a body, particles nearest to the body are slowed down and in their turn retard the motion of particles in layers farther away. This is what produces drag; if it is severe enough, it sets up eddies and turbulence which add enormously to resistance. Perfect streamlining should produce no turbulence and result in so little drag that the fluid layers glide smoothly over each other in a pattern known as laminar flow. No man-made vessel has ever achieved such perfection, but it seems that the dolphin has. No dolphin model, no matter how accurate, nor even the dead animal itself towed through the water, can reproduce this effect in the laboratory, but high-speed photographs of dolphins underwater show that their shapes are constantly changing (ESSAPIAN 1955). At speed the skin surface is thrown into fleeting folds and ripples which seem to be produced not by direct muscular action but in response to changes in pressure on different parts of the body. If the ridges correspond to areas of reduced pressure, and the indentations to localized increases in pressure on the skin, they could inhibit turbulence as fast as it begins.

There may also be microscopic effects. Underneath the smooth surface of the skin in most cetaceans there is a well-developed system of dermal ridges, something like those which produce our fingerprints (PURVES 1963). On the dolphin, these run obliquely upwards on the back, fore and aft along the flank, and are almost absent on the belly. This corresponds with the pattern of water flow and probably not only helps counteract turbulence but also provides propulsive force by accelerating the movement of fluid over the back. At high speed the resulting differences in pressure between back and belly could provide substantial lift.

Another boost to locomotion may be provided by lubrication. Water flows more easily through tubes when chemicals have been added to make the liquid slimy. Fish secrete mucus which covers their skin and oils their way through the water. The most copious producers of mucus are predators like tuna and bonito, which are amongst the fastest animals in the ocean. Cells in the smooth cetacean skin secrete droplets of oil that could produce similar changes in their boundary layers.

Any of these effects and others still undiscovered could be responsible for defeating Gray's paradox. Probably a combination of factors gives the oceanic dolphins their extraordinary hydrodynamic advantage.

Great Killer Whales (*Orcinus orca* 51) have been timed at 38 kph (20.5 knots), Bridled Dolphins (*Stenella attenuata* 73) at 43 kph (23.2 knots) and Shortfin Pilot Whales (*Globicephala macrorhynchus* 50) at 49 kph (26.5 knots). Acceleration was very rapid and under pressure the true maximum speeds of the fastest cetaceans are probably far higher, perhaps even in excess of 56 kph (30 knots).

Small cetaceans and the young of larger species often get free or assisted rides. Calves frequently swim *en echelon* with their mothers, just below and beside the dorsal fins of the larger animals. By placing themselves slightly behind the point of maximum diameter of their parents, the young enjoy what is known as the Bernoulli Effect. The speed of water flow in the narrow channel between their bodies is increased, and the pressure in that area is correspondingly decreased, which brings about a positive attraction between them, increasing thrust (or decreasing drag) on the smaller body; the result could be more than a 25 per cent increase in efficiency (LANG 1966).

Some small cetaceans get a free ride by taking up their position directly in front of a large whale and enjoying the positive thrust provided by its motion. We have seen Bottlenose Dolphins (*Tursiops truncatus 76*) doing this with Great Right Whales (*Balaena glacialis 1*). The action is similar to surfing in that the dolphin needs only to position itself in the forward slope of an advancing wave and plane, but this simple explanation cannot account for what actually happens (WOODCOCK 1948); dolphins riding the bow wave of a ship can be anywhere from 30 cm to 2 m (1–7 ft) away from the stem, are often stacked several layers deep and can frequently travel some distance to the side of the bow (HAYES 1953). Scholander (1958) discovered that a dolphin could be pushed along by burying its flukes in the forward portion of the wave and that, in his experiment, the most effective posture was to bend the flukes up so that their blades were set at an angle of 28° from the horizontal. The wave shape was such that water was being thrust not only forward, but upward and outward, so that a dolphin could roll over on its side or travel out of the direct line of the ship and still enjoy its benefits. Different kinds of vessel produce different patterns of thrust at their bows (NORRIS & PRESCOTT 1961). A slow-moving boat with a deep, blunt prow produces a wave whose pressure is directed predominantly downward, and to take best advantage of this, dolphins need to ride fairly deep, in front or just slightly to the side of the vessel, and to lean up into the pressure field by putting their tail flukes downwards.

A faster boat with a shallow draft and sharper prow forces water upwards in a high wave. To take advantage of this, dolphins need to tilt their flukes up and to place their bodies in an angle of positive attack, much like that of a surfer; the best lift is experienced to the side, or even slightly behind, the bow.

Bowriders choose the point where the force due to the pressure field produced by the ship equals the drag on their bodies; they must sense these pressures directly and seek out the spot which provides the maximum advantage (FEJER & BACKUS 1960). If it is occupied they may jostle for position, but most commonly the dolphins simply change the point of equilibrium by altering their own body shape to change the effects of drag; a group of dolphins riding together all adopt slightly different and changing postures, each placing itself at its own null point. In a choppy sea which sets the ship pitching, the thrust becomes too erratic to be useful and the cetaceans give up and leave the bow altogether.

Modern high-speed vessels tax the dolphins' ability to the full and it is difficult not to assume that they enjoy the challenge. The faster the boat, the more it is possible to hear the bowriders' excited high-pitched squeals.

The bow of a moving vessel, however, is one of the best places for getting a close look at many otherwise elusive cetaceans and the fact that they come to the bow at all can be useful in identification.

The following species often bowride:

La Plata River Dolphin (*Pontoporia blainvillei 33*)
Roughtooth Dolphin (*Steno bredanensis 39*)
False Killer Whale (*Pseudorca crassidens 52*)
Spray Porpoise (*Phocoenoides dalli 48*)
Whitebeak Dolphin (*Lagenorhynchus albirostris 55*)
Pacific Whiteside Dolphin (*Lagenorhynchus obliquidens 57*)
Dusky Dolphin (*Lagenorhynchus obscurus 58*)
Blackchin Dolphin (*Lagenorhynchus australis 60*)
New Zealand Dolphin (*Cephalorhynchus hectori 67*)
Spinner Dolphin (*Stenella longirostris 70*)
Striped Dolphin (*Stenella coeruleoalba 72*)
Spotted Dolphin (*Stenella plagiodon 74*)
Common Dolphin (*Delphinus delphis 75*)
Bottlenose Dolphin (*Tursiops truncatus 76*).
  These occasionally do so:
Great Killer Whale (*Orcinus orca 51*)
Common Porpoise (*Phocoena phocoena 43*)
Atlantic Whiteside Dolphin (*Lagenorhynchus acutus 56*)
Hourglass Dolphin (*Lagenorhynchus cruciger 59*)
Grey Dolphin (*Grampus griseus 68*)
Bridled Dolphin (*Stenella attenuata 73*).
  These rarely bowride, but may do so:
Northern Rightwhale Dolphin (*Lissodelphis borealis 63*)
Piebald Dolphin (*Cephalorhynchus commersonii 64*).
  We know of no baleen whale which ever bowrides.

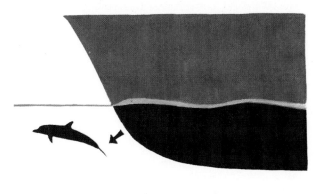

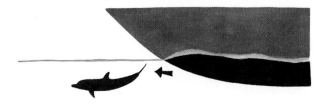

Diagrams of the thrust provided at the bow of ships of different shapes, showing the postures adopted by bowriding dolphin

Breathing

All cetaceans breathe air. The first indication of the presence of a great whale is usually the sight of its 'blow', which not only gives away its position from a great distance, but can also reveal its identity. The blow is a cloud of vapour produced largely by condensation when warm breath comes into contact with cooler air. It is naturally distinct in polar areas, but is equally dramatic in warmer climates, partly because the air in a whale's lungs is expelled very quickly and when a gas which has been under pressure expands, it cools. This process of adiabatic cooling results in condensation, even in the tropics. Another factor which may contribute to the visibility of a blow is the possibility that the exhaled air carries with it particles of a foamy emulsion which fills the nasal cavities and sinuses, where it probably absorbs excess nitrogen. This would also help account for the distinctly ripe and fishy smell of a whale's breath.

The height of blow depends partly on the size of the animal, but there are also consistent differences between the columns of vapour produced by great whales of separate species. The baleen whales have double blowholes and in those relatively slow-moving species which feed near the surface the blast is sufficiently leisurely for the streams of exhaled air to remain distinct, producing a double or V-shaped spout.

All the rorqual whales (Balaenopteridae) have single spouts, which can be difficult to tell apart, particularly on a windy day, but it is sometimes possible to identify the species from its blast alone.

A Fin Whale exchanges 3,000 times a human's meagre volume of air in less than two seconds, half the time we take. All the spent air is exhaled under enormous pressure from the diaphragm and chest muscles in a blow which lasts little more than half a second. The next inhalation follows immediately, lasting about a second and producing a splendid cool, round tubular sound.

All the rorqual whales are surface-feeders and do not dive very deep or for very long, and so three or four breaths at the surface are usually sufficient to replenish their oxygen debt before the next five- or ten-minute dive. Sperm whales on the other hand seldom dive for less than thirty minutes at a time and so spend longer at the surface and breathe more often, roughly once for each minute they spend underwater. A whale which has been seen to breathe four times a minute for ten minutes can be expected to surface again, in almost the same place, roughly forty minutes later.

Despite the fact that some species submerge for more than an hour, surviving all this time on a single spell of breathing, their lungs are not particularly large. Human lungs form 7 per cent of body weight, but in no cetacean is the proportion greater than 3 per cent. The difference lies in relative efficiency. We inhale no more than half a litre (about one pint) at a time, despite the fact that our lungs have a volume of more than four litres (a little over a gallon). Cetaceans fill their lungs to capacity every time, and they change up to 90 per cent of this air supply with each breath.

This alone cannot account for a whale's ability to hold its breath for up to twenty times as long as any terrestrial animal.

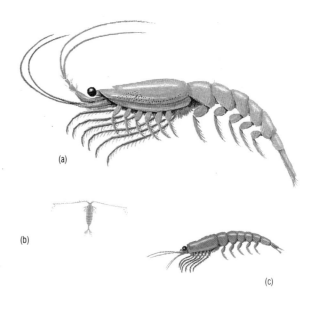

(a) Lifesize Lobster Krill *Euphausia superba*
(b) Enlarged Planktonic Form *Calanus sp.*
(c) Lifesize Krill-like *Thysanoessa sp.*

Humans carry some oxygen dissolved in their blood, but a diving whale goes down with a huge reserve (over 40 per cent of its total oxygen supply) locked up in its muscles. Whale meat is so full of oxygen-rich myoglobin that in some species it is almost black in colour.

Sperm and Bottlenose whales (*Hyperoodon* spp.), which dive for the longest periods, also go down to the most astonishing depths and return rapidly from pressures as great as 300 atmospheres without suffering from any of the compressed-air diseases that can kill human divers. Whales do not breathe compressed air but go down with just one lungful, which holds scarcely enough nitrogen to produce problems such as the 'bends', but they avoid the risk of absorbing even this small amount by means of an extraordinary adaptation. As the pressure increases, they simply allow their chests to cave in, so that below 100 m (328 ft) the lungs have collapsed and all the air they contain has been forced into the windpipe and nasal passages where no further nitrogen can be absorbed. Beyond this critical point, they can go on diving in complete safety for as long as they can survive on the oxygen already in their tissues. For the Great Sperm Whale (*Physeter macrocephalus 36*) this can mean 90 minutes or more at depths of up to 3,000 m (10,000 ft).

Whales, however, have nothing left over for emergencies. Humans that normally exchange little more than 15 per cent of their lung capacity can, under stress, take a deep breath and pick up enough extra oxygen for a special effort. Whales whose lungs are already filled to capacity cannot do this. They can only get more air by breathing more rapidly, which means coming to the surface more frequently.

Cetaceans under pressure also 'pant', but never with their mouths open. They cannot breathe through their mouths. The food and air passages, particularly in toothed whales, have become totally distinct by a special development of the larynx. In most mammals a muscular epiglottis closes the windpipe while food or drink is passing. Water under pressure could easily be forced into the lungs of deep-diving animals who open their mouths to feed at depths. Most cetaceans, therefore, have an epiglottis which reaches right across the throat and plugs directly into the inner end of the nasal passages, effectively sealing off the air system from the digestive system.

The blowhole is surrounded by thick lips of highly elastic tissue which normally keep it tightly closed. In baleen whales there are two blowholes lying behind a raised ridge or 'cut-water', which prevents their being flooded during breathing; in Great Sperm Whales (*Physeter macrocephalus 36*) the single blowhole is S-shaped; and in most other toothed whales it is a simple slit or crescent. The blowhole is only opened to breathe, and in every case this is a deliberate act.

Feeding

Water conducts heat twenty-seven times more effectively than air, and an underwater animal further accelerates cooling by swimming. A human loses enough heat to become unconscious after being submerged for only three hours in water at 15°C (60°F), and after fifteen minutes in water close to freezing point. Cetaceans deal with this problem partly by their insulating blubber and partly by their sheer size; the larger an animal, the smaller its surface area, and therefore its heat loss, in relation to its body weight. Big animals lose relatively little heat compared with small ones and therefore need relatively less food. Young whales take in up to 13 per cent of their body weight each day, but in adults of the larger species this falls to less than 3 per cent.

On land the largest animals are all herbivorous. They have solved their nutritional needs by going to the lowest and most productive end of the food chain and eating plants which get their energy directly from the sun. At sea plant foods are less accessible and cetaceans are all totally carnivorous, despite reports to the contrary (see *Sousa teuszii 41*). At the base of the marine food pyramid are creatures which are numerous enough to burst into seasonal 'bloom' like terrestrial vegetation. These are the 'drifters', the plankton, and they nourish most of the largest whales.

Water cooled by Antarctic ice sinks to the seabed and slides on to the ocean floors, while warmer water flows in the opposite direction and wells up at the Antarctic convergence, bringing sediment and nutrient to the surface. In the long, sunny days of the southern summer this grows a bountiful crop of marine algae, which in turn nourish the animal plankton bloom. One thousand kg of phytoplankton produce 100 kg of zooplankton, which in turn become only 10 kg of whale meat. Each hectare (2.47 acres) of southern ocean produces about 1,200 kg (over 1 ton) of animal protein a year (more than twice as productive as the best pasture land) and in the few short summer months of plenty many of the great whales grow fat enough to travel and breed right through the winter without having to eat again.

Therefore it is not surprising that at least one group of cetaceans evolved to deal specifically with plankton. The baleen whales modified their whole front ends to hold and house a sophisticated filter apparatus. They fall into two main groups: 'gulpers' (Blue, Fin, Piked and Humpback), who take huge bites of food and squeeze water out at the sides of their mouths; and the 'skimmers' (Great Right and Bowhead), who swim along with their mouths open, filtering constantly until enough food has accumulated on the baleen to be scraped off and swallowed. Sei and Grey whales do a little bit of both.

The Blue Whale specializes almost totally in the southern hemisphere on krill (*Euphausia superba*), crustaceans with a maximum length of 75 mm (3 inches). They swarm in lens-shaped shoals, anything from a few square metres to several hectares in size, mainly in the upper brightly lit layers of water where phytoplankton are most abundant.

It has been estimated that the big baleen whales were taking roughly 300 million tons of krill from the line of the convergence that encircles the Antarctic continent before they were decimated by whalers earlier this century. Since then there has been a rapid increase of other krill-eaters such as penguins, seals and the little Piked Whales (*Balaenoptera acutorostrata 7*), which elsewhere generally eat shoaling fish.

The smaller diameter of the baleen fringes of Fin Whales (*Balaenoptera physalus 5*) makes it possible for them to exploit the considerably smaller *Thysanoessa*, several species of which abound above submarine ridges just outside the Antarctic area. In lower latitudes and in the northern hemisphere, Fin Whales also take large quantities of fish such as herring, mackerel and capelin.

Humpback Whales have relatively stiff, coarse baleen and feed much as Fin and Blue whales do in high latitudes, but also spend a good deal of their time in shallow water, where they take bottom fauna. The Grey Whale feeds almost entirely on benthic (sitting-at-the-bottom) amphipod crustaceans. Sei Whales have the finest fringes and, though they feed on fish and krill when available, they also eat tiny crustaceans like *Calanus*.

Calanoid crustaceans are generally found at lower latitudes than either *Euphausia* or *Thysanoessa*, a fact reflected in the distribution of the Sei Whale, which seldom ventures as close to the ice as Fin or Blue whales do. The Right and Bowhead whales habitually eat the smallest plankton. They seem to have evolved in the northern hemisphere, where krill are scarce, and to have moved south and begun to extend their diet only comparatively recently.

The Odontocetes grasp their food in various ways with their teeth and include fish-eaters, squid-eaters and flesh-eaters.

The only true flesh-eater is the Great Killer Whale (*Orcinus orca 51*), which consistently feeds on seals and sealions and other cetaceans. There are reports of Killers consuming Common Porpoises, Spray Porpoises, Striped Dolphins and bits of Grey and Piked whales.

The pelagic dolphins are typical fish-eaters. They tend to have long beaks with many small sharp teeth well suited for grasping relatively small and slippery prey. Common Dolphins (*Delphinus delphis 75*) and the genus *Stenella* are primarily fish-feeders, but all take squid when it is available.

In teeth and diet they represent a generalized, relatively primitive condition.

The porpoises (Phocoenidae) have developed more specialized spatulate or chisel-shaped teeth that provide an efficient shearing mechanism for eating relatively large smooth fish. The river dolphins (Platanistidae) have some flattened molarlike teeth and eat armoured catfish. Squid-eaters either have just a few teeth at the front of both jaws (pilot whales, *Globicephala* spp.) or no upper teeth at all (the Great Sperm Whale, *Physeter macrocephalus 36*) or have lost all but one or two pairs of teeth on their lower jaws (beaked whales, *Ziphiidae*). Sperm whales manage perfectly well without teeth until they are more than ten years old.

The ancestors of modern whales presumably had normal external ears designed for detecting airborne sounds. In the water these became redundant, because in water sound is picked up as effectively by the skull or jawbones. The ancient whales may have continued to make and respond to airborne sounds, but before long natural selection must have singled out those capable of making sounds that could be useful underwater. At first these were probably simple signal systems, but the speed with which the ancient Archaeocetes were displaced, and the range of acoustic specialization in living species, suggest that they may have gained a very early competitive advantage over the ancestral forms developing some form of echolocatory food-finding system.

The baleen whales produce a wide variety of underwater sounds, including narrow-beam pulses in both Blue and Piked whales, which could be useful in finding food (BEAMISH & MITCHELL 1971 & 1973). Acoustic scans employed by at least these two filter-feeders seem to use frequencies which correlate well with the sizes of their favoured foods. Amongst toothed whales the sonic pulse systems are more directional and there is no doubt that the vast majority of all species use these not only for detecting their food, but for making fine distinctions between food items on the basis of their echoes.

Since most cetaceans swallow their food whole, they lack the powerful jaw muscles present in most terrestrial mammals which chew their food. Without these muscles there is no need for the processes on the jaw to which they were once attached. Baleen whales that do no more than open and close their mouths have jaws reduced to simple arched rods with a slight swelling at the head end. Cetaceans also lack freely-movable tongues. Those of some toothed whales have short free tips, but in baleen whales the tongue is nothing but a massive swelling (in an adult Blue Whale it can weigh as much as a full-grown elephant) which covers the bottom of the mouth.

The tongue in some toothed whales is very brightly coloured. The Great Killer Whale (*Orcinus orca 51*) and the False Killer Whale (*Pseudorca crassidens 52*) both have vivid pink-and-white mouths which may have something to do with attracting prey. It is possible that shiny teeth could act as lures in the same way as the dangling tassels of angler fish, and it has been suggested that some deep divers such as the Great Sperm Whale (*Physeter macrocephalus 36*) may have bioluminescent organisms living on or around their teeth which glow to attract squid in the darkness of the abyss (GASKIN 1967).

Social Behaviour

One difficulty with cetacean social behaviour is that it is hard to get any clear idea of the boundaries involved. Cetologists may define the size and shape of the community characteristic of a given species; this gives some idea of the degree of sociability, but it is at best a very rough estimate. Our whole notion of 'herds' amongst cetaceans is artificial (PAYNE 1971). It could be totally inappropriate for animals which are predominantly acoustic. Whales that appear to be travelling alone could well be part of a social unit whose other members are out of our sight but not beyond the whales' own hearing.

Fin Whales (*Balaenoptera physalus 5*), for instance, produce a low-frequency sound at 20 Hz which is distinctly audible, even to humans, at a distance of 75 km (46 miles). The speed of sound in water varies directly with temperature and pressure, decreasing with depth until it reaches a band of water of higher temperature, which in polar waters may occur near the surface but in low latitudes is most often found at depths of around 1,100 m (3,600 ft). In such bands the speed of sound increases again and its range is multiplied enormously, transmitted for great distances without much acoustic loss, like a signal in a submarine cable. The 20-Hz Fin Whale signals can under these circumstances easily travel for 840 km (520 miles). Other frequencies may travel even further.

Acoustic signals are thought of as bringing individuals together, perhaps for mating, but could equally well be a way of keeping a group spread out. Payne suggests that the great whales commonly have what he calls 'range herds', which may span an entire ocean; the 20-Hz sound signal loses no energy by reflection off the sea floor and has very low attenuation with distance, losing only 3 decibels over 9,000 km (5,600 miles), and lies below the level of storm-generated noise. It has provided Fin Whales with direct access to, and contact with, others of their kind on the other side of an ocean, at least until propellor-driven ships began to foul the open channels with a high level of interference in the form of ambient 20-cycle sound.

Baleen whales tend to form loose aggregations, coalescing at certain seasons into more closely knit breeding groups which are involved in intense social activity. Amongst toothed whales there is a complete range of social structure, from the beaked whales (Ziphiidae), most of which are evidently solitary, to the true oceanic dolphins (Delphinidae), which may form congregations of over 100,000 individuals; in between, Stenidae, Phocoenidae and Globicephalidae form smaller groups ranging from six to sixty individuals.

Large groups are heterogenous, but many of the smaller ones can be separated into three types on a demographic basis (EVANS & BASTIAN 1969). The first of these is the *nuclear group* consisting of a single adult male, who may be accompanied by a female. The second is the larger *nursery group* of a number of adult females and their young. The third is the *bachelor group* which contains a variable number of adult or sub-adult males. The triple array is an arrangement common to many ungulates in which the males remain apart from the harem and nursery organizations except during the breeding season. The resemblance may have its basis in ecology. Both cetaceans and ungulates 'graze' or 'browse' over a wide area in which food is patchily distributed. Under these circumstances, it is advantageous to break the breeding community up into smaller, more viable, more mobile groups.

With the essentially matriarchal (OHSUMI 1971) Great Sperm Whales (*Physeter macrocephalus 36*) the fundamental unit is the nursery group of between ten and twenty mothers, nursing young and immature calves of both sexes. This group is joined in autumn by fully grown males who return from polar feeding grounds to take possession of a nursery and turn it into a harem. The females become the centre of sexual behaviour and males fight for and defend the area in their vicinity. Rival males threaten each other with tail slaps, breaching and explosive claps of their jaws. Fighting takes the form of butting, biting and raking with the teeth, with possession of the harem for the duration of the season as the prize. Usually there is only one large adult male in the harem herd, but he may sometimes tolerate the presence of one or two subordinate males.

In communities of small toothed whales there are very rigid social hierarchies. Bateson (1974) studied a community of seven long-beaked *Stenella* dolphins at Sea Life Park in Hawaii. He found that formal organization was most clearly evident in threat behaviour, which was transitive; if A threatened B, he was never threatened back; B threatened C and was never threatened back; C never threatened A. When the dolphins were at ease they circled slowly in a formal vertical pattern, with the most dominant animal nearest the surface and the most subordinate at the deepest level. This pattern has since been confirmed for wild animals.

On the move, small and closely related groups of dolphins adopt well-defined geometric formations, depending on what they are doing. A *navigating formation* is wedge-shaped, with dominant animals – presumably the most skilled and experienced echolocators – in the lead and young animals protected in the centre. When such an array comes up against something unfamiliar, it stops and one of the dominant individuals goes forward alone to reconnoitre. *Parade formations* occur during unimpeded passage through clear water on long journeys and may take the form of open squares, hollow circles or single files. During feeding, formations are usually less formal, but a few species co-operate in special *hunting formations* which are well-defined relationships directed at the capture of certain kinds of food.

Bottlenose Dolphins have been seen feeding in pairs in a tidal creek near Boboy Sound in Georgia (HOESE 1971). They come into the salt-water marsh there at low tide and, working as co-ordinated couples, rush at shoals of small fish in the shallows and sweep them with the force of their combined bow wave up on to a muddy bank. The dolphins then shoot out on to the mud slope themselves, sometimes coming completely clear of the water, snap up the stranded fish and slide back in. Bottlenose Dolphins in the Black Sea have been observed coralling fish with the aid of two or more individuals acting as 'sheepdogs' or sentinels while the rest of the group take turns in feeding (MOROZOV 1970).

Carnivores, because they have to solve problems in the course of making a living, have the most to gain from the development of co-operation and various forms of social assistance during and after the hunt. Great Killer Whales (*Orcinus orca 51*), which feed on other brainy cetaceans, need to be particularly astute and are most often recorded as co-operating. They even organize their groups into respiratory units which ensure that no member is ever breathing alone. Family groups may remain intact for life and also learn to work together in other highly effective ways. They have been seen herding salmon into a tight circle in Blackfish Sound in western Canada and holding them there while each takes a turn in feeding (SPONG 1874). We ourselves have seen a group co-operate in tilting an ice floe in the Antarctic so that the Weddell seal sitting on it was forced to slide down into a carefully positioned waiting mouth on the other side.

There is no doubt that such animals are acting as a group with skill and foresight. Their behaviour may be determined up to a point by instinctive responses to certain kinds of prey, but the techniques employed clearly depend on learning and the practice of particular patterns of co-operation. It is highly refined social behaviour, very far removed from the free-for-all of an attack by predatory fish on a shoal of sardine. Killer Whales in action clearly remain in contact with each other throughout the hunt and, by signal or demonstration, modify their behaviour to take advantage of changes in the situation.

All female cetaceans take great care of their offspring, keeping them under constant surveillance until they are weaned, and continuing to shelter them in times of danger right up to the following pregnancy. If necessary, mothers sometimes even deal out summary punishment. Bottlenose Dolphins have been seen chastising their young by swimming on their backs, lifting the infants with their flippers and holding them wriggling in the air above the surface until they become subdued (TAVOLGA 1966). Frequently other females, particularly those which have not yet borne any young themselves, act as 'nursemaids', taking care of the calves.

Succouring behaviour is less common, but still widespread, and certainly occurs in all cetacean families, and possibly even in all species. CALDWELL & CALDWELL (1966) identify three types. The first, *standing by* a stranded or injured animal, was recorded by Aristotle and was certainly well-known to old whalers who called it 'heaving to' or 'bringing to a slow' and used it to ensure the capture of whole groups of Great Sperm Whales (*Physeter macrocephalus 36*) around an injured member (see page 175). The second is *excitement*, defined as 'evidence of hyperexcitability or distress'. There are many records of harpoon lines bitten in two and boats crushed by excited bystanders. Sometimes the succouring animal places its own body between the attacking boat and the injured individual, or pushes the damaged group member away from the danger (PILLERI & KNUCKEY 1969). The third involves *supporting* an ill or injured animal and helping it to get to the surface to breathe. This is most common in females and probably began with mothers and 'midwives' assisting newborn calves to take their first breath. Later it extended to any individual in difficulty.

The most serious disaster that can befall a cetacean is any incapacity which makes it difficult or impossible to swim and therefore to breathe. Minor injury or concussion, from which a terrestrial animal would normally recover, can be fatal for a cetacean. Under these circumstances, it is hardly surprising that most, if not all, species have a powerful, possibly innate, tendency to come to the aid of others in distress. And it is entirely appropriate that this behaviour pattern should involve the simple invariable response of helping an ailing animal to get to the surface.

One of the stimuli which sparks the response seems to be a distress call. There are several accounts of animals coming to the aid of an individual that was clearly out of sight: for example, a report of a group of Great Sperm Whales turning suddenly to go to the side of another which had been harpooned 5 km (over 3 miles) away (DULLES 1973). In the days before explosive grenades, the whalers knew that a securely harpooned but not badly injured whale was the best possible lure for enticing others within shooting range. They record that this device worked on all Great Sperm Whales inside a circle with a radius of 6 km (ROBBINS 1899).

It is not however necessary for the stricken animal to call for help. On one occasion a Bottlenose Dolphin (*Tursiops truncatus 76*) caught in the wild was being transferred into a holding pen in Florida when it struggled, struck its head on a post and, falling into 2 m of water, sank unconscious to the bottom. Two dolphins already in the pen immediately came to its aid and lifted it to the surface, where it began to breathe. They continued supporting it until it was sufficiently recovered from the injury to swim unassisted (SIEBENALER & CALDWELL 1956).

It seems that supporting behaviour is initiated by the ineffectual struggles or laboured breathing of a drowning animal. A diver in the Caribbean was rescued repeatedly by a group of False Killer Whales (*Pseudorca crassidens 52*) every time they heard him breathing through a slightly waterlogged snorkel (PORTER 1977). There are a number of reports of small cetaceans of several species carrying stillborn calves or dead group-members around until their bodies fell apart from decomposition. These reports raise the suspicion that such behaviour is an automatic pattern which is so important to these aquatic animals that it is built into their basic repertoire and is not subject to control or modification at a higher level. Yet it becomes increasingly difficult, in the face of experiences such as that of George Hunt with a Bottlenose Dolphin called Sissy, to ignore the possibility that some animals, at least, know precisely what they are doing.

'John Lilly wanted to make a film of a dolphin rescuing a human being in the water. So George gets in the water and pretends to be in distress. Sissy comes over and rescues him by pushing him to the side. Lilly is filming this, but when he looks at the camera he finds the cap is still on the lens. So he takes the cap off the lens and sends George back into the water. When George pretends to be in distress again, Sissy beats him up.' (BATESON 1974)

Play occupies a great deal of time in adult and young cetaceans. We all know that play is a pleasurable activity which might imitate some of the serious activities of life but is not concerned with serious goals. It seems to be confined to the higher vertebrates (the birds and mammals) and is particularly associated with those that have large brains and a large capacity for intricate but adaptable behaviour patterns.

A community of Indopacific Humpback Dolphins (*Sousa chinensis 40*) in South Africa on a normal day in a sheltered bay spent three times as long playing as it did feeding (SAAYMAN et al 1972). Amongst young animals the proportion of time spent in play is even higher, with 'toys' such as feathers and stones becoming the focus for long and involved games, but these 'unproductive' activities are by no means confined to immature individuals. There is a wonderful aerial photograph of a bachelor herd of adult male Great Sperm Whales dashing across the surface of the North Pacific in pursuit of one of their number with a full-grown tree grasped crosswise in his mouth like a puppy with a bone (NISHIWAKI 1962).

Many theories of play emphasize its functional aspect, suggesting that it is exploratory, testing patterns of movement and response in ways which prepare an individual for the serious tasks of adult life, but in the ocean elaborate preparations for acquiring food or avoiding predators are not needed.

Cetaceans unquestionably have big brains and the frequency with which they use them in patterns that can only be described as play suggests that they frolic with their minds as readily as they do with their bodies. This tendency toward mental playfulness may in itself have been partly responsible for the enlargement of their brains.

Many captive animals will perform readily for no reward other than the performance itself. Some even do so spontaneously without any training at all. Spinner Dolphins (*Stenella longirostris 70*) characteristically spin about their long axes when leaping into the air. Bottlenose Dolphins (*Tursiops truncatus 76*) never normally do this, but a female placed in a display tank at Marineland of the Pacific with a Spinner Dolphin watched her companion leap to her usual cue just once, and then immediately copied the aerobatic roll (BROWN et al 1966).

Breeding

In most mammals the period of gestation corresponds roughly to the size of the offspring. Horses carry their young for eleven months, rhinoceroses for eighteen months and elephants for twenty-two months. The calves of the great baleen whales are the largest in the world; that of the Blue Whale (*Balaenoptera musculus 6*) may be up to 7.6 m (25 ft) in length and weigh as much as 7,000 kg (8 tons), yet none of their gestation periods is longer than twelve months. Cetacean calves have to be able to fend for themselves from their first breath and so are born with open eyes, alert senses and sufficient muscular coordination to follow their mothers immediately. This combination of a short pregnancy with very rapid development in the womb is expensive in terms of the mothers' energy and there must be good ecological reasons for it. The answer seems to lie in the availability of food.

Animals the size of the big baleen whales are successful only because of the existence of concentrated supplies of planktonic food, and these supplies are intermittent; they 'bloom' roughly once in twelve months. So those periods in the life of a great whale, such as mating, parturition, lactation and weaning, when the greatest demands are made on it, all happen at those times of plenty. Eight of the ten species of baleen whale have gestation periods between ten and twelve months. All of them spend the season of plenty in polar waters, concentrating largely on feeding. Then they return fat and well fed to warmer waters for mating. Pregnant females are once again in peak condition when they return to tropical breeding grounds a year later to give birth and start nursing. A lactation period of roughly six months means that calves are weaned on the feeding grounds where they can eat as much as they need.

The period of gestation in the other species of mysticete, the rare Pygmy Right Whale (*Caperea marginata 3*) and the relatively common Tropical Whale (*Balaenoptera edeni 9*) is unknown. Both live in temperate or warm waters and it is possible that their life histories are not as tightly tied to the annual peaks dictated by polar plankton. A number of female Tropical Whales caught between October and November in the southern hemisphere held embryos at very different stages of development (OHSUMI 1979). This suggests that they have no well-defined breeding season.

Great Sperm Whale (*Physeter macrocephalus 36*) males spend their summers in rich polar waters, but the females remain in lower latitudes. Gestation in this species lasts for fourteen to sixteen months, so that calves are born just after the adult males leave the tropical breeding grounds the following year and peace is restored as harem herds revert to their nursery status. Lactation continues for over a year, which may ensure that females do not ovulate and become impregnated with the first return of the breeding bulls and can devote their full attention to the care and protection of growing young.

Gestation periods amongst the smaller toothed whales vary from eight to sixteen months. Lactation is equally variable, but in general lasts about as long again as the period of pregnancy.

The process of birth in baleen whales has been seen only fleetingly and the evidence suggests that calves may be born head-first in the usual mammalian fashion. Amongst toothed whales, however, a breech presentation seems to be more normal; in all cases observed in captive animals, the young emerged tail-first. For an air-breathing animal being born underwater this makes sense. The process of giving birth may take some time and a young dolphin with its head protruding could run the risk of taking its first breath underwater and being drowned. As it is the calf's tail may project from the vulva for hours before the rest of the body appears, but the final steps happen very quickly. The umbilical cord is broken, the calf without air in its lungs has a negative buoyancy and tends to sink, but the mother (and sometimes other female helpers) nudges it gently to the surface, usually within ten seconds. Something in the air initiates the voluntary opening of the blowhole and the calf takes its first breath.

The calves of all species take their first feed soon after birth. The mother's nipples protrude from their mammary slits under the pressure of milk and she usually turns on her side to give the calf easier access. Suckling takes place largely underwater between breaths, so it cannot be prolonged. The mother forces the milk out under muscular pressure. All the calf has to

do is to gulp down the rich, concentrated food with a fat content of more than 40 per cent (compared to just 2 per cent in human milk). The large baleen whales produce as much as 600 litres (158 gallons) of milk a day and the calves often double their weight in the first week.

By the time weaning takes place, calves are usually more than half grown and are feeding actively on their own. Sexual maturity is reached when they are roughly 85 per cent of their full size, which in larger species takes at least five years. Full physical maturity and maximum length are not attained until the animals are much older. A Great Sperm Whale's growth is not complete until it reaches about twenty-eight years (for cows) or thirty-five (for bulls).

In baleen whales females are invariably larger than their mates, but there are no other signs of sexual dimorphism. There are no physical indications of readiness to mate and as far as we know no cetacean produces or would be able to respond to a sexual odour. This leaves only behavioural and sound signals for communicating sex and may be the reason why some great whales have developed such elaborate songs. Amongst toothed whales, with their great acoustic sensitivity, receptivity may be communicated by sound or it may be something which a dolphin can 'see' with the aid of its sonar. Trainers working with captive animals report that these have no difficulty in distinguishing the sex of humans in the water, react differently to each one and seem even to be aware of menstrual cycles. Sexual dimorphism is however common in odontocetes. The males of most species are larger than the females and many of them have additional secondary sexual characters such as pronounced teeth or melons.

The most exaggerated sexual differences are those of the Unicorn Whale (*Monodon monoceros 34*) in which males have enormous spiral tusks. These may have a number of functions (see page 163), but the fact that only the males possess them suggests that they have something to do with sexual display. The whales seldom injure each other with their tusks in disputes over females, but in several other species the teeth are clearly used in fights with rival males. Beaked whales (Ziphiidae) have females without teeth who nevertheless manage to feed perfectly well, but their males have one or two pairs of greatly enlarged teeth which are certainly wielded as weapons. The bulls all bear conspicuous scars whose depths and spacing show that they have been inflicted by the 'battle teeth' of rivals. In some Delphinid species, such as the Grey Dolphin (*Grampus griseus 68*), scarring is so common and severe that it has become a characteristic by which this cetacean can be recognized at sea.

Courtship in all cetaceans is elaborate. There are boisterous patterns of behaviour such as the lunging display of a 'surface-travelling group' of Humpback Whales (*Megaptera novaeangliae 10*), or the resounding head-on collision of Shortfin Pilot Whales (*Globicephala macrorhynchus 50*); but as a rule the preliminaries to mating involve prolonged and gentle mutual caressing. The gregarious species are always touching and teasing each other in ways that are obviously sexually stimulating, but in true foreplay there is very much more intense nuzzling, nibbling, rubbing and stroking. In some species this sequence ends in the assumption by one or both sexes of a specific pre-copulatory posture which acts as a visual signal or releaser. In Bottlenose Dolphins (*Tursiops truncatus 76*), the male throws his body into a sinuous S-shaped curve (see page 277).

Cetaceans seem to spend an inordinate amount of time in sexual activity. This may be generated by boredom in captivity, but observers in the wild tend to confirm it. Dolphins engage in love-play with almost every creature in sight – with mothers, brothers, fathers, daughters, cousins or aunts. There is even one record of a Bottlenose Dolphin masturbating with a herring (BROWN 1979).

A freedom of sexual expression and emancipation of sex from a purely seasonal procreative activity usually indicates a high level of behavioural organization and development. If this is so the sheer quantity as well as the quality, sensitivity and complexity of sexual behaviour in cetaceans puts them very high up the evolutionary tree.

Sounds

Maritime literature is full of stories of mysterious sounds at sea. In the days before steam it was possible to hear everything that happened on a ship, to listen to the timbers talking and hear the complaint of sheets under tension in the wind. These sounds were familiar to sailors, who noticed them only when they stopped, but there were other calls in the quiet of the night which were less familiar and which led to a belief in haunted ships and the dreaded sirens' songs.

The constant clatter of powered vessels obscured the sounds and the fears for a while, but both reappeared during World War II when hydrophones were first deployed in an attempt to track enemy submarines. Those manning listening posts soon learned to recognize natural sea sounds such as croaking fish, snapping shrimp or the crash of surf on a distant shore, but there were other sounds so unexpected in character that the listeners found it hard to believe they were not made by ghosts in their machine or evidence of some diabolical new underwater weapon. It was not until well after the war that science caught up with the ancient mariners, who had known for centuries that it was possible to track cetaceans by their characteristic 'song'. Nineteenth-century whalers knew, and could distinguish between, the voices of Right, Bowhead, Humpback, Grey, White and Pilot whales (ALDRICH 1889).

By 1951 SOFAR (sound fixing and ranging) stations had been set up around the world and were beginning to add to the whalers' knowledge. Many of the oddest sounds seem to have been produced by cetaceans. A widespread low-frequency 'moan' at about 20 Hz in the background almost anywhere in temperate waters has now been identified (SCHEVILL 1964) as the voice of the Fin Whale (*Balaenoptera physalus 5*), perhaps with occasional choruses by the vanishing Blue Whale (*B. musculus 6*). Low-frequency 'thumps' between 100 and 200 Hz, which crop up so often in hydrophone records that they have come to be known to analysts as the 'A train', were identified only in 1976 as emanating from the Piked Whale (*B. acutorostrata 7*) (WINN & PERKINS 1976). A strange 'boing' about four seconds long at a frequency of 100 Hz has been recorded in the Pacific and still remains to be identified (WENZ 1964).

Known baleen-whale sounds seem to fall into four basic categories:

i. Low-frequency moans up to thirty seconds long, with fundamental frequencies between 20 and 200 Hz, either pure tone, as in the 20-cycle sounds of Fin Whales, or more complex with a strong harmonic structure.

ii. Short thumps or knocks also under 200 Hz, but less than a second long, now known to be produced by Great Right, Bowhead, Grey, Fin and Piked whales.

iii. Chirps and whistles which change frequency rapidly but are always above 1,000 Hz and less than one tenth of a second long. These may be pure tones or involve harmonics, and seem to be produced by most baleen whales.

iv. Clicks with a frequency as high as 30 kHz, lasting less than one hundredth of a second. These have now been recorded for Grey, Fin, Blue, Sei, Tropical and Humpback whales.

The 'thump trains' of Piked Whales, the moans of Fin Whales and the whistles of Humpback Whales all have distinctive frequencies and repetition rates which make it possible for human listeners, and therefore presumably whales, to recognize individual animals over great distances. A Blue Whale's whistle recorded at 188 decibels is the loudest sound ever known to be produced by any living source and, with power exceeding that even of a passing jet plane (usually between 140 and 170 decibels), will certainly travel considerable distances underwater (CUMMINGS & THOMPSON 1971). Even the relatively small Piked Whale has a song recorded at 152 decibels (BEAMISH & MITCHELL 1973). The acoustic range of high-amplitude, low-frequency moans produced by Fin Whales may be great enough to span an entire ocean (PAYNE & WEBB 1971).

We still know little about the function of sound in baleen whales, but it is difficult to over-estimate the value of such signals in a three-dimensional environment, in which visibility is necessarily restricted. They could provide information about identity, position, reproductive state, population size, the availability of food and the presence of predators. Singing Humpback Whales, for instance, simply because they are singing, can be assumed to be solitary, male, ready to mate, uninterested in food and undisturbed by predators. The song, now known to vary with time and place, tells even human listeners that the animal producing it is, for instance, part of the western Atlantic 'herd', singing near Bermuda, in April 1970 (THOMPSON et al 1979).

In the Humpback repertoire, single units of sound are combined into sequences or phrases, in turn linked into unbroken patterns to provide basic 'themes'. A series of these forms a 'song', lasting anywhere between six and thirty minutes long, probably the longest and most complex in the animal kingdom. A ritual collection of songs, separated by no more than a brief pause between each, can last for more than twenty-four hours. It is already clear that Mysticete vocalizations identify species and individuals, co-ordinate social structures by bringing animals together or by spacing them out,

and provide information about their physiological and behavioural state.

Some of the more powerful Mysticete sounds produce echoes from large reflective bodies such as submarine banks or pinnacles. In darkness or in murky water these must be useful to navigating whales, but there is no good evidence as yet that any baleen whale has evolved an efficient sonar apparatus. Most operate at frequencies lower than 2 kHz. The situation amongst toothed whales is completely different.

In 1947 Arthur McBride, Curator of the Marine Studios in Florida, discovered that Bottlenose Dolphins (*Tursiops truncatus 76*) were able to evade his nets even where visibility was virtually nil (McNALLY 1977). He theorized that they were using a system of echolocation similar to that discovered in bats. In 1956 William Schevill and Barbara Lawrence published the first proof of this talent in Bottlenose Dolphins which produced creaking sounds while locating fish held silently under muddy water (SCHEVILL & LAWRENCE 1956). Regular discoveries add fresh evidence of increasingly sophisticated sonar systems used by a growing list of Odontocetes.

The denser the medium, the faster sound waves travel in it. The speed of sound in water is roughly four times as high as it is in air. The distance a sound travels in either medium depends on its wavelength or frequency. High-pitched sounds travel only a fraction as far as low-pitched sounds of the same power. So, for long-range communication most animals use low-frequency, long wavelength sounds like the 20-Hz transoceanic moan of the Fin Whale. But a 20-Hz signal has a wavelength of almost 75 m (250 ft), which means that it will pass unimpeded over most obstacles, bouncing back only off something like an oil tanker or a seamount which has a diameter greater than 75 m (250 ft). The sonar systems of toothed whales concentrate on the short-range higher frequencies. Dolphins in tests locate fish less than 20 mm (.75 inch) long, so they must be using sound of a frequency near 100 kHz. Some cetaceans produce sounds with, and are presumably equipped for detecting the echoes from, frequencies higher than 200 kHz, with which they can distinguish objects as small as vertical wires 0.35 mm (less than .015 inch) in diameter (PENNER & MURCHISON 1970).

Most toothed-whale sonar systems operate with a steady stream of intense click sounds, generally between 30 and 60 kHz. They can vary the rate of clicking (up to 1,000 per second) for building more accurate echo pictures and can change the frequency of their transmissions, moving the energy peak up and down. Some can even produce two different frequencies simultaneously, and the most efficient of these can flatten, shorten or heighten the sound beam in order to focus it on a target. A few can manipulate sonar probes precisely enough to send a secondary exploratory beam off at right angles to the main one (EVANS 1973).

Echolocation in toothed whales fall into four categories:

i. **Low-frequency, narrow band,** with peak energy below 4 kHz (e.g. the Common Porpoise).

ii. **Low-frequency, broad band,** with peak energy between 16 and 20 kHz (e.g. the Great Killer Whale).

iii. **High-frequency, broad band,** with peak energy between 30 and 60 kHz (e.g. the Bottlenose Dolphin).

iv. **Ultrasonic, broad band** with peak energy above 80 kHz (e.g. the Indus River Dolphin).

These species also have lower-frequency sounds for communication, and some of them may operate in more than one of these modes, depending on what they are doing. All of them achieve greater acuity in any mode by 'scanning', by sweeping their sonar beams over the target with movements of their heads or bodies as they listen. This also changes the angle at which the returning echoes strike the head, and therefore the degree to which each frequency penetrates and is heard, providing very precise information about the nature of the object.

After training a blindfold female Bottlenose Dolphin (*Tursiops truncatus 76*) to recognize a copper plate by its acoustic properties, William Evans of the Naval Undersea Center in San Diego presented her with glass, plastic and aluminium imitations of the same size and shape. She immediately dismissed these as counterfeits. He then tested her with an aluminium plate whose thickness had been calculated to have exactly the same sonic reflectivity as copper, but she still picked out the copper correctly. To do this she had not only to perceive the basic features of the echoes but also their precise frequency composition. What makes this performance even more impressive is that, to do it all, she had to remember the frequency mix in the copper echo, analyse the sound from the aluminium copy, and then compare the two for subtle proportional differences. She completed this sophisticated exercise in a matter of seconds (EVANS & POWELL 1966).

Most bioacoustic experts agree that the echolocation clicks of toothed whales are created by implosive movements of air in the whales' nasal passages, but the exact methods of sound production and projection remain mysterious. Sound is produced either by the larynx, or by vibration of the nasal plugs, or by muscular action in other parts of the system which constricts air streams and produces vibration. Whatever the source of the sound, in all species it is clearly produced with the blowhole closed and somehow projected forward through the tissue of the head. In many species, such as the Bottlenose Dolphin and the pilot whales the skull and upper jaw are hollowed on top to produce a concave surface in which rests a complex structure of fat and oil. It seems highly likely that sound waves produced in the nasal passages are reflected off the curved bone of the head and, on their way out, focused into a concentrated beam by the lens-shaped tissue of the melon. This structure has reached its greatest refinement in the head of the Great Sperm Whale (*Physeter macrocephalus 36*), to guide it in the absolute darkness of the abyss. The fact that the head shape is intimately involved in projecting echolocatory sounds is demonstrated by a recent discovery that it is possible to determine the size of a Great Sperm Whale's head (and therefore its length) by measuring the interval between the two component sounds in its click (MOHL et al 1976).

Returning echoes are picked up by all parts of the body and travel effectively through the bones of the head. The ear channels are reduced to pinholes and in some cases plugged with wax. But cetaceans still need to locate the source of sounds by responding to the difference in time taken for them to reach each of the ears. So the inner ears are isolated from the skull in a cushion of bubbly foam; sound is picked up instead through the windows of fat in the hind part of each side of the lower jaw. In the same way that a fatty melon projects sound out, so it, and extra fat in channels through the jaws, conduct sound waves directly to the ossicles of each ear. The result is a system so sensitive that a dolphin in a large tank can hear a teaspoonful of water being poured into it anywhere and still turn and fix that spot precisely.

Many toothed whales also communicate directly with each other by clear pure tone whistles, which not only vary from species to species, but seem to be personal to each individual. The fact that the frequency and intensity of 'conversations' by whistle increases when animals are assembling for a hunt suggests that they may be involved in a complex exchange of information and intention, in many ways like human language. This had led to attempts to understand the cetacean system and to teach our language to selected small toothed whales. Neither has been successful.

The best-known overtures are those of John Lilly (LILLY 1961), based on a series of tests dealing with the apparent ability of Bottlenose Dolphins (*Tursiops truncatus 76*) to produce sounds in air with the blowhole open in imitation of human speech (LILLY et al 1968). Captive dolphins in an experimental chamber with their blowholes exposed were read a long list of human speech sounds, both as random phonetic units and in the form of simple English words and phrases. Fish rewards were offered to the dolphins to encourage them each time they produced air sounds. The human and dolphin sounds were then compared and it was found that they showed many similarities in their physical structure. In response to human-sound stimuli, the dolphins were producing sounds quite unlike their own natural ones in the frequency, number and spacing of the bursts of sound involved. They were mimicking the human experimenters. Lilly's opponents have strongly criticized the dolphin responses, questioning their alleged 'voice' and 'accent' and their comprehension. It has not yet been conclusively proved that dolphins can learn English and use it meaningfully, but Lilly's work does show that a dolphin can learn without any material reward to listen to a human, work out what the human wants, adjust its sound-producing mechanism to those needs, pitch its voice at the necessary and totally artificial level required, and make the noise the human wants exactly when it is requested. Cetaceans have shown themselves to be very much more adaptable than we are. They have changed the rate, frequency, style and even the physical medium of their communication system to operate in our habitual mode and are producing humanoid sound emissions in abundance, while we have yet to learn to speak a single delphinoid sound.

This could change with several research programmes now under way, each intent on producing a mechanical intermediary, a sort of translator designed to slow down the dolphin rate of communication or speed up the human one until they become compatible and mutually intelligible. But it may be that we still lack any sensible answers simply because we have been asking the wrong questions. If there are any complex cetacean languages, it is possible that they are not constructed from simple sonic units like ours, but rely more on an amalgam of subtle signals, rich in emotional overtones and sexual innuendo. We are only now beginning to catalogue and define the elaborate human system of body language and gesture which still accompanies our vocal communication. It is true that we can now operate without it; humans regularly converse and convey complex ideas without meeting face to face; but we may be wrong in assuming that the evolution of cetacean systems has followed a similar single sensory bias. In the open ocean, free of gravity and many of the restrictions which weigh heavily on our bodies and on our minds, they may have been able to develop something very different. We may be doing them a grave injustice by looking into the sunlit mirrors of the sea, and dismissing those who live there, simply because we cannot find there images of ourselves.

Intelligence

All who come into contact with cetaceans are impressed by their ability to imitate and learn – often, it seems, for no reward other than the sheer pleasure of doing so. These talents put whales and dolphins into a category with animals such as apes, bears and elephants, which are clearly highly adaptive and successful in coming to terms both with their natural environment and with the unnatural things expected of them in captivity or under domestication.

In the light of the large number of unsettling experiences now being recorded by those working with dolphins, it begins to seem unscientific *not* to consider the possibility that conscious awareness may be involved in some of them. There are many formal studies on classical learning, discrimination and problem-solving in the Bottlenose Dolphin (*Tursiops truncatus 76*) which conclude that its intelligence lies only somewhere between that of a dog and a chimpanzee. The design of these experiments, however, is so narrow and bears so little relation to the dolphin's natural life that the conclusions must be suspect. Everything we know about delphinoid awareness and sociability suggests that dolphins are likely to be bored by any programme which requires an isolated animal to perform a series of repetitive and meaningless tasks. Humans under similar circumstances score considerably less well than pigeons.

The most interesting insights into the potential of cetaceans are coming instead from work in which human experimenters deliberately try to be anthropomorphic. They treat their subjects as human mothers treat their babies, as if they were conscious creatures. Human mothers start with the assumption and the belief that complex responses are possible and deal with their children accordingly. It seems that when cetaceans are given similar treatment they often respond in ways which suggest that they too are conscious, conceptualizing creatures.

There are obvious risks involved in making such prior assumptions, but there are equally grave impediments to understanding implicit in any approach which denies all animals the possibility of mental experience. What we need, it seems, are a few reasonable rules for playing the anthropomorphic game. First of these perhaps should be: 'Allow animals the possibility of awareness, but do not make the mistake of assuming that it will be similar, or even comparable, to your own.'

Our evolution has been determined very largely by hand and eye. We operate almost entirely on a visual, linear basis which determines the way in which we think and speak, and we owe our dominance to an ability to make and use tools and to manipulate the environment for our own ends. Cetaceans have poor eyes and no hands at all. The sensory emphasis in their evolution has been acoustic, non-linear and non-manipulative, and yet they have acquired brains which both in size and complexity are very much like our own. Moreover, they achieved these structures almost 30 million years ago, when we were insignificant nocturnal insectivores. This is the crux of the matter and the ground on which all arguments for or against cetacean intelligence need to be based.

Brain size on its own is no measure of intelligence; elephants have brains which weigh four times as much as our own, but they are not necessarily four times as intelligent. The ratio of brain-weight to body-weight is a better measurement. Amongst cetaceans there is a range, beginning with ratios of 1:20,000 in the Blue Whale (*Balaenoptera musculus 6*), through 1:4,000 for the Great Sperm Whale (*Physeter macrocephalus 36*) and ending with less than 1:100 for many of the small toothed whales (GIHR & PILLERI 1969). The Bottlenose Dolphin's (*Tursiops truncatus 76*) ratio may be as low as 1:76, which compares very well with the average human ratio of about 1:50, but this comparison may be misleading because the body weights of aquatic animals, which live in conditions of zero gravity, are comparatively high.

The most complex part of any mammalian brain is the cerebral cortex, which seems to be the only component that differs in a significant way between humans and most other species. The cortex is the arbiter of higher behaviour, and the quality and quantity of 'grey matter' there is considered by most neurologists to be a valid measure of mental sophistication. In terms of cortical size, degree of folding and cellular organization, dolphins are the most highly evolved in the whole animal kingdom and are, in every anatomical way, comparable to ourselves. Differences that do exist in general brain architecture have to do with the obvious differences in life-style and behaviour between us and them. Our cerebral anatomy is similar, but our best-developed areas are those which deal with the elaboration of motor skills made possible by our hands, while cetaceans seem to concentrate on areas of social perception. Dolphins show marked development of those parts of the brain responsible for orientation, social skill, emotional self-control and perhaps even humour. Unlike us, they seem to have responded to social and sexual pressures rather than to the purely physical. Our dependence on tools, which now extends to books and computers, means that a large part of the mental capacity of a human culture exists outside the individual, whereas in non-manipulative dolphins it is still embodied in brain and behaviour. As far as our ability to act as social beings is concerned, we may be inferior to many cetaceans.

Such comparisons are largely invidious. It is perhaps sufficient to note that we are different creatures with different priorities, strengths and weaknesses. It is vital however to recognize that cetaceans are complex enough to make it probable that they have mental experiences, and that these in turn have important effects on their behaviour. Any less generous assessment makes it difficult to appreciate, and impossible to understand, some of their astonishing behaviour, particularly in the wild. At this moment, reports of this are isolated and largely anecdotal; but it is our hope that with tools such as this guide, and more typically cetacean tolerance, we may soon learn to come to terms with an intelligence in many ways comparable to our own.

Skulls of: Snubfin Dolphin *(Orcaella brevirostris 69) left* and Bowhead Whale *(Balaena mysticetus 2) right,* showing the position and relative size of the brain (not to scale)

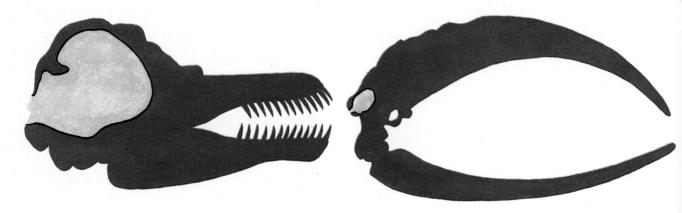

6
Status

Existing knowledge of cetacean populations is fragmentary. The figures most often quoted are derived from calculations made by the whaling industry which are at best questionable. The only certain result of the application of their mathematical models has been the progressive over-exploitation and decline of one species after another.

The concepts and traditions of the whaling industry have grown out of our knowledge of fish. There is little evidence that theories developed for obtaining statistical information about schools of cod can be applied successfully to herring or capelin, let alone to an altogether different class of animals that differs profoundly in physiology, behaviour and basic ecology. Whales are large mammals, but few marine-population dynamicists have ever looked at them in the same way as they would a grazing herd of elephant, and none has tried to create a model which considers them as intelligent individuals operating in a sophisticated social context. A fundamental difficulty is the lack of information about most cetacean species. The fishy-population theories assume a data base which simply does not exist. Information on growth, maturity, pregnancy and birth rates can be obtained from dead whales, but there is no real possibility of assessing the significance of these, or of calculating the effect of human interference, on a social structure that is still largely unknown. Estimates of whale populations are based largely on data derived from *sightings*, the number of live whales actually seen; *markings*, the number of identifiable individuals seen again; and *catch effort*, based on an arcane formula believed to represent the co-operative effort needed to find and kill whales. There are obvious shortcomings in all three measurements. Sightings cannot reflect the densities of whales in even one ocean area, because they are usually made by the whaling industry whose boats go to the places where they expect to find whales; resulting estimates are always too high. Markings are less suspect but of limited use because so few tagged whales are ever seen again. Catching effort is the least reliable measure, because it is impossible to ensure that even the same whaling fleet operates in precisely the same way on two separate occasions. To provide more accurate assessment, any system must improve the efficiency of identification. No census can work until it can be ensured that the same animals are not being counted again and again. We need to be able to recognize individual whales and to follow their movements and trace their development and growth in the social system; and we need to do so in ways which interfere as little as possible with that system.

Payne has shown that this is possible in his study of the Great Right Whale (*Balaena glacialis 1*) population which winters around the Valdez Peninsula in Patagonia. Humpback Whales (*Megaptera novaeangliae 10*) are being studied in the same way by groups keeping a close watch on populations wintering in the Caribbean and in Hawaii. The eastern Pacific population of the Grey Whale (*Eschrichtius robustus 4*) which travels to Baja California to breed, is the subject of further intensive research. These species lend themselves admirably to benign, non-intrusive study because they have conspicuous natural markings.

The rorquals and most smaller toothed whales present greater problems. There are occasional conspicuous individuals (such as albinos) that can be recognized easily, even from the air, which makes it possible to follow particular groups. Dedicated underwater work on communities of those species which stay in, or return to, given areas with reasonably clear water has shown that it is possible for a human observer to distinguish between individuals which at first glance look identical. But this painstaking approach is not suitable for all species in all areas.

Large whales have been marked with 'spaghetti tags', which consist of small stainless steel heads fired from crossbows, with a stop to limit the depth of penetration into the blubber and a colourful plastic streamer that can be seen from a distance. As commercial whaling is phased out, this may be the only practical long-term way of keeping track of baleen whales such as Fin (*Balaenoptera physalus 5*) and Piked (*B. acutorostrata 7*) whales. A refinement of this technique may be useful for marking small toothed whales which regularly present themselves at the bow of moving ships.

A few captive cetaceans have been equipped with radio locator beacons which send a signal to an aircraft or satellite. These have the advantage of providing information not only on position, but also on basic physiology. The beacons broadcast each time the animal surfaces (and the aerial tip is exposed), and can be programmed to measure depth of dive, water temperature, duration of dive, heartbeat, blood chemistry and a number of other factors. With miniaturization, it will soon be possible to implant transmitters durable enough to function for years and small enough to be fired from a gun or crossbow. This may be the only way we will ever learn what animals such as the Great Sperm Whale (*Physeter macrocephalus 36*) do when they are beyond our normal ken at depths approaching 3,000 m (10,000 ft).

Once commercial whaling has been effectively controlled and we have developed natural, non-intrusive methods of observing free-living populations, we have to turn our attention to whale habitats, because there are a number of ways in which we can affect the status of a species, or even exterminate it completely, without hunting a single animal. Bays and lagoons are notoriously vulnerable to human development and pollution, and species which breed in such areas are as vulnerable as the habitats they occupy. San Diego Bay in California was once an important breeding ground for Grey Whales (*Eschrichtius robustus 4*), but human activity there has driven them away. Parts of the Baltic Sea are now so polluted that cetaceans which were abundant there at the turn of the century have now completely disappeared.

In the face of indifferent despoliation of coastal waters and the intransigence of much commercial whaling, the future for most cetaceans is bleak; but there are signs that, provided with the right conditions, some whale populations do have the resilience to bounce back. We owe them that chance.

Distribution

In geological time there have been great changes in the position and distribution of continents, and in the number and size of oceans. These and the fluctuations in temperature which coincided with periods of glaciation seem to have produced bursts of cetacean evolution and brought about extensive redistribution of new and surviving species.

One of the main centres of distribution was the Indopacific Ocean. Species which still exist there and may be relatively little changed since the Miocene are the Snubfin Dolphin (*Orcaella brevirostris 69*), the Finless Porpoise (*Neophocaena phocaenoides 47*) and the Indopacific Beaked Whale (*Indopacetus pacificus 17*). The Ganges (*Platanista gangetica 29*), Indus (*Platanista minor 30*) and Yangtze (*Lipotes vexillifer 31*) river dolphins were probably then marine and have re-invaded freshwater.

Continental Africa today acts as a barrier, preventing many warm-water species from travelling through the cooler areas round the Cape of Good Hope into the Atlantic, but there must have been warmer times when such passage was possible. The La Plata River Dolphin (*Pontoporia blainvillei 33*) and the Amazon River Dolphin (*Inia geoffrensis 32*) now represent a comparable relict fauna in the tropical Atlantic Ocean. There is evidence that several more modern forms

Below: Isotherms showing the mean temperature of ocean waters for the warmest and coldest months of the year in each hemisphere.

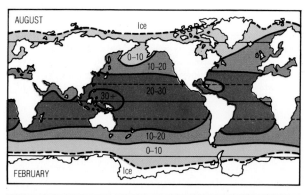

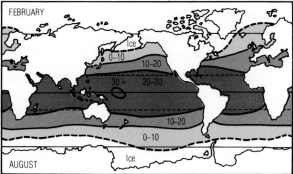

such as the humpback dolphins are now in the process of making such a transition round the Cape. There is a complex of several related forms of *Sousa* in the Indopacific and one slightly different variant (*Sousa teuszii 41*) in the eastern Atlantic.

The American continents formed another land barrier which restricted the movement of evolving cetaceans, but at times there was an open strait in central America through which species such as the Grey Whale (*Eschrichtius robustus 4*) and the Sei Whale (*Balaenoptera borealis 8*) probably moved.

As the oceans cooled, a number of formerly tropical forms adapted to changing circumstance and became so tolerant of the cold that they now enjoy a worldwide distribution. Prominent amongst these are Common Dolphins (*Delphinus delphis 75*), Great Killer Whales (*Orcinus orca 51*) and False Killer Whales (*Pseudorca crassidens 52*).

Some species are limited to warmer waters, moving away from the equator only when the isotherms relax and flow north and south in summer, but most temperature-sensitive cetaceans seem to be restricted more by the lower limits of their tolerance (or that of their prey) and their ranges end abruptly along lines formed by the 10°C or the 20°C isotherm in winter.

The fact that most polar forms still breed in the tropics suggests that even the hardiest species originated in warmer waters. Only the Unicorn Whales (*Monodon monoceros 34*), the White Whales (*Delphinapterus leucas 35*), and the Bowhead Whales (*Balaena mysticetus 2*) are polar breeders and all three are Arctic species. The existence of a circumpolar ocean in the Antarctic made it easier for southern forms to escape back to the tropics whenever necessary.

During the last million years there have been several cool spells, the most recent just 15,000 years ago, during the last glaciation. Average sea temperatures at this time were 6°C (10°F) cooler than they are today, which must have bent the isotherms far enough for many of the bipolar species to cross the equator and meet, particularly in the eastern Pacific, where cold currents from both north and south still flow quite close to the equator. As the weather warmed again the equator became a barrier once more, but it was breached so recently that it is probably too soon to state that many of the now isolated northern and southern forms have evolved into separate species; they will probably get together and breed again with the next ice age.

They may still form a common gene pool thanks to occasional strays which cross from one hemisphere to the other. The Northern and Southern Fourtooth Whales (*Berardius bairdii 12* and *B. arnuxii 13*) and the Rightwhale Dolphins (*Lissodelphis borealis 63* and *L. peronii 62*) have been given the status of separate species, but these could well be artificial distinctions. There is still a number of species of toothed whale (such as *Cephalorhynchus*) which occur only in the southern hemisphere, and there are several notable gaps in the north; Longfin Pilot Whales (*Globicephala melaena 49*) for

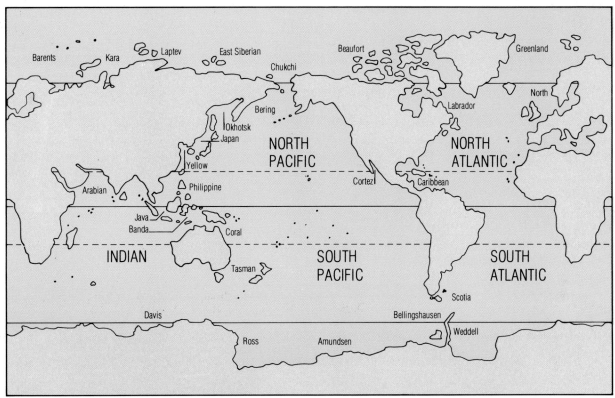

Map of the major named sea areas in each ocean

instance, are unknown north of the equator in the Pacific Ocean. Where species do occur in the north and not the south, they are usually specialized ones like the Spray (Dall's) Porpoise (*Phocoenoides dalli 48*), which is clearly an isolated and derivative offshoot of the southern Phocoenid family. The existence of the Gulf Porpoise (*Phocoena sinus 46*) in Mexico and its similarity to the southern Black Porpoise (*Phocoena spinipinnis 44*) suggest that it is a recent arrival and reached the northern hemisphere as a result of a partial bridge over the equator by a short-lived cold current.

The original Indopacific core stock is probably best represented today by the relatively unspecialized Japanese Beaked Whale (*Mesoplodon ginkgodens 22*). Other comparable species have changed little, but have colonized a range of habitats; Scamperdown Beaked Whale (*M. grayi 23*) now occupies the southern ocean, the Arch Beaked Whale (*M. carlhubbsi 21*) is North Pacific, and the Gulf Stream Beaked Whale (*M. europaeus 20*) has staked its claim to the North Atlantic. Each of the more specialized species seems to have its own ecological niche.

The large baleen whales which rely on summer blooms of plankton are forced to migrate and now travel considerable distances every year. The fact that the summer and its blooms occur at different times of the year in each hemisphere means

that these species synchronize with the tilt of earth's axis, swimming south in November and back north again in May. This rhythm makes it unlikely that any animals will cross over the equator to mix with their counterparts in the other hemisphere. They may share certain equatorial waters, but (except for rare stragglers) are never there at the same time. For these species, at least under present climatic conditions, the equator forms a real biological barrier.

The only toothed whales which regularly travel long distances are the adult male Great Sperm Whales (*Physeter macrocephalus 36*), which migrate to higher latitudes each summer. The deep-sea squid on which they feed are believed to live and breed where underwater mounts and ranges drop off steeply into the abyss. The little we do know of their distribution from whaling records suggests very strongly that in their movements they follow the submarine ridges. Those who summer in the Antarctic area of the Indian Ocean are funnelled in by the south-west Indian and mid-Indian Ocean ridges and meet their females somewhere near the Azores.

The seasonal movement of small toothed whales is much less co-ordinated. There are general north–south shifts with the seasons, but there are also inshore–offshore and east–west migrations, which depend not so much on climatic changes as on the presence and availability of favoured foods.

The Sea Guide

We still do not know exactly how many kinds of living cetaceans there are. For the purposes of this guide, we choose to believe that there are seventy-six species, but this is nothing more than a convenient starting point to identification.

Information about cetaceans is still so scarce that anything you see, recorded with suitable care, is important scientific evidence. The main purpose of this guide is to help you to understand what you see, help you to give a name to the animals involved and make your observations coherent, consistent and useful to the few professional cetologists, who cannot on their own keep watch on the vast world ocean and its shores.

Using the Guide

Modern scientific nomenclature dates back to 1758, the year in which the Swedish naturalist and physician Carolus Linnaeus published the tenth edition of his *Systema Naturae.* Since then scientific names have followed his binomial system, whereby the name of a species consists of two words, the *genus* (from the Latin meaning race, or class), which always has an initial capital letter, and the *species* (from the Latin for kind), which never has a capital. Both words must be Latin or latinized and are always set in italics or underlined, e.g. *Homo sapiens.* A genus may have any number of related species, but no species may belong to more than one genus.

This system has made it possible to avoid the confusion of multitudes of different local names. Zoologists everywhere have, by international agreement, adopted it as a single language, a single set of names for all animals, to be used on a worldwide basis. The names may provide valuable information about the animal or its habitat or the person who discovered or described it. So, in every case, we have given a direct translation of the Greek or Latin and tried to explain why the name was chosen.

Naming is organized in accordance with the International Code of Zoological Nomenclature. The first principle is that of priority, whereby the name of a species is the earliest name published in a way that meets the requirements of the Code. The surname of the author of a new species is commonly added to the scientific name along with the date of publication. If the species is now placed in a genus different from that in which the author originally placed it, the author's name is in brackets. In practice, however, the recognition of priority is far from simple. Publications are scattered over so many centres in so many languages that some are inevitably overlooked for a time. Thus a widely used name may later be found not to be the earliest and has to be changed. However, the Code provides that prior names unused for fifty years are, in general, not to be used; such names are referred to as *nomina oblita*, literally forgotten names. Cases where confusion is caused by strict application of the rules may be referred to an International Commission for resolution.

As more specimens are collected and examined, species that were originally thought to be distinct may turn out to be identical and have to be lumped together, while others, in which differences were not at first recognized, have to be split. Few animals keep both the generic and specific names which they were first given. This is particularly true of cetaceans which in many cases are known from only a few individuals washed up on some remote beach. The systematic changes which have been made tell so much about both the cetaceans and the cetologists involved that we have gone to some trouble to record them, in the section under each species headed *Classification.*

We have also given a cross section of vernacular names in a number of languages, partly to help with identification when speaking with whalers or local residents, but mainly because they contain useful information. For instance, *Globicephala melaena* is known in the Orkney Islands as the Caa'ing Whale, the islanders' way of saying 'calling whale'. Scientists discovered the voice of this whale only in the last twenty years, but the islanders have known about it for centuries. In order to locate schools of these animals, which they drive ashore in shallow bays for food, fishermen in the Orkneys still crouch with their ears pressed against the wooden gunwales of their boats, listening for the characteristic water-borne chorus of the highly vocal 'calling' or Caa'ing Whales.

We have given each of the seventy-six species identified in this guide a vernacular name in English. Most of the names are familiar; the majority are in accordance with those published by the two most recent authorities, Dale Rice in *A List of the Marine Mammals of the World* (1977) and the Scientific Committee of the International Whaling Commission in their *List of Smaller Cetaceans Recognized* (1975); others we have changed in an attempt to eliminate contradictions and to provide some degree of standardization.

We do not use 'dolphin' and 'porpoise' indiscriminately. The priority is clear. Aristotle, Pliny and Linnaeus all called the most common small cetacean in the Mediterranean *delphis*. We have to follow them and call *Delphinus delphis* a dolphin and, having done that, use the same name for all members of the family Delphinidae.

We treat the term 'porpoise' in a similar way. It comes from the Latin *porcus piscus*, hogfish, and was first used by the Romans to describe *Phocoena phocoena*. The members of the family Phocoenidae are anatomically and behaviourally distinct from the Delphinidae, so we use the name 'porpoise' only for Phocoenids, and we use it consistently for *all* of them.

We further restrict the use of both 'dolphin' and 'porpoise' to small cetaceans, those species less than 4 m (13 ft) long. Everything larger than that is known as a 'whale'.

We have eliminated most personal names from the vernacular list. If these ever had any significance they are still included in the reference to the author of the name. Otherwise they are redundant and uninformative to most people. Where no English vernacular name exists we have taken the liberty of inventing our own. In so doing we have followed three practical guidelines: we have selected a name which either describes a distinctive feature visible in the field *or* which identifies a characteristic habitat *or* which is a direct translation of either part of the binomial. We realize that not all choices will please everyone. It is difficult to break the habit of using a familiar name even if it is uninformative, but we hope that the new names will prove useful.

Identification

In addition to its use as a work of reference, this guide makes it possible for professionals and amateurs alike to put a name to cetaceans seen alive at sea or found stranded on beaches or in shallow water. A name is an essential prerequisite for making any further useful observation, and we know to our cost how difficult accurate identification can be. So we have designed this guide to meet precisely those needs, and to resolve those frustrations, which we ourselves have experienced during the last ten years in the field.

Running through the guide are three types of key, each containing clues to identification. The first, the wet key, deals with recognizing cetaceans by means of the fleeting glimpses one gets of live animals as they come briefly to the surface to breathe. The second, the dry key, is designed to help you identify stranded cetaceans at your leisure. The third is the map key which narrows the search by eliminating all species which do not occur in the ocean in which you happen to be. All naturalists develop a knack of identifying a bird by a single note of its call or a whale by the flash of its fin. Part of this comes from knowing what to expect, from being already a good way along in the process of elimination, but an even larger part depends on developing a set of ritualized search images, having in the mind's eye a simplified picture of each animal in which it is reduced to its most characteristic essentials. In our wet key, the species portraits and the accounts which form the body of this guide, we concentrate largely on these vital and distinctive field marks.

Live cetaceans sometimes make things easy for you by leaping entirely clear of the water or by rising up to look around them. Some allow you a good close look by coming up to ride the bow wave of a moving ship. These however are exceptions and the very fact that they do these things is in itself often enough to identify them. Most of the time you will have to be satisfied with a fleeting glimpse as they fill the lungs with air. When they appear at the surface to do this, note the following:

1. Try to estimate the animal's *size*. We use three categories, *small* for those under 4 m (13 ft) in length, *medium* for those between 4 and 10 m (13 and 33 ft) and *large* for those over 10 m (33 ft), from the tip of the upper jaw to the deepest part of the notch in the tail.

2. Note whether or not it has a *dorsal fin*. The size of the fin, its shape and its position on the animal's back are all useful characteristics.

3. Watch for the *blow*. If it is visible, describe or make a diagram showing the height and shape. Time the interval between spouts and count the number which occur before the animal dives for longer periods. If it has a fin, notice whether this appears together with, shortly after or long after the blow. Remember that wind conditions can alter this characteristic altogether.

4. Keep a sharp lookout for the *tail flukes*. Some species always hoist these into the air before sounding, some occasionally do so, and some never show the tail at all. Notice the shape of the tail and the condition of its trailing edge. Look for pattern, markings or barnacles on it.

5. Look out for distinctive patterns or *markings*. Eye spots, flank patches, saddle shapes or a blaze on the fin can all mean positive identification; but be careful not to be misled by highlights produced by the sun on smooth wet skin.

6. Make an assessment of the general body shape and *colour*. As a rule cetaceans are more brightly coloured than most texts allow; most descriptions have been taken from beached or boarded specimens, which begin to change colour within seconds of dying. We have made nearly all our observations from live animals and find that in many cases the ephemeral but nevertheless bright colours are useful field characteristics.

7. Assess the animal's *reaction* to you or your ship. Does it approach, avoid or ignore you? See if it tries to take advantage of the bow pressure wave. Watch to see if it reacts in any way to the wake at your stern.

8. Notice if it *jumps* clear of the water or arches high to breathe. If it does leap, is it in a smooth graceful arc, or does it spin, turn, somersault or re-enter with a splash?

9. Count the *numbers* of individuals involved. If possible, notice any disparity in size which will indicate the presence of immature animals or newborn calves.

10. If *more* than one species is involved, record that fact. Cetaceans, like anyone else, are sometimes known by the company they keep.

Sometimes one of these characteristics will be sufficient for positive identification. More often a combination will be necessary. Occasionally even the whole list will not be long enough to help you through the wet key. Then you will have to resort to the map key which lists known distribution records for all species and, by a process of geographical elimination, can help you decide for or against a suspect diagnosis. It might be helpful in this respect if you were able to record the surface water-temperature at the time of observation. Many species are very temperature-sensitive.

Finally, if all else fails, you may have to make a page-by-page search through all seventy-six species.

The diagrams of two generalized cetaceans overleaf illustrate and identify all the named body parts which occur in this guide and its keys.

MYSTICETE

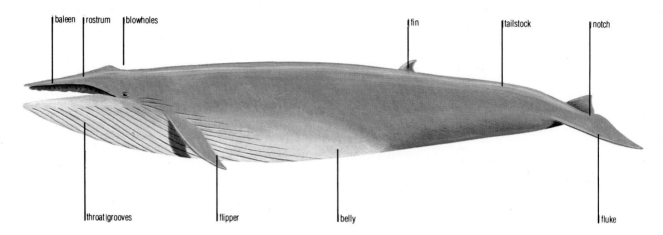

baleen · rostrum · blowholes · fin · tailstock · notch

throat grooves · flipper · belly · fluke

ODONTOCETE

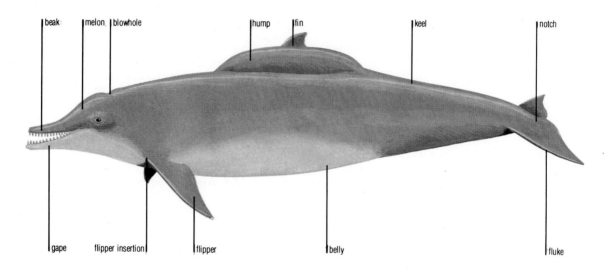

beak · melon · blowhole · hump · fin · keel · notch

gape · flipper insertion · flipper · belly · fluke

Typical Baleen Whale *above* and typical Toothed Whale *below,* showing parts identified in the text

Classification

All whales, dolphins and porpoises belong to a major assemblage, perhaps a sub-class, called the Cetacea, whose position in the Animal Kingdom is not in doubt. They are all air-breathing animals which have hair at least at some point in their lives, maintain a constant body temperature, bear their young alive and nurse them for a while. In other words, they are typical Mammals.

Kingdom:	Animalia	all animals.
Phylum:	Chordata	those with a notochord (the precursor of a backbone).
Subphylum:	Vertebrata	all animals with backbones.
Class:	Mammalia	those which suckle their young.

The Cetaceans are all exclusively aquatic and appropriately streamlined. Everything that might impede easy movement through the water has been lost or become internalized. They have spindle-shaped bodies, flipperlike forelimbs, no external digits or claws, no external ears, very few hairs, mammary glands enclosed in grooves, no sweat glands and a thick layer of subcutaneous blubber.

Their nostrils have moved from the front of the face to a more convenient point on the top of the head and, to accommodate this movement, the bones of the skull have been telescoped backwards. Whales are the only living animals other than elephants which have a brain larger than that of man.

Ancestral forms may have been small, but some modern species have become the largest animals the world has ever known, living or fossil.

In the guide we have drawn on all the latest taxonomic thinking and, where differences of opinion exist, we have chosen that alternative which seems to reflect best the relationship of living animals in the field. We have, for instance, adopted Nishiwaki's suggestion (1963) of separating the killer and pilot whales from the other Delphinidae and placing them in their own family of Globicephalidae.

We have followed the sequence suggested by Fraser and Purves who, in 1960, classified all Cetaceans according to the complexity of their air sinus systems. We begin with those species in which the system is least developed and end with those in which it is most evolved.

Cetaceans are subdivided into two Orders, **Mysticeti**, the baleen whales (from the Greek *moustax*, a moustache, and *ketos*, a sea monster) and **Odontoceti**, toothed whales (from the Greek *odous*, a tooth).

Mysticeti have no teeth as adults and carry instead up to 960 comblike plates which hang from the roof of the mouth and strain plankton or small schooling fish from the water. We recognize ten species.

Odontoceti have from 1 to 260 teeth, some of which may be concealed by the gums. We recognize sixty-six species.

Notes

1. Units
All measurements are made, not around the curve of the body, but in straight lines, as shown in the diagram on page 281 They are given in metric units, which are followed (in parentheses) by the customary non-metric equivalent. Weights are recorded in kilograms (kg) or in short tons (2,000 lb). Metric tons (1,000 kg) are never used. Distances are recorded in kilometres (km) and also in standard miles. Speed is measured in kilometres per hour (kph) and also in knots (nautical miles per hour).

2. Colours
As far as possible we have used only those colour terms suggested by KORNERUP and WANSCHER in the *Methuen Handbook of Colour* (1978), shown in the charts on page 25.

3. Names
Throughout the guide we use the technical and vernacular names as shown in the Species List on page 10, including the number of the species in our list. An additional list of outdated names and synonyms is given in Appendix 1 on page 278.

4. Maps
Each species in this guide has been given a diagrammatic map to indicate all those parts of the world ocean in which that animal *might* be seen. Some of the more conspicuous great whales, which go on regular and predictable migrations, have well-known ranges, but even these large species sometimes crop up in unexpected places. In the case of more elusive smaller Cetaceans, so little is known about many of them that their patterns of distribution tend to change with each new sighting. It is therefore misleading to draw maps which imply that a species is necessarily confined to those places in which it happens so far to have been seen. We have filled in some of the more obvious blank spaces between points of known occurrence and extrapolated to include areas in which we have reason to believe, from what we know of the animal's habits, favoured foods and temperature preferences, that the species does occur and could be seen.

No species will be found at all points shown on our maps, but it is unlikely to be seen anywhere outside the shaded area.

5. Keys
Using the Wet, Dry and Map Keys takes a little practice, but with them it is possible to identify most species from a glimpse at sea or from a fragment, such as a jawbone, baleen plate, vertebral column or parasite, washed up on the shore. Armchair enthusiasts will find that it is even possible to play this Whale Game at home, using the Keys to identify whales, dolphins or porpoises from untitled or incorrectly captioned photographs in books and newspapers.

ORDER A: MYSTICETI

The Baleen Whales

In all 10 species of baleen whale teeth are present, if at all, only as vestigial buds in the embryo. By birth even these have gone, to be replaced as the animals mature by the typical filter plates of baleen. The baleen, however, has nothing to do with teeth. It did not evolve from teeth. It does not even grow from the gums. It is an entirely new and extraordinary structure.

In 1959 the American cetologist Dale Rice examined 39 Sei Whales (*Balaenoptera borealis 8*) brought into a whaling station in California. He found 2, both adults, in which the baleen plates were less than 7 cm (about 2.5 inches) long and completely lacking in hairy fringes. These were clearly useless for straining plankton from water, but both whales were nevertheless in good condition. One was even lactating. He found the stomachs to be filled with anchovies; the whales were unable to filter-feed in the normal baleen-whale fashion, but succeeded in making a good living on fish and squid.

Look any horse in the mouth and you will find that it has 18 or 20 tiny transverse ridges on its palate. Even cats and dogs have a few. It is possible that baleen developed from these, and that, in its early stages, it served mainly to assist in holding food more securely in the mouth. The aberrant Californian Sei Whales show that this stage is possible, but it is a very long way from a little ridge on the roof of the mouth to the massive four-metre sheets that push the Bowhead Whale's palate up as high as the roof of a two-storey building. There is nothing in the fossil record to fill the gap and the origin of the Mysticetes remains a mystery.

Nevertheless, the pattern of baleen formation in each of the filter-feeding whales is sufficiently distinctive for it to be used as a characteristic for field identification:

For the sake of uniformity, each row of baleen plates on one side of the jaw is called a *series*. The count of the number of plates in each series is made at gum level on the outside and an average is taken for both series. In right whales of the family Balaenidae this count excludes the large number of very fine hairs at the ends of the baleen row. The filter fibres which form the fringe are called *bristles* and the *filter area* is the combined inner surface of both left and right series.

In Mysticetes the baleen and the whole front end of the animal have been modified in ways which directly reflect the kind of food it eats. Takahisa Nemoto of the Ocean Research Institute in Tokyo has classified the filter feeders into three types:

i. **Skimmers** who move along the surface with their mouths open, skimming and sifting through the plankton. These have the longest baleen plates and, naturally, the greatest exaggeration of the head which houses them. The head is more than 30 per cent of body length, triangular and highly arched, with huge scooplike lower jaws, e.g. *Balaena glacialis 1* and *B. mysticetus 2*.

RIGHT WHALE

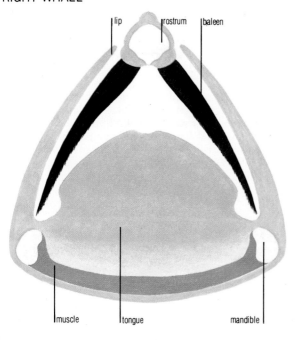

SEI WHALE

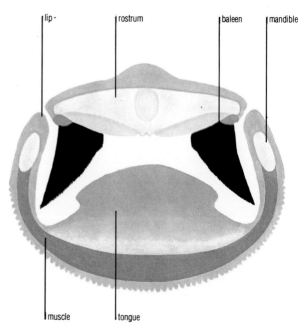

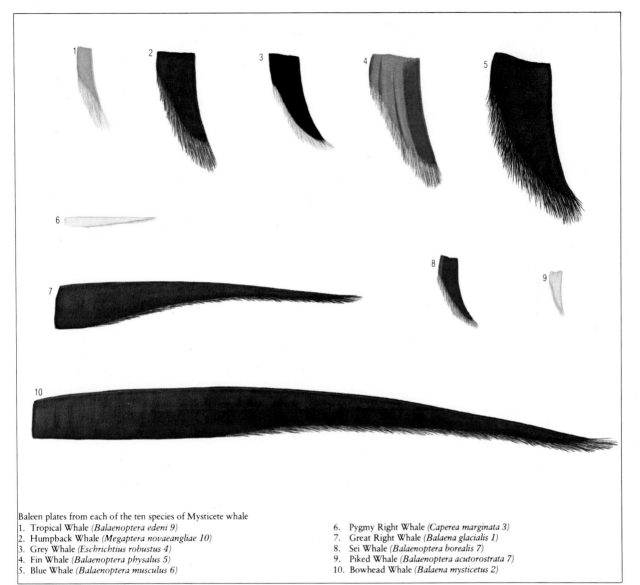

Baleen plates from each of the ten species of Mysticete whale
1. Tropical Whale (*Balaenoptera edeni 9*)
2. Humpback Whale (*Megaptera novaeangliae 10*)
3. Grey Whale (*Eschrichtius robustus 4*)
4. Fin Whale (*Balaenoptera physalus 5*)
5. Blue Whale (*Balaenoptera musculus 6*)
6. Pygmy Right Whale (*Caperea marginata 3*)
7. Great Right Whale (*Balaena glacialis 1*)
8. Sei Whale (*Balaenoptera borealis 7*)
9. Piked Whale (*Balaenoptera acutorostrata 7*)
10. Bowhead Whale (*Balaena mysticetus 2*)

ii. Swallowers who gulp at their food, usually rushing at it from the side or from below.

These have less development of the baleen and heads less than 25 per cent of body length, flat on the top, with upper jaws which fit into and between the lower ones, e.g. *Balaenoptera* species.

iii. Intermediates who do a bit of both, e.g. *Eschrichtius robustus 4.*

Even within these groups it is possible to recognize differences in the baleen and, from these, to predict what that whale most often eats, e.g. *Balaenoptera musculus 6* has comparatively well developed and fine baleen and feeds almost exclusively on those planktonic crustaceans known as krill,

B. acutorostrata 7 and *B. edeni 9*, which both have relatively short and coarse baleen, both feed on rather larger fish than their relatives.

The size and shape of the bristles on each baleen fringe are also indicative of an adaptation for dealing with a particular kind of floating food. Generally speaking, the finer the bristles the smaller the planktonic animals that can be trapped successfully.

The simple graph overleaf shows that the great whales have virtually shared out the ocean's bounty amongst themselves, each concentrating on, and specializing in, one clearly-defined section of the range of useful filter-feeding systems. There is little or no overlap; but where this does occur, particularly amongst the whales with finer bristles, the apparent conflict is resolved by the fact that the whales occur in different habitats, or at least occupy the same habitat in different seasons.

BALEEN DIMENSIONS

AVERAGE NUMBER OF BALEEN PLATES	MAXIMUM LENGTH (cm)	MAXIMUM WIDTH (cm)	MAXIMUM NUMBER OF BRISTLES	COLOUR OF BALEEN	SPECIES OF WHALE
260	240	30	70	dark olive grey	Great Right Whale *Balaena glacialis* **1**
350	450 very long	40	60	black, lighter bristle	Bowhead Whale *Balaena mysticetus* **2**
230	70	10	80 very many	ivory, dark bristles	Pygmy Right Whale *Caperea marginata* **3**
160 very few	50	25	40	medium grey, maize bristles	Grey Whale *Eschrichtius robustus* **4**
360	90	50 very wide	35	smoky blue grey or mustard, mustard bristles and some white	Fin Whale *Balaenoptera physalus* **5**
320	100	55 very wide	30	black	Blue Whale *Balaenoptera musculus* **6**
300	30	12	25	cream, pale cream or white bristles	Piked Whale *Balaenoptera acutorostrata* **7**
340	75	40	60	shiny black, fine white bristles	Sei Whale *Balaenoptera borealis* **8**
300	45	25	35	grey or pale, darker bristles	Tropical Whale *Balaenoptera edeni* **9**
330	64	15	35	deep grey or umber, lighter bristles	Humpback Whale *Megaptera novaeangliae* **10**

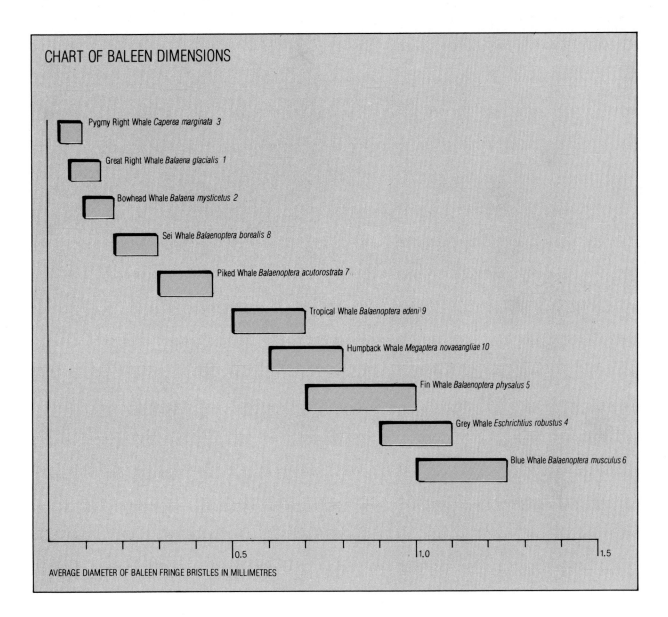

CHART OF BALEEN DIMENSIONS

Pygmy Right Whale *Caperea marginata* 3

Great Right Whale *Balaena glacialis* 1

Bowhead Whale *Balaena mysticetus* 2

Sei Whale *Balaenoptera borealis* 8

Piked Whale *Balaenoptera acutorostrata* 7

Tropical Whale *Balaenoptera edeni* 9

Humpback Whale *Megaptera novaeangliae* 10

Fin Whale *Balaenoptera physalus* 5

Grey Whale *Eschrichtius robustus* 4

Blue Whale *Balaenoptera musculus* 6

0.5   1.0   1.5

AVERAGE DIAMETER OF BALEEN FRINGE BRISTLES IN MILLIMETRES

61

Families of Baleen Whales

There are 3 families in the Order of the Mysticeti: Balaenidae which have no dorsal fin or throat grooves; Eschrichtidae which have no dorsal fin but have 2 short throat grooves; and Balaenopteridae which have a dorsal fin and many conspicuous throat grooves.

There is an exception to these rules, the Pygmy Right Whale (*Caperea marginata 3*) which has a fin and 2 short throat grooves. It is included at the moment in the family Balaenidae, but is perhaps odd enough to have a family of its own.

Family One   Balaenidae – the right whales
The head is disproportionately large and the rostrum and

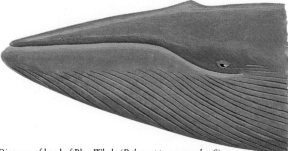

Diagram of head of Blue Whale (*Balaenoptera musculus 6*)

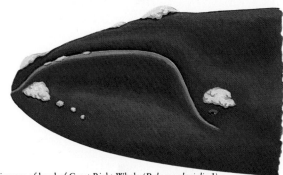

Diagram of head of Great Right Whale (*Balaena glacialis 1*)

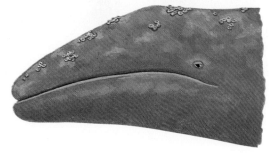

Diagram of head of Grey Whale (*Eschrichtius robustus 4*)

upper jaw are very long, thin and arched. The wide gap between the jaws is sealed by the huge lower lips which rise to cover the curtains of baleen which are suspended from the narrow palate.

There are 2 genera:
Balaena (with 2 species, the Great Right Whale and the Bowhead Whale) and *Caperea* (with a single species, the Pygmy Right Whale).

Family Two Eschrichtidae – the Grey Whale
The rostrum is narrower than that of the rorquals, but more gently arched than that of the right whales. The head is comparatively short and divided equally by the mouth. There is only 1 genus, *Eschrichtius* (with a single species, the Grey Whale).

Family Three Balaenopteridae – the rorqual whales
There is a moderate development of the baleen and a massive enlargement of the throat, made possible by the many pleats or grooves. The build of all the rorquals is slimmer and far less bizarre than that of the right whales, and the head is much broader and more flattened above.
There are 2 genera:
Balaenoptera (with 5 species, the Fin, Blue, Piked, Sei and Tropical whales) and *Megaptera* (with a single species, the Humpback Whale).

The 5 Mysticete genera have distinctive characteristics which make it possible to tell them apart fairly easily in the field, using the Wet Key overleaf.

Stranded cetaceans usually allow you the luxury of working out an identification at leisure. If, however, the animal is still alive or in danger of being taken by the tide you may have to work more quickly and this is where the Dry Key (overleaf) is likely to be most useful. In the case of older strandings, when the animal may be in an advanced state of decomposition or even have no flesh at all, you will have to abandon the key after 1. and turn instead to the sections on baleen or teeth for diagnosis.

Check the diagnosis on the Map Key but remember that dead whales, or parts of them, can drift for considerable distances at sea.

Map Key: The world ocean is divided, for convenience, into 5 major parts. In practice, the division between the South Pacific and the South Atlantic is a good one, preventing the passage between them of all but those species sufficiently at home in cold water to go far enough south to get round Cape Horn. The Cape of Good Hope is a much less effective barrier between the South Atlantic and the Indian Ocean; and there is no real barrier between the Indian Ocean and the South Pacific.

The equator forms a temperature barrier between the northern and southern sectors of the Atlantic and Pacific.

CHART OF FIELD CHARACTERISTICS

GENUS	FIN	SPOUT	FLUKES	HEAD	COLOUR
Balaena (Right Whales)	none	double, V-shaped	pointed, raised in diving	large, arched lip	deep grey black
Caperea (Pygmy Right Whale)	seldom seen	inconspicuous	never seen	small, more rounded	medium grey, lighter band on neck
Eschrichtius (Grey Whale)	none	single (diverging)	less pointed, sometimes raised	tapered, with barnacles	medium grey (mottled)
Balaenoptera (Rorquals)	clearly visible	single, tall	seldom seen	flat, with 1 or 3 ridges	dark grey light pleated throat
Megaptera (Humpback Whale)	clearly visible	single, bushy	serrated, often raised	flat, with many knobs	deep grey black, white flippers

CHART OF MAP KEY

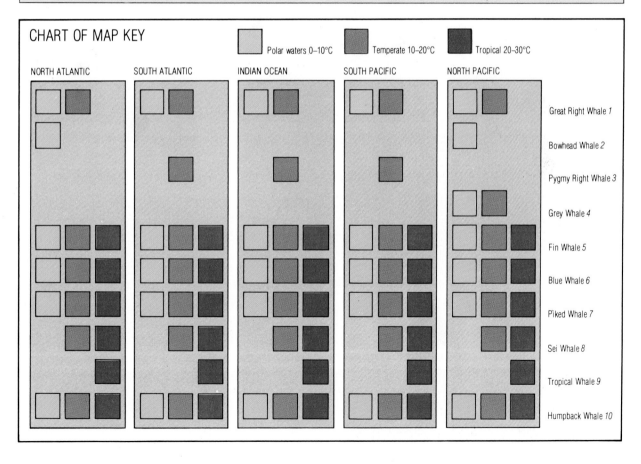

Polar waters 0–10°C   Temperate 10–20°C   Tropical 20–30°C

NORTH ATLANTIC   SOUTH ATLANTIC   INDIAN OCEAN   SOUTH PACIFIC   NORTH PACIFIC

Great Right Whale 1
Bowhead Whale 2
Pygmy Right Whale 3
Grey Whale 4
Fin Whale 5
Blue Whale 6
Piked Whale 7
Sei Whale 8
Tropical Whale 9
Humpback Whale 10

WET KEY

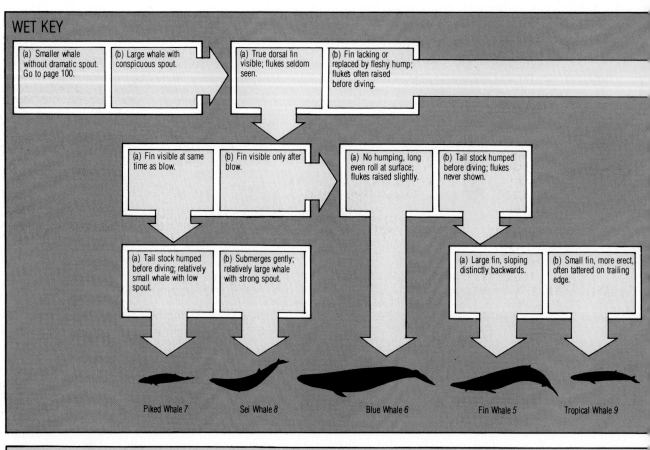

(a) Smaller whale without dramatic spout. Go to page 100.

(b) Large whale with conspicuous spout.

(a) True dorsal fin visible; flukes seldom seen.

(b) Fin lacking or replaced by fleshy hump; flukes often raised before diving.

(a) Fin visible at same time as blow.

(b) Fin visible only after blow.

(a) No humping, long even roll at surface; flukes raised slightly.

(b) Tail stock humped before diving; flukes never shown.

(a) Tail stock humped before diving; relatively small whale with low spout.

(b) Submerges gently; relatively large whale with strong spout.

(a) Large fin, sloping distinctly backwards.

(b) Small fin, more erect, often tattered on trailing edge.

Piked Whale 7   Sei Whale 8   Blue Whale 6   Fin Whale 5   Tropical Whale 9

DRY KEY

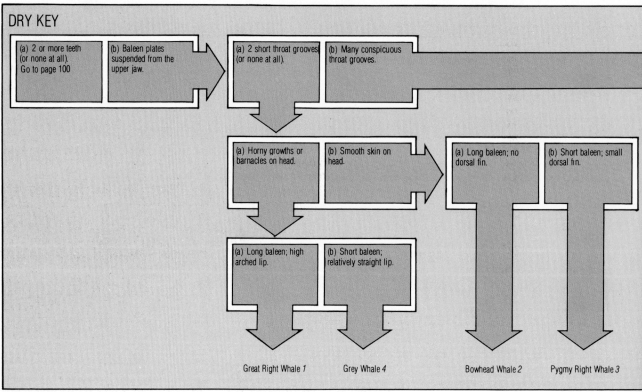

(a) 2 or more teeth (or none at all). Go to page 100

(b) Baleen plates suspended from the upper jaw.

(a) 2 short throat grooves (or none at all).

(b) Many conspicuous throat grooves.

(a) Horny growths or barnacles on head.

(b) Smooth skin on head.

(a) Long baleen; no dorsal fin.

(b) Short baleen; small dorsal fin.

(a) Long baleen; high arched lip.

(b) Short baleen; relatively straight lip.

Great Right Whale 1   Grey Whale 4   Bowhead Whale 2   Pygmy Right Whale 3

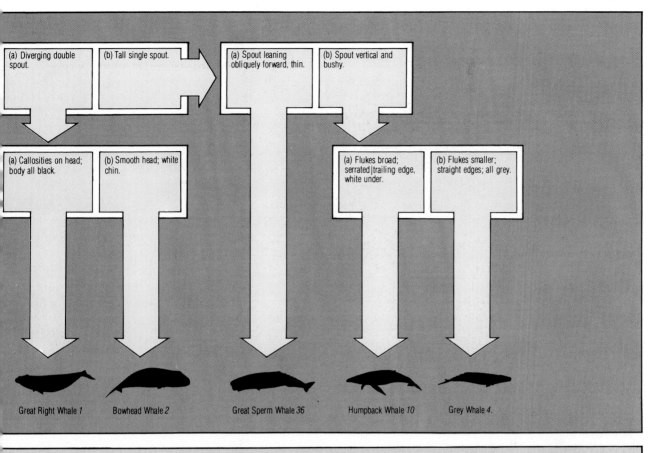

(a) Diverging double spout.

(b) Tall single spout.

(a) Spout leaning obliquely forward, thin.

(b) Spout vertical and bushy.

(a) Callosities on head; body all black.

(b) Smooth head; white chin.

(a) Flukes broad; serrated|trailing edge, white under.

(b) Flukes smaller; straight edges; all grey.

Great Right Whale *1*

Bowhead Whale *2*

Great Sperm Whale *36*

Humpback Whale *10*

Grey Whale *4.*

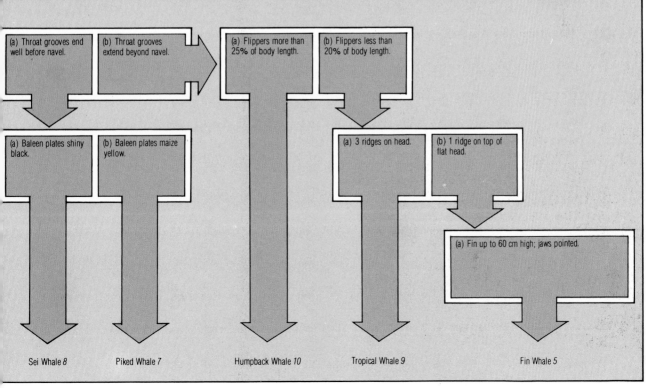

(a) Throat grooves end well before navel.

(b) Throat grooves extend beyond navel.

(a) Flippers more than 25% of body length.

(b) Flippers less than 20% of body length.

(a) Baleen plates shiny black.

(b) Baleen plates maize yellow.

(a) 3 ridges on head.

(b) 1 ridge on top of flat head.

(a) Fin up to 60 cm high; jaws pointed.

Sei Whale *8*

Piked Whale *7*

Humpback Whale *10*

Tropical Whale *9*

Fin Whale *5*

Family One – Balaenidae

In this family, established by John Edward Gray in 1825, the baleen apparatus is at its most extravagant. The head is correspondingly enormous, in some species up to almost 40 per cent of body length; and, to support this weight, all 7 neck vertebrae are fused into a single solid unit.

GREAT RIGHT WHALE

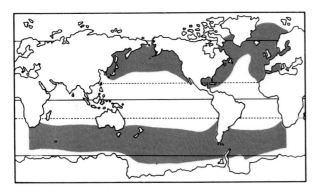

Classification Pliny the Elder described this species in *Historia Naturalis* as *balaena*, the true whale, to distinguish it from Aristotle's *physeter*, the sperm whale. In 1742 Hans Egede, a Danish missionary in Greenland, referred to it by its local name of *sildqval*. Linnaeus published his binomial system a few years later, describing the related Bowhead Whale, which he named *Balaena mysticetus*. A contemporary German naturalist, O. S. Müller, realized that the common black whale known to Norwegian whalers as *nordcaper*, differed sufficiently from the Bowhead to warrant its own name and in 1776 created the new species *B. glacialis*, from the Latin *glacies*, ice. The credit for the original description of this species is sometimes given to another German, Georg Borowski, but his work on natural history was not published until 1781.

In 1864 Gray at the British Museum decided that the Right Whale should have its own genus and invented *Eubalaena*, from the Greek *eu*, right. This initiative was largely ignored until 1908, when the American taxonomist J. A. Allen, resurrected it. For almost seventy years the Bowhead and Right whales were consigned to separate genera, but the actual differences between them are small, certainly no greater than those separating the five species of rorqual included in the genus *Balaenoptera* and it is now generally accepted that first thoughts were right. These two whales belong together.

Further confusion has resulted from the fact that there are also two quite distinct populations of Right Whales in the temperate areas of the northern and southern hemispheres. When the French physiologist Antoine Desmoulins received a complete skeleton, sent back from Algoa Bay in South Africa by the veteran collector Antoine Delalande, he had no local specimen with which to compare it and decided, in 1822, to describe it as a new species which he called *Balaena australis* from the Latin *auster*, south. The skeleton is still on view in the whale gallery of the Musée Nationale d'Histoire Naturelle in Paris and clearly differs in no substantial way from others collected more recently from both hemispheres. There appears to be no justification for considering the northern and southern Right Whales as distinct species, but they have been separated geographically for long enough to acquire slight differences that justify subspecific status. So the southern form is now known as *B. glacialis australis* (DESMOULINS 1822).

Attempts have been made to separate the North Atlantic

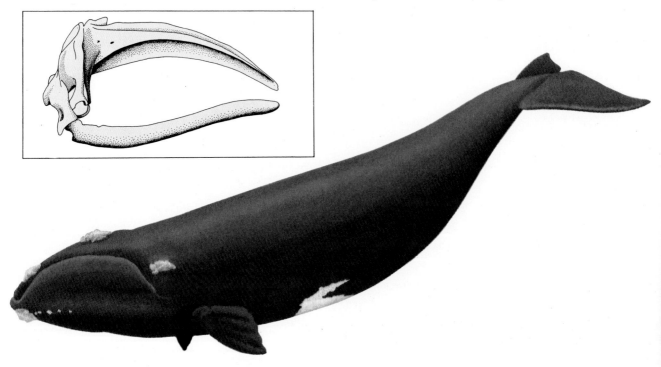

and North Pacific populations in the same way. Lacépède in 1818, on the basis only of a watercolour by a Japanese artist, proposed the existence there of *B. japonica*, and in 1864 Gray, looking at another illustration (by the Dutch explorer Temminck) decided that there must be two species in Japan, the second of which he called *B. sieboldii* after Karl von Siebold, the Professor of Zoology at Munich. However, more recent studies have failed to find any differences at all between right whales anywhere in the northern hemisphere.

Local Names This whale's slow speed and the fact that its body is so rich in oil that it floats, even when dead, led to Right Whale, i.e. the 'right' whale to hunt. The first systematic whaling was along the shores of the Bay of Biscay and so this whale is also known as the Biscayan right whale or the Biscay whale, *baleine de Biscaye* or *baleine de Basque* (French) and *ballena*, the whale (Spanish). Another popular early whaling ground off the North Cape of Norway in the summer led to *nordkaper* (Norwegian), *noordkaper* (Dutch) and *Nordkaper* (German). Others include *sebi kujira* (Japanese), *svarthval* (Danish), *cullamach* (Aleutian), *nastoiaschchii kit* (Russian) *liljehval* and *id* (Norwegian). We know it simply as the Great Right Whale.

Description Large; length averages about 15 m (50 ft) for both sexes, with a maximum of 18 m (60 ft); calves are 5–6 m (16–19 ft) at birth. Weight averages about 54,500 kg (60 tons), with a maximum of 96,000 kg (106 tons).

The body is stocky and fat, smoothly rotund without a trace of dorsal fin or any ridge along the back. The head is large, about 25 per cent of body length, with a long, narrow, highly arched upper jaw designed for the suspension of baleen plates more than 2 m (7 ft) long. This development is not as extreme as that of the Bowhead and, when seen from the side, the outline of the head runs smoothly back into the body with no suggestion of a neck.

There are no throat grooves, but there is a series of lumps or callosities on the head in front of the blowhole. These are crusty, horny outgrowths of the skin, as much as 10 cm (4 inches) high and usually infested with a colourful colony of barnacles, parasitic worms and whale lice. The largest section of this 'rock garden' perches on the tip of the upper jaw, but the shape, size and precise distribution of the callosities give each individual whale unique characteristics. Roger Payne, in his field study of the southern Great Right Whales in Patagonia, uses the patterns to keep track of his subjects and has found that they are unchanging over the years. Most callosities have sensory bristles pushing through them and tend to occur in the same areas as the whales' facial hair.

The colour is usually black above, often mottled with brown and disrupted by scars and patches, some undoubtedly caused by contact with the rough growths on other whales. There are usually irregular blotches of white on the chin and around the navel. Calves are often much lighter than adults, sometimes almost white. The baleen is light grey, darkening with age and can, when the whales are feeding near the surface, look yellowish.

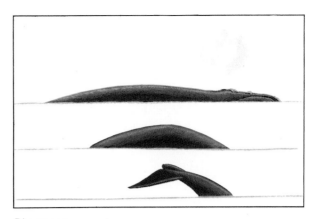

Dive sequence

Field Identification The smooth, finless back makes it unlikely that Great Right Whales will be confused with any other species except the Bowhead (*B. mysticetus*). The ranges of the two species now overlap only in the Bering Sea, where Great Right Whales occur in the summer and Bowheads in the winter.

In case of doubt, the following characteristics should be sufficient to tell them apart:

B.glacialis has callosities; is otherwise dark all over; neither sex shows any neck.
B.mysticetus has no callosities; has a bright white chin; males have a distinct constriction at the neck.

The blow is highly characteristic. The blowholes are widely separated and produce 2 distinct spouts rising up to 5 m (16 ft) in a V-shaped fan of mist. The usual breathing pattern is for the whale to cruise at the surface for 5–10 minutes, blowing roughly once a minute, and then dive for 10–20 minutes. On rare occasions dives may be longer; 60 minutes has been recorded, but is exceptional. Underwater observation in shallow water has shown that the whales sometimes submerge and remain motionless at the bottom for 10 minutes at a time.

During breathing the body is held high in the water and, on diving, the flukes nearly always show quite clearly. Only two other great whales reveal their tails in this way, the Great Sperm Whale (*Physeter macrocephalus 36*) and the Humpback Whale (*Megaptera novaeangliae 10*). If only the tail is seen, the 3 species may be distinguished as follows:

Balaena broad flukes; smooth edge, very pointed tips; deeply notched; dark below.
Physeter triangular flukes; smooth straight edge; small notch; dark below.
Megaptera broad flukes; highly scalloped edge; moderately notched; white below.

Great Right Whales are slow, seldom reaching as much as 10 kph (5 knots). They are usually easy to approach by ship and can be touched by a small inflatable boat before they move away or sound. Their behaviour at the surface may involve basking and rolling over on their backs or sailing with the broad tail flukes held up at right angles to the wind. In high winds (which may create enough wave noise to drown their normal voices) they seem to keep in contact by slapping the surface with their flippers or tails, or even by breaching. In leaps clear of the water they invariably land on their backs.

Stranding Great Right Whales are rarely stranded, because of their familiarity with shallow water, in which they spend much of their lives. There is little difficulty in identifying a dead or beached individual. One of the most interesting features of a recently dead whale is the fauna in its 'rock garden'. Whale lice, *Cyamus ovalis* and *C. erraticus*, are the most conspicuous parasites on the callosities and in the eyes, mouth, blowhole and genital grooves. In the southern whales *C. catadonti* has also been found. This is normally specific to the Great Sperm Whale (*Physeter macrocephalus 36*), which might mean that the two species form some kind of association (though it seems unlikely) where their ranges overlap. There are also several species of barnacle and sometimes a greenish-yellow coating produced by the parasitic diatom *Cocconeis ceticola*.

A skeleton should be equally easy to identify. The bones of the rostrum form a high arch in the skull, from each side of which hang 230–390 (average 260) narrow laminae or plates of dark olive-grey baleen. Each plate is up to 2.4 m (8 ft) long and has rougher bristles than those of the Bowhead.

There are 14 or 15 pairs of ribs and 56 or 57 vertebrae, the first 7 fused into a single unit.

One of the most astonishing facts about the Great Right Whale is that the testes of an adult male each weigh over 900 kg (1 ton), making them the largest in the animal kingdom.

Natural History Great Right Whales feed at or just below the surface, largely on shoaling planktonic crustaceans while moving at about 4 kph (2 knots) with their mouths open, closing the lips every few minutes to begin the process of straining through their copious fringes of fine baleen, and swallowing. In the northern hemisphere the most common food is the euphausid *Thysanoessa inermis* and the pelagic crustacean *Meganictyphanes norvegica*, while in the south it is usually the larger krill *Euphausia superba*. Sometimes the whales feed on bottom-living molluscs, standing on their heads in shallow water to do so.

The usual social group is a small herd of less than 6, most often a family unit. Mating occurs in early spring and is boisterous. Courtship begins with a series of breaches and then goes on to pushing and nuzzling, followed by stroking with flippers and caressing with flukes. Often a group of males will attend a receptive female, slapping their tails on the water as they manoeuvre for favourable positions.

Gestation lasts 9–10 months and a single calf is born in winter in a protected shallow bay. It suckles for a full year and spends another two or three in close touch with its mother

before she mates again. Roger Payne gives a vivid description of mother-infant play:

'I have watched many a calf boisterously playing about its resting mother for hours at a time, sliding off her flukes, wriggling up on to her back, covering her blowhole with its tail, breaching against her repeatedly, butting into her flank – all without perceptible reaction from the mother. When finally she does respond to the torment, it may be only to roll on to her back and embrace the infant in her armlike flippers, holding it until it calms down.'

One discovery to emerge from Payne's study in the calving ground off the Valdez Peninsula in Patagonia is that there are three distinct populations breeding there, each group returning once every three years and then melting away somewhere into the Southern Ocean until their turn comes round again at the end of the next calving interval.

Social cohesion is undoubtedly strong and was used by whalers. One calf was harpooned in the Bay of San Sebastian in northern Spain, whereupon the mother took it under her flipper and dragged it away until the line broke. Next day the body of the calf was found floating out at sea and was towed back to the village with the cow in close attendance. She remained there in the harbour with her dead calf for 6 hours despite being shot at and wounded several times.

The most common sound is a belch which lasts about a second at a frequency of 500 Hz. Moans have also been recorded between 160 and 235 Hz. Occasionally there are pulsed sounds with a duration of .06 second at 2,100 Hz. These occur mostly at night. There is no evidence yet of repeated vocalizations or songs, at least in Patagonia.

A recording of a northern Great Right Whale off Cape Cod included a regular clacking sound, at first assumed to be good evidence of echolocation; it turned out on analysis and direct observation to be nothing more than the noise of the flexible plates of baleen bumping into each other as a stream of water passed between them.

Status Following heavy whaling in the nineteenth century populations everywhere were reduced to critical levels. The species has now been protected for some years and, while still rare, there are signs of a slow recovery. There may now be 200 off the South African coast and an equivalent number wintering serially off Argentina. They tend to be scarcer in the northern hemisphere. The worldwide total may be as low as 2,000.

Distribution Once widespread throughout its range, this whale is confined to shallow coastal waters with local concentrations in Newfoundland, Madeira, Patagonia, Tristan da Cunha, South Africa, Crozet Island, Amsterdam Island, south-western Australia, New Zealand, Chile, Japan, the Aleutians and Alaska. There are migratory movements, involving a slow drift towards the equator in winter and away from it in summer months.

Sources BEST (1970) in South Africa, CLARKE (1965) in Chile, CUMMINGS et al (1972) sounds, MÜLLER (1776) original description, MÜLLER (1954) taxonomy, PAYNE (1976) behaviour, PAYNE & PAYNE (1971) sounds, SAAYMAN & TAYLER (1973) behaviour.

BOWHEAD WHALE

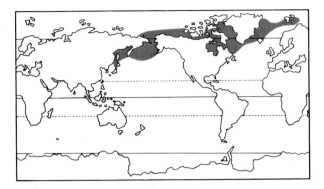

Classification Linnaeus called the Bowhead *Balaena mysticetus*, from the Greek *mustax*, a moustache and *ketos*, a sea monster.

There are 4 geographically isolated populations, but no recognized subspecies or races.

Local Names In the seventeenth- and eighteenth-century whaling boom this whale was so common that it was known as the common whale, *the* whale, or *la baleine* (French). Its abundance around Greenland led to great polar whale, arctic

whale, Greenland right whale, *Greenlandsvalur* (Icelandic), *Groenlandse walvisch* (Dutch), *Gronlandsval* (Swedish) and *wieloryb Grenlanzki* (Polish). The smooth finless back led to *sletbag* (Norwegian), *schilchteback* (Danish) and *glathvaler* (Icelandic). The bowshaped skull led to bowhead, *Bogenkop* (German) and *hokkyoku kujira* (Japanese). Arctic aboriginal peoples call it *akbek* (Greenland), *kakhlim* (Yakut), *ugamachcach* (Aleutian) and *akhgropik* (Chokotsk). Alaskan Eskimos, who battle now to be allowed to continue whaling on their remnant population, recognize 2 forms, *kairalik* and the smaller *ingotok* ('poggy' to ninteenth-century American whalers) but *ingotok* is probably an immature animal.

We continue to use the traditional name of Bowhead Whale.

Description Large; length averages 15 m (50 ft) for both sexes with a probable maximum of 20 m (65 ft). Reports of much greater lengths in the last century are probably exaggerated by measurement along curve of the body; calves are 3.5–4.5 m (11–15 ft) at birth. There are no reliable records of weight but it probably averages 90,000 kg (110 tons), with a maximum recorded of 110,000 kg (122 tons).

This is a thickset, very heavy whale, with huge curving upper jawbones in an immense head, up to 40 per cent of body

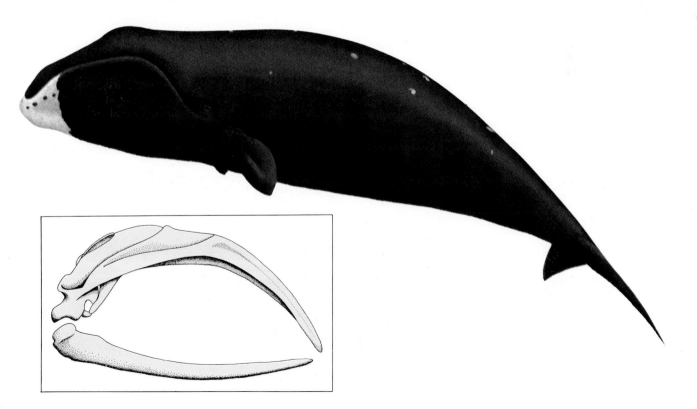

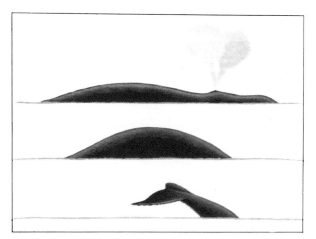

Dive sequence

The blowholes are widely spaced and the spout is a diverging double blast of spray, rising up to 7 m (23 ft). Bowheads usually breathe 4–6 times in about 3 minutes and then sound for up to 20 minutes. The dive is almost vertical, with tail flukes thrown high into the air before slipping smoothly beneath the water. Whales often surface again in the same place.

Bowheads are the only large whales routinely found in Arctic waters and any possibility of confusion with other species is minimized by the fact that all the others which could occur there have clearly visible dorsal fins.

Bowheads are easy to approach. Their only reaction to shipping is to lift the high dome of the jaw clear of the water to bring the eyes into position to see directly ahead. In this posture the white bib is exposed. Sometimes these whales may breach, throwing their heavy bodies clear of the water and falling back with a tremendous splash.

For some reason, Bowheads are very often found following the Unicorn Whale (*Monodon monoceros 34*).

Stranding Bowheads are rarely stranded, but identification of beached individuals is easy. The white chin and tail bands darken to black soon after death, but the body shape is unmistakable. There are a few whale lice (*Cyamus ceti*).

The skull is very large, with a long narrow rostrum that widens only near the eyes. Its height is greater than the depth of any other part of the body and provides suspension for the longest baleen plates of all filter-feeding whales. There are 300–360 plates (normally 350) on either side of the jaw, 4–4.5 m (13–15 ft) long, narrow and fringed with very fine feathery bristles. The longest plates are in the centre where the bow is deepest and all are dark grey or black with lighter fringes. In sunlight the bristles have a metallic green shine.

In many individuals there is a set of vestigial limb and pelvic bones where the hindlimbs used to be, now lying loose in the blubber unconnected to any part of the skeleton.

There are 53–55 vertebrae, the first 7 fused together.

length. The lips are very thick, eyes surprisingly small, set almost invisibly at the corner of the mouth. The back, like that of the Great Right Whale (*Balaena glacialis 1*), is smooth and finless. The flukes are broad, smooth-edged and deeply notched; there are no callosities or growths on the skin and no throat grooves.

The colour is overall velvet black, though the upper lip, tailstock, eyelids and flippers can be tinged with medium grey. A distinct and characteristic white (or sometimes yellowish) 'shirt front' or 'bib' on the chin, extends perhaps 2 m (6.5 ft) from the tip of the lower jaw. Running round this white zone, along the lip-line, may be a 'necklace' of dark spots; some individuals have a white band around the thinnest part of the tailstock. Calves are pale bluish black all over.

Field Identification The smooth, broad back is without a fin. Most adults show 2 distinct curves in profile, clearly visible even in the water; one starts on the nose and ends behind the bow of the head, the other encompasses the rest of the back. The young tend to be more stubby and uniformly barrel-shaped.

Natural History Like Great Right Whales, Bowheads are adapted for feeding on microplankton. The fine fringes on the inner margin of the baleen plates successfully trap all the

Feeding posture showing baleen plates

smaller shoaling crustaceans that abound along the edge of the Arctic icepack, most commonly the copepods *Calanus plumchrus* and *C. cristatus*. During feeding, Bowheads can be seen skimming along a plankton slick at the surface, with mouths open for long periods, waiting until a sufficient weight of crustaceans has accumulated on the baleen to justify the effort involved in swallowing. They have been known also to feed on pteropod molluscs (*Clione* spp.).

These whales are usually found singly or in small groups of 3 or 4, travelling at 5 kph (2–3 knots). When they were more plentiful it was common to see larger groups of up to 50 or even 100.

Little is known of their social behaviour. Mating occurs in early spring and copulation usually takes place between pairs hanging vertically in the water with their white chin patches showing above the surface. Gestation lasts 10–12 months and calves (occasionally twins) are born in mid-winter at the southern limit of the range. Nursing continues for almost a year, until the calf has doubled its length to about 7 m (24 ft). Mothers are said to tuck their calves under a flipper when danger threatens. They probably breed every other year.

The voice of the Bowhead is similar to that of the Great Right Whale (*Balaena glacialis 1*).

Status Bowheads were once so abundant that early whalers anchored at favourite haunts such as Spitzbergen and remained there throughout the season. The species began to become scarce in the seventeenth century and is now at a critical level everywhere; it may continue to decline even without further whaling. In 1978 a survey of the Chuckchi and Beaufort seas population placed Bowhead numbers between 1,783 and 2,865.

Little is known about other populations, except that they are low; 23 were seen going out of Baffin Bay into Lancaster Sound in 1976 and there have been isolated sightings from the Sea of Okhotsk and from the Greenland and Barents seas. The total world population is unlikely to be much more than 3,000.

Distribution There seem to be 4 remnant populations. The most abundant is in the western Canadian Arctic, moving from Banks Island and the Beaufort Sea in summer to the Chuckchi Sea and through the straits into the Bering Sea in winter. The second is in the Sea of Okhotsk, with a stray reported as far south as Osaka, Japan. The third moves between Baffin Bay and Hudson Bay in eastern Canada, perhaps travelling into the Labrador Sea in winter. The fourth, and least numerous, consists of a few tiny remnant groups in what used to be the main breeding grounds in the Greenland and Barents seas.

Like Great Right Whales, Bowheads hug shores and coastlines, favouring shallow bays and inlets, but also voyage along, and sometimes under, the edge of the Arctic iceshelf in deeper water. According to Eskimo sources, Bowheads can, when they need to breathe, smash their way through ice almost 1 m (3 ft) thick.

Sources BRAHAM et al (1979) in Alaska, GREENDALE et al (1976) in North Atlantic, JONSGARD (1968) review, LINNAEUS (1758) original description, NISHIWAKI (1970) in Japan, SCORESBY (1820) general.

PYGMY RIGHT WHALE

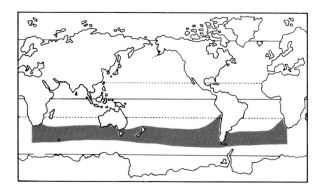

Classification During the world voyage of HMS *Erebus* and HMS *Terror* between 1839 and 1843, a huge natural history collection was made. Included in it were three unusual baleen plates found on a beach in Western Australia. These were presented to the British Museum and when Gray came to study them he recognized the plates (which were long in relation to their width) as being similar to those of the right whales, but considerably smaller and almost white, with black only on the outer edges. Gray classified them as having come from a new species he named *Balaena marginata* (from the Latin *margo*, *marginis*, a border).

By 1870 a skull complete with baleen had arrived at the British Museum from Kawau Island in New Zealand and Gray was able to see that it differed sufficiently from the Great Right Whale to be considered as a separate genus, which he decided to call *Neobalaena*. In 1864 he established a new genus *Caperea* (from the Latin *capero*, wrinkle) for an isolated and oddly wrinkled right tympanic bone, also from New Zealand.

In 1934 Australian zoologists showed that the baleen, skull and earbone belonged to a single species which, according to the principle of priority, had to be known as *Caperea mar-ginata.* It seems likely that this species is the only surviving offshoot of an early stock that took a slightly different evolutionary path from its relatives. No further species or subspecies are known.

Local names *Dwerg walvis* (Dutch), *Zwergglattwal* (German), *dvergretthval* (Norwegian), *balein franche-naine* (French), *kosemi kujira* (Japanese) and *gladkii kit* (Russian).

To distinguish it from the Great Right Whale, we call this species the Pygmy Right Whale.

Description Medium; length averages about 5 m (16 ft) for both sexes, with a maximum recorded of 6.4 m (21 ft); calves are about 2 m (6.5 ft) at birth. Weight averages about 4,500 kg (5 tons).

This is the smallest baleen whale, with a bow to the jaw like that of the Great Right Whale (*Balaena glacialis 1*), a distinct neck and a head roughly 25 per cent of body length. It is much thinner and more streamlined than the other members of the family and, unlike them, has a dorsal fin. This is small, triangular, recurved and set back two-thirds of the way to the tail. The flippers are narrow and slightly rounded at the tip and the flukes are broad with a well-formed notch. There are no callosities but there are two marked eye folds which look like dark bruises.

A further unusual feature for this family is the 2 clearly marked throat grooves. These escaped scientific notice until a live whale was filmed underwater in South Africa in 1967. As it swam and turned and showed the true convexity of its throat, the grooves became visible for the first time. They are almost certainly forerunners of the longer grooves found in the Grey Whale and the complex furrows which give the rorqual whales such enormous throat expansion. The fact that they went unnoticed for a century clearly illustrates the limitation of studies based only on beached whales in which

decomposition has produced distortion, or, in the Russian case, on freshly caught animals which had been inflated with an air hose.

The general colour is a deep blue grey, lighter beneath, with a darker band from the flipper to the eye and a lighter grey halter line across the back behind and between the flippers.

Field Identification Pygmy Right Whales are slow moving and inconspicuous and may be very much more common than is suggested by the few isolated live sightings.

The blowholes are paired, but the spout is barely visible and has no distinct shape. The whale tends to throw its snout up out of the water when breathing and spends only seconds at the surface before sinking out of sight, often without showing the back or fin at all. There are normally about 50 seconds between blows. Dives, which tend to be shallow, last 3–4 minutes. The tail flukes are not normally visible and no Pygmy Right Whale has ever been seen to leap or breach.

The swimming speed is slow, usually about 5 kph (3 knots) but the motion is peculiar. When these whales can be seen through or from below the surface, they move with an undulating wavelike pattern.

The most likely source of confusion is between the Pygmy Right Whale and the Piked Whale (*Balaenoptera acutorostrata 7*):

Caperea seldom shows fin when breathing; back also seldom seen; flipper dark; rounded head; no throat grooves; shy.
Balaenoptera shows fin when breathing; back humped when diving; white patch on flipper; sharp head; no throat grooves; attracted to ships.

Pygmy Right Whales have been seen together with Shortfin Pilot Whales (*Globicephala macrorhynchus 50*) and Sei Whales (*Balaenoptera borealis 8*).

Stranding Until recently this whale was known only from about 40 strandings on beaches in Australia, New Zealand, South Africa and the Falklands. The most popular site seems to have been Kangaroo Island in the Australian Bight.

On a recently beached animal the best sources of identification lie in the mouth. The baleen plates are ivory coloured, with a dark rim on the outer edge. They are about 70 cm (28 inches) long, slender and elastic with a very soft fine fringe. There is an average of 230 plates on each side of the jaw. The tongue is pure white and strangely feathered at the tip.

The skull is recognizably that of a baleen whale, with a lower jaw proportionately stronger and heavier than in any other species. The skeleton is most peculiar. Pygmy Right Whales have more ribs than any other whale; there are 17 pairs, and the ones nearest the tail have become extraordinarily wide and flat, presumably to provide additional protection to the internal organs, though it is not clear why this should have become necessary. As usual the first 7 vertebrae are fused, but the total number of 40–41 is less than in both species of *Balaena*. In addition the skeleton of the flipper is odd in having only 4 digits or phalanges instead of the more usual 5.

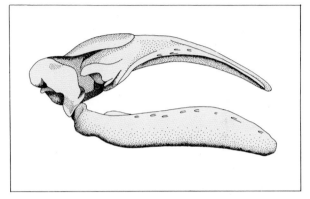

Above: typical breathing posture with the head thrown up out of the water
Below: skull

Natural History Hardly anything is known. Soviet whalers killed a few specimens for scientific purposes in the South Atlantic in 1970, from which we have learned little more than that their stomachs contained unidentified species of the tiny crustacean *Calanus*. On the few occasions these whales have been seen alive, they have been found, usually in pairs, in shallow bays. There is one sighting of 8 individuals together. Calves seem to be born in September or October and may suckle until they are 3.6 m (11 ft) in length.

Status It seems likely that difficulties in sighting and identification have made this species seem rarer than it actually is, but its status is unknown.

Distribution This whale's distribution is circumpolar in the southern hemisphere only, north of the Antarctic convergence and almost entirely south of a line which marks the limit of water cooler than 20°C.

Pygmy Right Whales are known so far from the Falkland Islands, the South Atlantic, South Africa, Crozet Island, South Australia, Victoria, Tasmania and New Zealand.

Sources DAVIES & GUILER (1957) stranding, GRAY (1846) original description, GRAY (1864) taxonomy, IREDALE & TROUGHTON (1934) taxonomy, IVASHIN et al (1972) feeding, ROSS (1975) in South Africa, ROSS et al (1975) live sightings.

Family Two – Eschrichtidae

A single species, the Grey Whale, was placed in this family on its own by Ellerman and Morrison-Scott in 1951. It is in many ways intermediate between the right whales and the rorquals.

There is no dorsal fin, but there are 2 short throat grooves. The body is less robust than that of the Balaenidae, but not as slender as that of the Balaenopteridae.

GREY WHALE

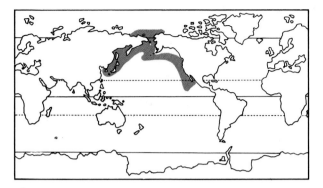

Classification The first scientific reference to the Grey Whale was made by an English naturalist, the Hon. Paul Dudley, in an essay published in 1725. He referred to it as the 'scrag' whale. In 1777 a prominent German veterinarian Johann Polycarp Erxleben called a specimen *Balaena gibbosa*, from the Latin *gibbus*, humped, and for almost two hundred years this name was applied to the Grey Whale.

In 1955 Miller and Kellogg of the Smithsonian showed that the animal examined by Erxleben was probably not a Grey Whale. They decided that, in the circumstances, the earliest published name for the Grey Whale was *Rhachianectes glaucus*, 'the grey swimmer along rocky shores', given by an American palaeontologist named Edward Drinker Cope, who was the first, in 1868, to describe a recent specimen in the Pacific. For a while that too was acceptable.

Then, as it became clear that living Grey Whales in the Pacific and sub-fossil finds in Europe were actually the same animal, which once had a much wider distribution, it was realized that priority for the species had to be given to a Swedish professor, Wilhelm Lilljeborg, who in 1861 had excavated a skeleton 250 m from the sea at Graso in upland Sweden, and had described it as *Balaenoptera robusta*. Gray at the British Museum appreciated that the bones could not belong to a rorqual whale and in 1864 created the genus *Eschrichtius* in memory of Daniel Eschricht, professor of zoology at Copenhagen, who had died the previous year.

Local Names Apart from the English scrag, whalers knew this whale as rip sack, mussel digger and, because females in breeding lagoons become aggressive in defence of their calves, as devil fish or *koku kujira* (Japanese). Because of its colouring it is known as *baleine gris* (French), *ballena gris* (Spanish), *grijze walvisch* (Dutch), *grayze walvis* (Flemish), *grähval* (Norwegian), *gräso val* (Swedish); and because of the knobbly humps on its back, it has been called *knabbelvisch* (Dutch), *Knotenfisch* (German) and *baleine à six bosses* (French). The native people along its coastal migration route call it *chick-akhluk* (Aleutian), *kentaen uiiut* (Chuckchi) and *antokhak* (Alaskan Eskimo).

Description Large; length averages 12.2 m (40 ft) for males, with a maximum of 15.3 m (50 ft), and 12.8 m (42 ft) for females, with a maximum of 15 m (50 ft); calves are 4.5 m (15 ft) at birth. Weight averages 26,000 kg (about 28 tons)

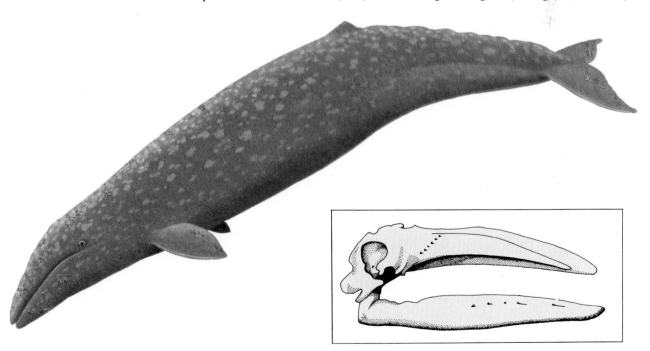

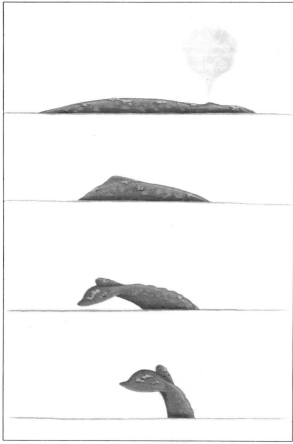

for males and 31,000 kg (about 34 tons) for females, with a maximum for both sexes of 34,000 kg (38 tons).

The Grey Whale is ungainly. Its head is bowed, but rather short and, when seen from above, sharply pointed. The profile is unmistakable: there is no dorsal fin, only a series of knuckles or bumps (usually 7–10, but sometimes as many as 15) along the midline of the lower back. The tail flukes are not large and are always abraded so that the tips are worn and rounded and the trailing edge visibly serrated. The species is strangely hairy; there are irregular rows of bristles on the top of the head and along the side of the lower jaw, with the greatest concentration growing in tufts on the tip of the snout. The eyes are small, circled by a skin-fold and on the throat there are 2 (occasionally 4) longitudinal grooves about 2 m (6.5 ft) in length.

The colour is basically dark grey, but varies. Most individuals are blotched and mottled with lighter flecks. Part of this dappling is due to discoloration of the skin, but much, particularly on the head, is caused by patches of whitish barnacles.

Field Identification The Grey Whale can be distinguished without difficulty from the other large whales without a fin, the Great Sperm Whale (*Physeter macrocephalus 36*) and the Great Right Whale (*Balaena glacialis 1*). The Grey Whale resembles the Sperm Whale in that it has knuckles or humps on the lower back, but the mottled grey colour is completely different. When swimming along just below the surface, the Grey Whale seems to be uniformly pale; in bright light it can look almost white.

The spout too is distinctive and loud. On still days it can be heard from more than one kilometre (at least half a mile) away. The blast is 3–4.5 m (10–15 ft) high and, unlike the Sperm Whale's, completely vertical. Although it emerges from twin blowholes, it usually appears in a single column, but it can sometimes be seen to be divided at the top. This separation is never as great as the divergence of the right whales' usual V-shaped blow.

Grey Whales have two characteristic breathing patterns. When making shallow dives of less than 30 m (100 ft) they blow 3 or 4 times at intervals of 10–20 seconds and then dive for 3–4 minutes, surfacing again about 300 m (1,000 ft) away. When diving more deeply, they take 5 or 6 breaths, disappear for longer periods of 7–10 minutes, and reappear roughly 600 m (2,000 ft) from the point of submergence. In both sequences, the whales spend approximately 15 per cent of their time at the surface. When undisturbed and resting, they may spend half an hour at a time basking in the sun. In the shallows of winter lagoons where the sun is hotter they rest on the bottom, rising to the surface every 10 minutes to breathe. The tail flukes usually only appear above the water before a deep dive.

Grey Whales are largely indifferent to shipping. In the breeding lagoons of Baja California they seem to accept, and even court, attention now being lavished upon them by whale-watchers. We have had our inflatable boats nuzzled by an inquisitive calf and, on one occasion, almost capsized by a friendly female who laid a full metre of her barnacled beak on

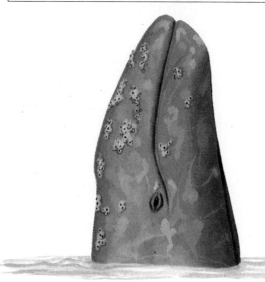

Above: dive sequence
Below: Grey Whale in the lookout position

our transom to be patted. A more common response to the approach of a boat is for the whale to stand with head lifted clear of the water in a pattern of behaviour which has been called 'spy hopping', 'pitchpoling' or 'spying out'. The whale's eyes are more than 2 m (6–7 ft) from the tip of the jaw and, to expose these, it beats its tail rapidly (or in shallow water even rests it on the bottom) and then rises up slowly. In the lookout position, maintained for as long as 30 seconds, it often turns deliberately through a full circle. Depending apparently on what it sees, the whale may go on with its business or it may breach, throwing itself half out of the water and splashing back 2 or 3 times in succession. We once counted 38 consecutive leaps in a manic sequence by a large male.

Grey Whales are sometimes seen with Bottlenose Dolphins (*Tursiops truncatus 76*). We have also seen Grey Whales being pestered by Great Killer Whales (*Orcinus orca 51*), who take the occasional calf. In a bay in Alaska we watched a pack of Killer Whales taking it in turns for half an hour to slide up and over the back of a female Grey Whale who continued to swim slowly on her way. The usual speed of the Grey Whale is about 7–10 kph (4–6 knots).

Stranding Their familiarity with shallow water means that Grey Whales seldom if ever strand themselves accidentally. The occasional dead whale presents no problems of identification. If death has been recent, it is worth looking for external parasites. Apart from barnacles, one of which (*Cryptolepas*

rhachianecti) is unique to the Grey Whale, there are many marine amphipods or whale lice, including one species (*Cyamus scammoni*) which knows no other habitat.

The skull is robust, rigid and very little bowed. Baleen plates are short and broad, 40–50 cm (16–20 inches) in length, grey with a narrow yellowish fringe. There are 160–180 (usually 160) plates on each side of the jaw, many of which are infested with barnacles. Often those on the right side are more worn than those on the left. The tongue is narrow and salmon pink with a grey tip.

There are 56 separate vertebrae and 14 pairs of ribs. The third to seventh pairs of ribs are double headed. The first finger of the flipper is missing, leaving 4 phalanges clearly visible as lighter lines in the dark skin of the paddle.

Natural History Unlike all other baleen whales, the Grey Whale seems to be specifically adapted for bottom-feeding. The sharp beak and short stiff baleen plates are suited to ploughing along the bottom, stirring up sediment and filtering the larger crustaceans, molluscs and bristle worms out of the turbid water. The tongue is muscular and large enough at 1,400 kg (3,000 lb) to provide ample suction. Almost all feeding is done in the summer months in the Arctic region where the major species involved are the amphipods *Amplisca eschrichti*, *A. macrocephala* and *Atylus carcinatus*. Each feeding whale is perpetually surrounded by clouds of sediment and can be seen surfacing with mud on the jaw tips. The

Mating menage with the female in centre and a supporting male behind her

consistently greater wear of baleen plates on the right and the almost total absence of barnacles along this jawline suggest that the whales normally swim on their right sides while feeding on the bottom.

Fish such as anchovy and smelt are sometimes taken, along with a quantity of marine algae, but these may be accidental inclusions. Evidence suggests that hardly anything is eaten on the long swim south to the breeding grounds and, apart from an occasional snack, little time is wasted in feeding on arrival there. An immature female in captivity (Gigi of the San Diego Oceanarium) ate over 800 kg (1,800 lb) of squid a day, gaining weight at the rate of over 1 kilogram an hour, until she became too big (at 6,350 kg or 7 tons) and too expensive to keep and was returned to the wild.

Grey Whales are not social animals, but migrate along common routes and meet on feeding and breeding grounds. Courtship is therefore complex and elaborate. In the shallow lagoons of Baja California, sometimes 50 km (30 miles) from the ocean, mature adults congregate in January. In the early morning there is much spyhopping and circling, intensified around midday as the whales break up into trios composed of two males and a single female. Only one male is involved in actual mating. He can usually be identified by a single flipper which is held up motionless above the surface of the water, presumably as a signal. The female approaches with a delicate touch display, caressing this male with her flippers until they come to lie belly-to-belly in very shallow water. There they stay for up to an hour, copulating several times, with each contact lasting about 2 minutes and ending with a massive orgasmic shudder. During all this time the other male remains in close attendance, taking up an upright position on the far side of the female and apparently forming a prop or wedge.

Gestation lasts exactly 12 months, so that calves are born in the same lagoons the following year. Females give birth, usually unattended, in water about 10 m (33 ft) deep. The 4.5 m (15 ft) calf weighs 700–1,400 kg (1,500–3,000 lb) at birth and is nursed for about 8 months. Mother and calf travel north together when the infant is about 2 months old and it is weaned in the rich Arctic feeding grounds where the mother breaks her 8-month fast. The calf remains with the mother until they return to the southern lagoons and, during this first year, she keeps a watchful eye on it, showing marked aggression on its behalf. There is one report of a female fighting off several Great Killer Whales while holding her calf out of harm's way by lifting it clear of the water on her flipper.

For many years the Grey Whale was thought to be silent because most of its vocalizations in the lagoons were masked by the constant background static provided by snapper shrimps, but recent recordings show that mother-young combinations are highly vocal. Grey Whales in the open ocean have also been found to produce a metallic-sounding pulsed signal with a frequency of 12 kHz, probably associated with echolocation.

Status Grey Whales were hunted so intensively by early American whalers that by 1874 Captain Scammon himself predicted that 'ere long it may be questioned whether this mammal will not be numbered among the extinct species of the Pacific'. For a while, at the turn of the century, it was feared that this had already happened, but under complete protection the Grey Whale population in the eastern Pacific seems to have stabilized at about 11,000. The western population, which feeds in the Sea of Okhotsk, has yet to recover and is still at a critical level.

Distribution Each year in the eastern Pacific Grey Whales undertake a 20,000-km (13,000-mile) trip between their feeding and breeding areas, the longest migration of any mammal. After four summer months in the Chukchi and Bering seas, the move south begins in late September and early October with pregnant females leading the way and other adults and yearlings following. They cross the Gulf of Alaska at a speed of about 185 km (115 miles) per day. They are first seen from land in late November and early December in Oregon and northern California, arriving opposite San Francisco in mid-December and San Diego at Christmas-time. The migration splits opposite Santa Barbara, with some whales taking the island route on to Guadaloupe and Socorro and the rest hugging the coast. Most whales go into the lagoons of Scammon and San Ignacio on the western shore of the Baja peninsula, but some go on to the area of Jalisco inside the Gulf of California.

The move north begins in February and overlaps near San Diego with the last few stragglers still coming south. The northern movement is slower (because of currents and the presence of young calves) with an average speed of 80 km (50 miles) per day. Females with calves tend to stay close inshore, but most whales follow a more westerly route north. The last wave leaves United States coastal waters in May, massing off the Olympic Peninsula in Washington before setting off on a circular navigation route to the Aleutians.

The western Pacific population is little known, but is said to leave the Sea of Okhotsk in October, arriving off the coast of Korea in late November. The whales probably breed in the waters south of Kyushu and migrate north again between March and May.

Sources ANDREWS (1914) monograph, DUDLEY (1725) first reference, ERXLEBEN (1777) taxonomy, EVANS (1974) review, GILMORE (1961) popular account, GRAY (1864) taxonomy, HUBBS (1954) natural history, KASUYA & RICE (1970) parasites, LILLJEBORG (1861) original description, MILLER (1975) general, MILLER & KELLOGG (1955) taxonomy, RICE & WOLMAN (1971) life history, SAMARAS (1974) courtship, SAUER (1963) courtship, WALKER (1975) general.

Family Three – Balaenopteridae

Gray created this family in 1864 to include all the rorqual whales, those which have a number of throat grooves. The tongue is soft and fleshy, well adapted for licking food off the filtering fringes. The row of baleen plates (except in the Tropical Whale, *Balaenoptera edeni 9*) is not divided at the tip of the jaw, but is continuous. The family name is based on the large winglike flippers, from the Greek *pteron*, a wing. All except the Humpback Whale (*Megaptera novaeangliae 10*) share a strong family resemblance, differing only in size, colour and the number of baleen plates and throat grooves.

FIN WHALE

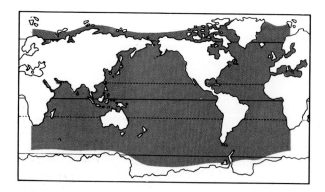

Classification Linnaeus called this whale *Balaena physalus* (from the Greek *phusalis*, a wind instrument or something, like a toad, which puffs itself up). He was probably guided by a description of *Finfisch* given by Friderich Martens, following an expedition to Spitzbergen in 1671. Lacépède pointed out the differences between this whale and all the right whales and established, in 1804, the separate genus *Balaenoptera*.

Lacépède called it *B. rorqual* after the Norwegian *rorhval*, the whale with pleats. In 1846 Gray created *B.australis* to describe a southern 'finner' seen on the voyage of HMS *Erebus* and HMS *Terror*. In 1865 Herman Burmeister described an Argentinian form as B.*patachonicus*. In 1903, following an expedition to the Antarctic, Emile Racovitza lumped all the specimens into a single species *B. physalus*.

Recently the suspicion has grown that there may be a different and larger form in the southern hemisphere meriting at least a subspecific rating. If so, priority rests with *B.p. quoyi* (FISHER 1829), from an animal from the Falklands named in honour of Jean Quoy.

Local Names Finback and finner, *finhval* (Norwegian), *finnhvaler* (Icelandic), *Finnval* (German) and *vinvisch* (Dutch). American whalers called it razorback from the acutely ridged tailstock. The throat pleats have led to *rohrval* (Danish), *rorval* (Swedish) and the common rorqual. *Kiit* (Russian), *capidolio* (Italian), *ballena boba* (Spanish), *vraie baleine* (French), *keporkarnak* (Greenland Eskimo), *reider* (Lapp), *mangidadakh* (Aleutian) and *nagasu kujira* (Japanese).

Description Large; length averages 21 m (70 ft) for males, with a maximum of about 25 m (82 ft), and 22 m (73 ft) for females, with a maximum of about 26.8 m (88 ft); calves are about 6.5 m (22 ft) at birth. Weight averages 35,000–45,000 kg (40–50 tons) for both sexes, with a reported maximum of over 69,500 kg (76 tons); calves are about 3,600 kg (4 tons) at birth.

Fin Whales are second only to Blue Whales (*B. musculus 6*) in length and weight. They are perhaps the fastest of the great whales; the head is wedge-shaped with a flat top marked only by a single median ridge ending at the blowhole. The flippers are comparatively small, about 12 per cent of body length; and the fin, placed about 65 per cent of the way back, is 60 cm

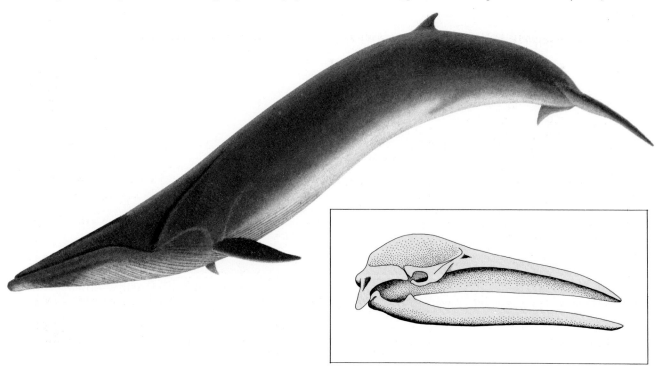

(less than 2 ft) high, leaning steeply backwards. There are 50–86 (average 64) deep grooves in the throat, beginning on the tip of the jaw and running back just beyond the midpoint of the body. From there back to the flukes, the Fin Whale is extraordinarily compressed from side to side, forming a sleek outline which, even when accurately portrayed, seems hopelessly exaggerated.

The colour pattern is unique. As in many other whales, the body of the Fin is countershaded, with a dark grey or umber-brown back and a light or white underside; but on the head this system is rotated through 90°. The colour seems to have shifted entirely to the left, leaving the right lower jaw, the right baleen plates and even the right side of the tongue, pale and unpigmented. There are also distinctive white areas on the underside of the flippers and flukes. This asymmetry may have something to do with feeding habits. Behind the head is a pale grey chevron on the back with arms pointing toward the tail; and, leading backwards from the eye, 2 lines: a dark one running up on to the back and a light one arching over to the insertion of the flipper and sometimes continuing up on to the flank. Fin Whales show none of the whitish mottling characteristic of the Blue Whale.

Field Identification All the rorquals are easily identified by the small dorsal fin placed well back on the body. The difficult part is distinguishing one species of *Balaenoptera* from another when only the back and the fin can be seen. Typically Fin Whales (*B. physalus*) rise obliquely to the surface so that the top of the flat head breaks water first. After breathing, there is a slow roll of smooth dark back bringing the fin into view. With Blue Whales (*B. musculus* 6) the roll lasts longer, until finally the tiny fin can be seen, whilst with Sei Whales (*B. borealis* 8), the fin appears almost simultaneously with the blow. A young Fin Whale and a Tropical Whale (*B. edeni* 9) of comparable size are almost impossible to tell apart in this way, except that the Tropical Whale's fin is a little more sharply pointed.

The breathing and diving sequence is almost invariable. First the blow is visible, a single tall column of spray 4–6 m (13–20 ft) high, widening at its crown into an ellipse. Then the long slow, fairly shallow roll ending with the fin, repeated 4 or 5 times at intervals of 10–20 seconds; in the last roll of the series the back is arched more steeply, rising at least twice the height of the fin above the water, before a deep dive usually lasting 5–15 minutes, but it can be longer. Fin Whales dive to depths of over 250 m (820 ft) and can stay down as long as 26 minutes. The tail flukes never show in surface rolls, but may just break the surface prior to sounding.

We have found that it is fairly easy to motor up to a Fin Whale in a small inflatable boat, line up on it with the first blow, follow the flash of the white underside beneath the surface and be close enough on subsequent blows actually to peer down into the huge blowholes. These are roughly rectangular and raised slightly above the back in the shelter of a curved waterguard of skin. At close range the slightly fishy smell of the whale's breath is apparent and it is possible to hear the deep rich whistling sound of the air intake. We feel certain in these situations, particularly when we have been

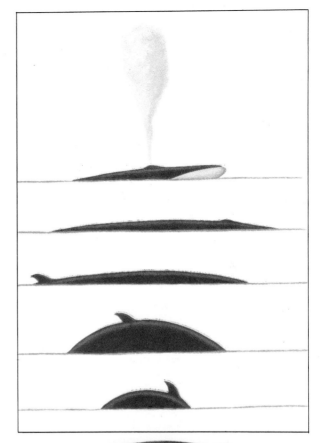

Above: dive sequence
Below: feeding posture with distended throat; note the white baleen plates on front right only

forward enough actually to touch the whale's back with our bows, that it is well aware of our presence, and it always seems clear that the giant mammals exercise deliberate caution and control the sweep of the great flukes in such a way that we have never been in danger of being overturned.

Fin Whales sometimes breach, falling back with a resounding splash, never re-entering smoothly headfirst as Piked Whales do. Fin Whales can move very fast, up to 40 kph (over 20 knots) and are so strong that, before diesel-powered catchers and explosive harpoons, they were beyond the reach of whalers.

The greatest source of confusion in the field is likely to be between Fin Whales, Sei Whales, and, in tropical regions, Tropical Whales, but there are differences:

B. physalus fin at angle of 50° from the back; visible long after blow; dark back; seldom scarred; one ridge on head; longest dives 5–15 minutes.
B. borealis fin angle 30°; visible simultaneously with blow; shiny back; often scarred; one ridge on head; short dives of 3–6 minutes.
B. edeni fin angle 70°, visible soon after blow; dark back; sometimes scarred; three ridges on head; fairly long dives of 4–10 minutes.

Stranding Fin Whales are occasionally beached. If this is recent, the white right-hand side of the lower jaw makes identification easy. Even when the skin has darkened the difference in colour of the baleen remains striking. There are 260–480 (average 360) baleen plates Each is short, less than 90 cm (3 ft) long, but larger and broader than those of any right whale. Those on the left of the jaw are blue grey in colour, while those of the front third on the right side are white. In all cases the feathery bristles are yellowish. It is said that Fin Whales in the North Pacific may have shorter and coarser baleen.

There are large numbers of presumably tactile hairs along both jaws, with a beard-like concentration on the tip of the lower one. There are few ectoparasites, although barnacles and whale lice (*Cyamus balaenopterae*) may be found.

The skull, as in all *Balaenoptera*, is birdlike and hardly arched. The brain weighs approximately 8.5 kg (over 18 lb). There are 60–63 vertebrae, those in the neck usually free, but sometimes the first 2 or 3 may be partly fused. The flippers have 4 fingers.

Natural History Fin Whales are generalist feeders. Their staple diet in the Antarctic is the ubiquitous krill (*Euphausia superba*); in the Aleutian area it is sardine (*Sardinella melaosticta*) and Alaskan pollack (*Theragra chalcogramma*); off Kamchatka the copepod (*Calanus cristatus*) is favoured; around the Kuriles it is squid (*Ommatostrephes sloani*); on the California coast anchovies; and in Newfoundland capelin.

Where swarming crustaceans or schools of small fish have been driven into compact masses, a Fin Whale will advance on them at speed and, as it approaches, roll on to its right side at the surface, left flipper in the air. Then with its mouth wide open and throat distended, the whale pivots on its submerged right flipper, making a massive lateral scoop, which is highly productive because the shoaling prey invariably try to escape by doubling back around the approaching whale rather than diving beneath it. The peculiar lopsided pigmentation on the Fin Whale's head makes sense: by turning on to its right side, the whale once again acquires the usual obliterative coloration (dark above and pale below) that helps to camouflage all animals living in an exclusively top-lit environment. The existence of this unique adaptation suggests that the Fin Whale prefers prey with good vision, i.e. fish rather than plankton. The two species which feed most heavily on krill (Blue Whales and Sei Whales) are the only ones in which the basic body colour is broken up by disruptive spotting, so that in the murky Antarctic waters they tend to look less like approaching predators than harmless spotty patches of plankton.

Fin Whales are the commonest baleen whales and tend to be more gregarious than other species. It is still possible to see concentrations of 100 or more on favourite feeding grounds. The normal social unit is a pod of 6–15 individuals, including one or more adult males. The age of maturity has been depressed by whaling to about 6 years for males (at 17 m or 57 ft long), and 7 years for females (18 m or 60 ft long).

Mating occurs in winter in warmer waters to the accompaniment of social play and ponderous courtship; gestation lasts almost a year and so the young tend to be born in the same areas the following year. Suckling lasts for 6 months, when the calf doubles its length to 12 m (40 ft). Females calve in alternate years. Fin Whales may live for 100 years.

During the 1960s a network of underwater listening posts was set up around the world and after their establishment widespread concern was expressed about a pattern of unusual and intense high-level, low-frequency sounds. These were repetitive bursts of pulsed sound, usually at 20 Hz and the military believed they were threatening. Eventually it was discovered that the mysterious noises were the normal vocalizations of Fin Whales.

Status There are probably 70,000–75,000 Fin Whales worldwide. Since protection in a number of areas, there seems to have been some recovery in populations decimated by whaling. The number in the North Pacific is estimated at 14,000, in the North Atlantic at 3,000–5,000 and in the southern hemisphere as a whole, at 70,000–80,000. From our own observations over the past decade we feel that the North Atlantic and South Pacific estimates are far too high. We suspect that the adopted values used in the calculation of recruitment rates (the number of whales being added each year to the populations) have been over optimistic.

Distribution Fin Whales are found in all oceans at all temperatures and in all depths, even in the Mediterranean. They tend to avoid the icepack and migrate towards the equator during the winter. Many travel up to 20,000 km (12,000 miles) a year to and from tropical waters, but this is not as regular or predictable as the Grey Whale migrations and it is possible that the northern and southern populations are not completely separated.

We once watched a large and clearly marked male in the Banda Sea off eastern Indonesia, who arrived at the equator with a northern group of whales one January. In April and June he was still there, feeding together with a group from the south; and in September he disappeared at the same time as the southern population moved down to the Antarctic for their summer feed. We suspect that it is not uncommon for Fin Whales to move from one pod, or even from one hemisphere, to another in this way. There is some evidence also, this time from whale-marking programmes, for latitudinal movement by as much as 50° east or west of the marked position.

Sources BROWN (1954) distribution, LINNAEUS (1758) original description, LAWS (1961) status, MITCHELL (1972) adaptive coloration, MITCHELL (1974) feeding behaviour, SCHEVILL et al (1967) sounds, VAN DER BRINK (1967) in Mediterranean, WALKER (1963) sounds, WATKINS & SCHEVILL (1979) feeding.

BLUE WHALE

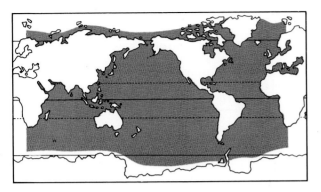

Classification Linnaeus named the largest animal the world has ever known *Balaena musculus*, which is sometimes seen as evidence of eighteenth-century humour: the Latin *musculus* means a little mouse, but it can also mean muscle, which is appropriate.

In 1864 Gray conceived the name *Sibbaldus borealis* for the celebrated 'Whale of Ostend', a giant animal found floating in the North Sea and towed to Ostend before a comprehensive tour of Europe. The name honoured Sir Robert Sibbald, who published the first natural history of Scotland in 1684. The Ostend Whale was clearly a Blue Whale, as was the animal stranded near Edinburgh and called *Balaena maximus*, another taken from the Firth of Forth and designated *Ror-*

qualis borealis and the famous 'sulphur-bottom' of the Pacific, *Sibbaldus sulfureus*.

It was again Racovitza, in 1903, who brought some order to this taxonomic confusion, putting the Blue Whale firmly into Lacépède's genus *Balaenoptera*.

It is possible that 3 distinct subspecies of Blue Whale exist, a smallish one in the northern hemisphere, a larger form that spends the southern summer in Antarctic waters, *B. musculus intermedia* (BURMEISTER 1871) and a possible Pygmy Blue Whale said to be confined to the area around Kerguelen and Crozet islands in the southern Indian Ocean, *B.m.brevicauda* (ICHIHARA 1976).

Local Names The most common English vernacular name is sulphur-bottom, which is based on the fact that in extended stays in colder water this whale picks up a film of yellow-green diatoms which conceal its natural hue. Many other names reflect its true colour: *baleine bleu* (French), *blaahaval* (Norwegian), *blahvalur* (Icelandic) and *ballena azul* (Spanish). Its size has led to: *grand rorqual* (French), *Riesenwal* (German), *bolshoi polosatik* (Russian), *umgulik* (Aleutian), *akhokhrikh* (Chukchi), *tunnolik* (Greenland Eskimo) and *takyshkok* (Chukotski).

Description Very large; length averages 25 m (82 ft) for males, with a maximum recorded of 31 m (102 ft), and 26 m (85 ft) for females, with a possible maximum of more than the

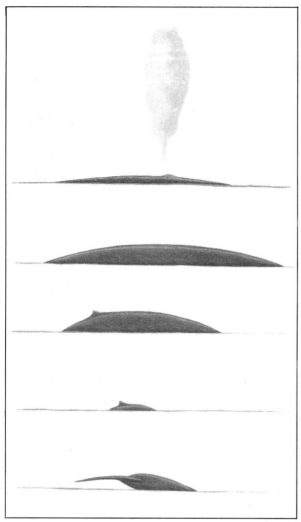

Dive sequence

The overall colour is marine blue grey, mottled with light grey and white. The flipper tips and undersides are much lighter. The shade of blue varies with individuals and probably darkens with age. The sulphurous mustard colour produced by gardens of diatoms seems to be most common in whales in the far northern Pacific.

The pygmy Blue Whales of Kerguelen Island in the Indian Ocean are said to be more silvery grey in colour, with a shorter tail and a proportionately longer and heavier trunk. They may also be extensively scarred.

Field Identification Despite their enormous weight, Blue Whales give an impression of sleek grace in water, making it easy to underestimate their size.

The blow is strong, blasting up in a single, thin column 6–12 m (20–40 ft) high. Breathing rhythms vary with activity, but the most familiar is several (up to 20), shallow dives at intervals of about 20 seconds, followed by a longer deeper dive of up to half an hour. Between some shorter dives, the whale surfaces almost horizontally so that the blowhole and much of the back appear at the same time. Usually the blowhole and part of the head surface first, the whale spouts, then reveals a long expanse of back sliding slowly over until the tiny fin emerges briefly just before the tail touches the surface.

The fluke exposure is fleeting, unlike the high, flapping dive of Great Right *1*, Humpback *10* or Great Sperm *36* whales, and serves as a useful distinction. Distinguishing Blue from Fin *5* whales is more difficult:

B. musculus broad U-shaped head; mottled blue back; tiny fin visible long after the blow; comparatively low roll; it often shows its flukes before diving.
B. physalus narrow V-shaped head; grey back; larger fin visible shortly after blow; it rolls high out of the water; it seldom shows flukes before diving.

Blue whales are shyer than other rorquals. They normally cruise at 6–8 kph (3–4 knots), but sound easily when disturbed and, when harried, accelerate rapidly to speeds of 20–30 kph (10–16 knots).

Stranding There are occasional solitary strandings. The baleen is the best clue to identification and unlike the Fin Whale's is all black. There are 270–400 (average 324) pure black plates on each side of the jaw. These are roughly triangular, about 100 cm (40 inches) long and 55 cm (20 inches) wide. In the pygmy race the plates may be shorter in relation to their breadth. In all Blue Whales there is a rudimentary moustache of 4 bristles and a sparse adolescent beard of 40 long hairs.

Crustacean parasites (*Balaenophilus unisetus*) often live in the baleen. On the skin there are a few barnacles and, around the mouth, eyes and genital slit, some whale lice (*Cyamus balaenopterae*). A common skin parasite is a strange crustacean called *Penella*, which protrudes like a small soft paint brush or algal frond from beneath the blubber. Most of these ectoparasites seem to be picked up in tropical waters, and, as

male record, but probably not as high as the 33.5 m (110 ft) claimed by some whalers; calves are about 7 m (23 ft) at birth. Weight averages 80,000–130,000 kg (90–144 tons) for both sexes, with a recorded maximum of 178,000 kg (196 tons); calves are about 7,250 kg (8 tons) at birth.

The Blue Whale's shape is long and streamlined, with the head forming less than 25 per cent of total length. The rostrum is broad and level and, from above, shaped like a slightly flattened Gothic arch. There is a single ridge extending from the sharply raised area of the blowholes almost to the snout. The fin is small, low, set very far back (about 30 cm or 1 ft high), triangular or hook-shaped. The flippers are relatively short, little more than 10 per cent of body length, and tapered. There are 64–94 grooves on the throat, extending for approximately 60 per cent of body length and ending beyond the navel.

the whales migrate to cooler areas, they tend to drop off.

In side view, the skull is very much like that of the Fin Whale, but it is broader above. There are 63–64 free vertebrae.

Natural History Blue Whales eat swarming planktonic creatures, but unlike Fin Whales are selective (i.e. stenophagous) and feed almost exclusively on a few species. In the Antarctic they seem to eat nothing but krill, with the accidental inclusion of a few small fish; in the North Pacific only the crustaceans *Thysanoessa inermis*, *T.longipes* and *Nematoscolis megalops*; and in the North Atlantic, the related species of *Temora longicornis* and *Meganyctiphanes norvegica*.

All these crustaceans concentrate in shoals in brightly lit waters, less than 40 m (130 ft) from the surface. In areas of turbulence or upwelling, krill reach a density of more than 15 kg/m^3 (about 1 lb/ft^3). Blue Whales swallow about 4,000 kg (over 4 tons) of this rich bisque each day, which in the Antarctic (where krill weigh about 1 g apiece) means 4 million shrimps.

The krill season lasts for about 120 days, after which the icepack covers the feeding grounds and the whales migrate towards the equator. There are subtropical and even tropical areas rich in plankton, which attract other baleen whales in winter months, but seem to be of no interest to Blues, who eat little or nothing in warmer waters. Because the Blue Whales feed largely at the surface, it is often difficult to decide whether they are cruising along in a series of shallow dives or actually eating. We have seen Blue Whales in the Sea of Cortez in Mexico, moving through patches of plankton on which Fin Whales were feeding, but it was impossible to see whether they were breaking their alleged tropical fast.

The social life of Blue Whales centres around close-knit groups of 3 or 4, who may join in larger associations for both feeding and breeding. Males mature at a length of 22.5 m (74 ft) and females at 23 m (76 ft); mating usually takes place in warmer waters. Courtship has never been seen. In proportion to the rest of its organs the Blue Whale's penis is the largest in the animal kingdom, measuring over 3 m (10 ft). Gestation lasts 11–12 months and calves are born in tropical waters outside the feeding season. Milk is rich and concentrated and, on a diet of 600 litres (about 130 gallons) a day, often doubles the calf's weight in a week. Lactation continues until calves are about 7 months old and over 15 m (50 ft) long. It is possible for females to breed every other year, but every 3 years seems to be more common.

Little is known of the Blue Whale's voice except that it produces ultrasonic bursts of sound while feeding. These are pulses of 21–31 kHz similar to those used by smaller toothed whales for echolocation. They could help to find concentrations of krill. Low-frequency moans lasting over 30 seconds and broken into three parts have been recorded off the coast of Chile.

Status Following the slaughter of 30,000 Blue Whales in the Antarctic season of 1930–31, the population has never recovered. The Antarctic population today may be 6,000–8,000; and there could be about 1,500 in each of the North Atlantic and North Pacific oceans. There are signs of slow recovery, but it could be a century before the Blue Whales reach numbers at which they are beyond danger of extinction.

In the meantime it is worth giving all claims for the discovery of new, and therefore unprotected, species or races the closest possible scrutiny. We cannot help feeling more than a little cynical about the fact that, in the 3 years following Tadayoshi Ichihara's announcement of the discovery of the pygmy Blue Whale at Kerguelen Island in 1960, the Japanese whaling industry killed 2,540 specimens.

Distribution Blue Whales used to be found worldwide. We have seen them in every part of the world ocean, even in the Arabian Gulf and in the Banda Sea on the equator, but they are undoubtedly tied to the polar feeding grounds. The best chance of seeing one is amongst the krill in Antarctica between December and February. Even at the height of this whale's abundance, there were no more than an average of one whale to every 50 km^2 (20 square miles) of ocean on the summer grounds; and in winter they were far more widely dispersed. So today it is easy for the remnant to disappear into the oceans almost without trace, and equally easy to understand why so little is still known of their behaviour and whereabouts during the breeding season.

It seems likely that the northern and southern populations make synchronous movements to and from tropical waters, arriving near the equator at different times of the year and seldom if ever meeting; but isolated individuals could cross the line into the other hemisphere. This is most likely to occur in the eastern Pacific, where the cold Humboldt Current sweeps right up to the Galapagos on the equator, only 20° of latitude from a possible feeding ground around Baja California in the north.

Sources BEAMISH & MITCHELL (1971) sounds, BUDKER (1959) general, CARRIGHAR (1978) life history, CUMMINGS & THOMPSON (1971) sounds, GULLAND (1972) status, ICHIHARA (1963) pygmy race, LINNAEUS (1758) original description, OMURA (1970) taxonomy.

PIKED WHALE (MINKE)

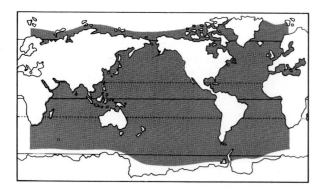

Classification When Buffon died in 1788 Lacépède took over his work and completed publication of the last 8 volumes of *Histoire Naturelle*. In the cetacean volume (1804) he created a new genus *Balaenoptera* and added to it a whale found in Greenland and described as *Balaena rostrata*, from the Latin *rostrum*, a beak. Lacépède examined a young whale stranded near Cherbourg in France in 1871 and because of the sharp shape of the head, called it *Balaenoptera acuto-rostrata*, from the Latin *acutus*, sharp, to emphasize the point.

Several subspecies have been proposed: *B.a. davidsoni* (SCAMMON 1872) for a short-snouted, high-finned specimen collected by Scammon in Puget Sound and now known from most of the Pacific, *B.a. thalmaha* (DERANIYAGALA 1963) of doubtful validity from Sri Lanka, and *B.a. bonaerensis* (BURMEISTER 1867) for an Antarctic variation which lacks the characteristic white spot on the flipper. There is immense variability in this species and it is likely that only the Antarctic form will be confirmed as a distinct and consistent variety.

Local names Lesser rorqual, sharp-headed finner, little finner, pikehead; summer whale, baywhale, *baleine à bec* (French), *dwerg vinvisch* (Dutch), *Zwergwal* (German), *vaagehval* (Norwegian), *vikval* (Swedish), *koiwashi kujira* (Japanese), *zalivov* (Russian), *agamakhchik* (Aleutian). The Norwegian *minkehval* has led to minkie, little mink, or minke whale which is widely accepted, but we find common names based on personal or proper nouns unhelpful and suggest a return to

the descriptive Piked Whale, derived from the Old English *pic*, a sharp point.

Description Medium; length averages 8 m (26 ft) for males, with a maximum of 9.4 m (31 ft), and 8.2 m (27 ft) for females, with a maximum of 10.2 m (33 ft); calves are about 3 m (10 ft) at birth. Weight averages 5,800–7,250 kg (6–8 tons) for both sexes, with a maximum of over 9,000 kg (10 tons); calves are about 450 kg (1,000 lb) at birth.

The Piked Whale is the smallest rorqual, less streamlined, more chunky than its relatives. The most distinctive feature is the narrow, acutely pointed, almost triangular rostrum, which is much sharper than that of the Fin Whale (*B.physalus 5*). There is a central ridge on the top of the flat head. The fin is in the last third of the back, as in the Sei Whale (*B.borealis 8*), but is taller and gives a more erect appearance. The flipper is pointed and measures approximately 12 per cent of total body length.

The throat is creased by 60–70 grooves running back for 47 per cent of the body length, about as far as the navel.

The colour is a bluish dark grey above and lighter below, with both eye and flipper insertion inside the darker area. The distinctive marking is a bright white patch or diagonal band across the middle of the upper surface of the flipper, the size and shape of which show enormous variation. There may be a distinct white patch on the right side of the upper jaw. Many adults have pale grey bracket marks, like gill slits, above the flipper and, in the Pacific at least, there are patches of light grey in the middle flank and just below the dorsal fin. These markings vary and may be inconspicuous or even undetectable. Part of the South Pacific population has no flipper mark.

Field Identification Piked Whales are more likely to be seen at close quarters than any of their relatives, because they seem to be curious about shipping and approach even moving vessels. They are fast swimmers and keep pace with a ship travelling at 24–30 kph (13–16 knots). Even at this speed they can dive down beneath the hull and surface again on the other side without losing ground.

The blow is low and indistinct, often invisible without a dark background. This may be because they start to exhale

while still half a metre underwater. While at anchor in Antarctic bays, we have often watched Piked Whales at close range and seen the blow beginning as a plume of white turbulence beneath the surface.

The usual breathing sequence consists of 5–8 blows at intervals of less than a minute, followed by a deep dive that may last as long as 20 minutes. The first exhalation following a long dive is noticeably louder than the others, sometimes producing a thinly visible blast no more than 2 m (6 ft) high, with a strong fishy smell. The fin always appears simultaneously with the blow and the tailstock is arched high into the air before sounding; the flukes are never shown unless the whale breaches. Piked Whales do breach, 2 or 3 times in a row, often falling back with a splash, but sometimes re-entering cleanly in a perfect dive.

Identification at close range presents few problems – the size, head shape and flipper patch are all distinctive – but at greater distances they could be confused with Sei Whales (*Balaenoptera borealis 8*) or even with one of the beaked or bottlenosed whales (such as the *Hyperoodon* spp. 15 and 16):

B. acutorostrata flat head; indistinct blow; fin visible at same time as blow; dark back; tailstock arched strongly prior to diving; never shows flukes.
B. borealis flat head; higher blow; fin visible with blow; dark back; submerges quietly; never shows flukes.
Hyperoodon spp. domed head; low bushy blow; fin visible long after blow; grey back; shows tail (without notch) when diving.

Stranding Piked Whales are often stranded and easily identified by their small size and the presence of the white flipper patch. The baleen is distinctive: there are 260–360 baleen plates (average 300), the largest 30 cm (12 inches) long and 12 cm (5 inches) wide. Fringes of all plates are fine and white, and most of the baleen is pale maize yellow, but many of the plates at the back of the jaw, particularly on the left, are black. In the southern form all the plates are said to be pale and always less than 300. Piked Whales in the Atlantic may also have a smaller number of plates.

There are usually 62 throat grooves. The skull is typical of the genus, though more pointed than in the larger species. There are 47–49 vertebrae. Many large baleen whales show little or no sign of the sternum (breastbone), but in Piked Whales it is relatively large and cross-shaped.

There are few ectoparasites.

Natural History In polar waters Piked Whales feed on planktonic crustaceans. In the Antarctic the species seems to be enjoying a population explosion, taking advantage of the absence of Blue Whales. Piked Whales, however, eat more fish more often than any other filter-feeding whale. In the North Pacific, Piked Whales live mainly on saffron cod (*Eleginus navaga*) and anchovy (*Engraulis mordax*); in the North Atlantic they take herring (*Clupea harengus*) and capelin (*Mallotus villosus*), and in southern temperate waters they are known to take large quantities of squid.

The mark on the right side of the jaw and the asymmetry of its baleen suggest that it might, like the Fin Whale 5, turn on to that side to feed at the surface, but most of the Piked Whales we have seen have used a gulping technique, involving a certain amount of splashing, sometimes even breaching, to scare fish into a compact huddle before the whale shoots up through the shoal from beneath with its mouth open. The existence of a broken beak tip from a blue marlin, embedded in the upper jaw of a Piked Whale captured in the Antarctic in 1972, suggests that the whale may have been competing for the same prey as that irascible fish.

Piked Whales are most often seen singly or in pairs, though in the Antarctic feeding grounds it is common to find up to 1,000 whales in a single area. As far as we know, Piked Whales live for about 50 years, reaching sexual maturity at about 6 years, when males are 7 m (23 ft) and females approximately 7.6 m (25 ft) in length. Females ovulate twice a year (in the northern hemisphere in February and August), so that any females that fail to become pregnant in the first mating season invariably succeed in the second. Gestation lasts for 10–11 months and calves are suckled for a further 6, making it possible for these whales to breed every 18 months – faster than any other Mysticete. This helps to account for the rapid rise in populations following the disappearance of the Blue Whale from many of its old haunts.

The voice of the Piked Whale has been described as a series of low-frequency grunts, thumps and ratchets. Most are trains of sound at 100–200 Hz which seem to make the call of each individual unique. They also produce pure-frequency pulsed sounds at 4–8 kHz involving series of clicks for 6–8 seconds at a time, possibly used for echolocation.

Status The world total for this species is probably about 200,000. After prolonged exploitation in the northern hemisphere, Piked Whales are now present only in small numbers. There are no reliable estimates, but a fair guess would be a few thousand in each of the North Atlantic and North Pacific oceans. In the Antarctic the Piked Whales have been direct beneficiaries of the reduction in Blue Whales. Krill abound and the Piked Whales are multiplying rapidly to fill the gap. The best estimates are based on sighting surveys and vary between 150,000 and 300,000 animals. The upper figure is probably too high, being biased by the tendency of Piked Whales to approach any boat.

Distribution Piked Whales occur worldwide. They tend to accumulate south of 55° south in the southern summer. They are found right up to the edge of, and sometimes marooned in little pockets of open water inside, the icepack. They favour shallow water, estuaries and tidal streams in warmer water, venturing into inland seas and rivers more often than any other baleen whales. They are rare in the tropics.

Sources ARSEN'EV (1961) in Antarctic, BEAMISH & MITCHELL (1973) sounds, BROWN (1960) marlin beak, JONSGARD (1961) in Norway, KASUYA & ICHIHARA (1965) in Antarctica, LACÉPÈDE (1804) original description, OMURA & SAKIURA (1956) in Japan, THOMPSON et al (1979) sounds, VAN UTRECHT et al (1962) behaviour, WINN & PERKINS (1976) sounds.

SEI WHALE

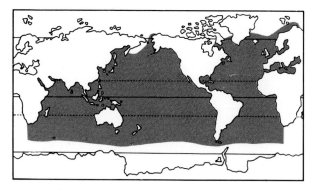

Classification René Primavère Lesson was naturalist to the Duperry Expedition which spent 3 years exploring the Pacific. In 1828, taking advantage of his field experience, he revised and updated Lacépède's volume on cetaceans and drew attention to the differences between the Fin Whale (*B.physalus 5*), the Piked Whale (*B.acutorostrata 7*) and a third close relative he called *B.borealis*, from the Latin *borealis,* of the north.

The type specimen for this species was one stranded in 1819 on the coast of Holstein in Germany and described by Carl

Rudolphi as *Balaena rostrata*, because he believed it to be a Right Whale. In 1823 Cuvier examined the same specimen in the Berlin Museum (where it remains) and identified it as a rorqual, *rorqual du nord*; Lesson, having seen the whale alive in the field, verified the diagnosis and latinized Cuvier's name for it.

There seem to be 2 variants, one in the north and a somewhat larger one in the southern hemisphere, first described by Flower from a specimen collected in Java (now in the museum at Leiden) and known as *B.borealis schlegelii* (FLOWER 1865).

Local Names Sei Whale (pronounced 'say') from the Norwegian *sejval* because it appeared off the Finnmark coast at the same time as the *seje*, a coalfish or pollack (*Theragra* spp.), which came to feed on the abundant plankton. Other names are sardine whale, coalfish whale, *iwashi kujira* (Japanese) *saidiaoni kit* (Russian). It is also known as Rudolphi's rorqual, Japan finner, *baleine noir* (French), *agalagitakg* (Aleutian), *noordische vinvisch* (Dutch) and *ivasevyi polosatik* (Russian).

Although there is no direct connection between the whale and the fish, we choose to follow tradition and call this species the Sei Whale.

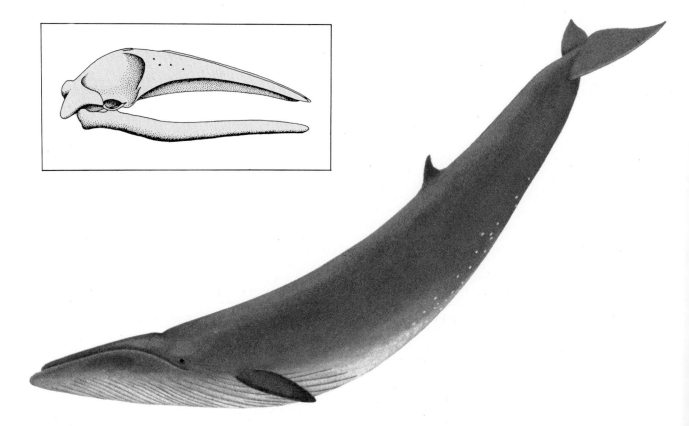

Description Large; length averages 15 m (49 ft) for males, with a maximum of 18.5 m (61 ft), and 16 m (52 ft) for females, with a maximum of 20 m (66 ft); calves are about 4.5 m (15 ft) at birth. Weight averages 12,000–15,000 kg (14–17 tons) for both sexes, with a maximum of 29,000 kg (32 tons); calves are about 900 kg (1 ton) at birth.

The Sei Whale is a typical rorqual, streamlined and flat-headed, but not as slender as the Fin Whale (*B.physalus 5*), nor as chunky as the Piked Whale (*B.acutorostrata 7*). It also falls roughly midway between them in size. The beak is as pointed as that of the Piked Whale, but is also slightly curved to allow room for baleen plates twice as long. Like the Fin Whale's, its tail is laterally compressed, forming a sharp upper and lower ridge that dips suddenly into the tail flukes. The dorsal fin is tall (sometimes 60 cm or 2 ft high), strongly hooked and situated further forward than that of either the Blue Whale (*B.musculus 6*) or the Fin Whale (*B.physalus 5*). Flipper size is less than in the other rorquals, at about 9 per cent of body length.

The colour is steely dark grey, the pleated throat and chest being lighter. (Compare with the Fin Whale and Piked Whale, in which the pale belly extends all the way to the tail.) There are no white markings on the flippers and no asymmetry in the head colouring. There are dark and light mottlings on flanks and belly, which, with the shiny surface of the skin, give the Sei Whale a distinctly metallic appearance in the water.

Field Identification The greatest similarities in shape and colour exist between the Sei and Blue whales, but their difference in size, and the Sei's taller fin, should distinguish them. It is more difficult, given only a fleeting glimpse, to distinguish Sei from Fin (*B.physalus 5*) or Tropical (*B.edeni 9*) whales.

Sei Whales feed close to the surface and usually rise almost horizontally to breathe. The head and a long expanse of back, including the fin, come into view at the same time and remain visible for longer than is customary for other species. The blow is an inverted cone-shape, much like the Fin or Blue whales' but not as high as either. About 3 m (10 ft) is usual. The breathing sequence is more regular than that of related whales, showing two common patterns. In our experience the most characteristic involves 2 or 3 blows at 20-second intervals, followed by a dive of 5–6 minutes. The other features 5 or 6 blows at intervals of 30–40 seconds prior to a dive of 15 or even 30 minutes. In the shorter dive sequence, the whales are seldom far from the surface and can usually still be seen from the raised deck of a ship. In neither case do Sei Whales arch their backs like the Fin Whale or show their flukes above the surface like the Blue Whale; they simply slip quietly away, leaving only a slick of smooth water.

The greatest difficulty in the field is the problem of telling Sei apart from the Tropical (*B. edeni 9*) whales. It was not until 1912 that whalers made any distinction. Some still have trouble, but there are several useful field characteristics which make positive identification possible:

B. borealis single ridge on head; large fin, less pointed, more sloping; dives quietly without a roll; uniformly dark appearance.

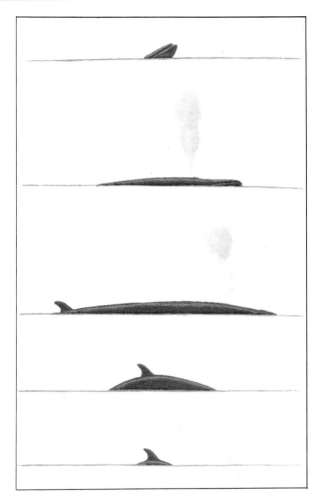

Dive sequence

B. edeni 3 rostral ridges; small fin, sharply pointed with tattered trailing edge; rolls high in water before diving; white undersides often visible.

After seeing both species many times, we can now identify them successfully, even at a distance, but without being certain of what it is that gives them away. Generally the Tropical Whale is more 'busy', with quicker, more erratic movements, almost like a salmon at the surface. Sei Whales seem more sedate, often lying motionless in the water, allowing our ship to get quite close before they submerge. In fact, Sei Whales are amongst the fastest cetaceans, and can swim off at over 50 kph (26 knots).

Stranding Sei Whales are found stranded less often than with Piked Whales but this may only reflect the fact that the Sei is now a rarer species. Confusion is possible between beached Sei, Tropical and Fin whales. The Tropical Whale has 3 longitudinal ridges, while Fin and Sei whales each have only 1.

The baleen is the best clue to discrimination between those two. Sei have 320–380 (average 340) baleen plates with a maximum length of 75 cm (26 inches). The plates are black, with a metallic sheen, but their most distinctive feature is the high number of very fine white bristles and hairs, all very soft to the touch. Sei have silky baleen fringe hairs, 40–60 per cm (100–150 per inch), while all other rorqual species have coarser bristles with less than 35 per cm (88 per inch).

Sei Whales seem to have only a few body hairs, concentrated around the blowhole or the tip of the lower jaw. The throat grooves are also distinctive; there are 38–60 (average 52), whereas both Fin and Blue whales never have less than 55 fine pleats. Sei and Tropical whales have roughly the same number of grooves, but those in the Sei end far short of the navel, extending for less than 45 per cent of body length, stopping just behind the flippers.

Few ectoparasites have been described, but the broken bill of a swordfish marlin was found in the neck of a male captured in the Antarctic in 1969.

The skull is very much like that of the Piked Whale, but the upper jaw is more visibly bowed. There are 56 or 57 vertebrae.

Natural History Sei Whales have catholic tastes and eat a variety of food, specializing in smaller organisms. When plankton is available, Sei Whales will eat almost any kind; *Euphausia superba*, *E.vallentini*, *Clausocalanus laticeps*, *Calanus tonsus* and *Parathemisto gaudichaudii* are only a few of more than 20 species of swarming crustaceans known to form part of their diet. In addition, they readily eat fish (sardine, capelin, Japanese anchovy and immature cod) or squid when the need or the opportunity arises. They take about 900 kg (1 ton) of assorted food each day, feeding most actively around dawn and dusk. They are primarily skimmers rather than swallowers, swimming along, rolling from side to side at the surface just as Right Whales do, but more erratically. We have seen Sei Whales in temperate waters, where they were clearly feeding on fish, adopt the Fin Whale tactic of approaching the prey on their sides, though, unlike the Fins, they did so for longer periods, cruising along with one flipper in the air for half a minute or more.

Sei Whales are usually found in small family groups of 4 or 5, sometimes forming larger congregations when feeding. They live for about 70 years, reaching maturity around the age of 10, when the males are 12 m (40 ft) and the females 13 m (43 ft) long. Mating can take place all year round, but seems to be commonest in autumn in warmer waters. Sei Whales seem to form firm pair bonds – we have often seen a pair together for long periods – and they may be monogamous. Gestation lasts for 12 months and lactation for 6, so a female may breed as often as every 2 years.

The only confirmed recording of Sei Whale voices features a train of metallic pulsed sounds at a frequency of 3 kHz.

Status The worldwide total is probably less than 80,000. Sei Whales were so extensively hunted when Blue and Fin whales became scarce that they too have declined to a level where protection is necessary. The highest estimate for the North Atlantic is less than 3,000, while the North Pacific cannot contain more than 20,000. The number in the southern hemisphere has been put as high as 80,000, but this is optimistic.

Distribution Sei Whales are widely distributed in all oceans, but they generally avoid the coldest areas close to the ice. They tend to be more tropical than the Fin Whale, but not as successful in warmer waters as the Tropical Whale itself. Sei Whales occur in the open ocean and in coastal waters, but usually remain beyond the 100 m (330 ft) line. They seldom venture into shallow bays and almost never enter rivers or estuaries unless they are in the process of stranding.

There is clear evidence of movement to and from the cooler circumpolar waters of the southern hemisphere in the warmest months, but there are no clearly defined migrations. Those summers in which Sei Whales appear in any numbers in polar waters in the northern hemisphere are still known to Icelandic whalers as 'Sei Whale years'. In some temperate areas they are year-round residents.

Sources BROWN (1969) swordfish bill, GASKIN (1976) general, KAWAMURA (1974) feeding, LESSON (1828) original description, RICE (1961) baleen, THOMPSON et al (1979) sounds, TOMILIN (1946) in Soviet Arctic.

TROPICAL WHALE (BRYDE'S)

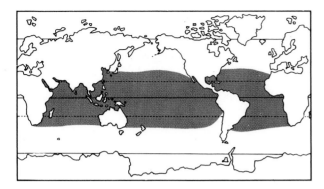

Classification In 1878 John Anderson, an enthusiastic Scots physician who was Superintendent of the Indian Museum in Calcutta, published an account of a whale skeleton collected in the Gulf of Martaban by Major A. G. Duff, the Deputy Commissioner of British Burma. It was a rorqual and Anderson called it *Balaenoptera edeni* in honour of Sir Ashley Eden, Chief Commissioner of Burma.

Nothing was heard of Eden's whale for many years, but in 1912 the Norwegian zoologist Olsen described another new rorqual, this time from the southern hemisphere. Olsen examined 12 specimens in Durban and Saldanha Bay, found them to be different from the Sei Whale (*B. borealis 8*), and called them *B. brydei* after J. Bryde, the Norwegian consul to South Africa, who built the first whaling factory in Durban in 1909. Olsen's preliminary report appeared in a Norwegian newspaper in 1912, but in 1913 he published a full and scientific account.

In 1957 Masaharu Nishiwaki identified an Eden whale in Japanese waters; and in 1959 Hideo Omura recorded Bryde's whale there also. It was not long before everyone realized that they were the same species.

It has been suggested that there may be two forms off the west coast of South Africa – a smaller coastal form and a larger pelagic race with a slightly different pattern of baleen; but nobody has gone so far as to give either variation a separate name. There may also be a smaller variety found locally in the Solomon Islands area.

Local Names Whalers call it, in honour of a pioneer in their industry, Bryde's whale (pronounced 'brew-der'), but, now that priority has been given to the 1878 description, if any person deserves to be honoured it is either Anderson or Eden. There is however a trend away from common names based on those of the authors or their friends and toward more informative descriptive or geographical terms. So we propose that this animal be known simply as the Tropical Whale.

Description Large; length averages 12 m (40 ft) for males, with a maximum of 14.3 m (47 ft) and 13 m (43 ft) for females, with a maximum of 14.6 m (48 ft); calves are about 4 m (13 ft) at birth. Weight averages about 12,000 kg (13 tons) for both sexes, with maximum of 20,000 kg (22 tons); calves are about 900 kg (1 ton) at birth.

In general shape and form Tropical Whales bear a close resemblance to Sei Whales (*B. borealis 8*). The body is slightly more slender, noticeably less muscular. The head is typically rorqual with a broad flat rostrum, but in addition to the median ridge characteristic of the genus, the Tropical Whale has 2 extra ridges, one along each side. These begin as shallow depressions level with the blowhole and run forward to the tip of the snout. The fin is in the Sei position, a little more than one-third of the way forward from the tail, but it is a different shape. The Tropical Whale's fin is never more than 45 cm (18 inches) tall, rather more erect, more pointed, than the Sei's, and often notched or even frayed on its curved trailing edge. The flippers are slender and pointed, about 10 per cent of total body length.

The colour is uniformly bluish dark grey, lighter in the region of the throat pleats. In many individuals there is a pale grey blotch on the flank just in front of the fin.

Field Identification A view close enough to pick out 3 ridges on the top of the head is sufficient to distinguish the Tropical Whale from all other rorquals; but one is seldom so fortunate and must usually look for other characteristics.

Tropical Whales are deep divers and when they surface to breathe often rise steeply in a way that exposes the head, and then shows a long expanse of back as they roll sharply over, humping the tailstock as Fin Whales (*B. physalus 5*) do

before diving. Like Fins, Tropical Whales seldom show their flukes, but the two can be distinguished by the larger fin of the Fin Whale, which is also set further back and does not become visible as soon after the blow.

The spout of the Tropical Whale is a typical tall thin rorqual blow, usually about 4 m (13 ft) high. The breathing sequence is seldom as regular as that of the surface-feeding Sei, consisting usually of 3 or 4 short blows at intervals of about 10–15 seconds, followed by a deep dive for 5–20 minutes.

Tropical Whales often approach ships out of curiosity, as Piked Whales (*B. acutorostrata 7*) do. The Piked Whale is usually easy to identify by its smaller size, much more pointed head with a single ridge and by the bright white band on each flipper. In warm waters, approached by a large whale which comes in to meet the ship at an angle, making adjustments in its course to match ours, we have little hesitation in identifying it as a Tropical Whale long before it gets close enough to show any specific details.

The greatest confusion clearly exists between Tropical and Sei whales. Even whalers have difficulty telling them apart and catches of one species are still often attributed to the other. Discrimination is possible in the field by some subtle distinctions:

B. edeni 3 ridges on head; fin small, sharply pointed, often notched; surfaces erratically; 4 m blow; rolls over with arched tailstock; white throat often visible; often approaches ships; more jerky, fishlike movement.

B. borealis single head ridge; fin large, less pointed, more sloping; breathes regularly; 3 m blow; sinks quietly below surface; dark, shiny appearance; never approaches ships; normally sedate movement.

Stranding Tropical Whales sometimes strand themselves, and identification is easy. The 3 ridges on the head are distinctive. The throat grooves are also useful: there are 40–69 pleats (average 53), but unlike those of the Sei Whale, they extend 58 per cent of body length, to the navel. Where the grooves end, there is often a band of darker grey across the belly. There are 250–370 baleen plates (average 300). These are short and wide, roughly 45 cm (18 inches) in length, with long, very stiff bristles. The plates are generally a shiny medium grey with dark bristles, but those nearest the tip of the jaw may be pale or even white. There is always a large gap in the front between the left and right rows of baleen.

The skull is typically rorqual; there are 54 vertebrae and 13–14 pairs of ribs, with the first pair being double headed.

Natural History Tropical Whales, as their habitat and coarse baleen suggest, eat a lot of fish. Off South Africa the staple is a pilchard (*Sardinops ocellata*); in New Zealand waters it is mullet; off Western Australia, anchovy (*Engraulis australis*) is favoured; while in the North Pacific it is *E. japonica.* There are plankton blooms in some areas of the tropics where cold water upwells and, when this does occur, Tropical Whales congregate to take advantage of swarming crustaceans such as *Euphausia lucens* and *Thysanoessa gregaria.*

Whenever we have seen Tropical Whales feeding they seem

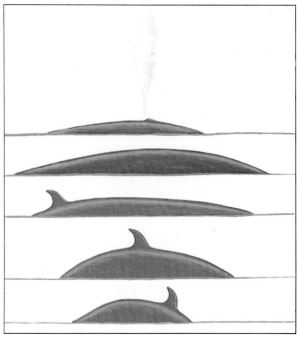

Dive sequence

to use a combination of techniques, sometimes rising up like Piked Whales and gulping at a shoal of fish, and sometimes making horizontal sweeps near the surface in the manner of Fin Whales. Feeding clearly takes place all year round.

Almost nothing is known about behaviour. They seem to associate in loosely-knit groups of 5–6; they probably mature after about 5 years at a length of close to 12 m (40 ft); and they almost certainly mate and breed all year round. More rarely, they form large concentrations, probably around unusual sources of food. On one occasion we saw 30–40 together off the southern coast of Madagascar.

The only known recording of the voice of this whale is of a pop lasting 0.4 second at a frequency of 124 Hz.

Status There are clearly local concentrations in all tropical waters which could add up to a sizable world total. One estimate puts this at about 20,000 individuals.

Distribution Tropical Whales are found primarily near the shore in most tropical and subtropical waters. There are regular concentrations off West Africa, South Africa, Malagasy, the Seychelles Bank, Western Australia, Fiji, Peru, the Bonin Islands and Hawaii.

There is some evidence of inshore-offshore migration, which is probably linked with the movement of favourite foods. The normal distribution of the species is clearly defined by the limits of the 20°C isotherm.

Sources AL ROBAAE (1969) in Iraq, ANDERSON (1878) original description, BEST (1960) in South Africa, BEST (1967) feeding, BEST (1973) status, CLARKE & AGUAYO (1965) in south-east Pacific, OLSEN (1913) early description, OMURA (1959) in Japan, THOMPSON & CUMMINGS (1969) sounds.

HUMPBACK WHALE

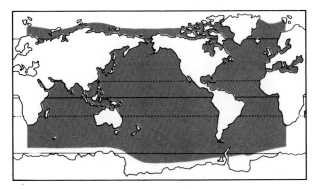

Classification A long chain of hearsay, uninterrupted for generations by any hint of original observation, began in the early eighteenth century with something called the '*pflockfish*'. In 1741 this was elaborated into Klein's '*balaena gibbo unico*' (the one-humped whale); and by 1756 it had matured (still without any of the authors catching even one glimpse of the animal, alive or dead) into Brisson's '*baleine de la Nouvelle Angleterre*'. The German naturalist Georg Heinrich Borowski, once again by proxy, dignified those earlier descriptions by inventing one of the new binomials in 1781, *Balaena novaeangliae.*

In 1846, Gray created the genus *Megaptera*, from the Greek *megas*, great, and *pteron*, a wing, for a whale with huge winglike flippers stranded at the mouth of the River Elbe. He gave it the species name *longipinna*, from the Latin *longus*, long, and *pinna*, a wing. In 1932 Remington Kellogg drew attention to Borowski's name, and since then all Humpback Whales have been known as *Megaptera novaeangliae.* If Humpbacks in the southern hemisphere should prove (as some cetologists suspect) to be different from those north of the equator, the southern form will be known as *M. n. australis* (LESSON 1828).

Local Names Humpback, hunchback and bunch whale (English); *bultrug* (Dutch), *hnufubakur* (Swedish), *gorbach* (Russian), and *buckelhval* (Danish); from the knobs and protuberances on its head and flippers it has been called knucklehead (English), *baleine à bosse* (French), *stubhval* (Danish), *knølhval* (Norwegian), *Knurrhval* (German), and *pletwal* (Polish). Northern aboriginal peoples know it as *aliama* (Aleutian), *kaipekak* (Bering Eskimo), and *keporkak* (Greenland Eskimo).

Description Large; length averages 14.6 m (48 ft) for males, with a maximum of 17.5 m (58 ft), and 15.2 m (50 ft) for females, with a maximum of 19 m (62 ft); calves are about 4.5 m (15 ft) at birth. Weight averages 30,000–40,000 kg (34–45 tons) for both sexes, with a maximum of 48,000 kg (53 tons); calves are about 1,300 kg (1.5 tons) at birth.

Although Humpback Whales are still classified in the family Balaenopteridae, they are unlike the rorquals. The body is robust, narrowing rapidly in front of the huge tail flukes. The head is broad and rounded, in some ways like that of the Blue

95

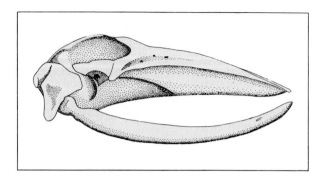

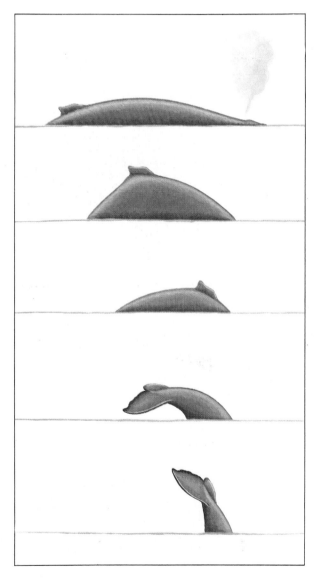

Above: skull
Below: dive sequence

Whale (*B. musculus 6*), but the median ridge is indistinct and has been replaced by a string of fleshy tubercles or knobs. Two further lines of these are arranged along the margins of the jaws; and there is a larger, more rounded, projection near the tip of the lower jaw. Each bump has a long coarse hair growing directly out of its centre.

The fin is small and varies in shape from triangular to sharklike. It is set two-thirds of the way back, in roughly the same position as that of the Fin Whale, but is mounted on a distinct fleshy step or platform unlike that of any other baleen whale.

The most characteristic features are the enormous flippers. They are almost a third of total body length (about 5 m or 16 ft long in an adult) and heavily scalloped on the leading edge. The trailing edge of the tail flukes is similarly serrated.

The colour is generally blackish with a white area covering the throat grooves. The flippers are almost pure white below and mottled black and white above. The underside of the flukes is marked with a variable pattern of white, making each whale recognizable at the surface as it throws its tail into the air before sounding.

Field Identification Humpback Whales at a distance can look a little like some rorquals, but the Humpback's habit of raising the tail flukes before sounding sets them apart. Great Sperm Whales (*Physeter macrocephalus 36*) also throw their tails in the air, but have no white markings on them at all.

The Humpback's blow is distinctive, seldom more than 3 m (10 ft) high, and is a broad, bushy balloon of spray. The usual breathing sequence involves 2–3 minutes at the surface, blowing once every 20–30 seconds, followed by a deep humpbacked dive for 3–28 minutes. The fin is seldom seen until the high rolling dive that brings the hump into view before sounding. In warmer water, the number of breaths taken between dives is reduced from an average of 6 to 2–3.

Humpbacks often leap clear of the water, usually in an arching backward flip which brings the pale pleats of the throat into view. On occasion these whales can be found lying motionless at the surface with one long flipper hoisted like a sail. When disturbed, or sometimes for no apparent reason, they slap the water hard producing a report like a rifle shot; or lobtail, bringing the tail down sharply in an even louder smack against the surface. All these sounds may have a signal function, keeping a scattered group of whales in touch, or warning each other of intruders.

In our experience Humpbacks show very little fear of boats, large or small. We have been able to motor close to these whales in our inflatable boats and have even had an adult come to scratch its back on the hull of our stationary ship. This fearless attitude is shown when the whales are busy on their polar feeding grounds or clowning in the warmer waters of the tropics. Everywhere the response and the experience are the same: groups of grotesque and beautiful monsters, filled with what seems like *joie de vivre,* breaching and falling, splashing and tailing, rolling, scooping, finning or bursting out together in great backward somersaults.

Stranding Possibly as a result of their familiarity with shallow waters, Humpbacks rarely strand. The occasional dead one presents few problems of identification. Out of water, these lithe acrobats become stocky and inflated as the sleek lines are destroyed by gravity and the relaxation of the great throat muscles.

Flippers, tuberosities on the head and the lump on the lower jaw are all distinctive. So too are the throat grooves: Humpbacks have fewer grooves, 14–24 (average 22), set more widely apart, than any rorqual.

The baleen is also characteristic. There are 270–400 plates (usually 330), each up to 65 cm (25 inches) long, dark grey or olive brown with light grey bristles.

The rough, knobbly skin provides great scope for ectoparasites. Humpbacks in cold waters are infested with up to 450 kg (half a ton) of the sessile barnacles *Coronula diadema* and *C. reginae*. One favours the lips and tail and is usually so deeply embedded in the skin that only the crown shows, while the other perches on the tubercles. A long-necked goose barnacle which never parasitizes the whale directly often sits on top of the barnacles. As the whales move into warmer waters, the barnacles tend to drop off, leaving the field clear for the whale lice, notably *Cyamus boopis* found only on the Humpback.

The skull differs noticeably from that of the rorquals in having a more curved lower jaw. There are 52–53 vertebrae and, in some individuals, remnants of hind limbs. A Humpback landed on Vancouver Island in Canada in 1919 had legs 1.2 m (4 ft) long.

Natural History Humpback baleen is coarse and stiff, excluding the possibility of feeding on smaller forms of plankton. But in the southern hemisphere the whales live mostly on swarming crustaceans, mainly species of *Euphausia*, *Munida* and *Thysanoessa*. In the northern hemisphere the various forms of krill are largely replaced by shoaling fish such as the capelin (*Mallotus villosus*), anchovy (*Engraulis mordax*) and cod (*Gadus morhua*). A few groups of Humpbacks even follow trawlers to take advantage of their spill.

Normally Humpbacks feed by lunging forward at the surface or by rushing on their prey from below, surfacing through the school with their mouths open. The Alaskan population have however developed a technical refinement involving the creation of a bubble net to trap and concentrate the prey long enough for them to grab it. To do this, the whales start 15 m (50 ft) below the surface, weaving a net of bubbles by forcing air out through their blowholes as they swim upwards in a tight spiral, finally surfacing open-mouthed right amongst the food. It may be possible for a whale to make a net with the most efficient grade of mesh by selecting the bubble size it uses, or for two whales to collaborate on a net 30 m (100 ft) or more in diameter.

The normal social unit seems to be a small family group of 3 or 4, often loosely tied by sound signals to other more distant groups of similar size. In animals like these, whose calls may travel for hundreds of kilometres, the normal human concept of a herd (that is a gathering of individuals all visible to us at the same time) breaks down altogether. For all we know, every Humpback in the entire north-west Atlantic Ocean

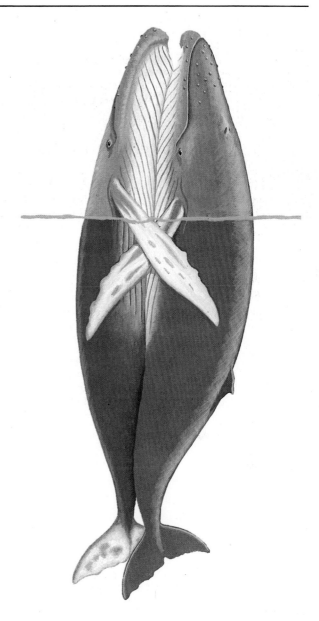

Pair of Humpbacks in mating posture

could be part of a single social system.

Humpbacks mature in less than 10 years, when males are 11 m (36 ft) and females 12 m (40 ft) long. Mating takes place on communal breeding grounds in warmer waters, usually in shallow bays within the 100 m (330 ft) contour. Courtship is playful and splashy, often social, involving an energetic group that races along the surface at breakneck speed, churning the water up into turbulent knots of breaching, slapping whales. Sometimes the confusion ends in a single pair rising, with their flippers interlaced, belly-to-belly above the surface, clasping each other and holding that position for 30 seconds or more until they shudder and subside again.

Gestation lasts for 11–12 months and calves nurse until they are almost a year old and 8 m (26 ft) long. During this time it is common to see a mother and her calf together with a third whale, a mysterious escort, who is sometimes an adult male. There are records of both animals acting protectively toward the infant, in one case of a mother taking her young calf under a flipper to protect it.

New mating frequently takes place soon after birth, so Humpbacks can breed every other year.

Intensive observation in the clear water of winter breeding grounds off the Hawaiian Islands is beginning to provide detailed information which makes the Humpback the best known of all baleen whales; but we are still far from understanding even the rudiments of their complex social behaviour.

Humpbacks produce the longest and most varied songs in the animal world. These are intricate fabrics of sound, ranging from pure high-frequency whistles to low and resonant rumbles which can even be heard above the surface. On one occasion near Tonga we found ourselves surrounded by underwater reverberations that made the blue breeding lagoon thrum almost painfully despite the fact that there was not a whale in sight.

At first, each song seems to consist of random grunts, groans, moos, rasps and twitters, but analysis shows that there are long, organized sequences. Each sequence normally lasts 10–15 minutes and may be repeated over and over again, without pause, for hours. It is made up of short sound units combined into phrases which form unbroken patterns or themes. These recognizable themes are subject to individual interpretation, but always arranged into cycles characteristic of each population, so that all Humpbacks in one area sing only the local song. Evidence shows that these songs evolve with time. Each year the song is a little different, but every change is picked up and incorporated in the current pattern and in the appropriate local dialect by all singers in a given population.

There is now a vast library of recorded songs, mainly from Bermuda and Hawaii, but we still know little about just who sings, or why. Singing is more common in, and perhaps even largely confined to, the breeding season; it usually seems to be a solitary whale, possibly a male, who sings. The song may function as sexual display, advertising the presence of a breeding male and keeping a family group together, but the complexity of the cycle suggests that there is more to it than that. In addition to the ritual announcement, there may be new information or the preservation of old in something like a simple folklore. Before any conclusions can be reached, it will be necessary to know exactly which individual is singing and to establish its age, sex and relationship to all those within

Humpback breaching, typically landing on back

hearing range; and then to document their direct response to the singer and the song. A start has been made by Roger and Katy Payne and their co-workers.

Status The world total probably lies somewhere between 4,000 and 6,000 individuals. Recent estimates show that the original population of hundreds of thousands of Humpbacks has been reduced to remnants of less than 2,000 in the North Pacific, even less in the North Atlantic, and certainly no more than another 2,000 in the southern hemisphere.

Despite the cessation of commercial whaling on Humpbacks, there is a new threat posed by growing competition between the animals and fishermen in over-exploited areas such as the codbanks of Newfoundland.

Distribution Humpback Whales follow fairly well marked coastal migration routes between their polar feeding grounds and a few selected tropical coastal or island breeding areas. In the southern hemisphere, these lie in the Mozambique Channel, on the north-eastern and north-western coasts of Australia, around the New Hebrides, Fijian and Samoan Islands and off the coasts of Ecuador and north-eastern Brazil. In the northern hemisphere they concentrate around the Marianas and Hawaiian Islands, off the coast of Baja California, in the Lesser Antilles and around the Cape Verde Islands. There is probably little or no mixing across the equator.

Humpbacks swim at about 8 kph (4 knots), moving through about 15° of latitude a month. Young males lead the way, followed by mated pairs, with females and calves bringing up the rear. Leaving the winter ground, the newly pregnant females depart first, followed by the immatures and males, with the females that have calves staying longest in warmer waters.

The time to see Humpbacks in Hawaii is from December to April; in the West Indies from January to March; and off Bermuda in April and May. Not all whales are involved in all migrations, we have seen individuals and pairs a long way from the traditional breeding grounds in winter; and the odd whale that seems to have decided not to travel up to the ice, but to remain all year in the tropics.

Sources BOROWSKI (1781) original description, CHITTLEBOROUGH (1965) breeding, DUNN (1978) general, EARLE (1979) behaviour, HERMAN & ANTINOJA (1977) in Hawaii, KELLOGG (1932) taxonomy, KRAUS & KATONA (1977) tail catalogue, LIEN & MERDSOY (1979) entanglement in nets, PAYNE & PAYNE (1979) sounds, PAYNE & McVAY (1971) sounds, WINN ET AL (1970) sounds, WOLMAN & JURASZ (1977) status.

ORDER B: ODONTOCETI

The Toothed Whales

The toothed whales differ from all other mammals in having only one nostril. The usual two nasal passages are present and separate at the base of the skull, but on their way up to the surface on the top of the head they join, or one of them becomes diverted. In addition the simple air cavities or sinuses usually found in the cheek bones of most mammals have become specialized in the toothed whales, spreading out into a maze of interconnected air- and foam-filled passages. There is a progressive series running from a relatively simple layout of this air sinus system in the beaked whales, to the extraordinary complexity of the system in true dolphins. These developments reflect an increasing ability to adapt to the ocean environment and to make the best possible use of it at all depths. So we have used this system as the basis for our arrangement of the 66 species listed here, starting with the ones least specialized in this respect and ending with the most advanced ones.

All Odontocetes have teeth, at least at some stage in their lives. There may be as many as 260 in some species of long-beaked dolphins, or as few as the one tooth which has become a spiral tusk in the Unicorn Whale (*Monodon monoceros 34*).

All cetacean teeth have only one root; they are simple pegs set in a single socket. All the teeth usually look alike, with no differentiation into incisors, canines and molars; and there is only one set, with no possibility of replacement once they are broken or lost.

It is possible to identify most toothed whales by the number, shape and position of the teeth.

The chart on pages 102/103, which gives the average total number of teeth and the complete range of numbers occurring on each side of each jaw, will make it possible to short-circuit a search for the appropriate species. Other characteristics must then be used to confirm this purely dental diagnosis.

Families of Toothed Whales

There are 8 families in the Order Odontoceti:

Family Four Ziphiidae
The 'ziphids' or beaked whales (page 108).
Medium-sized whales with long beaks, 2 or 4 teeth on the lower jaw, 2 grooves forming a V-shape on the throat; and a small fin placed far back on the slender body. There are 18 species.

Family Five Platanistidae
The river dolphins (page 148).
Small dolphins with very long slender beaks, many teeth in both jaws, and large broad flippers. There are 5 species.

Family Six Monodontidae
The White and Unicorn whales (page 162).
Medium whales with high rounded foreheads, no dorsal fin, and rounded flippers which turn up at the tip. There are 2 species.

Family Seven Physeteridae
The sperm whales (page 168).
One large and two small whales with square heads, fin low or missing; and teeth normally only in the lower jaw. There are 3 species.

Family Eight Stenidae
The coastal dolphins (page 180).
Longish snouts and dorsal fins. A family of convenience for 4 odd small dolphins.

Family Nine Phocoenidae
The porpoises (page 190).
Small whales with no beak, short jaws armed with spade-like teeth, and a low dorsal fin. There are 6 species.

Family Ten Globicephalidae
The killer and pilot whales (page 204).
Small and medium whales with very high fins, blunt heads, notched tails, and a few strong, curved teeth in both jaws. There are 6 species.

Family Eleven Delphinidae
The dolphins (page 222).
Large number of small and active dolphins with prominent beaks; many teeth in both jaws, large tapering flippers, most with well-developed dorsal fins. There are 22 species.

These 8 families contain 34 genera with a tentative total of 66 species. These differ considerably, even within the family categories, and no simple system can do justice to the variety involved. The following keys, however, provide at least a starting point for identifying toothed whales at sea or stranded on a beach.

Map Key Six of the 8 families have worldwide distributions, but geographical clues could help with the identification of members of: Monodontidae, which are confined to the Arctic; and Platanistidae, each species of which occurs in one river system.

CHART OF TEETH

AVERAGE TOTAL NUMBER OF TEETH	RANGE ON ONE SIDE OF UPPER JAW	RANGE ON ONE SIDE OF LOWER JAW	SHAPE AND PATTERN	SPECIES	No.
2	1	0	spiral tusk	Unicorn Whale (Monodon monoceros)	34
2	0	1	spindle-shaped	Goosebeak Whale (Ziphius cavirostris)	14
2	0	1	pear-shaped	Northern Bottlenose Whale (Hyperoodon ampullatus)	15
2	0	1	pear-shaped	Southern Bottlenose Whale (Hyperoodon planifrons)	16
2	0	1	on tip of jaw	Indopacific Beaked Whale (Indopacetus pacificus)	17
2	0	1	on tip of jaw	Skew Beaked Whale (Mesoplodon hectori)	18
2	0	1	on tip of jaw	Wonderful Beaked Whale (Mesoplodon mirus)	19
2	0	1	15% from tip	Gulf Stream Beaked Whale (Mesoplodon europaeus)	20
2	0	1	20% from tip	Arch Beaked Whale (Mesoplodon carlhubbsi)	21
2	0	1	25% from tip	Japanese Beaked Whale (Mesoplodon ginkgodens)	22
2	0	1	30% from tip	Scamperdown Beaked Whale (Mesoplodon grayi)	23
2	0	1	35% from tip	Bering Sea Beaked Whale (Mesoplodon stejnegeri)	24
2	0	1	35% from tip	Splaytooth Beaked Whales (Mesoplodon bowdoini)	25
2	0	1	50% from tip	Dense Beaked Whale (Mesoplodon densirostris)	26
2	0	1	50% from tip	North Sea Beaked Whale (Mesoplodon bidens)	27
2	0	1	50% from tip	Straptooth Beaked Whale (Mesoplodon layardii)	28
4	0	2	1 large, 1 small	Northern Fourtooth Whale (Berardius bairdii)	12
4	0	2	1 large, 1 small	Southern Fourtooth Whale (Berardius arnuxii)	13
10	0	2–7	at front of jaw	Grey Dolphin (Grampus griseus)	68
24	0	8–13	curved	Dwarf Sperm Whale (Kogia simus)	38
30	0	9–16	curved	Pygmy Sperm Whale (Kogia breviceps)	37
32	8–11	8–10	conical	White Whale (Delphinapterus leucas)	35
36	7–11	8–12	curved	Shortfin Pilot Whale (Globicephala macrorhynchus)	50
38	7–11	8–12	more on lower jaw	False Killer Whale (Pseudorca crassidens)	52
40	8–12	8–12	curved	Longfin Pilot Whale (Globicephala melaena)	49
44	8–13	10–13	more on right side	Pygmy Killer Whale (Feresa attenuata)	53
44	10–13	10–13	large curved	Great Killer Whale (Orcinus orca)	51
48	0	18–30	very large curved	Great Sperm Whale (Physeter macrocephalus)	36
56	12–19	12–17		Snubfin Dolphin (Orcaella brevirostris)	69
62	15–21	14–21	spade-shaped	Finless Porpoise (Neophocaena phocaenoides)	47
66	14–18	17–19	spade-shaped	Black Porpoise (Phocoena spinipinnis)	44
76	17–23	16–20	spade-shaped	Spectacled Porpoise (Phocoena dioptrica)	45
76	20–21	18–18	spade-shaped	Gulf Porpoise (Phocoena sinus)	46

AVERAGE TOTAL NUMBER OF TEETH	RANGE ON ONE SIDE OF UPPER JAW	RANGE ON ONE SIDE OF LOWER JAW	SHAPE AND PATTERN	SPECIES	No.
88	19–28	19–28	spade-shaped	Spray Porpoise (Phocoenoides dalli)	48
92	22–28	22–28	spade-shaped	Common Porpoise (Phocoena phocoena)	43
92	19–21	26–27		Tasman Whale (Tasmacetus shepherdi)	11
92	20–27	20–27	ridges on crown	Roughtooth Dolphin (Steno bredanensis)	39
96	22–25	21–25		Melonhead Whale (Peponocephala electra)	54
98	20–26	18–26		Bottlenose Dolphin (Tursiops truncatus)	76
98	22–28	22–28		Whitebeak Dolphin (Lagenorhynchus albirostris)	55
108	25–30	26–30		Benguela Dolphin (Cephalorhynchus heavisidii)	66
112	26–30	26–30		Atlantic Humpback Dolphin (Sousa teuszii)	41
112	28	28		Hourglass Dolphin (Lagenorhynchus cruciger)	59
116	24–32	26–32		New Zealand Dolphin (Cephalorhynchus hectori)	67
116	28–30	28–31		Chilean Dolphin (Cephalorhynchus eutropia)	65
116	29–30	29–30	larger in front	Ganges River Dolphin (Platanista gangetica)	29
116	29–30	29–30	larger in front	Indus River Dolphin (Platanista minor)	30
116	25–34	26–33		Amazon River Dolphin (Inia geoffrensis)	32
118	29–30	29–30		Piebald Dolphin (Cephalorhynchus commersonii)	64
120	30	30		Blackchin Dolphin (Lagenorhynchus australis)	60
122	23–32	23–32		Pacific Whiteside Dolphin (Lagenorhynchus obliquidens)	57
128	28–34	26–35		Estuarine Dolphin (Sotalia fluviatilis)	42
128	32–38	31–36		Indopacific Humpback Dolphin (Sousa chinensis)	40
128	28–36	30–36		Dusky Dolphin (Lagenorhynchus obscurus)	58
132	30–40	30–40	more on upper jaw	Atlantic Whiteside Dolphin (Lagenorhynchus acutus)	56
136	32–36	31–36		Yangtze River Dolphin (Lipotes vexillifer)	31
148	30–37	28–37		Spotted Dolphin (Stenella plagiodon)	74
154	35–45	35–44		Bridled Dolphin (Stenella attenuata)	73
172	40–44	39–43		Shortsnout Dolphin (Lagenodelphis hosei)	61
184	43–47	43–47		Southern Rightwhale Dolphin (Lissodelphis peronii)	62
200	40–53	40–51		Northern Rightwhale Dolphin (Lissodelphis borealis)	63
200	43–50	43–49		Striped Dolphin (Stenella coeruleoalba)	72
200	43–58	43–58		Helmet Dolphin (Stenella clymene)	71
200	40–57	40–58		Common Dolphin (Delphinus delphis)	75
220	48–60	48–60		La Plata River Dolphin (Pontoporia blainvillei)	33
224	46–65	46–65		Spinner Dolphin (Stenella longirostris)	70

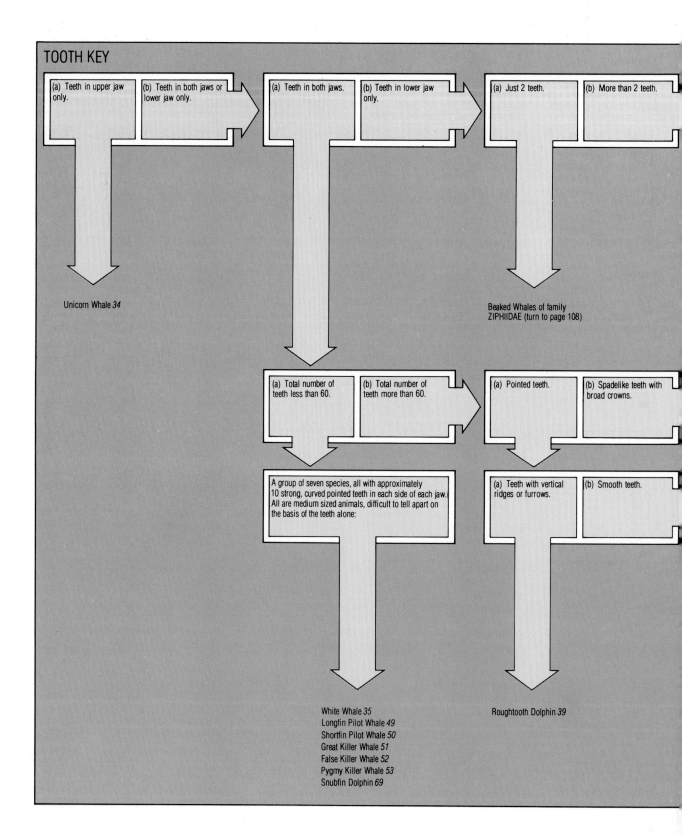

TOOTH KEY

(a) Teeth in upper jaw only.

(b) Teeth in both jaws or lower jaw only.

(a) Teeth in both jaws.

(b) Teeth in lower jaw only.

(a) Just 2 teeth.

(b) More than 2 teeth.

Unicorn Whale 34

Beaked Whales of family ZIPHIIDAE (turn to page 108)

(a) Total number of teeth less than 60.

(b) Total number of teeth more than 60.

(a) Pointed teeth.

(b) Spadelike teeth with broad crowns.

A group of seven species, all with approximately 10 strong, curved pointed teeth in each side of each jaw. All are medium sized animals, difficult to tell apart on the basis of the teeth alone:

(a) Teeth with vertical ridges or furrows.

(b) Smooth teeth.

White Whale 35
Longfin Pilot Whale 49
Shortfin Pilot Whale 50
Great Killer Whale 51
False Killer Whale 52
Pygmy Killer Whale 53
Snubfin Dolphin 69

Roughtooth Dolphin 39

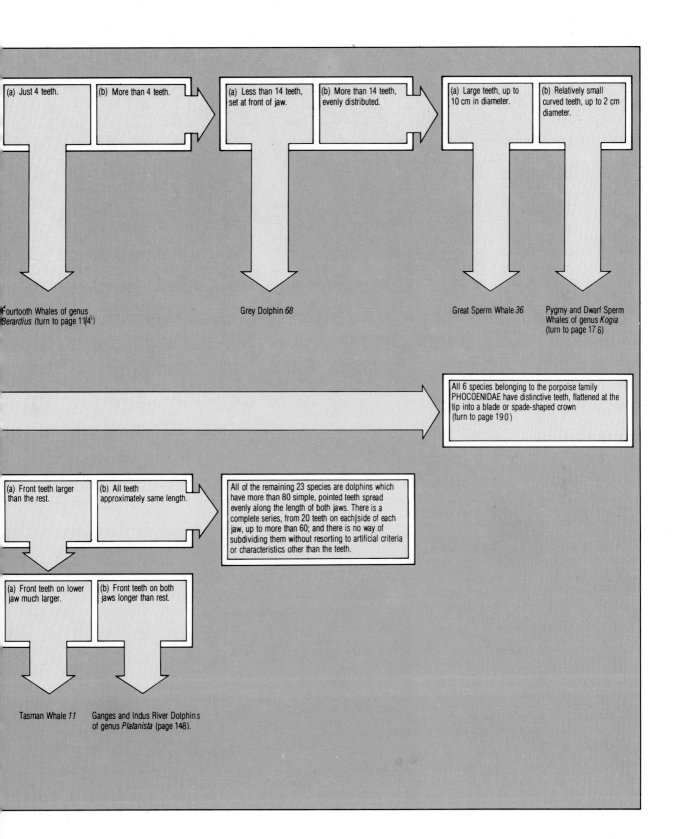

(a) Just 4 teeth.

(b) More than 4 teeth.

(a) Less than 14 teeth, set at front of jaw.

(b) More than 14 teeth, evenly distributed.

(a) Large teeth, up to 10 cm in diameter.

(b) Relatively small curved teeth, up to 2 cm diameter.

Fourtooth Whales of genus *Berardius* (turn to page 114)

Grey Dolphin *68*

Great Sperm Whale *36*

Pygmy and Dwarf Sperm Whales of genus *Kogia* (turn to page 176)

All 6 species belonging to the porpoise family PHOCOENIDAE have distinctive teeth, flattened at the tip into a blade or spade-shaped crown (turn to page 190)

(a) Front teeth larger than the rest.

(b) All teeth approximately same length.

All of the remaining 23 species are dolphins which have more than 80 simple, pointed teeth spread evenly along the length of both jaws. There is a complete series, from 20 teeth on each side of each jaw, up to more than 60; and there is no way of subdividing them without resorting to artificial criteria or characteristics other than the teeth.

(a) Front teeth on lower jaw much larger.

(b) Front teeth on both jaws longer than rest.

Tasman Whale *11*

Ganges and Indus River Dolphins of genus *Platanista* (page 148).

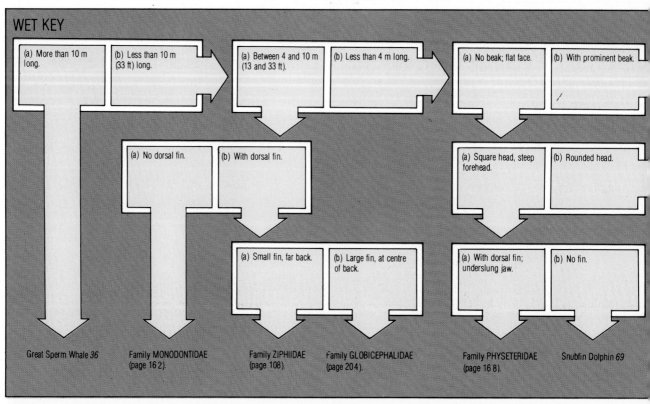

WET KEY

(a) More than 10 m long.

(b) Less than 10 m (33 ft) long.

(a) Between 4 and 10 m (13 and 33 ft).

(b) Less than 4 m long.

(a) No beak; flat face.

(b) With prominent beak.

(a) No dorsal fin.

(b) With dorsal fin.

(a) Square head, steep forehead.

(b) Rounded head.

(a) Small fin, far back.

(b) Large fin, at centre of back.

(a) With dorsal fin; underslung jaw.

(b) No fin.

Great Sperm Whale *36*

Family MONODONTIDAE (page 162).

Family ZIPHIIDAE (page 108).

Family GLOBICEPHALIDAE (page 204).

Family PHYSETERIDAE (page 168).

Snubfin Dolphin *69*

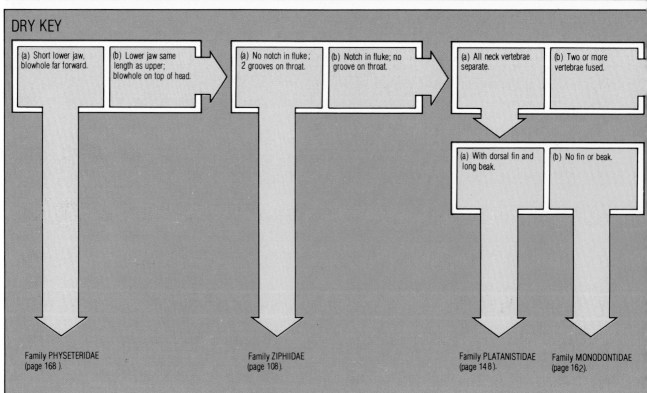

DRY KEY

(a) Short lower jaw, blowhole far forward.

(b) Lower jaw same length as upper; blowhole on top of head.

(a) No notch in fluke; 2 grooves on throat.

(b) Notch in fluke; no groove on throat.

(a) All neck vertebrae separate.

(b) Two or more vertebrae fused.

(a) With dorsal fin and long beak.

(b) No fin or beak.

Family PHYSETERIDAE (page 168).

Family ZIPHIIDAE (page 108).

Family PLATANISTIDAE (page 148).

Family MONODONTIDAE (page 162).

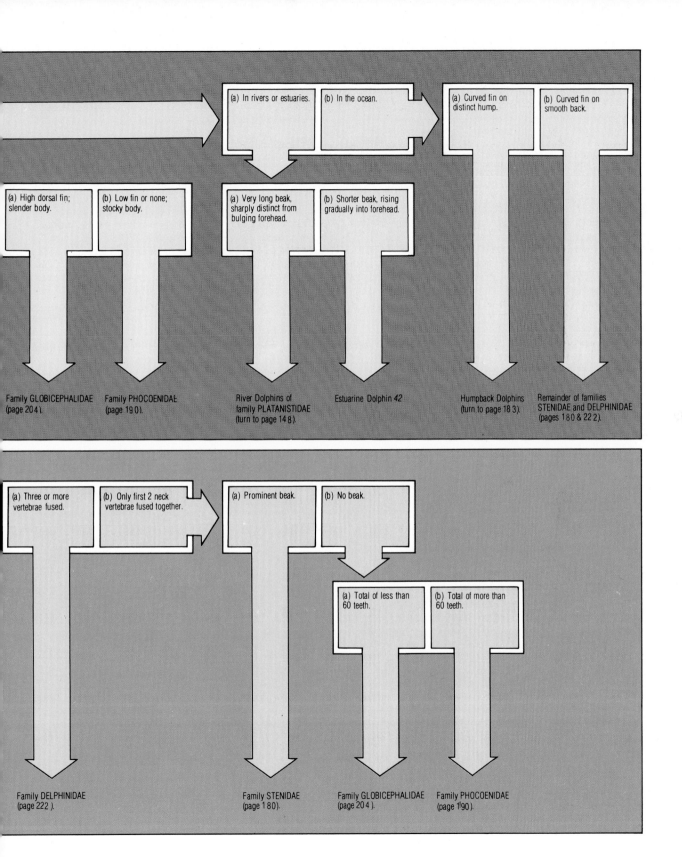

(a) In rivers or estuaries.

(b) In the ocean.

(a) Curved fin on distinct hump.

(b) Curved fin on smooth back.

(a) High dorsal fin; slender body.

(b) Low fin or none; stocky body.

(a) Very long beak, sharply distinct from bulging forehead.

(b) Shorter beak, rising gradually into forehead.

Family GLOBICEPHALIDAE (page 204).

Family PHOCOENIDAE (page 190).

River Dolphins of family PLATANISTIDAE (turn to page 148).

Estuarine Dolphin 42.

Humpback Dolphins (turn to page 183).

Remainder of families STENIDAE and DELPHINIDAE (pages 180 & 222).

(a) Three or more vertebrae fused.

(b) Only first 2 neck vertebrae fused together.

(a) Prominent beak.

(b) No beak.

(a) Total of less than 60 teeth.

(b) Total of more than 60 teeth.

Family DELPHINIDAE (page 222).

Family STENIDAE (page 180).

Family GLOBICEPHALIDAE (page 204).

Family PHOCOENIDAE (page 190).

107

Family Four–Ziphidae

This family was established in 1865 by Gray to include all medium-sized whales with a pointed beak and a single pair of grooves which converge on the throat. The length varies from 4 m (13 ft) in *Mesoplodon*, to 12.8 m (42 ft) for the largest female fourtooth whales of the genus *Berardius*. In all species the single blowhole is crescent-shaped, with the arms pointing forward; and there is a relatively small dorsal fin, usually placed behind the midpoint of the body, 55–65 per cent of the distance towards the tail. There is either a very small notch or no break at all in the trailing edge of the flukes.

The 6 genera and most of the 18 species differ chiefly in the arrangement of their teeth. In most cases the number of teeth has been secondarily and often drastically reduced leaving just 4 functional teeth in the genus *Berardius*, and only 2 in the genus *Mesoplodon*. The exact shape and position of those teeth which do remain provide useful characteristics for identification.

The bones of the skull are asymmetrical, except in *Berardius*; the first 3 or 4 of the neck vertebrae (cervicals) are generally fused with one another, and several of the ribs are double-headed. In some species a cartilage extends from the ribs to connect with the sternum (breastbone) and is visible even in a dried skeleton.

Wet Key assuming that the search has been narrowed down to a whale of moderate size, greater than 4 m (13 ft) long and less than 13 m (42 ft) long, with a small fin placed well back, an inconspicuous blow and a head with a narrow beak, follow the key overleaf.

Dry Key all 6 genera in the family are readily recognizable by their teeth alone. Distinction between the species of *Berardius* and *Hyperoodon* can be made on geographical grounds. In each genus 1 of the 2 species is confined to the northern hemisphere and the other to the south. The many species of *Mesoplodon* are distinguished by the precise position of the single pair of teeth on the jaw (see page 127).

Map Key the Goosebeak Whale (*Ziphius cavirostris 14*) and all the species of *Mesoplodon* have wide distribution, particularly in the southern hemisphere, and geographical clues are of limited use.

In the northern hemisphere the search may be narrowed in this way:

1. There are no *Berardius* species recorded in the Atlantic.

2. There are no *Hyperoodon* species recorded in the Pacific.

3. There are no records of *Indopacetus* in the Atlantic.

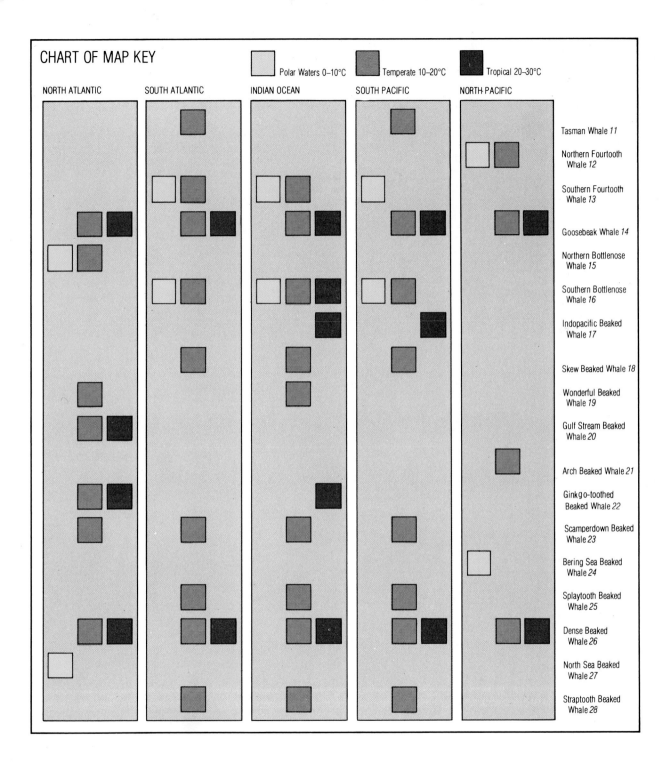

CHART OF MAP KEY

Polar Waters 0–10°C   Temperate 10–20°C   Tropical 20–30°C

NORTH ATLANTIC   SOUTH ATLANTIC   INDIAN OCEAN   SOUTH PACIFIC   NORTH PACIFIC

Tasman Whale *11*

Northern Fourtooth Whale *12*

Southern Fourtooth Whale *13*

Goosebeak Whale *14*

Northern Bottlenose Whale *15*

Southern Bottlenose Whale *16*

Indopacific Beaked Whale *17*

Skew Beaked Whale *18*

Wonderful Beaked Whale *19*

Gulf Stream Beaked Whale *20*

Arch Beaked Whale *21*

Ginkgo-toothed Beaked Whale *22*

Scamperdown Beaked Whale *23*

Bering Sea Beaked Whale *24*

Splaytooth Beaked Whale *25*

Dense Beaked Whale *26*

North Sea Beaked Whale *27*

Straptooth Beaked Whale *28*

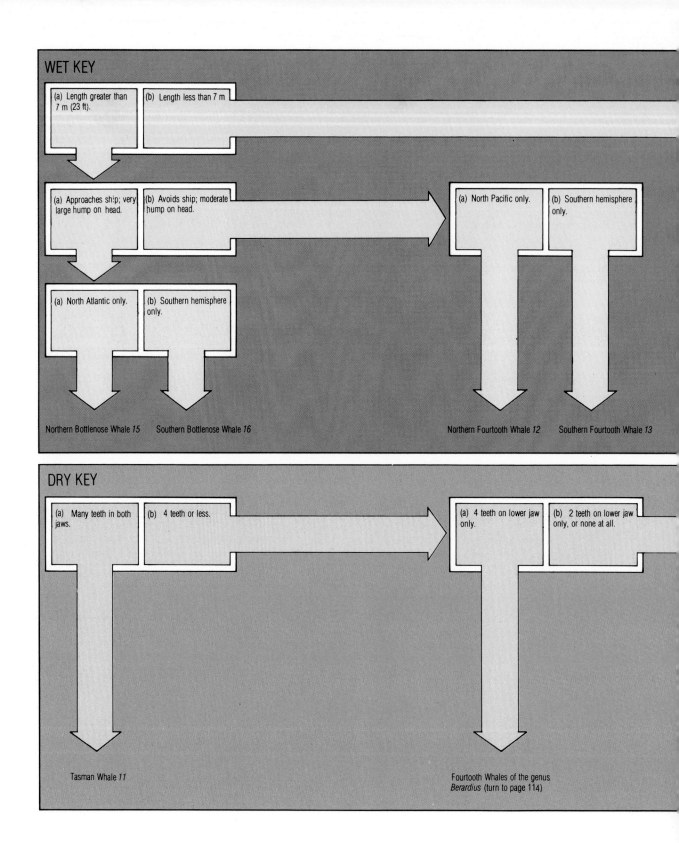

WET KEY

(a) Length greater than 7 m (23 ft).

(b) Length less than 7 m

(a) Approaches ship; very large hump on head.

(b) Avoids ship; moderate hump on head.

(a) North Pacific only.

(b) Southern hemisphere only.

(a) North Atlantic only.

(b) Southern hemisphere only.

Northern Bottlenose Whale *15*

Southern Bottlenose Whale *16*

Northern Fourtooth Whale *12*

Southern Fourtooth Whale *13*

DRY KEY

(a) Many teeth in both jaws.

(b) 4 teeth or less.

(a) 4 teeth on lower jaw only.

(b) 2 teeth on lower jaw only, or none at all.

Tasman Whale *11*

Fourtooth Whales of the genus *Berardius* (turn to page 114)

110

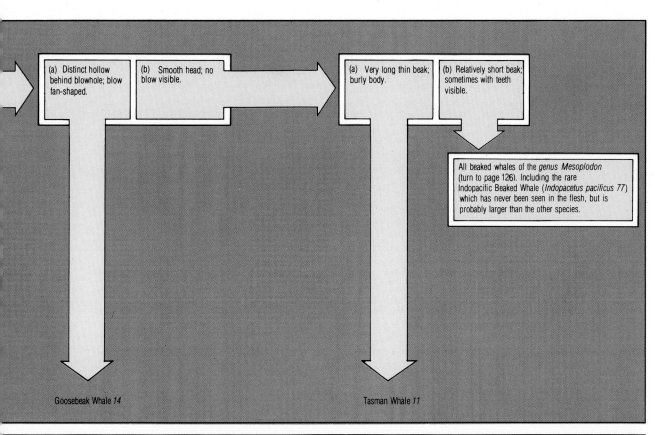

(a) Distinct hollow behind blowhole; blow fan-shaped.

(b) Smooth head; no blow visible.

(a) Very long thin beak; burly body.

(b) Relatively short beak; sometimes with teeth visible.

All beaked whales of the *genus Mesoplodon* (turn to page 126). Including the rare Indopacific Beaked Whale (*Indopacetus pacificus 77*) which has never been seen in the flesh, but is probably larger than the other species.

Goosebeak Whale *14*

Tasman Whale *11*

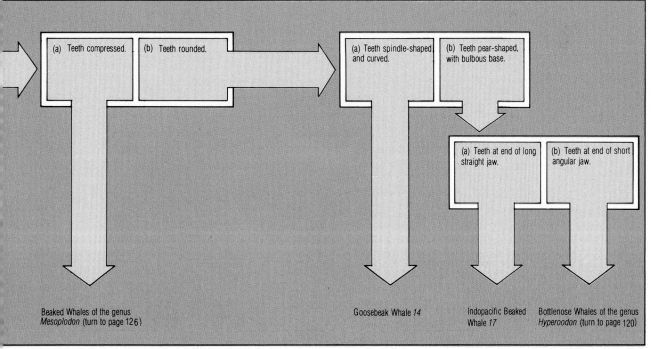

(a) Teeth compressed.

(b) Teeth rounded.

(a) Teeth spindle-shaped and curved.

(b) Teeth pear-shaped, with bulbous base.

(a) Teeth at end of long straight jaw.

(b) Teeth at end of short angular jaw.

Beaked Whales of the genus *Mesoplodon* (turn to page 126)

Goosebeak Whale *14*

Indopacific Beaked Whale *17*

Bottlenose Whales of the genus *Hyperoodon* (turn to page 120)

111

TASMAN WHALE

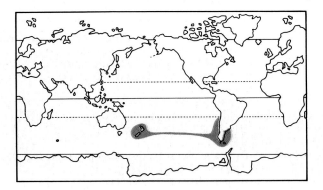

Classification This species was unknown until December 1933, when one whale was found stranded on the beach at Ohawe on the west coast of North Island, New Zealand. The skeleton was collected by G. Shepherd, Curator of the Wanganui Museum, and passed on to his colleague Walter Oliver of the Colonial Museum in Wellington. The type specimen, an almost complete mounted skeleton, remains in the Wanganui Public Museum. Oliver decided on the basis of the peculiar teeth to put the whale into a new genus *Tasmacetus*, after the sea in which it was found (which is itself named for the

explorer Abel Tasman), and the Latin *cetus*, a whale. The specific name *shepherdi* honours the finder.

In the last few years specimens have been found in Chile and the Argentine, but they seem to be identical to the New Zealand whales and there has been no attempt to create subspecies.

Local Names There are few common names, which is not surprising since this species is known only from 8 separate beached individuals. The only names used in the literature are Tasman beaked whale and Shepherd's beaked whale. In accordance with our decision to use the name 'beaked whale' only for members of the genus *Mesoplodon*, we call this species simply the Tasman Whale.

Description Medium; length averages about 6 m (20 ft) for both sexes, with a known maximum of 6.6 m (almost 22 ft). Weight is estimated to be 2,200–2,700 kg (5,000–6,000 lb).

The body form of the Tasman Whale is very much like that of the other ziphid whales, although it is more robust than any species of *Mesoplodon*. There is a bulging melon in front of the single blowhole, but this is not as well marked as that in either species of *Berardius*. The beak is untypically long and slender. The fin is small and rounded and positioned rather

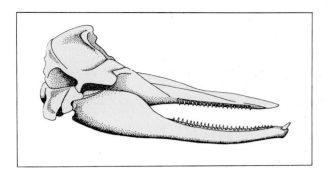

identify it immediately as one of the family Ziphiidae; but the teeth are unique. There are 2 large teeth (4 cm or 1.5 inches long) with bulbous bases and conical crowns on the tip of the lower jaw, like those of the Goosebeak Whale (*Ziphius cavirostris 14*). Behind these, unlike in any other member of the family, there are a large number of small but functional peglike teeth. These are separated from the large pair by a gap of about 4 cm (1.5 inches), followed by 26 or 27 evenly-spaced conical teeth on the lower jaw; and another 19–21 similar teeth on the upper jaw. The wear on all these shows that they are used, and not simply buried in the gums as are the rudimentary extra teeth of some young Goosebeak Whales.

less than two-thirds of the way back. The flippers are small, but the flukes are large and lack a median notch. There are 2 distinct grooves on the throat.

It is difficult to determine the true colour from beached individuals, but the back seems to be a dark grey brown, the flanks lighter and the belly almost white. There may be curved pale grey bracket marks on the cheeks.

Field Identification The Tasman Whale may never have been seen alive. The only possible sighting is an observation made in 1964 from a cliff top near Christchurch in New Zealand by William Watkins of the Woods Hole Oceanographic Institution in Massachusetts. Watkins watched for a few minutes as a whale with a beak surfaced briefly in the disturbed water of the bay below, and he got the distinct impression of a long thin rostrum and a suggestion of gill-like markings on its cheeks.

All the beaked whales are notoriously difficult to distinguish at sea, but it should be worthwhile, at least in New Zealand waters, looking out for one with an unusually attenuated jaw. It is reasonable to assume that the Tasman Whale, like its relatives, rises beak-first to breathe, has an inconspicuous blow, never shows its tail and is probably shy of shipping.

Stranding All the information we have on Tasman Whales comes from strandings. So far 8 individuals have been recorded, 6 of these from New Zealand. Identification is simple. The throat grooves and the lack of a notch in the tail

Natural History Very little is known. The stomach contents of one beached individual included bottom fish and a few squid. On one occasion 2 males were stranded together, implying some kind of social cohesion. The only female amongst the New Zealand animals carried a foetus in March.

Status The Tasman Whale must be described as rare.

Distribution The New Zealand finds were made at Ohawe near Wanganui on North Island, on New Brighton Beach and on Summer Spit near Christchurch on South Island and in Mason Bay on Stewart Island in the far south. Local distribution would therefore seem to cover all coasts, Pacific as well as those in the Tasman Sea.

For most of the first 40 years of the Tasman Whale's short recorded history it was believed to occur only around New Zealand, but in 1973 Roger Payne and James Mead found a recently beached specimen on the Valdez Peninsula in Patagonia and packed the 2-ton animal laboriously out piece by piece. Since then one other specimen has turned up in southern Chile and it seems at least likely that there is some connection between New Zealand and South America, perhaps along the current of the West Wind Drift. It is even possible that the distribution is circumpolar in the southern hemisphere and that the Tasman Whale will turn up one day in South Africa as well.

Sources McCANN (1964) records, MEAD & PAYNE (1975) in Argentina, OLIVER (1937) original description, WATKINS (1976) possible sighting.

NORTHERN FOURTOOTH WHALE

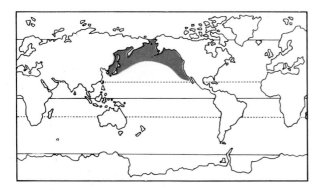

Classification On a pioneering expedition to Alaska in 1882, the Norwegian-American naturalist Leonhard Hess Stejneger found a 4-toothed skull at Stare Gavan on the eastern shore of Bering Island. Stejneger was at that time Curator of the mammal department of the United States National Museum and when he came to describe the skull as a new species, he honoured Spencer Baird, another Alaskan pioneer who had just been appointed Secretary of the Smithsonian Institute. The genus was clearly *Berardius*, created for a skull from New Zealand by Duvernoy in 1851.

Although there are obvious differences in size, shape and marking between this northern whale with 4 teeth and a similar whale in the southern hemisphere, they may be merely geographically-isolated populations of the same species. If this view prevails, the southern form, which was the first to be described, has priority and the northern subspecies will be known as *B. arnuxii bairdii*.

The whale several Japanese authors have been describing as

Hyperoodon rostratus is not a bottlenose whale at all, but clearly *Berardius bairdii*.

Local Names Baird's beaked whale, Japanese porpoise whale, *sovernyi Berardius* (Russian), and *tsuchi kujira* (Japanese). It was recognized by the Aleutians as *chiduk*, and by the Pribilof people as *cha-dakh*. This species is sometimes known as the giant bottlenose whale, but we have chosen to use the more descriptive name of Northern Fourtooth Whale.

Description Medium; length averages 10.3 m (34 ft) for males, with a maximum of 12 m (40 ft), and 11.2 m (37 ft) for females, with a maximum of 12.8 m (42 ft); calves are about 4.5 m (15 ft) at birth. Weight averages about 9,000 kg (10 tons) for both sexes, with a maximum of over 11,380 kg (12.5 tons).

Although the southern form is a medium-sized whale, this Northern Fourtooth Whale is appreciably larger and ought, as far as size is concerned, to be grouped with the great whales. It is certainly the largest living ziphid. The body is long and cylindrical, but the flippers and flukes are proportionately smaller than those of *B. arnuxii*. The head too is a little smaller, taking up about 12 per cent of total body length.

The beak is conspicuous, with a lower jaw extending almost 10 cm (4 inches) beyond the tip of the upper, and a large pair of protuding front teeth. The fin is triangular, 30 cm (12 inches) high with a completely straight trailing edge and is set well back on the body.

The colouring is largely a bluish dark grey, often with a brown tinge. The undersides are generally lighter and there are variable patches of pure white. These occur as blotches on the throat, between the flippers, and around the navel and

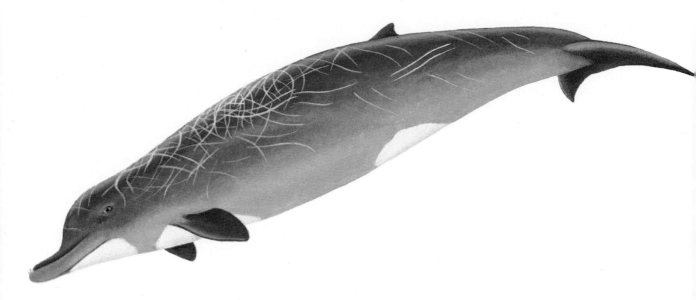

Breathing posture of Northern Fourtooth Whale, with whole beak exposed and teeth visible

anus. In extreme cases they may all run together to form an extended white belly, or be hardly visible at all. Females tend to be lighter in colour. There are many tooth scars on the beaks, particularly of males, and oval sucker scars on the belly, which seem to be caused by a parasitic crustacean (*Livoneca ravnaudi*).

Field Identification Northern Fourtooth Whales occur in small groups which characteristically rise to breathe with their heads stuck out of the water at an angle that makes the beaks distinctly visible. At first glance there is a strong resemblance to the Bottlenose Dolphin (*Tursiops truncatus 76*), but the greater size soon dispels doubts on this account. When the distance is not too great, we have even found it possible to pick out the large protruding teeth of a surfacing whale.

The blow is low and wide and a characteristic breathing sequence involves rising 3 or 4 times at 10–20-second intervals before disappearing in a dive about 20 minutes long. When harassed the whales have been known to submerge for over an hour.

In our experience, the Northern Fourtooth is fairly elusive and shy of ships, but can sometimes be found basking at the surface. On one occasion in Alaskan waters we found several whales floating together in this fashion with one individual hanging upside down so that its flukes projected 2 m (6 ft) into the air. When the group became aware of us, this whale reversed its position and stood bolt upright with 2 m of its other end staring directly at our ship as we approached.

The back shape and the position of the fin has led to confusion of this species with the Piked Whale (*Balaenoptera acutorostrata 7*), but the behaviour of the species is so distinct that closer observation should soon resolve confusion. A glimpse of the head or flipper (respectively pointed and white-banded in the Piked Whale) should be sufficient to tell them apart.

Stranding Northern Fourtooth Whales are found stranded, but less often than the southern form. This may however be due simply to the lack of records from the more remote parts of the Aleutians and Kamchatka. Identification of a beached animal should be easy by its teeth. The front pair are 9 cm (3.5 inches) long, flattened from side to side and roughly triangular. Behind these by 20 cm (8 inches) are a second, less compressed, pair no more than 5 cm (2 inches) high. Both sexes have teeth, but those of the females are slightly smaller.

On the throat are 2 shallow grooves, each 60 cm (2 ft) long, almost meeting beneath the chin to form a V-shape. There may also be 2 further small grooves parallel to, and outside, the main ones.

Typical external parasites include ship barnacles, acorn barnacles, whale lice and pendulous stalks of *Penella*.

The skull is symmetrical and similar in shape and form to that of *Berardius arnuxii*; there are 46–49 vertebrae, the first 3 of which are fused into a single unit. There is a well developed sternum of 5 separate bones.

Natural History Fourtooth Whales seem to be deep divers, feeding largely on squid (particularly *Gonatus fabricii*), but the northern species at least has fairly catholic tastes. It is known to take octopus, lobster, crab, rockfish, herring and even starfish and sea cucumber.

The usual social unit is a breeding group of 6–30, often led by one very large male. To judge by heavy scarring on the heads and backs of most males, there is a good deal of aggression and rivalry between males for the leadership of harems. Sexual maturity is reached when males are about 9.4 m (31 ft) and females 10 m (33 ft) in length. Mating takes place in mid-summer in the warm waters off Japan and California. Gestation generally seems to last about 10 months, but there are reports of pregnancies as much as 17 months long.

Status Northern Fourtooth Whales have long been a mainstay of the Japanese coastal whaling industry. Small numbers were taken with hand harpoons in the early days, but with improvements in technology the catch increased to a maximum of 382 in 1952. With declining numbers and greater emphasis on other species, the catch has now fallen again. Relatively large groups are still seen in the western Pacific, but the status of the species remains uncertain. It ought to be protected until more information is available.

Distribution This species has a peculiar back-to-front migration. It spends the summer months in warmer waters, appearing off the eastern coast of Honshu in May and around Hokkaido in June and July. In California it is most often seen from June to August, and off British Columbia in September. Then, as autumn approaches, the whales move north towards the Okhotsk and Bering seas, spending the winter months in cold waters around the Aleutian Islands. This pattern of movement must be connected with a seasonal abudance, probably of squid, in the north in winter.

The Northern Fourtooth Whale is entirely confined to the North Pacific and is usually found only in deeper water beyond the 1,000-m (3,300-ft) line.

Sources KASUYA (1977) growth, MITCHELL (1975) status, OMURA (1955) in Japan, STEJNEGER (1883) original description.

SOUTHERN FOURTOOTH WHALE

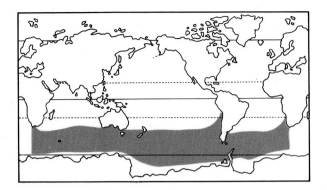

Classification In 1846 the French corvette *Rhin* under the command of Captain Bérard returned from an extended Pacific voyage. On board were the ship's surgeon M. Arnoux and a strange skull he had found on a beach near Akaroa in New Zealand. The specimen was presented to the Musée Nationale d'Histoire Naturelle in Paris, where it eventually came to the attention of Georges-Louis Duvernoy, an anatom-ist who worked there with Cuvier. Duvernoy was an authority on monkeys and crocodiles, but he realized that this skull, with just 4 teeth on its lower jaw, was odd and bore no relation to any other living whale. He was not sure that it even came from a living whale; in the paper published in 1851 he hedged his bets by describing it as *vivant ou fossile*. Duvernoy nevertheless had no hesitation in ascribing it to a new genus and species, *Berardius arnuxii* named after the ship's captain and surgeon. Duvernoy by some mischance omitted an 'o' from Arnoux but under the Rules the original spelling has to be retained.

The species is known from a total of less than 50 specimens; 6 specimens with just 2 teeth were once thought to be juveniles but have now been identified as a different species, the Skew Beaked Whale (*Mesoplodon hectori 18*).

Local Names In the literature this whale is variously described as Arnoux's beaked whale, New Zealand beaked whale, smaller ziphid whale, and southern porpoise whale. We see little to commend any of these and suggest that this species be known as the Southern Fourtooth Whale.

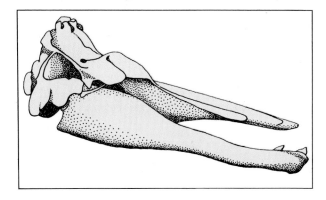

Description Medium; length averages about 9 m (30 ft), with a maximum of 10 m (33 ft); calves seem to be about 3.5 m (11–12 ft) at birth. Weight averages about 6,400 kg (7 tons), with a recorded maximum of 7,750 kg (8.5 tons).

The Southern Fourtooth Whale is similar to the northern form (*Berardius bairdii 12*), but not as long, although the head, flippers and flukes are proportionately larger. The head is 15 per cent of the total body length and has a well-marked, buffer-like melon and a pronounced beak.

The lower jaw protrudes beyond the upper, revealing the foremost pair of teeth and giving the whale a distinct resemblance to an old man relaxing without his upper dentures. There are 2 grooves on the throat which almost intersect beneath the chin to form a V-shape.

The flippers are broad and rounded; the fin is roughly triangular; set very far back; and the flukes are large, with the faintest suggestion of a notch.

The colour is a thunder blue grey with sometimes a slight brownish tint. The flukes, flippers and back are all darker. Older males seem to bleach a little, turning whitish on the back between the head and the fin. Both males and females bear a large number of pale scars which are clearly made by the 2 leading teeth of other Southern Fourtooth Whales. These wounds seem to be the result of sidelong slashes because one of the parallel tracks is always far deeper than the other. There are also a number of oval scars, usually around the anus, which are produced either by lamprey suckers or by a parasitic crustacean.

Field Identification Little is known of the habits of this whale. We have never seen a live one, but imagine that its behaviour must be rather like that of its northern relative.

The Southern Fourtooth Whale probably rises to breathe at an angle so that the beak breaks water first, and produces a diffuse low blow. Like the larger whales, it is said to cruise for a while at the surface, taking several short breaths in a series before diving. The dive is almost certainly deep and vertical and we would expect the broad tail flukes to be raised well into the air each time the animal sounds. It is likely to be shy of shipping.

Stranding At the moment the Southern Fourtooth is known largely from strandings, mostly in New Zealand but also from Australia, South Africa, South Georgia, the Falklands and Argentina.

Identification presents no problem. The spindle-shaped body, throat grooves and un-notched tail betray it as a ziphid whale. The teeth are unique to this genus; there are just 4, all on the lower jaw. The front pair are laterally compressed and large, about 7.5 cm (3 inches) in height. Behind them is a gap of 10–20 cm (4–8 inches) and then the second pair of smaller, roughly triangular, teeth. Neither pair erupts until the whales are a few years old, and the teeth do not reach their full size until sexual maturity, when they become identical in both sexes. In older individuals the teeth are greatly abraded, sometimes flattened enough to be flush with the gum.

There are 47 or 48 vertebrae, the first 3 of which are fused.

Natural History Squid beaks have been found in the stomachs of stranded animals, but the abrasion of the teeth suggests that they must also feed on molluscs with rough external shells.

Several of the females so far examined have been pregnant and, from them, it would appear that gestation lasts for about 10 months, with calving taking place in spring or early summer (September–December).

Nothing is known about Southern Fourtooth Whales' social behaviour, but they probably do not form large groups.

Status This species is clearly not common. A few whales have been taken by Antarctic whaling expeditions.

Distribution Most of the beached individuals have been found in New Zealand; the type specimen came from Banks Island and others have been stranded near Porirua on the west coast of North Island; at Titai Bay in the Cook Strait, in Lyall Bay and Karamea Bight on South Island and on Chatham Island in the east.

Others have been found on the Falklands, in Arroyo del Pescado near Buenos Aires in Argentina, in South Africa, in the Antarctic and on the coast of Chile. Distribution would seem to be circumpolar in the southern hemisphere, extending from a latitude of about 33° south to the edge of the icepack. On one occasion in Graham Land in the Antarctic, a live Southern Fourtooth Whale was found trapped in an ice pool along with 120 Piked Whales (*Balaenoptera acutorostrata 7*) and 60 Great Killer Whales (*Orcinus orca 51*).

Sources DUVERNOY (1851) original description, McCANN (1975) review, RICE & SCHEFFER (1968) taxonomy, TAYLOR (1957) in Antarctica.

GOOSEBEAK WHALE (CUVIER'S)

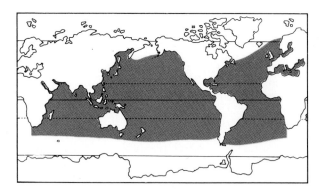

Classification In 1804 Raymond Gorsse excavated a fossil skull near the mouth of the River Galegeon. He sent it to the Musée Nationale d'Histoire Naturelle in Paris. Cuvier published details of the skull in his monumental *Recherches sur les Ossements Fossiles* in 1823, describing it as an extinct whale, for which he created the genus *Ziphius*, from the Greek *xiphos*, a sword, and species *cavirostris* from the Latin *cavus*, hollow, and *rostrum*, a beak.

In 1826 a whale was found stranded near Genoa in Italy and named *Delphinus desmaresti*; in 1850 one from Corsica became *Hyperoodon doumetii*; *Petrorhynchus capensis* turned up in South Africa in 1865; *Delphinorhynchus australis* near Buenos Aires in the same year; and *Epiodon chathamensis* off New Zealand in 1872. In that year Sir William Turner in Edinburgh described a whale from the Shetland Islands and realized that he was dealing with a live specimen of Cuvier's fossil. He also realized that many of the new beaked whales being so enthusiastically described from beaches all over the world were identical and ought all to be attributed to *Ziphius cavirostris*. Over the next decade he published three further papers in an attempt to stem the taxonomic tide. Turner succeeded at last in getting the genus

Ziphius universally accepted, but outrageous new species such as *savii*, *novaezealandiae* and *grebnitzkii* kept on pouring in right into the early twentieth century.

Today all synonyms have been subsumed under Cuvier's *Ziphius cavirostris* of worldwide distribution.

Local Names Cuvier's whale, *dolfijn van Cuvier* (Dutch), *kuiverov kliuvoryl* (Russian), *ziphius de Cuvier* (French), *ballena de Cuvier* (Spanish), *akago kujira* (Japanese) and *chumchugagakh* (Aleutian). We use the descriptive name Goosebeak Whale, which draws attention to the animal's ziphid affinities without actually calling it a beaked whale, which name we reserve for the genus *Mesoplodon*.

Description Medium; length averages 6.4 m (21 ft), with a maximum (for females) of 7 m (23 ft); a record of 8.5 (28 ft) seems exaggerated or possibly confused with the Bottlenose Whale (*Hyperoodon ampullatus 15*); calves are about 2.1 m (7 ft) at birth. Weight averages 3,000 kg (3.5 tons), with a maximum of 4,500 kg (5 tons).

A whale with the typical spindle-shaped body of all ziphids, the Goosebeak is perhaps a little stouter than most, but not as heavily built as the fourtooth whales of *Berardius*. The head is relatively small at 10 per cent of body length and not only ends in a distinct neck, but has a most unusual and characteristic scooped-out hollow just behind the blowhole. There is a stubby beak which, coupled with the short cleft of the mouth, gives it a gooselike profile. In adult males the points of 2 large teeth on the tip of the lower jaw protrude.

The flippers are small and rounded and, in Goosebeak Whales at least in the Pacific, fold back into marked depressions or 'flipper pockets' on the flank. The fin is relatively tall (up to 40 cm or 16 inches) and sweeps back in a sharklike curve. The actual tail is surprisingly small. Unlike most other ziphids, Goosebeak Whales have a tiny (1-cm or half-inch) notch in the centre of the broad tail flukes.

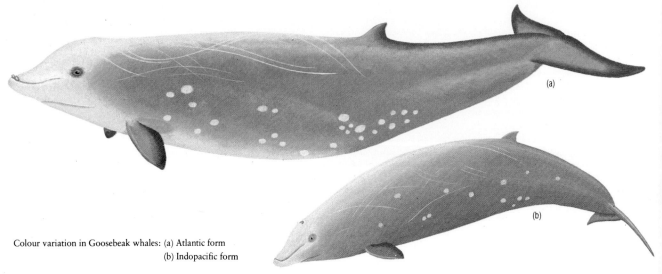

Colour variation in Goosebeak whales: (a) Atlantic form
(b) Indopacific form

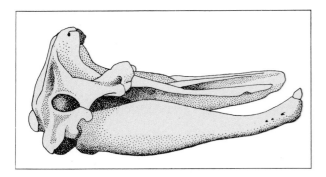

The colouring is peculiar and has doubtless contributed to the rash of 'new' discoveries. Almost every Goosebeak Whale looks a little different from the others. In the Indopacific, sienna is a common basic colour, grading all the way from mustard brown to darkest umber. In most individuals the backs are darker than the bellies, but in many the pattern becomes totally reversed so that an individual with a pale maize back might have a black stomach. Both variations also commonly occur with a head that is almost white. This is usual for older males, but it can occur in either sex at any age.

In the Atlantic various shades of grey or smoke blue seem to be more common, though these too may be combined with the pale pattern on the head. The eye is usually included in this light area and is often marked by a black patch or ring. Juveniles tend to be lighter than their parents.

All individuals have some scar marks. Oval white patches are most common around the belly and are caused, it seems, by lampreys and by the females of the parasitic crustacean *Livoneca ravnaudi*; but the very characteristic double-track scars produced by the teeth of other Goosebeaks are confined largely to the backs of adult males.

Field Identification The Goosebeak is not uncommon in deep water. All our sightings have been of groups of whales, travelling at a leisurely pace of 5–6 kph (3 knots). Every breathing sequence begins with a view of the rounded forehead (the beak is never seen), followed by an almost immediate blow, which is unhurried and usually forms a low and inconspicuous fan of spray. After the spout clears, the back rolls gently over, providing a good view of the curved fin before the whale sinks gently out of sight. The normal rhythm seems to involve a series of blows at intervals of about 20 seconds, between which the whale can be seen cruising just below the surface, then a deeper dive in which the tail is raised as the whale plunges almost vertically down.

On rare occasions Goosebeak Whales may breach, leaping clear of the water and falling clumsily back again. They seem on the whole to be rather shy of ships and we have found them difficult to approach. The possibility of confusion with almost every other species of ziphid exists, but if the beak cannot be seen and the animals in question are clearly operating as a large and cohesive social group in warm water, then the chances are that you are seeing Goosebeak Whales.

Stranding Almost all our knowledge of Goosebeaks comes from strandings, which occur regularly on all tropical and temperate shores. When the whales involved are adult males, identification is simple. They have 2 large blunt teeth on the tip of the lower jaw. These are up to 8 cm (3 inches) long, oval in cross section and forward-leaning. In females the teeth never erupt, but remain embedded in the rough and knobbly gums. Many individuals also have 15–40 tiny vestigial teeth, the size and shape of old-fashioned gramophone needles, deep in the gums of both upper and lower jaws.

There are 2 deeply incised throat grooves which are more widely separated on the chin than those of the fourtooth whales of *Berardius*.

The skull is broad in relation to its length and marked on its underside with Cuvier's 'sword'. The lower jaw is heavy. There are 47 vertebrae, of which the first 3 or 4 are fused.

Natural History Goosebeaks seem to live mainly on squid and deep-water fish caught during their long dives, lasting anything up to 30 minutes, but they also eat crabs and starfish.

Solitary males with white heads are sometimes seen, but the normal social unit seems to be an extended family pod of around 15 individuals. Both sexes mature when roughly 5 m (17 ft) long and, as befits a tropical species, show no marked breeding season. Calves seem to be born all year round after an unknown gestation period.

Status Goosebeak Whales are found beached more often than any other ziphid. Despite their social habit, mass strandings are unknown. The whales struggle ashore singly, on beaches all over the tropical and temperate world, more often in some places than others. Most of the strandings in New Zealand have taken place on the east coast of Otago; but, for some reason still unknown, Genoa on the Ligurian coast of Italy is popular. However, as Francis Fraser points out: 'these may not necessarily provide evidence of a natural concentration... but may merely be the peripheral component of a great, dispersed, oceanwide community.' About 20 whales, most of them males, are taken each year by the Japanese coastal stations, and an occasional Goosebeak is known to have been caught from St Vincent in the Caribbean. These operations present little or no threat to their survival.

Distribution Strandings are known from Florida, Ireland, Britain, Sweden, Spain, the Mediterranean, Brazil, Argentina, South Africa, Australia, New Zealand, Chile, Siberia, Japan, the Midway Islands, Hawaii, Alaska, Canada, California and Mexico.

Distribution is clearly worldwide in deeper waters, usually those outside the 1,000-m (3,300-ft) contour. There is some evidence of a movement into higher latitudes in the summer months, but Goosebeak Whales seem to be clearly confined by the 10°C isotherm, seldom venturing into colder water.

Sources CUVIER (1823) original description, ERDMAN (1962) in Puerto Rico, FRASER (1974) status, GALBRAITH (1963) on Midway, MITCHELL (1968) in North Pacific, NORRIS & PRESCOTT (1961) description, OMURA (1972) taxonomy, TURNER (1827) taxonomy.

NORTHERN BOTTLENOSE WHALE

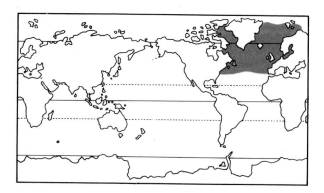

Classification In 1717 an unusual whale was stranded above the bridge on the River Blackwater near Maldon in Essex, England. It was described by a local historian called Dale as a 'bottle-head' or 'flounders-head' whale and it figures in a work on British Zoology in 1766 as 'The Beaked Whale of Essex'. The first full scientific description of it came a few years later from Johann Reinhold Forster, a German-British clergyman and explorer who later took part in Captain Cook's second world voyage. In 1770 he added a footnote to his translation of Peter Kalm's account of a journey into North America, which tells of seeing 'cetaceous fish of the dolphin kind ... called by the sailors bottle-nose ... everywhere in the ocean from the Channel to the very neighbour-

hood of America'. Forster decided that Kalm could not have meant the Bottlenose Dolphin (*Tursiops truncatus 76*), but must be referring to something like the Essex whale. He revived the earlier description of it, included a drawing, and suggested that 'Perhaps it would not be improper to call it *Balaena ampullata* Forster', from the Latin *ampulla*, a flask.

The fact that Forster was mistaken about Kalm's sighting, which certainly *was* of Bottlenose Dolphins, and had himself never seen a specimen of the Bottlenose Whale, does not invalidate his name.

In 1804 Lacépède, completing Buffon's natural history, included in it a description of a skull in the Museum at Caen taken from a whale stranded near Honfleur at the mouth of the Seine. He called it *Hyperoodon butskopf*, taking the species name from the German vernacular for 'steep head', and the genus from the old Greek *hyperoe*, above plus *odous*, gen. *odontos*, a tooth. The generic name is somewhat misleading, because this whale has its large teeth on the lower jaw, but Lacépède was dealing with one of the many toothless skulls and was referring in his description to the tiny vestigial teeth sometimes located in the upper jaw.

The connection with the Essex whale was made, and the full binomial finally put together in 1902 as *Hyperoodon ampullatus*. Some taxonomic confusion has occurred as a result of an early Danish description of a whale which was thought to be different and has come to be known as *Hyperoodon rostratus* (MULLER 1776). All specimens from

the North Atlantic have now been shown to be identical to *H. ampullatus* and those in the North Pacific are now seen to be misidentifications of the Northern Fourtooth Whale (*Berardius bairdii 12*). There are as yet no confirmed reports of this species anywhere in the Pacific.

Local Names From the bulbous, flask-like container of oil on the head of older males this whale has been called bottlehead, *hocico de botella* (Spanish), *buytlkonos* (Russian), *grand souffleur à bec d'oie* (French), *bottlenosen* and *andehval* (Norwegian), *andhvaler* (Icelandic), *dögling* and *naebhval* (Danish), *näbhval* and *nabbad gomtand* (Swedish), *butskop* (Dutch) and *Butskopf* (German). The Greenland Ekimos call in *anarnac*.

We choose to follow tradition and call this species the Northern Bottlenose Whale.

Description Medium; length averages 9.1 m (30 ft) for males, with a maximum of 10 m (33 ft), (there is one doubtful record of an 11.5-m or 38-ft male), and 7.3 m (24 ft) for females, with a maximum of 8.5 m (28 ft); calves are about 3 m (10 ft) at birth. Weight averages about 3,600 kg (4 tons) for males, and about 3,000 kg (3.5 tons) for females, with a possible maximum of 5,400 kg for one very large male; (reports of 9,000-kg or 10-ton animals seem to be exaggerated).

The Northern Bottlenose Whale has a heavy-set, rounded body and a conspicuous head. The forehead or melon is bulbous in all adult animals and is most pronounced in older males. In all individuals it rises steeply from a sharply-defined beak reminiscent of, though much larger than, that of the Bottlenose Dolphin (*Tursiops truncatus 76*). The jaws are of equal length.

The maxillary bones which support the melon have enormous crests and fall away rapidly to make room for the nasal passage which leaves the blowhole lying in a visible depression on the top of the head. There is a noticeable neck line. The eyes, which lie behind the corner of the mouth, look small and bright.

The fin is sickle-shaped, lies two-thirds of the way back and is seldom more than 30 cm (12 inches) high. There is no notch in the tail flukes.

Colour varies a great deal. The back is normally a dark greenish sienna, grading to smoke grey on the belly, but there is a marked change with age. Calves are a uniform umber brown and lighten progressively with age, beginning with marbling and spotting on the flanks and ending (in some older individuals) altogether cream coloured, with distinctive white heads. The flippers, flukes and fin all remain dark and there is often a pale bracket or gill mark across the back of the neck.

Field Identification Northern Bottlenose Whales are usually easy to identify. They are fascinated by ships and shipping, or by anything that produces an unusual sound, which makes them all too easy to kill. They are attracted to any loud noise and will readily approach a ship stopped in deep water with its generators running. On occasion we have been able to bring them alongside, diving backwards and forwards beneath our vessel, by pounding on the steel hull with a hammer.

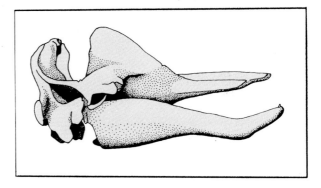

Above: dive sequence.
Below: skull

When excited in this way, they often lobtail, raising their flukes high and slapping them explosively down on the surface. A group doing this produces a sound like a fusillade of rifle shots. Very rarely an individual, usually young, will leap completely clear of the water.

The whales rise quite steeply to blow, often showing the blunt forehead and the beak. The blow is a strong, globular cloud of spray, rising 1–2 m (3–6 ft) and dense enough to be seen from a distance. Bottlenose Whales cruise on the surface between blows, riding high in the water at about 4–5 kph (2–3 knots) with the head, back and fin exposed at the same time. The head is distinctive and there is no possibility of confusion with the Piked Whale (*Balaenoptera acutorostrata 7*), which has a similar fin. In the case of older males, the white on the head is clearly visible.

Usually the whales spend several minutes at the surface and then lift the tail flukes into the air, diving almost vertically for anything up to 30 minutes. The Northern Bottlenose Whale is said to be the longest diver of all cetaceans, submerging for as much as 2 hours at a time, but these records were set under stress at the end of a whaler's line and cannot, even if true, be regarded as normal behaviour.

The shape of the head and even the pattern of the blow might lead to confusion with Great Sperm Whales (*Physeter macrocephalus 36*), but the distinctive fin of the Bottlenose is usually enough to set the species apart. When watching from a distance, it is worth looking for the lift of the tail preceding diving; this is much more emphatic in the Great Sperm Whale, which also has a distinct notch in the centre of the flukes.

Stranding Northern Bottlenose Whales frequently are stranded, sometimes in groups. The fin, the lack of a notch in the tail, and the presence of 2 throat grooves are sufficient to identify the whale as a ziphid. The head, and the overall size (if it is an adult) should identify an anonymous beaked whale as a Bottlenose; but it is not always that easy because the most distinctive feature, the teeth, are unfortunately often hard to find or else missing altogether.

Typically, an adult male Northern Bottlenose Whale has just 2 teeth on the tip of the lower jaw. These are 4–5 cm (1.5–2 inches) long, shorter than those of the Goosebeak Whale (*Ziphius cavirostris 14*) or the Northern Fourtooth Whale (*Berardius bairdii 12*), and bulbous at the base. Unlike those of any other ziphid, the teeth have enamel caps. Frequently these teeth, even in males, are so deeply embedded in the gum that they cannot be seen. With females, this is always the case. Sometimes the teeth of the oldest males fall out altogether, leaving only a telltale socket in the gum. Rarely, the whole position becomes confused by the presence of an additional pair of teeth behind the first ones. In these cases, the whales can be distinguished from fourtooth species by the fact that the 2 pairs of teeth are close together, rather than separated by a gap of several centimetres, as they are in *Berardius*. Like the Goosebeak, the Bottlenose Whale occasionally has up to 40 rudimentary vestigial teeth set deeply in the gums of both jaws. There are 43–46 vertebrae, 3 of which are fused.

Natural History Northern Bottlenose Whales live largely on squid, particularly *Gonatus fabricii*. They may also take herrings (*Clupea harengus*) and some, most often the males, feed at least partly on starfish.

There are a number of solitary males, but Bottlenose Whales are normally gregarious and intensely social, most often found in groups of 4–10. Larger congregations are rare. The usual social unit seems to be composed of a large male and a group of females with young. There are many records of care-giving behaviour, in which members of a group remain with, or come to the aid of, a wounded whale. The whalers take advantage of this behaviour, keeping a wounded animal alive on a line while they pick off the rest of the group one by one.

Sexual maturity is reached between 9 and 12 years of age, when males are 7.3 m (24 ft) and females 6.7 m (22 ft) in length. Mating takes place during spring and early summer; gestation takes approximately 12 months with calves born the following April or May. Nothing else is known of reproductive behaviour, but it has been suggested that adult males may rush at each other in dominance disputes, crashing their melons together.

Northern Bottlenose Whales produce a wide variety of sounds. Intermittent pulsed sounds, consisting of trains of up to 50 clicks in several frequencies, have been recorded; as have whistles 3–16 kHz and a number of chirping calls.

The enlarged maxillary crests, which give the melon its squarish shape, could act as acoustic baffles. If they do, then the oldest males with the most massive crests have the best developed sonar abilities. A similar configuration exists in the Indus River Dolphin (*Platanista minor 30*) which swims on its side and uses side-scanning sonar to help find food on the bottom. It is possible that at least the males of the Bottlenose Whale feed in the same way, and it may be reasonable to assume that it is the dominant male, with his special sensitivity, who is responsible for finding food for the entire harem.

Status The present population is unknown, but Edward Mitchell of the Arctic Biological Station in Canada considers that this species is 'the most critically depleted of all the small cetaceans currently or formerly exploited'. Commercial whaling of the Northern Bottlenose began in 1877, and every year since then a number has been taken, usually by the Norwegians. At the turn of the century as many as 3,300 were taken in a single season, but the catch is now in the tens. At least part of the reason for this decline has to be the increasing scarcity of the Northern Bottlenose Whale.

Distribution Northern Bottlenose Whales are restricted to the cooler Arctic and temperate waters of the North Atlantic. They most commonly occur in deep offshore waters; but strandings are known from Canada, Greenland, Iceland, Ireland, Scotland, England, Holland, Denmark, France and Norway. There is a seasonal movement away from the Arctic ice in autumn, as far south as Rhode Island in the west, and to the Azores and the coast of Portugal in the east. A possible winter sighting off the Cape Verde Islands and an occurrence in the Mediterranean have yet to be confirmed.

Sources ANON (1978) review, BENJAMINSEN (1972) biology, BENJAMINSEN & CHRISTENSEN (1979) natural history, CHRISTENSEN (1976) status, FORSTER (1770) original description, FRASER (1974) taxonomy, KALM (1770) voyage, LACÉPÈDE (1804) taxonomy, MITCHELL (1975) status, MITCHELL & KOZICKI (1975) stranding, WINN et al (1970) sounds.

SOUTHERN BOTTLENOSE WHALE

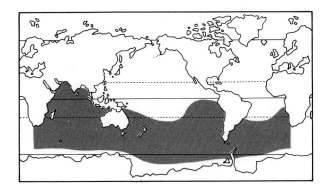

Classification Sir William Flower was perhaps the last of the old school of comparative anatomists, generalists such as Cuvier and Buffon who could afford to think in terms of entire natural histories. Flower was Conservator of the Museum of the Royal College of Surgeons and Director of the British Museum (Natural History), and during his tenure of both positions introduced sweeping changes in policy and display.

While he was involved in one of his reorganizations of the collections in the British Museum, he came across part of a water-worn and mutilated whale skull found on Lewis Island in the Dampier Archipelago of Western Australia. He tidied it up most effectively by creating a new species to house it – *Hyperoodon planifrons* from the Latin *planus*, flat, and *frons*, front. In the century since then, nothing has changed.

Local Names With only a dozen known specimens, there has been little need for common names. Those in the literature include: Flower's bottlenose whale, flatfront bottlenose, flathead bottlenose, and Antarctic bottlenose. We call this species the Southern Bottlenose Whale.

Description Medium; length averages 7.6 m (25 ft) for males, with a maximum of 9 m (30 ft), and 6.7 m (22 ft) for females, with a maximum of 7.3 m (24 ft); calves are about 2.75 m (9 ft) at birth. Weight averages about 3,600 kg (3 tons) with a possible maximum of 4,000 kg (4.5 tons).

H. planifrons lives up to its name. It is flat fronted; the melon on the head has developed, at least in the older males, to such an extent that the forehead rises vertically from the beak and sweeps back in a broad curve to the flat top of the head; making this southern whale even more bottle-nosed than its northern relative.

The body shape is similar, somewhat cylindrical, with the greatest girth just behind the flippers, then tapering off to the tail. Neither a glimpse at sea nor a diagrammatic lateral view can give a true impression of how sleek and tubular these whales really are. Behind the bulbous head, the body seems to be absurdly long, finally broadening into a surprisingly large tail fluke. The flippers too are relatively large. The fin, which is higher than that of the northern species (up to 40 cm or 15 inches), less robust and with a tendency to curl a little at the tip, is placed rather nearer to the tail.

The colouring seems to be a metallic deep grey, lightening to bluish on the flanks. The forehead, back, flippers and flukes

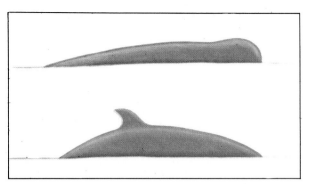

Dive sequence

are dark, but the throat and belly are rather pale. Sightings of live animals are rare, but it is likely that in life the colours are warmer and browner, fading to blues and greys only after death. There are sometimes tooth scars on the backs of adult males.

Field Identification We cannot speak from first-hand experience. The Southern Bottlenose Whale does not seem to share the curiosity of its northern relative; there are no confirmed reports of it approaching ships in the same fearless way.

Like the northern form, it probably rises steeply to breathe, showing the melon and the beak above the surface. The blow is similar, low and strong and globular instead of finely sprayed. The blowhole, back and fin all become visible simultaneously, and often remain so, as the whale surges along at the surface between dives.

The Southern Bottlenose breathes every 10–20 seconds for several minutes and then lifts its flukes and dives, disappearing for 5–15 minutes. It seems to be a deep diver and can probably, like the Northern Bottlenose, submerge for much longer periods.

It appears that the Southern Bottlenose Whale may form groups of 30–40. In these circumstances, they could be confused with the pilot whales (*Globicephala melaena 49* and *Globicephala macrorhynchus 50*). Both have prominently rounded heads which appear above the surface, but the fin of the pilot whales is placed in the centre of the back and is very much more broadly based. The Southern Bottlenose Whales are likely also to appear less glossy black and more mottled blue grey or brown in colour.

Stranding Almost everything we know about the Southern

Bottlenose Whale has been learned from a dozen strandings. Identification of adult males is relatively simple, but toothless females and young present problems. When teeth are present, they are placed right on the tip of the lower jaw and there is normally only 1 pair, larger than those of the Northern Bottlenose, conical and 5 cm (2 inches) long. Those of the females are deeply embedded in the gums.

There are 47 vertebrae, with all the first 7 bones in the neck fused into a single unit. The first 7 of 9 pairs of ribs are double headed.

Natural History As far as we can tell from the few stomachs that have been examined, Southern Bottlenose Whales feed entirely on squid and cuttlefish. They may well be more social than the northern form and, being more tropical, possibly less tied to a fixed breeding season. Nothing is known of their behaviour.

Status There are a few reports of Southern Bottlenoses, probably large solitary males, being seen in the Antarctic by whaling fleets, and at least one record of a kill there. Apart from these, a handful of strandings and a few unconfirmed sightings off the west coast of South America, we know nothing of this whale's status. Pending further study, it must be classified as rare.

Distribution The Northern Bottlenose Whale is confined to cold waters, but the scattered strandings of the southern species indicate that, in the Indian Ocean at least, it even crosses the equator.

Strandings are known from Winchester on South Island and from East Cape Beach on North Island in New Zealand, from Port Victoria on the Cape York Peninsula and the more westerly Dampier Archipelago in Australia, on the coast of Chile, several points in the La Plata Estuary in Argentina, on the Falkland and South Orkney islands, from the west coast of South Africa, and, most surprisingly, in the harbour of Colombo in Sri Lanka. This apparently tropical distribution may be misleading in that the whales continue to confine themselves to cool water, which is known to well up strongly in several places in the northern Indian Ocean.

We predict a similar northern spread in the eastern Pacific, perhaps even as far as the Galapagos Islands on the equator.

Sources DERANIYAGALA (1960) in Sri Lanka, FLOWER (1882) original description, FRASER (1945) anatomy, RICE & SCHEFFER (1968) distribution, TOMILIN & LATYSHEV (1967) in Antarctica.

INDOPACIFIC BEAKED WHALE

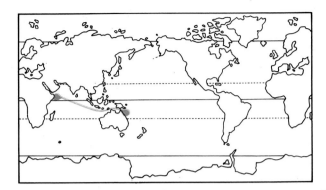

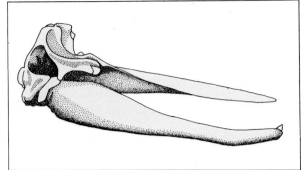

Classification The only evidence of this whale is 2 skulls. The first was found, considerably eroded, on a beach at Mackay in north-eastern Australia in 1822. It was presented to the Queensland Museum by E. W. Rawson and remains there. In 1926 H. A. Longman published a brief account of it in a general paper about cetaceans known from the Queensland coast. He thought it might be related to the Wonderful Beaked Whale (*Mesoplodon mirus 19*), but as that species occurs in the North Atlantic, decided instead to call it *Mesoplodon pacificus*.

Despite the presence of a pair of long teeth on the tip of the male lower jaw and the lack of the usual high maxillary crests, the large size of the skull and the existence of an extra pair of vestigial teeth prompted Charles McCann in New Zealand to suggest that it was nothing more than a female Southern Bottlenose Whale (*Hyperoodon planifrons 16*). These doubts have now been resolved by the discovery in 1955 of a second skull which is unquestionably female.

The second specimen was found in Somalia on the north-east horn of Africa, on the floor of a fertilizer factory near Mogadiscio, by a visiting Italian, Dr Ugo Funaioli. He traced it to a beach near Danane and took it back to the University Museum in Florence. In 1968 Maria Loisa Azzaroli examined it there and recognized the skull as confirmation of the existence of the rarest living beaked whale.

Joseph Curtis Moore, the greatest living authority on beaked whales, was impressed by the length of the beak and the shallowness of the tooth sockets and decided in 1968 that it warranted not only its own species, but also a separate genus. In recognition of its existence in two oceans he decided to call it *Indopacetus pacificus*.

Time, and the discovery of an Indopacific Beaked Whale with flesh on its bones, may restore this species to the genus *Mesoplodon,* but for the moment *Indopacetus* (MOORE 1968) stands as an appropriate monument to the man who has brought more order to the beaked whales than exists in almost any other group of cetaceans.

Local Names There are obviously no local names for this species. It has been variously described in the literature as Longman's beaked whale, Pacific beaked whale and Indopacific beaked whale. We prefer to reserve the use of the term 'beaked whale' for the genus *Mesoplodon*, but make an exception in this moot case and follow Moore in calling it the Indopacific Beaked Whale.

Description Nobody has ever knowingly seen an Indopacific Beaked Whale in its entirety, either living or dead.

The size of the skull suggests that it may be a large animal, probably around 7 m (23 ft) in length, which makes it inter-mediate between the beaked whales and the larger ziphids.

Field Identification Until more information is available, it is impossible to identify this whale, but it will be worth keeping watch in the Indopacific for any large beaked whale that does not seem to fit into a recognized species. Captain Morzer Bruyns, an inveterate whale spotter, believes that he saw a group of rust-brown whales with slender beaks in the Gulf of Aden; and more recently Ken Balcomb of Washington State took a photograph of 25 unusually large beaked whales on the equator at 165° west, near Christmas Island. These may both have been sightings of this species.

Stranding The distinguishing characteristics of the skulls are the 2 teeth on the tip of the lower jaw and a peculiar hoodlike formation of the lachrymal (cheek) bones.

Status and Distribution The Indopacific Beaked Whale is rare and its distribution is unknown, probably tropical.

Sources AZZAROLI (1968) second skull, LONGMAN (1926) original description, McCANN (1964) taxonomy, MOORE (1968) taxonomy.

Genus Mesoplodon

This is a large and fascinating genus of medium-sized whales, known primarily from strandings. They may not in fact be rare, but are so widely distributed in deep water, so inconspicuous and so shy of shipping, that their appearance and behaviour in the wild are almost totally unknown.

On the beach all beaked whales will be found to have 2 short deep grooves forming a V-shape on the throat, a low sharklike fin set well back on the spindle-shaped body, short rounded flippers which are often supplied with a corresponding depression or 'flipper pocket' in the body wall and fairly broad tail flukes which are normally un-notched, but may in certain species have an inconspicuous nick in the centre.

Functional teeth are found only in adult males. Those of females seldom emerge from the gum and can usually be seen only on a clean skull. A single pair of large teeth is placed on the lower jaw and their shape and position differ from species to species. There may rarely be additional vestigial teeth buried in the gums.

The genus *Mesoplodon*, derived from the Greek *mesos*, middle, *ploe*, floating, and *odous*, gen. *odontos*, tooth (literally 'a tooth floating somewhere in the middle of the jaw') was published by the French palaentologist Paul Gervais in 1850.

In 1830 Johann Wagler proposed the genus *Nodus* for a beaked whale (probably the North Sea Beaked Whale 27) collected at Le Havre, and in 1849 Daniel Eschricht suggested *Micropteron* for another specimen of the same species from the coast of Denmark. Both of these names have priority over *Mesoplodon*, but they have been overlooked for so long that they have become *nomina oblita* (forgotten names).

A further generic name *Dioplodon* was proposed by Gervais himself (for what he believed to be the Dense Beaked Whale 26) in the same paper as that in which he first published *Mesoplodon* (in a description of the Gulf Stream Beaked Whale 20). Under the Code, the first reviser, that person who first points out that two names refer to the same taxonomic unit, has the right to choose the one they feel to be most appropriate. *Mesoplodon* was chosen in this way.

There are 11 recognized species. This number bears testimony to the pioneer work of the American zoologist Joseph Curtis Moore, who has spent a large part of his life at the Chicago Field Museum of Natural History sorting out the taxonomic confusion in this genus. The species are arranged here, following his criteria, in sequence from the most primitive to the most evolved, assuming always that there has been a progressive movement of the teeth away from the tip of the jaw, and that they show a tendency to become larger and to lean more markedly backwards in more recent species.

All species of *Mesoplodon* are extremely difficult to distinguish at sea. The general shape, size, position of the fin and behaviour are all, as far as we know, much the same.

These keys form a superficial attempt to provide some basis for identification of live beaked whales as well as those found stranded on the shore. They might help to short-circuit a search, but colour and marking are variable, so care should be taken to use the Wet Key in particular with discretion.

Wet Key (overleaf) Geographical characteristics are included here, but our knowledge of the distribution of this genus comes almost entirely from a few strandings and these may not accurately reflect the true ranges on any of these species.

Note Skew Beaked Whale (*M. hectori 18*) and Splaytooth Beaked Whale (*M. bowdoini 25*) are known from too few specimens to be certain of any external characteristics at all and are therefore excluded from this key.

Dry Key (overleaf) Even with a beached specimen available for examination at leisure, female and juvenile beaked whales are notoriously difficult to tell apart. Full classification of these will probably have to wait for a complete anatomical analysis; but if the animal has teeth, as most adult males do, then this key can lead to a positive identification in any part of the world. All characteristics used in the key relate to the teeth.

Map Key Zoogeography of the genus:

1. North Atlantic: North Sea Beaked Whale (*M. bidens 27*), Gulf Stream Beaked Whale (*M. europaeus 20*), Wonderful Beaked Whale (*M. mirus 19*).

2. North Pacific Bering Sea Beaked Whale (*M. stejnegeri 24*), Arch Beaked Whale (*M. carlhubbsi 21*), Japanese Beaked Whale (*M. ginkgodens 22*).

3. Pantropical: Dense Beaked Whale (*M. densirostris 26*), Straptooth Beaked Whale (*M. layardii 28*).

4. Circumpolar in South: Scamperdown Beaked Whale (*M. grayi 23*), Splaytooth Beaked Whale (*M. bowdoini 25*), Skew Beaked Whale (*M. hectori 18*).

Note *M. mirus* (*19*) may also occur in the southern hemisphere. *M. ginkgodens* (*22*) may be found in the tropical Indian Ocean. *M. layardii* (*28*) is found also in cooler waters.

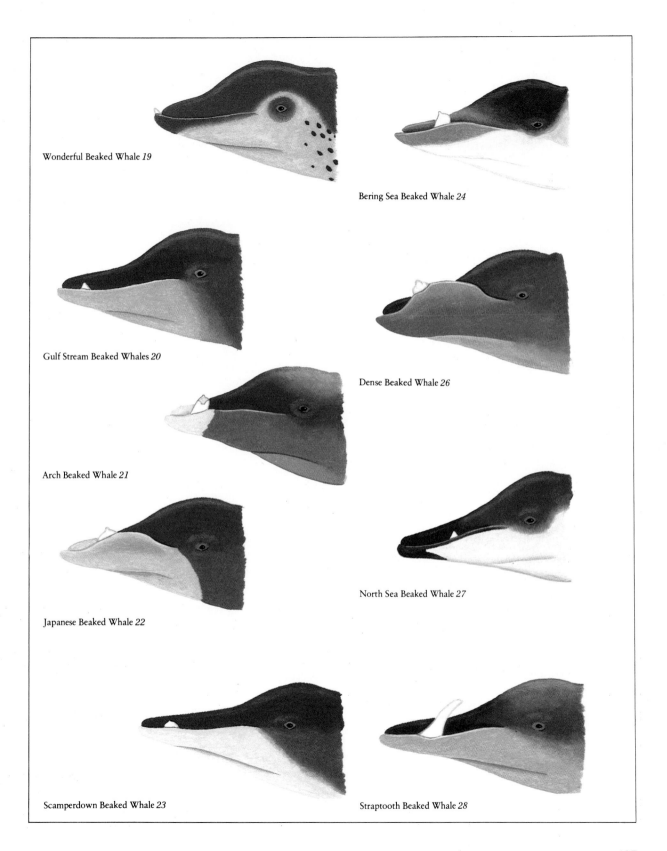

Wonderful Beaked Whale *19*

Bering Sea Beaked Whale *24*

Gulf Stream Beaked Whales *20*

Dense Beaked Whale *26*

Arch Beaked Whale *21*

North Sea Beaked Whale *27*

Japanese Beaked Whale *22*

Scamperdown Beaked Whale *23*

Straptooth Beaked Whale *28*

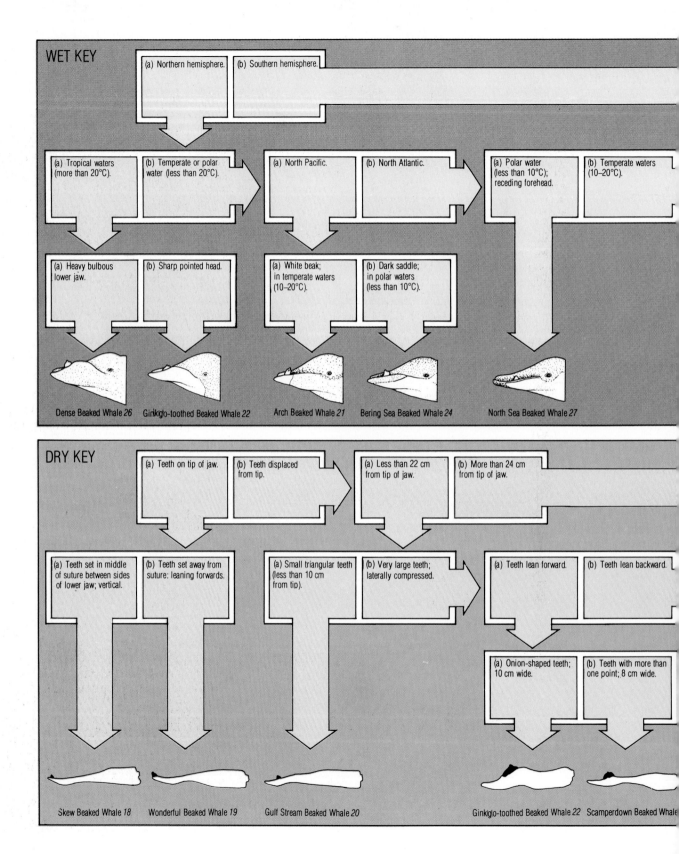

WET KEY

(a) Northern hemisphere. (b) Southern hemisphere.

(a) Tropical waters (more than 20°C). (b) Temperate or polar water (less than 20°C).

(a) North Pacific. (b) North Atlantic.

(a) Polar water (less than 10°C); receding forehead. (b) Temperate waters (10–20°C).

(a) Heavy bulbous lower jaw. (b) Sharp pointed head.

(a) White beak; in temperate waters (10–20°C). (b) Dark saddle; in polar waters (less than 10°C).

Dense Beaked Whale *26*   Ginkiglo-toothed Beaked Whale *22*   Arch Beaked Whale *21*   Bering Sea Beaked Whale *24*   North Sea Beaked Whale *27*

DRY KEY

(a) Teeth on tip of jaw. (b) Teeth displaced from tip.

(a) Less than 22 cm from tip of jaw. (b) More than 24 cm from tip of jaw.

(a) Teeth set in middle of suture between sides of lower jaw; vertical. (b) Teeth set away from suture: leaning forwards.

(a) Small triangular teeth (less than 10 cm from tip). (b) Very large teeth; laterally compressed.

(a) Teeth lean forward. (b) Teeth lean backward.

(a) Onion-shaped teeth; 10 cm wide. (b) Teeth with more than one point; 8 cm wide.

Skew Beaked Whale *18*   Wonderful Beaked Whale *19*   Gulf Stream Beaked Whale *20*   Ginkiglo-toothed Beaked Whale *22*   Scamperdown Beaked Whale

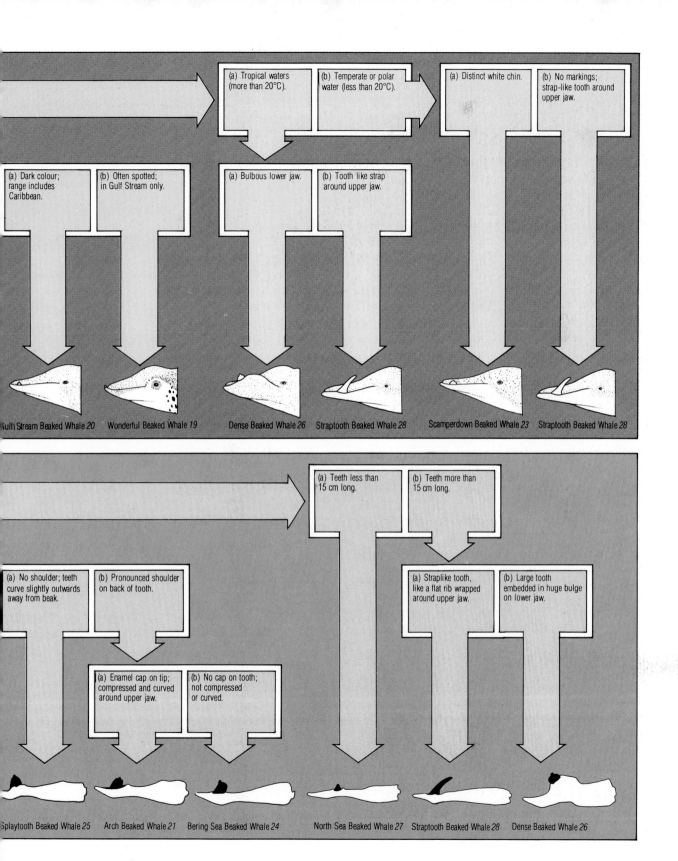

(a) Tropical waters (more than 20°C).

(b) Temperate or polar water (less than 20°C).

(a) Distinct white chin.

(b) No markings; strap-like tooth around upper jaw.

(a) Dark colour; range includes Caribbean.

(b) Often spotted; in Gulf Stream only.

(a) Bulbous lower jaw.

(b) Tooth like strap around upper jaw.

Gulf Stream Beaked Whale 20

Wonderful Beaked Whale 19

Dense Beaked Whale 26

Straptooth Beaked Whale 28

Scamperdown Beaked Whale 23

Straptooth Beaked Whale 28

(a) Teeth less than 15 cm long.

(b) Teeth more than 15 cm long.

(a) No shoulder; teeth curve slightly outwards away from beak.

(b) Pronounced shoulder on back of tooth.

(a) Straplike tooth, like a flat rib wrapped around upper jaw.

(b) Large tooth embedded in huge bulge on lower jaw.

(a) Enamel cap on tip; compressed and curved around upper jaw.

(b) No cap on tooth; not compressed or curved.

Splaytooth Beaked Whale 25

Arch Beaked Whale 21

Bering Sea Beaked Whale 24

North Sea Beaked Whale 27

Straptooth Beaked Whale 28

Dense Beaked Whale 26

129

SKEW BEAKED WHALE (HECTOR'S)

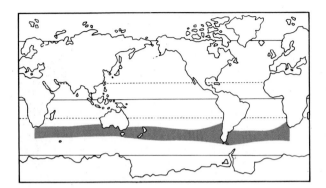

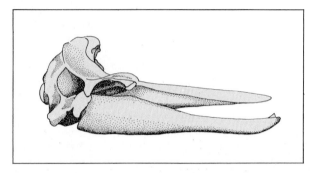

Classification In 1862 a skull was taken from a whale stranded in Porirua Harbour in Cook Strait, New Zealand; in 1866 when a similar whale was captured in nearby Titai Bay the entire skeleton was collected. Both specimens were given to the Colonial Museum in Wellington, where the Curator, Sir James Hector, identified them simply as belonging to a 'smaller ziphid whale'. The skulls were sent to the British Museum as part of an exchange of material and examined there by Gray, who recognized them as juveniles and assumed that they were fourtooth whales, but nevertheless found them distinctive enough to warrant the creation of a new species, *Berardius hectori*. In 1873 another whale was captured in Titai Bay in New Zealand. Hector classified this one himself as *Mesoplodon knoxi*.

Gray died in 1875 and Flower, looking again at the skulls of *Berardius hectori*, in the light of Hector's subsequent discovery of *Mesoplodon knoxi*, decided that they were also beaked rather than fourtooth whales and in 1878 reclassified them all as *Mesoplodon hectori*. Almost a century later, despite the discovery of another whale with similar teeth in the Falklands in 1952, one cetologist still insisted that the 4

known specimens were all fourtooth whales, and merely juveniles of the well-known Southern Fourtooth Whale (*Berardius arnuxii 13*). The dispute was settled conclusively only in 1967 when 2 more specimens were stranded at the mouth of the Lottering River in South Africa, and a fully adult animal turned up in Tasmania. These made it possible for Moore to establish *Mesoplodon hectori* as a true beaked whale, rare but a species in its own right.

Local Names This whale has usually been known as Hector's beaked whale or the New Zealand beaked whale. The first is uninformative and the second, given the new finds in South America and South Africa, inappropriate. Nothing is known about its habits or appearance, so we have chosen a common name for it which reflects its only known peculiarity – the huge asymmetry of the skull – and we call it the Skew Beaked Whale.

Description Despite the existence now of at least 7 specimens in museum collections, nothing is known of the external appearance. Most of the material only came into the hands of zoologists as clean dry bones. The best recent chance of a description was lost with the South African specimens, which were found soon after stranding, but unfortunately the only soft parts saved were two flukes and a single flipper.

We can only assume that the Skew Beaked Whale is dark coloured, of normal beaked whale size and shape and with the usual small rounded flipper and notchless tail.

More information is urgently needed. It is a good idea to look all beaked whales in the mouth, watching for a male with a pair of roughly triangular teeth about 3 cm (just over 1 inch) high, set back about the same distance from the tip of the lower jaw. The tooth sockets lie right on the suture which connects the sides of the lower jaw to each other. Only one other species, the Wonderful Beaked Whale (*Mesoplodon mirus 19*) has teeth like this on the front of the jaw, and they are set more widely in sockets to the sides of the central suture.

Distribution Now known from strandings in the Falklands, South Africa, South Tasmania, and New Zealand, this species must have a circumpolar distribution in all temperate waters of the southern hemisphere.

Sources FLOWER (1878) further description, FRASER (1950) skull, GRAY (1871) original description, HAMILTON (1952) in Falklands, HECTOR (1873) taxonomy, KNOX & HECTOR (1871) first account, McCANN (1962) review, ROSS (1970) in South Africa.

WONDERFUL BEAKED WHALE (TRUE'S)

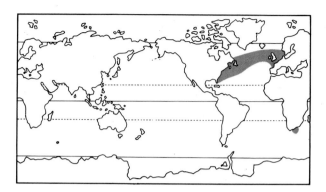

Classification Frederick William True, an American mammalogist and author of the classic *The Whalebone Whales of the Western North Atlantic* (1904), described a female stranded in 1912 on Bird Island shoal outside Beaufort Harbour in North Carolina. It is obvious that the whale impressed him enormously. He took a cast of the entire body; another of the head alone; preserved the skull and the skeleton; wrote a meticulous account with all the necessary weights and measures; and called it *Mesoplodon mirum*, from the Latin *mirus*, wonderful.

In 1941 Frederick Ulmer changed the gender of the species to conform with that of the genus *Mesoplodon mirus.*

Local Names This species has always been known as True's Beaked Whale. But we prefer to honour his species name and call it the Wonderful Beaked Whale.

Description Medium; length averages 5 m (17 ft); calves are about 2 m (6 ft) at birth. Weight averages about 1,300 kg (1.5 tons).

The body differs sufficiently from those of other species of beaked whales to be distinctive. The head is relatively small, with a bulging forehead and a short neck; there is a depression (like that of the Goosebeak Whale *Ziphius cavirostis 14*) in the top behind the blowhole. The flippers are small and placed unusually low and far forward, again reminiscent of the Goosebeak. The fin is small and curved, but behind it there is an unusually pronounced ridge along the top of the tailstock. The flukes can have a small median notch, unlike those of other beaked whales. Some illustrations show rounded tips to the tail flukes, but we believe this to be abnormal and is the result of natural wear in very old individuals, or of beach damage to dead animals.

The colour is generally a bluish dark grey above, with lighter patches on throat and anal area. One possible live sighting suggests that colour can vary to an overall smoky grey or maize. True's original description also mentions the purple and yellow tints on the belly. Animals found stranded in the eastern Atlantic sometimes have a light patterning of

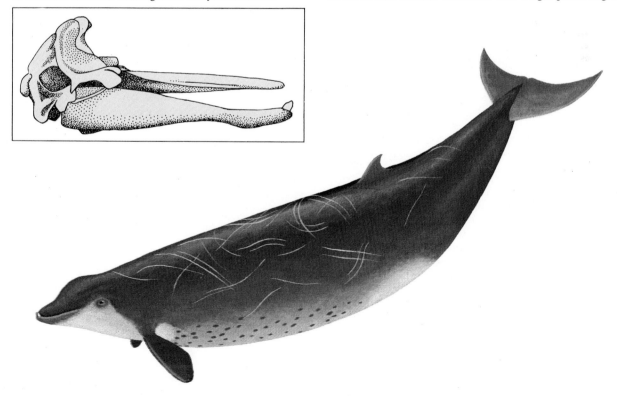

hazel or sienna spots on the lower flanks. Spotting is less noticeable on animals from the western Atlantic. Raked markings, clearly made by the teeth of another Beaked Whale, are common on the sides and backs of adult males.

Field Identification Wonderful Beaked Whales are difficult to identify. They appear to cruise at about 5 kph (3 knots), taking a number of breaths at 10-second intervals, swimming just beneath the surface between blows. The spout is barely visible. They are shy of shipping and dive rapidly when disturbed. The tail flukes are not seen even prior to deep diving.

Stranding A beached whale can be identified without difficulty by its teeth. There is just 1 pair 5 cm (2 inches) long, triangular and compressed from side to side, leaning forwards. At close quarters they can be seen protruding from the lips of a live or recently dead animal. The teeth are set back about 5 cm (2 inches) from the tip of the jaw and roughly the same distance apart. The other beaked whale with teeth on the end of the jaw (the Skew Beaked Whale *M. hectori 18*), has the teeth set closer together. Females and juveniles show no visible teeth, but beneath the gums may have smaller versions of the larger teeth and tiny vestigial teeth in shallower sockets.

There are 46 vertebrae, the first 3 fused together. The first 7 pairs of ribs are double headed, 5 firmly joined to the floating breastbone by heavy cartilage; often visible on the skeleton of a beached animal.

Natural History The staple food is squid, with an occasional deep-water fish. The natural social unit is a mated pair or a mother alone with her calf. Calves seem to be born in the spring (March in the northern hemisphere).

Status It is impossible to assess the numbers of the Wonderful Beaked Whale but it is probably relatively common in the western North Atlantic.

Distribution Strandings occur on both sides of the North Atlantic temperate area, but are twice as common on the coast of North America. Judging from stranding data, the centre of distribution seems to be in the western mid-Atlantic, somewhere around 40° north. It is significant that all of the strandings in the eastern Atlantic have taken place on the west coasts of Ireland and the Orkney Islands, as though the whales were carried there by the Gulf Stream. However this simple and satisfying pattern of distribution is totally destroyed by the fact that a Wonderful Beaked Whale was washed ashore on the South African coast near the Wilderness in 1960. It would be possible and convenient to assume that this individual was a meaningless straggler, a freak, were it not for the fact that 2 more were found at the mouth of the Maitland River near Port Elizabeth in South Africa in 1969, one a juvenile, the other a pregnant female, suggesting that there may be a separate southern-hemisphere population with a breeding centre in the Indian Ocean.

Sources McCANN & TALBOT (1964) in South Africa, MOORE (1966) in North America, ROSS (1969) in South Africa, SERGEANT & FISHER (1957) in Canada, TALBOT (1960) in South Africa, TRUE (1913) original description.

GULF STREAM BEAKED WHALE (GERVAIS'S)

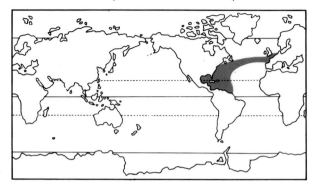

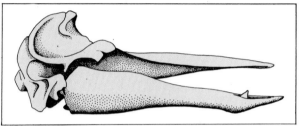

Classification In 1855 Paul Gervais included a skull (found in 1848 in the English Channel) in one of his natural histories as *Dioplodon europaeus*, a name so quickly forgotten that by 1866 Eugène Deslongchamps tried again with *Dioplodon gervaisi*. Flower at the British Museum in 1878 put the skull, together with several others in dispute, firmly into the genus *Mesoplodon*.

No second specimen has ever been found in Europe, the one area in the world in which meticulous records are kept, and in which few stranded whales escape official notice. More than a dozen have accumulated in North America and the Caribbean, and were given almost as many different names as there were localities and authors, until Moore identified them all as *Mesoplodon europaeus*. *M. gervaisi* is now also considered to be synonymous with *M. europaeus*.

Local Names The name European beaked whale has become ridiculous, Gervais' beaked whale is uninformative, Antillean beaked whale is better, but we have chosen to use the one name which unites the apparent centre of distribution with the area of historical discovery, the Gulf Stream Beaked Whale.

Description Medium; up to 6.7 m (22 ft) long; a calf of 2.2 m (7.5 ft) is recorded. Weight is perhaps as much as 2,700 kg (3 tons).

This seems to be the largest species of *Mesoplodon*. More than any of the others, it gives the impression of being laterally compressed, taller than it is deep. The head is proportionately small, has a rounded forehead and tapers to a relatively narrow beak. The flippers seem to be inserted particularly low down on the side of the body. The fin is small and its shape varies from sharklike to bluntly triangular. There is no notch in the tail.

The colouring is uniformly dark marine blue or black with a slight lightening on the undersides. In some animals (male and female) there is a vivid irregular white blotch around the anal area. Many individuals are also heavily marked with tooth scars.

Field Identification We know of no sighting of a Gulf Stream Beaked Whale alive in the wild. They are probably shy and inconspicuous, rising gently (probably beak first) to blow and sliding back beneath the surface. It should be worthwhile keeping watch in the Caribbean for anything large enough and dark enough, with a small fin set well back on a robust body. Confusion could occur between this species and the Goosebeak Whale (*Ziphius cavirostris 14*): a solitary 'Goosebeak' whose blow is not strong enough, or whose fin is not tall enough, would be worth looking at for the sharper narrower beak that could identify it as a Gulf Stream Beaked Whale.

Stranding Beached females and young present the same problems as all beaked whales. A male can be identified by the single pair of teeth set back 7–10 cm (3–4 inches) from the tip of the lower jaw. This distance represents 30 per cent of the length between the tip of the jaw and the corner of the mouth in a live animal, and 15 per cent of the total length of the lower jaw bone. Each tooth is about 10 cm (4 inches) tall, triangular and sharply pointed, compressed and leaning slightly for-ward. Sockets lie within the area in which the mandibles are joined. In females they are either absent or buried deeply in the gum.

There are the usual deep grooves meeting in a V-shape on the throat. The first 3 of 47 vertebrae are joined.

Natural History Gulf Stream Beaked Whales apparently live on squid. A female and newborn calf were stranded together on Jamaica in February 1953, so it seems that breeding either takes place all year round in warm water or is seasonal for a population that migrates south to the Caribbean in winter.

Status This species is perhaps not uncommon in the warmer areas of the western North Atlantic.

Distribution Strandings in New York, New Jersey, North Carolina, Florida, Texas, Cuba, Jamaica and Trinidad suggest a wide distribution along the shores of the western North Atlantic, with a possible centre in warmer water somewhere in the Caribbean or Sargasso seas.

The existence of the single type specimen in the English Channel implies a connection along the warm water highway of the transatlantic Gulf Stream. This would give the Gulf Stream Beaked Whale a range which overlaps slightly in the north with that of the Wonderful Beaked Whale (*Mesoplodon mirus 19*).

Sources FRASER (1953) in Trinidad, GERVAIS (1855) original description, MOORE (1960) taxonomy, MOORE (1966) distribution, RANKIN (1953) in Jamaica.

ARCH BEAKED WHALE

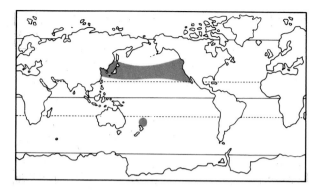

Classification In 1945 a male beaked whale was stranded alive at La Jolla in California. Carl Hubbs of the Scripps Institute of Oceanography believed it to be a specimen of the Splaytooth Beaked Whale (*Mesoplodon bowdoini 25*), previously only known from the southern hemisphere. In 1950 another male was found dead, but fresh, on the beach at Drake's Bay in Marin County, California. This was identified by Robert Orr of the California Academy of Sciences in San Francisco as a Bering Sea Beaked Whale (*M. stejnegeri 24*). Orr felt that the La Jolla specimen was of the same species. In 1958 a third male was captured at sea 120 km (65 nautical miles) south-east of Ayukawa, Japan. The skeleton was described by Masaharu Nishiwaki and Toshiro Kamiya of the Ayukawa Museum of Whales and Whaling, who followed

Orr in identifying it as yet another *Mesoplodon stejnegeri*.

In the early 1960s Moore began meticulous studies of the genus. He decided that, of the 12 animals then known from the Pacific coast, 8 certainly belonged to the subarctic species *M. stejnegeri*, but that the La Jolla and Drake's Bay specimens, as well as two others from Gray's Harbour in Washington and San Simeon Bay in California, and including the Japanese catch, represented a new and different species. The most complete specimen was that from La Jolla and in 1963 Moore called the species *M. carlhubbsi*.

Local Names Moore also provided a descriptive common name, the Arch Beaked Whale.

Description Medium; length can be up to 5.2 m (17 ft). Weight is estimated at 1,500 kg (1.7 tons).

The size and shape are typical of the genus. The throat grooves are well marked; flippers seem to be relatively slim and elongated and have well-marked 'flipper pockets' in the body wall. There is no notch on the tail.

The colour is overall black, possibly with a bluish tint in life. There is a lighter area on the hump of the head, at least in adult males. The most conspicuous marking is a vivid white area on the beak, covering both jaws and ending just short of the eye.

The skin is thin and easily broken; the animals so far described have had a tangle of threadlike scars on their backs and flanks in addition to the usual oval lamprey or crustacean marks and the raked cuts made by the teeth of other whales.

JAPANESE BEAKED WHALE (GINKGO-TOOTHED)

NISHIWAKI & KAMIYA 1958

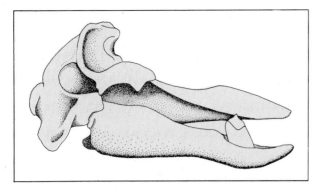

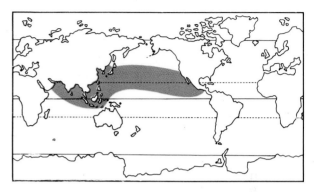

Field Identification Arch Beaked Whales must be easier to identify than most species of *Mesoplodon* if it is true that all individuals have white beaks, and if they lift their heads clear of the water prior to breathing. There are no grounds for assuming that they are any less shy of shipping or any more conspicuous in their behaviour than related species.

Stranding Despite the early confusion between this species and the Bering Sea Beaked Whale (*M. stejnegeri 24*), the teeth are distinctive. The single large pair in a male is displaced approximately 15 cm (6 inches) from the top of the lower jaw; which is about 20 per cent of the length of the dry jawbone, but a little less than half of the distance between the chin and the angle of the mouth in a living animal. The teeth are up to 15 cm (6 inches) high, very flat and wide (10 cm or 4 inches across), with a prominent bulge on the hind edge near the tip. There is a cap of enamel rising to a single sharp point. The teeth lean markedly backwards and curve inwards around the cylinder of the upper jaw.

There are 46 vertebrae, the first 2 fused. The first 7 of 11 pairs of ribs are double headed, the last 2 pairs are unusually short.

Natural History Nothing is known.

Status This species can only be described as relatively rare.

Distribution. With about 10 known specimens, it is difficult to reach any firm conclusion. Almost all the stranded animals have been found on the west coast of North America, between 32° and 47° north. The single animal captured near Japan suggests they may spread right across the North Pacific in temperate waters, south of the range of the Bering Sea Beaked Whale (*M. stejnegeri 24*), and largely north of the Japanese Beaked Whale (*M ginkgodens 22*).

A skull discovered in 1969 in the Bay of Plenty on North Island, New Zealand has been attributed to *M. carlhubbsi*, but it could be a Splaytooth Beaked Whale (*M. bowdoini 25*). If it is the former, then this species will be represented in the southern hemisphere as well.

Sources HUBBS (1946) type specimen, MOORE (1963) original description, NISHIWAKI & KAMIYA (1959) in Japan, ORR (1950) in California, ORR (1953) in California, ROEST (1964) in California.

Classification The type specimen was stranded on Oiso Beach in Sagami Bay near Tokyo in 1957. It was examined there by Nishiwaki and Kamiya of the Japanese Whale Research Institute. In 1958 they published their original description of the whale, an adult male, and noted with obvious delight that the pair of huge teeth were shaped exactly like leaves of the sacred 'ginkgo' tree, *Ginkgo biloba*. In 1963 a second whale with leaflike teeth was washed ashore at Ratmalana near Colombo in Sri Lanka. The skull, fin, flukes and a plaster cast of the head were identified by Deraniyagala as a new species, *Mesoplodon hotaula*. The third came ashore on the public beach at Delmar in Southern California. It was collected by Raymond Gilmore of the Natural History Museum in San Diego and in 1965 he and Moore suggested that this animal and the one in the Indian Ocean were identical to the new Japanese Beaked Whale.

Local Names Ginkgo-toothed beaked whale, *ichó kujira* (Japanese – *Ichó* is the old name for the ginkgo tree), *hotaula* (Sinhalese). We choose to call it the Japanese Beaked Whale.

Description Medium; length can be up to 5.2 m (17 ft). Weight is estimated at about 1,500 kg (1.7 tons).

The shape is typical, but the head is distinctly different. The upper jaw is very narrow with a sharp point, and the lower jaw wraps itself around this spike, sending up heavy flaps of skin which touch the rostrum and almost enfold the enormous teeth.

The fin is small, the flippers short and narrow, but the throat grooves are deep and prominent. There is a suggestion of a notch in the centre of the tail flukes.

The colouring seems to be deep marine blue, turning very rapidly to black as the skin dries and the whale dies. Adult males appear to have some, probably highly variable, white on the beak. All Japanese Beaked Whales seen so far have had a number of white spots on the belly and flanks which could be the result of ectoparasites on the skin.

135

Field Identification The tropical habitat of the Japanese Beaked Whale might make identification possible, at least for older males. Once the Goosebeak Whale (*Ziphius cavirostris 14*) has been eliminated by its greater size, its tendency to lift its tail on diving and its occurrence in larger groups, the two predominantly tropical beaked whales differ somewhat about the head: the Dense Beaked Whale (*M. densirostris 26*) has a very exaggerated bulbous jaw; while that of the Japanese Beaked Whale, despite the fleshy flanges arising from the mandible, has a far more pointed appearance, which could be visible at sea.

Stranding The teeth of adult males are distinctive. The 2 large ones on the lower jaw are about 18 cm (7 inches) from the tip,

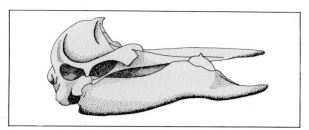

a distance of roughly 25 per cent of the total jaw length, or a little more than half of the gape in a living animal. This puts them behind the flange of bone which joins the two sides of the lower jaw.

Each tooth is shaped very much like a ginkgo leaf (or an onion). They measure 10 cm (4 inches) from the base to the pointed tip and are as wide as they are high. Both teeth are heavily enveloped in a bony prominence of the mandible and tend to lean slightly forwards.

The first 4 of the 48 vertebrae are fused; and the first 7 of the 10 pairs of ribs articulate with the spine by means of double heads.

Natural History Nothing is known.

Status The Japanese Beaked Whale must be considered as relatively rare.

Distribution Strandings in southern California, southern Japan and Sri Lanka suggest a wide distribution throughout the warm waters of the tropical Indopacific. We have, at this stage, limited the extent of the mapped distribution to waters surrounding the known points of occurence, but expect this range to be extended by new strandings or sightings.

There are as yet unconfirmed reports of at least 2 further *M. ginkgodens* being taken on long lines by Japanese deep-sea operations in the waters near Taiwan. These would not only confirm the distribution, but show that this species at least feeds on sizable fish as well as on squid.

Sources DERANIYAGALA (1963) in Sri Lanka, MOORE & GILMORE (1965) in California, NISHIWAKI & KAMIYA (1958) in Japan.

SCAMPERDOWN BEAKED WHALE (GRAY'S)

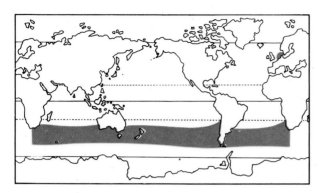

Classification This whale illustrates how a single good sighting or stranding in a little known group of animals can not only double the available information on that species, but also shed new light on its entire genus.

In 1874 a school of 28 beaked whales stranded at Waitangi Beach on Chatham Island east of New Zealand. Skulls were collected from 3 animals and sent to the Canterbury Museum in Christchurch. The founder and Director of the Museum, Sir Julius von Haast, examined them in 1875, noticed their resemblance to a specimen that had recently come to him from Saltwater Creek, just north of the Banks Peninsula, and decided that together they constituted a new species. In 1876 he named it after Gray, who had died the previous year, and briefly toyed with the idea of a new genus as well, which was tentatively named *Oulodon.* However Flower decided that it was a *Mesoplodon.*

Flower also discovered several other specimens in the British Museum collections from New Zealand which seemed to be different enough to warrant new names. He called them *M. haasti* and *M. australis,* but these have now been recognized as the same whale and have all been lumped together as *M. grayi.*

Local Names Southern beaked whale, Scamperdown whale (after an early location in New Zealand), but usually referred to in the literature as Gray's beaked whale. We prefer to call it the Scamperdown Beaked Whale.

Description Medium (on the small side); length averages 3.6 m (12 ft), with a maximum of 4.2 m (14 ft). Weight averages about 1,000 kg (about 1 ton).

With over 20 separate strandings known from New Zea-

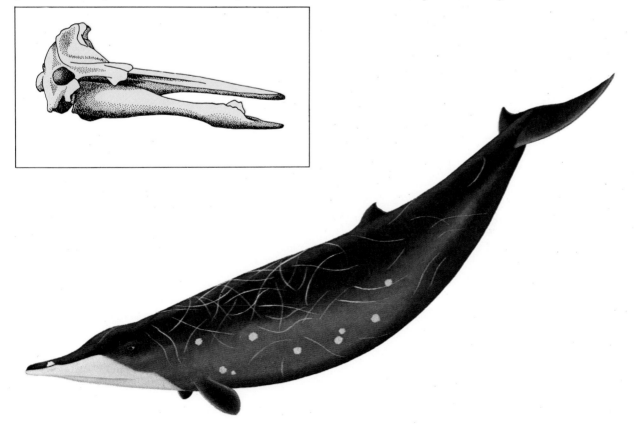

land alone, we are in a better position to describe the Scamperdown Beaked Whale than any other species. It is the smallest of the group, with the usual body shape but a tendency to be both slender and laterally compressed. The head is distinctive. There is a small melon bulge in front of the blowhole, but the forehead recedes almost to the point of being entirely flattened and runs directly into a long slender beak. The teeth are not as large as those of several other species, but protrude far enough from the tapered jaw to be visible in some living animals.

The throat grooves are well marked; the flippers are short but nevertheless the widest in the genus; and the dorsal fin is relatively large and sharply pointed.

The colour is overall deep grey, almost black, grading to dark grey on the undersides. There is a variable amount of white on the throat and the lower jaw. Pale spots and scars are scattered over most of the body with an unusually high proportion of these markings on and around the slender head.

Field Identification It should be relatively easy to identify this species. There is every reason to believe that it is highly social. The early mass stranding and several more recent sightings suggest that it commonly occurs in groups of 6 or more, and that these may be more active and more conspicuous at the surface than other beaked whales.

Scamperdown Beaked Whales have been described shooting up out of the water at an angle of 30° until all but the tail is exposed and then falling back with a splash. They may do this in reaction to the approach of a ship. We saw a group of at least 10 animals in the southern Indian Ocean making low arched leaps as they moved away from our vessel in almost perfect single file. We thought at first they were Southern Rightwhale Dolphins (*Lissodelphis peronii 63*), which characteristically behave in this way, until we were able to see their larger size and that they had typical Mesoplodon dorsal fins. They were leaping serially, each one rising at least once every 10 seconds, probably faster than their normal breathing rhythm. No blows were visible.

In 1968 2 beaked whales which answer to this description were observed for several hours off Napier breakwater in New Zealand by Frank Robson. They were breathing once every 30 seconds.

Stranding This species is frequently stranded and is unusually easy to identify. Males and females have one pair of large teeth displaced about 20 cm (8 inches) from the tip of the jaw.

These have a serrated edge with one or more sharp points and lean slightly forwards. Their size is apparently independent of body size; quite large teeth are found in the jaws even of immature males. The height of the teeth is about 10 cm (4 inches) and the width is normally 80 per cent of the height.

In addition to this pair of prominent teeth, both males and females have a number of smaller teeth in both jaws. Vestigial teeth, usually buried deep in the gums, are a feature of many beaked whales; but Scamperdown Beaked Whales commonly have up to 26 extra teeth, usually on the upper jaw behind the point of origin of the large teeth, breaking through the gum far enough to be functional.

Natural History Scamperdown Beaked Whales seem to be highly gregarious, which may be characteristic of this species alone, or simply made more evident in these animals by their tendency to be more active at the surface than their larger relatives.

One of the New Zealand strandings was a calf less than 2 m (6 ft) long. The fact that this stranding took place in March suggests that calving may normally occur in the spring.

Despite the frequency of stranding, there is nothing in the literature to show that a single stomach or any of its contents were ever examined.

Status Scamperdown Beaked Whales are clearly relatively common. The frequency with which they strand may be an accurate reflection of their greater abundance or may simply be the result of their more coastal way of life.

Distribution This species has been found stranded at Chubut in Argentina, on the Atlantic and Indian Ocean coasts of South Africa, in Victoria and at the mouth of the Murray River in Australia, in Tasmania and throughout New Zealand.

The range is clearly circumpolar in all cool temperate waters of the southern hemisphere, but this simple distribution is complicated by the fact that the Scamperdown Beaked Whale has now turned up in the northern hemisphere. A single animal was found stranded at Loosduinen in Holland. The Scamperdown Beaked Whale either extends throughout the Atlantic or it has a northern form.

Sources BOSCHMA (1950) in Holland, McCANN(1964) review, VON HAAST (1876) original description.

BERING SEA BEAKED WHALE

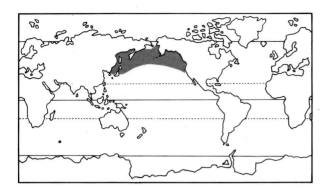

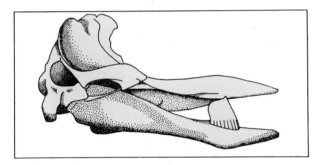

Classification In 1883 Leonhard Stejneger, a Norwegian who eventually became Curator of the United States National Museum, was doing pioneer work on the fauna of Alaska. He sent to the United States National Museum a beach-worn immature whale skull which lacked a lower jaw. It was nevertheless interesting enough to catch the eye of an even younger zoologist just beginning his museum career. Frederick William True was working on a history of the Commander Islands (Komandorski) at the Russian end of the Aleutian chain and in his account of Bering Island he included a description of the skull washed ashore there and named it *Mesoplodon stejnegeri*. Nobody knew what the teeth of this beaked whale looked like until 1904, when an adult male was stranded on South Beach near Newport in Oregon. The skull enabled True to complete the picture he had begun to draw a generation earlier. He included the first full description of the species in a magnificent account of the whole ziphid family published in 1910.

During the following 50 years another 7 specimens were recovered from Alaska, Canada, the United States and the coast of Japan. Some of these were identified as northern representatives of the Splaytooth Beaked Whale (*M. bowdoini* 25) of the South Pacific, but in 1968 Moore firmly established *M. stejnegeri* as the dominant subarctic beaked whale in the North Pacific. Today the species is known from a dozen individuals.

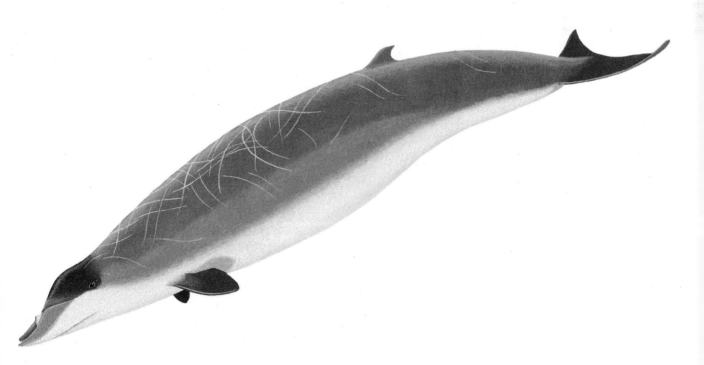

Local Names *Kigan agaliusiak* (Aleutian), *kvov-kvov-e-akht-le* (in Maka), Stejneger's whale or sabretooth. In view of its point of discovery and apparent centre of distribution in the deep cold waters of the far North Pacific, we prefer Moore's name of Bering Sea Beaked Whale.

Description Medium; length is about 5 m (16 ft), with a maximum of about 6 m (20 ft). Weight is estimated as 1,200 kg (1.3 tons).

Owing to confusion with the Splaytooth Beaked Whale (*M. bowdoini 25*) and the Arch Beaked Whale (*M. carlhubbsi 21*), many of the published descriptions of this species are at variance. Those which show a predominantly dark animal with a bright white beak are almost certainly derived from the La Jolla whale now known to be *M. carlhubbsi*. The Bering Sea Beaked Whale has the usual spindle-shaped body, small rounded flippers and a moderately large dorsal fin set two-thirds of the way back on the body. It is distinctive in having a well-developed keel or ridge along the back, running from the fin to the flukes. Characteristic markings include some whiteness around the lips and an umber-brown saddle running across the blowhole on an otherwise light grey or brownish body.

There are numerous scratch marks on the skin, both tooth scrapes and oval parasitic scars.

Field Identification This species is difficult to identify except on geographic grounds. Any beaked whale in the North Pacific without the white beak characteristic of the Arch Beaked species (*M. carlhubbsi 21*) is almost bound to be the Bering Sea Beaked Whale.

Stranding The teeth are distinctive. In adult males a large pair are set 20 cm (8 inches) back from the tip of the jaw, 30 per cent of the total jaw length and half the gape in a living animal.

The teeth are 20 cm (8 inches) high, 10 cm (4 inches) wide and relatively stout, over 2 cm (about 1 inch) thick, not as compressed as those of other beaked whales. Each tooth leans slightly backwards, with a round shoulder behind and with the dentine on the front raised into a sharp point or cusp. The leading edge of the tooth is therefore almost vertical and often worn to a smooth, blunt finish.

The width of the mandible increases rather suddenly just behind the teeth. The first 3 of 46 vertebrae are fused; and the first 7 of 10 pairs of ribs are double headed.

Natural History Bering Sea Beaked Whales are apparently sometimes taken by whalers from Japanese coastal stations; their stomachs are said to contain both squid and salmon.

The whalers' reports indicate that this species is usually encountered in small groups of 2 or 3 animals.

Status The Bering Sea Beaked Whale is probably relatively rare.

Distribution This species is known from strandings at Akita Beach on Honshu in Japan, at St Paul Island in the Pribilofs, from the Copper River area and the Kenai Peninsula in Alaska, on Vancouver Island, at Yaquima Bay in Oregon, and from the mouth of the Waatch River in Washington.

The distribution seems to lie entirely between 40° and 60° north in the Pacific, overlapping only slightly in the south with the range of the Arch Beaked Whale (*M. carlhubbsi 21*). In this respect the Bering Sea Beaked Whale occupies the same position, the same subarctic niche, in the Pacific as the North Sea Beaked Whale (*M. bidens 27*) does in the Atlantic.

Sources MOORE (1965) review, NISHIMURA & NISHIWAKI (1964) in Japan, NISHIWAKI & KAMIYA (1959) in Japan, TRUE (1885) original description, TRUE (1910) taxonomy.

SPLAYTOOTH BEAKED WHALE (ANDREW'S)

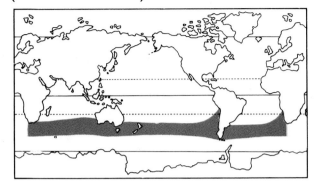

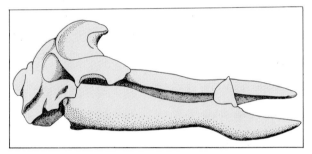

Classification Sometimes the circumstances which bring new species to light are so circuitous, that the failure of any of a number of vital connections can result in their being displaced altogether. There must be species of cetacean still undescribed solely for lack of the appropriate accident.

In 1904 the American Museum of Natural History in New York purchased the mounted skeleton of an adult male beaked whale, along with a number of other specimens, from Henry Ward's Natural Science Establishment. Roy Chapman Andrews, a 23-year-old naturalist, studied the skeleton carefully and concluded that it was new to science; he established that it had been stranded on Brighton Beach near Canterbury, New Zealand. He called it *M. bowdoini* in honour of James Bowdoin, an eighteenth-century American amateur zoologist who was Colonial Governor of Massachusetts and First President of the American Academy of Arts and Sciences.

Today there are at least 6 specimens of *M. bowdoini* known from New Zealand and 1 each from Tasmania and western Australia.

The specimen recorded from the Sea of Japan is now known to be *M. carlhubbsi 21*; and the other discrepant northern-hemisphere record from the west coast of North America has been shown to be either *M. carlhubbsi* or *M. stejnegeri 24*.

Local Names In the literature this species is called Bowdoin's or Andrew's whale; to some taxonomists familiar with its skull, it is known as the deepcrest beaked whale. We choose instead to acknowledge the one diagnostic feature of this species and call it the Splaytooth Beaked Whale.

Description Medium; length averages 4 m (13 ft) for both sexes. Weight averages 1,100 kg (1.2 tons).

The shape is similar in most respects to the Bering Sea Beaked Whale (*M. stejnegeri 24*), but smaller. Females may be larger than males. The colour is said to be a darkish grey, grading to light grey on the underside. Nothing else is known of this whale's appearance, which means that identification will be virtually impossible in the field.

Stranding Identification of a beached specimen should be reasonably easy. The teeth are very similar to those of the Bering Sea Beaked Whale (*M. stejnegeri 24*). They are 20 cm (8 inches) from the tip of the lower jaw, up to 15 cm (6 inches) high, 9 cm (3.5 inches) wide, lean slightly backwards and have a sharp point of denticle on the top of the leading edge. They have, however, no shoulder on the back edge of the tooth. They also differ radically in the fact that both large teeth curve noticeably outward away from the centre of the beak.

In this respect the beaked whales of the Pacific, which have superficially similar teeth, all displaced roughly 20 cm (8 inches) from the tip, can be distinguished by close examination of a beached animal or a clean skull.

Natural History Nothing is known.

Status Nothing is known.

Distribution Strandings are known in New Zealand from New Brighton near Christchurch, Waitofara Beach near Wanganui, from Manawatu Heads, Cook Straits and Steward Island and from Bunbury in south-western Western Australia.

The range appears from these records to be confined to the cool temperate waters of the central Indopacific. This almost certainly reflects the existence there of beaches that are both suitable for stranding and near enough to population centres for the stranding to be noticed and recorded. It would be surprising if the distribution did not extend to the eastern Pacific and perhaps also into the South Atlantic.

We predict that the Splaytooth Beaked Whale will soon be discovered in southern Chile or Patagonia.

Sources ANDREWS (1908) original description, OLIVER (1922) in New Zealand, MOORE (1963) taxonomy.

Cross-section of the lower jaws of: *M. carlhubbsi 21*, *M. stejnegeri 24* and *M. bowdoini 25*

DENSE BEAKED WHALE

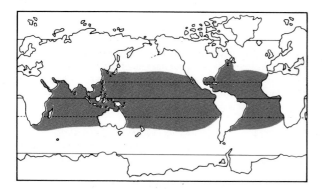

Classification Henri Marie Ducrotay de Blainville took over Cuvier's chair of comparative anatomy in Paris and published his own dictionary of natural history in 1817. In it he outlined his new system for the identification of animals by their external appearance, but he also included internal characteris-

tics where these were relevant. For one new species all he had was 22 cm (9 inches) from the tip of the upper jaw of an unknown small whale. This small piece of rostral bone was extraordinarily heavy, 34 per cent denser even than elephant ivory, making it the densest structure ever produced by any vertebrate. De Blainville named it simply *Delphinus densirostris*, from the Latin *densus*, dense, and *rostrum*, a beak.

The rest of the whale only came to light in 1846 when Gray of the British Museum, in his report of the voyage of HMS *Erebus* and HMS *Terror*, described a skull collected in the Seychelles Islands in the Indian Ocean. The skull had a heavy bone structure which reminded Gray of Cuvier's Goosebeak Whale (*Ziphius cavinostris 14*), so he called it *Ziphius sechellensis*.

After Gray's death in 1875 Flower reviewed everything known about the ziphid family, concluding that de Blainville and Gray were dealing with the same animal, which he identified as a beaked whale and called *Mesoplodon densirostris*.

This species is so distinctive that there has been no confu-

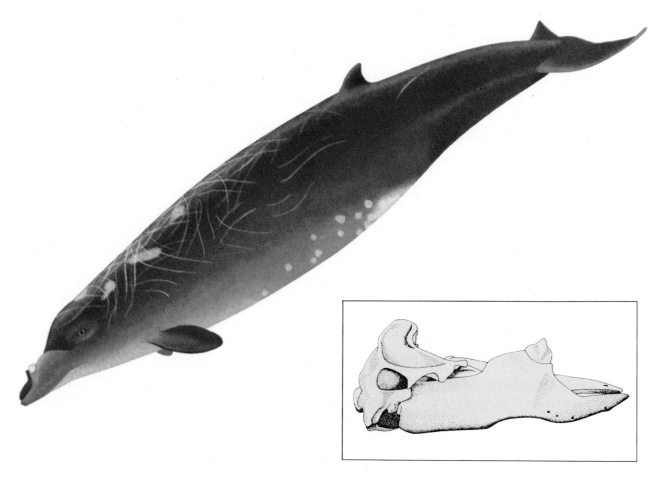

sion in the century since then, save for one brief attempt by a zoologist to classify three beaked whales stranded alive on Midway Sound as *Nodus densirostris*.

Local Names This species is usually known as Blainville's beaked whale, but his description of the rostrum has proved so apt of the mandible also, that it seems inevitable this animal should be called the Dense Beaked Whale.

Description Medium; length averages 4.5–4.8 m (15–16 ft). Weight averages about 1,000 kg (about 1 ton).

The general body form and shape are similar to those of other beaked whales, but the head is strikingly different. The entire middle third of the mandible is dominated by a huge tooth that rises up above the top of the beak and is enveloped and supported by a massive bony protruberance. This alters the whole shape of the jaw, giving the mouth a high arching contour which sweeps up over the rostrum and only dips down again in front of the eye, making it virtually impossible for the whale to see forwards at all.

The flippers are short and the throat grooves inconspicuous. The dorsal•fin is relatively large and noticeably curved backwards to a point. There is no notch in the tail flukes, which sometimes even bulge outwards and backwards in the centre.

The colour is a bluish dark grey, with a slightly lighter grey throat and chest. The anal area is often splashed almost white. All Dense Beaked Whales seem to be marked with paler blotches, most of which are the result of parasites. There is some evidence also of scarring produced by the teeth of rival males.

Field Identification If any adult males are present, there should be no difficulty in identifying a group of Dense Beaked Whales. Several times, on calm days in the tropical Indian Ocean, we have seen small groups (always less than 6) moving along together at the surface. They invariably seem to lift the beaks up until the rostrum is clear of the water before blowing. In this position, the high contour of the lower jaw is distinctly visible in the single large male in each group, rising vertically like leather blinder flaps on a horse's bridle. Even the smaller animals, presumably females and young, show a curve at the back of the mouth.

The blow is indistinct, but on a calm day can be seen to shoot forwards at a sharp angle. The whales spend several minutes at or near the surface, breathing at 15- or 20-second intervals, before diving together for longer periods which may end in their disappearance. The fin is prominent and clearly shown at the end of a long curve of back with every breath. We never saw the tail flukes raised above the surface.

The chances are that any beaked whale seen in warm tropical waters will be *M. densirostris*, so it is worth looking specifically for the distinctive bulging jaw line.

Stranding If males of almost any age are involved, identification is not difficult. The single gigantic pair of teeth is displaced 30 cm (1 ft) from the tip of the jaw. This is half the

length of the jawbone and, in a live animal, more than two-thirds of the length of the gape. Each tooth is almost 20 cm (8 inches) high, but all the root and most of the body are enclosed in a heavy bulge of bone that rises from the jaw and usually only a small part of the tooth tip protrudes, facing slightly forwards. The teeth of female whales are small and totally buried in the gum, but the lower jaw still has a marked bulge. There are 47 vertebrae. The first 7 of 11 pairs of ribs are double headed and, in addition to the normal chest ribs, there is often an extra pair of slimmer ribs attached to the last neck vertebra.

Natural History Analysis of the stomach contents of one stranded animal show that, at the time, it was feeding entirely on squid. Our sightings, and others by Captain Morzer Bruyns, suggest that the Dense Beaked Whale is normally social, living in small family units of 3–6 animals.

Nothing is known of reproductive behaviour.

Several reports of the stranding of live animals describe them producing 'roars', 'lowing sounds', and 'sobbing groans'. A recording was made of a male beached in Florida, who produced a pulsed sound as well as audible chirps and whistles.

Status The Dense Beaked Whale is known from little more than 20 museum specimens, but is nevertheless probably relatively common.

Distribution This is the only beaked whale known to strand on oceanic islands in the tropics. There are records from the Atlantic side of Abaco in the Bahamas, Madeira, the Seychelles, Lord Howe Island in the Tasman Sea and Midway Island and Formosa in the North Pacific. Coastal stranding has taken place near Halifax in Nova Scotia, Annisquam in Massachusetts, Southport on Long Island, Corson's Inlet in New Jersey, near Beaufort in North Carolina, Charleston in South Carolina and in Florida. In South Africa it is known from Shelly Beach near Cape Recife and in Australia from the coast of Queensland.

The Dense Beaked Whale is the only member of the family apart from the Goosebeak Whale (*Ziphius cavirostris* 14) which regularly crosses the equator. The Dense Beaked Whale is not yet known from the South Atlantic, but we predict that it will be found there.

Distribution is clearly worldwide, in all tropical and subtropical waters, normally extending no further from the equator than about 35° of latitude in either hemisphere. The northward projection of its range in the western Atlantic, as far as Nova Scotia at 45° north, can be attributed to the warming effect of the Gulf Stream.

The Dense Beaked Whale seems to occur in deep offshore waters more commonly than some of its relatives.

Sources BLAINVILLE (1817) original description, CALDWELL & CALDWELL (1971) sounds, GALBREATH (1963) on Midway, KASUYA & NISHIWAKI (1971) on Formosa, MOORE (1958) in Bahamas, MOORE (1966) distribution, PRINGLE (1952) in South Africa, RAVEN (1942) in Nova Scotia.

NORTH SEA BEAKED WHALE

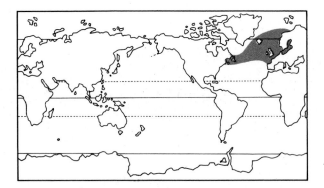

Classification This was the first beaked whale to be described. In 1800 a male was stranded on the Moray Firth in north-eastern Scotland and its skull was collected and preserved by James Brodie of Elginshire. It came to the attention of James Sowerby, a travelling English watercolour artist who was part of an extraordinary dynasty of naturalists. In 1804 he published a delightful collection of illustrations called *The British*

Miscellany, including an excellent portrait of the whale skull and a reconstruction of the entire animal. Sowerby captioned it *Physeter bidens*, using Linnaeus's generic name for the sperm whale and adding the Latin for 'having two teeth'.

In his new dictionary of 1817, de Blainville changed the name to *Delphinus sowerbensis*. In 1850 his successor Paul Gervais made the species type of his new genus *Mesoplodon*. This is how all the beaked whales, even those with teeth as far forward on the jaw as it is possible to have teeth, come to be known as whales with 'teeth in the middle of the jaw'.

It was Flower who finally brought Sowerby's original species name forward to complete the binomial of *Mesoplodon bidens*.

The skull which Sowerby drew is now in the Museum of the University of Oxford.

Local Names *Dauphin du Havre* or *dauphin de Dale* (French), *Flosser* (German), *spitsdolfijn* (Dutch), *remnezub soverbi* (Russian), *spidshvalen* (Norwegian) and *Sowerby's nabbwal* (Swedish). We prefer Moore's name of North Sea Beaked Whale.

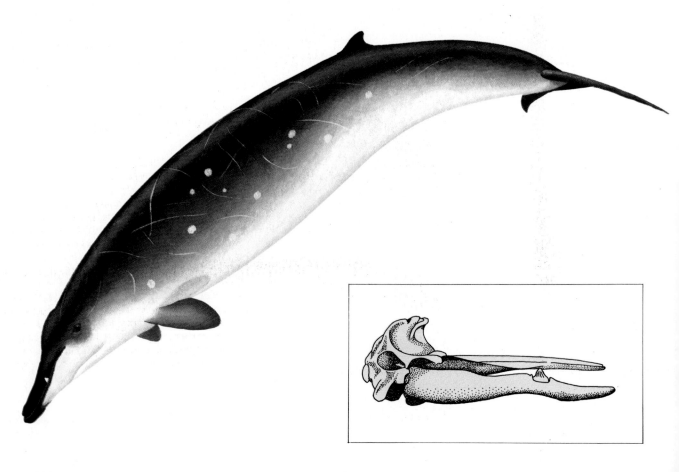

Description Medium; length averages 5 m (16–17 ft), with a possibly exaggerated maximum of 6.7 m (22 ft) reported for one specimen. Weight is perhaps as high as 1,300 kg (3,000 lb).

The general body proportions are like those of most beaked whales, but the North Sea Beaked Whale gives the impression of being sleeker and more streamlined. The head is distinctive. Immediately in front of the off-centre blowhole, there is a definite bulge, not large enough to be called a melon, but sloping rapidly off into a concave forehead and a long slim beak. The throat grooves and flipper pockets are well developed and the tail flukes, although they lack a median notch, are more concave than in any other species of *Mesoplodon*. The colour is mostly a bluish dark grey, but younger whales tend to have lighter bellies. All individuals have some white on the lower jaw and, as they grow older, become more and more conspicuously scarred, mostly with the oval white marks of parasitic attachments.

Field Identification As their name suggests, North Sea Beaked Whales occur well north of a latitude of 50°. No other species in the Atlantic is likely to be seen so near the Arctic circle. Further south there is a possibility of confusion with the Wonderful Beaked Whale (*M. mirus 19*). A good close view may reveal a white tooth tip jutting up above the lip line in adult male North Sea Beaked Whales, but failing this, the species are probably indistinguishable at sea.

We have twice seen a pair of North Sea Beaked Whales off the southern coast of Iceland. Their breathing patterns were similar. The beak and head break the surface first so that the rostrum is clearly visible, but the mandible remains submerged. The blow is gentle and inaudible even at close quarters. After the head disappears, the smooth round curve of the back slides slowly over, raised surprisingly high above the water for a beaked whale. Then, finally, the small fin and a portion of the keeled tailstock appear briefly. We have never seen the flukes.

This characteristic sequence is so much more like that of a large whale e.g. the Piked Whale (*Balaenoptera acutorostrata 7*) and, in our experience, so unlike that of other beaked whales, that it might be diagnostic of the North Sea species.

Stranding A beached male North Sea Beaked Whale is identifiable by a smallish pair of teeth set in the middle of the lower jaw. This does not mean, as some descriptions imply, that they are in the centre of the gape. In a live animal, the tooth is quite near the back of the mouth opening. Each tooth is usually 30 cm (1 ft) from the tip of the jaw, about 10 cm (4 inches) high and rises to a sharp point of denticle which faces slightly towards the back of the mouth. The roots of the tooth are long and point obliquely forwards. Females have smaller teeth of similar construction, or none at all. In many specimens there are additional small vestigial teeth which may be found on either jaw, but are seldom set in sockets. There are 46 vertebrae.

Natural History Squid and small fish have been found in the

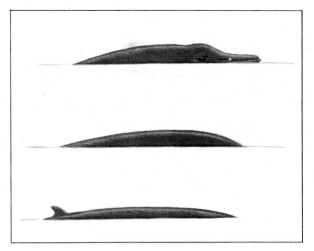

Dive sequence

stomachs of North Sea Beaked Whales. The famous 'Whale of le Havre' (captured alive in 1825) was kept alive for 2 days, it is said, 'on soaked bread and other alimentary substances'.

A foetus 1.57 m (62 inches) long was found in a whale stranded in December 1892. It was near full term, indicating perhaps that the whales migrate south in front of the advancing ice in winter, and calve at this time.

The voice of a stranded North Sea Beaked Whale has been described as 'like a cow's'.

Status This species is probably relatively common. It is the most commonly stranded beaked whale, or at least the one most often reported on beaches. There are dozens of records from the coasts of western Europe and Scandinavia.

Distribution Numerous strandings have been reported from Norway, Sweden, Denmark, Holland, Belgium, Baltic Germany, the north coast of France, the North Sea coasts of Britain, and the west coast of Ireland. There is one dubious record from Sicily. In the western Atlantic there are relatively few records: one at Trinity Bay, one at Notre Dame Bay in Newfoundland, and a third on Nantucket Island in Massachusetts. These seem to indicate that this species, unlike the other 2 North Atlantic beaked whales, has its centre of distribution in the east, possibly somewhere in or near the North Sea.

The habitat of the North Sea Beaked Whale is clearly in the cooler parts of the ocean, perhaps even right up to the edge of the ice. It may not be as restricted to truly deep waters as several other species of *Mesoplodon*, but occupies a subarctic, predominantly coastal, niche much like that of the Bering Sea Beaked Whale (*M. stejnegeri 24*) in the North Pacific.

Sources BEDDARD (1900) stranding, GERVAIS (1850) taxonomy, MOORE (1966) distribution, SOWERBY (1804) original description, VAN DER BRINK (1967) in Europe.

STRAPTOOTH BEAKED WHALE

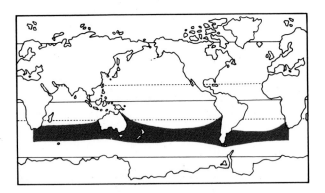

Classification The pleasure of describing the most bizarre whale in the whole of this strange family fell to John Edward Gray towards the end of his long career at the British Museum.

In 1865 Edgar Leopold Layard, Curator of the South African Museum in Cape Town, sent Gray a set of drawings of a skull in his collection. Gray was astounded and had no qualms about immediately publishing a note proclaiming the dis-covery of a new species of ziphid whale which he called *Ziphius layardii*. A few years later the skull itself was presented to the British Museum and Gray was able to see that it was not a Goosebeak Whale at all, but a beaked whale. In 1871 he changed the name to *Dolichodon layardii*.

The second specimen turned up on Chatham Island east of New Zealand and Hector of the Colonial Museum in Wellington had equally little hesitation in identifying it and including it, correctly, in Paul Gervais's genus of *Mesoplodon*.

In the century since then, more than 50 of these extraordinary whales have been stranded right across the temperate southern hemisphere. In various stages of development, some have looked sufficiently different to warrant the creation of the new species *M. floweri*, *M. guntheri*, *M. thomsoni* and *M. traversii*. However all are now known as *M. layardii*.

Local Names Straptooth Beaked Whale.

Description Medium; length averages 5 m (16–17 ft), but some of the larger skulls suggest a possible maximum of around 7 m (23 ft). Weight is estimated at about 1,250 kg (2,750 lb).

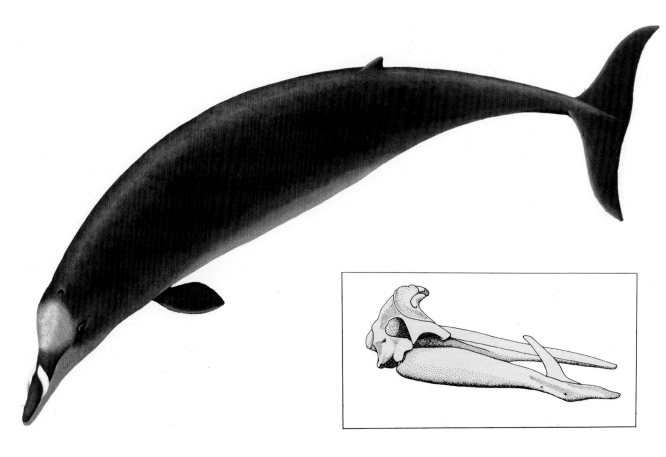

Rolling dive of Straptooth Beaked Whale, showing one flipper above the water

This may be the longest species of beaked whale. Its body is sleek and streamlined, laterally compressed, with a marked keel along the top of the tailstock. The flippers and fin are slightly smaller than those of other southern-hemisphere species. The head is small, the forehead long and gently sloping all the way down to a long, slender beak. These features are characteristic of beaked whales in general and each is familiar from at least one other species, but all take second place to this whale's astonishing teeth.

Male Straptooth Beaked Whales have taken the progressive displacement and growth of the single pair of teeth to absurd limits. In an adult male, such as Layard's first specimen, the tips of the large flat teeth grow upwards and backwards like inverted ribs until they almost meet outside the mouth above the upper jaw. The whale ends up with a strap like a muzzle across its beak which makes it impossible to open the mouth more than a centimetre or two.

The colouring is dark grey with a lighter grey on the underside. Some older males have a white blaze on the top of the head. Despite the peculiar, apparently non-functional, development of the teeth, males still seem to manage to leave tooth scars on each other's skin.

Field Identification Males of this species are easy to identify. The Straptooth breathes like other beaked whales, by breaking the surface first with the beak and the head. If there is an adult male present, and there usually is in small family groups, his broad enamel strap shines out like a plastic marker. There is no mistaking it.

We have seen this species in the southern Indian Ocean basking at the surface on calm sunny days. Their usual reaction to an approaching ship is to sink slowly beneath the surface, almost without a ripple, while the vessel is still more than 100 m (330 ft) away. Sometimes however, one of the larger whales will dive with a deliberate lateral roll, bringing one flipper up out of the water as it turns. The tail flukes do not show. Usually the group submerges for 10–15 minutes, surfacing again some 400 m (1,300 ft) further away; but a closer approach in a small boat is possible.

Stranding This species is frequently stranded, particularly in New Zealand. The teeth of males are displaced a full 30 cm (11 inches) from the tip of the jaw. Each is very long, up to 35 cm (14 inches), 4 or 5 cm (2 inches) wide, covered with enamel and tapering exactly like a rib toward the tip. The teeth grow up and out and then tilt backwards at an angle of about 45°. On the tip is a small sharp denticle which is often bent at right angles to the rest of the tooth. In young males, growing teeth seem at first to curve outwards away from the beak, like those of the Splaytooth Beaked Whale (*M. bowdoini 25*), but the jaw in that species is considerably more robust.

Natural History Straptooth Beaked Whales live almost entirely on squid; although how the large males with their very restricted gape manage to catch or swallow anything remains a mystery. They must function rather like the long pointed attachments that make it possible to get into tight corners with a vacuum cleaner. A female stranded in New Zealand in September had just given birth, showing perhaps that parturition normally takes place in the spring. The calves are about 2.2 m (87 inches) long at birth and are probably suckled for almost a year.

Status This species is relatively common in the southern hemisphere.

Distribution Most of the recorded strandings have taken place in New Zealand, on Chatham Island, or the east coast of South Island between Otago and Cook Strait and in Hawke Bay and Hauraki Gulf on the east coast of North Island. In Australia they are recorded on Cape Yorke Peninsula in North Queensland, in Encounter Bay near Adelaide, Little Bay near Sydney and in Tasmania.

Other records from South Africa and the Falkland Islands show that the distribution of Straptooth Beaked Whales is circumpolar in the southern hemisphere, in relatively cool water. There are several sightings by whaling expeditions as far south as the Antarctic convergence, but the range seems to be largely between 30° and 45° south.

Sources GASKIN (1971) in New Zealand, GRAY (1865) original description, HECTOR (1873) taxonomy, McCANN (1964) records.

Family Five – Platanistidae

In 5 separate great river systems on 2 continents there now live 5 distinct long-snouted dolphin species which look enough alike to be regarded as a single family. In 1863 Gray named this assemblage after *Platanista*, the genus found in the Indian subcontinent, but there is still no real consensus. Many taxonomists believe that the similarity is the result of convergence owing more to the influence of similar environments than to any family relationship. There ought perhaps to be at least 3 separate families.

Whatever their ancestry, all these dolphins are small and have long slender beaks sharply demarcated from bulging foreheads. Their dorsal fins are relatively low and their flippers broad and visibly fingered. The jaws are very long and narrow, with many small teeth in 2 parallel rows. All the cervical vertebrae are separate, giving a noticeable neck and greater freedom of movement for the head than is usual amongst cetaceans. They can turn their heads sideways as well as up and down.

Living most of the time in turbid muddy waters, where visibility is almost nil, the eyes of most river dolphins have become much reduced. *Platanista* has no lenses at all and is effectively blind, but compensates with an elaborate and refined sonar system.

Of the 4 genera:
Platanista occurs in the Indian subcontinent,
Lipotes in China,
Inia in tropical South America and
Pontoporia in temperate South America.

The geographical isolation of the genera makes identification easy and keys unnecessary. A few species of oceanic dolphin enter river systems and at least one, the Estuarine Dolphin (*Sotalia fluviatilis 42*) of the Amazon, may spend its entire life cycle in freshwater, but the appearance and behaviour of these is distinctly different. The true river dolphins are slower, less inclined to leap, and instead of a classic curved fin tend, when they dive, to show a distinct and angular hump.

Each of the 5 species in this family can be identified with certainty by its habitat alone:

1. In the Ganges and Brahmaputra river systems of India, Bangladesh and Assam: Ganges River Dolphin (*Platanista gangetica 29*).

2. In the Indus River and its tributaries throughout Pakistan and into north-western India: Indus River Dolphin (*Platanista minor 30*).

3. In the Yangtze and Kiang river systems of China, including Lake Tungt'ing: Yangtze River Dolphin (*Lipotes vexillifer 31*).

4. In the Amazon and Orinoco river systems of Brazil, Bolivia, Peru, Colombia and Venezuela: Amazon River Dolphin (*Inia geoffrensis 32*).

5. In the lower reaches of Rio de la Plata and the associated coasts of Argentina, Uruguay and Brazil: La Plata River Dolphin (*Pontoporia blainvillei 33*).

GANGES RIVER DOLPHIN

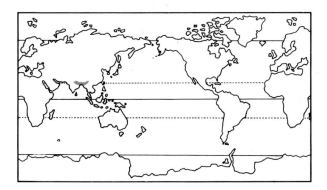

Pair of Ganges River Dolphins in precopulatory display; and rolling over at surface in copulation

Classification Pliny the elder wrote in *Historiae Naturalis 'In Gange Indiae platanistes vocant, rostro delphini . . .'* Pliny's source is unknown, but elsewhere he uses the term *platanistes* for a kind of fish. In Roman times it was, at least after Pliny's publication of this volume in AD 77, common knowledge that in the River Ganges there was a fish with a beak like a dolphin. It was not until the nineteenth century that anyone again took official notice of that strange beast in the Ganges. Then, suddenly, 2 different authors both published scientific descriptions of a new dolphin. Priority and credit are usually given to Heinrich Julius Lebeck, about whom little is known except that he was probably Dutch, grew up on the Malabar coast and once served as mint master in Batavia (now Djakarta).

Lebeck's account was published in Germany in 1801. The other paper did not appear in the English version of the journal *Asiatick Researches* until 1803, and was written by William Roxburgh, a physician and well-known botanist, who was Superintendent of the Botanical Garden in Calcutta.

In 1969 the Brain Anatomy Institute of the University of Berne organized an expedition to Pakistan and Assam with the express intention of studying the river dolphins. They captured a pair of the animals and transported them to Switzerland as the first step in a series of intensive studies that have made the Institute's Director, Georg Pilleri, the foremost authority on the entire family. Pilleri discovered that Roxburgh's 1803 paper was in fact a reprint from the Indian edition of the same journal originally published in Calcutta in 1801.

Roxburgh also called the Ganges River Dolphin *Delphinus gangetica*. In 1828 René Lesson classified it as *Susu platanista*, going back to Pliny for the species name and adopting a genus based on the Bengali name *susuk*. A few modern taxonomists still know it as *Susu gangetica*, but priority is now generally given to Johann Wagler who, in 1830, tried one further Plinian permutation and made *Platanista* a genus.

Local Names *Susuk* (Bengali), *soosa* (Hindi), *sunsar* (Sindi), *sisumar* (Sanskrit) and *hiho* (Assamese), all of which are apparently onomatopoeic, based on the sound the animal makes as it surfaces to breathe. We choose to describe all the freshwater species as 'river dolphins' and to distinguish each by the name of the major river system in which it is found, and so this is the Ganges River Dolphin.

Description Small; length averages 1.5 m (5 ft) for males, with a maximum of 1.8 m (6 ft), and 1.7 m (5.5 ft) for females, with a maximum of 2.45 m (8 ft); calves are about 75 cm (30 inches) at birth. Weight averages 35 kg (77 lb) for males, with a maximum of 60 kg (132 lb), and 44 kg (97 lb) for females, with a maximum of 84 kg (185 lb).

The Ganges River Dolphin is a small and surprisingly angular animal. The beak is very slender and in an adult female may be as much as 45 cm (18 inches) long, 20 per cent of total body length. The forehead rises steeply from the beak into a small head which ends in a definite constriction at the neck. The body is small and plump, the flippers are large and almost rectangular in shape, and the flukes are very pointed and notched at the centre. Instead of a true fin, there is a long dorsal keel beginning in a raised angular process behind the middle of the back and running all the way to the flukes. There is a similar, shorter keel on the underside of the tailstock.

The colour is a uniform medium grey, grading to light grey on the belly.

Field Identification Apart from the geographical isolation, everything about the Ganges River Dolphin is distinctive.

They are deft swimmers, perfectly at home in strong river currents, usually slow moving but capable of short bursts of speed. Unlike all other cetaceans, which may swim on their sides for short manoeuvres, the river dolphin habitually does so, apparently returning to the upright position only to breathe. In deeper parts of the river this posture is invisible, but in shallow water the dolphins can sometimes be seen swimming along with one broad-fingered flipper in the air and the other clutching at the mud on the bottom, helping to propel the animal along.

There are 3 characteristic modes of breathing. In the first only the melon is visible above the surface and the dolphin exhales with a soft sigh. In the second the animal stretches the head up so that the beak lies on the water line and takes a longer, louder breath. In the third and most active pattern it rises at an angle, showing the entire beak and head above the surface, blowing with a distinct double sound and bending the body sharply so that the tip of the keeled fin shows at the top of a triangular hump before the dolphin dives. The dolphins always roll upright from the usual side-swimming position, breathe, and then somersault down on to their sides again, completely reversing their direction of travel.

An average dive lasts 30–45 seconds, with a minimum of 10 seconds and a maximum of 3 minutes. Perhaps due to the partial decomposition of stomach contents, or to the passage of air through a complex sinus system, the breath of this river dolphin smells unusually bad. On still days in a backwater occupied by a group of dolphins, the air is distinctly foetid.

In turbulent water, or when disturbed by a boat, or sometimes for no apparent reason at all, Ganges River Dolphins leap. They rise out of the water, usually in an upright position, curl over and return head first, sometimes letting the body fall over backwards as they do, so that the upper side of the tail slaps down on the surface with a loud noise. This may well be a warning signal to other dolphins in the area and is usually the only time the tail flukes are seen.

Stranding There are no records of stranding. A dead animal could be identified very easily by its distinctive shape and by the long beak with up to 30 teeth in each side of each jaw. The blowhole is a simple longitudinal slit and the eyes, which have no lenses, are tiny and beadlike.

A unique feature of the skull is the presence of 2 high bony plates, extensions of the maxillary bones, which project upwards and outwards as a crest, almost meeting in front of the blowhole. There are 49–51 vertebrae, all freely articulated, with those in the neck area being relatively large and long. Five of the 10 pairs of ribs are double headed.

Natural History Ganges River Dolphins feed mostly on fish, particularly the catfish *Wallago attu* and *Saccobranchus fossilii*, but also take shrimps (*Palaemon carcinus*) and crabs directly from the muddy bottom. The array of sharp teeth in the long beak makes it possible for the dolphin to grab and hold even quite sizable fish. Pilleri reports seeing a dolphin chasing a carp (*Labeo rohita*) at high speed along the surface. The largest fish found in any stomach was a catfish 35 cm

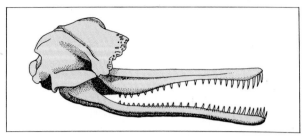

(over 1 foot) long.

Feeding seems to take place mainly during the evening and after dark, which is probably connected more with the habits of the prey than those of the predator, which is active throughout the 24 hours. The dolphin's success in murky water is undoubtedly a result of its skill as an echolocator. The domelike process on the skull forms a highly sensitive sound transmitter and receiver, brought into play as a side-looking sonar system when the dolphin swims along on its flank, sweeping the area ahead of it by nodding the head up and down. While doing this, the jaws are often opened almost at right angles and make a lightning snap around the prey.

Ganges River Dolphins are often seen in pairs, but sometimes congregate into larger feeding groups of 6 or more, usually at favoured river junctions. Mating usually takes place in the autumn, when pairs can sometimes be seen together, face-to-face, rising up out of the water with their flippers interlaced, holding that position by frantic tail work while they copulate; and then falling over and rolling over together at the surface still conjoined. Gestation lasts for about 9 months with calves born between April and July of the following summer.

At all times, while scanning and feeding, the dolphins produce pulsed trains of sound of 45–50 kHz sometimes as high as 380 kHz. There is little doubt that they are highly effective echolocators.

Status Dams and irrigation systems are breaking the rivers of India and Assam up into isolated areas of water and destroying the normal distribution of the dolphins. Some animals are caught accidentally in fishing nets and quickly released, but in Bangladesh they are deliberately hunted for meat and oil.

Distribution The Ganges River Dolphin was once found in all parts of the Ganges, Karnaphuli and Brahmaputra river systems, from the deltas right up into the foothills of the Himalayas. During the monsoon season of late summer, the dolphins still take advantage of the heavy rains to extend their range up into smaller streams and tributaries, retreating to the larger rivers in the dry season.

Their density today is lowest in the delta and estuary areas where human population is highest.

Sources ANDERSON (1878) early monograph, HAQUE et al (1977) general, KASUYA (1972) growth, LEBECK (1801) original description, MIZUE et al (1971) sounds, PILLERI (1970) behaviour, PILLERI (1978) taxonomy, POULTER (1970) sounds, ROXBURGH (1801) true original description.

INDUS RIVER DOLPHIN

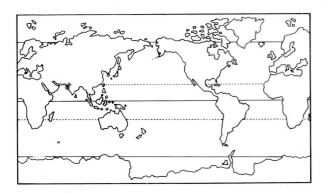

Classification In 1853 David Wallich collected the skull of a dolphin from the Indus and presented it to Sir Richard Owen at the Royal College of Surgeons. Owen was familiar with Roxburgh's specimen from the Ganges and, finding the crests on the new skull to be lower and of a slightly different shape, decided that the Indus dolphins were a variety of *Platanista gangetica* which he called *minor*. In 1859 Edward Blyth at the Indian Museum in Calcutta described 'the skull of a *susu* from the Indus, presented by the late Sir Alexander Burns' as a new species which he called *Platanista indi*.

When Pilleri and his associates first began their investigations they used the species name *gangetica* interchangeably for dolphins from both the Ganges and the Indus. Then in

1971 Pilleri published a detailed analysis of skeletal material from both rivers and concluded that there were sufficient differences to warrant the establishment of separate species. He adopted Blyth's *Platanista indi.*

In 1976 the Dutch taxonomist Peter van Bree pointed out that Owen was the first to describe the difference between the dolphins and that the correct name for the Indus River Dolphin must be *Platanista minor.* Most cetologists agree with van Bree. Owen's type specimen however was destroyed by an air raid on London in 1942 and Blyth's skull has been missing for more than a century, so in 1977 Pilleri proposed that one of the skulls in his collection be considered as the neotype: 'During the past few years attempts have been made to replace the name *Platanista indi* by *Platinista minor* and give Owen (1853) priority for the Indus dolphin. Apart from the dubiousness of such attempts on the part of a not particularly well qualified colleague ... any change in the name is by now completely unnecessary and would run counter to the stability of the zoological system.' Pilleri's view nevertheless remains a minority one.

Local Names There are numerous local names, depending on the dialect in use in each part of the river. We call this species simply the Indus River Dolphin.

Description Small; with dimensions identical with those of the Ganges River Dolphin (*P. gangetica 29*). The external appearance of the Indus River Dolphin is indistinguishable from that of its relative in the Ganges; the lower bony crests on the skull should lead to a less pronounced melon but this is a characteristic which is neither constant nor easy to observe. Pilleri has found that this difference in the basic shape of the skull is reflected in a flattening of the frontal lobes of the brain in the Indian species.

These dolphins seem to have a tendency to swim in circles, more often than not anticlockwise. This may have something to do with an anatomical peculiarity of the blowhole, which is displaced to the left of centre and has a higher ridge along its right hand edge. When the dolphin breaks the surface, it is rolling from an upright position back on to its right side and the prominent ridge on that side of the blowhole is likely to divert water away from, rather than into, the open nostril.

Natural History After years of continuous observation of captive Indus River Dolphins, Pilleri and his associates conclude that the animals remain in perpetual motion and never pause to rest, either on the bottom or at the water surface. They seem, however, to respond to changing weather conditions and, even in the laboratory, show marked reduction in activity and feeding during the approach of storm fronts and in response to fluctuations of barometric pressure. Normally, each dolphin eats 2–3 kg (5–7 lb) of fish a day, sometimes regurgitating the heads and backbones.

Like the Ganges River Dolphin, the Indus species is sometimes found singly, often in pairs and occasionally in larger feeding concentrations. There is some evidence that this species may be more social. Jhabar people catch the dolphins with hoopnets (*kularee*) thrown by a man standing on a wooden tripod in mid-river. The captive animal is then tethered by its flipper or tail to the tripod and soon attracts other dolphins which remain close enough to it for them also to be caught by the fisherman.

The breeding season begins in the spring and involves prolonged chases between pair members which sometimes leave toothmarks on the flanks and tails of both sexes. In quieter moments the dolphins rub their sides together or stroke each other's flippers and flanks with their beaks or tails. Mating takes place in shallow water, the dolphins lying stomach-to-stomach with their beaks and flippers interlaced. This activity often attracts other male bystanders, who may join in and take their turn. Young calves are first seen in early April, so the gestation period is probably 12 months. Calves can be distinguished from adults not only by their size, but by their habit of leaping almost clear of the water in an exaggerated version of the normal breathing pattern each time they surface to blow. When feeding they remain attached to the teats even when their mothers submerge, and they seem to be weaned after as little as 3 months of lactation. At all ages the river dolphins are apparently less playful and curious than their marine relatives, although young are sometimes attracted to passing boats.

In most of the Indus, underwater visibility is restricted to less than 4 cm (1.5 inches) by mud and sediment held in suspension. Normal eyes in this situation are almost useless and the dolphins seem to have adapted accordingly. Their eyes have no lenses, the optic nerve is very thin and eye-muscle nerves are entirely lacking. Although the retina remains, it is almost impossible for such an eye to pick up images. The best it can do is to distinguish between night and day and, if there is any light, possibly determine its direction. This may be all the dolphins need. A total absence of light will tell them when it is time to move into the shallows to feed and, because they swim habitually on one side or the other, the detection of light only by the eye nearest the surface will tell them which way is up and help them to maintain stability.

The Indus River Dolphin compensates for its lack of vision with great acoustic sensitivity. The usual sonar signal consists of a series of short single clicks at a dominant frequency of about 80 kHz. The rate of repetition varies from 10 to over 150 clicks per second depending on activity. These click trains are clearly used for echolocation and are dramatically affected by the introduction of foreign objects into the dolphin's environment. Pilleri found that his captives normally produced 20–40 clicks per second during calm swimming, but that this rate rose to 90 clicks per second when they were actually exploring. They were able to detect a single lead shot just 4 mm (.15 inch) in diameter from a distance of 1.5 m (5 ft) and, when taking bearings on it, would hover in the water making scanning movements with their heads, always ending up with the object at an angle of approximately 30° in front of and below their throats. This highly directional sonar signal seems to originate from the larynx and clearly concentrates largely on the area below the beak. The pattern of the sound field is quite different from that of marine dolphins such as the Bottlenose (*Tursiops truncatus 76*) and is produced by reflection of the signal from the underside of the huge domed crests of the maxillary bones above the beak. The net effect is to set up a particularly sensitive area in front of and below the river dolphin exactly where a fish would best be placed to be picked up by the wide gape. These dolphins have shown that they can easily distinguish their favourite species of fish from an array of similar sizes offered to them many metres away; indicating that they are capable not only of differentiating between frequency patterns, but of remembering these distinctions for long periods of time.

In addition to the sonar signals, Indus River Dolphins also seem to produce communication sounds which last about 0.4 seconds at frequencies ranging from 800 Hz to 16 kHz.

Status The construction of barrages which break up the natural range, and the diversion of water for irrigation systems, both severely threaten the survival of this species.

A survey made in 1974 suggests that there may then have been only 450–1,000 dolphins left in the entire river system.

These numbers, taken together with the fact that about 100 dolphins are caught each year, puts the species at great risk. It would seem imperative that, along with the developments necessary to meet pressing human needs, at least 2 suitable areas be set aside to ensure the survival of these dolphins.

Distribution The Indus River Dolphin was once widespread throughout all the slower-moving parts of all 3,200 km (2,000 miles) of the Indus system. Now that the river has been fragmented by barrages, the dolphins are limited largely to the area between Sukkur and Taunsa, between the latitudes of 24° and 34° north.

Sources BLYTH (1859) taxonomy, GIHR et al (1972) effects of weather, HERALD (1969) field study, HOLLOWAY (1974) status, KASUYA & NISHIWAKI (1975) distribution, OWEN (1853) original description, PILLERI (1970) behaviour, PILLERI et al (1971) sounds, PILLERI & GIHR (1971) rediscovery, PILLERI (1972) brain, PILLERI et al (1976) echolocation, PILLERI (1977) taxonomy, VAN BREE (1976) taxonomy.

Below: breathing and diving sequence showing side-swimming posture underwater

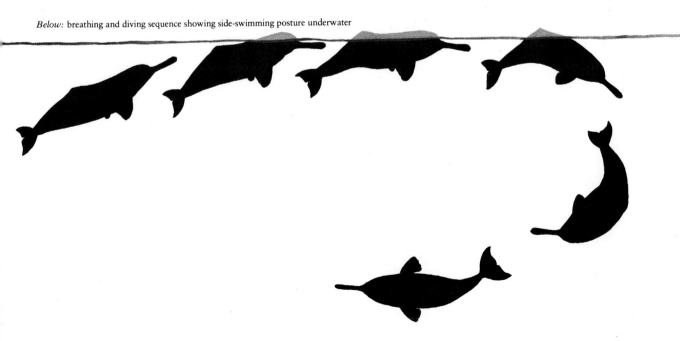

YANGTZE RIVER DOLPHIN

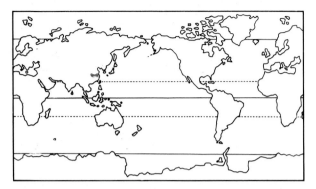

Classification Long known in China, where it is revered as the reincarnation of a drowned princess, this dolphin only came to the attention of the West when a visiting American, Charles M. Hoy, killed one on the shores of Lake Tungt'ing in 1914. He preserved the skull and took it back with him to the United States where he sold it to the Smithsonian Institution.

Gerrit Smith Miller, Curator of Mammals in the United States National Museum, published a description in 1918 of what was obviously a new genus and species of river dolphin. He named the genus *Lipotes* from the Greek *leipo*, left behind,

in reference to its relict status in a small area of China. For the species name he chose *vexillifer* from the Latin *vexillum*, a banner, and the suffix *-fer*, to bear, because he was told by Hoy that the Chinese name translated as 'flag-bearer' and referred to the flaglike appearance of the dorsal fin above the surface of the water.

Local Names The Chinese know this dolphin as *bai ji* or *pei c'hi*, which has nothing to do with flags or banners. It means 'the greyish-white dolphin'. We ignore the mistranslation and refer to this species simply as the Yangtze River Dolphin.

Description Small; length averages 2–2.4 m (7–8 ft). Weight averages 70–80 kg (155–180 lb).

Little was known about this dolphin until the work of the Academia Sinica in Hunan was made available to the West in 1980. There are just 5 skulls in western museums. Until recently all the known illustrations were based on a life-size model in the American Museum of Natural History of a specimen collected by Clifford Pope on the Third American China Expedition of 1931. There is another such model in the British Museum.

The body shape is similar to that of *Platanista*, the other Asian river dolphin, but the Yangtze River Dolphin has a

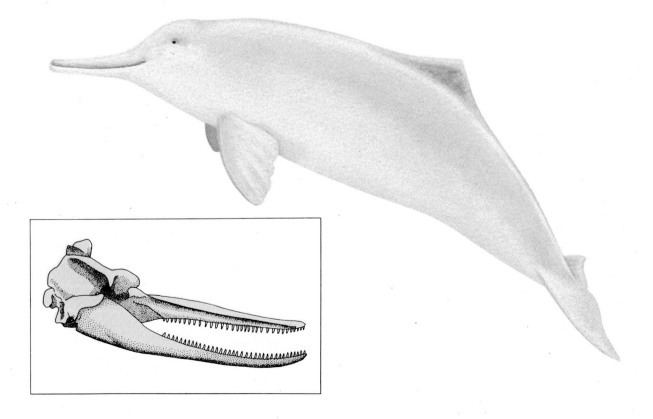

slimmer, more pointed beak which turns distinctly upwards at the tip like that of a duck, more rounded flippers and proportionately larger tail flukes. The fin does not remotely resemble a flag, being solid and fatty, little more than a roughly triangular process or keel along the lower back. The tiny eye is placed surprisingly high on the head and there is a prominent ear opening roughly where the eye would normally be on another dolphin.

The colouring is said to be pale smoky grey, turning almost to white on the stomach.

Field Identification There are no other freshwater cetaceans in China. This species seems to behave much like its relatives, moving rather slowly as a rule and rising to breathe once every 40 seconds. It has a high-pitched blow, a little like a sudden sneeze. It is shy and stays away from boats and river banks, diving on the approach of a boat. The tail flukes are seldom seen.

Stranding There are no records of stranding and it would be unlikely to occur. A dead animal can be identified readily by its shape and by the set of up to 34 uniform peglike teeth on each side of both jaws. Unlike those of *Platanista*, these teeth are the same length all the way along the jaw.

The skull is highly asymmetrical, with an over-developed right side which squeezes the longitudinal slit of the blowhole across to the left. There is, in addition, a most unusual pair of large floating bones or ossified muscles placed one on either side of the blowhole, which apparently help to keep it tightly closed.

Details of the internal anatomy suggest that it might be more closely related to the Amazon River Dolphin (*Inia geoffrensis 32*) than it is to the other Asian species.

Natural History Yangtze River Dolphins seem to be primarily fish eaters – 'a bucketful' of catfish was taken from the stomach of the first specimen – but they probably also use their long thin beaks for probing in the mud after freshwater shrimps. Feeding takes place during the night and early morning.

The usual social unit seems to be a group of 2–6 which may, like other river dolphins, merge into larger congregations at popular feeding sites or when conditions of drought force the animals into closer proximity. During the rainy summer season, the dolphins are said to leave the lakes and muddy mainstream and to venture into the clear water of small tributaries to breed. No details are known of reproductive behaviour.

The eyes are barely functional and the dolphins probably rely on sonar for finding food. Charles Hoy reported that the dolphin he shot 'gave a cry like that of a water buffalo calf' and there are other local accounts of 'peculiar roaring sounds' at night.

Status Population densities everywhere in the middle and lower reaches of the Yangtze are as low as 1 dolphin to every 4 km of river. The fishermen of Hunan believe that 'ill fortune descends on those who molest' their dolphins, but further down stream and in the Yangtze delta a few were taken for medicinal purposes until 1975 when all river dolphins in China were protected by law. Several however still die accidentally on fish hooks and in nets.

Distribution Western specimens were all collected in Lake Tungt'ing in northern Hunan, 1,000 km (more than 600 miles) from the mouth of the Yangtze Kiang (Ch'ang Chiang), but the dolphin has now abandoned that lake and occurs most commonly between Yichang and the river mouth at Shanghai. It does not seem to enter salt water.

Sources BROWNELL & HERALD (1972) review, CHEN et al (1980) ecology, ZNOU et al (1980) physiology, HINTON & PYCRAFT (1922) anatomy, HOY (1923) popular account, MILLER (1918) original description, PILLERI & GIHR (1976) history, POPE (1940) expedition, SHOU CHEN-HUANG (1962) status, SOWERBY (1936) photograph, VAN BREE & PURVES (1975) skull.

Dive sequence of Yangtze River Dolphin

AMAZON RIVER DOLPHIN

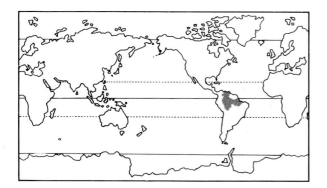

Classification This is probably the only cetacean ever to have been regarded as part of the rightful spoils of war. After his occupation of Portugal in 1807, Napoleon Bonaparte personally despatched Étienne Geoffroy St Hilaire, Professor at the Musée Nationale d'Histoire Naturelle in Paris, to take whatever was worth having from Portuguese museums. He discovered, in Lisbon's Museu da Ajuda, the skull and skin of a dolphin unfamiliar to him. The catalogue showed that it had been collected around 1790 by Alexandre Rodriguez Ferreira in the upper Amazon; and, because the only freshwater dolphin then known to science was the one from the Ganges, St Hilaire took this specimen back with him to Paris. Cuvier took an obviously cursory look at the plunder and classified it as *Delphinus rostratus* along with the Asian river dolphins.

When Henri de Blainville took over Cuvier's chair he also took a longer and more careful look at this specimen. He appreciated that it was different, decided in 1817 to call it *Delphinus geoffrensis* after its most recent liberator; and in 1826 despatched the museum's travelling naturalist Alcide d'Orbigny to South America on the Castelnau Expedition with instructions to find additional specimens. On the Rio Guapore in the Bolivian Amazon, d'Orbigny finally succeeded after great difficulty in catching a river dolphin. This fresh specimen looked so different from the museum skin, which had been painted to simulate its natural colour, that he decided it must be a different animal and named it *Inia boliviensis*, basing his new genus on the Guarayo Indian name for the dolphin.

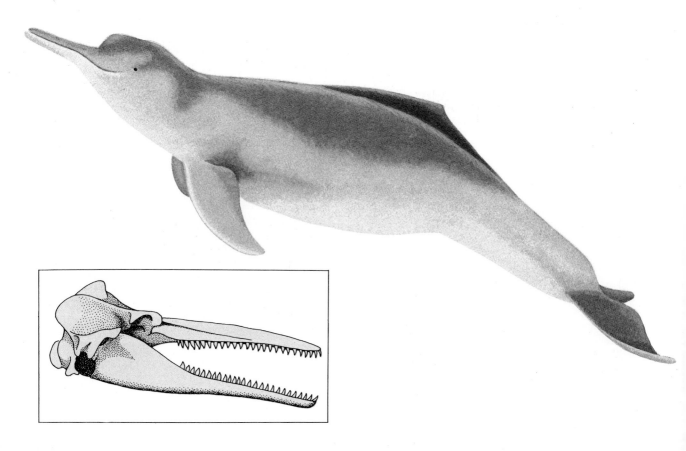

Three Amazon River Dolphins supporting an injured animal and carrying it to the surface

In 1855 Paul Gervais concluded that both St Hilaire's and d'Orbigny's specimens were not only the same animal, but were also identical with a third specimen brought back from Brazil by the German naturalists Spix and von Martius in 1831 and named *Delphinus amazonicus*. Gervais lumped them all together as *Inia geoffrensis*, and they have remained that way for over a century.

In 1968, and again in 1976, Georg Pilleri and his team from the Brain Anatomy Institute in Berne made expeditions to the Beni region of Bolivia and captured a total of 10 river dolphins. A detailed study of these has led Pilleri back to d'Orbigny's original distinction and to a resurrection of *Inia boliviensis* as a separate species. He bases his decision on the fact that the Bolivian animals seem to have less robust skulls, a few more teeth and a smaller number of bones in each finger. Using techniques as microscopic and mathematical as Pilleri's, it is possible to identify geographical variations of almost any animal, but many taxonomists feel that these do not constitute valid specific differences.

The best interim solution seems to be to recognize that there is variation within the vast Amazon area and that this species might be split into perhaps 3 separate subspecies. In the main Amazon basin there is *Inia geoffrensis geoffrensis*; in the upper waters of the Madeira, south-west of the Amazon, *I. g. boliviensis* (D'ORBIGNY 1834), and in the Orinoco river system, north of the Amazon, *I. g. humboldtiana* (PILLERI & GIHR 1977).

Local Names The Guarayo call this dolphin *inia*, but there are many other names, including *sisi* (Chapucara), *ihui* (Baure), *puchca* (Jtonama), *cochoicama* (Pacaguara), *pathi* (Movima), *nituya* (Canichana), *aico* (Moxo) and *uyara* (Chavante). The Portuguese settlers know it as *bouto* or *boto* and to the Spanish speakers it is *bufeo*. In English it has somewhat confusingly been called the pink porpoise, but we prefer to know it, in all its guises, simply as the Amazon River Dolphin.

Description Small; length averages 1.8 m (6 ft) for males, with a maximum of about 2.7 m (9 ft), and 1.8 m (6 ft) for females, with a maximum of about 2.4 m (8 ft); calves are about 80 cm (30 inches) at birth. Weight averages about 60 kg (132 lb), with a maximum of about 100 kg (220 lb).

The average size is not much greater than that of the Indian species, but the maximum length and weight are both higher, giving the impression of an altogether more burly animal. It is likely that most of the animals captured for measurement in the Amazon have been less than fully grown.

The beak is less pointed, more sturdy and dolphinlike. The head has a distinct melon and is highly mobile; the neck constriction is even more marked than in any of its relatives. The flippers are very large, curve to a point and have a wavy finger line along the trailing edge. The dorsal fin is a long fleshy keel rising to its greatest height behind the midpoint of the body, but is nowhere as pointed or triangular as that of *Platanista* or *Lipotes*. The ear opening is large, but the eyes are very small, although clearly more functional than those of the Asian river dolphins. The larger cheeks however prevent downward vision and could account for the fact that this species often swims upside down.

The colouring is characteristic and at times almost unbelievable. Young Amazon River Dolphins are a bluish dark grey, but as they mature the grey tends to be replaced by a ruddy colour which gradually spreads from the undersides up on to the back. Some older dolphins keep a bluish-grey mantle along the head and keel, but many are completely flesh or shell pink. We have often been startled, in some quiet black water lagoon away from the main stream, by the sudden appearance of a vivid, almost cosmetic, pink hump alongside our boat. It seems to us that dolphins in black rivers like the Negro and Japura are the most shocking pink, those in the muddy Solimoens are intermediate, while dolphins living in clear white water tributaries like the Tapajos, tend to be altogether darker. It is possible that the skin colour, at least along the back, may be influenced by light, becoming tanned and darker in the sun. All the pink colours disappear soon after death.

Field Identification The only possible confusion which can arise is between the Amazon River Dolphin and the freshwater representative of the ocean dolphin family, the Estuarine Dolphin (*Sotalia fluviatilis 42*). Both species occur together throughout the length and breadth of the river

Dive sequence

system. We have seen them right up the Rio Maranon, some distance beyond Iquitos in Peru, over 4,000 km (2,600 nautical miles) from the sea; but there is never any problem in telling them apart.

The Estuarine Dolphin is smaller and behaves much like its marine relatives; rolling over at the surface to show a curved sharklike fin; often leaping out of the water, and being altogether more active and more playful than the true river dolphins.

The Amazon River Dolphin is slower, larger and more decorous in its behaviour. The first sight of a long beak and domed forehead breaking the surface of muddy water in the delta, moving slowly and horizontally along as it breathes, is reminiscent of an alligator or cayman. We find that it often takes several hours to convince newcomers to the river that what they are seeing is not a reptile at all, but a mammal. Later in the evenings, when the dolphins are more active – their strong spouts become visible in the cooling air and they bend higher up out of the water to show the full blush of their colouring – there is little room for doubt.

Most of the time only the melon and the blowhole appear above the water, followed by part of the long dorsal keel, just before the dolphin submerges; but in deeper water or when actively feeding, it lifts the beak up level with the surface and then seems to throw the head down, bending almost double and showing a pyramidal pink hump in a jack-knife before making a vertical dive. The normal breathing interval is every 30–40 seconds, but it can vary between 5 and 120 seconds. The blow is slow and deliberate, ranging from a 2-second sighing sound to a shorter sneezelike snort; the *bouto* of the Portuguese name is a reasonable imitation of the shorter sound. We have learned to associate the long 'glide-blow' with a leisurely dolphin showing only its melon and the shorter 'roll-blow' with a more active animal. We have only rarely seen one jump clear of the water.

The Amazon River Dolphin often associates with the Estuarine Dolphin and is frequently accompanied by a black cormorant, presumably because they all feed on the same kinds of fish. The Amazon River Dolphin is largely indifferent to small boats, often surfacing right alongside us as we paddle quietly along, but it sometimes seems to be positively attracted to the sound of an outboard engine or of an oar slapping on the water. In several parts of the river the dolphins are said to co-operate with local fishermen, coming to their call and helping to herd fish from deeper water into their seine nets in the shallows.

Stranding There are no records of stranding. These dolphin

are very much at home in the shallows. During the flood season, when the rivers overflow their banks and flood the *varzea* (floodland), the dolphins travel up to 100 km (60 miles) from the main channel. We have found small groups splashing quite comfortably amongst the buttress roots of giant forest trees in water barely deep enough to cover them.

Identification of a dead Amazon River Dolphin is easy. The shape and colour are distinctive and there is a highly characteristic arrangement of about 50 short sensory bristles on the lower jaw and another 30–40 on the top of the beak. All of them point towards the tail. The teeth too are distinctive. The front ones are sharp and conical, while those at the back are flattened, like molars, and obviously adapted for chewing. This is a characteristic unique amongst cetaceans, who generally swallow their food whole, and seems to have arisen in this species to help it deal with some of the most common Amazon catfish, which have heavily armoured skins.

In dolphins of the main stream, there are normally 26–28 teeth on each side of both jaws (a total of about 110), but the Bolivian subspecies more commonly has a larger number of teeth, perhaps 33 to a side (giving a possible total of 132), while dolphins in the Orinoco have as few as 25 in each half row (or a total of little over 100).

The skull is asymmetrical, with the blowhole displaced to the left, and there are sometimes more teeth on the right side of each jaw than there are on the left. The skull we illustrate is of a dolphin from Manaus on the upper Amazon. All the vertebrae, including those of the neck, are free and there are always 13 pairs of ribs. The sternum is a single massive plate of bone.

Natural History Amazon River Dolphins usually feed on fish 10–20 cm (4–8 inches) long, although we have sometimes seen a dolphin at the surface juggling with a much larger meal, nodding its head up and down to get the fish into the best position for swallowing. Dissection of captured specimens has shown that their stomachs contain up to 5 kg (11 lb) of assorted fish, usually characins (including the piranha) and armoured catfish. The intestines are very long and thin and it seems likely that the large heads and bones of most fish are simply regurgitated.

Dolphins are most often seen swimming in deep shady water near the banks of quiet tributaries (where fish tend to gather), or at points where a stream joins the main river, producing a visible line of demarcation between the different coloured bodies of water. This is where most of the feeding appears to take place, although the presence of crabs and shrimps in some dolphins' stomachs suggests that they may also use their sensory bristles to nuzzle crustaceans out of the muddy river bottoms. We have on occasion seen dolphins in shallow water swimming upside down, perhaps for this very purpose. Although the eye is small, the oculomotor nerve is still well developed in this species and there seems little doubt that they see quite well, perhaps even having colour vision. Quite often a dolphin surfacing near one of our boats will lift its beak and eyes up out of the water and apparently give us a good visual examination.

Amazon River Dolphins are often found in pairs, distributed throughout the Amazon basin at a density of roughly one pair per square kilometre of water (4–5 animals per square mile). Little is known of their reproductive behaviour, but many seem to give birth between July and September in the Amazon.

In most parts of the river, people treat the dolphins with elaborate caution and respect, believing that at night they turn themselves into beautiful women who roam the banks in search of hapless men to seduce and drown, but in areas where the taboos have broken down they are sometimes hunted and when caught, are tethered in the shallows to attract other dolphins. There are several reports of dolphins coming to the aid of injured companions. On one occasion an adult followed for an hour behind a boat carrying a captive calf.

Although the Amazon River Dolphins seem on the whole to be less playful than most marine species, we have seen younger animals in a quiet lagoon involved in what looked like a game with the empty floating pod from a Brazil nut tree. Each in turn would hold the pod in its jaws and swim with it underwater while being chased by the others. It is probably a mistake to assume that the generally more leisurely pace of this species indicates a lesser intelligence.

The sounds of this dolphin are well known. It is clearly an echolocator, producing trains of broad-band clicks in single, double or treble combinations at a rate of 30–80 per second. These are highly directional, producing a narrow cone-shaped sonar beam directly in front of the beak and have a complex harmonic structure of 25–150 kHz. When clicking, the dolphin moves its head to and fro in a pattern of auditory scanning made possible by the flexibility of its neck. In captivity it has been shown that the dolphins can detect a copper wire 1 mm (.03 inch) in diameter. In addition to these sonar clicks, there are at least 10 other common sounds, including an audible screech that may be used as an alarm call.

Status This species is common. It is difficult to spend a day anywhere in the Amazon basin without seeing it. It has in the past been protected by local superstitions, including the belief that retaliatory blindness results from looking at a lamp burning oil from the dolphin, but as settlers without these old taboos come to live along the river banks, a great number of dolphins are being killed. Many of these are lost because they sink after being shot. It may not be too long before they become as scarce as the now rare river manatee (*Trichechus inunguis*).

A further threat is posed by the increasingly large number of dolphins being captured alive for exhibition. In the last decade

Above: head of Amazon River Dolphin showing characteristic hairs
Below: hump of Amazon River Dolphin preceding dive

almost 100 were taken to the United States alone, but at the latest count only 17 of those remain alive.

Distribution The dolphins occur everywhere, from the channels of the Amazon delta up to headwaters not far from the Andes. During those seasons when the river falls, the dolphins are confined to the main stream and its major tributaries, but between January and May, when the rivers rise as much as 10 m (over 30 ft), the streams become hundreds of kilometres wide and whole areas of riverside and even canopy forest are opened up for aquatic habitation. Fish move into this *varzea* to breed and the dolphins follow them to feed. One of the major mysteries is how they manage to navigate through the forests and find their way unerringly back to the river banks. When the waters fall, as they do in a matter of days, they trap thousands of fish in isolated pools, but the dolphins are seldom if ever caught.

There is complete and continuous connection between the Amazon of Brazil and the upper Madeira in Bolivia and it is difficult to understand how or why the population in the latter area could have become isolated and sufficiently distinct to warrant the suggestion that they may have acquired separate specific status. It is easier to appreciate distinctions arising in the Orinoco river system. There is a connection between the Amazon and the Orinoco through the Casiquiare canals, but dolphins apparently rarely make the transition.

Sources ALLEN & NEILL (1957) general, CALDWELL et al (1966) sounds, CURTIS (1963) captivity, DE BLAINVILLE (1817) original description, FERREIRA (1791) first specimen, LAYNE (1958) behaviour, LAYNE & CALDWELL (1964) behaviour in captivity, NORRIS et al (1972) sounds, PENNER & MURCHISON (1970) echolocation, PILLERI (1969) general, PILLERI & GIHR (1977) in Bolivia and Orinoco.

LA PLATA RIVER DOLPHIN

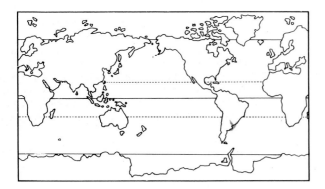

Classification This is one of the many species to have been discovered by an amateur, Christophe Paulin de la Poix, Comte de Freminville. He dabbled in archaeology, but was first and foremost a yachtsman who organized his own expeditions under sail to Spitzbergen, the Caribbean, West Africa and South America. At the mouth of the Rio de la Plata, near Montevideo, in 1842 he collected an unusual looking dolphin and took the skull back with him to Paris.

At the Musée National d'Histoire Naturelle, Gervais had just succeeded de Blainville. Gervais and d'Orbigny decided jointly in 1844 that the skull belonged to a new species *Delphinus blainvillei.*

At the time their paper was published, Gray was just beginning his report on the voyage of HMS *Erebus* and HMS

Terror. In it he described a complete specimen of the Blainville dolphin which was clearly no relation of the Common Dolphin, so in 1846 he created a new genus for it. He called it *Pontoporia blainvillei* from the Greek *pontos*, a sea, and *poria*, a crossing, or a way of travelling, because it was the first member of the new family of river dolphins to be found in freshwater and in the open sea.

In the meantime, the French had made a further expedition to *Amerique Meridionale* and returned with a specimen from the banks of Lagoa dos Patos on the southern coast of Brazil. This allowed Gervais and d'Orbigny to reclassify their first skull and, not yet having received Gray's paper, they called it *Stenodelphis blainvillei*, from the Greek *stenos*, narrow, presumably referring to the long narrow beak.

For more than a century the French genus was used in much of the literature, but Gray's priority is now recognized and all the river dolphins in the region of the Plate estuary are today known as *Pontoporia blainvillei.*

Local Names Fishermen on the coast of Uruguay know this dolphin by the Spanish names of *tonina* or *Franciscana*. We choose, in spite of its frequently marine habitat, to call this species the La Plata River Dolphin.

Description Small; length averages 1.5 m (5 ft) for males and 1.6 m (5.25 ft) for females, with a maximum of 1.8 m (6 ft) for both sexes; calves are about 50 cm (20 inches) at birth. Weight averages 36 kg (80 lb) for males and 45 kg (100 lb)

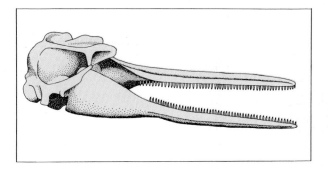

for females with maximum for both sexes of about 50 kg (110 lb); calves are about 7 kg (15 lb) at birth.

This species is an altogether smaller animal than the Amazon River Dolphin (*Inia geoffrensis 32*). The beak is very long and narrow with a large number of uniform teeth. The head is domed and narrows to a conspicuous neck. The blowhole is crescent-shaped, like that of most marine dolphins, instead of the longitudinal slit common to other freshwater species. Unlike other members of the family, the La Plata River Dolphin also lacks the long fleshy dorsal keel, but has a true fin, tall, curved and placed on the centre of the back. The eyes are still small, but better developed than those of even the Amazon species. It cannot be coincidental that this animal happens to live in the least turbid water.

The colour is soft, buffy ochre brown, grading to a paler mustard brown on the belly. A few older individuals become so pale and bleached that they are known in the estuary as 'white ghosts'.

Field Identification The partly marine habitat of the La Plata River Dolphin brings it into contact with several saltwater species and raises the problem of identification at sea.

Like the other freshwater species, this one is relatively inconspicuous. It is a quiet breather, seldom rolling or splashing and, in anything but very calm conditions, is almost impossible to detect. It breathes once every 30–40 seconds as a rule, but can dive for longer periods.

The usual speed is 4–7 kph (2–4 knots), but it will sometimes come to the bow of small boats. Its curiosity often brings it close enough to boats and to the shore for the very long beak to be seen and to leave identification in no doubt.

Stranding There are no records of stranding, but dolphins drowned in nets deployed by local shark fishermen are sometimes washed ashore. Identification is easy because of the long beak which looks like that of a garfish. In it there are 50–60 sharp, slender teeth on each side of both jaws, making a total of up to 240. This is more than can be found in any other cetacean, with the exception of an occasional particularly well-endowed Spinner Dolphin (*Stenella longirostris 70*). The neck vertebrae are all unfused and the first 4 pairs of ribs are double headed.

Natural History La Plata River Dolphins feed on squid and fish, particularly the species *Porichthys porosissimus* and *Cynoscion striatus*. They also clearly probe the mud and into crevices in rocks with their long beaks, because the stomach contents of several captured animals have contained shrimp and octopus beaks.

These dolphins live in small, tightly-knit family groups of 3 or 4. One report describes the attempts of a female to free her calf from the mesh of a shark net: she held the calf by the tail, gripping it tightly enough to leave her tooth marks in the flesh and continued to struggle until she too became enmeshed in the net and drowned.

Little is known of reproductive behaviour except that these dolphins reach maturity at a length of about 1.4 m (almost 5 ft) and that calves seem to be born between October and January (early and mid-summer) each year.

The La Plata River Dolphin is presumably an echolocator, but the fact that this species is frequently caught in broad mesh nets suggests that it relies less on this sense than its relatives in muddier river water.

Status Several hundred (one estimate puts the number as high as 1,500) La Plata River Dolphins are taken each year along the coasts of Uruguay and southern Brazil. Most of these are caught accidentally by shark nets in the Los Cerros area of Uruguay, but some fishermen may also set gill nets deliberately for the dolphins. The meat and oil are used locally. While nothing is known of the population size, this relatively large catch must be a matter of grave concern. The dolphins seem to be becoming less common, but may be saved by the fact that the coastal shark fisheries are closing down in favour of operations from larger boats farther offshore.

Distribution This species still qualifies as a river dolphin by the fact that it is found in the lower reaches of the Rio Paraguay and Rio Uruguay and throughout the partly saline La Plata river estuary.

During summer, it travels north and south along the coasts of Uruguay and Argentina, entering lagoons, but apparently never venturing more than 40 km (21 nautical miles) from the shore. The northern limit of this long narrow 3,000-km (1,600-nautical-mile) range seems to be the edge of Sao Paulo state in Brazil at about 25° of latitude; and the southernmost records are those from the Valdez Peninsula at about 43° south.

Sources BROWNELL (1975) biology, BROWNELL & NESS (1970) general, FITCH & BROWNELL (1971) feeding, GERVAIS & D'ORBIGNY (1844) original description, GRAY (1846) taxonomy, KENYON (1971) status, PILLERI (1971) distribution, PILLERI (1971) behaviour, PRADERI (1979) in Uruguay, VAN ERP (1969) in Uruguay.

Family Six–Monodontidae

This family, created by Gray in 1821, contains just 2 genera, each with 1 species. Both are arctic animals, confined to the area between the icepack and the 10°C (50°F) isotherm.

Each of these two medium-sized whales is distinctive, but they have much in common. Their body forms are similar, with rounded foreheads, flat faces, and constrictions at the neck which reflect the free articulation of all cervical vertebrae and the great mobility of the head. Neither has throat grooves or a dorsal fin. The flippers of both are short, broad and rounded, with a tendency to curl upward at the tips. Both species produce calves that are very much darker than the adults, but neither presents any real problems of identification:

Map Key Both species are found only in the Arctic.

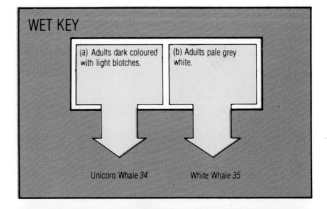

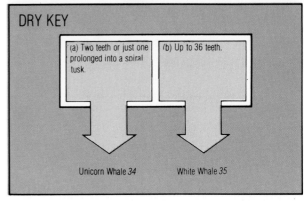

UNICORN WHALE (NARWHAL)

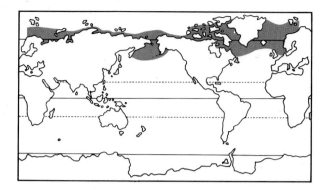

Classification Linnaeus never saw one of these whales, but he was familiar with the tusk and with the description of early explorers. He included it in the 1758 edition of *Systema Naturae* and called it 'one-tooth, one-horn' i.e. *Monodon monoceros* from the Greek *monos* single, *odous*, gen. *odontos*, a tooth, and *keras*, a horn.

Local Names *Kaipuuliak* (Umkchi), *kallilugruk* (Alaskan Eskimo), *kelleluak-kakortok* (Greenland Eskimo) and *tugalik* (Inuit). *Illhval* (Icelandic), *edinovog* (Russian), *eenhornis* (Dutch), *itsu-kaku* (Japanese), *lighval* (Norwegian). The Norwegians also call it *narwhal* because it has the blotched appearance of a body, long drowned, floating bloated at the surface, and this gruesome label has been widely adopted in *narhvalus* (Icelandic), *Narwal* (German) and *narval* (French). We have revived the historical and more evocative name of Unicorn Whale.

Description Medium; length averages 4.7 m (15–16 ft) for males excluding the tusk, with a possible maximum of 6.2 m

(over 20 ft); the longest known tusk was another 2.7 m (9 ft); females average 4 m (13 ft), with a possible maximum of 5.1 m (17 ft); calves are about 1.5 m (5 ft) at birth. Weight averages about 1,600 kg (1.8 tons) for males, with a maximum of 1,800 kg (2 tons), and about 900 kg (1 ton) for females, with a maximum of 1,600 kg (1.8 tons); calves are about 80 kg (180 lb) at birth.

The body shape is cylindrical, with a blunt head and a tiny mouth showing no sign of a beak. The flippers are small and rounded, with a tilt at the top. There is no dorsal fin, but there is a series of low bumps, no more than 5 cm (2 inches) high along the midline of the lower back.

Calves are a dark blue grey colour at birth, but this changes with age to dark olive brown and breaks up into blotched leopard-spotting in adults. Patches of white first begin to appear around the anus and spread up the flanks as the whale grows. At maturity the belly is completely white, while the back, sides and the upper surface of the flukes are variegated. The contrast between dark back and pale belly is most marked in old males, the ones with the largest teeth.

In the males alone, 1 of 2 simple teeth grows out through a hole in the upper lip to form the amazing spiral tusk.

Field Identification The only other medium-sized whale in Arctic waters is the White Whale (*Delphinapterus leucas 35*) which is all white or very pale grey, so identification is not a problem. Unicorn Whales are found in small groups, breaking the surface with their distinctive blotched backs every 40–50 seconds. The blow is low and indistinct, but, when breathing, these whales have the habit of tossing their heads sharply up above the surface showing, if the animal is an adult male, the conspicuous tusk. In both sexes the series of low bumps on the back produces a distinct and visible ridge as the animal moves through the water. Females and young are sometimes mis-

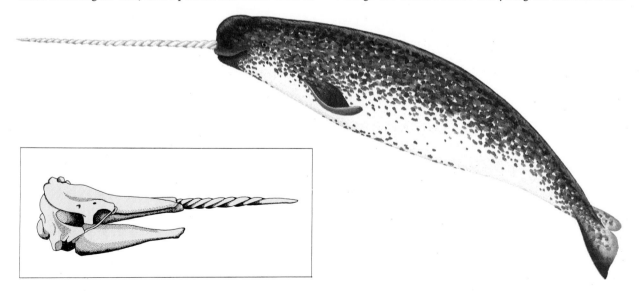

taken for seals, but all seals, even the grey seal (*Halichoerus grypus*) which looks spotted on land, tend to become sleek and black in the water.

As a rule, Unicorn Whales are shy and difficult to approach by boat. The only time we have managed to get a really good look at one on the surface was when we found an adult male squabbling noisily with several walrus (*Odobenus rosmarus*) at an ice hole.

Stranding This species is rarely stranded; a dead Unicorn Whale should be easy to identify by its colour and by its teeth. In embryonic animals there are 2 pairs of teeth in the upper jaw. The hind ones always remain rudimentary, buried in the gum, but the front pair go through some extraordinary changes. The left tooth keeps growing in a spiral which, in an adult male, breaks through the upper lip and may continue until it is well over 2 m (7 ft) long. Occasionally the right tooth develops in the same way to produce a double tusk, but this is rare. The abundance of skulls with 2 horns in museum collections is produced by the preference of collectors for these oddities. They are nowhere common. It is said that when the great Victorian anatomist Sir Richard Owen was first shown a skull with 2 tusks in a Dutch Museum, he firmly declared it to be a fake.

Sometimes females may also have 1, or even 2, shorter tusks. In all cases, male or female, left or right, the teeth are embedded 20–30 cm (more than 1 ft) deep in the skull and grow in a sinistral spiral, which is an anti-clockwise curl when looking (as the whale does) down the tusk toward the tip. The average weight of one of these horns is about 10 kg (over 20 lb), and on the living animal it is filled with a spongy core rich in blood vessels. There are between 50 and 55 vertebrae, all separate.

Natural History Stomach contents reveal that Unicorn Whales eat squid, crabs, shrimps and fish. The most common species of fish seem to be flounders or flatfish and Arctic cod (*Boreogadus saida*). The tusks are always worn smooth at the tip and may sometimes be used to dig for food. Divers working on a rig near Baffin Island in the Canadian Arctic have seen male Unicorn Whales ripping long trenches in the sea floor. This tusking worries members of the oil industry, who are concerned for their pipes, but it may not be a regular or important part of the whales' behaviour and is certainly not essential to their survival. The females feed quite effectively without entrenching tools.

Unicorn Whales certainly occur around the icepack and may from time to time be forced to break their way through thin ice to breathe. It has been suggested that the tusks may have developed for this purpose, but it seems more likely that they serve as secondary sexual characteristics, emphasizing masculinity and playing a prominent part in aggressive and courtship displays. Mating seems to take place in early spring. Gestation lasts for 15 months and lactation for another 18–20, which means that calves can only be produced, at the most, once every 3 years.

The usual social unit is a group of 6–10 centred on an adult male. During periods of migration, groups may amalgamate into very much larger travelling herds.

Unicorn Whales are highly vocal, producing clicks, squeals, growls, and whistling sounds. The clicks are narrow band pulsed sounds with a frequency of 15–24 kHz. These could be sonar pulses, but they seem to show no variation with approach to obstacles. They are often heard through the hulls of wooden ships as 'growling sounds'. Many of the calls are clearly communicative; mothers are known to keep in contact with their calves by means of a soft low tone.

Peter Beamish of the Marine Ecology Laboratory in Nova Scotia has come up with a fascinating notion for the adaptive significance of Unicorn teeth. He noticed that the tusks of captive males throbbed in a disturbing way when the whales were producing their highest frequencies, and he suggests that they may function as wave guides which channel the sounds and focus them into tight directional beams. It is possible that the animal with the longest tusk, or the one best able to place the tip of its tusk closest to an opponent's head, could produce considerable discomfort in animals such as these with highly sensitive hearing. This opens up the possibility of rival male Unicorn Whales fighting acoustic duels, jousting and lashing at each other with their sonic lances.

Status Some estimates of the total world population place it as high as 20,000, but this must soon dwindle as a result of catches greater than the natural annual increase. Inuit people have always taken Unicorn Whales by harpoon from kayaks in deep water or by driving them ashore in shallow bays. The red meat was fed to sled dogs, the sinews used for sewing and the skin and blubber saved for a delicacy known as *muktuk*. Today, sleds have been replaced by snowmobiles, harpoons by high-powered modern rifles, and the whales are taken only for the curio value of their ivory.

Unicorn Whales have already disappeared from the northeastern end of their range in Novaya Zemlya and Zemlya Frantsa Iosifa (Franz Josef Land), presumably as a result of over-hunting, and those of the Canadian and Greenland Arctic areas could well go the same way. There are legal limits to the catch, but as many as 3 or 4 are hit and lost for every whale successfully taken.

Distribution Unicorn Whales were once found throughout the deep water area of the high Arctic, but today the distribution is patchy, with isolated concentrations of whales that migrate along the continental coasts synchronously with the seasonal pulse of the icepack. They do not enter rivers as readily as the White Whale (*Delphinapterus leucas 35*).

Unicorn Whales are now rare around Iceland and have not been seen in the shallow Beaufort Sea or in southern Hudson Bay. The normal southern limit of their range seems to be along the coast of Labrador in the Atlantic and across the Aleutian chain in the Pacific, but there are reports of isolated strandings from the coasts of Britain and the Netherlands.

Sources DART (1969) economics, DAVIS & FINLEY (1969) status, FORD & FISHER (1978) sounds, KEMPER (1979) status, LINNAEUS (1758) original description, MANSFIELD et al (1975) in Canada, REEVES (1977) general, SERGEANT (1979) in Canada, WATKINS et al (1971) sounds, YABLOKOV (1979) in Soviet Union.

WHITE WHALE (BELUGA)

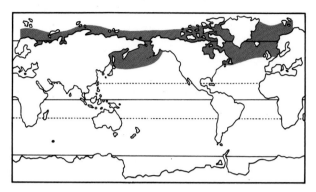

Classification Peter Simon Pallas was a German author and naturalist who travelled extensively in Asia. Between 1768 and 1774 he lived in Russia, became a confidant of the

Empress Catherine, founded the Museum at St Petersburg and made several expeditions to Siberia. On one of these he watched people on the Sea of Kara at the mouth of the Ob River harpooning a perfectly white whale. Pallas described both the hunt and the animal graphically and classified it as *Delphinus leucas* from the Greek *leukos*, white.

During the next century white whales were reported from the Orkney Islands, Greenland and Canada and described variously as *Balaena albicans*, *Catodon candicans* and *Phocoena albus*. Lacépède, in 1804, drew particular attention to the lack of a dorsal fin and devised the new genus *Delphinapterus* from the Greek *apterygos*, without wings. Flower, in 1885, recognized the priority of Pallas's name and put the binomial together as *Delphinapterus leucas*.

It has been suggested that in the Sea of Okhotsk *D. l. leucas* is replaced by a larger subspecies *D. l. dorofeevi* (BARABASH & KLUMOV 1935); and in the Barents Sea by a smaller version

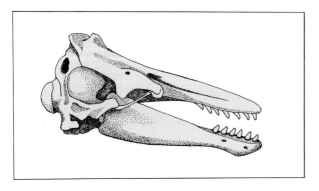

D. l. marisalbi (OSTROUMOV 1935). There is however little hard biometrical evidence to justify these divisions in the light of the wide and highly complex distribution of this whale.

One disquieting note was introduced in 1822 when the skull of a young White Whale was presented to the British Museum by Captain P. P. King of the Royal Navy after a survey voyage. The problem was that his survey was made in New Holland, which happens to be along the tropical coast of Western Australia. Not knowing what else to do with it, John Edward Gray called it *Delphinus kingii*. It is now known as *Delphinapterus kingii*, but suspicions remain that the specimen was simply mislabelled in 1822.

Local Names Aboriginal names include *pechuga* (Ainu), *bechurinka* (Kuril), *iina* (Koryak), *pukhzak* (Chukotsk), *puuliak* (Chukchi) and *zatcha* (Kamchatka). Most Indo-European names refer to the white colour: *marsouin blanc* (French), *hvidvisk* (Norwegian), *vitval* (Swedish), *shiro iruka* (Japanese), *Weisswal* (German) and *witvis* (Dutch). In Russian it is known as *beluga* (white one), and for some time now that has been the most common name in English and several other languages. The same name is, however, also given to the great white sturgeon (*Acipenser* sp.) and to its caviar and, on occasion, also to the Common Dolphin (*Delphinus delphis 75*) and the Bottlenose Dolphin (*Tursiops truncatus 76*).

To avoid unnecessary confusion, we prefer to know it simply and distinctively as the White Whale.

Description Medium; length averages 4.26 m (14 ft) for males, with a possible maximum of 6 m (20 ft), and 3.9 m (13 ft) for females, with a possible maximum of 5 m (17 ft); calves are about 1.2 m (4 ft) at birth. Weight averages 640 kg (1,400 lb) for males, with a possible maximum of 1,300 kg (3,000 lb), and 400 kg (890 lb) for females, with a possible maximum of 900 kg (2,000 lb); calves are about 45 kg (100 lb) at birth.

The White Whale is similar in general shape to the Unicorn Whale (*Monodon monoceros 34*), but smaller and more rotund. In relation to the plump body, the head looks small and is very rounded. There is the beginning of a beak below the steep forehead and a marked constriction at the level of the mobile neck. The flippers are short and wide and always curl up at the rounded tips. There is no dorsal fin, but where it

would normally be in a dolphin there is a short raised ridge just a few centimetres high. The tail flukes are deeply notched and frequently asymmetrical.

The colour varies enormously with age. Calves are liver coloured at birth and remain so throughout the first year. During the second year they become a deep marbled blue grey; and over the following 3 years this slowly fades as pigment is lost from the skin until, at the age of about 6, the entire body is a creamy white colour. In adult whales, traces of pigment may remain on the edges of the flippers and flukes.

Field Identification It is probably easier to identify this species than any other. The colour, the lack of a fin and the limited distribution in the Arctic alone, make it highly unlikely that White Whales will be confused with any other species. To make it even simpler, White Whales have a highly characteristic way of moving. They swim in a slow and stately fashion at the surface, with a gentle undulating movement, breathing once or twice a minute. The blow is steamy and about a metre high, but tends to be thin and often indistinct. Dives usually last from 5 to 15 minutes, although a White Whale which swam up the Rhine in 1966 was seen (perhaps under pressure) to submerge for as long as 70 minutes.

Stranding This species is rarely stranded. A beached whale is easily identifiable by its shape and colour and by its teeth. There are up to 11 (normally 10) sturdy, conical teeth on each side of the upper jaw and up to 8 or 9 similar ones on each side of the lower jaw. A total of 32 teeth is common. Sometimes a few of the hindmost teeth in an adult whale have more than one cusp; as though they were about to become specialized as grinders. This may have some connection with the high proportion of crustaceans in the White Whale's diet. The skull we illustrate is that of an immature whale from our own collection.

The blowhole is displaced slightly to the left and there are 50–51 separate vertebrae.

Natural History White Whales are most often found in shallow water feeding along the bottom. They live on a mixed diet of about 25 kg (55 lb) per day of crustaceans and schooling fish, most often capelin (*Mallotus villosus*), char (*Salvelinus alpinus*), sand lance (*Ammodytes americanus*) and several species of cod. The calves feed largely on shrimps, crabs and annelid worms (*Nereis vivens*).

Like the Unicorn Whale (*Monodon monoceros 34*), White Whales venture right up to the ice, but they seem to spend more time actually under the pack. The broad top of the head forms an excellent cushion for pushing up amongst the floes to breathe. White Whales have been seen to break their way through solid ice as thick as 10 cm (4 inches).

Social life is based on pods of up to 10 whales centred on a female with several young of various ages. They can often be seen swimming along in single file behind her. Mothers are highly protective of their young and are invariably caught with them by Inuit hunters. There are also exclusively masculine groups of 3–15 which merge with the harem groups only during the breeding season. During migrations from the feeding grounds in the north, White Whales sometimes congregate in vast autumn herds which are hundreds or even thousands strong.

Sexual maturity is reached between the fifth and eighth years and mating usually takes place in spring. Gestation lasts 14 months and calving occurs in the warmer shallow waters of estuaries and rivers in mid-summer. Although the breeding cycle is normally 2 years long, suckling may continue for more than a year, extending the calving interval to 3 years. Many White Whales seem to live for 50 years or more.

They are often harried and eaten by Great Killer Whales (*Orcinus orca 51*). In an experiment in Bristol Bay, Alaska a group of White Whales was kept away from a salmon fishery area by broadcasting the recorded sounds of Killers.

The voice of the White Whale itself is remarkable and can be distinctly heard even above the surface. An approaching group produces a pattern of squeals in a bewildering variety of keys, which led early mariners to call the whales 'sea canaries'. In addition, they produce a well-modulated bell tone which is unique amongst cetaceans. Typical whistles range from 3 to 9 kHz, but there are also short pulses of click sounds which almost certainly are used in echolocation. There is some evidence that White Whales use their sonar abilities to help them locate air holes in the ice. As well as all these resonant sounds, White Whales also produce loud reports by clapping their jaws suddenly together in what seems to be a very clear threat.

Status The tendency for White Whales to gather in large groups when migrating, makes fairly accurate aerial counts possible. Some recent estimates put the number in the Beaufort Sea at 4,000–5,000; in eastern Canada and Greenland at 10,000–14,000; in the Barents, Kara and Laptev seas at 7,000–10,000; in eastern Siberia and Chukchi at 1,000–2,000; and in the Sea of Okhotsk around 6,000. The world total is 26,000–32,000.

Inuit people have taken White Whales for hundreds of years. They were always particularly easy prey when trapped by ice (a condition known as a *savssat*) and forced to breathe at isolated holes where hunters waited for them. Today's modern equipment makes them vulnerable at all times. There is an annual kill of about 3,000 whales, but so many are struck and lost that this might easily be as much as 7,000, which is probably twice as high as the natural replacement rate. It is a melancholy admission, but the one thing which may eventually save the White Whale from over-exploitation is the fact that mercury levels in the meat are now so high that marketing is forbidden anywhere in the West.

Distribution White Whales are found in all shallow waters, rivers and estuaries of the Arctic. They seem to be limited only by temperatures higher than about 15°C (60°F). Groups of White Whales live throughout the year in the St Lawrence River; some travel over 1,100 km (700 miles) up the Yukon in summer; and in 1966 one individual (nicknamed 'Moby Dick') created a considerable stir by swimming right up the Rhine into the centre of Germany.

The southern limits of this whale's range seem to be at Massachusetts or Connecticut in the western Atlantic and off Honshu Island in Japan.

Sources BELKOVICH (1960) aerial survey, FISH & MOWBRAY (1962) sounds, FISH & VANIA (1971) reaction to killers, GEWALT (1976) monograph, GUREVICH (1979) status, KLEINENBERG et al (1969) review, LACÉPÈDE (1804) taxonomy, MORGAN (1979) sounds, PALLAS (1776) original description, SERGEANT (1973) biology.

Family Seven – Physeteridae

Gray created this family in 1821 to include both the Great Sperm Whale and its Pygmy and Dwarf relatives. The species have in common a spermaceti organ or 'case', which is fitted into a depression on the toothless upper jaw; an underslung lower jaw with large teeth; and a comparatively simple air sinus system, but apart from these few features they have little in common.

The 2 genera differ most markedly in their overall size and the relative size of their heads. The Great Sperm Whale (*Physeter macrocephalus 36*) is the largest of all toothed whales, with an enormous head almost 35 per cent of total body length. The smaller species (*Kogia breviceps 37* and *K. simus 38*) are amongst the smallest of whales, with conical heads which form only 15 per cent of body length. In addition, both species of *Kogia* have blowholes situated on top of the head instead of on the end of the snout and a distinct curved dorsal fin where *Physeter* has none.

It would probably be best if the *Kogia* were placed in a family of its own, Kogiidae, but until there is any real consensus, we continue to group Dwarf and Pygmy Sperm Whales with their gigantic though distant relative.

Map Key All 3 species are distributed worldwide, but only the large male Great Sperm Whales (*Physeter macrocephalus 36*) venture into colder polar waters.

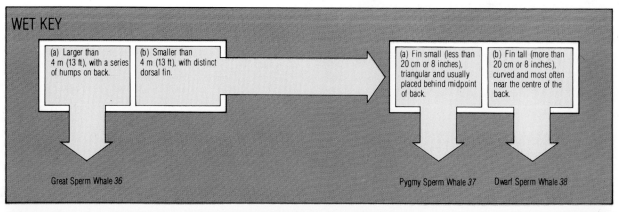

WET KEY

(a) Larger than 4 m (13 ft), with a series of humps on back.

(b) Smaller than 4 m (13 ft), with distinct dorsal fin.

(a) Fin small (less than 20 cm or 8 inches), triangular and usually placed behind midpoint of back.

(b) Fin tall (more than 20 cm or 8 inches), curved and most often near the centre of the back.

Great Sperm Whale *36*

Pygmy Sperm Whale *37*

Dwarf Sperm Whale *38*

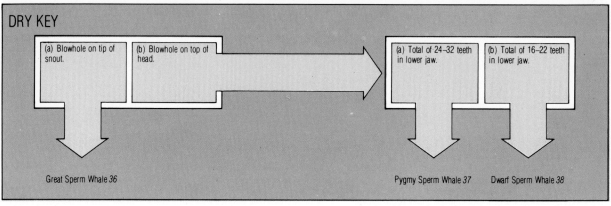

DRY KEY

(a) Blowhole on tip of snout.

(b) Blowhole on top of head.

(a) Total of 24–32 teeth in lower jaw.

(b) Total of 16–22 teeth in lower jaw.

Great Sperm Whale *36*

Pygmy Sperm Whale *37*

Dwarf Sperm Whale *38*

GREAT SPERM WHALE

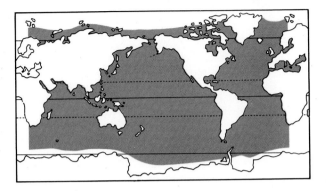

Classification In the tenth edition of *Systema Naturae*, Linnaeus established the genus *Physeter*, from the Greek *phuseter*, a whirlpool, or a wind instrument, and included in it 4 related spouting species: *microps*, *tursio*, *catodon* and *macrocephalus*. Most recent taxonomists have assumed that the 4 names are synonymous and that they arose as the result of differing, inaccurate and sometimes fanciful, descriptions by early authors. In 1911 Oldfield Thomas chose *catodon*, which derives from the Greek for 'teeth only in the lower jaw'.

In 1938, however, Hilbrand Boschma complained that the original description of *Physeter catodon* was so vague that it was unidentifiable and that it ought to be rejected in favour of *Physeter macrocephalus*. He produced an 1866 publication on zoogeography by an English naturalist called Murray, who had chosen *macrocephalus*, which comes from the Greek for 'big headed'. For a while this in turn enjoyed priority, but in 1966 Philip Hershkovitz, veteran taxonomist in the Field Museum in Chicago, objected to the recognition of Murray's authority, saying that it was 'merely part of an uncritical classification of mammals included in the appendix to his book ... compiling names without dates, bibliographical

references, or regard for priority'. However, in 1974 2 Dutch taxonomists discovered a paper published in 1857 which clearly opted for *Physeter macrocephalus*, which is at the moment the accepted form.

Whatever its true name may be, there seems to be no races or subspecies of the Great Sperm Whale.

Local Names The generic name of *Physeter* comes directly from Aristotle and was therefore adopted also by Pliny. Its nearest equivalent in modern local names is probably the Russian *bolshoi plevum*, the great spouter. The presence in the whale's head of a reservoir of clear liquid which sets to a solid white wax on cooling, led to analogies with semen and the name of *spermaceti* (literally, whale semen); hence sperm whale, *spermacethval* (Danish), and *spermatsetoryi* (Russian). Another common name derives from the old Gascon *cachau* or the Catalan *quachal*, large teeth, and has today become *cachalot* (French), *kaskelot* (Swedish), *cachalote* (Spanish) and *capidoglio* (Italian). Further names include *Pottwal* (German), *buthvalue* (Icelandic), *hunshval* (Norwegian), *makko kijira* (Japanese), *olbrotowick* (Polish), *agidagikh* (Aleutian), *kigutilik* (Greenland Eskimo), *koiapchak* (Koryak) and *trumpo* (in Bermuda). We continue to use the old name sperm, instead of cachalot, but dignify it with the name of Great Sperm Whale.

Description Large; length averages 15 m (50 ft) for males, with a maximum of 20 m (65 ft) in the past, and 11 m (36 ft) for females, with a maximum of 17 m (56 ft) in the past; calves are about 4 m (13 ft) at birth. Weight averages 36,000 kg (40 tons) for males, and 20,000 kg (22 tons) for females, with a maximum of 38,000 kg (42 tons) in the past.

The profile of the Great Sperm Whale is unmistakable. The enormous head with its blunt snout and the relatively small underslung jaw have come to symbolize all great whales in the

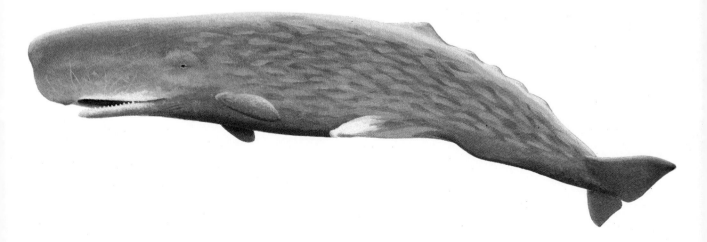

minds of many people. With the head forming as much as one-third of total body length, and considerably more than one-third of its mass, this whale has been aptly described as the owner of 'the biggest nose on record'.

Behind the huge rectangular head case, the body form is equally distinctive. There is no true dorsal fin, but, about two-thirds of the distance down the back, flesh and fibre are raised into a distinct dorsal hump which looks something like a low fatty fin. Beyond this are a series of knuckles or lumps; the number differs, but there usually seem to be 4 or 5. Some larger males also have up to 6 smaller knuckles in front of the main dorsal hump. Many females have been found to grow a distinct callus on the forward slope of the hump. This varies in size and shape, but it is not pathological and could be some kind of secondary sexual characteristic.

The flippers are short and stubby, apparently functioning largely as brakes, but the tail flukes are broad and powerful. Their area is greater than in any other whale and they provide rapid acceleration. On the underside of the tailstock, opposite the line of knuckles on the lower back, is a raised keel running into the centre of the flukes near the tail notch. This keel ends suddenly at its forward end, producing an angular notch in which the anus is located.

There are no body hairs at any stage of development. The entire skin surface is corrugated, giving the animal a shrivelled appearance. The overall colour is normally a steely dark grey, with a light brownish underlay. The skin round the lips is usually white and there are often white blotches on other parts of the head, at the navel, alongside the hump, or splashed in random streaks along the flank and tail. On some whales the white markings on the head are arranged into a distinct whorl. The frequency and area of the pale patches increase with age and it is possible for older males in particular to be completely white. In 1957 a pure white adult male, exactly like the mythical Moby Dick, was taken in Japanese coastal waters. It was apparently not an albino.

The skin of most Great Sperm Whales, especially in the head area, is patterned with circular scars which can only be sucker marks from tentacles of giant squid. We have measured the disc-shaped scars on several stranded whales and found that some of them are more than 12 cm (almost 5 inches) in diameter, which means that the arm which carried the sucker must have been about 60 cm (over 2 ft) in diameter. There are some reports of whales bearing sucker marks more than 20 cm (8 inches) in diameter, which could make their owners as much as 45 m (150 ft) long.

Field Identification It is relatively simple to identify this species. The long, blunt head is always the first to appear above the surface, often at an angle, to expose the terminal blowhole. The head is highly asymmetrical and the single nostril is situated well to the left of the midline, producing a spout with a bias unlike that of any other whale. Seen from the front or the back, the blow is directed away to the whale's left; and when viewed from the side, the blast shoots up 3–5 m (10–16 ft) at a forward angle of 45°. The first exhalation after a deep dive is like an explosion which can be heard almost a kilometre (half a mile) away. Each following breath lasts

about 3 seconds on the exhalation and 1 second for the next intake of air. The whale usually spends about 10 minutes at the surface, breathing deeply every 10–15 seconds before diving. There is an old whalers' rule of thumb which predicts that for every foot of a Great Sperm Whale's length, it will breathe once at the surface and spend one minute submerged during the subsequent dive. In our experience, this works remarkably well. A 50-ft (15-m) male does blow about 50 times and then disappears for roughly 50 minutes; while a 30-ft (10-m) female can be expected to reappear again about 30 minutes after the last of her 30 breaths.

After the final blow of a series at the surface, the whale draws its head under and a cloud of spray persists as the long back bends down to expose the hump and the knuckles along the spine. The dive is almost vertical and the broad tail flukes are always thrown well up into the air. When only the hump and raised tail can be seen from a distance, there is a possibility of confusion with the Humpback (*Megaptera novaeangliae 10*), which also arches its back and lifts its flukes before diving. When in doubt, these are the most useful distinctions:

Physeter Blowhole on tip of smooth head; angular spout; blows more than 20 times; rounded hump; flukes all dark.
Megaptera Blowholes set back on raised area of knobbly head; vertical spout; blows less than 10 times; triangular hump; flukes with white markings underneath.

The usual surface speed of the Great Sperm Whale is a leisurely 6 kph (about 3 knots), but it is capable of at least 40 kph (over 20 knots) in certain circumstances. Time spent at the surface is devoted largely to breathing, but sometimes Great Sperm Whales float motionless on the water, resting. We have seen them drifting, tail down, with their noses sticking up out of the water, or lying on their sides with one flipper and one wing of the fluke showing above the surface. It seems possible that these whales may even be sleeping. We have been able to bring our ship alongside and almost touch them before they take fright and sound. It is likely that many of the collisions which occur between ships and whales take place under these circumstances and have nothing to do with 'enraged whales, full of greed and fierceness, that ply the oceans looking for ships to sink', as a medieval bestiary put it.

As a rule it is more difficult to approach solitary males, but we have found that groups of females and young found floating at the surface in tropical waters are less wary. On several occasions we have put down small boats and managed to manoeuvre amongst such a herd until, not apparently as a result of anything we have done, the whole pod dives simultaneously. Very often they surface, once again together, about half an hour later in almost the same place.

After a particularly deep dive, Great Sperm Whales ascend with a rush and may shoot through the surface in a complete breach, falling back with a splash that can be heard 4 km (2 nautical miles) and seen 28 km (15 nautical miles) away.

Stranding Great Sperm Whales are unfortunately frequently stranded, often in whole herds. Identification is not a problem. There is no other large whale with a lower jaw that seems

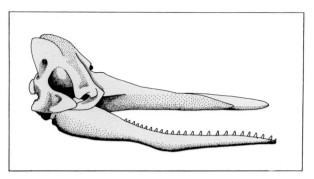

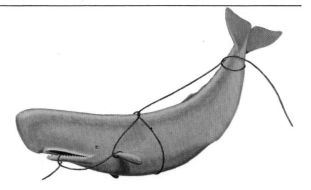

Great Sperm Whale as it was found entangled in submarine cable at 997 m (3,270 ft) off Ecuador in 1931. Other Great Sperm Whales have been found so entangled at 1,135 m (3,720 ft)

so puny and inadequate for an animal of its size. Even in an adult whale 15 m (50 ft) long, the jaw is barely 20 cm (8 inches) wide at the tip. The teeth are conical, oval in cross section, have no enamel and begin to emerge from the gum only when the whale is about 10 years old. Eruption is not complete until a male is 16 m (52 ft) and a female 11 m (36 ft) long, and has 18–29 teeth on each side of the mandible, fitting snugly into sockets in the upper palate. There can be a total of up to 22 very much smaller maxillary teeth embedded in the upper jaw; they may grow large enough to erupt through the gums and become visible. Occasionally there are double teeth and the mandibles are bent or in some way deformed.

On a beached whale it is possible to see features seldom visible in the water, including a number of pleats on the chin.

The most common external parasites are diatoms, which give the skin a greenish glow in polar waters, but disappear in the tropics. There are colonies of ship barnacles, concentrated mainly on the flukes and around the mouth; and in some areas whale lice are common. There are several species of louse, 2 at least of which are peculiar to this whale, *Cyamus catadontis*, which is found most often on larger males, and *Neocyamus physeteris*, which is more common on females and young. This parasitic distinction is certainly caused by the fact that males migrate into polar waters, while the females remain with their young all year round in the tropics.

The skull consists of a rounded cranium enclosing the spherical 10-kg (22-lb) brain, which is displaced backwards leaving a wide shelf of bone curving upward at the sides to form what the old whalers called 'Neptune's sledge'. The soft tissues of the massive nose sit in this chair, forming the 'case' of muscle and fibre which encloses a body of clear white spermaceti wax surrounding the nasal passages. It is now known that these tubes are voluntarily filled with water when a Great Sperm Whale dives and that it can, by controlling the amount or distribution of water of different temperature from different depths, change the density of the wax and alter the whole buoyancy of its body.

The skull is asymmetrical, much larger on the right than the left, with the left nasal bone missing altogether. There are 50 vertebrae. The first neck vertebra is free, but the next 6 are fused into a solid mass. The first 8 of 11 pairs of ribs are double headed and the last pair are very much reduced in size. There is quite often a vestigial hind-limb bone, a femur, articulating with, or fused to, the rudimentary pelvis.

During digestion, perhaps initiated by the sharp beak of a

squid and encouraged by a flow of bile, a dark sticky resinous mass builds up in the stomach of some whales. This becomes squeezed into a bolus in the intestine, where it picks up more squid beaks and detritus, growing as new strata are added to its surface, until the whole lump is excreted; it floats on the ocean surface or breaks up into smaller aromatic pieces which eventually drift ashore. This is ambergris. It consists largely of non-volatile alcohols and is found most often in the tropics and is still valued for its ability to intensify and stabilize fragrances and for its action as an antispasmatic drug. It is also found in the alimentary canals of 1 or 2 per cent of all Great Sperm Whales taken commercially, usually in small quantities, but once in a lump weighing 420 kg (925 lb) in the gut of a 13-m (43-ft) male taken at the British Antarctic base.

The frequency with which Great Sperm Whales strand makes it possible to arrive at tentative conclusions about this strange and lethal behaviour pattern. Frank Robson of New Zealand has made meticulous studies of mass strandings which show that they usually involve a close-knit harem herd. He has watched several such strandings in progress and each began with just one whale coming ashore. This individual apparently produces a loud and sustained distress call which is near the limits of human sensitivity, but which has a disturbing effect on any dogs which may happen to be on the beach and on the rest of the whale herd which mills around offshore. Invariably, one or more individuals detach themselves from such a group and strand near the first whale; and then the pattern is repeated again and again until the entire group lies helpless on the shore. On 18 March 1970, 59 Great Sperm Whales stranded in this way at Okitu beach near Gisborne on the North Island of New Zealand. All were females and young, including a newborn calf. Another stranding at nearby Muriwai beach on 29 October 1974 involved 72 whales, again mostly females and young, but this time including the harem-leading bull. Familiarity with the pattern made it possible for Robson, when a further stranding seemed imminent at Napier, to forestall any additional beaching of a herd that swam uneasily just offshore, by killing the whale already lying on the shingle and thus preventing her from transmitting the call that normally summons the rest to their deaths.

It seems that, whatever the initial cause of a single stranding (illness, parasitic infection, disorientation during a storm, confusion produced by a gently-sloping beach with inadequate echoes, stray calves and panic in shallow water are all possible contributory factors) in harem herds at least all subsequent beaching is the result of social cohesion. In contrast, when a herd of bachelor bulls is in similar difficulties, any individual fortunate enough to float free swims away.

Natural History Adults eat up to a ton of squid each day, specializing in the large deepwater species such as *Moroteuthis robusta*, but at least one whale's stomach is reported to have held 28,000 tiny surface squid. Over 40 species of cephalopods of various sizes are known to be eaten, plus a variety of other marine animals which cannot all be accidental inclusions. Amongst these are the longnose skate (*Raja rhina*), snapper, lobsters, jellyfish, angler fish, cod, ocean perch and 4-m (14-ft) long sharks. Random sampling of stomach contents has also turned up boots, wire, buckets, plastic bags, deep-sea sponges and quantities of sand.

We now know that Great Sperm Whales in open water regularly descend beyond 1,000 m (3,300 ft). One large male was followed down to 2,250 m (7,400 ft), but even this may not be near the whale's limits. The presence of bottom-dwelling sharks in the stomach of a whale captured in an area where the bottom depth was more than 3,000 m (10,000 ft), suggests that Great Sperm Whales can and do go to even more extraordinary depths to feed. Even more incredible is the discovery that they descend at a speed of 7–8 kph (4 knots) and come back to the surface at about 9 kph (5 knots). At these speeds a round trip to a depth of 1,000 m (3,300 ft) takes no more than 15 minutes and yet the whales can stay down for 45 minutes. The duration of the dive and the fact that the whales frequently surface close to the spot where they submerged suggest that they lie almost motionless at their target depths, waiting in ambush for the fleet but luminous giant squid. It seems that they accomplish this by drawing water into the huge nasal passages (the right one is 5 m long and as much as 1 m in diameter) and cooling the surrounding spermaceti wax just enough to increase its density to a point where they have neutral buoyancy. In this state, they can lie at any depth, converse energy and catch giant squid.

Cross section through the head of Great Sperm Whale

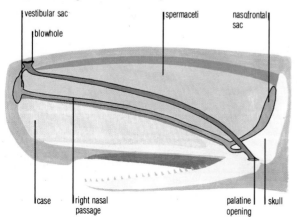

vestibular sac   spermaceti   nasofrontal sac

blowhole

case   right nasal passage   palatine opening   skull

Location of prey in the dark depths may be facilitated by its luminescence, but the Great Sperm Whales' sonar system is probably more important than sight for hunting. There is at least one record of a completely blind adult in good condition captured alive with a well-filled stomach.

Great Sperm Whales reach puberty when they are about 10 years old and 12 m long (40 ft) in the case of males, 9 m long (30 ft) in females. Females may become pregnant at this age, but the young males are forced out of breeding groups into bachelor herds and seldom breed until they reach full maturity and gather their own harems at about 25 years of age. Until that time, they consort in loose bachelor groups which travel and feed together. We once saw a pod of immature males surfing together in huge rollers off the Cape of Good Hope.

Adult males and females have lifestyles so distinct that they might be separate species. The males leave tropical waters each summer and voyage into the highest latitudes, where the largest solitary bulls are seen right up to the ice. Groups of younger males congregate in cool water on the perimeter of the polar zone, but females and young seldom venture more than 40° from the equator. In winter the sexes meet in warmer waters and the biggest males clash in their annual struggles to form and hold a harem. Most large bulls bear the scars of these encounters in which they ram each other or lock jaws in combat, twisting over and over at the surface until one or other of the rivals submits and swims away, often with teeth broken off at the gum.

Most harems consist of 20–30 adults, many of which may be pregnant or lactating, so the number of females available for breeding is usually very much smaller. Gestation lasts for 14–16 months and lactation for another year or even 2, following which there is a resting phase of another 9 months, so that the entire breeding cycle may last as long as 4 years.

Usually there is only one calf, but twins are known. While giving birth, the mother often stands vertically in the water with her head exposed while other adult females gather round her in a supportive group. We once came across such a 'maternity ward' in the Indian Ocean and watched for 2 hours while the 'midwife' whales in the harem formed a tight protective ring around the central female, eventually taking turns to nudge the newborn calf to the surface to breathe.

Such supportive behaviour is common in harem herds and is something that whalers have ruthlessly exploited. Members of a herd will often gather round an injured whale, all facing inwards towards the stricken individual, tails hanging out and down; they stay as long as the central whale remains alive, while the hunters circle round and pick them off one by one.

There are several eye-witness accounts of a similar, but more aggressive display when a number of Great Sperm Whales group themselves, heads outwards, in a circle around their youngest calves in response to an attack by Great Killer Whales (*Orcinus orca 51*). The Great Sperm Whales sometimes clap their jaws in an explosive threat sound that travels even above the water for a distance of several kilometres. On rare occasions threat can turn to outright attack. In 1896 the Clyde Line steamer *Seminole* rammed a sleeping Great Sperm Whale off Florida and, before it died, 5 other adults arrived and charged at the ship, ramming it repeatedly until the steel bow plates bent sufficiently to produce serious leaks. In 1820 the American ship *Essex* rammed a large male basking at the surface in the South Pacific and he turned and hit the ship several times until it sank; only 1 lifeboat with 3 crew aboard reached the shores of Peru and lived to tell the tale.

The fundamental social group is the 'nursery school' of mature females and nursing calves with an average number of 20 or 30. Bachelor herds are usually smaller, with a maximum of 20 younger males, and harem herds seldom number more than a total of 80 adults and young, but sometimes Great Sperm Whales gather into very much larger congregations which have been seen travelling abreast on a front more than 20 km (10 nautical miles) long. There is one record of such a group of more than 1,000. There is also some evidence to show that aggregations follow a lunar rhythm, with whales grouping together and migrating as the moon waxes, reaching their greatest concentration over oceanic ridges under a full moon. It is possible that these movements and their timing have something to do with the life cycle of certain squid which breed where underwater mountain ranges fall steeply away.

Beached whales produce a roar which can be heard for several kilometres, and social groups in the water produce audible squeaks; but the most characteristic sound is a monotonous series of clicks or pulse-burst sounds at the rate of 20–80 per second. These are ideally adapted for long-range echolocation and analysis has shown that each pulse carries a sonic signature characteristic of the individual producing it. The pattern of this sound is shaped by its passage through the reverberation chamber of the spermaceti organ, so that the space between the clicks is directly proportional to, and gives an accurate indication of the size of, the organ, and therefore of the length and age of the whale. Recordings made at sea show that Great Sperm Whales start producing these sounds about 5 m (17 ft) below the surface and that they use them, not only to locate their prey, but to keep in touch, holding station roughly 100 m (330 ft) apart and coming back to the surface to breathe simultaneously. The click sounds have been found to fall into repetitive sequences called 'codas', which may have a communication function.

Status There is no agreement about the present level of Great Sperm Whale populations, but declines in the age of pregnancy and maturation indicate that these whales are under sufficient pressure to alter their basic physiology in ways designed to speed up breeding. Some of the best estimates suggest that there may be 350,000 in the southern hemisphere and another 175,000 in the north. These figues are based on approximations which may well be hopelessly optimistic.

Since the first recorded commercial capture of a Great Sperm Whale off the American coast in 1712, this species has been a mainstay of the industry. Before 1850 there was an American fleet of 729 vessels, almost all engaged in killing Great Sperm Whales and the killing has continued ever since, with respites only during the world wars. In recent times the world catch reached a peak of over 30,000 in 1963, but has been falling under the influence of controls ever since.

Distribution This species favours the edges of ocean trenches

Above: dive sequence
Below: members of Great Sperm Whale pod gathering around injured member in the 'Marguerite Formation'

and points where strong currents flow in opposite directions.

Both sexes migrate, moving in autumn towards the equator and in spring towards the poles. Males as a rule travel further and faster than the females and young. In theory the population in each hemisphere is distinct, but we suspect that there is considerable mixing (even of the males) in equatorial areas such as the Galapagos, where cold-water currents and abundant food exist all year round.

Sources BACKUS (1966) eating shark, BERZIN (1971) monograph, BEST (1967–1970) in South Africa, BOSCHMA (1938) teeth, CALDWELL et al (1966) behaviour, CLARKE (1979) buoyancy, HEEZEN (1957) in cables, HOLM & JONSGARD (1959) lunar influence, HUSSON & HOLTHUIS (1974) taxonomy, LINNAEUS (1758) original description, MOHL et al (1976) sonar probes, NISHIWAKI (1962) photographs, OHSUMI (1958) white male, OHSUMI (1966) in North Pacific, ROBSON & VAN BREE (1971) in New Zealand, ROBSON (1976) stranding, STEPHENSION (1975) stranding, STIRLING (1934) ambergris, WATKINS (1977) codas, WATKINS & SCHEVILL (1977) sounds.

PYGMY SPERM WHALE

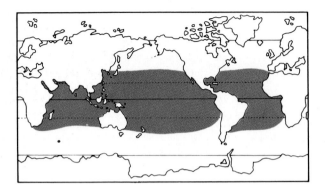

Local Names Lesser sperm whale and lesser cachalot (English), *cachalot pigmée* (French), *zwergpotvis* (Dutch), *Zwergpottwal* (German), *malyi kashalot* (Russian), *dwerg spermhval* (Norwegian), *zaru kaburi* (Japanese) and *wongu* (Telugu Indian).

Description Small; length averages 3 m (10 ft) for both sexes, with a maximum of 3.4 m (11.5 ft); calves are about 1.2 m (4 ft) at birth. Weight averages 363 kg (800 lb) for both sexes, with a maximum of 408 kg (900 lb); calves are about 55 kg (120 lb) at birth.

The Pygmy Sperm Whale has a swollen nose filled with spermaceti, like its larger relative, but the proportion of head to body is quite different. In the Great Sperm Whale (*Physeter macrocephalus 36*) the head forms more than one-third of total body length, but in this species the ratio is closer to 15 per cent. The Pygmy has a somewhat conical head which, with its tiny underslung jaw, gives it much the appearance of a blunt-nosed, bottom-feeding shark.

The flippers are short and broad, located far forward, and the flukes are typically dolphinlike, with a deep notch. The dorsal fin is small and curved and usually placed about two-thirds of the distance toward the tail. The body tapers rapidly off behind the fin, becoming narrow and compressed, with prominent keels above and below the tailstock, running on to the flukes and finally dipping into the tail notch.

The colour is steely medium grey, with a distinct pink tinge in life. In water, Pygmy Sperm Whales sometimes look almost purple. The darker colour on the back fades to a pale grey on the belly. Between the eye and the flipper there is a pale grey or white bracket mark, often called a 'false gill'. In front of the eye there is sometimes another pale marking, usually circular in shape. Scarring is rare.

Field Identification It is difficult to identify this species, which has given it a false reputation for rarity. The frequency of

Classification In 1818 Antoine Delalande and Jules Verreaux collected and prepared the first complete skeletons of Right and Humpback whales. Delalande died in 1823 and Jules, just 16, recruited his brothers Edouard and Alexis to join him. Between them they sent a total of over 150,000 specimens back to Paris, including the first recorded specimen of a new species of whale. In 1838 de Blainville described a skull from the Verreaux collection, noted its small size but superficial resemblance to the Great Sperm Whale (*Physeter macrocephalus 36*) and decided to call it *Physeter breviceps* from the Latin *brevis*, short. Eight years later Gray found a further specimen in the collection brought back by HMS *Erebus* and HMS *Terror* and decided that it was different enough from the Great Sperm Whale to warrant its own genus, which he named *Kogia*.

The next 3 specimens to be discovered were given entirely new genus and species names and, a few years later, another 2 of each were proposed by several more authors. Gray recognized that there were too many names and set up several tentative synonymies, but it was Hector in New Zealand who finally cleared up the confusion in 1878 by bringing all the then known specimens together under *Kogia breviceps*.

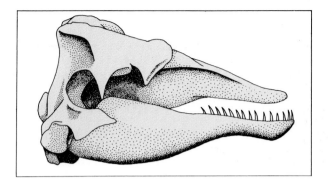

sightings seems to be increasing in proportion to the number of observers.

The best guide to field identification is size; these whales are smaller even than some Bottlenose Dolphins (*Tursiops truncatus 76*). Pygmy Sperm Whales are slow and deliberate in all their movements. They rise slowly to the surface to breathe, produce an inconspicuous blow, and seldom roll forcefully over or jump. They may occasionally breach in the same way as a Great Sperm Whale, falling back tail first, but are far more likely to be found hanging motionless in the water with the back of the head exposed and the tail hanging down loosely.

We have twice come across small cetaceans resting at the surface in this way and found them difficult to identify until, startled by our proximity (perhaps waking suddenly from sleep) they defecate and dive through a rust-coloured stain that spreads slowly over the water. This reaction and the colour of the faeces seem to be consistent enough to be regarded as diagnostic.

From observations made on specimens briefly held captive, it appears that Pygmy Sperm Whales fold their flippers flat against the body while swimming.

They are certainly shy of shipping, but a close view of the head should be sufficient to distinguish the species from all other cetaceans except the Dwarf Sperm Whale (*K. simus 38*). The Pygmy and the Dwarf are best distinguished as follows:

K. breviceps Up to 3.4 m (11.5 ft) long; fin less than 20 cm (8 inches) high and usually set well back.
K. simus Up to 2.7 m (9 ft) long; fin more than 20 cm (8 inches) high, strongly curved and most often situated near midpoint of the body.

Stranding Pygmy Sperm Whales are often stranded, either singly or in pairs of a mother and calf. During the century following discovery only 50 specimens were found, but this number has been increasing rapidly. Fifty have been found on the North Island of New Zealand alone.

Identification of a beached animal presents few problems, although there is the danger that it might seem at first glance to be a stranded shark. The shape of the head and mouth and the presence of sharp curved teeth on the lower jaw are

distinctive for this genus, and the 2 related species are easily separated by the number of teeth:

K. breviceps 12–16 (rarely 9–11) teeth on each side of lower jaw; none on upper jaw.
K. simus 8–11 (rarely 12–13) on each side of lower jaw; sometimes up to 3 pairs of tiny vestigial teeth on upper jaw.

The blowhole is displaced to the left, a little farther forward than is characteristic of most small cetaceans. The rostrum is extraordinarily short, making the skull almost as wide as it is long. From the top or bottom it forms a perfect isosceles triangle. The nasal bones have been completely suppressed and the dorsal surface of the brain case has a cuplike depression in which the spermaceti organ rests. This is as complex as that of the Great Sperm Whale, which suggests that the Pygmy Sperm Whale may also dive to considerable depths and make use of this apparatus for controlling its buoyancy.

There are 56 vertebrae, with all 7 bones in the neck fused into a solid mass. Eight of the 13 pairs of ribs are double headed and 4 are joined to the sternum by persistent cartilage.

Natural History Analysis of the stomach contents of beached animals shows that Pygmy Sperm Whales feed on squid, fish and crabs. Some of these are deep-water species, but several of the crabs live on the shore and shallow bottom, suggesting that these whales may not be as rigorously confined to deep water as their giant relative.

The usual social unit seems to be a school of 3–5; but many sightings have been of solitary individuals. Nothing is known of social or reproductive behaviour beyond the fact that gestation lasts about 9 months, calves seem to be born in the spring, and are probably nursed for about 12 months.

One animal held briefly in captivity in Napier, New Zealand in 1964 showed marked aggressive behaviour, charging and snapping at those who tried to feed it.

A recording made from an animal stranded in Florida, showed evidence of pulsed sounds of a 'click train' type which could be used for echolocation.

Status There are no estimates of the worldwide population, but it ought perhaps to be described as uncommon, rather than rare. A few are taken by harpoon from Japanese coastal stations, and an occasional one may be taken by the aboriginal industry on Lomblen Island in Indonesia, but these activities probably represent little or no threat to the species.

Distribution This species is apparently confined to the warmer seas of the world. Most frequent reports of strandings come from South Africa, south-east Australia, New Zealand and the south-eastern United States. There are few records from the South Pacific and none at all from the South Atlantic, but there is no reason to assume that Pygmy Sperm Whales do not occur there. This species may migrate from tropical into slightly more temperate waters during the summer months.

Sources ALLEN (1941) in Atlantic, CALDWELL et al (1966) sounds, DE BLAINVILLE (1838) original description, FITCH & BROWNELL (1968) food, GRAY (1846) taxonomy, HANDLEY (1966) review of genus, HECTOR (1878) taxonomy, ROBSON (1976) in New Zealand, ROSS (1979) in South Africa.

DWARF SPERM WHALE

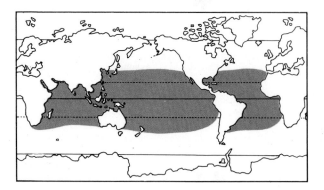

Classification At a time when every new specimen of Pygmy Sperm Whale (*Kogia breviceps 37*) was being classified as a separate species often in its own genus, Owen at the Royal College of Surgeons received the skeleton of a young female whale collected in India by his colleague Sir Walter Elliot. He recognized its affinity to the Great Sperm Whale (*Physeter macrocephalus 36*) and described it as *P. simus* from the Latin *simus*, snubnosed. Later he amended the genus to *Euphysetes.*

Hector in one great effort in 1878 successfully eliminated all the spurious species which had arisen as a result of descriptions of individual differences, sexual variation and immature characteristics and lumped the whole lot together under the single species of *Kogia breviceps*. In 1902 Frank Beddard recognized 2 distinct forms, *K. breviceps* and the slightly smaller *K. simus*. A 1936 survey of all the specimens in Japanese collections came to the same conclusion.

There are still diehards who feel that there should be only 1 species of *Kogia*, but most cetologists now accept that there are 2 forms which are anatomically distinct.

Local Names The recognition of this species is too recent for there to be many established local names, but, Japanese fishermen have long distinguished this species as *uki kujira*, the floating whale, from its habit of lying motionless at the surface. It is identified in the literature as Owen's pygmy whale or as the rat whale because of its peaked profile, but we prefer to call it the Dwarf Sperm Whale.

Description Small; length averages 2.4 m (8 ft), with a maximum of 2.7 m (9 ft); calves are about 1 m (3.3 ft) at birth. Weight averages 154 kg (340 lb), with a maximum of 272 kg (600 lb); calves are about 46 kg (100 lb) at birth.

The Dwarf Sperm Whale has an abbreviated, slightly bulbous head, like that of its relative the Pygmy Sperm Whale (*K. breviceps 37*), but is never quite as square at the front. There is considerable variation in the head shape of individuals in both species, with juveniles having a softer, more rounded, puppylike face and the adults becoming more angular. The jaw is also understated and underslung, giving the

Dwarf Sperm Whale a sharklike profile which is accentuated by the large curved dorsal fin situated in the middle of the back. The flippers are broad and short, the tail is compressed and the flukes are deeply notched.

The colouring is similar to that of the Pygmy Sperm Whale, medium grey above and paler below, with a pink tinge that can become quite bright on the belly. There is a pale, almost white, bracket mark or false gill, which is much less curved than that of the Pygmy species, but no white spot in front of the eye has been recorded. There is little or no scarring.

Field Identification It is perhaps even more difficult to identify this species than the Pygmy Sperm Whale. Dwarf Sperm Whales are shy and unobtrusive, but are said to be easy to approach when basking. When seen at close quarters, the tall curved dorsal fin makes this species distinct from the Pygmy, but it is possible that this feature is variable and may not be a totally reliable field characteristic. Some reports suggest that the fin might not always occur at the middle of the back, but could sometimes be displaced toward the tail.

When the fin is classically tall and curved, there is the additional possibility of confusion with 2 other species, the Pygmy Killer Whale (*Feresa attenuata 53*) and the Melonhead Whale (*Peponocephala electra 54*). All are dark coloured, have a blunt head and a sharklike fin. They are best distinguished in the following ways:

Kogia Fin less than 30 cm (12 inches) high, with slightly concave trailing edge; white false gill marking on head; broad square flippers; and a flat face.
Feresa Fin 30–40 cm (12–15 inches) high, with a markedly concave trailing edge; no white markings visible; rounded flippers; long tapered face.
Peponocephala Fin more than 40 cm (15 inches) high, with a notched and wavy trailing edge; white belly extending far enough up flank to be visible in water; pointed flippers; and a curved parrotlike face.

We have yet to see Dwarf Sperm Whales at sea, but have been told (by Japanese fishermen) that they do not normally produce the red faecal stain which seems to be characteristic of the Pygmy Sperm Whale.

Stranding In this species stranding is fairly frequent and identification at least as far as the genus *Kogia* presents no problems. Distinction between the 2 species is possible by the number of teeth. The Dwarf Sperm Whale seldom has more than 11 on each side of the lower jaw, compared with 12 or more in the Pygmy species. The Dwarf also has several short creases or grooves on its throat, which are altogether lacking in the Pygmy Sperm Whale. Some Dwarf individuals may have 3 small vestigial teeth on each side of the upper jaw.

The skulls of both species are superficially similar, although that of the Dwarf is generally smaller and flatter. The mandibles are unusually delicate for a toothed whale, often paper thin and translucent. There are 56 vertebrae, with the first 7 in the neck fused so that there appear to be only 3.

Natural History In addition to the usual squid, 18 kinds of fish have been found in the stomachs of Dwarf Sperm Whales. All of these are known to be species living at depths greater than 250 m (800 ft). There is little doubt that, like its huge relative, the Dwarf Sperm Whale dives deep and spends long periods submerged.

Nothing is known of its social or reproductive behaviour beyond the fact that it is usually seen in groups of 2–7 individuals, and reaches maturity at a length of 2.1 m (7 ft).

Status This species must be relatively uncommon.

Distribution Dwarf Sperm Whales are known from strandings in the central eastern United States, South Africa, India, Sri Lanka, south Australia, Japan, Hawaii and Baja California. None is recorded from the South Pacific or the South Atlantic, but it is unlikely that they do not occur there.

This species may be slightly more common in the tropics than the Pygmy Sperm Whale and seems to be less often encountered in shallow water. Sightings off the coast of Japan suggest that it frequents the edge of the continental shelf.

Sources FITCH & BROWNELL (1968) food, HANDLEY (1966) review, OGAWA (1936) taxonomy, OWEN (1866) original description, YAMADA (1954) taxonomy.

Family Eight—Stenidae
The coastal dolphins

This family is a rather awkward, and probably temporary, assemblage of 4 species with superficial similarities. It was established by Fraser and Purves of the British Museum in 1960 to house those species whose external appearance resembles the classic dolphins, but whose air sinus systems betray a more primitive, and a less specialized anatomy.

All are small cetaceans with a more or less typical dolphin shape and a pronounced beak, but beyond that they have little in common. Distinguishing between them in the field presents few problems.

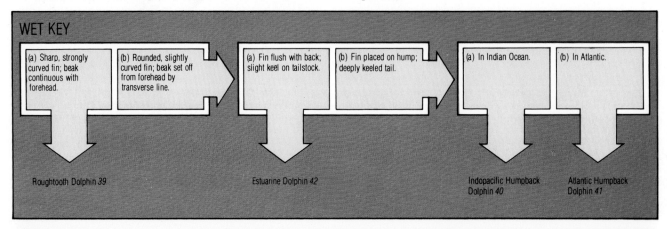

WET KEY

(a) Sharp, strongly curved fin; beak continuous with forehead. / (b) Rounded, slightly curved fin; beak set off from forehead by transverse line. → Roughtooth Dolphin 39

(a) Fin flush with back; slight keel on tailstock. / (b) Fin placed on hump; deeply keeled tail. → Estuarine Dolphin 42

(a) In Indian Ocean. → Indopacific Humpback Dolphin 40 / (b) In Atlantic. → Atlantic Humpback Dolphin 41

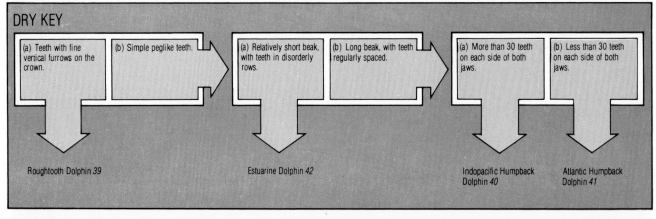

DRY KEY

(a) Teeth with fine vertical furrows on the crown. / (b) Simple peglike teeth. → Roughtooth Dolphin 39

(a) Relatively short beak, with teeth in disorderly rows. / (b) Long beak, with teeth regularly spaced. → Estuarine Dolphin 42

(a) More than 30 teeth on each side of both jaws. → Indopacific Humpback Dolphin 40 / (b) Less than 30 teeth on each side of both jaws. → Atlantic Humpback Dolphin 41

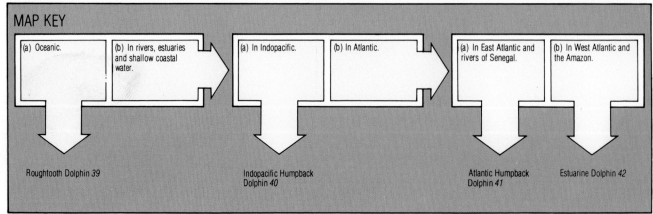

MAP KEY

(a) Oceanic. / (b) In rivers, estuaries and shallow coastal water. → Roughtooth Dolphin 39

(a) In Indopacific. → Indopacific Humpback Dolphin 40 / (b) In Atlantic.

(a) In East Atlantic and rivers of Senegal. → Atlantic Humpback Dolphin 41 / (b) In West Atlantic and the Amazon. → Estuarine Dolphin 42

ROUGHTOOTH DOLPHIN

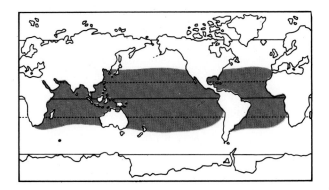

Classification In the early nineteenth century Cuvier examined the skull of a dolphin stranded at Brest on the Channel coast of Brittany in France. His description of this part of the specimen was published in 1823 and is beyond reproach, but he then went on to create an extraordinary monster, which he called *Delphinus frontatus*, by combining the skull with the skin of an Amazon River Dolphin (*Inia geoffrensis 32*) which had somehow become associated with it in the collection. The origins of the Amazon skin remain mysterious, because at that time the only specimen of *Inia* in the Paris Museum was the one looted from Lisbon in 1810. It was not until 1826 that the museum despatched its own collector to South America to find another specimen.

The true owner of the skull was only rescued from oblivion by a happy accident. When it was first stranded on that beach at Brest, an artist named van Breda drew a colour portrait of it which he called *dauphin à long bec*. This somehow came to the attention of Lesson, just back from his voyage to the Pacific aboard *La Coquille*, and the young naturalist had the courage to contradict Cuvier and in 1828 renamed the Brest dolphin *Delphinus bredanensis* after its artist.

The genus *Steno* was created by Gray in 1846 for a long, thin-beaked dolphin featured in his report on the voyage of

HMS *Erebus* and HMS *Terror*, which he called *Steno compressus*, from the Greek *stenos*, narrow. This was probably the same species as the dolphin from Brest, but it was not until 1955 that Miller and Kellogg put the binomial *Steno bredanensis* together in its currently accepted form.

There is a possibility that a related species or subspecies, which is very pink on the belly and has much darker spots, exists in the Indian Ocean. This has been tentatively identified as *S. perniger* (BLYTH 1848) or *Stenopontistes zambezicus* (RIBEIRO 1936).

Local Names In France this species is still known as *dauphin à long bec* and in Holland as *snaveldolfijn*, but the most popular and apposite common name is the one based on its uniquely furrowed teeth. We therefore call it the Roughtooth Dolphin.

Description Small; length averages 2.4 m (8 ft) for males, with a maximum of 2.75 m (9 ft), and 2.2 m (7.5 ft) for females. Weight averages 130 kg (285 lb), with a possible maximum of 160 kg (352 lb).

The body shape is different from that of most other species. Its proportions are perfect and it should be beautiful, but somehow it is put together in a way that makes it ungainly. The long beak runs directly into a sloping forehead which continues in a clear sweeping line all the way through to the tail. The beak is very slender, giving the whole head the sharp conical, streamlined look of a cetacean Concorde. In many ways the outline is reminiscent of one of the sleeker marine dinosaurs or ichthyosaurs, but the dolphin has peculiar bulging eyes. The flippers and dorsal fin are smoothly curved and pointed, almost identical in shape and size, and the same balanced contours are repeated on the flukes. Adults, however, lose something of this aesthetic appeal by developing thickenings or keels on the upper and lower surfaces of the tailstock.

The colour is dark grey with a ruddy underlay which shows through as a pinkish hue on the white belly. The throat, chin

181

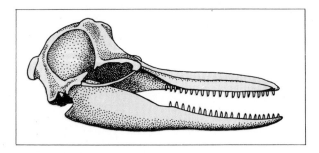

and the tip and sides of the beak are white. There are always numerous streaks, and star-shaped yellow or white scars all over the body, which are probably the result of injuries, tussles with squid and the attachment of external parasites.

Field Identification It is usually easy to identify Roughtooth Dolphins, which are attracted to fast-moving vessels. We normally get our first glimpse of a school as they come angling rapidly in toward us, leaping in smooth flat curves as they accelerate to match speed with our ship before taking up station on the bow wave. To do this, they need to travel at about 28 kph (15 knots), which they seem to manage effortlessly. After riding the bow in tiers 3 or 4 animals deep for several minutes, they invariably peel off simultaneously, diving under the keel to reappear some distance back in our wake, leaping again and again in the turbulent water.

When travelling normally, Roughtooth Dolphins break the water cleanly with the top of the head and the sharklike fin, usually every 7–10 seconds. They sometimes school with tuna and have been taken, along with Bridled Dolphins (*Stenella attenuata 73*) and Spinner Dolphins (*Stenella longirostris 70*), in purse-seine nets. We have seen Roughtooth Dolphins associating with both Bottlenose Dolphins (*Tursiops truncatus 76*) and Shortfin Pilot Whales (*Globicephala macrorhynchus 50*).

The shape of the fin and the marks on the body raise the possibility of confusion with both Bottlenose and Spotted (*Stenella plagiodon 74*) dolphins. The following characteristics should be useful in telling these 3 genera apart:

Steno Long conical beak, continuous with forehead; few large and irregular markings.
Stenella Long beak, sharply set off from head by transverse line; many small regular spots.
Tursiops Stubby beak, sharply set off from head by transverse line; no spots.

Under most circumstances it is possible to make a positive identification of Roughtooth Dolphins at sea by looking for a white tip and white sides on the narrow pointed beak. At very close quarters, the narrowness of the head can be seen to accentuate the eye sockets, giving these dolphins a somewhat disturbing goggle-eyed appearance.

Stranding There have been mass strandings in Indonesia and Florida, but it usually occurs in groups of 3 or 4. Once death and sunlight have blackened the skin, the best clues to identifi-

cation are the shape of the beak and the peculiarity of the teeth. Roughtooth Dolphins usually have 20–27 teeth on each side of both jaws, with fine vertical ridges or furrows forming a very distinctive roughness on the crown. It is normally possible to feel this texture on all parts of teeth exposed by the gums, but sometimes the wrinkles can be difficult to detect.

The skull is distinctively narrow, and there are 66 vertebrae. Five pairs of ribs are double headed and 5 are joined to the sternum.

Natural History Stomachs of stranded dolphins in West Africa contained fish and squid. Several examined in the Gulf of Mexico had been feeding on the blanket octopus (*Tremoctopus violaceus*).

In our experience, schools are normally fairly large (50 or more), but very little is known of their social behaviour. Females stranded in West Africa in May were carrying almost full-term foetuses, so calving probably takes place in midsummer. Recordings made of captive Roughtooth Dolphins show that they are effective echolocators, producing trains of brief click sounds with a broad and even spectral distribution. This narrow beam of sound projects ahead of the dolphin and is directed by scanning movements of the head.

Several Roughtooth Dolphins have been kept in captivity at the Oceanic Institute of the University of Hawaii. They seem to be even more receptive of training than the usual Bottlenose Dolphins, so 2 were tested for creativity in a series of experiments in which only entirely novel patterns of behaviour were rewarded. Very quickly getting the idea, both dolphins independently invented tail slaps, tail walks, tail waves, beaching, breaching, corkscrews, backflips, porpoising, swimming upside down and spitting, all without specific instruction or example.

Status Once thought to be rare, and known only from occasional strandings, Roughtooth Dolphins are being seen more and more often as more people begin to take an interest in marine mammal identification. They may turn out to be quite common.

Apart from those caught in tuna nets, a few are taken each year by the small whaling industry on St Vincent in the Caribbean, but this represents no threat to their survival.

Distribution Strandings are known from Virginia, Florida, Cuba, Holland, Portugal, the Mediterranean, Senegal, the Ivory Coast, Brazil, Argentina, Tristan da Cunha, South Africa, Aden, India, Java, Japan, Hawaii, California and the Galapagos. It would seem that Roughtooth Dolphins occur worldwide in all tropical and subtropical waters and that they prefer deeper water, being found most often at the edge of the continental shelf.

Sources CADENAT (1959) in West Africa, CALDWELL et al (1971) at St Vincent, CUVIER (1823) taxonomy, LESSON (1828) original description, MILLER & KELLOGG (1955) taxonomy, NORRIS (1976) open ocean dive, NORRIS (1976) general, NORRIS & EVANS (1967) sounds, PRYOR et al (1961) learning, SLIJPER (1962) general.

INDOPACIFIC HUMPBACK DOLPHIN

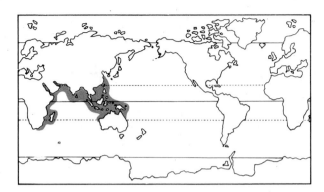

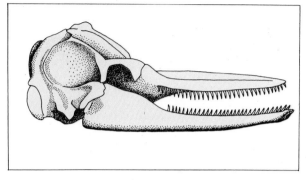

Classification Per Osbeck published in 1757 and in 1765 reports of snow white dolphins at play in the China Sea and trapped in nets set for fish in the Canton River. He described them as *Delphinus chinensis*. The first museum specimens were captured a century later by Robert Swinhoe in the Fuchow River and 1,200 km (750 miles) up the Yangtze at Hankow.

In 1829 Cuvier classified a new lead-coloured dolphin from the Bay of Bengal as *Delphinus plumbeus*. Sir Walter Elliot collected a similar dolphin along the Bengal coast near Madras in 1865, but as this was spotted, Owen decided to call it *D. lentiginosus*, from the Latin for freckled.

Finally at the turn of the century Charles Hose captured several pale dolphins at the mouths of the Sarawak and Lutong Rivers. He sold them to the British Museum, where in 1901 Lydekker described them as a new species belonging to the genus of the smaller Amazon dolphin *Sotalia borneensis*.

One of these specimens was redescribed more than half a century later as the type specimen of the Shortsnout Dolphin (*Lagenodelphis hosei 61*).

Eventually all 4 species of dolphin from China, Borneo and India were placed in the genus *Sotalia*, but in 1960 Fraser and Purves kept *Sotalia* for the South American estuarine species and revived Gray's *Sousa*, which was based on the Indian vernacular name for river dolphin and created by him in 1866 for Owen's Bornean species. So, in 1960, there seemed to be 4 valid species: *Sousa chinensis*, *S. borneensis*, *S. lentiginosa* and *S. plumbea*.

However the species seem to overlap and blend imperceptibly into each other. No definitive study has yet been made, but it seems likely that all the forms are no more than individual, sexual, age and geographical variations of a single species. Anatomically, it is impossible to tell them apart. It seems prudent therefore to recognize only 1 species, *S. chinensis*, with 3 possible subspecies:
S. c. chinensis (OSBECK 1765) for the white dolphin, including the Bornean form; *S. c. lentiginosa* (OWEN 1866) for all the freckled forms; and *S. c. plumbea* (CUVIER 1829) for the darker variants.

Local Names Chinese or Bornean white dolphin, speckled or freckled dolphin, and lead-coloured dolphin. The Bornean variety is known as *la maing* (in Burma), *darfeel* (in Kuwait) and *malar* (in Sind). The freckled subspecies is known as *kabara nulla* (in Sinhalese) and as *bolla gadini* (in Telugu India). To cut across confusion, we suggest all forms should be called the Indopacific Humpback Dolphin.

Description Small; length averages 2 m (6.5 ft) for both sexes, with a possible maximum of 3.1 m (over 10 ft); calves are 90 cm (35 inches) at birth. Weight averages 85 kg (187 lb), with a maximum of 139 kg (306 lb); calves are about 25 kg (55 lb) at birth.

The shape is almost as variable as the colour. Calves have a classic dolphin form, much like that of the Bottlenose Dolphin (*Tursiops truncatus 76*), but as they mature, fatty tissue accumulates on the back, forming a narrow longitudinal hump. This intrudes between the back and the unchanged dorsal fin which is perched incongruously on top. Males and some females also develop large keels above and below the tailstock.

The beak is long and cylindrical, there is a slight melon and the flippers are short and rounded. The dorsal fin is roughly triangular, curving backwards in calves, but becoming softer and more rounded later. In older individuals with prominent humps the fin is often so flexible that it flaps at the tip.

The colour ranges from deep lead grey to ivory white, in a variety of patterns from unmarked to heavily spotted. Calves of all forms are uniform pale cream. In the South China Sea many dolphins keep this colour into maturity. In the Bay of Bengal and sometimes across the Arabian Sea to the coast of East Africa adults also remain light coloured, but develop a pattern of yellow, pink, grey and ruddy spots or freckles, mainly on their backs. Across the entire range certain adults seem to become completely dark, leaving a light area only on the belly, but when these dolphins age they acquire white blazes on the tip of the beak and on the ends of the flippers and fin. Scars are often prominent.

Field Identification All Humpback Dolphins breathe in a most distinctive way, which makes identification simple. The overriding impression is of slow, measured movement. First the

183

Colour variation in Indopacific Humpback Dolphins: (a) adult male, (b) juvenile, (c) spotted adult from East Africa

Typical Humpback Dolphin breathing posture, cruising horizontally at surface with beak showing

rodlike beak breaks water, followed by the melon and the hump. Then, while the dolphin blows, it cruises horizontally for a moment with the long beak just resting on the surface, but sometimes with the whole head lifted completely clear of the water, when the large hump and relatively small fin are clearly visible. Finally it ducks the head down, rolls the hump a little higher and slides from view. When undisturbed this deliberate pattern may be repeated several times, with the dolphin remaining at the surface for 3–5 seconds over each breath. At the end of a sequence the dolphin bends the hump at an acute angle, arching the back very steeply, and shows the entire tail as it dives almost vertically, disappearing for a period of 1–5 minutes.

We have been able to approach within 20 m of a group of Humpback Dolphins behaving in this way, but find that any attempt to get closer invariably leads to their diving, dashing off underwater in all directions and reappearing at the surface some distance away. Sometimes, before fleeing, one of the group will sit up vertically in the water with its whole head exposed. These dolphins are apparently neither afraid of, nor attracted to, larger boats, never bowriding, but sometimes swimming about beneath an anchored vessel.

Indopacific Humpback Dolphins often associate with Bottlenose Dolphins (*Tursiops truncatus* 76) in shallow water, small groups apparently integrating fairly easily with larger schools of Bottlenoses. We have also seen them feeding together with Spinner Dolphins (*Stenella longirostris* 70) just outside fringing reefs off the East African coast.

Stranding Humpback Dolphins are rarely stranded, being very much at home in shallow water. They can even heave themselves over mudbanks to get to channels of deeper water.

A dead adult should be easy to identify by its hump, but failing that the number of teeth is a useful clue. All Indopacific Humpback Dolphins have 30–38 simple peglike teeth (usually 31–32) on each side of both jaws, a total of at least 120. Bottlenose Dolphins (*Tursiops truncatus* 76), the species most likely to be confused with a humpless Humpback, never have more than 26 teeth in each side of both jaws, a maximum total of 104 teeth. There are 51 vertebrae.

Natural History Indopacific Humpback Dolphins feed exclusively in shallow water, often in mangrove swamps, on a wide assortment of fish, molluscs and crustaceans, generally after dark.

The usual social unit is a group of 2–20 (average 8 or 9), who move together in an orderly way. Young tend to be more playful, leaping into the air and twisting for no apparent reason. Sometimes a mother and nursing calf are found on their own and, occasionally, a solitary adult, usually a male, can be seen.

Courtship begins with one of a pair (we presume the male) floating on his side and beating rhythmically on the water with his exposed flipper. He follows this up by swimming alongside the female, rocking in the water as he goes. There ensues a flurry of chasing, leaping, rubbing, fluke stroking, inverted swimming, biting and clasping; ending with copulation, which takes place belly-to-belly with both partners standing vertically in the water.

Graham Saayman of the University of Cape Town reports a spectacular display, seen on the coast of South Africa, in which the dolphins swim upside down, burst out of the water still inverted, turn a full back somersault and re-enter, right side up but facing in the opposite direction.

Newborn calves have been seen in March and April north of the equator, but nothing else is known about periods of gestation or lactation.

Indopacific Humpback Dolphins produce directional clicks and creaks with a frequency of up to 25 kHz, clearly involved in echolocation. They also make a high-pitched whistle which, in groups of animals, sometimes builds up into a harmonic scream that seems to have a signal function.

Status Too little is known about this species to assess the size of its population, but it seems to be fairly common and in no apparent danger. A few are taken each year for human consumption in the Red Sea and the Persian Gulf and a few are netted in Kuwait, where their oil is valued chiefly for treating the wooden decks of dhows.

Distribution Indopacific Humpbacks are coastal, preferring areas in which there are lagoons, estuaries or mangrove swamps. They are seldom seen more than 20 km (12 miles) out to sea, but there is no reason to assume that they do not or cannot make ocean crossings. There is no evidence of migration, although it is possible that those at the northern and southern limits of the range might move closer to the tropics in the colder winter months.

Taking all 3 subspecies together, these dolphins are known from the coasts of South Africa, East Africa, Malagasy, Somalia, Aden, Oman, Kuwait, Iran, Pakistan, India, Sri Lanka, Malaysia, Thailand, Vietnam, China, North Borneo and northern Australia.

Sources AL ROBAAE (1970) in Kuwait, FRASER & PURVES (1960) revision, GRAY (1866) genus, LYDEKKER (1901) in Borneo, MORZER BRUYNS (1960) in Indian Ocean, MORZER BRUYNS (1971) general, OSBECK (1757) in China, PILLERI & GIHR (1972) behaviour, SAAYMAN et al (1972) behaviour, SAAYMAN & TAYLER (1979) behaviour, TIETZ (1963) in South Africa, ZBINDEN et al (1977) sounds.

ATLANTIC HUMPBACK DOLPHIN

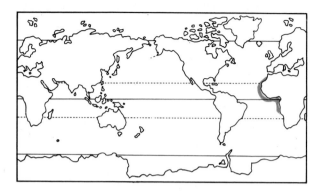

Classification In some respects cetology is like space travel. A favoured few have had the privilege of actually going out there and seeing things while the vast majority, including most specialists, have had to rely on second-hand observations. The result of this is that faulty observations sometimes get handed down and uncritically accepted by one generation after another.

The improbable suggestion that this species is herbivorous was first made in 1892 and was even repeated in a recent and otherwise excellent book on dolphins. The confusion began in the Bay of Warships in the Cameroons, West Africa, in 1892. Edward Tëusz collected a skull there and sent it back to the Jena Natural History Museum in Germany, where Willy Kükenthal described it and correctly identified it as a new species of the genus that was then known as *Sotalia*. He called it *Sotalia teuszii*. Tëusz also sent a description of the animal which gave it some highly unusual characteristics. He claimed that its stomach contained nothing but leaves, mangrove seedlings and quantities of sea grass. Kükenthal accordingly entitled his original paper *Ein Pflanzenfressender Delphin aus Kamerun*. Ever since then, most of the relevant authorities have spoken with awe of 'the one cetacean believed to feed exclusively on vegetable matter', or have bent over backwards to account for the existence of plants in the gut. The most

popular explanation has been that they represent the stomach contents of vegetarian fish which the dolphin has in its turn consumed and digested.

For a long time this paradoxical species was known only from that one skull, but between 1956 and 1959 several specimens were collected from the coast of Senegal by Jean Cadenat. He was puzzled, but not really surprised, to discover that their stomachs contained nothing but fish, including the herring *Ethmalosa dorsalis* and a species of mullet.

The solution to the dilemma lies in the original notes supplied to Kükenthal by Tëusz. After his botanical observations he points out that the animal also had a very thick skin, no dorsal fin, and nostrils (sic) which protruded as tubular prolongations. There never was a dolphin which looked like that, but there is another marine mammal which lives in the river estuaries of West Africa and fits this description perfectly, the manatee (*Trichechus senegalensis*), an aquatic relative of the elephant, which really does eat sea grasses and mangrove shoots. The only mystery which remains is how Tëusz managed to get the right skull out of the wrong body.

In 1960, Fraser and Purves placed the species in *Sousa*. There is still some question about the validity of the species; it is very much like *Sousa chinensis 40* and could be considered a geographical variant, but for the moment the fact that it has fewer teeth and more vertebrae than its relatives in the Indian Ocean, is considered sufficient justification for maintaining it.

Local Names Cameroon dolphin. To compare and contrast it with the Indopacific Humpback Dolphin, we call this species the Atlantic Humpback Dolphin.

Description Small; length averages 2.15 m (7 ft) for both sexes, with a maximum of about 2.5 m (8.5 ft). Weight averages about 100 kg (270 lb), with a maximum of 139 kg (306 lb).

The Atlantic Humpback closely resembles its Indian Ocean counterparts. Adult males have the same long hump, like a pack strapped to the middle of their backs, and similar fleshy keels above and below the tailstock.

Calves are a very light creamy colour, which darkens in adults to a pale slate grey, leaving white only on the chest and throat. The eyes are black.

Field Identification This species is easy to identify; it presumably surfaces like its relatives, rising beak first into the air after a dive and forging steadily along at the surface, with head and hump all showing together.

The Atlantic Humpback Dolphin is the only cetacean known to enter rivers anywhere in West Africa.

Stranding This species is rarely stranded. It has fewer teeth than the Indopacific forms. The normal count seems to be 26–30 on each side of both jaws, making a possible maximum of 120. The skull is broader than that of *S. chinensis* and there are 2 extra vertebrae in the tail region, making a total of 53.

Natural History Virtually nothing is known except for the now clearly established fact that this dolphin is definitely not vegetarian, but eats several varieties of fish. The few recorded sightings of live animals suggest that it occurs in small schools of 5 or 6.

Status Little is known, but this dolphin is apparently fairly common around the mouths of the Senegal and Gambia rivers. A few are taken by local fishermen with beach-seine and shark nets.

Distribution The Atlantic Humpback Dolphin is confined to coastal waters of tropical West Africa from Mauritania south to Angola. Current records are from Mauritania, Senegal, Cameroon, Nigeria and Angola.

Sources CADENAT (1956) in Senegal, CADENAT & PARAISO (1957) in Senegal, FRASER (1949) taxonomy, PILLERI & GIHR (1972) review.

ESTUARINE DOLPHIN (TUCUXI)

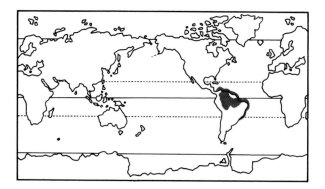

Classification A skin and part of a skull collected from the upper Amazon near Pebas were enough for Gervais at the Paris Museum to be certain that he had a new species, described in 1853 as *Delphinus fluviatilis*, from the Latin for belonging to a river. Two years later the Castelnau Expedition brought back another specimen from the same area which was almost white. This one Gervais called *D. pallidus.*

In 1858 a German collector called Kappler sent 3 dolphin skeletons from the Maroni River in Surinam to the Stuttgart Museum. One of these went to the Natural History Museum at Louvain, where it was described in 1864 by Pierre van Bénéden as *D. guianensis.*

Meanwhile, Gray had received a specimen from Santarem in the lower Amazon, which he described in 1856 as *Steno tucuxi*, based on the local Indian name. Ten years later he published his catalogue of the British Museum collection in which he created the genus *Sotalia* for van Bénéden's dolphin, calling it *S. guianensis*, but strangely failing to recognize that his own Amazon dolphin belonged with it.

When van Bénéden received a similar but more complete specimen from the Bay of Rio de Janeiro in 1875, he had no hesitation in calling it *S. brasiliensis*; and in 1880, with Gervais, transferred the 2 upper Amazon species *fluviatilis* and *pallida* to *Sotalia*. Finally, in 1884, Flower transferred Gray's species to *Sotalia.*

It is now becoming clear that *fluviatilis, pallida* and *tucuxi* are colour and age variants of the same species, which is common throughout the Amazon, for which *fluviatilis* is the prior name.

The dolphins that stray from the rivers into coastal salt waters are slightly larger and may have a few more teeth, but these differences are probably not great enough to warrant their recognition as separate species. The best solution, at least until a definitive study is made, is to regard them as subspecies, *S. f. fluviatilis* in the Amazon and its tributaries, *S. f. guianensis* (VAN BÉNÉDEN 1864) in the Orinoco and associated coastal areas and a third, *S. f. brasiliensis* (VAN BÉNÉDEN 1875) along the coast between the Amazon and Santos in Brazil.

Local Names *Tucuxi* or *pirayaguara* (Tupi and Yagua Indian), *bufeo, bufo, bofo, boto* or *bouto* (Portuguese- and Spanish-speaking settlers in the Amazon). Some cetologists use these names in the literature, but this can lead to confusion because they tend to be indiscriminately applied along the rivers to both *S. fluviatilis* and *Inia geoffrensis 32*. We prefer to restrict the term 'river dolphin' to members of the family Platanistidae, and so we have decided to call this species the Estuarine Dolphin.

Description Small; length averages 1.4 m (4.5 ft), with a possible maximum of 1.8 m (6 ft) for animals from Rio de Janeiro. Weight averages 36 kg (80 lb) for both sexes, with a maximum of about 50 kg (110 lb).

With the possible exception of the Gulf Porpoise (*Phocoena sinus 46*), this is the smallest living cetacean. It is a robust animal, shaped somewhat like a Bottlenose Dolphin (*Tursiops truncatus 76*), but smaller, with a more rounded fin and a beak less sharply demarcated from the head. The beak itself is short and distinctly ducklike, curving up slightly at the tip. The forehead is gently rounded and the fin is roughly triangular. The flippers are large and spatulate.

The colour is highly variable. The basic pattern is a soft garnet or medium grey with a brownish tinge, becoming maize coloured on the throat and belly. The southern subspecies may have more ochre flares on its flanks and patches of mustard on the fin. The Guiana form seems to be uniformly darker, ranging from black to dull medium grey. Many individuals have 2 bars of a paler hue extending diagonally up on to the flanks. The lower jaw and throat sometimes show a pink blush which fades rapidly after death. All Estuarine Dolphins seem to grow paler with age, with those in the dark rivers of the Amazon becoming altogether creamy white.

Field Identification In the rivers of the Amazon basin the only possible source of confusion is with the Amazon River Dolphin (*Inia geoffrensis* 32) which is far larger, pinker, slower and lacks a distinct dorsal fin. Estuarine Dolphins are more like typical marine dolphins in their behaviour, breaking through the surface in a rush, breathing rapidly and rolling directly over before diving. They also seem to be more social, occurring in schools of up to 20, which more often move together than the ponderously independent *Inia*. They are perhaps a little shyer than the large river dolphins, more wary of boats and more likely to leap clear of the water when disturbed by the sound of an engine or the passage of a wake. When breaching, *Sotalia* usually turn on their sides in the air and flop back down on their flanks.

When undisturbed Estuarine Dolphins breathe roughly once every 30 seconds, though they sometimes submerge for as long as 80 seconds at a time. The blow is far quieter than that of the river dolphins, little more than a delicate puff which can hardly be heard more than 15 m (50 ft) away.

Stranding There are no records of stranded Estuarine Dolphins, but a dead one is easy to identify by its teeth. There is some variation amongst the subspecies, but all fall within the range of 26–35 on each side of both jaws. The Amazon subspecies usually has 28–31, the Guiana form 31–33 and the southern coastal variation 32–35. There are usually a few more teeth on the upper jaw than the lower, while those on the mandible tend to be more disorderly, lying in ragged patterns rather than straight lines. There are 56 vertebrae and the first 5 pairs of ribs are double headed and joined to the sternum.

Natural History The teeth of Estuarine Dolphins often show considerable wear. This clearly has something to do with their diet, which consists of prawns, crabs and heavily armoured catfish. We have often seen an animal surface in the current and remain there, chewing at its food in full view until the item was sufficiently softened or suitably aligned for swallowing. *Inia* and *Sotalia* frequently feed together at points where tributaries flow into the main rivers, working their way upstream along the interface between the bodies of water which sometimes mix rather reluctantly.

The normal social unit seems to be a closely knit group of 6 or 7, who move and breathe and feed more or less together. Nothing is known of reproductive behaviour, but calves seem to be born in February or March when the water level is high and the rivers burst their banks and invade the low-lying forest areas. The calves are two-tone, black above and pinkish below, with a sharp line between the two.

Underwater recordings of Estuarine Dolphins reveal a pure single-tone call, which must have some communication function, as well as repeated trains of rapid clicks at a very high intensity. Each click seems to consist of a double sound produced at the rate of about 960 per second. These trains are highly directional and, when being transmitted at maximum speed, could range on targets as close as 15 cm (6 in) away. This is exactly the length of the beak, which means that in muddy water where visibility is nil, the dolphins can focus their sonar down to objects which are close enough to touch.

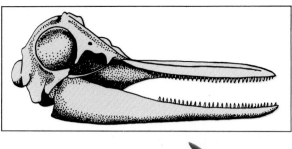

Above: skull
Below: Estuarine Dolphins often breach and fall back into the water on their sides

Status In the decade since we first went to the Amazon, the population of this species seems to have declined.

James Layne of the University of Florida estimated that *Inia* were twice as common as *Sotalia*. This may have been true for the area where he worked on the border of Brazil and Peru, for that time of the year, but it is by no means true of the river as a whole. We have spent a considerable amount of time exploring the Amazon and its tributaries from the mouth to a point 4,300 km (2,600 miles) from the sea and, as far as we can tell, there are slightly more *Sotalia*. The smaller species is commoner in the delta, but numbers decline inland, until *Inia* predominate in the upper areas.

Estuarine Dolphins nowhere enjoy as much protection by taboo as their mysterious pink relatives, and are often taken in drift and gill nets and marketed for medicinal purposes. In the *macumba* market at Belem near the river mouth, strings of dried dolphin vulvae are sold as magical charms.

Distribution The Amazon subspecies occurs throughout the basin, from a point 200 km (125 miles) out at sea, where freshwater finally gives way to salt, to the rapids in each of the great river tributaries. The Guiana form is similarly widespread in the Orinoco system and also extends its range into shallow waters along the northern coast of South America from Punta de Gallinas in Colombia to Paramaribo in Guiana. Little is known about the third subspecies, except that it is very common in the Bay of Rio de Janeiro and probably occurs as far south as Santos in the province of São Paulo. In the north it connects up with the Amazon overflow.

Sources GERVAIS (1853) original description, GRAY (1866) taxonomy, HERALD (1967) in captivity, LAYNE (1958) behaviour, NORRIS et al (1972) sounds, VAN BENEDEN (1864) Guiana form, VAN BENEDEN (1875) Rio form, VAN BENEDEN & GERVAIS (1880) taxonomy.

Family Nine – Phocoenidae
The porpoises

We have tried to resolve the totally unnecessary confusion between 'dolphins' and 'porpoises' by restricting the use of the latter term to this family alone, and by using it to describe *all* members of this family. However few other authors have been so rigorous. Unqualified references to the 'common porpoise' in Europe usually mean *Phocoena phocoena 43* but the same name in North America might equally well describe the Bottlenose Dolphin (*Tursiops truncatus 76*); in New Zealand it will probably refer to *Cephalorhynchus hectori 64.* As far as we are concerned, the classic usage has priority and 'porpoises' are members of the family Phocoenidae, established by Auguste Bravard in 1885 to include all very small beakless whales, having small, roughly triangular dorsal fins or none at all, and typically spadelike teeth with 2 or 3 lobes on the crowns. Between 3 and 7 of the neck vertebrae are fused.

The Finless Porpoise (*Neophocaena phocaenoides 47*) differs radically in external form from the 4 species of the genus *Phocoena*, but anatomically it is very similar. The third genus *Phocoenoides* is so distinct in anatomy, behaviour, marking and habitat that it could well be, and perhaps should be, separated from them and placed in its own family.

Discrimination between the 6 species of porpoise in the field is most easily accomplished on a geographical basis before turning to the characteristics of live or dead animals:

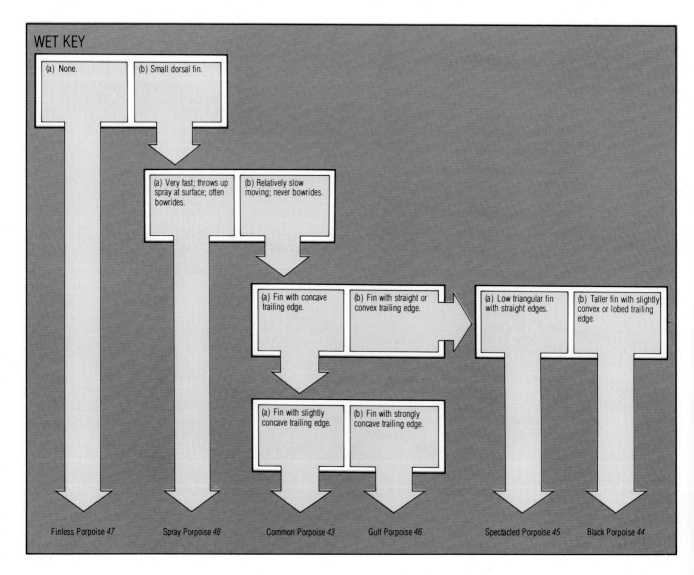

WET KEY

(a) None.

(b) Small dorsal fin.

(a) Very fast; throws up spray at surface; often bowrides.

(b) Relatively slow moving; never bowrides.

(a) Fin with concave trailing edge.

(b) Fin with straight or convex trailing edge.

(a) Low triangular fin with straight edges.

(b) Taller fin with slightly convex or lobed trailing edge.

(a) Fin with slightly concave trailing edge.

(b) Fin with strongly concave trailing edge.

Finless Porpoise 47

Spray Porpoise 48

Common Porpoise 43

Gulf Porpoise 46

Spectacled Porpoise 45

Black Porpoise 44

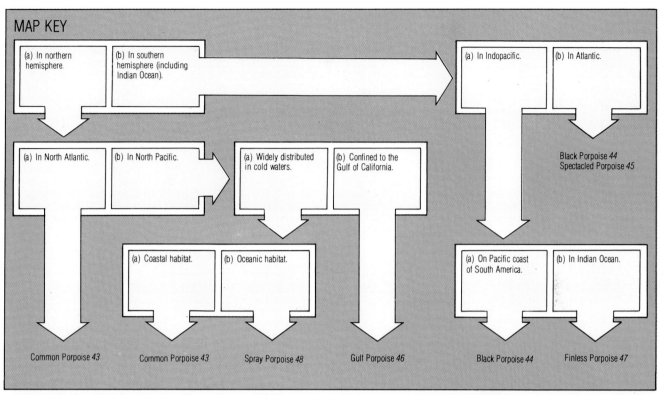

MAP KEY

(a) In northern hemisphere.

(b) In southern hemisphere (including Indian Ocean).

(a) In Indopacific.

(b) In Atlantic.

(a) In North Atlantic.

(b) In North Pacific.

(a) Widely distributed in cold waters.

(b) Confined to the Gulf of California.

Black Porpoise *44*
Spectacled Porpoise *45*

(a) Coastal habitat.

(b) Oceanic habitat.

(a) On Pacific coast of South America.

(b) In Indian Ocean.

Common Porpoise *43*

Common Porpoise *43*

Spray Porpoise *48*

Gulf Porpoise *46*

Black Porpoise *44*

Finless Porpoise *47*

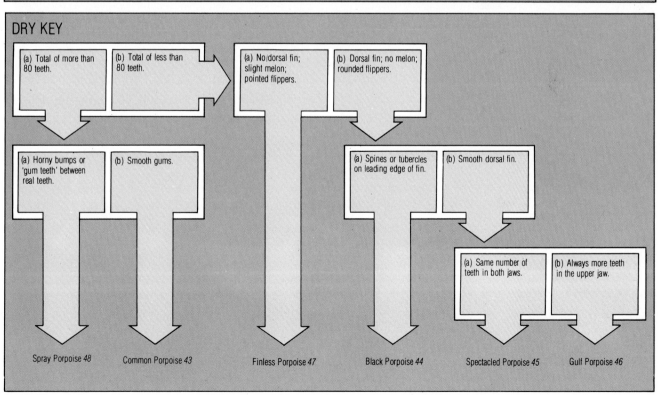

DRY KEY

(a) Total of more than 80 teeth.

(b) Total of less than 80 teeth.

(a) No dorsal fin; slight melon; pointed flippers.

(b) Dorsal fin; no melon; rounded flippers.

(a) Horny bumps or 'gum teeth' between real teeth.

(b) Smooth gums.

(a) Spines or tubercles on leading edge of fin.

(b) Smooth dorsal fin.

(a) Same number of teeth in both jaws.

(b) Always more teeth in the upper jaw.

Spray Porpoise *48*

Common Porpoise *43*

Finless Porpoise *47*

Black Porpoise *44*

Spectacled Porpoise *45*

Gulf Porpoise *46*

191

COMMON PORPOISE

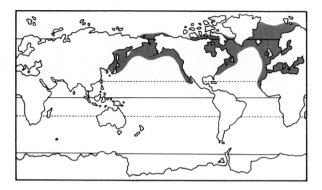

Classification This species has always been the most abundant cetacean in European waters and was one of the few named by Linnaeus in 1758. He was obviously aware of its seal-like appearance and, to distinguish it from the Common Dolphin (*Delphinus delphis 75*), called it *D. phocoena*, from the Greek *phoke*, a seal.

In the first edition of *La Regne Animal* in 1817, Cuvier established the genus of *Phocoea*. This spelling retains priority over variations such as *Phocena* and *Phocaena*.

Remote populations of this widely distributed species may have been isolated for long enough to become slightly different. The whole question needs more study, but the most likely candidates for subspecific status would be those in the North Pacific (which would be known as *P. p. vomerina* GILL 1865) and the Black Sea population (*P. p. relicta* ABEL 1905).

Local Names This was the first cetacean to be called 'porpoise', from the Latin name *porcus piscus*, a pigfish, in common use in ancient Rome. That led to herring hog (in England), puffing pig (in Newfoundland), *Meerschwein* (German), *zee vark* (Dutch), *marsouin* (French), *swinia*

morska (Polish) and *morskaja svinia* (Russian). Other vernacular names include *ise* (Norwegian), *tummler* (Yiddish), *tumler* (Danish), *tumblare* (Swedish), *toninha* (Portuguese), *handfiskar* (Icelandic), *marsopa* (Spanish), *mutur* (Turkish), *jurascuka* (Latvian), *nezumi iruka* (Japanese), *aladak* (Aleutian) and *tselkh-koo* (in Alaska). In place of the often used Harbour Porpoise, we prefer to call this species simply the Common Porpoise.

Description Small; length averages 1.4 m (4.5 ft), with a maximum of 1.8 m (6 ft); calves are about 75 cm (30 inches) at birth. Weight averages 41 kg (90 lb), with a maximum of 90 kg (200 lb); calves are about 5 kg (11 lb) at birth.

The Common Porpoise is small and chunky, rather stoutly built for its size. There is normally no trace of a beak, although the Black Sea population is said to have a slightly longer snout. The flippers are oval in outline and relatively small. The dorsal fin is broadly based, low and roughly triangular, with a somewhat concave trailing edge which gives it a curved point. The fin is situated almost in the middle of the back and sometimes has a row of small tubercles on the bottom of the leading edge. Similar tiny lumps are sometimes found on the edges of the flippers. The flukes are distinctly notched.

The usual colouring is very dark grey, almost black, on the back and both surfaces of the flippers and flukes. There is a patch of medium grey, sometimes slightly bluish, on the flank behind the rather small eye. The transition area between the dark back and the light belly is often speckled. The flipper lies entirely within the pure white area of the belly, which extends forwards to the throat, and there is a dark grey line leading from the flipper insertion to the angle of the jaw. There is some evidence to suggest that older individuals may become a little lighter in colour.

Field Identification Common Porpoises are seldom difficult to

192

identify. They are almost always found in small groups in shallow water or river estuaries, feeding or playing together. They seldom swim or dive in formation but usually create a complex pattern of interaction, cutting across each other's path and ruffling the water with sudden spurts or changes of direction. The Yiddish *tummler*, which is used for this species in parts of Germany and Denmark, expresses it perfectly. A *tummler* is an irrepressibly rowdy actor, who dashes on stage and, through some outrageous act, throws the entire production into disarray. The only thing we have never seen a porpoise do is leap out of the water, but we believe they sometimes do so.

Porpoises roll easily and slowly over at the surface when breathing, rising with a characteristic single puff about once every 15–20 seconds, then diving for 3–6 minutes.

As a rule Common Porpoises are timid and rather wary of swimmers or boats, but we have found that it is possible to get quite close to them on calm days when they are basking in the sun-warmed layers at the surface. They are very much more restless and easily disturbed on days when the wind blows. They apparently never bowride, but sometimes a small group will gambol alongside a slow-moving vessel before cutting away at an angle.

It is unlikely, given their characteristic shape and habitat, that they will be confused with any other species.

Stranding In spite of being so much at home in shallow water, Common Porpoises are often stranded. Identification of a beached individual is simple from its general shape, but in cases of decomposition, the teeth are highly characteristic. Instead of being conical and pointed like those of most dolphins, they are flattened at the tip into tiny spatulae (or spades) with crowns which are sometimes split. There are 22–28 on each side of both jaws, with a usual total of 92. The first 6 of 68 vertebrae are completely fused.

Natural History Common Porpoises live mainly on smooth fish, such as herring (*Clupea harengus*), whiting (*Gadus merlangus*) and mackerel (*Scomber scombrus*), taking about 4–5 kg (9–11 lb) per day. Sometimes this is supplemented with squid or shrimps.

This species matures very quickly, the females being able to breed when only 14 months old. Males reach maturity in their third year at a length of about 1.25 m (4 ft). Mating takes place in July and August, and begins with an elaborate courtship in which the pair swim along side by side as the male caresses the female with his flukes, in turn presenting his abdomen to be nuzzled. Gestation lasts for 10–11 months and calves are nursed for another 8 months. While suckling, the female rests at the surface on her side so that the calf may breathe easily while feeding. She usually becomes pregnant again in the following season.

Porpoises are normally gregarious, living in small, hierarchical groups of 10–15. They are highly vocal and demonstrative, splashing at the surface or swimming rapidly around in circles in what looks like some sort of greeting ceremony when they meet porpoises from other groups. Rarely, perhaps in preparation for a migratory movement, a number of groups

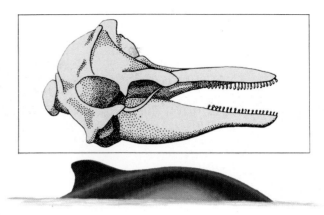

Above: skull
Below: Common Porpoise rolling at surface

will amalgamate into a school of several hundred.

There are several cases of Common Porpoises supporting an ill or injured group member and bringing it up to the surface to breathe; and one instance in Scotland in which a porpoise (presumably the mother) followed a boat carrying a calf that had been captured in a fishing net, and continued the pursuit for an hour until the calf was released, whereupon the two swam away together.

Vocalizations include a narrow-band low-frequency call and an echolocation click up to 1,000 times per second.

Status Common Porpoises are becoming a little less common than they were. There was a substantial porpoise catch made every year along the coast of Norway as early as the eleventh century, and they continued to be widely and enthusiastically eaten throughout Europe in medieval times. Henry VIII of England held regular porpoise feasts. For centuries the Danes captured hundreds of animals each November as they made their way out through the narrow straits between Funen and Jutland just before parts of the Baltic froze over. There used to be a population of 15,000 in the Baltic each summer, but pollution by insecticides has taken a very heavy toll.

More than 1,000 are still taken each year in Greenland and Iceland; and about as many again die each season in the salmon drift nets of Newfoundland. A certain number also fall foul of trawl and gill nets off the Pacific coasts of the United States and Canada. A few are taken by Japanese coastal stations and by opportunist fishermen.

Distribution Common Porpoises are still widespread in all cooler shallow waters of the North Atlantic and Pacific, and seem to be largely limited to areas with a mean temperature of less than 15°C (60°F). The species is known from the Mediterranean and Black Seas and often ventures considerable distances up major rivers. One was once recorded 320 km (200 miles) up the River Maas in Holland.

Sources AMUNDIN & AMUNDIN (1974) field study, ANDERSON (1969) succorant behaviour, DE LATTIN (1967) zoogeography, GASKIN (1974) review, LINNAEUS (1758) original description, MERCER (1973) colour, SCHEFFER & SLIPP (1948) in Pacific, SERVICE (1896) nurturant behaviour, VAN HEEL (1963) in Baltic.

BLACK PORPOISE (BURMEISTER'S)

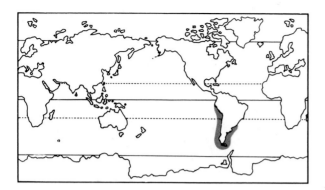

Classification Until very recently, cetology was an old-fashioned discipline, practised in a handful of centres by a few remarkable men. Each of these held supreme sway over a great collection, either founded or substantially augmented by themselves.

In South America the Museo Argentino de Ciencias Naturales in Buenos Aires housed a centre of cetology, built almost single-handed by Herman Karl Conrad Burmeister, a German entomologist (Professor at Cologne), who retired and settled in Argentina where he became an authority on the local fauna and Director of the Museum. He was a great naturalist who made meticulous notes and superb drawings

and so when an unusual cetacean was captured alive by fishermen at the mouth of the Rio de la Plata in 1865, he recorded exactly what it looked like.

It was flat faced, dark and seal-like, and on the leading edge of the dorsal fin it had a strange spiny bump. Burmeister called it *Phocaena spinipinnis*, from the Latin *spina*, with spines, and *pinna*, a wing, or a fin.

Local Names *Marsopa espinosa* (Spanish). It is usually referred to in the literature as Burmeister's porpoise, but we prefer to call it simply the Black Porpoise.

Description Small; length averages 1.5 m (5 ft), with a possible maximum of 1.8 m (6 ft). Weight averages 50 kg (110 lb), with a possible maximum of 70 kg (154 lb).

The Black Porpoise has the same general body form as the Common Porpoise (*Phocoena phocoena 43*). The head is not so round, and a little smaller and more flattened across the forehead between the tip of the jaw and the blowhole, and the flippers are larger. The fin is altogether different, set far back, with its leading edge long and straight, leaning very much backwards; the trailing edge, unlike in almost any other small cetacean, is convex rather than concave; on the base of the fin are several small tubercles, the foremost of which is sometimes elongated into a sharp spine which gives this porpoise its

specific name. In older individuals there are prominent keels above and below the tailstock.

The colour is deep grey to black. By the time this porpoise has been dead for even a few minutes it is completely black, but in life there is probably a lighter grey area on the belly and, in some individuals, a pale grey moustache-shaped marking around the anus. There may also be a broad dark line sweeping from the flipper around beneath the chin and returning on the other side.

There is a distinct possibility of confusion in the field with the rare and equally elusive Chilean Dolphin (*Cephalorhynchus eutropia 65*). That dolphin is about the same size and colouring, but has a far more triangular fin and none of the tubercles characteristic of this porpoise.

Field Identification Despite the Black Porpoise's discovery more than a century ago, no scientist has yet described one alive in the field. Less than a dozen specimens have been collected, all of them taken dead from fishing nets or discovered in fish markets.

We presume that its behaviour is like that of other porpoises in that it breathes inconspicuously, breaking the surface without fuss and seldom if ever leaping clear of the water. It would be easy to overlook, but once seen should be difficult to confuse with any other animal.

The Piebald Dolphin (*Cephalorhynchus commersonii 64*) occurs in the same area and has a lobed fin which looks something like that of the Black Porpoise, though more rounded on its leading edge; but the dolphin has an unmistakable white band across its back and is altogether a more lively, extrovert animal.

Stranding There is no evidence of stranding, but it can presumably happen. It is worth looking very closely at all small cetaceans found anywhere on beaches in South America. Black Porpoises should be readily recognizable by their peculiar dorsal fins, but failing that, the teeth could be useful for identification. They are typical spade-shaped porpoise teeth, but there are fewer of them than in any other member of this genus, 14–18 on each side of the upper jaw and 17–19 on each side of the lower. Common Porpoises (*P. phocoena 43*) and Spectacled Porpoises (*P. dioptrica 45*) have the same number of teeth in both jaws, and Gulf Porpoises (*P. sinus 46*) always have more teeth in the upper jaw. Only the Black Porpoise consistently has more in its lower jaw.

There are 68 vertebrae, of which only the first 3 in the neck are fused, as opposed to the first 6 in the Common Porpoise (*P. phocoena 43*).

Natural History Nothing is known except that one stomach analysis showed that the animal was eating both fish and squid. A 44-cm (18-inch) foetus found in the uterus of one porpoise was said to be near full term.

Status The Black Porpoise is usually referred to as rare; but Natalie Goodall, who is doing pioneer work on the cetaceans of Tierra del Fuego, has collected 4 sightings in the past few years and believes that this species could be quite common in the Straits of Magellan and the Beagle Channel. She reports that 4 porpoises were taken there in a fishing net in 1976.

Along the coast of southern Chile, north and south of Valdivia, a large number of small cetaceans is taken each year in fishermen's nets. These are sometimes eaten locally or sent to the fish-meal plant in Valdivia, but most of them are used for bait. It is possible that anything up to half of these catches could be of the 'rare' Black Porpoise.

In 1962 Robert Clarke found one of these porpoises in a fish market at Chimbote in Peru. Each year in Peru up to 114,000 kg (250,000 lb) of dolphin meat is officially sold in public markets. The species involved are unknown, but it is possible that many are Black Porpoises.

It is even possible that the so-called rare Black Porpoise is in fact one of the commonest cetaceans off the coast of Chile and Argentina. More work is urgently needed.

Distribution The Black Porpoise is definitely known from only a few scattered records, but is probably distributed in all cold coastal waters from about 33° south on the east coast of Uruguay; through Patagonia and Tierra del Fuego, round the Horn into southern Chile and up the cold current on the west coast to about 5° south of the equator in Peru. It is probably restricted to the shallow waters of the continental shelf, but because this widens on the Atlantic side of South America, we predict that the species will also be found in the Falkland Islands.

Sources ALLEN (1925) early description, BROWNELL & PRADERI (1976) status, BURMEISTER (1865) original description, CLARKE (1962) in Peru, GOODALL (1979) in Argentina & Chile, HAMILTON (1941) anatomy, NORRIS & McFARLAND (1955) taxonomy, PILLERI & GIHR (1972) anatomy.

SPECTACLED PORPOISE

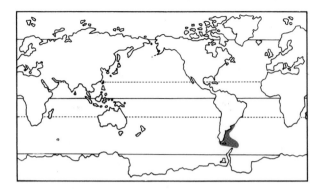

Classification The original discovery of this striking porpoise was made in Argentina at the turn of the century when a specimen was captured by José de Gaetano. A foetus taken from it is still in the museum at Buenos Aires, but the porpoise itself disappeared before it could be fully described.

In 1912 another individual was found stranded at Punta Colares on the Rio de la Plata and Fernando Lahille at the museum bottled the entire specimen in spirits. He was particularly struck by the black rings around the eyes and called it

Phocaena dioptrica from the Spanish for two eyes, or spectacles.

Nothing has changed since then except for a reversion to the original spelling of *Phocoena*.

A small cetacean with equally striking black and white markings was caught in Bahia de Talcahuano in southern Chile in 1893 and identified by Rudolph Philippi as *Phocaena obtusata*. It has been suggested that this could be a specimen of *Phocaena dioptrica*, which would extend the range of the species into the Pacific, but the individual was immature and is now thought to be a juvenile Chilean Dolphin (*Cephalorhynchus eutropia 67*).

Local Names *Marsopa de anteojos* (Argentinian). We stick to the excellent descriptive name of the Spectacled Porpoise.

Description Small; length averages 1.65 m (5.5 ft), with a maximum of about 2.04 m (6.5 ft). Weight averages 50 kg (110 lb), with a possible maximum of 84 kg (185 lb).

The Spectacled Porpoise differs markedly in shape from the Common Porpoise (*P. phocoena 43*). It is more fishlike, with a smaller, narrow head and the bulk of the body evenly distributed rather than concentrated in front of the fin. The flippers

are small and rounded, placed relatively close to the head. The flukes are sharply pointed and the fin is perfectly triangular, a little larger and more rounded at the tip in males than in females.

The markings are dramatic, black above and white below, with a sharp dividing line running around the nose, above the eye and rising up the side near the tail so that the tailstock in older animals becomes almost, sometimes completely, ringed in white. The underside of the flukes is white with grey lines radiating from the notch and a grey border. The lips are black and there is a broad black ring around each eye which exaggerates its size and looks very much like a pair of dark glasses. In many individuals there is a medium-grey line running from the gape of the mouth back to the point of flipper insertion and out along its leading edge to the tip. This is the only porpoise which has white flippers, but these cannot alone be used as field characteristics because there is some variability: every so often a Spectacled Porpoise is seen with completely black flippers.

Field Identification Spectacled Porpoises and Black Porpoises (*P. spinipinnis 44*) are found in the same waters off Uruguay and Patagonia, but there should be little difficulty in telling them apart. Both have black backs, but it is usually possible to see white showing at or near the water surface on the sides of the Spectacled species, which also has a much more triangular fin, whose trailing edge is straight, rather than convex or lobed.

There are no good field descriptions of live Spectacled Porpoises, but we presume that they live in small groups (strandings are always solitary) and lead relatively inconspicuous lives in shallow coastal waters. As far as we know, they do not leap and never bowride.

Stranding All specimens (less than 15) in collections have come from strandings. Identification of a beached porpoise of this species is simple if it is fresh, but if the eye rings are not visible, the teeth could be useful. There are 17–23 rather small spade-shaped teeth on each side of the upper jaw and 16–20 on each side of the lower jaw; but whatever the count (and the most common seems to be 21 in the upper, 17 in the lower), there are always more above than below. In Black Porpoises (*P. spinipinnis 44*) the reverse is true, there are always a greater number of mandibular teeth.

There are 68 vertebrae, of which the first 5 in the neck are fused, compared with 6 in the Common Porpoise (*P. phocoena 43*); and only 3 in the Black Porpoise (*P. spinipinnis 44*). Nine of the 13 pairs of ribs are double headed and the last 4 pairs are extraordinarily wide and flat, very much like those of the Pygmy Right Whale (*Caperea marginata 3*).

Natural History All that is known is that Spectacled Porpoises eat both fish and squid. The foetus taken from the first female to be found was just 48 cm (18 inches) long, but was already near full term.

Status Natalie Goodall in Tierra del Fuego has found a number of stranded Spectacled Porpoises and has seen at least 1 live animal in the Beagle Channel. She feels that they are probably relatively common. Tangle nets laid on the intertidal flats on the northern coast of Argentinian Fuego captured at least 2 in 1978. There may be similar catches on the coasts of Uruguay and Patagonia, but at the moment they do not represent any threat to the survival of the species, which may be far less rare than the late discovery or the lack of scientific specimens might suggest.

Distribution At the moment this is the only species of *Phocoena* known to occur around remote oceanic islands which lack suitable intermediate stepping stones, such as those provided by the Aleutian chain. One of the first known specimens beached itself, still alive, on the shore at a whaling station in South Georgia, 2,000 km (1,200 miles) from continental South America.

Apart from that possible stray, the species seems to be confined largely to the cold inshore waters of the Falkland Current.

Sources BROWNELL (1975) review, GOODALL (1978) records, GOODALL (1979) records, HAMILTON (1941) taxonomy, LAHILLE (1912) original description, PRADERI (1971) taxonomy.

GULF PORPOISE

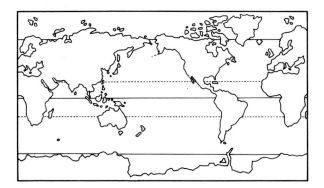

Classification In 1950 Ken Norris of the University of California at Santa Cruz found a single bleached porpoise skull above the high tide line on a beach at Punta San Felipe in the Gulf of California, now in the University's Museum of Vertebrate Zoology at Berkeley. In 1958, with several more skulls to hand, Norris and William McFarland of Cornell University published the first full description of their new porpoise and called it *Phocoena sinus*, from the Latin *sinus*, a bay of the sea, or a gulf.

Local Names Mexican fishermen in the Gulf, who see this species often, know it as *cochito* or *vaquita* (the little cow); it is also sometimes called *duende*, a name given to creatures

inhabited, according to local belief, by a supernatural spirit. We call it the Gulf Porpoise.

Description Small; length averages 1.35 m (4.5 ft), with a maximum of 1.5 m (5 ft); calves are about 60 cm (24 inches) at birth. Weight averages 36 kg (80 lb), with a maximum of 55 kg (120 lb).

The Gulf Porpoise is the smallest of its kind, if not the smallest of all living cetaceans. It is very much like the Common Porpoise (*P. phocoena 43*) in general body shape, which is why it was only recently discovered. The slightly smaller size is reflected in a small head, also a little flattened and broader in proportion to its length than that of related species. When seen from the side, the rostrum curves gently, dipping downwards at the nose.

The flippers are proportionately larger than those of the Common Porpoise and the fin is slightly higher, although roughly the same shape, with a sharp point and a concave curve on the trailing edge.

The overall colour is a medium to dark grey with a hint of brown in it. The belly, throat and chin are all white and the dark flippers seem to be inserted almost on the dividing line. The flanks appear to be a little lighter than the back and there is a faint suggestion of a stripe, widest at the flipper insertion and petering out somewhere near the corner of the mouth.

Field Identification It is fairly easy to identify Gulf Porpoises,

because this is the only species of porpoise in the Gulf of California.

On a recent expedition there we found 4 porpoises in shallow murky water just outside a mangrove lagoon south of Pico de Johnstone on the north-east coast of the Gulf. They were apparently feeding on bottom fish, each animal quartering its own area, rising a little higher in the water than the Common Porpoise would, but blowing with the same familiar loud and abrupt puff before sinking again for 20–30 seconds. The group was very close to the shore and, by approaching from the land, we were able to come within 10 m (33 ft) of the animal nearest the beach. Its fin had a much more rakish look, more sharklike, than that of any Common Porpoise, but the head, which was raised into full view each time the animal seemed to be swallowing something, had the same blunt, beakless profile. The colour of the back on 3 of the 4 porpoises was medium grey, but the fourth, and smallest one, was distinctly brown. It is possible that they darken with age. Our observation of this group continued until one of us moved too suddenly and all 4 took fright, racing off through the shallows in several different directions before reappearing several minutes later, as a group again, in deeper water some distance offshore.

Stranding Gulf Porpoises seem very comfortable in shallow water and have been seen 'inch-worming' their way across mudbanks to get to deeper water, but stranding may occur. There should be no difficulty identifying a dead animal. The teeth are small, but still typical porpoise teeth, flattened at the tip into miniature shovel shapes. The number and distribution are like those of the Spectacled Porpoise (*P. dioptrica 45*), with more in the upper jaw (20–21 each side) than the lower jaw (18 to a side).

There are 62–65 vertebrae, fewer than in any other porpoise and, like the Black species (*P. spinipinnis 44*) further south, only the first 3 in the neck are fused.

Natural History Gulf Porpoises are known to feed on fish such as grunt (*Orthopristis reddingi*) and croaker (*Bairdiella icistius*), but they probably also take shrimps and occasionally squid.

Little is known of their social behaviour. There are reports of schools of up to 40, but they seem to be most often seen in twos and threes. Calves are apparently born in early summer, May or June.

Status This species must be classified as becoming increasingly rare.

Mexican fishermen in the gulf used to take many porpoises, perhaps hundreds each year, in the gill nets they set for sharks. That industry has now closed, but a few porpoises still get caught in small-scale netting for *totoaba* (a seabass) or become entangled in shrimp trawls. Even these small operations are now ceasing, but this will not necessarily do the porpoise any good. The fishermen are leaving because the fish are no longer abundant and this scarcity has less to do with over-fishing than it does with the diversion of the Colorado River for irrigation projects. Nutrients which once flowed into the head of the Gulf, no longer do so and an entire ecosystem is dying.

Distribution The Gulf Porpoise seems to be confined to the Gulf of California. It has been most common in the closed northern end of the gulf, but is known to occur as far south as the Tres Marias Islands in the southern entrance. There are no confirmed sightings further down the mainland coast of Mexico.

Sources BROWNELL (1976) status, FITCH & BROWNELL (1968) feeding, NOBLE & FRASER (1971) taxonomy, NORRIS & McFARLAND (1958) original description.

FINLESS PORPOISE

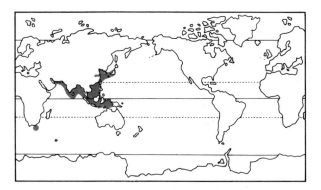

Classification This porpoise was described in 1829 by Cuvier from a skull brought back to Paris by the normally reliable collector Jean Dussumier. Cuvier called it *Delphinus phocaenoides*, the 'dolphin that is like a porpoise'. In 1846 Gray created the new genus of *Neomeris* for this species and remarked that there were 2 skulls in Paris, the type specimen (No. 3086) and another (No. 3087) also collected by Dussumier, on the coast of Malabar in 1837. Most workers have insisted that No. 3087 must be the true type, since, apart from No. 3086, there are no records of this species from South Africa, or anywhere nearer Africa than the west coast of India. The suggestion is that Cuvier's original specimen must have been mislabelled. Gray's genus was in fact invalid because it was preoccupied by a genus of worm (COSTA 1844). So, in 1899, Theordore Palmer replaced it with *Neophocaena*.

In 1971, on an expedition to Pakistan, Pilleri and his co-workers produced the first good observations of this species in the field. They also collected 12 specimens and made an exhaustive anatomical study, comparing them with 17 others collected from the eastern end of the range in China, Korea and Japan. Pilleri concluded that there were 2 separate species and called the eastern one *Neomeris asiaeorientalis*. In 1973 van Bree published a short admonitory paper in which he corrected the genus and relegated Pilleri's new species to a subspecies *Neophocaena phocaenoides asiaeorientalis*. He

went on to refer to it as a synonym for *Delphinus melas*, a species described over a century ago by Coenraad Temminck. Pilleri was outraged and in 1975 he and Gihr went even further and split the Chinese and Japanese specimens of this porpoise into 2 separate species, *Neophocaena asiaeorientalis* from the Chinese rivers, with 3 or 4 pairs of sternal ribs and a short ridge in place of the fin on its back, and *N. sunameri* from the coast of Japan, with 4 pairs of sternal ribs, little or no dorsal ridge, and a broader set of flukes. At the moment, the prevailing taxonomic climate is against undue splitting and most cetologists while allowing that the eastern form of the Finless Porpoise differs enough to be described as a separate subspecies *N. phocaenoides asiaeorientalis* (PILLERI & GIHR 1971), feel that the data presented for *sunameri* are insufficient to warrant recognition of it even as a subspecies, let alone as a species in its own right.

Local Names *Bhulga* (Mahr people of India), *molagan* (Tamils), *tabi* (Sindi of Pakistan), *hai-chu* (Chinese) and *sunameri* (Japanese). For a long time and in most of the Western literature, this species has been known as the black porpoise or the black finless porpoise. Its true colour is however a light blue grey, so we prefer to call it simply the Finless Porpoise.

Description Small; length averages 1.4 m (4.5 ft), with a maximum of 1.8 m (6 ft). Weight averages 30 kg (66 lb), with a possible maximum of 45 kg (100 lb).

The Finless Porpoise differs from other members of the family in more than the lack of a dorsal fin. It has a full square forehead produced by a melon of fatty tissue which provides just the hint of a beak. This soft flat face and the small round belly give even adult Finless Porpoises an infantile tadpolelike appearance. The body is deep, and a little behind the point where a fin would normally be placed there is a distinct dent in the profile. Beyond this the skin of the back is thrown up into a low ridge of tubercular projections 7–10 cm (3–4 inches) wide at the front, narrowing rapidly and finally disappearing on the tail. The shape and length of this ridge seem to differ,

diminishing in the eastern parts of the porpoise's range and perhaps disappearing altogether in Japan. The flippers are large and pointed and the flukes deeply notched.

In all the literature, for almost 150 years, the colour of the Finless Porpoise has been described as black or plumbeous. It becomes so very soon after death, but in life it is a light grey with a soft blue tinge. The lips, throat and area between the flippers tend to be a little lighter. The eyes are often pink and there is an odd dark marking, like a bib or chinstrap, across the lower jaw. In some this is clearly visible, whilst in others it fades imperceptibly into the white area on the throat.

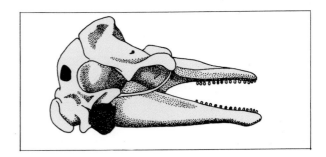

Field Identification Finless Porpoises are very simple to identify. They usually occur in or near river mouths and mangrove swamps. They are most often seen alone or in pairs, just touching the surface with their blowholes while breathing. The lack of a dorsal fin makes it look as though the back is completely submerged, but in fact enough reaches the surface to show that there is no fin. The flukes never appear above the water, and we have yet to see this species leap.

Following 3–4 abrupt breaths, these porpoises dive for 45–75 seconds, often surfacing 100 m (330 ft) away. Underwater they are surprisingly quick and lively, swimming just beneath the surface with sudden, darting or circling movements, like those of feeding tuna. Finless Porpoises are found quite often in the company of Indopacific Humpback Dolphins (*Sousa chinensis 40*), with which there is no possibility of confusion; but there is a real risk of mistaking the Snubfin Dolphin (*Orcaella brevirostris 69*) for this porpoise. The dolphin occurs in the same area, but is larger and has a small stubby fin.

Stranding Finless Porpoises are rarely stranded but a dead one is easy to identify, if not by the tubercles on its back where the fin should be, then by its typical spade-shaped teeth. There are no other species of porpoise known from anywhere in the Indian Ocean.

There are 14–21 (usually 15) flattened teeth on each side of both jaws. The skull is equally characteristic, with 2 most unusual, almost circular holes in the occipital bones on each side of the back of the head. The cranium is large and the mean weight of the brain at 466 g (over 1 lb) is unusually high for an animal of this size. A human with the same body weight has a brain which weighs about 700 g (1.5 lb).

There are 59–64 vertebrae, of which the first 5 in the neck are fused. There are 13 pairs of ribs.

Natural History Analyses of the stomach contents of captured Finless Porpoises show that they feed mainly on crustaceans. All the stomachs contained the remains of several kinds of prawn and shrimp (most often species of *Penaeus* or *Palaemon*) together with squid, cuttlefish, and a few small fish. It is said that when as many as 10 of these porpoises are found together, they sometimes hunt co-operatively, entirely surrounding a school of fish.

Although usually seen in pairs, groups of 5–10 Finless Porpoises are not uncommon. In 1959 a total of 17 were taken in a single seine net on the South Kamara coast of India,

and as many as 50 have been seen together on rare occasions.

Nothing is known of their courtship or mating behaviour. Calves in south-east Asia are born between August and October and in the Yangtze between February and April, when the river is high. During their first months the young spend long periods riding on their mothers' backs, clinging to the very area marked with the tubercules peculiar to this species. The balance and streamlining in this position are perfect, making it possible for the adult to swim rapidly, dive and come up to blow with the infant still firmly fixed in place (PILLERI & CHEN 1980).

Finless Porpoises are almost certainly efficient echolocators and we have heard a birdlike twittering sound coming from a group of 3 or 4 animals which surfaced together in a mangrove creek.

Status The present numbers are unknown and the status should probably be given as no more than locally common. A few Finless Porpoises die accidental deaths each year in set nets and shore seines in India. In China, somewhat larger numbers are taken deliberately, by gun or hook.

Distribution Finless Porpoises seem to be confined to shallow muddy estuaries in the tropical north Indian Ocean, with the possibility of local winter migrations into rivers in step with the movements of shrimps.

This species has been reported from Iran, Pakistan (including 65 km or 40 miles up the Indus River), India, Singapore, Sumatra, Borneo, the East China Sea (including the Yangtze River as far as Lake Tung T'ing), Korea and the Izu Peninsula in Japan. Our own records extend that range eastwards to the river deltas along the Asmat or Casuarina coast of Indonesian New Guinea (Irian Jaya).

The locality of the type specimen in South Africa remains disputed, but it is not impossible that the Finless Porpoise could be found along the east and even the southern African coasts. A sighting has been claimed in New Zealand, but that seems unlikely.

Sources ALLEN (1923) review, CUVIER (1829) original description, DAWSON (1960) catches in India, GIBSON-HILL (1949) in Malaysia, GIBSON-HILL (1949–1951) in Sarawak, MIZUE et al (1968) sounds, PALMER (1899) taxonomy, PILLERI & CHEN (1980) behaviour, PILLERI & GIHR (1972) in China, PILLERI & GIHR (1975) in Japan, PILLERI et al (1976) colour, VAN BREE (1973) taxonomy.

SPRAY PORPOISE (DALL'S)

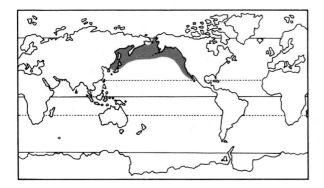

Classification William Healey Dall, served as quartermaster to Captain Charles Scammon. Dall set out on survey work of his own in Alaska aboard the *Humboldt* and in 1873, off Adak in the Aleutians, collected the first specimen of a species which now bears his name.

In 1885 True began to work his way through the collections of the United States National Museum. One look at Dall's specimen was enough to make him print a report of the discovery of 'A new species of porpoise from Alaska', which he called *Phocaena dalli*.

Other sightings and specimens quickly accumulated and it became apparent that there was considerable variation in the pattern of this pied porpoise. In 1909 Andrews, aboard the *Albatross* on a cruise to the Far East, saw Dall's porpoise in both the east and west Pacific. Off the coast of Japan he found individuals with more white on their flanks, white patches on both surfaces of the flukes, and deep keels on their tailstocks. He collected a specimen, decided that it was a new species with belonged with Dall's in a genus of their own, *Phocoenoides*; he named his species *Phocoenoides truei*.

Unfortunately all the characteristics of the Japanese porpoise which so impressed Andrews, are now known to occur also in Dall's Porpoise. True's porpoise is today generally regarded as either a colour phase of *P. dalli* or at best a doubtful subspecies, *P. dalli truei*.

Local Names White-flanked porpoise, *belokrylka* (Russian) and *isi-iruka* (Japanese). Sometimes known as True's Porpoise, this species is usually called Dall's Porpoise, but we prefer the more descriptive Spray Porpoise.

Description Small; length averages 1.8 m (6 ft) for males, with a maximum of 2.36 m (7.5 ft), and 1.8 m (6 ft) for females, with a maximum of 2.2 m (7 ft); calves are about 1 m (3.5 ft) at birth. Weight averages 123 kg (270 lb) for both sexes, with a possible maximum of 160 kg (350 lb); calves are about 25 kg (55 lb) at birth.

The Spray Porpoise is so little like any other species in the family that, were it not for the teeth, it might now be classified separately. The head is small and rounded with no sign of a beak; the lower jaw extends slightly beyond the upper. The flippers and flukes are about the usual size for a porpoise, i.e. two-thirds of body length and weight. The body is larger and heavier than that of the true porpoises, particularly around the middle. The fin is placed a little forward of the centre of the back and is higher and more nearly vertical in front than that of any other porpoise. The trailing edge has a distinctive double angle, which gives it a backward curve at the tip. The tailstock is heavily keeled, both above and below.

The colours are harlequin black and white in a number of variations. The basic pattern is black above and white below, but the shape and extent of the upside-down saddle of white on the belly and flank seem to be individual. In some porpoises it stops well behind the flippers, while in others the flippers are inserted within the white flank area. In many animals, the margin between the colours on the side is smudged with horizontal flowlines, as though the porpoise had swum away before its paint was quite dry. A few individuals have black anchor-shaped markings around the anus. There are ovoid patches of white on both upper and lower surfaces of the flukes of most individuals, and there is usually some white also on the dorsal fin. There may be other blotches of white on the black areas or vice versa, and there have even been reports of completely black Spray Porpoises.

Field Identification Added to the distinctive shape and colour of this species are behaviour patterns which make it quite unmistakable. Spray Porpoises actively seek out and bowride most moving vessels. To get into position at the bow, they literally throw themselves through the water, homing in directly on the ship, dashing along at the surface. The first sight of them is usually confined to a moving curtain of spray thrown up by their rapid approach. At this speed, the head and back produce a bow wave, thrown forward like a 'rooster tail', leaving behind it a hollow cone which makes it possible for the animal to breathe while still beneath the surface.

Once on station at the bow, Spray Porpoises behave in an equally characteristic fashion, darting in and out of the wave with quick jerky movements. This active zig-zag makes them the one species almost too difficult for Japanese crossbow artists to tag.

Left to themselves Spray Porpoises usually only move this fast while feeding, but they do seem to delight in speed for its own sake, sometimes making short rapid runs, throwing up spray for no apparent reason. Under normal circumstances they breathe roughly every 20 seconds, rolling slowly over at the surface with the sharp angle of the keel on the tailstock exposed so that, from a distance, they look like black and white squares rotating in the water.

Spray Porpoises are sometimes found together with Pacific Whiteside Dolphins (*Lagenorhynchus obliquidens 57*) which could cause confusion. Both species swim vigorously, but the dolphins have much longer, more curved dorsal fins and nearly always leap out of the water as they travel. Spray Porpoises very seldom jump. We have also seen them in the company of Shortfin Pilot Whales (*Globicephala macrorhynchus 50*) and Humpback Whales (*Megaptera novaeangliae 10*), with which there is no possibility of confusion.

Stranding Spray Porpoises have been found stranded. Freshly beached specimens are easily identified by their markings, but these soon become obliterated as the entire body darkens after death. Then the typical waisted porpoise teeth and the characteristic body shape should be sufficient, but failing these clues, this species also has some useful anatomical peculiarities. First and most evident of these are the strange 'gum teeth', rigid protuberances on the gums between the real teeth, which probably help the porpoise to grasp slippery foods like squid.

Many individuals also carry colonies of the yellowish diatom *Cocconeis ceticola* growing on the skin around the blowhole and on the trailing edges of fin, flippers and flukes.

The skull is broad and flat with a relatively short rostrum. There are 19–28 rather small teeth on each side of both jaws. The teeth start spade-shaped, but in adults may become rounded at the tip, retaining only the characteristic waist between the roots and the crowns. There are on average 92–98 vertebrae (30 more than in the Common Porpoise *Phocoena phocoena 43*), with all 7 neck bones fused into a single unit. Twelve of the 18 pairs of ribs are double headed.

Natural History Spray Porpoises feed on fish and squid, particularly the common cold-water squid *Loligo opalescens*. Hake (*Merlucius productus*) are also commonly found in their

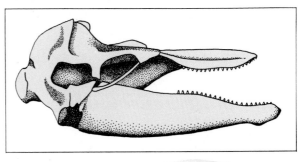

Above: skull
Below: porpoise producing typical 'Rooster Tail' of spray at the surface

stomachs, which is interesting because these fish normally live at depths of over 120 m (400 ft). Each porpoise seems to take about 15 kg (33 lb) of food every 24 hours, largely at night.

This species normally lives in small groups of 10–15 but we have several times seen as many as 100 travelling, evenly spaced out in a long single file. In 1953 a giant school of many thousand was seen off the coast of Japan. The school was estimated to be 8 km long and 2.5 km wide (5 × 1.5 miles).

Spray Porpoises seem to reach maturity when males are 8 years and females 7 years old. Both mating and calving take place all year round, with gestation estimated at 10–11 months. Lactation may continue for as long as 24 months.

The few recordings made of vocalizations show that these porpoises produce short pulsed sounds with frequencies up to 12 kHz. They are probably echolocators.

Status Spray Porpoise is still common, but is in urgent need of protection. At one time an estimated 10,000 died each year during Japanese gill-net operations for salmon off the coasts of Kamchatka. There are no recent figures of mortality in that area, but it is known that several thousand porpoises are taken – in the most inhumane way with harpoons and floats – each winter by Japanese fishermen for human consumption.

Distribution Unlike the other porpoises, this species is found both inshore and in deep oceanic waters. The range extends from Baja California across the Pacific to Japan, but is confined to colder northern waters with a temperature of less than 15°C (60°F).

There are spring migratory movements up beyond the Aleutian chain into the Bering Sea and an autumnal migration back south again to more coastal waters for the winter.

Sources ANDREWS (1911) True's porpoise, BENSON & GROODY (1942) review, HOUCK (1976) taxonomy, KASUYA (1978) life history, MIZUE et al (1971) ecology, MOREJOHN (1979) natural history, NORRIS & PRESCOTT (1961) catches, TOMILIN (1957) in Pacific (west), TRUE (1885) original description.

Family Ten–Globicephalidae
The pilot and killer whales

In 1866 Gray set up this family for species once included in the Delphinidae, but differing from them in having blunt, beakless heads and fewer teeth. For some reason Gray's suggestion fell into disfavour until in 1963 Masaharu Nishiwaki revived the family and characterized the 4 (or possibly 5) aberrant genera as being more than 2.5 m (8 ft) long, having blunt beakless heads, less than 15 teeth on both sides of both jaws and 3 or more fused neck vertebrae.

We find this separation both convenient and convincing and totally sympathize with Nishiwaki's reluctance to complicate cetacean taxonomy with the introduction of superfamilies or subfamilies. We feel that obvious, visible, external characteristics of form and behaviour should be given as much importance in classification at this level as more esoteric features such as the relative sophistication of the air sinus system. If the porpoises (Phocoenidae) and the coastal dolphins (Stenidae) deserve full family status, then we see no reason not to deal with Globicephalidae in the same way. In the field pilot and killer whales are very obviously distinct from other dolphins.

Map Key All members of the family are distributed worldwide and geographical clues are therefore of little use, but the following facts might be helpful:

1. Only the Great Killer Whale (*Orcinus orca 51*) occurs consistently in waters cooler than 10°C (50°F) or ever approaches the ice.
2. The Longfin Pilot Whale (*Globicephala melaena 49*) has not yet been found anywhere in the North Pacific.

Wet Key All members of the family are predominantly black, with white markings and a prominent fin.

Dry Key Once markings have been obliterated by darkening of the skin, the best clues to the identification of beached specimens, which may be immature, are the flippers and teeth.

Note In some classifications, the Melonhead Whale (*Peponocephala electra 54*) is included amongst the pilot and killer whales. It used to be considered as belonging to the genus *Lagenorhynchus* and many cetologists still feel that it rightfully belongs there. Although it does have the blunt head, 3 fused neck vertebrae, and the markings typical of Globicephalidae, it also has at least 20 teeth on both sides of each jaw. It could be included in the true dolphin family, but it is in many ways intermediate and so, on the basis of visible field characteristics alone, we include it here as an additional member of this family.

In the Keys it would be considered a small whale, difficult to distinguish from the Pygmy Killer Whale (*Feresa attenuata 53*), except that its flippers are pointed.

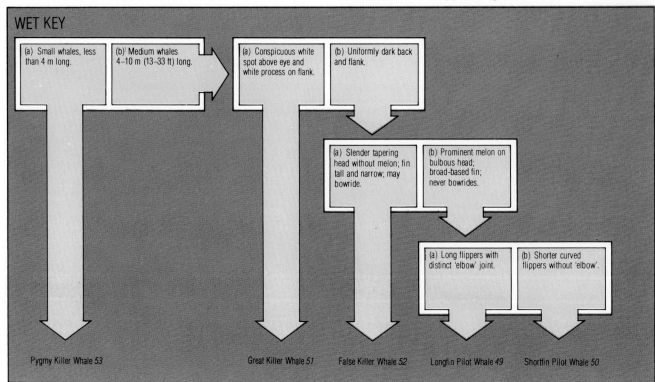

WET KEY

(a) Small whales, less than 4 m long.

(b) Medium whales 4–10 m (13–33 ft) long.

(a) Conspicuous white spot above eye and white process on flank.

(b) Uniformly dark back and flank.

(a) Slender tapering head without melon; fin tall and narrow; may bowride.

(b) Prominent melon on bulbous head; broad-based fin; never bowrides.

(a) Long flippers with distinct 'elbow' joint.

(b) Shorter curved flippers without 'elbow'.

Pygmy Killer Whale 53   Great Killer Whale 51   False Killer Whale 52   Longfin Pilot Whale 49   Shortfin Pilot Whale 50

DRY KEY

(a) Oval, paddle-shaped flippers; usually 12 teeth in both jaws.

(b) Long, narrow flippers.

(a) Flippers with distinct hump or 'elbow'

(b) Flippers thin and sickle-shaped.

(a) 10–13 teeth, often more on right side than left; neck vertebrae fused.

(b) 7 to 9 teeth on left and right of both jaws; more than 3 neck vertebrae fused.

(a) Flippers relatively short; more teeth on lower jaw (usually 8 above and 12 below).

(b) Flippers very long; same number of teeth (usually 10) in both jaws.

Great Killer Whale 51

False Killer Whale 52

Longfin Pilot Whale 49

Pygmy Killer Whale 53

Shortfin Pilot Whale 50

LONGFIN PILOT WHALE

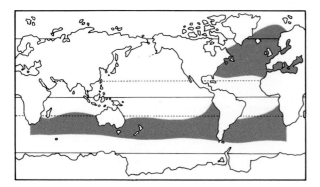

Classification Ever since the Middle Ages the residents of Orkney, Shetland and Faroe Islands in the North Atlantic have encouraged schools of small cetaceans, which they know as 'caa'ing' whales or *grindhvalur*, to beach themselves on sandy shore lines.

In 1806 Thomas Traill collected one of 92 whales stranded at Scapay Bay on Pomona in the Orkneys. He published a brief description of them in 1809 under the name of *Delphinus melas*, from the Greek *melas*, black. In 1828 Lesson created the genus *Globicephala* (sometimes given in the masculine form as *Globicephalus*), from the Latin *globus*, round, and the Greek *kephalos*, a head, to include a number of medium-sized whales with pot-shaped heads. Traill's species was one of these and for a while it was known as *Globicephalus melas*, but when it was appreciated that *Globicephala* was the generic name with priority, the species also had to be altered to its specific feminine form and in 1898 it became *Globicephala melaena*.

In 1834 Smith described a specimen beached at Slangkop near the Cape of Good Hope as *Phocaena edwardii*. In 1866 Gray realized that it was similar to Traill's whale and transferred it to *Globicephala*. It seemed to differ from the northern form in having a greyer belly and a white eyebrow. These may be valid distinctions, but they are no longer seen to be sufficient for the creation of a separate species. If, on further study, the southern race can be shown to be genuinely different, then it will be known, after appropriate adjustment of the gender and spelling, as *G. m. edwardii* (SMITH 1834).

Local Names *Caa'ing* or calling whale (in the Orkneys), pot-head, blackfish and bagfin (English), *calderon* (Spanish) or *chaudron, deducteur* or *conducteur* (French), *grindy* (Russian) and *gondo kujira* (Japanese). The name Pilot derives from its habit of swimming line astern with one individual in the lead, or from a belief that it guided fishermen to shoals of herring. We choose the descriptive name of Longfin Pilot Whale.

Description Medium; length averages 6 m (20 ft) for males, with a maximum of 8.5 m (28 ft), and 4.8 m (16 ft) for females, with a maximum of 6 m (20 ft); calves are about 1.8 m (6 ft) at birth. Weight of males can be up to 3,800 kg (4.25 tons) and of females up to 1,800 kg (2 tons); calves are about 100 kg (225 lb) at birth.

Longfin Pilot Whales vary enormously with age and sex. Calves of both sexes have a narrow head which tapers, much like that of the False Killer Whale (*Pseudorca crassidens 52*); but as they mature the head fills out and becomes square and bulbous. In adult males the melon grows into a pronounced shiny black pot shape. There is no constriction between the head and the body and no beak at any stage, although the upper lip protrudes slightly.

Although the body is long, it is relatively slender and narrow along the tailstock where it is compressed to form substantial dorsal and ventral keels. The absence of a neck makes the flippers appear to be directly attached to the head. They are very long, about 20 per cent of total body length, bent sharply into an angular 'elbow' about halfway down their length, and sharply pointed. The fin is equally distinctive, relatively high, but so broad at the base that it seems low. It is placed forward of the midpoint of the body and sweeps strongly backwards from a leading edge that is thicker in males than in females. There is a report of at least one animal, seen in Newfoundland in 1964, in which the fin was triangular.

The colour is mainly black or very deep grey, but on the throat, chest and belly there is a white or pale grey anchor-shaped marking. In most individuals there is a medium grey saddle-shaped patch directly behind the fin which is conspicuous at close quarters, but often difficult to see in the field. There may also be small white blazes beneath the chin and on the undersides of the flippers. Calves are more brownish grey with a white mottling.

Field Identification The most distinctive field characteristic is the strongly curved, long-based fin, set well forward on the whale's back. This, coupled with the broad, round foreheads of all adult animals, makes identification, at least as far as the genus, relatively simple. Longfin Pilot Whales can be distinguished from Shortfin Pilot Whales (*G. macrorhynchus 50*) by their longer flippers and the fact that the heads of adult male Shortfins are often set off from the body by a dorsal notch in the neck at the position of the blowhole.

Both species normally travel in compact schools, slowly and steadily near the surface, rising to blow roughly once every 1 or 2 minutes. The dome of the head appears first, followed very quickly by a strong blast about 1.5 m (5 ft) high, which is clearly visible under most conditions. Then the head and the back and the entire fin remain in sight as the whale glides forward before submerging. Prior to a long dive, the body and fin are raised more deliberately and the flukes show clearly. The whales apparently have sufficient control over their buoyancy to sink straight down without arching or diving. Most dives are 30–60 m (100–200 ft) deep, but Pilot Whales frequently go to very much greater depths, perhaps as much as 1,000 m (over 3,300 ft). This species is said to stay

down for as long as 2 hours, but even if that were possible, it would be unusual. The duration of a normal feeding dive is 5–10 minutes.

Longfin Pilot Whales are largely indifferent to ships, seldom come close and never bowride, but schools can be approached to within 50 m (160 ft) by even a large vessel. In smaller boats we often manage to manoeuvre amongst a school and come within a boat length (6 m or 20 ft) of an individual before it sounds.

We once came across a group in mid-Atlantic resting motionless at the surface. When they became aware of us, several pitchpoled (sitting up vertically in the water with their heads exposed as far as the flippers) and held this position for up to 30 seconds. These same individuals then subsided and slapped their tails and flippers on the water several times before the whole school dived. Breaching is rare, but we have seen juveniles leap clear of the water in a moving school, throwing themselves completely over in a backward somer-

sault. The normal swimming speed is roughly 4–6 kph (2–3 knots), but in a panic Longfin Pilot Whales are said to exceed 50 kph (25 knots).

We have seen them with Common Dolphins (*Delphinus delphis 75*) and Bottlenose Dolphins (*Tursiops truncatus 76*), with which there is no possibility of confusion, but they can be mistaken at sea for False Killer Whales (*Pseudorca crassidens 52*). Both species are dark, with prominent fins and 'elbowed' flippers. They can best be distinguished as follows:

Globicephala square head; robust body; broad-based, back-curved fin; grey saddle patch; seldom breaches; never bowrides.
Pseudorca tapered head; relatively slender body; narrow, pointed fin; back all black; often breaches and bowrides.

Stranding Social bonds amongst a group of Longfin Pilots are so cohesive that whatever happens to one seems to affect them

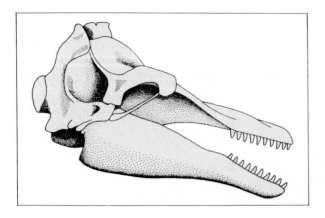

all, and stranding is very common. One group of over 1,000 once hurled themselves ashore on Lofoten Island in Norway. A school is easily stampeded by the injury or stranding of any of its members, something which the whalers in the Faeroes have been quick to exploit; but large numbers of these whales frequently beach themselves without human assistance.

The number of whales stranded may in itself be enough to identify this species. If more than 20 medium-sized whales are involved, they are almost certain to be Globicephalidae and if the stranding takes place anywhere in the cooler waters of the North Atlantic, they must be Longfin Pilot Whales.

Identification of the genus should be simple from its external appearance, but it may take an expert and a laboratory preparation to identify the species of a decomposed or young individual. Adult Longfin Pilot Whales can be separated by their elbows and sometimes by their teeth. All members of the genus have 7–12 strong, slightly curved teeth on each side and usually near the front of each jaw. A Longfin Pilot Whale will usually have a total of 20–22 teeth in its upper jaw, while the Shortfin usually has no more than 18 slightly larger teeth. There are 58–60 vertebrae, of which 6 are fused into a highly compressed unit. Six pairs of ribs are double headed.

Natural History Each mature Longfin Pilot Whale consumes about 34 kg (75 lb) of mixed fish and squid daily. The most common food is squid, particularly *Illex illecebrosus*, and the most favoured fish seem to be cod, horse mackerel and turbot.

Societies range from small groups of half a dozen to large schools of 40–200. There is at least one report of a herd 3,000 strong. The structure of the group depends on activity, and varies from travelling schools, which move along on a broad front usually with large males in the lead, through erratic feeding schools to 'loafing groups' in which the whales lie about in disarray with fins and flippers showing, apparently sleeping with their bodies in close contact. Herds are probably hierarchical and polygamous, with young males (who are often more scarred than older ones) bearing the brunt of aggression. Cohesion is so strong that fishermen in Novia Scotia once hesitated to kill any group member for fear that the leaders would sink their boats. Jaw-clapping, which produces a sharp explosive sound, has been heard in threats.

Longfin Pilot Whales seem to mature at about 6 years, although only females breed at this age. Males wait until they are nearer 12. Courtship is said to be violent, with a pair rushing at each other and clashing their melons together. Pregnancy lasts for 16 months and births take place throughout the year, with a possible peak in the spring. Lactation continues for another 20 months, although during the second half of this period, the calf may take some solid food.

The sound repertoire is amazing. Apart from an assortment of squeaks, a variety of contoured whistles, as well as chirps, pops, buzzes, snores, whirs and grating sounds, a Longfin Pilot Whale can even smack the lips of its single nostril. Many of these noises are clearly social and communicative, continuous even in a loafing group, but some must be involved in echolocation.

Status Records of the Faeroes hunts have been kept since 1584 and show that in the first 300 years a total of 117,456 whales were caught. About 1,500 are still taken each summer in hunts announced by the lighting of special bonfires which bring a large number of islanders and their boats together, beating tin pans, shouting and yelling, throwing special stones attached to leather thongs into the water again and again, until they succeed in stampeding a passing school into particular shallow bays where the whales beach themselves or can be killed in the shallows with knives, spears and lances. In Newfoundland in recent years similar hunts have taken place without the traditional and technological restraints of the islands. In 1956 alone, 10,000 were killed and that population at least seems now to have collapsed. In the North Atlantic as a whole, numbers have been substantially reduced, but there has been little or no hunting in the southern hemisphere where the whales (perhaps representing a separate subspecies) are still fairly common.

Distribution The North Atlantic population is known from Greenland, Iceland, the Barents and North seas, south to the coast of the north-eastern United States and to the Mediterranean. These whales seem to be most at home in deeper waters 13°–30°C (55°–85°F), with a preference for the cooler areas. Their place seems to be taken over in the tropics by the related Shortfin Pilot Whales.

There seems to be a break in the distribution at the equator, with the southern form taking up a similar range in the South Atlantic, South Pacific and Indian Oceans. Coastal records there are from the Cape, New Zealand and Australia, and oceanic ones from almost everywhere in the cool waters of the Benguela, Falkland and Humboldt currents, north of the Antarctic convergence.

There are no recent catches and no confirmed sightings anywhere in the North Pacific, although illustrated records from tenth-century Japanese manuscripts seem to show that the species occurred there at that time.

Sources BROWNELL & BOICE (1965) triangular fin, DAVIES (1960) in southern hemisphere, JOENSEN (1976) in Faeroes, SERGEANT (1962) biology, SMITH (1834) taxonomy, TARUSKI (1979) sounds, TRAILL (1809) original description, WILLIAMSON (1945) in Faeroes.

SHORTFIN PILOT WHALE

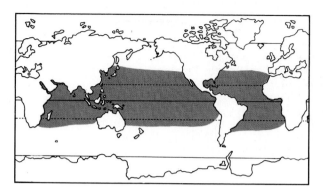

Classification Following René Lesson's creation of the genus *Globicephala* in 1828, a number of specimens began to appear from various parts of the world. Several of these came back to London where John Edward Gray was busy compiling his report on the collection made during the voyage of HMS *Erebus* and HMS *Terror*.

In 1846 Gray described several new pilot whales including one 'from the South Seas' which he named *Globiocephalus Macrorhynchus*, from the Greek *makros*, large, and *rhynchos*, a beak. The animal lacks a beak altogether, but Gray was a museum man, used to making relative assessments of unfleshed bones, and this animal does have an unusually large head for a dolphin of its size.

A century later, in 1950, Francis Fraser altered the species name to *macrorhyncha* to match the feminine gender of *Globicephala*, which is the proper generic form; but it now appears that this is wrong. The specific name is not an adjective, but a noun in aposition and, according to the Rules, must retain its original masculine gender. So, awkward though it may sound, we must keep the androgynous *Globicephala macrorhynchus*.

In 1846 Gray also described *G. sieboldii* from the skeleton and drawing of an animal stranded near Nagasaki and brought back to Europe from Japan by the German anatomist Karl Siebold. This name is now regarded as synonymous with *G. macrorhynchus*, although some cetologists believe that animals found in the North Pacific might be different enough to warrant their recognition as the subspecies *G. m. sieboldii* (GRAY 1846). In 1869 Edward Cope described a pilot whale taken from Baja California by Scammon as *G. scammonii*; but this is simply another *G. macrorhynchus*.

Local Names Generally referred to as the Pacific pilot whale in order to distinguish it from the Atlantic species, but these

labels ignore the existence of either form in the southern hemisphere. We prefer instead to call it the Shortfin Pilot Whale.

Description Medium; length averages 5.5 m (18 ft) for males, with a maximum of 6.75 m (22 ft), and 4.25 m (14 ft) for females, with a maximum of 5 m (17 ft); calves are about 1.4 m (4.5 ft) at birth. Weight can be up to 3,000 kg (3.3 tons) for males, and up to 1,500 kg (1.6 tons) for females; calves are about 60 kg (132 lb) at birth.

The Shortfin Pilot Whale is very much like its long-flippered relative (*G. melaena 49*) in general body shape. The only major morphological difference is that the flippers in this species are usually shorter, 15–17 per cent of total body length. This is not easy to see and may not be as consistent as some taxonomic statistics imply, but the shape of the flippers is distinctive. The Longfin Pilot Whale has a marked bend or 'elbow' halfway along its flipper, whereas the flipper of the Shortfin species is smoothly curved into a sickle shape.

A further distinction lies in the size and shape of the head, which seems to be larger and more robust even though the body of the Shortfin Pilot Whale is marginally shorter and lighter. This difference is particularly marked in adult males, whose pot-shaped melons rise steeply from the blowhole near the angle of the neck and sometimes protrude so far that they overhang the mouth by as much as 10 cm (4 inches).

The fin is set far forward, broad based and strongly curved. It sometimes gives the impression of being taller and less pointed than that of *G. melaena 49*. The keel on top of the tailstock is very marked in males.

The colour and marking in both species is similar, although in Shortfin Pilot Whales the contrast between the dark back and the lighter pattern beneath is less marked. The blaze on the belly is still shaped like a kedge anchor with its blades opening out in front of the flippers, but instead of being white, it is pale grey and much more difficult to see. Many individuals look completely black. The grey saddle patch behind the dorsal fin is present and tends in this case to be *more* conspicuous than it is in the Longfin Pilot Whale.

Field Identification Shortfin Pilot Whales travel in highly social groups at a sedate 8 kph (4 knots). Adults rise evenly to breathe, showing the top of the head first and producing an explosive blow. After a long dive the blast sounds like a sharp high-pitched whistle. Although the melon breaks the surface every time the whale breathes, the mouth is never seen. Calves plunge along next to their mothers, throwing their whole heads up out of the water as they swim.

This species is usually indifferent to shipping. When we approach a herd moving along a broad scattered front, a small segment of the line simply submerges as we steam across, and surfaces again, without disruption, behind us. In small boats we can often get within an oar's length of such a travelling school; the whales simply roll over on to their sides to get a better look at us.

In the tropics loafing groups of up to 40 are common, bobbing at the surface with their heads up or lying on their backs with their flippers in the air. They seem to be positively buoyant. It is even possible that they might sleep at these times, maintaining nothing more than an occasional sculling movement of the flukes to keep them floating. When disturbed, one or more will invariably pitchpole or spyhop, rising high up out of the water with the head thrown well back, peering at us around the sides of the melon, because it is impossible for them to see anything directly ahead. In this position, in a heat haze or with the sun at their backs, they look disturbingly like the cowled figures of a group of monks in black robes; early Italian mariners actually called this whale *monaco*, a monk.

Shortfin Pilot Whales are often found in the company of Bottlenose Dolphins (*Tursiops truncatus 76*) and Pacific Whiteside Dolphins (*Lagenorhynchus obliquidens 57*), presumably feeding together on squid. There is no possibility of confusion with either of these long-beaked species, but in warmer waters there is a distinct possibility of confusion with a school of the equally social False Killer Whales (*Pseudorca crassidens 52*). Both are shiny black in the water, with prominent fins, but the False Killers are more extrovert, often leaping clear of the water in their haste to get into the bow wave of a moving vessel. Shortfin Pilot Whales never bowride. At close quarters the comparatively slender tapered head and the longer, narrower fin of False Killer Whales are distinctive. There is also a superficial resemblance to the Pygmy Killer Whale (*Feresa attenuata 53*) and the Melonhead Whale (*Peponocephala electra 54*), but both species are considerably smaller and have much more pointed fins.

Stranding Entire schools frequently strand on remote tropic shores for no apparent reason. They are usually found in close concentration on the coast, but sometimes a herd is scattered into several groups dispersed along a beach as though radiating out away from some source of panic offshore. Shortfin Pilot Whales have no difficulty breathing while stranded and unless they die of overheating or sunstroke, usually survive until the following tide, when they invariably drown. Their compressed body shape makes it impossible for them to lie on their bellies. As the tide retreats, they topple over on to one side and when the water returns it covers their blowholes long before it is deep enough for them to right themselves. They cannot move and they cannot turn their heads. The only reaction left to the animals is to thrash the rising water with their tails until they retch and die.

Beached pilot whales are simple to identify to genus level as *Globicephala*, but the species is more difficult, although the flippers are a good guide and teeth can be helpful. Shortfin Pilots have fewer, larger teeth than their relatives. There are usually 8–9 at the front on each side of both upper and lower jaws. With recently beached animals it may be possible to see a dark chevron marking just behind the blowhole (with the arms of the V facing forward) and a number of fine grooves, in whorls and loops like giant fingerprints round the circumference of the body.

The first 6 of 57–59 vertebrae are fused into a single compressed unit.

Natural History Shortfin Pilot Whales feed largely at night, most often on squid, with the opalescent squid (*Loligo*

Shortfin Pilots cruising at surface and diving

opalescens) a favourite in Pacific waters. An adult may take as much as 45 kg (100 lb) a day.

The normal social unit is a school of between 10 and several hundred. The bonds between individuals in a group, as shown by mass strandings, are strong. Ken Norris tells of shooting 1 of 15 whales in a group off Southern California and having 2 others literally take the dead animal away from the ship so that he never saw his intended specimen again. On several occasions a Shortfin Pilot Whale has been seen lifting an injured group member up to the surface to breathe by balancing the body across its blowhole. At Marineland of the Pacific, when the female of a pair died in 1960, the male spent 5 hours carrying the body to and from the surface with him by holding her flipper in his mouth.

Female Shortfin Pilot Whales reach maturity at the age of 6, and males at 10 or 11. Courtship seems to begin with a pair butting heads together underwater with great force until the male attains an erection. The pair then swim slowly together, with the female upside down and ahead of the male, her body strongly arched, rubbing her genital slit between his flippers until they slide into position and mate. Gestation lasts 15–16 months and the breeding cycle takes 3 years.

Shortfin Pilot Whales are enormously vocal. In the field we find that the approach of a school is always accompanied by a staccato popping sound which can be heard distinctly, even above the water. Underwater, or with an ear pressed to the wooden gunwale or pontoon of an inflatable boat, it is usually possible to hear a chorus of birdlike twitters in several different keys. A wide range of other sounds, including echolocation clicks, has been recorded from whales in captivity.

Status Shortfin Pilot Whales seem to be common and in no great danger from hunting. Early whalers caught large numbers of Shortfin Pilots when they could not get Great Sperm Whales. Today Shortfin Pilots are hunted extensively only in Okinawa and on the Izu Peninsula in Japan, where up to 800 are driven ashore each year. Another 200–300 'blackfish' are taken each year, usually by harpoon, off the island of St Vincent in the Lesser Antilles where they are consumed locally as 'island bacon'.

Distribution Apart from a single stray recorded in Alaska, this species occurs only in tropical and subtropical waters of the Atlantic, Pacific and Indian oceans. There is some evidence of local migrations associated with the movement and abundance of squid, but there is no reason to suppose that northern- and southern-hemisphere populations are distinct.

Sources BROWN (1960) in captivity, BROWN (1962) in captivity, CALDWELL et al (1971) in St Vincent, FRASER (1950) taxonomy, GILMORE (1962) review, GRAY (1846) original description, KRITZLER (1952) in captivity, NORRIS & PRESCOTT (1961) behaviour, RACK (1964) in Caribbean, VAN BREE (1971) taxonomy.

GREAT KILLER WHALE (ORCA)

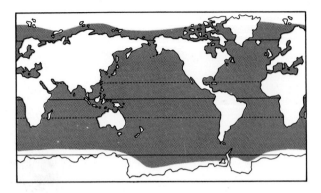

Classification There is no type specimen. Linnaeus based his original description on the accounts of early mariners, choosing to name it *Delphinus orca*, literally the demon dolphin, from the Latin *orcus*, lower world.

Although it is the largest of the dolphinlike group, this whale differs markedly from them, and so in 1860 the new genus *Orcinus* was created specifically for it by Leopold Fitzinger.

Kellogg in 1940 transferred the species to *Grampus* and in 1942 Scheffer revived the nineteenth-century name *Grampus rectipinna* for a second species which, also according to Kellogg, had a longer fin. Both revisions have now been questioned and abandoned, and all Great Killer Whales are included in a single worldwide species.

Local Names Because of its swordlike fin this whale is called *epée de mer, epaulard* and *orque gladiateur* (French), swordfish (old English) *swaardvis* (Dutch), *Schwertwal* (German). Its predatory habit has led to killer or trasher (English), *vaghund (Norwegian), tandthoye* (Danish), *fann-fiskar-hydengen* (Icelandic); other names include *agluk* (Aleutian), *nookur* (Kurile), *habyrna* or *huyding* (Icelandic), *stourvaga* or *spekkhugger* (Norwegian), *svinka* or *kasatka* (Russian), *sakamata* or *sadshi* (Japanese), *innatu* (Korean), *fakan*

Giant Killer Whales 'sky hopping' and 'porpoising'

(Lapp), *ardursak* (Greenland Eskimo) and *kosatka drava* (Czech).

Description Medium; length averages 8 m (27 ft) for males, with a maximum of 9.75 m (32 ft), and 7 m (23 ft) for females, with a maximum of 8.5 m (28 ft); calves are 2–2.4 m (8 ft) at birth. Weight can be up to 7,200 kg (8 tons), usually 700 kg/m for males, and 500 kg/m for females.

This is a heavy-bodied whale, with a blunt round head, smooth streamlining, a tall fin, and unusually large (20 per cent of body length) paddle-shaped flippers.

The colour is basically black above, sharply distinguished from a white underside extending from the chin to a point beyond the anus, with a white process reaching back up on to the flank behind the fin. There is also a conspicuous white spot above and behind the eye. Both sexes have a pale grey saddle patch directly behind the fin. In calves the black areas are greyish for most of the first year and the white areas tend to be tinged with buffy yellow. Pure black animals have been seen, and an albino was captured in British Columbia in 1970.

It has been suggested that Killers in the southern hemisphere have larger melons and smaller eye patches. We have seen such an individual on the equator, but we have found no geographical correlation with any particular shape or marking. There is sufficient natural variation in the shape of the eye patch, the extent of the grey saddle and the shape of the fin, to make almost every individual recognizable from a distance.

Field Identification The most useful field characteristic is the tall fin which in adult males may be almost 2 m (6 ft) high. Even in females and immature males it is longer and more pointed than that of any other cetacean. The male fin is erect, sometimes even forward leaning, while the female's is curved and sharklike. Both show clearly each time the whale rises up out of the water to blow.

The usual breathing pattern involves a series of up to 5 short dives of 10–30 seconds, followed by a longer dive of 1–4 minutes. Most dives are fairly shallow, but in experimental conditions whales have been recorded at a depth of over 300 m (1,000 ft).

Apart from the pronounced fin, the best field mark is the white spot behind the eye. In most circumstances this stands out in bright contrast to the glossy black body. The grey saddle patch is usually conspicuous at close quarters, but it is

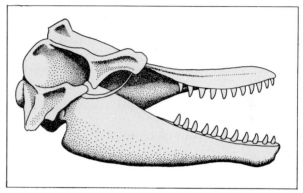

variable, and in certain lights can be difficult to see.

Killers are generally unconcerned by shipping and are usually easily approached. They are capable of speeds exceeding 50 kph (27 knots), but we have only seen one, an immature male, bowride. A more common response is for the whole group to spyhop or pitchpole, which involves standing vertically with the head and body (as far as the flippers) held up above the surface. In this position the eyes are exposed, giving the whales a clear view of their surroundings. Sometimes an approaching ship may give rise to lobtailing. This may lead to breaching. On a few rare occasions, we have seen a pod move rapidly off porpoising along on the surface.

If adult males (with their long fins) are present, Great Killer Whales are unlikely to be confused with any other species. If a pod consists only of females and young there is a possibility of confusion with Grey Dolphins (*Grampus griseus 68*) and False Killer Whales (*Pseudorca crassidens 52*). These differ from *Orcinus* as follows:

Grampus has a more slender body and a more tapered head; grey or white with many visible scars.
Pseudorca has a more slender body and a more tapered head; solid black with no visible markings.

Stranding In this species stranding is uncommon, but does take place, usually involving males. Mass strandings have been recorded from Vancouver Island and (in 1955) from a sloping beach near Wellington, New Zealand.

The characteristic shape makes beach identification relatively easy, even after darkening of the skin has obliterated the striking markings. Where decomposition is advanced, or only bones remain, identification is simplified by several distinctive skeletal characteristics. The skull is broad and chunky, with 10–13 (usually 11) strong, sharp teeth on each side of both jaws. The teeth are oval in section, curve inwards and backwards at the tip, and interlock when the jaws close. In adults they may be as much as 12 cm (almost 5 inches) long, but only the last third protrudes from the gum and is covered with enamel. The total length of an adult skull is 60–120 cm (24–48 inches), and anything greater than 100 cm (40 inches) is bound to belong to a male.

There are usually 52 vertebrae, the first 3 or 4 fused together. The first 6 or 7 of the 12 ribs are always double headed.

Natural History The basic social unit is the pod, which appears to be an extended family of 5–20 members. Usually 20 per cent of these are adult males, another 20 per cent are calves, the remainder females and immature males. The group is cohesive and travels close together, or in contact, along a broad front seldom exceeding 1–2 km. There is a high degree of co-operation in the hunt and ample evidence of communal concern.

Killers are predators feeding on a wide variety of prey. Analyses of stomach contents show squid, bony fish, skates, rays, sharks, seals, sealions, sea birds and walrus. Killers also eat other whales. Common Porpoises (*Phocoena phocoena* 43), Spray Porpoises (*Phocoenoides dalli* 48) and White Whales (*Delphinapterus leucas* 35) all feature in their diet, and there are records of groups attacking and killing adult Piked Whales (*Balaenoptera acutorostrata* 7) and Grey Whale calves (*Eschrichtius robustus* 4). The killers seem to be particularly fond of the tongues of the large baleen whales, ripping these out from carcasses that have been inflated by whalers, and perhaps even attacking live great whales with similar intent.

There are several accounts of a group which co-operated with Australian whalers hunting Humpbacks, in return for the tongues of the whales successfully captured.

In captivity Killers eat about 45 kg (100 lb) a day, but their appetites can be enormous. Eschricht claimed to have found 13 porpoises and 14 seals in the stomach of one male, with yet another seal hung in its throat.

Small prey is certainly swallowed whole, while larger meals are ripped apart. We have seen a group in the Galapagos dismember a 5 m (16 ft) manta ray by throwing it into the air and, on another occasion, an adult male sealion, weighing close to 300 kg (over 600 lb), tossed several metres up out of the water and deftly caught again. Even fully-grown polar bears are not immune.

Almost anything in the sea seems to be at risk and, on occasion, even terrestrial animals. In Patagonia the whales often follow seals right up into water too shallow for either to continue swimming. In 1937 on Johnstone Island in British Columbia a male almost succeeded in catching an Alsatian dog by hurling itself half out of the water on to a rock shelf from which the dog was barking.

In the Antarctic we watched 2 Killer Whales tilt an ice floe, by lifting it on their backs, so that a sleeping Weddell seal slid down directly into the waiting jaws of a third whale.

There is not one authentic report of a Great Killer Whale ever having harmed a human in any way without provocation. Today it is common, though nevertheless demeaning, for trainers in marine shows to place their heads into the enormous mouths of captive Killers, and to ride on their backs; but it must have taken a great deal of courage for the first diver, in a seal-like black wetsuit, to enter the water with wild whales before it was established that they unaccountably exclude man from their otherwise omnivorous taste for warm-blooded prey.

Little is known of reproductive behaviour. Gestation lasts for 12 months. Calves are born in shallow water in autumn or early winter. Males reach maturity at a length of 6 m (20 ft) and females at about 5 m (16 ft).

Great Killer Whales produce a narrow band, low-frequency clock sound with a pulse length between 0.5 and 1.5 milliseconds, quite unlike that made by any other dolphin. It probably functions as an echolocator, finding food in murky waters. Killers also have several distinctive calls, some within our hearing range.

Status This species is still common, but it is threatened by unnecessary killing. The US Navy is reported to have killed hundreds with machine guns and depth charges in 1955 at the request of Icelandic fishermen.

Several are taken each year off the Norwegian coast, by the herring fleet. The industry claims that the whales are devastating fish stocks, but if it is true that there is now direct competition for a dwindling resource, then the source of the problem is almost certainly human over-fishing. About 50 are taken each year by Japanese coastal stations, and over 1,000 were killed by Soviet pelagic whaling operations in the Antarctic in 1979.

A lucrative and growing trade involving the capture of live Killer Whales for display has recently come under control, at least in Canadian and American coastal waters.

Distribution This species occurs in all parts of all oceans, limited only by the edge of the icepack. Great Killer Whales prefer coastal areas and cooler waters and are most often seen in shallow bays and estuaries, but we have come across a pod on the equator in very deep water, 750 km (400 nautical miles) from the nearest land.

The species shows an irregular pattern of migration, probably governed more by the availability of favoured food than by a preference for water or climatic conditions. When they do travel, pods cover approximately 100 km (about 68 miles) per day.

Sources BALDRIDGE (1972) killing Grey Whales, BIGG et al (1975) census in Canada, CHANDLER et al (1977) US census, ERICKSON (1978) radio tracking, ESCHRICHT (1862) stomach contents, HANCOCK (1965) killing Piked Whales, MEAD (1962) co-operation with whalers, NORRIS et al (1961) observations, SIVASUBRAMANIAN (1964) in Ceylon, WELLINGS (1944) in Australia, WILLIAMS (1964) relations with man.

FALSE KILLER WHALE

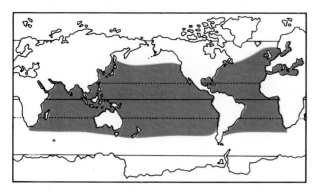

Phocaena crassidens from the Latin *crassus*, thick, and *dens*, a tooth. He decided that it was probably extinct, but qualified his conclusion by adding 'until it should be proved that it still existed in our seas'.

Sixteen years later 100 of these 'extinct' whales beached themselves on the Bay of Kiel in Baltic Germany. Johannes Reinhardt examined several and concluded that Owen's fossil had come back to life. In 1862 he published the first description of its external appearance and, because of its resemblance to the Great Killer Whale (*Orcinus orca 51*), named it *Pseudorca crassidens*, from the Greek *pseudos*, false.

In the succeeding century nothing has changed, and no subspecies have been proposed or recognized.

Classification This species was discovered as a fossil on land long before anyone realized that it was still to be found at sea.

In 1846 the sub-fossil skeleton of a whale was dug up in the Lincolnshire fens near Stamford, England. Owen called it

Local Names Thicktooth grampus (English), *Dickzachniger butzkop* (German), *swarte zwaardwalvis* (Dutch), *okikondo* (Japanese), *faux orque* or *pseudorque* (French) and the False Killer Whale.

Description Medium; length averages 5.4 m (18 ft) for males, with a maximum of 6 m (20 ft), and 4.6 m (16 ft) for females, with a maximum of 5.4 m (18 ft); calves are about 1.5 m (5 ft) at birth. Weight can be up to 2,200 kg (2.5 tons) for males and up to 1,100 kg (1.25 tons) for females; calves are about 80 kg (175 lb) at birth.

The external resemblance to the Great Killer Whale is only superficial; the backs and fins of females look a little alike in the water, but everything else about them is different. The False Killer Whale is long and slender with a head more rounded than that of the Great Killer, but not nearly as bulbous as that of either of the pilot whales (*Globicephala* spp.). Its relatively slender but nevertheless swollen snout juts out beyond the lower jaw by 10 cm (4 inches) or more. The mouth opening is large. The flippers are pointed and narrow in comparison with the broad paddles of the Great Killer Whale. They are shorter than those of both pilot whales, being roughly 10 per cent of total body length, and have a distinct hump or 'elbow' at the midpoint, very much like those of the Longfin Pilot Whale (*Globicephala melaena 49*). The dorsal fin is narrow and strongly curved, it has been called 'cucumber shaped', and is set almost in the centre of the back. It is tall and prominent, about the size and shape of a female Great Killer Whale's, but by no means as exaggerated as the fin of an adult male.

The body of the False Killer is uniformly deep grey or black, except for a thin light grey blaze on the belly. This marking is anchor-shaped, similar to that on the underside of both pilot whales, but smaller and more muted. It seems to be most readily visible on animals in the Pacific. Calves are altogether lighter, with a larger pale area on the belly.

Field Identification False Killers are as social as the pilot whales and, at a distance, difficult to distinguish from them, but at close quarters the differences are obvious. This species comes readily to the bows of moving vessels, leaping in graceful flat arcs. False Killers are positively attracted to ships, but too slow to enjoy the bow wave of anything moving faster than about 25 kph (12 knots). These are the largest whales ever likely to be seen in a bow wave and will readily ride in front of smaller ships for minutes on end, but have to content themselves with sporting in the stern wave of a larger, faster vessel. After leaving the bow, they can often be seen leaping in the wake some distance behind. Such behaviour in a whale of this size is often enough in itself for positive identification.

When undisturbed by shipping False Killer Whales cruise in co-ordinated groups, blowing once every 15–20 seconds, or twice as often in the case of calves. When breathing, they tend to show much more of themselves than do the pilot whales, rising so that the back, fin, part of the flank and all of the head are exposed. They very often do this with their mouths open, so that the large white teeth are clearly visible, making them look intimidating. They also frequently lobtail.

On every occasion in which we have come close to a group we have been able to detect their piercing whistles from 200 m (660 ft) away, sometimes even above the sound of our outboard engines. James Porter of the University of Michigan describes the effect: 'The noises were astonishingly diverse,

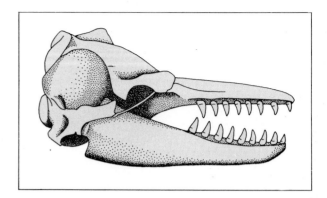

much more varied than the sounds of human speech, both in pitch and intensity. Each whale seemed to be making different sounds. The cacophony gave the impression that whatever they were "saying", they were not all "saying" the same thing at the same time.'

Where sightings are fleeting, the possibility exists of confusion with several other species: the Great Killer Whale (*Orcinus orca 51*), Pygmy Killer Whale (*Feresa attenuata 53*), Shortfin Pilot Whale (*Globicephala macrorhynchus 50*) and, to a lesser extent, the Melonhead Whale (*Peponocephala electra 54*). All are dark, have prominent fins and lack beaks, but a second look should make discrimination possible on the following grounds:

Pseudorca more than 4 m (13 ft) long; narrow tapered head; high curved fin; long pointed flippers with elbow; no markings visible.

Orcinus more than 4 m (13 ft) long; wide pointed head; very high fin; oval paddle-shaped flippers; bright white spot behind eye and white flank patch.

Globicephala more than 4 m (13 ft) long; square bulbous head; broad-based fin; long pointed flipper with elbow; white visible on throat.

Feresa less than 4 m (13 ft) long; narrow pointed head; pointed fin with wavy trailing edge; short round-tipped flippers; pale grey markings often visible on flank.

Peponocephala less than 4 m (13 ft) long; very pointed head; simple curved fin; short pointed flippers; white goatee marking on chin.

We have twice seen False Killer Whales together with Grey Dolphins (*Grampus griseus 68*), but there is no possibility of confusion between these species.

Stranding False Killers are often stranded. One of the most informative and best documented strandings ever to take place involved this species. In July 1976, 30 False Killer Whales swam into shallow water on the shore of the Dry Tortugas Islands off Florida. Three days earlier the same group were stranded briefly in Pine Island South, 260 km (160 miles) away. On both occasions the centre of attention was the lead male who was seriously wounded and bleeding

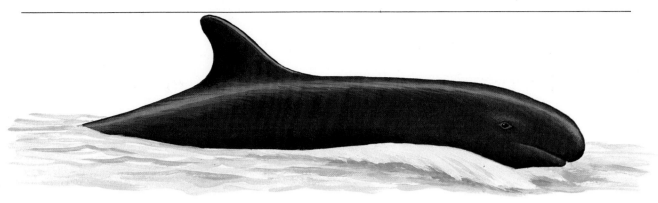

Typical posture of False Killer Whale surging along the surface

from one ear. He was supported continuously by at least half the whales who formed living wedges on either side, holding him up and keeping his head toward the beach. Tidal flux in the Tortugas is very low and at all times during the following 3 days, all the whales had the option of leaving and swimming freely away at any time. Despite the fact that many developed severe sunburn blisters and were clearly uncomfortable in the heat of the day, not one individual left, or could be persuaded to leave by human intervention. When attempts were made to push some of the whales ashore, they became highly agitated and could not be restrained from returning to contact with the group on the beach. Not, that is, until the night of the third day, when the large male died. Then the formation broke up and by dawn and the following tide all the whales had swum safely away. On any other coast with a normal tidal range, this would have been another inexplicable mass stranding, fatal for the entire group by the end of the first ebb.

Identification is usually very easy. Even when the characteristic shape has been completely obliterated by advanced decomposition, the teeth are unmistakable. They are large and stout, circular in cross section (the Great Killer Whale's teeth are oval) and up to 25 mm (1 inch) in diameter. There are usually 7–10 teeth on each side of the upper jaw and 9–12 on each side of the lower. Average numbers are 8 and 10, but there are always more in the lower jaw.

All 7 of the neck vertebrae (out of an overall total of 50) are fused. 6 of the 10 pairs of ribs are double headed.

Natural History False Killer Whales feed partly on squid, but their strong teeth and large gape make it possible for them to catch sizable fish such as bonito (*Sarda lineolata*), tuna and mahi-mahi (*Coryphaena* sp.). These are all predators in their own right, and catching them requires a formidable turn of speed. We have seen False Killers feeding on bonito, burst through the surface with a fish held crosswise in their mouths, carried up by their own momentum until the entire front half of their bodies, including the flippers and fin, was exposed above the water.

In captivity these whales have prepared large fish by shaking them until the head and entrails break free, then peeling and discarding the skin from a fillet before swallowing the remainder. There is even a record of an adult holding a fish

steady in her mouth while her weaning calf chewed small portions off it. These examples of food manipulation may be commonplace amongst land mammals, but they are rarely seen in cetaceans. There are well authenticated records, from both the Atlantic and the Pacific, of False Killer Whales stealing fish from the lines of fishermen.

Schools of False Killers are normally quite large, but tend to be secondarily subdivided into small family groups of 4–6. Maturity is reached between the ages of 8 and 12, breeding seems to occur at all times of the year, and gestation is known to last a little over 15 months.

Apart from the audible, drawn-out, high pitched sounds that can be heard above water and are probably used in communication, False Killer Whales produce several other sounds in which the skull and the melon seem to act as transducers. False Killers are certainly echolocators.

Status This species is probably relatively common. There used to be a traditional hunt organized by Arab whalers in the Gulf of Oman for the teeth of False Killer Whales. These were at one time traded all the way across Asia and Alaska to certain North American Indian tribes. Today a few are taken each year when schools are driven ashore at Goto Island near Nagasaki, Japan. Otherwise there is little exploitation.

Distribution False Killer Whales are found worldwide, in all tropical and temperate seas. They are sometimes seen close to coasts in cooler water, but over most of their range tend to be oceanic.

There is some evidence that they gather in large numbers for local migrations, either for feeding or breeding. False Killer Whales almost certainly pay no attention to the equator, crossing it at will.

Sources BROWN et al (1966) behaviour, BUSNEL & DZIEDZIC (1966) sounds, MIZUE & YOSHIDA (1961) in Japan, OWEN (1846) original description, PILLERI (1967) behaviour & sounds, PORTER (1977) stranding, PURVES & PILLERI (1978) anatomy, REINHARDT (1862) taxonomy.

PYGMY KILLER WHALE

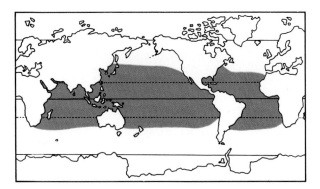

Classification In 1827 Gray identified a skull of unknown origin as *Delphinus intermedius*. Later he had second thoughts and renamed it *Grampus intermedius*. By 1846 he was much more familiar with cetaceans and changed his mind yet again, deciding that *Orca intermedia* was probably more appropriate. In 1870, still worrying about the oddity of the single skull, he created for it the entirely new genus of *Feresa*. In 1875 a second specimen appeared from 'somewhere in the South Seas', and in the last paper he ever published Gray named it *Feresa attenuata* from the Latin *attenuatus*, reduced.

In 1952 Munesato Yamada discovered a third specimen in Japan, a complete skeleton of an animal caught near Taiji on Honshu Island. Yamada identified it with *Feresa intermedia*,

but at about this time it was discovered that that old species name was in 1827 preoccupied by another *Delphinus intermedius*. So in 1956 a new name, *Feresa occulta* from the Latin *occulere*, to conceal, was chosen for both Gray's original and Yamada's new specimen.

Then a complete animal was found beached at Yenn in Senegal, 5 more stranded themselves at Luderitz in south-west Africa, 1 was discovered in Hawaii, 2 in the Gulf of Mexico, more in South Africa, Costa Rica, St Vincent in the Caribbean, and in 1963, 14 specimens were captured, still alive, near Oshima in Japan and herded into a harbour on the Izu Peninsula. With all these it became apparent that there was sufficient diversity within the species to allow for the small differences observed by the authors involved. Today all the known specimens are grouped together, according to Gray's final thoughts on the subject, as *Feresa attenuata*.

Local Names Slender Pilot Whale and Pygmy Killer Whale.

Description Small; length averages 2.28 m (7.5 ft) for males, with a maximum of 2.75 m (9 ft), and 2.13 m (7 ft) for females, with a maximum of 2.4 m (8 ft). Weight averages 170 kg (375 lb) for males, with a maximum of 225 kg (500 lb), and 150 kg (330 lb) for females, with a maximum of 200 kg (440 lb).

The Pygmy Killer Whale is an interesting amalgam. Its body is slender and tapers rapidly behind the fin, like that of the

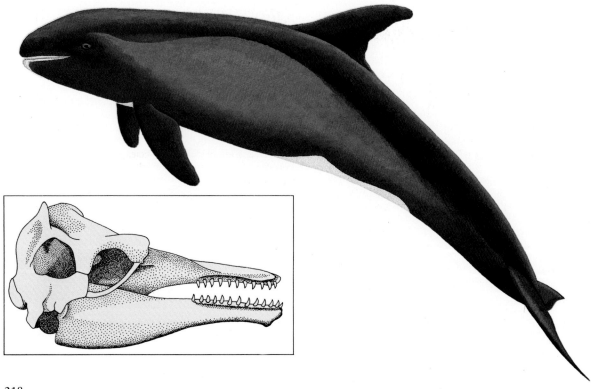

pilot whales (*Globicephala* spp.); its head is compressed and narrows to a point, like that of the False Killer Whale (*Pseudorca crassidens 52*); and its dorsal fin is curved and pointed, like that of the Bottlenose Dolphin (*Tursiops truncatus 76*), but high enough to topple over at the tip, like that of the male Great Killer Whale (*Orcinus orca 51*). The flippers are its own – small (about 12 per cent of total body length), gently curved, rounded at the tip and thrown into indentations on the trailing edge. In many there are similar irregularities on the trailing edge of the dorsal fin.

The colour is black, with an often conspicuous light grey flank patch separated from the back in life by a wavy upper margin. This grey area darkens rapidly after death and soon disappears altogether. As on the pilot whales, there is an anchor-shaped pale grey patch between the flippers, but the shaft is very short and sometimes tapers to nothing on the belly. There is however a large white anal patch, strongly tinged with pink in life, which may extend as far back as the tail. The lips have a narrow white margin which expands on the tip of the lower jaw to form a very distinctive and variable white goatee marking, which may in some animals become quite bushy. Scarring is fairly common.

Field Identification Pygmy Killer Whales look like typical Globicephalidae in the water, dark and blunt headed, with a prominent fin. They occur in small groups, moving fairly sedately, breathing roughly once every 10 seconds, each time lifting the body high enough in the water for the whole head to be seen distinctly. In this behaviour they resemble False Killer Whales (*Pseudorca crassidens 52*), but are much smaller and never seem to leap, or approach a ship, or ride a bow wave. With the chin exposed during breathing, the goatee is often distinct and is probably the best field characteristic.

Like several other members of this family, the Pygmy Killers seem to feed largely at night and spend a good part of sunny days lazing at the surface in loafing groups. The only time we have managed to get a close look at this species was when we encountered such a group in mid-Indian Ocean, lying in a loose circle with their heads toward the centre. When we were still 100 m (330 ft) away, one of the loafers sat bolt upright in the water like a Pilot Whale, which we assumed it was until we got a little nearer and could assess the smaller size and see the goatee. The spy hopper then turned head down, beat his flukes on the water and the whole group submerged. They surfaced again 3 minutes later 500 m off and swam away.

Its relatively small size separates this species from most other members of the family, but there is a possibility of confusion with the Melonhead Whale (*Peponocephala electra 54*). Both are about the same size, shape and colour and are best distinguished in the field as follows:

Feresa fin up to 40 cm (15 inches) high, with wavy trailing edge; head narrow and smoothly pointed; grey flank marking and white goatee.
Peponocephala fin up to 25 cm (10 inches) high, with smooth trailing edge; head narrow and curved into 'parrot beak'; pure black above the water.

Stranding Recently stranding has been fairly common. Identi-

Pygmy Killer Whale in 'spy hopping' posture, showing white 'goatee' marking on chin

fication is simple in a fresh specimen, but becomes more difficult later. Pygmy Killer Whales could be mistaken for juvenile False Killer Whales (*Pseudorca crassidens 52*) and are best separated from them by flipper shape (the False Killer has a characteristic elbow) and by the teeth. This species has slenderer teeth and more of them. There are 10 or 11 on each side of the upper jaw and 12 or 13 on each side of the lower. The skull is markedly asymmetrical and in some animals there may be fewer teeth on the smaller right hand side of both jaws.

One feature which is likely to be noticed only in a stranded Pygmy Killer Whale, is that it has a deep groove on the belly, running from the anus forward beyond the navel.

There are 68–71 vertebrae, of which only the first 3 are fused. Six pairs of the ribs are double headed.

Natural History Very little is known. One of the Japanese captives and another in Sealife Park Oceanarium in Hawaii fed on small fish, taking about 10 kg (22 lb) each day. The usual social unit seems to be a small group of around 10, but at least one school of 50 has been seen off Hawaii. Calving appears to occur in the spring.

An interesting sidelight on Pygmy Killer Whale behaviour is that several of those examined in captivity have been unusually aggressive, both towards other cetaceans and to human handlers. this is in marked contrast to other species.

Status It seems likely that this species is less rare than was once thought. After a century in which only 2 specimens came to light, we have in the last 20 years been bombarded with sightings and strandings. Either there has been a population explosion, or else records simply multiply in accordance with the number of those keeping them.

Distribution This species seems to occur worldwide in all deep tropical and warm temperate waters. The Pygmy Killer Whale has been recorded so far from Texas, Florida, St Vincent, Senegal, south-west Africa, mid-Indian Ocean, Japan, Hawaii, Mexico and Costa Rica.

Sources BEST (1970) in South Africa, GRAY (1827) original description, GRAY (1875) second specimen, JAMES et al (1970) in Texas, NISHIWAKI (1966) taxonomy, PERRIN & HUBBS in Pacific, PRYOR et al (1965) in captivity, YAMADA (1954) in Japan.

MELONHEAD WHALE

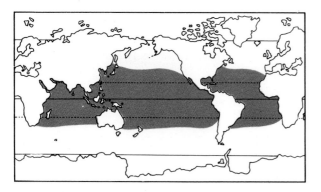

Classification This species does not quite fit with dolphins, pilot or killer whales. For the moment it has its own genus and is tagged on at the tail end of the Globicephalid family, but it could equally well be inserted at the head of the Delphinids, or even set apart in a family of its own.

The first known specimens are 2 skulls described by Gray in his 1846 report on the collections of the HMS *Erebus* and HMS *Terror*. He identified the skulls as members of a new genus of 'flask-beaked' dolphins which he called *Lagenorhynchus*. This species he named *electra* from the Greek *elektra*, amber, presumably from the colour of the bone. A third skull was found in Hawaii in 1848 and a fourth in Madras in 1869. Two specimens came from West Africa; the author Robert Cushman Murphy found one in mid-Atlantic in 1912; and 4 more were collected on the island of Solor in Indonesia by the German zoogeographer Max Weber in 1923.

In 1963 a live specimen was caught at Sagami Bay on Honshu in Japan and doubts were expressed about the genus by Nakajima and Nishiwaki. In 1964 Norris examined a juvenile caught alive in Hawaii and found that he had similar reservations. Then, as with the Pygmy Killer Whale (*Feresa attenuata 53*), what had for more than a century been a very rare animal, suddenly appeared in abundance. More than 500

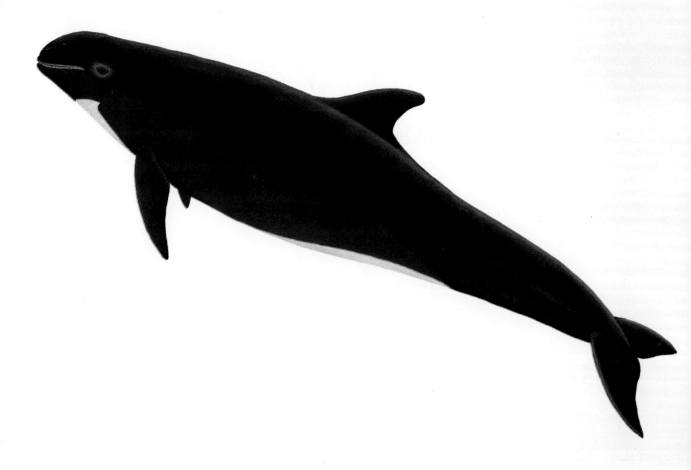

swam into Suruga Bay in Japan in 1965 and 250 were caught and studied. A further 200 were trapped in Taiji Bay in 1980. Nishiwaki and Norris compared morphological notes and decided that what they had was an animal which warranted a genus of its own. They decided on *Peponocephala* from the Greek *peponis*, a melon, and *kephalos*, a head.

Most cetologists today accept this classification but some still feel, on purely anatomical grounds, that this species rightfully belongs where Gray first put it, with the *Lagenorhynchus* dolphins.

Local Names This animal has been referred to as little killer whale and many-toothed blackfish, but we prefer to adopt the literal translation of its new generic name and call it the Melonhead Whale.

Description Small; length averages 2.2 m (7.5 ft), with a maximum of 2.75 m (9 ft). Weight averages 160 kg (350 lb), with a maximum of about 200 kg (440 lb).

The external appearance is quite unlike that of any of the *Lagenorhynchus* dolphins. This species does not have their clearly defined beak, it is longer and more slender, and has none of the typical dolphin saddle, cape or flank markings. It is instead superficially very much like a small Longfin Pilot Whale, although the melon on its head is not nearly as pronounced or pot shaped. The head is narrow and tapering, like that of the False Killer Whale (*Pseudorca crassidens 52*), but the bump of its melon gives it a curved profile somewhat reminiscent of a parrot's beak. The flippers are relatively long, about 20 per cent of total body length, smoothly curved and sharply pointed. The dorsal fin is central and shaped very much like that of the Bottlenose Dolphin (*Tursiops truncatus 76*). Melonhead Whales are uniformly deep grey or black on their backs and flanks, with no trace of saddle or flank patches. The usual Globicephalid shield or anchor-shaped patch is present between the flippers, but it is pale grey rather than white and tails away around the navel. There is a large pale blotch around anal and genital areas. The lips are thin white lines and there is no goatee, but there sometimes seems to be a lighter ring around the eyes.

Field Identification We have never seen a Melonhead Whale in the wild, but understand that when simply breaking the water with blowhole and fin, it might be difficult to distinguish at a distance from the Bottlenose Dolphin (*Tursiops truncatus 76*). Like that species, this one arches quite strongly when diving, rolling over to expose the keel on the tailstock. At close quarters the absence of a beak would clear up any confusion.

It is more likely that difficulty will be experienced in distinguishing this blunt-headed, small, dark whale from the Pygmy Killer Whale (*Feresa attenuata 53*). The Melonhead however has a lower fin, no patch on the chin and a pointed rather than a rounded flipper. Melonhead Whales apparently look around with their heads out of the water, but they do not sit up as high as other Globicephalids; they are said to jump in a low flat arc when moving at normal speed. They have not been seen to bowride.

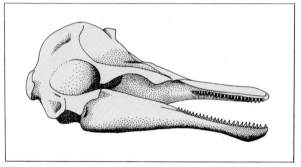

Above: Melonhead Whale in lookout posture, showing parrot beak and white lips
Below: skull

Stranding The occasional beached Melonhead is very easy to identify. It looks like a small Longfin Pilot or Killer Whale, black all over soon after death, but the teeth are unmistakable. They are small and pointed and there are twice as many of them as can be found in the mouths of any other Globicephalid. The normal total is just under 100, with 21–25 on each side of both jaws. There is also a comparatively large number of vertebrae, about 82, with the first 3 fused into a single unit.

Natural History Almost nothing is known. They probably feed on fish. Maturity is reached at a length of about 2.1 m (7 ft), which represents an age of approximately 4 years. Gestation lasts 12 months and calves are born all year round. The normal social unit is probably a group of 20–30, but Japanese records show that schools of as many as 500 do occur.

Status Nothing is known, but the possibility exists that this species may not be as rare as was once assumed.

Distribution The Melonhead Whale seems to be found in all tropical and subtropical waters. Records so far are from St Vincent, in mid-Atlantic, Senegal, India, Malaysia, Indonesia, New Guinea, north-eastern Australia, Japan, Hawaii, the Society Islands and Mexico.

Sources BRYDEN et al (1977) general, CALDWELL et al (1976) in St Vincent, DAWBIN et al (1970) field notes, GOODWIN (1945) in Atlantic, GRAY (1846) original description, NAKAJIMA & NISHIWAKI (1945) taxonomy, NISHIWAKI & NORRIS (1966) taxonomy, PERRIN (1976) distribution, VAN BREE & CADENAT (1968) in Senegal.

Family Eleven – Delphinidae

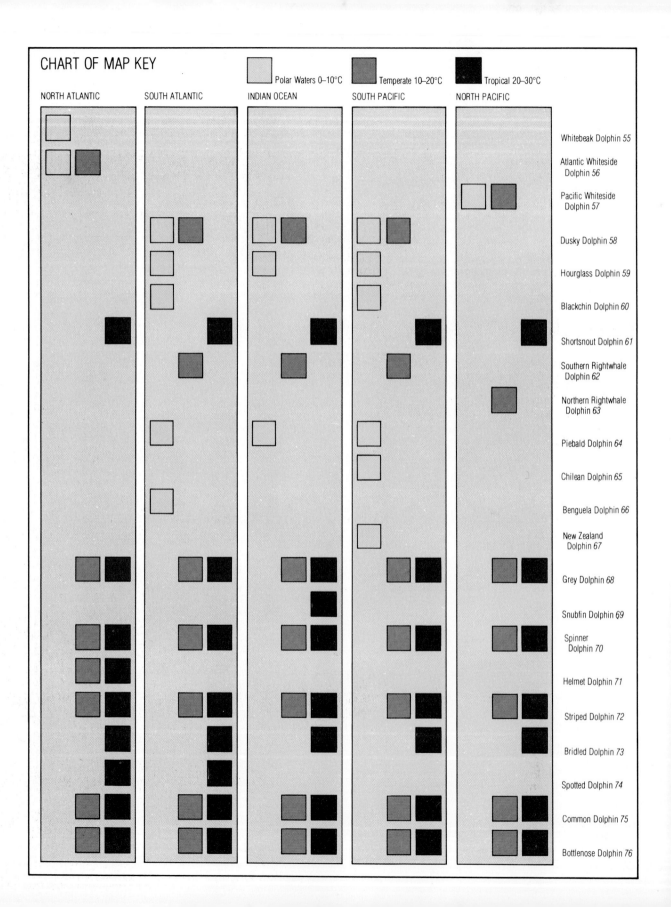

CHART OF MAP KEY

Polar Waters 0–10°C   Temperate 10–20°C   Tropical 20–30°C

NORTH ATLANTIC   SOUTH ATLANTIC   INDIAN OCEAN   SOUTH PACIFIC   NORTH PACIFIC

Whitebeak Dolphin 55

Atlantic Whiteside Dolphin 56

Pacific Whiteside Dolphin 57

Dusky Dolphin 58

Hourglass Dolphin 59

Blackchin Dolphin 60

Shortsnout Dolphin 61

Southern Rightwhale Dolphin 62

Northern Rightwhale Dolphin 63

Piebald Dolphin 64

Chilean Dolphin 65

Benguela Dolphin 66

New Zealand Dolphin 67

Grey Dolphin 68

Snubfin Dolphin 69

Spinner Dolphin 70

Helmet Dolphin 71

Striped Dolphin 72

Bridled Dolphin 73

Spotted Dolphin 74

Common Dolphin 75

Bottlenose Dolphin 76

These are the classic dolphins, all those smaller cetaceans with beaklike snouts and slender, streamlined bodies. The family was created in 1821 by Gray as his first action in a life devoted to building up what was then the largest and best catalogued zoological collection in the world. Many authors, Gray among them, make the Delphinid family much more comprehensive, but in this book we have placed the porpoise (Phocoenidae), the estuarine dolphins (Stenidae), the river dolphins (Platanistidae) and the pilot and killer whales (Globicephalidae) in their own families, partly on anatomical

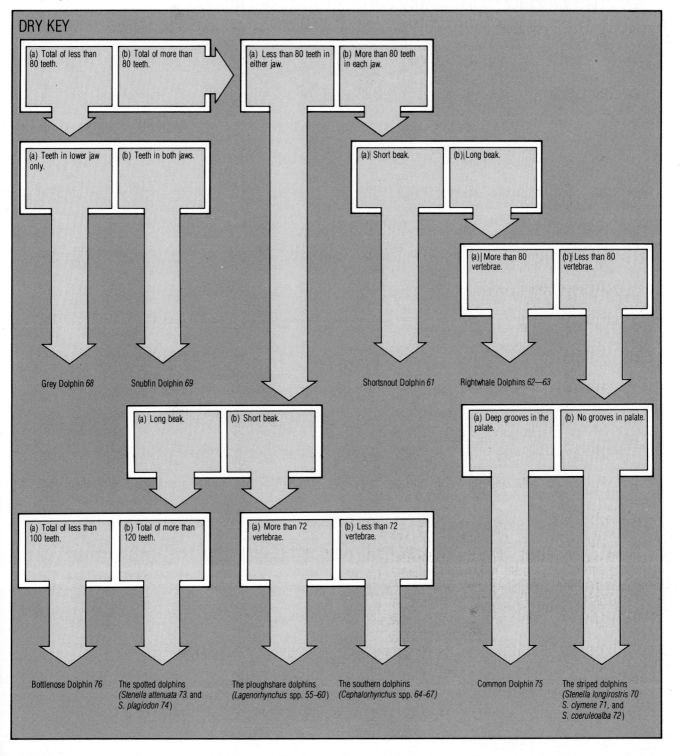

DRY KEY

(a) Total of less than 80 teeth.   (b) Total of more than 80 teeth.

(a) Less than 80 teeth in either jaw.   (b) More than 80 teeth in each jaw.

(a) Teeth in lower jaw only.   (b) Teeth in both jaws.

(a) Short beak.   (b) Long beak.

(a) More than 80 vertebrae.   (b) Less than 80 vertebrae.

Grey Dolphin *68*   Snubfin Dolphin *69*

Shortsnout Dolphin *61*   Rightwhale Dolphins *62—63*

(a) Long beak.   (b) Short beak.

(a) Deep grooves in the palate.   (b) No grooves in palate.

(a) Total of less than 100 teeth.   (b) Total of more than 120 teeth.

(a) More than 72 vertebrae.   (b) Less than 72 vertebrae.

Bottlenose Dolphin *76*   The spotted dolphins (*Stenella attenuata 73* and *S. plagiodon 74*)

The ploughshare dolphins (*Lagenorhynchus* spp. *55-60*)   The southern dolphins (*Cephalorhynchus* spp. *64-67*)

Common Dolphin *75*   The striped dolphins (*Stenella longirostris 70 S. clymene 71,* and *S. coeruleoalba 72*)

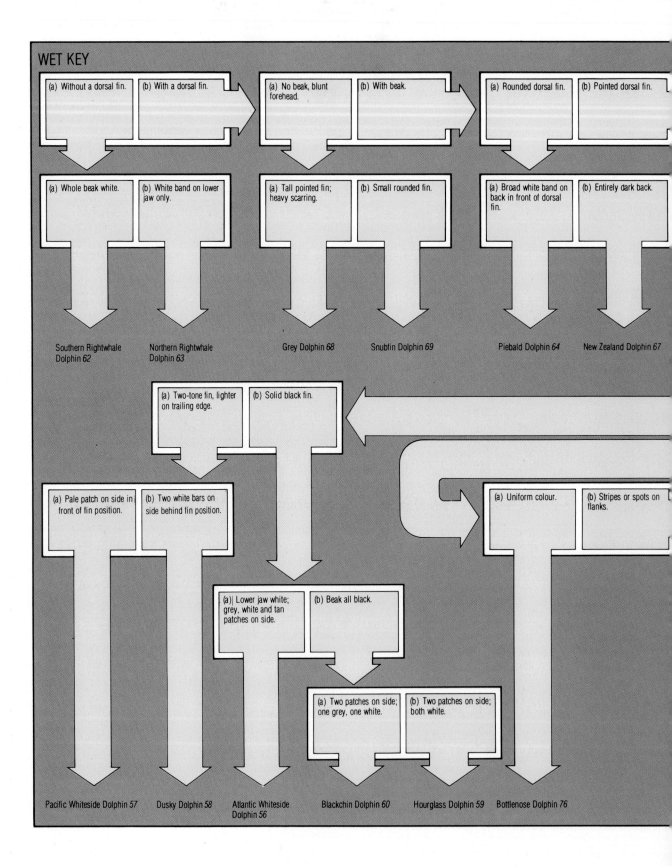

WET KEY

(a) Without a dorsal fin.

(b) With a dorsal fin.

(a) No beak, blunt forehead.

(b) With beak.

(a) Rounded dorsal fin.

(b) Pointed dorsal fin.

(a) Whole beak white.

(b) White band on lower jaw only.

(a) Tall pointed fin; heavy scarring.

(b) Small rounded fin.

(a) Broad white band on back in front of dorsal fin.

(b) Entirely dark back.

Southern Rightwhale Dolphin 62

Northern Rightwhale Dolphin 63

Grey Dolphin 68

Snubfin Dolphin 69

Piebald Dolphin 64

New Zealand Dolphin 67

(a) Two-tone fin, lighter on trailing edge.

(b) Solid black fin.

(a) Uniform colour.

(b) Stripes or spots on flanks.

(a) Pale patch on side in front of fin position.

(b) Two white bars on side behind fin position.

(a) Lower jaw white; grey, white and tan patches on side.

(b) Beak all black.

(a) Two patches on side; one grey, one white.

(b) Two patches on side; both white.

Pacific Whiteside Dolphin 57

Dusky Dolphin 58

Atlantic Whiteside Dolphin 56

Blackchin Dolphin 60

Hourglass Dolphin 59

Bottlenose Dolphin 76

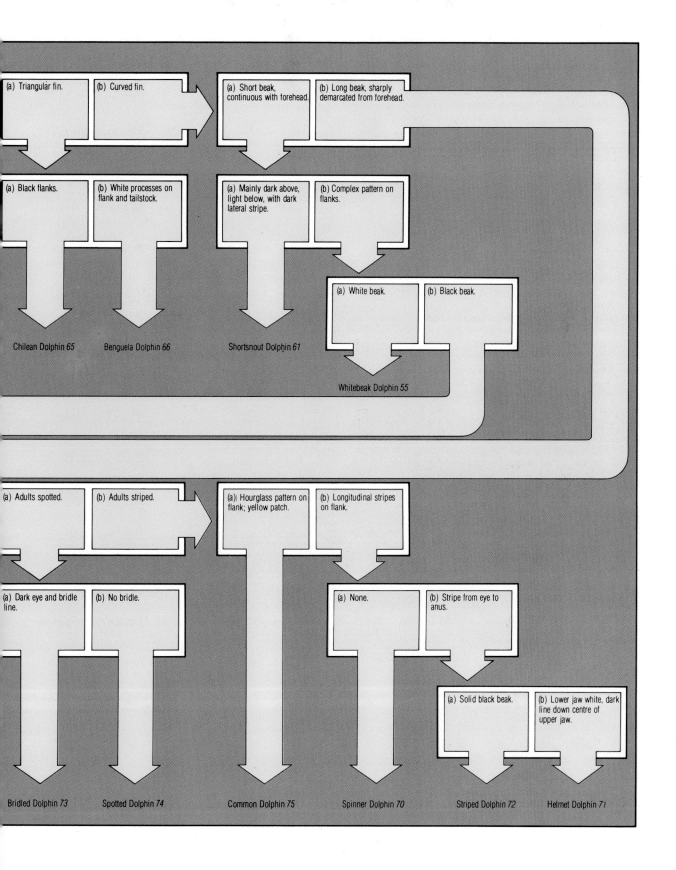

(a) Triangular fin.

(b) Curved fin.

(a) Short beak, continuous with forehead.

(b) Long beak, sharply demarcated from forehead.

(a) Black flanks.

(b) White processes on flank and tailstock.

(a) Mainly dark above, light below, with dark lateral stripe.

(b) Complex pattern on flanks.

(a) White beak.

(b) Black beak.

Chilean Dolphin 65

Benguela Dolphin 66

Shortsnout Dolphin 61

Whitebeak Dolphin 55

(a) Adults spotted.

(b) Adults striped.

(a) Hourglass pattern on flank; yellow patch.

(b) Longitudinal stripes on flank.

(a) Dark eye and bridle line.

(b) No bridle.

(a) None.

(b) Stripe from eye to anus.

(a) Solid black beak.

(b) Lower jaw white, dark line down centre of upper jaw.

Bridled Dolphin 73

Spotted Dolphin 74

Common Dolphin 75

Spinner Dolphin 70

Striped Dolphin 72

Helmet Dolphin 71

grounds, but mainly on the basis of visible physical and behavioural differences which we believe not only simplify cetacean study but make good biological sense.

It was our original intention to exclude the Grey Dolphin (*Grampus griseus 68*) and the Snubfin Dolphin (*Orcaella brevirostris 69*) in the same way, but we have been persuaded by others, better qualified than we are, that aberrant though they may be, these species belong here rather than on their own.

Apart from these odd animals, all the remaining 7 genera with their 20 species are small whales less than 4 m (13 ft) long with prominent beaks more or less sharply demarcated from their foreheads, just 2 fused neck vertebrae and an increasingly elaborate pattern of stripes, bands and spots. They are the most abundant and the most evident of cetaceans, seldom making deep dives, but surfacing several times each minute. All are called dolphins (not whales or porpoises) and none of them should be confused with the dolphin fish or mahi-mahi (*Coryphaena hippurus*).

There are enough of them to make identification tricky, but all species are distinctive in some way, as shown in the Wet Key on pages 226/227.

Map Key The range of species present in each habitat is apparent at a glance. For positive discrimination between those listed, check with the species description, but:

1. The only species which occur in cold water belong to *Lagenorhynchus* and *Cephalorhynchus*.
2. *Cephalorhynchus* is confined to the southern hemisphere.
3. The 2 rightwhale dolphins (*Lissodelphis* spp.) occur in temperate waters only, one in each hemisphere.
4. The Shortsnout Dolphin (*Lagenodelphis hosei 61*) and the Snubfin Dolphin (*Orcaella brevirostris 69*) are unknown outside tropical waters.
5. All the remaining species are widely distributed in tropical, temperate and cooler waters and many cross the equator.

Dry Key The species in several Delphinid genera are still in a state of taxonomic confusion. While they can often be separated on geographical grounds or on the basis of their colour patterns, their anatomy is virtually identical. The Key, page 225, therefore, may work only as far as generic level.

Genus Lagenorhynchus

During the second half of the eighteenth and the first part of the nineteenth century, all dolphins and many small whales were automatically put into Linnaeus's genus *Delphinus*. This practice gradually changed under the influence of Gray who had the advantage of a collection that made it possible for him to make taxonomic sense of the variety of cetaceans. In 1846 a dolphin with a short beak, curved a little like an old-fashioned ploughshare, was beached at Great Yarmouth in England and collected there by a Mr Brightwell. It had a white beak and when it was delivered to Gray he called it simply *Delphinus albirostris* from the Latin *albus*, white, and *rostrum*, a beak.

A few months later Gray found several specimens from the southern hemisphere with similar skulls. With these he had a range large enough to be certain that they differed from the classic *Delphinus* and so he created a new genus *Lagenorhynchus* from the Greek *Lagenos*, a flask, and the Greek *rhynchos*, a beak, with *Lagenorhynchus albirostris* the type species.

Members of the genus have some similarity in the field to the Common Dolphin (*Delphinus delphis 75*) the Bottlenose Dolphin (*Tursiops truncatus 76*) and the longbeak dolphins (*Stenella* spp.); but they can be distinguished as follows:

Lagenorhynchus short flat beak; thin stripe from flipper to angle of jaw; prominent white pattern on flanks.
Tursiops short robust beak; no stripes; uniform grey flanks.
Delphinus longer beak; thick stripe from flipper to middle of lower jaw; hourglass pattern on flanks.
Stenella long slender beak; variable stripe from flipper to eye; dark stripes or spots on flanks.

There are 6 recognized species of *Lagenorhynchus*. Two occur only in the North Atlantic:

L. albirostris 55 fin all black; 2 distinct white flank patches; beak with white tip; often bowrides.
L. acutus 56 fin part grey; 1 yellowish flank patch; beak all dark; seldom bowrides.

One is found alone in the North Pacific:
L. obliquidens 57 two-tone fin; 2 flank patches, both grey.

There are 3 species in the southern hemisphere temperate and polar zones. Two are widespread:
L. cruciger 59 2 white flank patches, in front of and behind fin; flipper and eye within broad black flank patch.
L. obscurus 58 1 white flank patch behind fin; narrow line from flipper to eye.
And the third is confined to the area on the tip of South America:
L. australis 60 2 flank patches, 1 grey in front of fin and 1 white behind it; narrow line from flipper to eye.

L. albirostris 55 and *L. acutus 56* are the largest species, reaching almost 3 m (10 ft); the others are all less than 2 m (6.5 ft) long.

(a) Whitebeak Dolphin *Lagenorhynchus albirostris* 55
(b) Pacific Whiteside Dolphin *Lagenorhynchus obliquidens* 57
(c) Blackchin Dolphin *Lagenorhynchus australis* 60
(d) Hourglass Dolphin *Lagenorhynchus cruciger* 59
(e) Dusky Dolphin *Lagenorhynchus obscurus* 58
(f) Atlantic Whiteside Dolphin *Lagenorhynchus acutus* 56

WHITEBEAK DOLPHIN

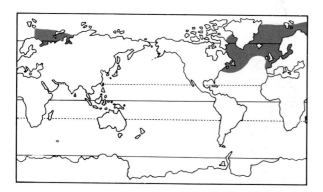

Classification This species was described in 1846 by Gray and became the type for the genus (see above).

There are no regional variations or subspecies.

Local Names *Dauphin à nez blanc* (French), *Weisschnauziger springer* (German), *hvidnaese* (Norwegian) and *belorylyi delfin* (Russian). It is also known in Newfoundland as squid hound. We retain the traditional name of Whitebeak Dolphin.

Description Small; length averages 2.75 m (9 ft), with a maximum of 3.2 m (10.5 ft); calves are about 1.2 m (4 ft) at

birth. Weight averages 200 kg (450 lb), with a maximum of 275 kg (600 lb); calves are about 40 kg (88 lb) at birth.

This is the largest species in the genus, with a very robust body. The beak is short but distinct and the fin is very tall and curved. The trailing edge of the flipper is unusually straight. There are distinct keels both above and below the tailstock.

The distinctive white or pale grey beak is usually visible on all adult animals in the eastern North Atlantic, but it may darken and be less conspicuous in some dolphins of western North Atlantic waters. The fin, flukes and flippers are uniformly dark, but there is a variable patchwork of white, pale grey, dark grey and black along the flanks. Usually this consists of a dark cape across the back in front of the fin, extending down to join a dark flank patch behind the flipper; a pale saddle behind the fin, which is reflected on the narrow tailstock and in a chinstrap; and a solid line from the flipper to the angle of the jaw. There are however individual differences in this pattern which often blur the margins between these areas.

Field Identification The white beak, where it occurs and can be seen, is diagnostic; but the most useful field characteristics are the 2 distinctive white or pale grey patches on the flanks. These can always be seen as the dolphin rolls to breathe, one in front of and below the fin, and the other behind the fin and

extending up on to the back. In many individuals the pale saddle behind the fin is light enough to blend with the second white patch and form a much larger bright area. Both patches are clearly visible from above, even from an aircraft.

Whitebeak Dolphins are powerful swimmers and sometimes rush along the surface throwing up their own bow waves. They seldom leap clear of the water and only occasionally ride the bow waves of ships, usually choosing larger vessels travelling at least 30–40 kph (15–20 knots). We have never been able to attract these dolphins to small boats or to get close to them underwater.

They are the only dolphins in the far North Atlantic. In slightly warmer water they overlap with the Atlantic Whiteside Dolphin (*L. acutus 56*) with which they can be confused. The best way to tell them apart is to look for the patterns on their sides. Despite its name, the Whiteside Dolphin does not have a white side. It has a cream or maize-coloured patch along its side behind the fin, quite different from the 2 bright, and much more white, patches on the flanks of the Whitebeak Dolphin. In addition, the Whiteside Dolphin always has a black upper and a white lower jaw.

Stranding There are some, usually solitary, strandings. The bright flank patches disappear very soon after death, leaving a uniformly black back and side above a white belly. If the white beak is present, it persists for longer and can be a useful clue to identification. Failing this, the strong keels on the laterally flattened tail are characteristic, but in a badly decomposed animal, even these will have vanished and all that is left are the teeth.

Whitebeak Dolphins have fewer teeth than any other member of the genus, usually 22–25 relatively large ones on each side of both jaws. There are sometimes more teeth on the upper jaw and, in some individuals there may be an additional 2 or 3 teeth in each row, smaller than the others and concealed beneath the gums at the point of the jaw. There are 88–93 vertebrae; and 5 pairs of ribs with double heads.

Natural History Whitebeak Dolphins feed mainly on squid, octopus, cod, herring, whiting and capelin. Some animals

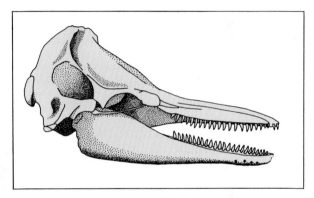

Above: Whitebeak Dolphin at the surface, showing the characteristic double white patch on its flank
Below: skull

have also been found with hermit crabs and several species of marine snail in their stomachs. These dolphins are gregarious, gathering in schools of up to 1,500, which move together in a broad migratory wave. During feeding and mating the schools seem to fragment into more compact social units of 6–30. Pairing takes place in autumn in the southern part of the range and most calves are born on the northern feeding grounds in mid-summer, after a gestation period of about 10 months.

Status Whitebeak Dolphins are fairly common in the colder Atlantic waters. Some are taken accidentally in nets off Iceland and a few are caught commercially each year in Norway.

Distribution The Whitebeak Dolphin is the most northerly of its genus, ranging from the ice in the Greenland and Barents seas to the Davis Strait and the North Sea in summer. In winter it migrates as far south as Cape Cod in the western Atlantic and the Bay of Biscay in the east.

Sources GRAY (1846) original description, SAEMUNDSSON (1939) feeding, TOMILIN (1967) distribution.

ATLANTIC WHITESIDE DOLPHIN

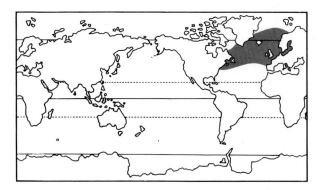

some other, purely skeletal feature in mind. A few years later the Brookes collection was sold and the skull ended up at Leiden Museum in the Netherlands. There, in 1841, Schlegel unwittingly described it again, naming it *Delphinus eschrichtii* after Daniel Eschricht. In 1846 Gray placed it in his new genus *Lagenorhynchus*.

Local Names Jumper (Newfoundland), *Springer* (Germany), *springhval* (Norwegian) or *leiftur* (Icelandic). *Dauphin à flancs blancs* (French), *witzijdolfin* (Dutch) and *hvidskaering* (Danish). To contrast it with a similar species in the Pacific we call this the Atlantic Whiteside Dolphin.

Description Small; length averages 2.4 m (8 ft), with a maximum of 3 m (10 ft); calves are about 1.05 m (3.5 ft) at birth. Weight averages 190 kg (420 lb), with a maximum of 250 kg (550 lb); calves are about 34 kg (75 lb) at birth.

This is the second largest species in the genus, only marginally smaller than the Whitebeak Dolphin (*L. albirostris 55*). It is equally robust, with a body strongly compressed into dorsal and ventral keels on the tailstock, but narrowing less abruptly

Classification This species, with several others, first appeared in 1828 in a pictorial publication of Gray's called *Spicilegia Zoologica.* The illustration was of a skull found in the Faeroe Islands and kept in Brookes Museum in London. Gray called it *Delphinus acutus* from the Latin for sharp, or pointed, an apt description of the particular shape of the dolphin's dorsal fin, but having only the skull to work with, he presumably had

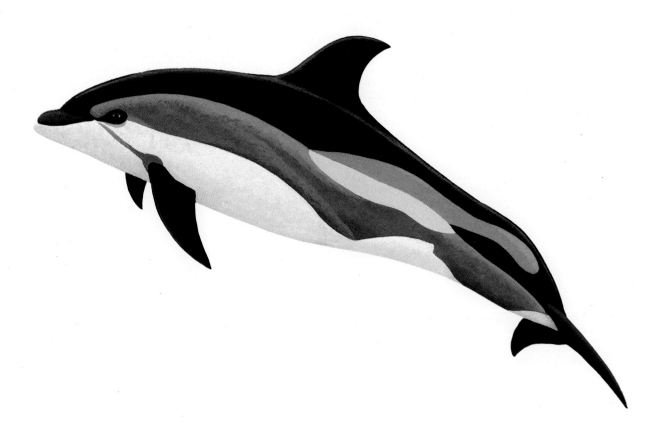

at the tail than the Whitebeak's. The beak is small, but very well defined, with a deep groove marking it off from the rest of the head. The flippers curve backwards strongly and the fin is tall and narrows at the top to a very sharp point.

The colour is predominantly black or deep grey on the back, with a white belly which extends rather high up the sides, well beyond the flipper insertion. Between the dark back and the light underside is a medium grey band which stretches the length of the body and is broken only by this dolphin's most distinctive feature – a maize-yellow, oval patch on the flank behind and below the fin. Half of this lies on the grey band and looks rather bright, almost white in certain lights (the 'whiteside'), and the remainder is overlaid by the black cape on the back and is a subdued buffy ochre colour. There is a dark stripe from the flipper to the corner of the mouth and a black ring around the eye. The beak is black above and white below.

Field Identification Whiteside Dolphins are distinctive in the field, much more active than Whitebeak Dolphins (*L. albirostris 55*), moving rapidly in large acrobatic troupes, of which about a third seem to be airborne at once. They are fast swimmers, breathing several times each minute, leaping almost clear of the water as they do so, or throwing up a bow wave with their heads. They seem to be wary of shipping, usually going on about their own business or travelling away at an angle from the ship's course. We have never seen one come to the bow, but have been told that they may do so. We have, on several occasions, seen them together with Longfin Pilot Whales (*Globicephala melaena 49*).

When leaping or rolling at the surface to breathe, the lower brighter part of the yellow flank marking is usually clearly visible. The upper darker portion can only be seen in good light and at close quarters. The sharp curved tip of the fin is also distinctive and both characteristics are useful for distinguishing this species from the Whitebeak Dolphin (*L. albirostris 55*) where their ranges overlap in the area just north of the Gulf Stream:

L. acutus single patch on flank, behind fin; upper beak black; fin very pointed; flipper inserted on white belly area.

L. albirostris 2 patches on flank, in front of and behind fin; whole beak usually white; fin more rounded; flipper inserted on edge of dark flank marking.

Stranding Solitary strandings are fairly common, and there are records of schools of 30–40 beached together. Once the flank markings have darkened after death, little remains to give any clue to identification by external characteristics. The teeth however are distinctive. In each half of each jaw are 30–40 small pointed teeth, making a total of at least 120 (average 132 teeth). Very often there are more along the upper jaw than the lower one. There are 78–82 vertebrae. Six of the 15 pairs of ribs are double headed.

Natural History Atlantic Whiteside Dolphins eat both squid and fish, concentrating mainly on herring at certain times. The normal social unit seems to be a group of up to 50 of all ages and sexes, but very much larger aggregations occur, particularly at the northern limits of the range. Schools of 1,000 or more have been recorded. Mating takes place in the summer. Gestation lasts for 10 months and most calves are born in April or May.

Status This species still seems to be fairly common, although Whitesides are sometimes taken together with Pilot Whales in drives along the coast of Newfoundland. Larger numbers, up to 1,500, are still taken each year in Norway by harpoon or by trapping groups in the narrower fjords with the aid of nets.

Distribution Atlantic Whiteside Dolphins occur mainly in cool northern waters between the Gulf Stream and the more northerly latitudes inhabited by the Whitebeak Dolphin (*L. albirostris 55*). The southern limits of both species in winter are similar, but the Whiteside Dolphin does sometimes occur as far south as Portugal and there is a record of a stray animal in the Adriatic Sea.

Sources GRAY (1828) original description, JONSGÅRD & NORDLI (1952) in Norway, SERGEANT & FISHER (1957) distribution, TOSCHI (1965) in Adriatic.

PACIFIC WHITESIDE DOLPHIN

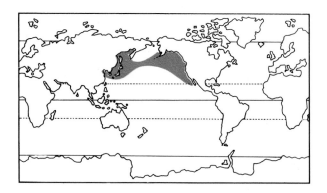

Classification Theodore Nicholas Gill, Librarian to the Smithsonian Institution, is best remembered in biology for his elegant taxonomic work on fishes, but at least once he strayed across the class boundary and applied his talents to cetaceans.

In 1865 he classified 3 skulls collected near San Francisco in 1855 by W. A. Trowbridge as *Lagenorhynchus obliquidens* from the Latin *obliquus*, slanting, and *dens*, a tooth.

Local Names *Kama iruka* (Japanese) and *belobokii delfin* (Russian). In the literature this species is sometimes described as hook-finned porpoise or white-striped dolphin. We have decided on balance to continue with a name which has become widely accepted and call this the Pacific Whiteside Dolphin.

Description Small; length averages 2.1 m (7 ft), with a maximum of 2.4 m (8 ft); calves are about 1 m (over 3 ft) at birth. Weight averages 90 kg (200 lb), with a maximum of 140 kg (308 lb); calves are about 15 kg (33 lb) at birth.

Pacific Whiteside Dolphins have extremely short beaks and in profile show a rounded snout, like that of a porpoise. The fin is high and strongly hooked, curving backwards so that the tip is almost horizontal. In juveniles it tends to be more triangular. The tailstock is not markedly keeled.

The colouring is distinctive: the basic pattern is a deep grey back sharply marked off from a white belly, the dark flanks broken up by a variable pattern of pale grey; there is usually a large light ovoid patch in front of the fin above the flipper extending forward to meet the eye (the 'whiteside'). Above the

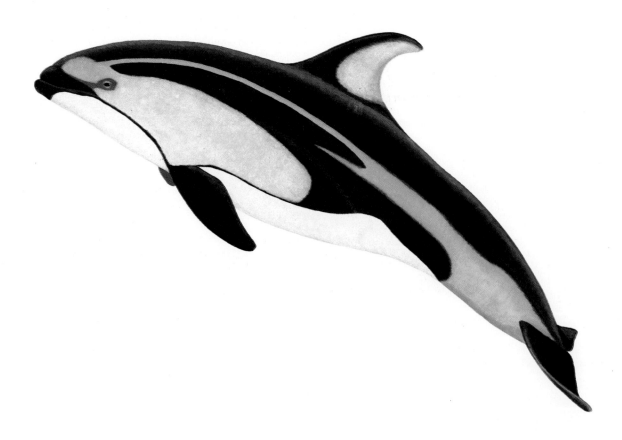

eye and running down the length of the body is a narrow stripe of the same pale shade as the 'whiteside', which broadens out in the anal area into an irregular shape which varies in individuals. The posterior half of the hooked fin may bear a similar pale grey blazé and there is always a black ring around the eye.

Field Identification These dolphins are fast, powerful swimmers, sometimes cutting through the water with just the fin showing, like a marauding shark's. They breathe about once every 20 seconds, often in a clean low leap; but the young in particular are tremendous jumpers, spinning on their axes or even turning a complete somersault before dropping back into the water with a resounding smack. They throw up quantities of spray which sometimes makes a school visible long before the dolphins themselves can be seen.

Pacific Whitesides of all ages are enthusiastic surfers, sliding down ocean waves and seldom wasting an opportunity to try the bow wave of a passing ship. We have seen them abandon a shoal of fish in mid-meal and come racing over to our vessel, often muscling their way in and displacing other riders from the bow. When the ship is travelling at about 25 kph (12 knots), they sometimes keep their station for 10–15 minutes at a time, riding so effectively that 45 seconds often pass between tailbeats. While at the bow, they are easily identified by the 2 pale longitudinal stripes down the sides of their backs. No other species has markings quite like these. When seen from the side, or from a distance, these narrow bands are less conspicuous.

We have seen Pacific Whitesides schooling with Shortfin Pilot Whales (*Globicephala macrorhynchus 50*), Northern Rightwhale Dolphins (*Lissodelphis borealis 62*), Common Dolphins (*Delphinus delphis 75*), and Spray Porpoises (*Phocoenoides dalli 48*). There is a possibility of their being confused with the last 2 of these species, but they differ as follows:

L. obliquidens very short beak; fin strongly curved, white stripes down back; light pattern on side in front of fin; often leaps and bowrides.
D. delphis long beak; fin slightly curved; dark back; yellow patch on side behind fin; sometimes leaps and bowrides.
P. dalli no beak; fin curved only at tip; dark back; bright white patch below fin; never leaps or bowrides.

We have seen Pacific Whitesides in what seem to be feeding associations with Humpback Whales (*Megaptera novaeangliae 10*), Sei Whales (*Balaenoptera borealis 8*), sealions, cormorants and pelicans. We once followed an Arctic Humpback Whale for over an hour, during which time 4 of these dolphins apparently never left their stations above and slightly behind the whale's huge flippers. In this position, they seemed to be getting some hydrodynamic advantage, cruising along effortlessly like surfers in a wave.

Stranding Pacific Whitesides are usually stranded individually. The distinctive markings disappear soon after death. Teeth however are often sufficient for positive identification.

There are 23–33 on each side of each jaw (usually 30 to a row), providing a total of approximately 120 small pointed teeth; compared with at least 200 in the Common Dolphin (*Delphinus delphis 75*), and never more than 100 waisted ones in the Spray Porpoise (*Phocoenoides dalli 48*). There are 73–78 vertebrae; and 6 pairs of double-headed ribs.

Natural History Pacific Whiteside Dolphins feed on squid (most often *Loligo opalescens*), and on fish such as hake (*Merluccius productus*) and anchovy (*Engraulis mordax*). They each eat about 9 kg (20 lb) a day.

It is a highly gregarious species, sometimes seen in schools of 1,000 or more, spread out over an area of 10 km² (4 square miles). They are more often found in groups of up to 50, possibly forming a distinct genetic association and certainly close knit. When one is ill or injured, the others will seldom leave its side. One Pacific Whiteside Dolphin was seen in the Sea of Japan still supporting on its fin the partly decomposed body of a calf that must have been dead for at least a week.

Mating takes place in autumn and involves a courtship display in which the female takes the initiative, swimming beneath the male and rubbing against his flippers with her flukes. He responds by nuzzling her or nipping her on the tail, and copulates by hooking his own tail under hers from below. Calves are born about 9 months later, during the following summer and are unusual in having several long tactile hairs at the base of the beak. They soon lose these and during most of their nursing period can be seen riding *en echelon* with their mothers, taking up a position just beside and below the dorsal fin, where they get a bit of a boost from her movement through the water.

Pacific Whitesides are known to echolocate with a pulsed sound of up to 80 kHz. They also produce, probably for purposes of communication, a high-pitched whistle, unique to each individual.

Status Numbers are difficult to estimate, but this species is certainly still common with something like 30,000 in the western North Pacific and perhaps double this number in total. They are hunted by Japanese coastal fishermen in the East China and Japan seas and taken accidentally in the North Pacific purse-seine fishery, but are apparently difficult to drive and do not panic easily.

Distribution Pacific Whiteside Dolphins are found only in colder waters of the North Pacific, from Amchitka in the north-west to Baja in the south-east. They are usually seen in deep water (1,000–2,000 m or 3,300–6,600 ft) up to 160 km (100 miles) offshore. There seem to be local migrations inshore in the winter months.

Sources BROWNELL (1965) colour variation, GILL (1865) original description, KASUYA & MIYAZAKI (1976) behaviour, OHSUMI (1972) in Japan, WALKER (1964) general.

DUSKY DOLPHIN

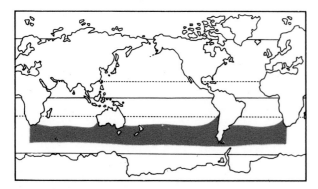

Dusky Dolphin cruising at the surface, showing the two-tone dorsal fin and brush stroke marking on its flank

Classification This is another species first described by Gray in *Spicilegia Zoologica*. The drawing in this case was based on a skull and stuffed skin from the Cape of Good Hope. Gray called it *Delphinus obscurus* from the Latin *obscurus*, dusky. He later changed the name to *Electra*, but it was left to True in 1889 to transfer the species to yet another Gray genus, *Lagenorhynchus*.

In 1832 HMS *Beagle*, with Charles Darwin on board, captured a dolphin off the coast of Patagonia. In 1836 George Waterhouse of the British Museum called this animal *Delphinus fitzroyi*. The illustration prepared by Captain Robert Fitzroy of the *Beagle* shows a dark dolphin with 2 light brush strokes of pale pigment arising from the tailstock and pointing upwards at the fin. The resemblance in every respect to *L. obscurus* is so strong that, had the finder been anyone of less consequence than Darwin himself, it would probably long since have been subsumed in Gray's earlier species.

The consensus today is that *L. fitzroyi* (WATERHOUSE 1836) from South America and *L. superciliosus* (LESSON & GARNOT 1826) from Tasmania are no more than local variants of the widespread *L. obscurus,* first found in South Africa.

Local Names The literal translation of Gray's species is the Dusky Dolphin.

Description Small; length averages 1.8 m (6 ft), with a maximum of 2.1 m (7 ft); calves are about 60 cm (2 ft) at birth. Weight averages 115 kg (250 lb), with a maximum of 140 kg (308 lb); calves are about 5 kg (11 lb) at birth.

Dusky Dolphins are smaller than any of their northern relatives. They have the same sleek shapes, but the fin is a little more vertical, a little less curved. Their beaks are short and poorly defined.

The colouring is simple, but the pattern is complex. Basically, these dolphins have a deep grey back above a pure white belly and, between them, a wide margin of lighter grey in 2 segments. The first of these is a smooth pale grey flank patch which starts in a point on the beak, touches the flipper and ends near the anus. In some parts of the wide distribution this patch is almost as dark as the back and elsewhere it is light

enough to merge with the white of the belly. Sometimes, as in Fitzroy's specimen, the eye is included entirely within this area. The second segment is even more variable. It is usually a very light grey, paler than the flank patch, and takes the form of a bold brush stroke beginning on the tailstock somewhere behind the anal region and sweeping forwards and upwards towards the fin. In some animals a single stroke is visible, but in others this splits like the tails on a comet. Occasionally this marking is even split into 2 distinct and separate brush strokes, one above the other. The flukes, flippers and beak are all uniformly dark, although in a few cases the white of the belly may extend up to cover the lower jaw. The dorsal fin, however, is always two-toned, with a paler trailing edge.

Field Identification Dusky Dolphins are fast, energetic swimmers finding no difficulty overtaking and riding at the bow of a ship moving at 35 kph (17 knots), but they seem to take particular pleasure in small boats. They usually appear out of nowhere, suddenly surfacing around a boat, cruising gently alongside, sometimes lifting their heads or even leaping up to get a better look inside. With all this activity, they never seem to become boisterous in the manner of porpoises, but manifest an easy warmth and dignity which is very hard to define, but quite unmistakable.

From a distance they look dark, even black, but in a good light at close quarters the pale brush strokes on the tailstock and the lighter aft portion of the fin are conspicuous. When they leap the white belly seems very bright. When breathing normally at the surface, which they do 4 or 5 times each minute, they push up a little bow wave just ahead of the blowhole.

In New Zealand and South Africa there is nothing else quite like Dusky Dolphins, but off the coasts of South America there is the possibility of confusion with both the Blackchin Dolphin (*L. australis 60*) and the Black Porpoise (*Phocoena spinipinnis 44*). These species can often be distinguished, but the dolphins are so much alike that discrimination may be impossible:

L. obscurus high two-tone fin with concave trailing edge; single or double pale brush markings on tailstock; white throat and chin.

L. australis high black fin with concave trailing edge; single white marking on tailstock; chin black as far back as the eye.

P. spinipinnis low black fin with convex trailing edge; uniformly black body.

Colour variation in Dusky Dolphins
Above: the 'Fitzroy' form
Below: the most common pattern

Stranding Dusky Dolphins are sometimes stranded; with a recently beached animal it may be possible to see the characteristic markings, but an old stranding on the tip of South America presents problems. The Dusky Dolphin and the Blackchin Dolphin (*L. australis 60*) are identical in death. They even have the same number of teeth, 28–32 small sharp ones on each side of each jaw, making a total of about 120. There are some records from New Zealand which suggest that Dusky Dolphins there might have as many as 180 teeth.

Natural History Dusky Dolphins eat both fish and squid, and seem to take advantage of their coastal habitat to hunt in amongst rocks or reefs for bottom-dwelling species.

They have been recorded in congregations as large as 300, but can usually be seen in schools of 20 or less. These social units seem to be age groups rather than family groupings. All the associations are intense, with group members invariably coming to each other's aid in times of stress or injury. There are several moving accounts of Dusky Dolphins battling to release companions entangled in nets, desperately trying to push them up to the surface to breathe; and one report of a mother who spent a week searching for her drowned calf, persisting until she herself died.

Mating takes place in spring, often at the surprising depth of 10 m (33 ft). Gestation lasts about 9 months and calves are born in mid-winter at the northern (warmer) limit of the dolphin's range. The calves are unusually small, and soon after birth take up their position *en echelon* with the mother, riding just below and in front of the dorsal fin, matching her every movement as though they were tethered together.

Status Precise numbers are unknown, but locally Dusky Dolphins are common. A few sometimes become entangled in nets, but these are largely incidental to other fisheries.

Distribution The Dusky Dolphin's range is circumpolar in the southern hemisphere alone, from about 58° to 30° south.

Dusky Dolphins are recorded from cooler and temperate inshore waters off Argentina, the Falkland Islands, South Africa, Kerguelen Island, South Australia, Tasmania, New Zealand, the south central Pacific and Chile. They migrate northwards during the winter, returning south in October.

Sources BROWNELL (1965) in New Zealand, BROWNELL (1974) distribution, FLOWER (1885) taxonomy, GASKIN (1968) in New Zealand, GRAY (1828) original description, ROBSON (1976) behaviour, TRUE (1889) taxonomy, WATERHOUSE (1838) Fitzroy's specimen.

HOURGLASS DOLPHIN

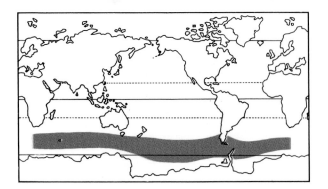

Classification By 1822 three corvettes belonging to Louis XVIII were out on world voyages, *La Coquille* with Lesson as resident naturalist and the companion ships *Uranie* and *La Physicienne* with zoologists Jean René Quoy and Jean Paul Gaimard. The voyages each took several years and brought back valuable specimens and sightings. In the cold Antarctic waters between Australia and Cape Horn, Quoy and Gaimard saw numbers of dolphin with striking black and white markings which seemed to be cross-shaped. Their report of 1824 includes a plate with a stylized representation of the animal, which they called *Delphinus cruciger*, literally, the cross-bearing dolphin from the Latin *crux*, a cross and *gero*, to bear. In 1824 Lesson was still at sea, but on his return in 1826 he published a report in which he too told of seeing this dolphin, west of the Falkland Islands. His description and

illustration are a little more accurate and, from the 2 conspicuous white patches on its side, he decided to call it *Delphinus bivittatus*.

A few years later d'Orbigny succeeded in bringing back a skull from Cape Horn which he and Gervais described in 1847 as *Delphinus cruciger*, recognizing the priority of Quoy and Gaimard. Finally, in 1880, Gervais and van Bénéden transferred the species to *Lagenorhynchus*.

During the British Antarctic Expedition of 1901–04 aboard the *Discovery* and the *Terra Nova*, Wilson described and figured a black and white dolphin which was later named *Lagenorhynchus wilsoni* (LILLIE 1915), but this was almost certainly also *L. cruciger*.

Local Names *Dauphin à museau court* (French) or *delfin cruzado* (Spanish), but it is better and more accurately known as the Hourglass Dolphin.

Description Small; length averages 1.6 m (5.5 ft), with a maximum of 1.8 m (6 ft). Weight averages about 100 kg (220 lb), with a possible maximum of 120 kg (264 lb).

The Hourglass Dolphin is the smallest in the genus. Its shape is much like the others, streamlined in a robust way, with a very short back and a tall, curved fin. The fin is usually strongly concave on its trailing edge, but we have seen several which are far more nearly triangular.

The tailstock is conspicuously keeled.

The patterning is unique. The back, flukes, flippers and

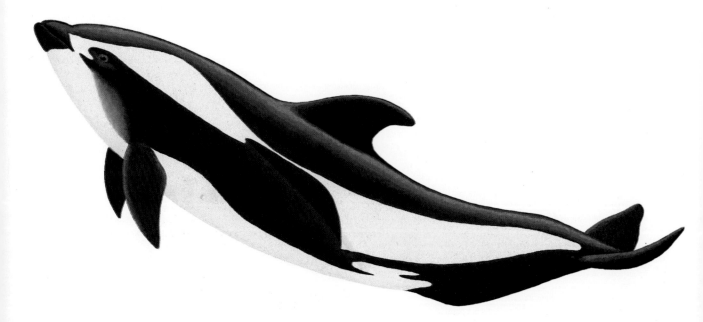

A pair of Hourglass Dolphins sporting alongside a small boat, showing typical markings

beak, like those of the whiteside dolphins in the northern hemisphere, are black. The sides and the belly are pure white, interrupted by an irregular black stripe down the flank which stretches from the eye to the tail and is thrown into a number of highly variable folds and tatters. In most individuals these leave 2 more or less distinct white patches stranded high up on the side, in front and behind (and below) the fin. In some animals the black side stripe might extend down on to the belly, meeting between the flippers to divide the ventral white area into 2 distinct sections. Both jaws are always black.

Field Identification There is little chance of overlooking or mistaking this species. Apart from its striking markings (the white flank patches are visible under all circumstances at sea), the Hourglass Dolphin is the only one consistently found as far south as the Antarctic convergence. We have seen it in the South Atlantic all the way down to the ice in summer.

It also has a distinctive way of moving through the water, undulating in a smooth wave motion which, from a distance, makes it look remarkably like a flock of penguins. Hourglass Dolphins are avid bowriders, easily overtaking a ship moving at 25 kph (12 knots) and sporting in fervent little groups around smaller slower boats. Most often we find them leaping in pairs, showing all of their vivid markings.

In slightly warmer waters around Cape Horn there is a possibility of confusion with the Blackchin Dolphin (*L. australis 60*). They can be most easily distinguished by the fact that the flank patch in front of the fin of the Hourglass Dolphin is white rather than grey. Because this patch is so dark in the Blackchin Dolphin it often seems to have only one patch, the whiter one behind the fin.

In cold waters of the western South Pacific, there is a faint possibility of confusion with the New Zealand Dolphin (*Cephalorhynchus hectori 67*), which also has a black back and white side patch, but its fin is rounded and lobed instead of tall and pointed.

Stranding Hourglass Dolphins are rarely stranded, but a few have been found in Tierra del Fuego. On a recently beached specimen, the markings are striking and unmistakable, but these darken soon after death to a much more uniform black. Then the teeth can prove useful. All counts so far made report exactly 28 small pointed teeth on both sides of both jaws, making a total of 112. This may be the only way to distinguish a skull of this species from that of the Blackchin Dolphin (*L. australis 60*), which usually has a total of 120, and the Dusky Dolphin (*L. obscurus 58*), which can have 128 or more.

Natural History Almost nothing is known. We have seen Hourglass Dolphins feeding at the surface on fairly large fish. The usual social unit seems to be a small family group of less than 6, but up to 14 have been reported. On one occasion near the Falkland Islands, we saw 3 Hourglass Dolphins amongst a large school of Longfin Pilot Whales (*Globicephala melaena 49*).

Status There are no records of the status of this species, but Hourglass Dolphins are apparently relatively common in cold southern waters.

Distribution They seem to be largely confined to waters of less than 5°C (40°F). They have been reported from a number of oceanic areas on, and south of, the Antarctic convergence in the South Atlantic and South Pacific. There are no records yet from the south Indian Ocean, but their distribution is probably circumpolar and we would not be surprised if, sooner or later, they were found there as well.

In summer they occur all the way to the edge of the icepack in Antarctica, and in winter follow the ice north, being seen more often on the coasts of the Falkland Islands and off the tip of South America.

Sources GOODALL & POLKINGHORN (1979) distribution, NORMAN & FRASER (1948) general, QUOY & GAIMARD (1824) original description.

BLACKCHIN DOLPHIN (PEALE'S)

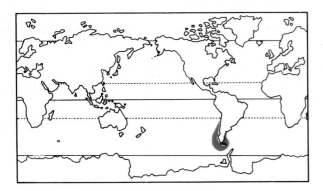

Classification In 1839 Titian Peale, naturalist on USS *Vincennes* off the coast of Patagonia, saw an unusual dolphin which he illustrated but was apparently unable to collect. In the 1848 publication of the report on the expedition, he captioned his painting *Phocaena australis.*

In 1866 Cope published a description of skull No. 3887 in the United States National Museum, noting that it had been collected by USS *Vincennes* off South America on the 1838–42 expedition. He called it *Sagmatius amblodon,* but it has never been possible to confirm the provenance of the type specimen. Charles Pickering, a fellow naturalist of Peale's aboard *Vincennes,* said later that he had no record or recollection of the capture of such an animal.

It was not until the 1930s that Peale's dolphin was seen again at sea and 1941 before an undoubted specimen was finally collected in southern Chile. This matches Peale's description and produced a skull exactly like Cope's mysterious No. 3887, so Kellogg of the Smithsonian classified it as *Lagenorhynchus australis.*

In the last 30 years there have been numerous sightings of this dolphin and several further specimens have been added to the great collections, but there is still no real taxonomic consensus about it. Most cetologists feel that it is a good species, but some still consider it conspecific with *L. cruciger 59* or *L. obscurus 58,* and one at least believes that Cope was right to put it into the separate genus of *Sagmatius.*

We have seen this animal at close quarters several times and we do not hesitate to include it here as a valid species.

Local Names Usually known in the literature as Peale's Porpoise, but we prefer the more accurate and descriptive name of Blackchin Dolphin.

Description Small; length averages 2 m (6.5 ft), with a poss-

ible maximum of 2.3 m (7.5 ft). Weight averages 115 kg (250 lb), with a maximum of about 136 kg (300 lb).

The Blackchin Dolphin, like all members of its genus, has a short beak; but in this species it seems to be a little more clearly defined from the forehead. The dorsal fin is fairly large and moderately hooked. The flippers are relatively small.

The colouring is deep grey above and white below, with the intrusion on the flank of 2 further intermediate shades. On the tailstock is a bold brushstroke of very pale grey, sweeping up to a sharp point directly beneath the fin. The shape and position of this stripe are almost identical with a similar feature on the tail of some Dusky Dolphins (*L. obscurus 58*). On the flank above the flipper is a larger, darker, more ovoid, light grey area which begins directly behind the eye and tapers away toward the anus. The fin, flukes, flippers and the entire head, including the eye and the chin, are all dark; there is a thin dark line running from the point of insertion of the flipper to the eye.

Field Identification It is difficult to identify a Blackchin Dolphin at a distance, but at close quarters there is no mistaking this species. It is a very friendly little dolphin, coming readily to the bow of a large vessel or jumping alongside smaller boats. Under these circumstances, the markings are distinct. The most noticeable are the almost white spike pointing forwards on the tailstock and the bright white patch in the 'armpit'. On a dark animal, or in a poor light, it can be difficult to see the light grey area above the flipper. The best way to distinguish between this species and the Dusky Dolphin (*L. obscurus 58*) is to remember that the latter has a two-toned fin, no armpit patch and, in South America at least, always seems to have a double white spike on the tailstock.

The dark chin of the Blackchin Dolphin is not in itself very noticeable, but it is a useful means of distinction from the Hourglass Dolphin (*L. cruciger 59*). which always has a bright white chin in addition to the equally white areas on its side.

Stranding This species is found stranded particularly in Tierra del Fuego. Identification of a recently beached animal should be possible by its markings, but once it has darkened these become virtually invisible. The teeth are not a great help, as the number is roughly intermediate between that of the Hourglass Dolphin (*L. cruciger 59*), which has a total of 112, and the Dusky Dolphin (*L. obscurus 58*), which usually has 128 or more. The Blackchin seems to have exactly 120, but not enough specimens have been examined for this to be accepted as a taxonomic rule.

Natural History Little is known except that one of the few specimens taken had octopus in its stomach, which implies that it feeds, part of the time at least, on the bottom, close inshore.

We occasionally see single animals, but the normal social unit seems to be a family group of 3 or 4. There are some records of as many as 50 together.

The Blackchin's vocalizations include low-frequency clicks, centred around 3–5 kHz; as well as a low-level pulsed tonal sound. No whistles or squeaks have been heard.

Status Nothing is known, but the Blackchin Dolphin is probably relatively common in its limited range. Goodall has recorded 107 sightings in a 4-year survey of ships operating off Tierra del Fuego.

Fishermen at the crab factories in southern Chile and Argentina sometimes take dolphins to use as bait in their traps. The numbers used in this industry are growing and the practice represents a severe threat to this dolphin's survival.

Distribution Blackchin Dolphins seem to be limited to cold coastal waters; in Chile as far north as Valparaiso, in Argentina to about the Gulf of San Matias and in the waters of the Falkland (Malvinas) Islands. Sightings have been recorded off the Cape of Good Hope as far south as 57°.

Sources COPE (1866) taxonomy, GOODALL (1979) catches, GOODALL & POLKINGHORN (1979) distribution, KELLOGG (1941) taxonomy, PEALE (1848) original description, SCHEVILL & WATKINS (1971) sounds.

SHORTSNOUT DOLPHIN (FRASER'S)

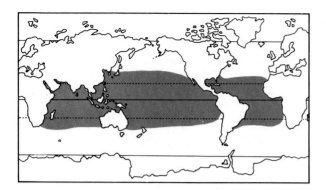

Classification In 1955 Fraser came across a skeleton in the British Museum labelled simply 'white porpoise'. Records indicated that it had been bought from the biological supply house of Gerrards in London in 1895. Further research revealed that it had been captured that same year at the mouth of the Lutong River by Charles Hose, a resident of Sarawak. The specimen came to the museum with several others captured in the same area and identified by Richard Lydekker in 1901 as *Sotalia borneensis* (now known as *Sousa chinensis 40*); but it was clearly different. Fraser decided that it had affinities with both the Common Dolphin (*Delphinus delphis*

75) and the ploughshare dolphins (*Lagenorhynchus* spp.), but was sufficiently distinct to be placed on its own. So in 1956 he created the new intermediate genus *Lagenodelphis* for this single aberrant dolphin and named it *L. hosei* after the finder.

Suddenly, 15 years later, within the space of no more than 5 weeks, the species was rediscovered alive, and in large numbers, in 3 widely separated areas.

On 27 January 1971, there was a stranding on Cocos Island in the east Pacific, between 17 and 19 February 1971 more specimens were found near Durban in South Africa, and on 1 March 1971 another beaching occurred in New South Wales, Australia. There were further finds in the South Pacific during May 1972 and several sightings of large schools in mid-ocean in the next few years. All of these discoveries have confirmed Fraser's diagnosis and turned what was once the rarest of cetaceans, known from a single skeleton collected in the last century, into a relatively common tropical species.

Local Names If ever a species deserved to be known after its finder, it is this one; but we rigorously pursue our policy of eliminating proper nouns, and change Fraser's dolphin, to the more descriptive Shortsnout Dolphin.

Description Small; length averages 2.3 m (7.5 ft), with a maximum of 2.6 m (8.5 ft). Weight averages 90 kg (200 lb),

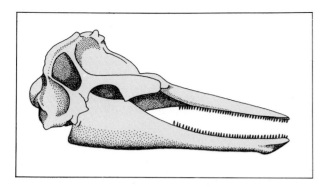

distinctive, and reminiscent of the Striped Dolphin (*Stenella coeruleoalba 72*). Both are tropical species, but can be distinguished as follows:

Lagenodelphis short, pointed snout; robust body; small fin, pointed at tip; single broad flank stripe.

Stenella long, distinctive beak; slender body; tall fin, broader at the base; several stripes in various patterns.

There is also a possibility of confusion with the Common Dolphin (*Delphinus delphis 75*), but that species also has a very long snout and, instead of a single stripe, an hourglass pattern of yellow on its flanks.

Stranding This species is frequently stranded. A Shortsnout Dolphin should be readily recognizable by the combination of its robust body and the surprisingly large number of teeth in its abbreviated beak. These are small, pointed, oval in cross section and there are 40–44 on each side of the upper jaw, and 39–43 on each side of the lower jaw. This total of at least 160 (more often 172), clearly separates this species from all other dolphins with short snouts.

Natural History Shortsnout Dolphins seem to be deep divers, feeding on squid and fish (particularly *Ichthyococus elongatus*) that are seldom found near the surface.

They have been seen in very large schools of up to 500, and are probably largely oceanic.

Nothing is yet known of their reproductive behaviour.

Status Shortsnout Dolphins are probably relatively common in deep tropical waters. Twenty-five animals were recently taken in purse-seine nets on one day in the east Pacific.

Distribution This species is now known from St Vincent in the Caribbean, from the east coast of South Africa, from Sarawak, Taiwan, Japan, eastern Australia, Clipperton Island, the Phoenix Islands and Cocos Island in the east Pacific. There are no records from any waters cooler than 20°C (68°F).

with a maximum of about 136 kg (300 lb).

This species has an even shorter snout than those of the ploughshare dolphins (*Lagenorhynchus* spp.), but tiny as it is, it is nevertheless a beak, which makes the profile quite different from the truly beakless flat-faced porpoises. The body is rounded and rather robust, with comparatively small flippers, flukes and fin. The dorsal fin is slender, roughly triangular, but sharply hooked right at the tip. There are marked keels both above and below the tailstock.

The colour is mainly medium grey above and pinkish white below, with 2 parallel stripes running the full length of the body on the margin between the dark back and the light belly. The upper of these bands is cream coloured or pale grey, beginning above and in front of the eye, and petering out on the tailstock. The lower, more dramatic, band is blackish grey, darker than the back, and runs from the eye to the anus. There may be an additional black band from the mouth to the flipper. The throat and chin are white, but the tip of the lower jaw is usually black.

Field Identification This is surprisingly easy to identify for a species that went unnoticed for so long. The most distinctive feature in the field is the shortness of all appendages. The first impression is of a smoothly rounded, typical dolphin body with an abrupt pointed snout, equipped with flippers and flukes which seem inadequate for its size.

Despite these apparent shortcomings, it is an aggressive swimmer, bursting up to breathe in a cloud of spray. Shortsnout Dolphins have a blowhole which is noticeably left of centre. They have not been seen bowriding, but apparently often leap as they travel alongside a vessel.

When seen clear of the water, the dark lateral stripe is

Sources CALDWELL et al (1976) in Atlantic, FRASER (1956) original description, MIYAZAKI & WADA (1978) in west Pacific, PERRIN et al (1973) in east Pacific, TOBAYAMA et al (1973) in north Pacific.

SOUTHERN RIGHTWHALE DOLPHIN

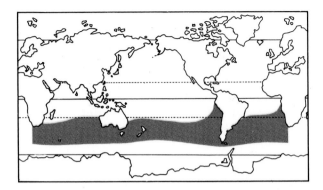

Classification During the French expedition to Australia of 1800–4 the naturalist aboard *Geographe*, François Peron, saw a unique finless dolphin somewhere south of Van Diemen's Land (Tasmania). On his return to Paris he submitted a manuscript report with a description of it to Lacépède, who included it in his natural history as *Delphinus peronii*. In 1826 Lesson included the species in *Delphinapterus*, together with the equally finless White Whale; but that association was never very comfortable. In 1841 Constantine Wilhelm Lambert Gloger, a German ornithologist and expert in geographical variation, who believed that variation was never accidental but took place with design and for good reason, found the aberrant form of this dolphin fascinating and proposed for it a new genus *Lissodelphis* from the Greek *lissos*, smooth.

All this seems to have taken place on the basis of nothing more than Peron's original sighting and description, but by the middle of the nineteenth century a number of actual specimens had been brought back to Europe by whaling and Antarctic expeditions to Chile, Cape Horn and the South Seas, and the dolphin's character and classification were confirmed.

Local Names *Tunina sin aleta* or *delfinliso* (Spanish). In most other languages it has been compared, because of its smooth finless back, with the Great Right Whale (*Balaena glacialis 1*). To contrast it with a related northern form, we call it the Southern Rightwhale Dolphin.

Description Small; length averages 1.8 m (6 ft), with a possible maximum of 2.4 m (8 ft). Weight averages 60 kg (132 lb), with a maximum of about 82 kg (180 lb).

The Rightwhale Dolphins are unique in form. Neither has any trace of a dorsal fin; their backs curve smoothly and evenly over from the tip of the snout to the tail. The fin is thought by most experts on hydrodynamics to function principally as a stabilizer, keeping the cetacean upright when swimming underwater. The Great Right Whale (*Balaena glacialis 1*) and the White Whale (*Delphinapterus leucas 35*) get by without one, because neither normally does much more than rise slowly to the surface and sink again. These dolphins are, however, fast-swimming oceanic animals and would seem to be in need of stabilizing. They may have found their own solution. In all other dolphins the height of the body is greater than its width, but in Rightwhale Dolphins the reverse is true. They are flattened from top to bottom and, having flippers set right at the edge of the widest part of their bodies, seem to be perfectly balanced and in no danger of losing stability, even at high speed.

The southern species is a little smaller than its northern relative (*L. borealis 63*) and slightly more stocky. It has the same smooth, torpedolike lines, but the beak seems to be stouter, with the lower jaw protruding slightly beyond the upper. Hermann Melville described it: 'Though his entire back down to his side fins is of a deep sable, yet a boundary line, distinct as the mark on a ship's hull, called the "bright waist", that line streaks him from stem to stern, with two colours, black above and white below. The white comprises part of his head, and the whole of his mouth, which makes

The smooth, high, arching leap of a pair of Southern Rightwhale Dolphins disturbed by a ship

him look as if he had just escaped from a felonious visit to a meal-bag.' We need only add that the flukes are always white below and can sometimes also be white above, while the flippers are completely white, both above and below. In exceptional cases, the flippers can be greyish, with a dark tip or trailing edge. The eyes are always set within the bluish-black area of the back. One pure white animal has been reported from the south-western Pacific.

Field Identification There is absolutely no question of mistaking this species for any other dolphin, but it is easy to confuse with penguins or sealions, moving along in the same smooth series of rather rapid low angle leaps.

When swimming slowly, Southern Rightwhale Dolphins expose only the shiny black of their backs, but as soon as they sense a ship, they invariably put on speed and begin to swarm away in a tightly concentrated formation. As they leap, the vivid white of the head, flippers and belly are clearly visible. There are no aerobatics – no twists or turns or somersaults – but the whole group seem to leap in concert, and to do so at such short intervals, that they create a considerable flurry at the surface. This disturbance, plus the fact that they are often seen from behind as they flee, makes it possible to continue to confuse them with sealions or furseals even at quite close quarters. It is necessary to look very closely for the characteristic dolphin tail.

Some schools of Southern Rightwhale Dolphins seem less wary than others and may remain for a short while, moving near a ship rather than immediately turning tail. Under these circumstances they leap higher out of the water than a fleeing school and much higher than any Northern Rightwhale Dolphin (*Lissodelphis borealis 63*) we have seen.

On one occasion in the southern Indian Ocean we surprised a school apparently resting at the surface with just the tips of their heads showing. Their immediate response was to sound and we assumed at first that we had seen a shoal of large fish. Then they broke surface again, directly ahead of our vessel which was moving at 25 kph (12 knots) and we could see that they were Southern Rightwhale Dolphins. The group scattered as we continued to pursue them, but 5 stayed with us

and went on bowriding for a short while. That was the only time we ever saw this generally timid animal react positively to shipping.

Stranding Southern Rightwhale Dolphins are rarely stranded, but beached individuals are usually unmistakable. Apart from the characteristic body form and pattern, Rightwhale Dolphins have distinctive heads. The skull is long, with a very slender beak reminiscent of some of the freshwater dolphins. There are 43–47 tiny pointed teeth on each side of each jaw, making a total of at least 172, and often as many as 180. There are usually 90 vertebrae, and the first 5 of 14 pairs of ribs are double headed.

Natural History Southern Rightwhale Dolphins seem to live well offshore, feeding on both fish and squid.

The groups we have seen usually number between 30 and 100, but very much larger schools have been reported. In 1964 herds of up to 1,000 were seen east of South Island in New Zealand; and in 1968 over 1,000 were filmed together 320 km (200 miles) off St Paul Island in the southern Indian Ocean.

Status This species was once thought to be rare, but is probably fairly common in low latitudes.

Distribution The Southern Rightwhale Dolphin is a deep-water species, seldom seen near land. The range is circumpolar in the southern hemisphere only, with most sightings being made in the cold subantarctic waters of the West Wind Drift. Where cold currents such as the Humboldt and the Benguela move northwards, Southern Rightwhale Dolphins seem to follow them, at least in winter, into higher latitudes along the western coasts of South America and South Africa. There have been reports of this species from Japan, but they seem unlikely.

Sources FRASER (1955) taxonomy, GASKIN (1968) in New Zealand, LACÉPÈDE (1804) original description.

245

NORTHERN RIGHTWHALE DOLPHIN

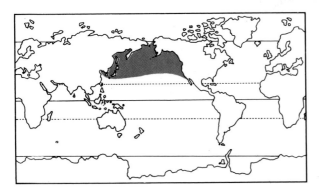

Classification The Southern Rightwhale Dolphin was well known, both to whalers and in the literature, by about 1840, but it was not until 1848 that the northern form was discovered. Credit goes to Peale, who took the first specimen 320 km (200 miles) off the mouth of the Columbia River in the north-eastern Pacific. He did not apparently preserve the animal, but described and identified it as *Delphinapterus borealis* from the Latin *borealis*, of the north. Some years later, Gloger's genus was accepted for both southern and northern forms and the species became *Lissodelphis borealis.* For more than a century it was considered rare, with barely half a dozen specimens in all the world's collections, but in 1976 James Stephen Leatherwood and his colleagues at San Diego added 175 sightings to the known records and showed that this species was relatively common.

In 1936 it was reported that some individuals being caught off Kinkasan in Japan were different from ordinary specimens and Ogawa suggested that they might be stray *L. peronii 62* from the southern hemisphere; but Nishiwaki has now shown that there are variations in the colour form of the northern species and that the one seen in Japan could possibly be a subspecies *L. b. albiventris.*

A skull collected on the west coast of North America in 1849, and identified by Gray as a ploughshare dolphin with an unusually large number of teeth, which he called *Lagenorhynchus thicolea*, is certainly a specimen of *Lissodelphis borealis.*

Local Names *Semi iruka,* the cicada dolphin (Japanese). We distinguish this from the southern form simply as the Northern Rightwhale Dolphin.

Description Small; length averages 2.1 m (7 ft), with a possible maximum of 3.1 m (over 10 ft). Weight averages 70 kg (154 lb), with a maximum of about 90 kg (200 lb).

This is a truly beautiful dolphin with the clean slender shape of a drop of dark liquid. Like its southern relative (*L. peronii 62*), it is wider than it is high and has no trace of a dorsal fin. There is however a marked flattening of the tailstock to produce a fairly strong keel. The beak is more slender and better defined than in the southern species, and the body is longer.

The colouring is distinctive. The back is a deep, slightly metallic, black, sharply separated from a pure white belly. The flippers are black and the white belly patch is shaped like an hourglass with a constriction at the navel. In the Japanese subspecies, the white underside extends much further up the flank and only the tips of the flippers remain black. It has not yet been established whether this difference is genetically determined or falls within the normal range of variability in the basic pattern. In some individuals there is a paler grey area on the forehead, and in most a distinct white band across the bottom of the lower jaw. All juveniles seem to be very much lighter, almost brown, on their backs. One albino is known from Japan.

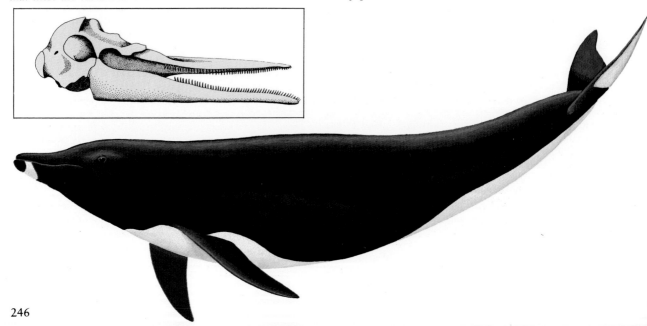

Northern Rightwhale Dolphins leaping in smooth low arcs as they travel away from approaching ship

Field Identification Northern Rightwhale Dolphins are no less distinctive in the water than their southern relatives. When undisturbed, they hang motionless in the water or move slowly along at the surface, breathing once every 20–30 seconds, barely exposing their smooth black backs. Under these circumstances, they can be very difficult to see and very easy to overlook or dismiss as a shoal of fish; fortunately for whale-watchers, these dolphins are easily startled. When disturbed, they erupt into a flurry of low-profile leaps, showing little of their heads. They arch out of the water together, sometimes slapping their flukes or flopping down on their bellies, but most often entering cleanly and bouncing out again a few moments later in another graceful arc. They are fast swimmers, easily outpacing a vessel travelling at 30 kph (15 knots) and occasionally drop back to take advantage of the bow wave. They have even been seen riding the head wave of a migrating Grey Whale (*Eschrichtius robustus 4*). When pursued, they scatter and dive, disappearing for 6 minutes or more.

Under most circumstances, it is difficult to see any of the white markings making it easy to confuse this dolphin with furseals or sealions on the move. Both show the same kind of smooth low leap when travelling at speed, but the tail flukes of the dolphin are distinctive. When a group can be seen moving across the bows or on a parallel track, the white chest area just in front of the flippers does become visible.

Schools most often seem to be acting in concert, drawing together into a dense mass when alarmed, leaping simultaneously so that it is possible to make a fairly accurate assessment of their numbers. Most of the group will be in the air at any given moment in a leap and all return to the water without fuss or histrionics.

Northern Rightwhale Dolphins have been seen in the southern part of their range schooling with Shortfin Pilot Whales (*Globicephala macrorhynchus 50*), and further north with Pacific Whiteside Dolphins (*Lagenorhynchus obliquidens 57*). In company with the latter, they come more frequently to bowride. They may also occur with Common Dolphins (*Delphinus delphis 75*), Grey Dolphins (*Grampus griseus 68*), and Spray Porpoises (*Phocoenoides dalli 48*). There is even one report of Rightwhale Dolphins schooling with a shoal of large mackerel.

Stranding There are occasional solitary strandings. A beached

Northern Rightwhale Dolphin presents no problems of identification. The shape and pattern are diagnostic and the teeth are distinctive. The skull is very narrow, with long slim jaws housing at least 40 small sharp teeth on each side. The average total is greater than 180. Most sources give 43 or 46 as an upper limit to the number in each row, but in our experience this often rises to 51 or 53. The skull we illustrate is one from the collection in the British Museum with a total of 218 teeth. There are 88–90 vertebrae, and 6 of the 15 pairs of ribs are double headed.

Natural History It seems that this species is a deep diver, feeding largely at night on squid (*Loligo opalescens*) and lantern fish. One stomach examined also contained a number of pelagic barnacles.

Groups of 30–40 are most common, usually seen moving in tight V-formation, but occasionally strung out in a more relaxed 'chorus line'. Large schools of several hundred do occur.

Little is known of reproductive behaviour, except that they apparently reach maturity at a length of about 2 m (6.5 ft) and produce calves in April or May.

Recordings made in the field show that this species echolocates with rapid trains of clicks at a high frequency of over 40 kHz. They also produce some broad-spectrum low-rate pulsed sounds in addition to a repertoire of frequency-modulated yelps, whistles and moans.

Status A number, perhaps as high as several hundred each year, is taken by Japanese coastal stations and in purse-seine fisheries. Northern Rightwhale Dolphins are nevertheless relatively common in parts of their range.

Distribution Northern Rightwhale Dolphins are known only from the cooler waters of the North Pacific, ranging from Japan and the Sea of Okhotsk in the west, to the Bering Sea, Alaska and the coasts of Washington and California in the east. This is primarily a deep-water offshore species, which undertakes some northward movement in the spring and makes a corresponding migration back south in the autumn.

Sources LEATHERWOOD (1979) natural history, LEATHERWOOD & WALKER (1976) status, NISHIWAKI (1966) taxonomy, NORRIS & PRESCOTT (1961) behaviour, PEALE (1848) original description.

PIEBALD DOLPHIN (COMMERSON'S)

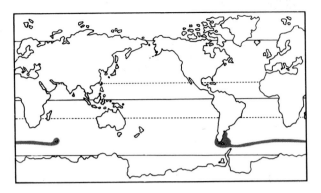

Classification In the middle of the eighteenth century, with King Louis XV on the throne of France and the Linnaean revolution sweeping through natural history, demanding that all living things be neatly indexed; Georges Louis Leclerc, Comte de Buffon, was appointed Keeper of the Jardin du Roi and charged with cataloguing the King's Museum. Buffon turned this relatively simple task into an elaborate account of the whole of nature and did everything he could to encourage further collecting. One of the results of his enthusiasm was the first French voyage round the world in the mid-eighteenth century, an expedition under Baron Louis Bougainville with the botanist Philibert Commerson.

Commerson saw a dolphin with conspicuous black and white markings and described it in an unpublished manuscript addressed to Buffon. In 1804 Lacépède referred to Commerson's sighting in the Straits of Magellan and named it *Delphinus commersonii*. In 1836 Cuvier, describing a similar animal from the Cape of Good Hope, called it *D. cephalorhynchus* from the Greek *kephalos*, a head, and *rhynchos*, a beak. Gray seized on this apt description of a dolphin whose whole head looks like a broad beak, and in 1846 used it as the name for a new genus *Cephalorhynchus*.

The full binomial *Cephalorhynchus commersonii* was finally assembled in 1922 by Sir Sidney Harmer, the Director of the British Museum.

Local Names Commerson called his dolphin '*le Jacobite*' because of its black and white costume. In Spanish it is known as *tunina overa*. Other names include skunk dolphin and puffing pig, but we prefer the simple and descriptive name of Piebald Dolphin.

Description Small; length averages 1.35 m (4.5 ft), with a maximum of 1.65 m (5.5 ft). Weight averages about 50 kg

(110 lb), with a possible maximum of about 66 kg (145 lb).

The Piebald Dolphin is a robust little animal with a body shaped more like a porpoise than a true dolphin. It has no melon, but a broad, flat, almost triangular head which seems to be composed entirely of mouth and beak. The flippers are small and rounded, and the dorsal fin is a smooth low oval lobe set behind the midpoint of the back.

The markings are dramatic: the body is basically a deep grey, but thrown right across the back in front of the fin is a white or very pale grey cape which wraps around the belly, leaving only a black spot in the anus area. On the throat and chin is another white spot of roughly similar size. The undersides of both flippers and flukes are black.

Field Identification With the rounded black fin and the vivid white shawl across its shoulders, there is no mistaking this species. It rolls easily and smoothly over at the surface, breathing 4 or 5 times each minute.

We have never seen Piebald Dolphins bowride, but they are certainly not timid, running alongside ships, jumping clear of the water from time to time. In the Falklands and in protected bays in the Fuegian channels, we often find that our boats are followed in by a small group of these friendly dolphins, that sometimes come near enough to the propellors to give us cause for concern. On several occasions in little more than a metre of water, we have had them swimming close enough to touch, in amongst our legs as we land.

Stranding Usually only single animals are involved in strandings. Identification of a recently beached Piebald Dolphin is no problem. Even when the skin darkens, the shape is distinctive. There are 29 or 30 (very rarely as many as 32) peglike teeth on each side of both jaws.

Natural History Very little is known. Piebald Dolphins feed on krill, cuttlefish, squid, shrimps and small fish. They are most often found in social units of less than 6, but we have seen at least one group of more than 30 and there are several records of schools of over 100.

This species seems to have a lot of trouble with predation by Great Killer Whales (*Orcinus orca 51*) and it is possible that their markings have significant survival value in that they divide the body visually into 2 parts with little apparent connection. This disruptive camouflage could help conceal them from a predator which hunts at least partly by sight, and it would be particularly effective in water containing small ice floes.

Status This species seems to be relatively common. About 100 are taken each year in gill nets in southern Argentina and used

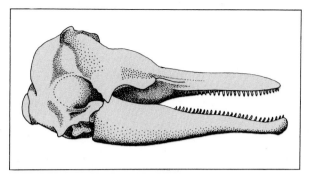

Above: skull
Below: Piebald Dolphin rolling at the surface, showing white cape in front of fin

both for baiting crab traps and for human consumption. A similar number are caught deliberately in Tierra del Fuego or incidentally in tangle nets set for Patagonian blenny (*Eleginops maclorinus*).

Distribution Piebald Dolphins are known mainly from cold, shallow inshore waters 42°–56° of latitude off the tip of South America. There are records from both Chilean and Argentinian Tierra del Fuego, as far west as Isla Desolacion; north to the coast of Patagonia and eastwards out to the Falkland Islands.

Piebald Dolphins may also occur around South Georgia, Tristan da Cunha and Gough islands because there are some surprising records from as far afield as Kerguelen Island in the southern Indian Ocean. Two specimens were apparently captured there in 1954 although their skulls have now vanished; Peter Best of the Marine Mammal Laboratory in Cape Town reports seeing live animals there more recently.

Sources ANGOT (1954) at Kerguelen, BROWNELL (1974) distribution, BROWNELL & PRADERI (1979) taxonomy, FRASER & PURVES (1960) taxonomy, FROST & BEST (1976) in Indian Ocean, GOODALL (1979) status, HAMILTON (1952) distribution, HARMER (1922) taxonomy, HART (1935) in South Georgia, LACÉPÈDE (1804) original description.

CHILEAN DOLPHIN (BLACK)

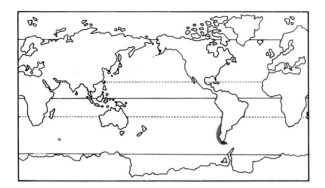

Classification The first specimen of this species was collected from the southern coast of Chile by George Dickie. Gray illustrated it, without comment, in his 1846 report of the collection of HMS *Erebus* and HMS *Terror*, calling it *Delphinus eutropia* from the Greek *eu*, well or right, and *tropidos*, a keel.

Between 1893 and 1896 at least 5 further specimens were collected near Valparaiso and the Rio Valdivia in Chile. They were studied in the National Museum in Santiago and described by Perez Canto and Rudolph Philippi variously as *Phocaena albiventris* and *P. obtusata*.

Local Names In Chile it is known as *delfin negro* and in English it has been called both black dolphin and whitebelly dolphin. These names are too much like too many others to be truly distinctive, so we recommend that this species be known as the Chilean Dolphin.

Description Small; length averages 1.2 m (4 ft), with a possible maximum of 1.5 m (5 ft). Weight averages 45 kg (100 lb), with a maximum of about 60 kg (132 lb).

Chilean Dolphins are like the other members of their genus in being small, stocky animals, with heads and beaks which merge imperceptibly into each other. The flippers are small and rounded at the tip, and the dorsal fin is very low, backward leaning and triangular with a blunt apex. The tailstock is keeled both above and below.

The colouring is pure black, darker than the back of the Piebald Dolphin (*Cephalorhynchus commersonii 64*). On the belly are 3 patches of white: one on the throat, one behind the flippers, and a third in the anal area. The last two may be either very much reduced, or large enough to overlap. There is a pale and very thin white line around the lips on both jaws. In a few individuals there may be a pale blaze mark around the blowhole.

Field Identification Chilean Dolphins appear totally black in the water. The variable white markings on the belly are difficult to see, which makes it possible, even likely, that this species will be confused with the Black Porpoise (*Phocoena spinipinnis 44*). Both are timid, relatively slow-moving animals, but the dolphins have a slightly more undulating motion in the water, much more like a furseal's. The fins too are distinctive, that of the porpoise being more lobed on the trailing edge.

The best field characteristic of the Chilean Dolphin, when it can be seen, is probably the broad flat forehead.

Stranding The rare strandings provide a method of certain identification. There are 28–31 small, round-tipped teeth on each side of both jaws, totally unlike the waisted, shovel-shaped teeth of the equally black porpoise.

Natural History Almost nothing is known. We have only been able to discover that this species eats cuttlefish and shrimps, and that it is most often seen in groups of about 6. There is one record of a school of 30 from the Straits of Magellan.

Status This species must be considered as relatively rare. Along the Chilean coast, both north and south of Valdivia, these dolphins are caught, along with the Black Porpoise (*Phocoena spinipinnis 44*) in nets set for fish. The meat is used to bait traps in a growing fishery for southern king crab (*Lithodes antarctica*).

Distribution Chilean Dolphins are known only from cold, shallow, inshore waters along the southern coast of Chile, between latitudes 33° and 55° south. In summer months they can often be seen in the channels of Tierra del Fuego.

Sources AGUAYO (1975) status, CABRERA (1961) distribution, GOODALL & POLINGHORN (1979) distribution, GRAY (1846) first illustration, GRAY (1849) original description.

BENGUELA DOLPHIN (HEAVISIDE'S)

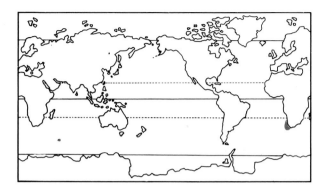

Classification In 1828 the Conservator of the Museum of the Royal College of Surgeons, William Clift, received several cetaceans for the museum and recorded for a specimen from the Cape of Good Hope that it came from the collection of Captain Heaviside, a prominent naval surgeon whose personal accumulation of anatomical material had been sold at auction earlier that year. Gray illustrated the specimen in his *Spicilegia Zoologica* of 1828 and named it *Delphinus heavisidii*. In fact there are no cetaceans in Heaviside's collection and the dolphin skin and skull came back to England in the hands of a Captain Haviside, an employee of the British East India Company, who carried the extensive Villet collections from the Cape in 1827. The error in attribution was eventually discovered, but the original spelling must stand.

Local Names There have never been any satisfactory names for this species. We suggest that it be known, after the cold-water current in which it is found, as the Benguela Dolphin.

Description Small; length averages 1.2 m (4 ft), with a maximum of about 1.4 m (4.5 ft). Weight averages 40 kg (88 lb), with a possible maximum of 55 kg (120 lb).

This is a very small, compact little dolphin with the typical broad flat head of its genus. There is no distinct beak, just a large, wide mouth set in a shortened head, with a lower jaw extending slightly beyond the upper one. The flippers are oval-shaped, smaller and narrower than those of the Piebald Dolphin; the dorsal fin is broad-based and triangular.

The colour and pattern are very much like those of the

Chilean Dolphin (*Cephalorhynchus eutropia* 65), black above and white below; but the white belly in this species extends upwards in 3 major lobes which invade the dark area of the flank. The first of these lies in front of the flippers and the second immediately behind them; the third is longer and more slender, reaching obliquely backwards up on to the tailstock. When seen from beneath, the white underside forms a continuous pattern shaped in the front like a rounded cross of Lorraine, and behind like a blunt trident.

Field Identification Following the original specimen, another was captured in 1856 and then there were no further reports until 1965 when a Benguela Dolphin was stranded near Cape Town. In 1969 3 more were caught north of Blaauwberg on the Cape coast; together these represent the entire history of our knowledge of this species. The last 3 animals were observed while still alive, but there are no good observations on record of the species in the field. It probably surfaces slowly and quietly like its relatives and does not show more than its head and back above the surface unless moving rapidly. It seems likely that at least the white process on the tail would be conspicuous in the water.

Stranding A beached specimen is easy to identify. There is nothing in South African waters like it. There are 25–30 slender, pointed teeth on each side of both jaws.

Natural History Benguela Dolphins feed on squid and bottom-dwelling fish. Recordings were made of the animals captured in 1969 and it was found that they produced low-level pulsed sounds around 8 kHz. These were largely short bursts of clicks, sometimes running together fast enough to produce a tonal cry.

Status This species can only be considered as rare.

Distribution From the few records it is assumed to be confined to the cold inshore waters of the Benguela current on the west coast of southern Africa, from the Cape Peninsula northwards to about Cape Cross in Namibia.

Sources BROWNELL (1979) distribution, GRAY (1828) original description, WATKINS et al (1977) sounds.

NEW ZEALAND DOLPHIN (HECTOR'S)

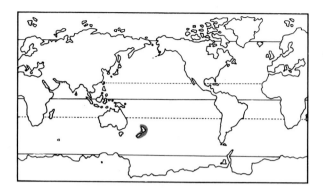

Classification In 1873 Sir James Hector, Curator of the Wellington Colonial Museum, New Zealand, described a dolphin shot in the Cook Strait as *Electra clancula*, assuming that it was a form of Dusky Dolphin (now called *Lagenorhynchus obscurus 58*). To be certain he sent the specimen off to the Belgian palaeontologist van Bénéden, who realized that it was something new and published details of it in 1861, naming it this time as *Electra hectori*. Finally in 1885 Hector himself was able to place his dolphin in correct taxonomic perspective as *Cephalorhynchus hectori*.

Hector and van Bénéden both described their specimen as having a plain black back, but they never saw a living animal. In life this dolphin's upper side is a medium grey with a pale grey or white disc on the forehead. So, when one was first described from life, it was assumed to be a different species and was given a different name, *C. albifrons*. Even as recently as 1946, Walter Oliver of the Wellington Museum was suggesting (from observations made at sea) that there must be at least a separate subspecies (*C. h. bicolor*), to accommodate the light-fronted and grey-backed dolphins that were being seen in New Zealand waters. Eventually it dawned on everyone involved that they were seeing only the *bicolor* variety and that nobody since Hector and van Bénéden had ever encountered the black-headed version. Today the separate species and subspecies have been abolished, leaving only *C. hectori*.

Local Names Having denied Commerson's and Gray's claims to vernacular names, we must deal similarly harshly with Hector. We therefore choose to call this species the New Zealand Dolphin.

Description Small; length averages 1.4 m (4.5 ft), with a maximum of 1.8 m (6 ft). Weight averages 40 kg (88 lb), with a maximum of about 60 kg (132 lb).

This is a fat little dolphin with a slightly more defined beak than the other species in its genus. The body is equally rotund and is topped by a backward-leaning, smoothly-oval lobe for a dorsal fin. The shape of this is identical with the fin of the Piebald Dolphin (*C. commersonii 64*). The flippers are also smoothly rounded.

The markings are variable, but distinctive. The ground colour of the back is a deep grey, which still shows on the nose, fin, flippers and flukes, but it is usually overlain by a medium-grey cape, which gives the bulk of the body a misty sheen. There is an even paler grey, sometimes almost white, egg-shaped patch on the forehead in front of the blowhole. In some individuals this is large enough to extend right down to the tip of the jaw and encompass the eye. The underside is white from the throat all the way back to the anal area, with an oblique, pointed peninsula extending up and back on to the tailstock. In most individuals this white belly is broken by a dark body belt which extends from the flank right round the chest between the flippers, leaving only a small white oval in the armpit. Many animals have a dark patch of a similar size and shape around the anus and a few have a scattering of dark spots all over the body.

Field Identification New Zealand Dolphins are generally quiet and unobtrusive, but sufficiently friendly to be very well known to all who operate small coastal boats. They congregate in small groups, often in the turbid waters of an estuary, rising quietly to blow 3 or 4 times at 10-second intervals, with only their rounded fins showing above the surface. These stand out distinctly from the paler colour of the back. When the dolphins dive, they disappear for 1–3 minutes, surfacing again a short distance away. When resting, a group may hang motionless at the surface.

These dolphins seem to delight in boats with a speed of around 15 kph (about 8 knots), running with and in front of them, bowriding in and out of most fishing ports in the area. New Zealand Dolphins seldom jump, but when moving at speed swim in an undulating wavelike manner, bobbing smoothly through the surface like seals. At a distance they look dark, but at close quarters the grey back, the pale forehead and the white process on the tailstock are all distinctive and unmistakable.

The fearlessness shown by this species sometimes extends even to playing with, and allowing themselves to be touched by, bathers in shallow water. There are several records from New Zealand of swimmers, particularly children, being befriended in this way.

Stranding Apparently only ailing individuals strand themselves. The markings on the back disappear soon after death, darkening to a uniform black, but a New Zealand Dolphin is still recognizable by its characteristic shape. There are 24–32 (usually 28 or 30) teeth on each side of both jaws, a number likely to be confused only with that of the Dusky Dolphin (*Lagenorhynchus obscurus 58*), which is larger and tends to have more than 30 teeth in each row of a longer, much narrower beak.

Natural History These dolphins feed on cuttlefish, shrimps and small fish, seeking them out close inshore and in the muddy outflows of river mouths.

The dolphins may congregate in large numbers at popular

feeding sites, but the usual social pattern is for groups of up to 10 to forage together, often some distance away from other schools similarly occupied.

Social cohesion is apparently strong. One dolphin was found swimming frantically up and down outside a net in which another had become entangled in shallow water. When the trapped animal was freed, they swam away together.

Little is known about reproductive behaviour, but this species seems to calve in mid-summer, producing infants perfectly pied like their parents.

Status A few individuals are deliberately taken for exhibition or accidentally in nets, but there is otherwise little to threaten this species which is clearly quite common in its area.

Distribution The New Zealand Dolphin is apparently confined to shallow coastal waters, principally on the shores of North Island and the east coast of South Island, New Zealand. The dolphins may migrate locally, moving northwards in summer, often entering and travelling some distance upstream in the turbid waters of rivers in flood.

There is one dubious record of this species from the South China Sea, but this was almost certain to have been the result of misidentification.

Sources ABEL et al (1971) distribution, BRUYNS & BAKER (1973) general, GASKIN (1972) in New Zealand, HARRISON (1960) in China Sea? HECTOR (1873) first specimen, OLIVER (1946) taxonomy, VAN BENEDEN (1881) original description, VAN BREE (1972) taxonomy.

GREY DOLPHIN (RISSO'S)

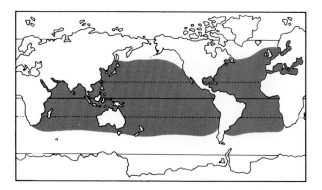

Classification In 1811 Cuvier received the stuffed skin and skull of a dolphin stranded at Brest in Brittany, with a full description, and drawing, of another beached near Nice in Provence. He saw no reason to associate the two and in 1812 identified the first as *Delphinus griseus* from the Latin *griseus*, grey; and the second as *Delphinus aries*, because the drawing showed that this dolphin had a creased forehead something like the horn boss on a ram's head.

The report of the Nice stranding came from an amateur naturalist known to history simply as M. Risso, but Cuvier referred to the animal several times as '*dauphin de Risso*' and this became not only the vernacular name, but was adopted specifically by several later authors, who identified specimens as *Delphinus rissoanus, Phocaena rissonus* and *Globicephalus rissii.*

In 1828 Gray created the genus *Grampus* for a number of species, including Cuvier's grey dolphin from Brest. His choice of this name has been criticized, and it is in some ways unfortunate and confusing, because it is also one of the popular names for the Great Killer Whale (*Orcinus orca 51*). The word grampus is usually seen to be derived from the French *grand poisson* or *gras poisson*. There was one brief attempt in 1933 to alter the genus to *Grampidelphis*, and there have been

a number of proposed new specific names for local variants, but all specimens are now classified as *Grampus griseus.*

Local Names Grampus, grey grampus, mottled grampus (English), *gramper* (Dutch), *dauphin de Risso* or *dauphin de Cuvier* (French), *avala* (Russian) and *sakamata kujira* (Japanese). To avoid confusion with the Great Killer Whale (*Orcinus orca 51*) and all others sometimes known as grampus, we call this species the Grey Dolphin.

Description Small to medium; length averages 3 m (10 ft), with a possible maximum of 4.25 m (14 ft); calves are about 1.5 m (5 ft) at birth. Weight averages about 300 kg (660 lb), with a possible maximum of 680 kg (1,500 lb).

Grey Dolphins have a unique combination of characteristics. Their body shape is reminiscent of pilot whales (*Globicephala* spp.), robust in front of the fin and tapering rapidly to a narrow tailstock behind it. There is no beak and the head is not as high or rounded in the melon as that of the pilots. It is instead split right down the centre of the forehead from the blowhole to the upper lip, by a crease or parting peculiar to this species. The rest of the head is rather porpoiselike, but the appendages are distinctly delphinid. The flippers are long and pointed and the fin is very tall, curved like that of the Bottlenose Dolphin but up to 50 cm (20 inches) high. The flukes are broad and deeply notched.

These dolphins are a uniform dark grey at birth and keep this colour throughout their lives on most of the fin, flippers and flukes. As they age, their colour fades to a light or pale grey, becoming almost white on the face, belly and the area of back directly in front of the fin. A few individuals keep a dark patch on the chin. In the oldest animals the tip of the fin also becomes bleached. There is however considerable variation in this lightening process; with some adults becoming almost as pale as a White Whale (*Delphinapterus leucas 35*) while others remain as dark as a False Killer Whale *52*.

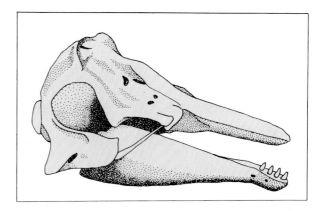

Above: Grey Dolphin in lookout posture, showing the prominent crease in the forehead
Below: Grey Dolphin at the surface, showing the high pointed fin and the extensive scarring on the back in front of the fin

All Grey Dolphins seem, sooner or later, to become dramatically scarred. As they grow their backs become laced with fine white lines. These are apparently produced by other Grey Dolphins; the depth and spacing of the lines correspond directly with the few strong teeth set well to the front of a Grey Dolphin's lower jaw. Most dolphins bear tooth marks of mates or rivals at some time, but none so conspicuously or abundantly as this species. Many individuals also have oval sucker or parasitic scars on their flanks and bellies.

Field Identification At close range Grey Dolphins are unmistakable. If the light is at all good, it is hard to miss the network of white scars on their grey backs. Even from a distance the scars stand out as distinct lighter areas in front of the fin.

They are active animals, sometimes rising gently to blow with just the back and fin showing, but most often porpoising along in a small tight group of about a dozen. They are usually fairly shy, swimming unhurriedly away from shipping, but they have been known to bowride in front of a large, slow vessel. We have become most familiar with the sight of them leaping clear of the water in the expanding wake of our ship.

On calm days in the deep water of mid-ocean we have twice found ourselves being stared at by a Grey Dolphin standing so high in the water that its flippers were totally exposed. In this position, with the head thrown back, the dolphin can see with both eyes simultaneously, giving the benefit (possibly unique amongst cetaceans) of stereoscopic vision.

The normal interval between blows seems to be about 15 or 20 seconds, followed, after 3 or 4 minutes at the surface, by a deep dive. Most dives last for a minute or two, but can apparently be prolonged for as much as half an hour.

We have seen Grey Dolphins together with Spinner Dolphins (*Stenella longirostris 70*), Northern Rightwhale Dolphins (*Lissodelphis borealis 63*) and Longfin Pilot Whales (*Globicephala melaena 49*). Grey Dolphins' long, high fins and less bulbous heads make them distinct from the latter.

At a distance there is a possibility of confusing Grey Dolphins with Bottlenose Dolphins (*Tursiops truncatus 76*) or False Killer Whales (*Pseudorca crassidens 52*).
Grampus pale grey back; extensive scarring; tall pointed fin; short blunt face.
Tursiops dark grey back; seldom scarred; relatively short pointed fin; long pointed beak.
Pseudorca dark back; never scarred; very tall rounded fin; slender tapered head.

Stranding Grey Dolphins are often stranded and a freshly beached individual is readily recognizable by its scars, by the long fin and by the groove in its head; but even without these characteristics, there is no mistaking its teeth. No other cetacean has a similar configuration. Normally there are no teeth in the upper jaw and only a few strong oval ones at the front (in the first fifth) of the lower jaw. Usually there are 3 or 4 on each side, but the numbers range from 2 to 7. In older animals, even this is reduced as teeth become extensively worn or drop out altogether. There may rarely be 1 or 2 extra vestigial teeth on the tip of the upper jaw, but these are seldom visible.

There are 68 or 69 vertebrae and 6 of the neck vertebrae are welded into a solid mass to which the seventh, very thin, one is also attached. There are 6 pairs of ribs with double heads.

Natural History As far as we know, Grey Dolphins live mainly on squid. The normal social units seem to consist of cohesive groups of 3–30. Larger schools have been reported.

Little is known of reproductive behaviour, except that calving takes place during winter months in warmer waters.

Status Grey Dolphins are relatively common in warmer waters. Substantial numbers are caught each year by the Japanese whaling stations, particularly in the East China Sea. A few are taken in Indonesia and from St Vincent in the Caribbean.

Distribution This species is known worldwide, from all deep warm waters 15°–25°C (60°–77°F).

Sources CUVIER (1812) original description, DAWBIN (1966) in Solomon Islands, GRAY (1828) taxonomy, IREDALE & TROUGHTON (1933) taxonomy, PILLERI & GIHR (1969) anatomy, WEBER (1923) in Indonesia.

SNUBFIN DOLPHIN (IRRAWDDY)

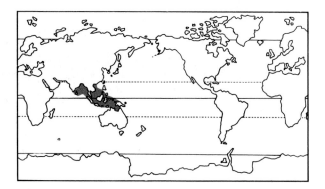

Classification In 1866 Sir Walter Elliot returned from India with several cetacean specimens, including a skull collected in the harbour of Vizagapatam on the Bay of Bengal. Owen compiled a brief report on the collection, tentatively identifying this as *Phocaena brevirostris* from the Latin *brevis*, short, and *rostrum*, a beak, but it was Gray who recognized its uniqueness and was the first to publish a description, creating for it a new genus, using the diminutive form of the Latin *orca*, a whale, to obtain *Orcaella*.

In 1868 John Anderson, Superintendent of the Indian Museum in Calcutta, found, high up the Irrawaddy River as much as 1,500 km (900 miles) from the open sea, a dolphin which Anderson in 1871 described as *Orcaella fluminalis*.

Later studies found no real differences between the Bengalese and Burmese specimens and the river form was reduced to subspecific status as *O. b. fluminalis* (ANDERSON 1878), but even this may be going too far. The taxonomic consensus at the moment is that there is only one form in salt and freshwater habitats alike, *O. brevirostris*.

Local Names In Malay this species is known as *lumba lumba*; each individual dolphin in its own area of river is given a personal name. The only English common name is Irrawaddy dolphin, but it occurs in several other Asian river systems, and travels in the open ocean as far afield as Australia. We describe it (from the characteristic shape of its dorsal fin) as the Snubfin Dolphin.

Description Small; length averages 2 m (6.5 ft), with a maximum of 2.3 m (7.5 ft); calves are about 90 cm (34 inches) at birth. Weight averages about 100 kg (220 lb).

This dolphin is very much like the White Whale

(*Delphinapterus leucas* 35) in general body form. It has the same blunt head, beakless but with a large melon and well developed bulging eyes, set off to the side; it even has similar rounded flippers. The Snubfin Dolphin, however, does have a dorsal fin, small and curved with a rounded tip; it is placed well behind the midpoint of the body, and beyond it a keel extends backwards on to the tail.

The colour is a bluish medium grey, slightly lighter on the underside. Anderson claimed that the freshwater form was streaked with light lines, but this effect seems to have been produced by scars on the specimen he collected.

Field Identification This species is quiet and inconspicuous, rising slowly to the surface so that only the rounded head protrudes, and then sinking quickly again after blowing. This procedure is repeated 2–5 times at 10-second intervals, and is followed by a deeper dive which takes the dolphin out of view for up to 3 minutes.

In the muddy waters of the rivers and in the equally turbid shallow coastal water of the estuaries, these dolphins are difficult to see. The best field characteristics are the globose head and the small snub fin. The blowhole is set off at an angle to the left, but there is insufficient blast to make this characteristic visible or useful.

There is a distinct possibility of confusion with the Finless Porpoise (*Neophocaena phocaenoides* 47) which occurs in much the same area and habitat. The porpoise however is very much smaller, more blue than grey, and has no trace of a dorsal fin.

Stranding The body shape should be sufficient to identify rare stranded members of this unusual species, but a skull on its own is equally distinctive. There are 12–19 small, conical teeth on each side of both jaws. There may be some disparity between upper and lower jaws, and teeth are often considerably worn or missing altogether. The Finless Porpoise (*Neophocaena phocaenoides* 47) has a similar number of teeth, but in that species they are distinctly spade-shaped. There are 63 vertebrae, of which only the usual 2 are fused.

Natural History Snubfin Dolphins feed on the bottom in shallow muddy water, catching fish and crustaceans. In the rivers they are strictly protected by fishermen who recognize individual local dolphins and claim that these co-operate with them by driving fish into their nets. There are frequent disputes in country courts and village councils between rival fishermen charging alienation of a resident dolphin's affection or suing for the recovery of fish captured with the assistance of a

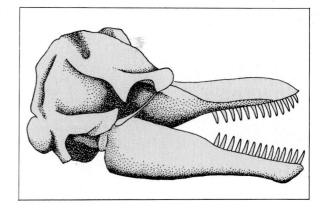

dolphin which does not 'belong' to the defendant.

These dolphins are usually seen individually or in small groups of 3 or 4, feeding or swimming together upstream or against the tide. Nothing is known of their social or reproductive behaviour except that calving apparently takes place in August off the Asian coast.

The sounds of the Snubfin Dolphin have not been recorded, but it is likely that, despite its large eyes, this species functions in turbid waters by efficient echolocation. It is interesting however that the young at least have a moustache of sensory bristles on their upper lips.

Status This species is strictly protected in the rivers and is still fairly common everywhere.

Distribution Snubfin Dolphins are known from the Ganges, Brahmaputra, Irrawaddy and Mekong rivers (often some distance upstream), as well as from shallow inshore waters along the coasts of India, Bangladesh, Burma, Singapore, Vietnam and much of the Indonesian archipelago.

These dolphins can live all their life in freshwater and muddy estuaries, but seem to travel also across the open waters of warm tropical seas. There have been several reports from the coasts on northern Australia and it seems likely that the Snubfin Dolphin will eventually also be found in the Moluccas, New Guinea and Irian Jaya.

Sources ANDERSON (1871) in Burma, ANDERSON (1878) taxonomy, DE LATTIN (1967) distribution, ELLERMAN & MORRISON-SCOTT (1951) taxonomy, GRAY (1866) original description, JOHNSON (1964) in Australia, LLOZE (1973) in Mekong, OWEN (1866) first report, PILLERI & GIHR (1973) anatomy.

Genus Stenella

Great confusion still exists concerning the classification of oceanic dolphins with long beaks.

The classic dolphin (*Delphinus delphis 75*) is set aside on its own because it has a distinctive anatomical characteristic, a deep groove on the palate on the inside of each tooth row.

All the remaining species (the numbers tend to fluctuate in an alarming way with each new revision) are now tentatively placed together in the genus *Stenella* (GRAY 1866). The name is a diminutive form of the Greek *stenos*, narrow, and refers to the long narrow beak which, in all forms, has just a short symphysis (join) between the slender halves of the lower jaw.

The teeth are small and pointed and their number varies between 28 and 65 in each row. Most species have a more or less distinct line running from the flipper to the eye, as opposed to a line from flipper to jaw in all *Lagenorhynchus* species 55–60 and in *Delphinus delphis 75*. Some have an additional bridle or flank stripe and others are conspicuously spotted.

During the century since the genus *Stenella* was introduced, at least 25 species have been described by almost as many authors. The numbers have been consistently reduced in recent years, but there is still no real consensus about which should be retained. The best and most comprehensive studies so far made are those by William Perrin of the National Marine Fisheries Service in La Jolla, California and it is his preliminary classification which we use here.

Perrin suggests that *Stenella* be divided into 3 main groups of species as follows:

1. **Spinner Dolphins:** with long snouts and an average of 50 teeth in each row. This group includes all those species which indulge in aerobatics, spinning and turning in the air as they breach. These are distributed worldwide and occur in a range of shapes and colours, but there seem to be intermediate populations which connect all the extreme forms and so Perrin regards them as conspecific and as belonging to the single species *S. longirostris 70*.

In recent years however it has become apparent that there is one form in the North Atlantic which probably breeds true and should be given separate specific status because of its unique and consistent markings, *S. clymene 71*.

2. **Striped Dolphins:** with intermediate snouts, a dark lateral stripe, and an average of 44 teeth in each row.

The second group also enjoys a range of colour forms and variants with a worldwide distribution, but all have in common a dark lateral flank stripe running from the eye to the anus. These are now considered as a single species, *S. coeruleoalba 72*.

3. **Spotted Dolphins:** with shorter snouts, spots, and an average of 37 teeth in each row.

In this group are a number of somewhat larger forms, all spotted to a greater or lesser degree. Their taxonomy is still confused, but there seem to be good reasons to assume the existence of 2 good species, one with a worldwide distribution and a band from flipper to mouth (*S. attenuata 73*), and the other restricted to the Atlantic with a faint band from flipper to eye (*S. plagiodon 74*).

(a) Spinner Dolphin (*Stenella longirostris 70*)
(b) Striped Dolphin (*Stenella coeruleoalba 72*)
(c) Helmet Dolphin (*Stenella clymene 71*)
(d) Bridled Dolphin (*Stenella attenuata 73*)
(e) Spotted Dolphin (*Stenella plagiodon 74*)

(a)

(b)

(c)

(d)

(e)

SPINNER DOLPHIN

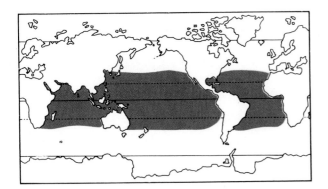

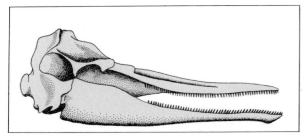

Classification In 1828 Gray in his *Spicilegia Zoologica* gave a brief description, without illustration, of a dolphin with a long beak. This was taken from a skull of unknown origin in the old Joshua Brookes Museum and Gray simply gave a tooth count and some measurements and called it *Delphinus longirostris*, from the Latin *longus*, long, and *rostrum*, a beak. Perrin believes that Gray may actually have been describing another species and that the application of his specific name to this one is questionable, but it has been used by so many authors for so long that to replace it would cause confusion.

The reduction of the 25 species of *Stenella* to 5 has brought under this species, as no more than local variants: *S. alope* (GRAY 1846) of Ceylon, which has a dark back and a yellow belly; *S. microps* (GRAY 1846) from the Pacific coast of Mexico, with a brown back; *S. roseiventris* (WAGNER 1853) from the Banda Sea, with a bright pink belly. These and a number of other still poorly identified variants still await possible subspecific classification.

Local Names Longsnout, small head, rollover and long-beaked dolphin. We prefer the descriptive name of Spinner Dolphin.

Description Small; length averages 1.8 m (6 ft), with a maximum of 2.1 m (7 ft); calves are 80 cm (30 inches) at birth. Weight averages 75 kg (165 lb), with a maximum of about 95 kg (210 lb).

There are so many variations in form and marking within this species that it is difficult to describe a typical specimen. In general the body is slender, the beak is long and thin and the

flippers are large and pointed. Everything else varies on a geographical basis. In the eastern Pacific for instance, there seem to be at least 3 distinct forms, each possibly a valid subspecies (see p. 258). Perrin identifies these as:

i. Costa Rican Form the most slender, attenuated form; with a very long rostrum and an almost vertical dorsal fin. This variety is usually medium grey above and pale beneath, with a light grey stripe from flipper to eye and a similar colour on the upper beak. It is most common along the coast of Central America.

ii. Eastern Form a stockier, darker variety, with an intermediate beak and a dorsal fin which leans markedly forward. Adult males of this form tend to have marked keels above and below the tailstock. The colouring is medium to deep grey above, grading through a broken spotted area on the flank to almost pure white on the lower belly. It is found up to 800 km (500 miles) from the west coast of Central America.

iii. Whitebelly Form a larger, more robust variety, with a long beak and a curved sharklike fin. There is no hump or keel. In this form the pattern is distinct, with a deep grey back sharply demarcated from a pure white belly, which extends some distance up on to the flank, well past the flipper insertion. The upper beak is black. This form is most common in mid-ocean, more than 800 km (500 miles) offshore.

Further west in the Pacific, around Hawaii, is an even larger form whose white belly is still more distinct and often separated from the dark back by a band of intermediate pale grey.

In the western Pacific and Indian Ocean there are brownish variants; in Indonesia, one with a pink blush on the belly; in the Bay of Bengal yellow bellies seem to predominate and in the Atlantic it seems that beaks often become distinctly shorter. All these areas still await the kind of quantitative survey made by Perrin in the east Pacific, before their varieties can even begin to be described and understood.

It seems that all of the wide variation in marking may be attributed to the presence, and to the relative dominance, of 2 independent pigment systems. The first of these is a 'dorsal field' system which is responsible for the dark cape, the eye patch, and the dark shades of back, fin and flukes. The second is a 'lateral field' system which produces intermediate shades (sometimes spots) on the flank and flippers. In the eastern Pacific forms, the Whitebelly shows a predominance of the dorsal field, while the Eastern is more influenced by genes controlling the lateral field.

Field Identification With such wide inherent variation it is difficult to use markings as field characteristics, but fortunately these are almost unnecessary because of the Spinner Dolphin's distinctive behaviour.

These dolphins appear throughout their range in large schools, many now somewhat wary of shipping as a result of harassment by tuna fishermen, but most are still sparked into

Local variations in colour and form of spinner dolphin:
(a) Costa Rican Form
(b) Whitebeak Form
(c) Eastern Form

a running frenzy by the approach of a boat. Usually the whole school explodes into action, towards or away from the vessel, churning the water up into a boiling foam with their rapid leaping movements. Most dolphins make a series of very long low jumps, but every few seconds one or more of the school hurl themselves high into the air, twisting their bodies into sinuous curves or spinning over and over again about their longitudinal axes. These acrobatics seem to be most common in the Pacific, where up to 7 barrel-rolls have been counted before the dolphin splashed back into the water once again.

There seems to be no good practical reason for these antics. Explanations which involve parasites or the need to escape

Spinner Dolphins in typical aerial postures

from predatory sharks or Great Killer Whales all sound somewhat contrived. Having seen these animals perform in small and large groups, in the open sea and shallow lagoons, through storms and mirror calms, having watched while one individual discovers and perfects a new manoeuvre and then seen others try to mimic it, we find it difficult not to conclude that the behaviour springs very largely from sheer *joie de vivre*.

Most Spinner Dolphins also delight in bowriding, often for prolonged periods, staying with a ship for half an hour or more. Looking down on them from the bow, it is easy to see the upright or forward-leaning fin, the grey back and, in most forms, the dark-tipped beak. The latter characteristic is a useful one for distinguishing this species from the Spotted Dolphin (*S. plagiodon 74*) and the Bridled Dolphin (*S. attenuata 73*), both of which school with the Spinner Dolphin, but have light tips to their beaks. The greatest source of confusion is likely to be with the Common Dolphin (*Delphinus delphis 75*), which has a very similar body form, but its fin leans backward and its side is marked with an hourglass pattern of yellow.

It is only the Spinner Dolphin which draws attention to itself with splendid and spectacular gymnastic displays.

Stranding In this species, stranding occurs naturally or can be provoked by stampeding a school into shallow water. A beached Spinner Dolphin is simple to identify by the fact that it has more teeth than any other cetacean. The range is from 46 to 65 tiny pointed teeth on each side of both jaws, with an average total of at least 210. The Striped Dolphin (*S. coeruleoalba 72*) has almost as many teeth, but is rather larger. There are 72 or 73 vertebrae.

Natural History Spinner Dolphins feed on small fish and squid, often several hundred feet down. These foods may be what draws this dolphin together with yellowfin tuna.

The species reaches maturity at a length of about 1.65 m (5.5 ft), has a gestation period of 10.5 months and a calving interval of a little over 2 years. Age is assessed by counting one dentinal layer per year.

The usual social unit is a large school of 30 to several hundred of all ages and sexes. There is some evidence to show that schools have separate identities, seldom if ever mix with others, and may even be genetically distinct. The behaviour of wild Spinner Dolphins is now being studied in Hawaii by Norris and his associates of the University of California.

Spinner Dolphins produce a wide range of click sounds, pulse bursts and squeals. Directional recordings have shown that most exchanges take place between individuals 10–15 m (33–50 ft) apart, and that there seems to be an intentional control of sound level depending on the distance involved in such communication.

Status Spinner Dolphins are widespread and common, but have been severely threatened by purse-seine fishing for tuna. This and several other species of dolphin school above yellowfin tuna and provide fishermen with a marker for setting their nets.

It is estimated that in the 1960s up to half a million dolphins, 10 or 15 per cent of which were Spinner Dolphins, were captured each year in the tuna nets and drowned. Intensive lobbying and research, with the introduction of new hauling techniques, have cut this incidental catch dramatically, but it still remains a problem. There are small drive hunts for Spinner Dolphins in the Solomon Islands, the Marquesas, New Guinea and Japan.

Distribution This species is found in all warm tropical waters of Indian, Pacific and Atlantic oceans. It is most common in deep water, but also known from inshore areas where the water is clear. In recent years, a satellite-based tracking system, using tiny radio transmitting markers, has been developed to plot the movements of dolphin schools.

Sources GRAY (1828) original description, HESTER et al (1963) spinning, PERRIN (1972) taxonomy, PERRIN (1972) colour, PERRIN (1977) reproduction, SCHLEGEL (1841) taxonomy, WATKINS & SCHEVILL (1974) sounds.

HELMET DOLPHIN

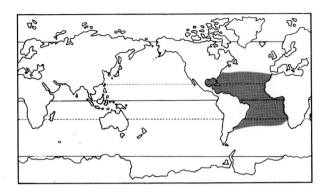

Classification Skull No. 350a in the British Museum, of unknown origin, looks a great deal like that of a Spinner Dolphin (*S. longirostris 70*), but has fewer teeth. In 1850 Gray, acting it seems on intuition, designated it a new species, *Delphinus clymene*, from the Greek *klymenos*, famous.

By 1975 it was widely considered to be little more than a minor, and probably local, variant of *S. longirostris.* Then in June 1976 a striking dolphin beached itself at Ocean City in New Jersey. It had distinctive markings and its skull proved to be identical with the one which Gray had singled out in 1850. At the Second International Conference on the Biology of Marine Mammals in Seattle in 1977, the New Jersey specimen was examined and its distinctness confirmed.

Local Names There are no local names. We suggest, because of the distinctive line from the blowhole to the tip of the beak that looks like the visor on a Norman suit of armour, the Helmet Dolphin.

Description Small; length averages 1.8 m (6 ft). Weight averages approximately 75 kg (165 lb).

The shape is similar to the Whitebelly form of the Spinner Dolphin (*S. longirostris 70*), except that its beak is relatively short. The fin is tall and leans slightly backwards and the tailstock is moderately keeled.

The markings are unique and more complex then those of any other species of *Stenella*. The basic body colour seems to

be a medium grey, overlain by a dark grey cape which covers the head and all of the back except for the tailstock. The flippers and flukes are equally dark, but the centre of the fin is paler than its margins. There is a light stripe from the flipper to the eye and a dark stripe running from the anus toward the eye. The belly is pinkish. The most distinctive and unusual marking is a black band along the beak, extending from the tip of the upper jaw to the melon and continuing as a pale but equally striking line to the blowhole. This is the noseguard of the helmet and, cutting it at right angles halfway along the beak, is a dark grey crosspiece. Both lips are dark.

Field Identification The Helmet Dolphin has never been well observed. We would however expect the marking on the head to be distinctly visible and suggest that all bowriding *Stenella* in the Atlantic be examined carefully with this in mind.

Stranding A beached animal of this species may be difficult to distinguish from the Spinner Dolphin (*S. longirostris 70*) once its skin has darkened, but a tooth count could give it away. The range seems to be 43–58 teeth on each side of both jaws, with a usual total of about 200, which is at least 20 fewer than the average Spinner Dolphin.

Natural History Nothing is known.

Status This species is probably relatively rare.

Distribution The Helmet Dolphin apparently occurs from the coast of New Jersey south to the Caribbean and east to the shores of tropical Africa. It has not yet been reported from the South Atlantic, but we predict that it will be.

Sources GRAY (1850) original description, PERRIN et al (1977) rediscovery.

Dorsal view of the head of the Helmet Dolphin to show the unique markings

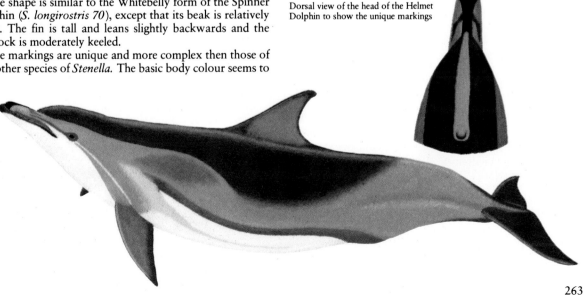

STRIPED DOLPHIN

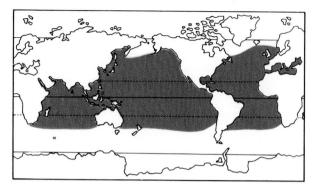

Classification In 1833 the German zoologist Franz Julius Meyen reported on a dolphin captured on the east coast of South America, near the Rio de la Plata. He remarked on its blue-and-white colouring and called it *Delphinus coeruleo-albus*, from the Latin *caeruleus*, dark blue, and *albus*, white. As other specimens turned up from Chile and the North Pacific, Gray and True described them variously as *Lagenorhynchus caeruleo-albus* and *Prodelphinus coeruleo-albus*.

Most cetologists today agree that this species, like the Spinner Dolphin (*Stenella longirostris 70*), has a wide range of continuous geographical variation. Much work still needs to be done on a worldwide basis, but for the moment the following have all been included:
S. styx (GRAY 1846), Atlantic with a dark back and a double line between the eye and the flipper. There may also be a form, seen off Durban, in which this line has 3 components.
S. euphrosyne (PEALE 1848), North Pacific, with a heavy flank stripe.
S. marginata (PUCHERAN 1868), North Atlantic, with a brown back and a short beak.

Local Names Longsnout, blue-white and streaker (English), *dauphin bleu-et-blanc* (French) and *suzi-iruka* (Japanese). We prefer to call this species the Striped Dolphin.

Description Small; length averages 2.4 m (8 ft), with a possible maximum of 3 m (10 ft); calves are 1 m (3.25 ft) at birth. Weight averages 100 kg (220 lb), with a maximum of about 130 kg (286 lb).

The Striped Dolphin is larger than the Spinner Dolphin (*S. longirostris 70*) and intermediate between it and the even bulkier spotted dolphins (*Stenella* spp. 73 and 74). It has a typical delphinid spindle-shaped body with a tall, curved dorsal fin. The beak is relatively short and runs into a smoothly curved melon which is perhaps more pronounced in this species than in other members of the genus. There are no marked keels on the tailstock.

The colouring is immensely variable. The type specimen from the South Atlantic was described as cerulean blue above and pure white below. There may well be specimens like this, but in our experience most forms are distinctly brownish on the back in life and darken to a deeper bluish hue only after death. There is a wide range of variation from very dark to relatively light shades and in most of them a sharp process reaches down from the cape in the region of the dorsal fin, pointing toward the eye. All variants seem also to have in common an even darker, sometimes blackish side stripe running from the eye along the flank and dipping down to the anus. In many this gives rise to an additional short branch stripe running backwards off the flank stripe from a point midway between the flipper and the fin. In addition, there is usually a dark band from the eye to the flipper, which may be single or have 2 or 3 components. The beak is always dark.

Field Identification In the field, the diagnostic dark stripe on the lower flank may become visible when these dolphins arch out of the water to breathe, but in practice the most distinctive field characteristic is the dark streak extending forward on to the flank from a point behind the dorsal fin. This is particularly dramatic on a bowriding animal.

Striped Dolphins are most often encountered in large schools which we have found to be somewhat wary of shipping. They will sometimes bowride, but seem to be easily frightened and to stampede away for no apparent reason. At any one time at least one-third of such a school will be in the air, making clean low leaps, with mothers and calves jumping in perfect formation. When pursued, the whole school often alters course very suddenly fleeing at right angles to their previous direction.

There are none of the wild acrobatics of Spinner Dolphins and little possibility of confusion with that species, but Striped Dolphins do look a great deal like Common Dolphins (*Delphinus delphis 75*) in the water. These characteristics may help to distinguish them:

Stenella pale side with dark point reaching forward from behind the fin; dark stripe from flipper to eye; slightly rounded fin, more pointed flippers.
Delphis hourglass pattern of yellow on side; dark stripe from flipper to chin; slightly rounded flippers, more pointed fin.

Stranding In this species stranding does occur and can easily be incited by herding a school into shallow water. Striped Dolphins are very easily identified by their markings, which seem to remain visible for some time following death, although the eye-to-flipper line tends to fade. Their larger size should be useful in distinguishing them from the Spinner Dolphin; and the greater number of teeth makes it possible to separate Striped Dolphins from the two spotted species (*Stenella* spp. 73 and 74). The teeth are small, heavily enamelled, sharply pointed and curve slightly inwards. There are 43–49 on each side of each jaw, compared with less than 40 in the spotted dolphins. There are 79 vertebrae and the first 5 pairs of ribs are double headed.

Colour variation in Striped Dolphins

Natural History Striped Dolphins feed mainly on small pelagic fish such as *Diaphus elucens* and *Erythrocles schlegeli*. They may also take squid and shrimps. Some animals have sucker marks around their mouths. The large schools (up to 3,000 have been reported) are usually broken up into age groups, with mothers and nursing young, immature animals, and adults all forming separate sub-sections. Dolphins of all ages school with yellowfin tuna.

They reach maturity at a length of about 2.1 m (7 ft) and calve at intervals of 3 years. Gestation lasts for 12 months and lactation for a further 9–18 months.

Status This species still seems to be common except in the West Pacific. Relatively small numbers of Striped Dolphins die in tuna nets, but a larger number are killed each year in spring and autumn drives on the coasts of Japan, particularly at the Izu Peninsula ports of Kawana and Futo, and on Iki Island. Schools of several thousand dolphins are often taken in their entirety. This annual catch of about 20,000 dolphins must have a serious effect, at least on populations in the west Pacific.

Distribution Striped Dolphins are known mainly from tropical and warm temperate waters in the Atlantic and Pacific, but may also be found as far north as the Bering Sea and Greenland. We can find no record of this species in the Indian Ocean, but have ourselves seen large schools south of Java and in waters east of the Seychelles.

This species is not often seen in coastal waters, seeming to prefer a deeper offshore habitat. There are marked local migrations, towards the equator in autumn and back to higher latitudes in spring.

Sources FRASER & NOBLE (1970) markings, KIMURA & PERRIN (1976) reproduction, MEYEN (1833) original description, MIYAZAKI (1976) behaviour, NISHIWAKI (1975) ecology, PERRIN (1968) in tuna nets.

BRIDLED DOLPHIN

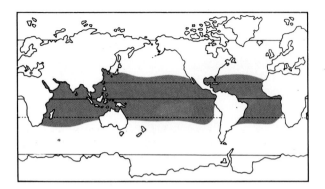

Classification No group of cetaceans is at the same time as plentiful or as little known as the spotted oceanic dolphins.

The first to try to bring order to the taxonomic confusion surrounding them was Gray. The earliest name given to a spotted dolphin seems to have been Gray's 1846 identification of a specimen captured near Cape Horn as *Delphinus attenuatus*, from the Latin *attenuatus*, reduced. This was later referred to as *Steno* and *Prodelphinus* but was finally fixed in *Stenella*.

Perrin has begun the long process of rationalizing the multitude of species names applied at various times since then to long-beaked dolphins with spots, and has concluded that there is one major species with a worldwide distribution (*S. attenuata*) plus another species (*S. plagiodon 74*) which seems to be restricted to the Atlantic Ocean.

The following variants must now be regarded as synonymous with *S. attenuata*:

S. graffmani (LONNBERG 1934) from coastal areas of the central east Pacific; dark and heavily spotted, with a small head and large flukes;

S. dubia (CUVIER 1812) a tropical form with no flipper stripe;

S. frontalis (CUVIER 1829) in warmer waters of the Atlantic; with a dark bridle, black spots on the belly and light spots on the back;

S. malayana (LESSON 1826) found in the Malay Archipelago and Indonesia; uniform dark grey with few spots and a long narrow snout. (It is possible that this variant is in fact a Humpback Dolphin.)

Local Names Spotted dolphin, narrow snout dolphin, Cape dolphin and Cuvier's dolphin (English), *gamin dauphin bridé* (French). We differentiate this dolphin from other spotted ones by drawing attention to its unique facial markings as the Bridled Dolphin.

Description Small; length averages 2.1 m (7 ft), with a maximum of 2.75 m (9 ft); calves are 90 cm (36 inches) at birth. Weight averages 100 kg (220 lb), with a maximum of about 140 kg (308 lb).

There is great variation in size, shape and colour, but most forms are fairly robust, with a long beak, a tall curved fin, large pointed flippers and a marked ventral keel on the tailstock. There is often a lower keel from the dorsal fin to the tail.

The colouring and markings vary not only with geography, but with age. All Bridled Dolphins are unspotted at birth and they almost double their size before dark spots begin to appear on the belly. The dorsal spots appear later and, as these become more marked, the ventral spots enlarge and merge, forming a uniform dark grey belly. There is enormous individual and local variation in this process, but most Bridled Dolphins seem to go through 5 well-marked phases:

i. Newborn dark grey back with soft edges; light belly; no spots.

ii. Two-tone sharply divided back and belly countershading; no spots.

iii. Speckled separate and distinct dark grey spots on belly.

iv. Mottled dark spots on belly merge; light spots on back.

v. Fused uniform dark grey underside; white tip to jaws.

In general, coastal forms tend to be larger and more heavily spotted than those which live some distance offshore.

Most Bridled Dolphins are deep slate grey above and paler, sometimes pinkish, beneath with dark fin, flippers and flukes. They have an equally dark band running from the flipper to the middle of the lower jaw; a black circle around each eye, with the eyes connected together by a bridle line across the beak; and a black beak with pink or pure white lips.

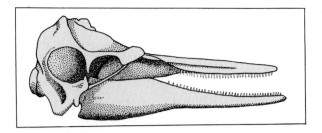

Field Identification Bridled Dolphins are fairly easy to distinguish in the field. At the bow, or even at a distance, some spotting is usually evident. They often run in front of a vessel, matching its speed easily; a trained animal was clocked in pursuit of a lure at 43 kph (21.4 knots), reaching that speed in just 2 seconds. When bowriding, which they sometimes do for minutes on end, they zigzag to and fro in front of the pressure wave, testing all its characteristics before peeling off and doubling back to let the ship go by.

When not involved with shipping, these dolphins travel in large schools without acrobatics or high leaps. Their usual breathing sequence involves a smooth roll at the surface several times each minute.

Bridled Dolphins can be, and usually are, confused with the other spotted species (*S. plagiodon 74*) where their ranges overlap in the Atlantic. These are the most evident differences:

S. attenuata slender body; uniform dark cape over back, without flank; marked bridle; dark flipper line.
S. plagiodon more robust body; lighter, more spotted back, with bright blaze on flank beneath the fin; no bridle; faint flipper line.

Young Bridled Dolphins, before their spots appear, can be confused with Common Dolphins and Spinner Dolphins, but both these species have longer darker beaks.

Stranding In this species stranding occurs singly and in groups. Freshly beached Bridled Dolphins should be identifiable by their markings alone, but once these have been obliterated, it takes a museum expert to distinguish one from a Spotted Dolphin (*S. plagiodon 74*). Both these species however are fairly easy to separate from the Spinner Dolphin (*S. longirostris 70*) and the Striped Dolphin (*S. coeruleoalba 72*) by their fewer teeth. The range in Bridled Dolphins is 35–40 tiny pointed teeth (average 38 or 39) on each side of both slender jaws. There are 78 vertebrae and only the first 2 pairs of ribs are double headed.

Natural History Unlike the Spinner Dolphin which feeds at some depth, the Bridled Dolphin is a surface feeder, taking horse mackerel and flying fish. It also eats a fish called *Oxyporhamphus micropterus* and the squid *Dosidicus gigas*, the species most favoured by the yellowfin tuna with which it is often associated.

Bridled Dolphins occur in large schools. In a survey made in the western Pacific, 37 was the smallest number found in any school and 1,381 the largest, with a mean of 281. There seems to be no segregation by age or sex. The entire group ranges together, travelling about 70 km (40 nautical miles) a day over a roughly circular home area, 320–480 km (200–300 nautical miles) in diameter.

This species reaches maturity after about 9 years at a length of approximately 2 m (6.5 ft). Mating takes place all year round and gestation lasts a little over 11 months. Lactation is usually over by the end of the first year, but may go on for as long as 2 years, prolonging the period of infant dependancy in a way which can give extra time for learning the species

system of communication. In such large societies, this could be elaborate. Calving intervals may therefore be as little as 2 years or as long as 4 years. There is good reason to assume that schools in different areas are genetically distinct.

When a school finds itself caught along with tuna in a purse-seine net, it first mills around until the artificial overcrowding produces what looks like a stress reaction. The dolphins simply sink tail first down into the folds of the net and lie there until they are hauled up to the surface or drown. This may be a sort of displaced sleep, an immobility produced by an overload of stimuli and could, in certain circumstances such as an attack by predators, be useful. It is however difficult to see survival value in simply sinking down through 3,000 m (10,000 ft) of deep ocean, unless the dolphins recover and swim away after reaching the safety of a certain depth.

Status This is the species which has suffered most from the incidental kill of dolphins in purse-seine nets. Roughly 80 per cent of an estimated half million killed in 1970 by United States trawlers alone, were Bridled Dolphins. This number was reduced in 1978 to something between 15,000 and 20,000, but that takes no account of unregulated catches by the fleets of other nations. There may be 2–4 million Bridled Dolphins still left in the tropical Pacific, but not even this population could long withstand such depredation.

Some thousands of Bridled Dolphins are also taken in drives on the Izu Peninsula of Japan and by a few aboriginal industries. On Malaita in the Solomon Islands, a necklace of dolphin teeth is still an essential part of a bride price and it takes 6 or 7 adult dolphins to make one necklace. The dolphins are captured in periodic drives by canoes which gather on the seaward side of a school and create a 'sound net' by cracking large stones together under water. With this sonic barrier, the group is driven into shallow water in a harbour or mangrove channel where they can easily be lifted out of the water. Reports of these drives show that as the cracking stones build up to a crescendo, the dolphins seem to lift their tails up in the air and try to bury their heads in the sand.

Distribution Bridled Dolphins are known from all deep, warm waters of the Atlantic, Pacific and Indian oceans.

Sources BEST (1969) in South Africa, CUVIER (1812) taxonomy, DAWBIN (1966) in Solomon Islands, GRAY (1846) original description, KASUYA et al (1974) reproduction, LANG & PRYOR (1966) speed, LESSON (1826) taxonomy, LONNBERG (1974) taxonomy, NISHIWAKI et al (1965) in Japan, PERRIN et al (1976) reproduction, PERRIN et al (1979) tuna kill, PERRIN (1970) colour patterns, SCHMIDLY & SHANE (1976) in Caribbean.

SPOTTED DOLPHIN

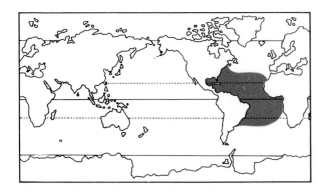

Classification In 1763 de Bougainville made an expedition to the Malouine (now known as the Falkland) Islands to found a settlement there. On the Abrolhos Bank off the coast of Brazil a dolphin was captured and described by Antoine Pernetty, the Dominican priest who acted as recorder to the expedition. In his contribution to a dictionary of natural history published in 1817, de Blainville included the *dauphin de Pernetty* and named it *Delphinus pernettensis.*

In 1866 Cope published a history of the Delphinid family in which he described, for the first time, a skull of unknown origin which he called *Delphinus plagiodon*, from the Greek *plagios*, slanting, and *odous,* gen. *odontos*, a tooth.

Both dolphins are now thought to be the same and are

included here under the latter species simply because it has been more widely used and accepted.

Local Names This species is generally known as the Spotted Dolphin.

Description Small; length averages 2.1 m (7 ft), with a maximum of about 2.4 m (8 ft). Weight averages 110 kg (242 lb), with a maximum of about 145 kg (320 lb).

The Spotted Dolphin is very similar in shape to the Bridled Dolphin (*S. attenuata 73*), but somewhat more robust, with a more sharply curved and pointed dorsal fin. It differs from the other spotted species in lacking both the bridle and the dark line from flipper to mouth. The spotting is extensive, usually dark on the light underside and light on the slightly darker back. There is no conspicuous cape on the back, but there is a pronounced pale blaze on the flank, slanting up on to the back behind the fin. The flippers, flukes and fin are an unspotted medium grey and the tip of the jaw and lips are usually pale grey or white.

Calves are born without spots and are grey above and pure white beneath. After a year spots begin to appear, first on the tongue, then on the head, then on the belly, moving gradually upwards until at the end of the second year they cover most of the body. The number of spots increases throughout life, making some older animals quite dark on the belly.

Field Identification. The spots and the white-tipped beak make this animal instantly recognizable as one of the 2 currently accepted species of spotted dolphin. Identification of the Spotted Dolphin depends a great deal on experience with both species at sea. When either spotted dolphin is glimpsed from a distance, or only seen rolling over at the surface to breathe, it is difficult to identify it, but we find that, as a rule, it is usually possible to see the light blaze on the upper flank of *S. plagiodon*. Identification at the bow is much more simple: *S. attenuata* has a lighter cheek with a very visible dark bridle and flipper line, while *S. plagiodon* has no lines on the head at all.

This species sometimes bowrides, often runs before ships and seldom leaps out of the water. When undisturbed it breathes quietly, showing first the tip of the snout, then the head, followed by the arched back and fin. It usually blows 3 or 4 times a minute, but may sometimes hyperventilate, taking up to 5 quick breaths before making a deep dive lasting a minute or more. The tail flukes normally never break the surface, but we have seen this species standing on its head in deep water, waving its tail in the air for no apparent reason.

Young unspotted *S. plagiodon* look very much like Bottlenose Dolphins (*Tursiops truncatus 76*) and are best distinguished from them by the fact that the latter have more robust heads, shorter beaks and are usually found closer inshore. Reports of mixed schools of the 2 species are usually due to misidentification of the young, and to the fact that in certain lights it can be difficult to see the spots even on an adult animal.

Stranding Spotted Dolphins are seldom stranded, but can be distinguished from beached Bridled Dolphins if the markings are still visible; darkened or decomposed animals are impossible to distinguish, even by their teeth. Both species usually have less than 40 teeth in each row, although the range for *S. plagiodon* lies between 28 and 37 teeth on each side of both jaws, which may be a little lower than *S. attenuata.* There are 68 or 69 vertebrae.

Natural History Spotted Dolphins feed near the surface on squid, herrings, anchovy and several kinds of carangid fish, including *Decapterus* sp. and *Selar* sp. This species is normally highly gregarious, living in groups of between 10 and several hundred, but there is one record of a young male which was apparently solitary and regularly sought the company of human divers off the island of San Salvador in the Bahamas.

Mating takes place in summer and involves a courtship in which a pair take turns in rubbing gently over each other's back at right angles, before standing vertically in the water opposite each other with their mouths open, or breaching, usually falling back tail first. Calves are born a little less than a year later.

Spotted Dolphins are apparently not as vocal as Bottlenose Dolphins (*Tursiops truncatus 76*), but have click trains which are probably used for finding food, pulsed growls, a chirp on a pure rising tone, and signature whistles which seem to be unique to each individual.

Status Very little is known, but this species is relatively common, at least in the western North Atlantic.

Distribution Spotted Dolphins are found mainly in offshore waters of North and Central America, from New Jersey in the north, through the Caribbean to Panama. There is at least one good record from west Africa and there is no reason to assume that the species is not equally widespread in warm waters of the South Atlantic. Spotted Dolphins are usually seen at least 20 km (12 miles) offshore, but may migrate longitudinally, moving in closer during calmer summer months.

Sources CALDWELL et al (1975) sounds, CALDWELL & CALDWELL (1966) review, COPE (1866) original description, DE BLAINVILLE (1817) taxonomy, PERNETTY (1769) early description, WOODCOCK & MCBRIDE (1951) bowriding.

COMMON DOLPHIN

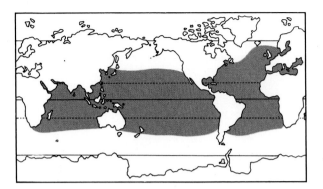

Classification This is the classic dolphin, both in the sense of serving as the model for its kind, and in the frequency with which it was represented in the art and literature of ancient Greece and Rome. Aristotle and Pliny the Elder described it in great detail, and it seems fitting that the first to classify it should have been the master himself. In the tenth edition of *Systema Naturae* Linnaeus named this animal *Delphinus delphis* from the Greek *delphis*, a dolphin, with the suffix *-inus*, being like.

This dolphin is widespread and a number of other forms, with a variety of names, resemble it. Further research may show that one (or more) of them deserves to be considered as a separate species, but for the moment the following variants are all considered as geographical forms of *D. delphis*:

D. bairdii (DALL 1873), North Pacific; with a longer rostrum, slimmer body; a completely grey or brownish tailstock; and without the otherwise characteristic grey lines on the flank. Consistent differences in the skull suggest that it should be considered at least as a valid subspecies.
D. capensis (GRAY 1828), South Atlantic; with a large rostrum and a darker back; having a very conspicuous dark line from chin to flipper and 1 grey line, instead of 2, along the flank.
D. dussumieri (BLANDFORD 1891), the Indian Ocean; with more teeth. Probably identical with *D. tropicalis*.
D. tropicalis (VAN BREE 1971), a possibly sympatric form in the Persian Gulf; with a far longer, narrower rostrum, a lower vertebral count and more teeth. Probably a valid subspecies and might even prove to be a separate species (see skull), but probably synonymous with *D. dussumieri*.
D. delphis ponticus (BARABASH-NIKIFOROV 1935), the Black Sea; with a distinct black line from eye to anus. Probably a valid subspecies.

There is clearly a wide range of variation, and, despite the fact that dolphins in different areas and schools form genetic entities which differ from each other in marking, pattern and colour, these variants seem to be part of the spectrum within a single species. More work is clearly needed.

Local Names Saddleback, crisscross dolphin and whitebelly

dolphin (English), *camus* or *bec d'oie* (French), *springhval* (Norwegian), *springare* (Swedish), *hofrung* (Icelandic), *warworn* (Russian), *angaigik* (Aleutian), *ardlusarsuk* (Greenland Eskimo), *tu kiak* (Kamchatka), *tyrtak* (Turkish) and *tobi iruka* (Japanese). In many languages simply *the* dolphin, *delfino* (Italian), *Delphin* (German) and *dolfijn* (Netherlands). We suggest that this species be known simply as the Common Dolphin.

Description Small; length averages 2.1 m (7 ft), with a maximum of 2.6 m (8.5 ft); calves are about 90 cm (36 inches) at birth. Weight averages about 82 kg (180 lb), with a possible maximum of 136 kg (300 lb).

Common Dolphins are sleek, streamlined and spindle-shaped, with a long beak, a moderately pointed fin, and pointed flippers. There is some variation of fin size and shape even within a single population, but most curve backwards.

The colour is deep grey above and lighter grey below, but is complicated by the most elaborate flank markings to be found on any cetacean. There is considerable variation in detail, although all forms seem to share in the possession of a criss-cross or hourglass pattern produced by the overlay of several complementary pigment systems. The ground colour is light or pale grey. Over this lies a buffy yellow or mustard-coloured saddle which covers the head, most of the back, and dips down below the eye in front of the fin. On top of both these systems is a dark cape thrown across the head and all the back, falling down behind the fin to cover the tailstock. The interaction and relative size and dominance of these pigment systems produces the characteristic hourglass or figure-of-eight marking on the flank, buffy yellow in front of the fin and light grey behind it. It is said that the yellow pattern in some areas becomes less conspicuous in winter.

There are also usually dark circles around the eyes, connected by a spectacle bridge across the base of the melon and bold lines running from flipper to jaw. Depending on geographical variation, there are also 1 or 2 broken, wavy grey lines running longitudinally through the pale belly colour on the lower flank, although these are apparently missing altogether in the Pacific subspecies tentatively known as *D. delphis bairdii*. All forms often have squid sucker marks on their chins and lower jaws.

Field Identification Common Dolphins are usually found in large active schools, often churning up a wide area of water. There seems to be more variety, more individuality, in their swimming style than in any other species except perhaps the Spinner Dolphin (*Stenella longirostris 70*). In any school it is possible to see dolphins rolling up to breathe, leaping out in smooth arcs to re-enter head first, splashing down on their heads and backs, pounding on the water with their chins and flukes, or zigzagging along just beneath the surface. They usually breathe several times each minute, but have been known to dive for as long as 5 minutes.

They readily come to bowride, shifting restlessly in the

pressure wave to find the best position, often rolling over on their sides to look up at humans. The speed of a ship seems to present them with no problems. A group were once seen at the bow of a destroyer in the Mediterranean travelling at 64 kph (32 knots). A school, often with calves travelling in tender, may bowride for 20 minutes or more.

At close quarters the yellow patch on the side is conspicuous, but even in poor light and at a distance it usually stands out as part of the clear crisscross pattern. This is the best field characteristic, both for recognizing Common Dolphins and for distinguishing them from Striped Dolphins (*S. coeruleoalba 72*), with which they occasionally school. Striped Dolphins (and other members of the genus *Stenella*) also have dark lines running from flipper to eye, whilst those on the Common Dolphin run forward from the flipper to the bottom of the lower jaw.

Stranding Common Dolphins are frequently stranded. The bright colours soon fade and the finer markings disappear after death, making confusion with some of the *Stenella* species likely. The tooth count of 40–57 on each side of both jaws, is similar to that of the Striped Dolphin (*S. coeruleoalba 72*). In many cases, where decomposition is advanced, the only way to tell them apart may be to look at the palate of a clean skull. The Common Dolphin has deep grooves running just inside the tooth rows, whereas these are shallow or missing altogether in all species of *Stenella*. There are 73 or 74 vertebrae. Four or sometimes 5 of the 14 pairs of ribs are double headed.

Natural History Common Dolphins are known to travel along above submarine ridges, diving down through the deep scattering layers of plankton to feed on lantern fish and squid.

271

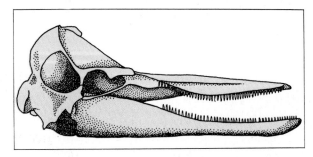

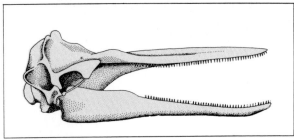

Above: skull of an adult *Delphinus delphis tropicalis* with 210 teeth
Below: skull of an adult *Delphinus delphis delphis* with 186 teeth

They routinely feed at about 40 m (132 ft), but have been recorded 280 m (920 ft) down. In the Pacific they feed largely on anchovy, but in the Atlantic take sardines, herrings and bottom-living crabs. While feeding at the surface (which they sometimes do), Common Dolphins have been seen to swim right out of the water, catching flying fish and bonito in mid-air. There is one record of a dolphin with the otoliths of 7,596 fish in its stomach.

Mating seems to take place at a depth of at least 10 m (36 ft) and gestation lasts for 10 or 11 months. Calves are born in summer and the interval between calves can be as short as 16 months.

Groups are normally large. There are some old reports from the Black Sea of schools 250,000 and 300,000 strong, and one more recently from Napier in New Zealand of a solid mass of Common Dolphins 27 × 44 km (17 × 27 miles). When travelling in such numbers, a school moves in crescent formation on a broad front, producing an awesome rushing sound that is audible a considerable distance away.

More commonly, a social unit consists of anything from 20 to a few hundred individuals, segregated by age and sex. There seems to be a well-defined hierarchy within each group, with the lead usually taken by adult males. There are numerous, well-founded reports of group members coming to the aid of weak or wounded individuals. Aristotle saw one support the body of a dead calf. A recent expedition in the Mediterranean saw a stunned animal being supported con-

stantly by 6 others, taking turns 2 or 3 at a time, to hold it up to the surface until it recovered and was able to join them as they all swam away. In the light of observations such as these, classic myths like the tale of the lyric poet Arion of Lesbos being carried to safety on the back of a dolphin no longer seem absurd.

There is at least one instance of dolphins coming to men for assistance. In 1967 a group of 50 Common Dolphins, many already injured by sharks, sought protection close to the hull of a fishery research vessel in the Gulf of Mexico. The 6 young calves with them were herded against the boat while the adults patrolled the fringes, making periodic rushes at a number of oceanic sharks which were harrying them. Observers saw a dolphin get his tail shredded in the jaws of a shark while doing this. The attack lasted for an hour, with the humans unable to do much to help, until a sudden violent rain squall seemed to provide the dolphins with the diversion they needed to escape.

Common Dolphins are known to echolocate, producing rapid pulsed sounds at a frequency of 100–150 kHz.

Status Common Dolphins are now scarce in the Black Sea, but elsewhere, despite continued catches, they still seem to be common. They have long supported extensive whaling industries in the Black Sea and on the coasts of Japan. At one time 130,000 a year were being taken with purse-seine nets in the Black Sea, but since 1966 the Russian part of this industry has closed, leaving a very much smaller catch to the Bulgarians and Turks. Elsewhere, Common Dolphins are taken on the coasts of Israel and the Azores, where the traditional sperm whalers are transferring their attention to a more manageable prey. This is the third most common species represented in the incidental catch by tuna fishermen in the Pacific.

Distribution Common Dolphins are found worldwide in all tropical and warm temperate waters, both coastal and deep water, though concentrations are usually greatest over relatively shallow banks. This species also occurs in some numbers as far north as Iceland and Nova Scotia in the Atlantic, possibly extending their range into these higher latitudes with the aid of the Gulf Stream.

There are no known habitual migrations, but Common Dolphins clearly travel a great deal, becoming very common in some areas one year and vanishing in the next.

Sources BANKS & BROWNELL (1969) taxonomy, BARABASH-NIKIFOROV (1935) in Soviet Union, BLANFORD (1891) taxonomy, CASPERS (1957) in Black Sea, DALL (1873) in North Pacific, GASKIN (1968) in New Zealand, GRAY (1828) taxonomy, HOUSBY (1971) in Azores, LINNAEUS (1758) original description, PILLERI (1972) in Pakistan, PILLERI & KNUCKEY (1969) epimeletic behaviour, SERGEANT & FISHER (1957) distribution, SPRINGER (1967) shark attack, VAN BREE (1971) in Somalia, VAN BREE & GALLAGHER (1978) taxonomy, VAN BREE & PURVES (1972) taxonomy.

BOTTLENOSE DOLPHIN

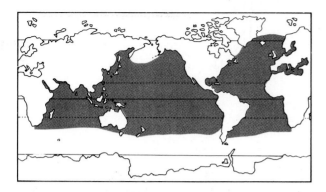

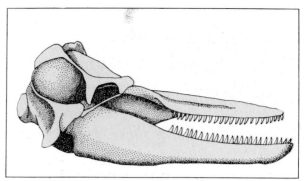

Classification This was well known to classical authors, but the first scientific description seems to be that of Lacépède, in 1804 from a mounted animal once held in the Maisons Alfort, a veterinary school near Charenton in Paris. This specimen has disappeared and Lacépède's name for it, *Delphinus nesarnack*, seems also to have been ignored. Under the Code it is a *nomen oblitum.*

In 1814 a solitary dolphin was stranded in Duncannon Pool near Stoke Gabriel, about 8 km (5 miles) up the River Dart in Devonshire, England. It was collected and described by George Montagu, who wrote a short paper on it for the Wernerian Natural History Society, calling it *Delphinus truncatus* from the Latin *trunco,* cut off, in reference to its abbreviated snout.

In 1843 Gray created a new genus for this species, calling it *Tursio* after the Latin for porpoise. The generic name was later discovered to have been preoccupied and was amended to *Tursiops* by adding the suffix derived from the Greek *ops,* a face.

A host of authors described local geographical variations of what is probably just one widely distributed species. The following species are included here under *T. truncatus* and, where they seem to merit it, given subspecific status:

T. aduncus (EHRENBERG 1832) from the Latin *aduncus,* hooked; based on strandings in the Red Sea of dolphins which seem to be smaller, darker and more slender, and to have a lower and more hooked dorsal fin. They may also have a few more teeth. This form, together with the following 7 alleged variants, may constitute a good tropical Indian Ocean subspecies, *T. t. aduncus:*
T. abusalem (RUPPELL 1842), Red Sea;
T. catalania (GRAY 1862), north-eastern Australia;
T. dawsoni (LYDEKKER 1909), off southern India;
T. hamatus (WIEGMANN 1841), Red Sea;
T. fergusoni (LYDEKKER 1903), Laccadive Sea;
T. gadamu (GRAY 1866), Bay of Bengal;
T. perniger (BLYTH 1848), also in the Bay of Bengal.
T. gilli (DALL 1873), based on Pacific specimens which are smaller and browner; they have a longer fin and a distinct pink patch around the anus. They may also have fewer and

larger teeth. This form, together with the following one, may provide a valid subspecies for the Pacific Ocean, *T. t. gillii.*
T. nuuanu (ANDREWS 1911), tropical east Pacific.
T. gephyreus (LAHILLE 1908), Argentina; with stouter mandible and fewer vertebrae.
T. pervimanus (VAN BENEDEN 1886), Adriatic; with more bones in one phalanx.

Local Names *Souffleur* and *grand dauphin* (French), *bolshoi delfin* (Russian), *Grosser Tummler* (German), *hando iruka* (Japanese), *oresvin* (Swedish), *peixe boto* (Portuguese) and *nezarnak* (Greenland Eskimo).

Description Small, becoming medium-sized in large males; length averages 3 m (10 ft), with a maximum of 4.2 m (14 ft); calves are about 1 m (3.5 ft) at birth. Weight averages 200 kg (440 lb), with a maximum of one extraordinary specimen of 650 kg (1,430 lb); calves are about 32 kg (70 lb) at birth.

Some adult animals weigh almost as much as pilot whales. They are robust in every way and yet still succeed in maintaining the streamlined grace of all other dolphins. The beak is short, usually only 7–8 cm (3 inches) long, wide and rounded, with a lower jaw which protrudes conspicuously beyond the upper. The line of the mouth is soft and curves upwards at the back to give this species its familiar, faintly amused, facial expression. The dorsal fin is tall, broad at the base and usually curved backwards. Dolphins from the tropical east Pacific seem to have narrower, more strongly curved fins. The tail-stock is moderately keeled.

The colouring is subdued and normally consists of a medium grey back above and pale or light grey flank and belly. Individuals in the Indian Ocean are sometimes darker and those in the Pacific, often more brown than grey. It is possible that strong sunlight might deepen the colour of the back. Calves everywhere tend to be slightly bluish. In living animals, particularly in the Pacific, the pale undersides are distinctly tinged with pink. There is a pale line drawn from the flipper to the eye and, in older individuals, some spotting becomes apparent on the belly. Adult dolphins may also have a white mark or callus on the tip of the lower jaw which, from above, makes it look as though they have white noses.

Additional body markings are claimed for some geographic forms. The Red Sea Bottlenose for instance, seems often to have 2 or 3 pale diagonal bands on its tailstock. It is difficult without further study to determine whether these are consistent enough to be diagnostic of the variant in question. Many individuals bear scars from the teeth of fellow dolphins and, occasionally, from sharks.

Field Identification Most people are familiar with the Bottlenose Dolphin from its film and television appearances, but it seldom obliges by adopting similar postures in the field. The over-riding impression of this species in the sea is the height and bulk of its fin and the strong, deliberate arch of its back as it dives after breathing. Bottlenoses are usually seen in small groups feeding in the same area, with each dolphin pursuing its own track, rising well up in the water 2 or 3 times each minute, but seldom showing either beak or flukes. Occasionally, before diving to avoid an approaching boat, the dolphins lobtail, flapping their flukes loudly on the water surface. Dives usually last for less than a minute, but some have been timed at as long as 10 minutes.

Throughout their wide range, Bottlenose Dolphins are astonishingly unafraid of man. They come readily to the bows of ships of all kinds and are conspicuous there because of their size. Even after years of seeing this species in captivity and of watching it in the wild, we still find ourselves surprised by the bulk and muscularity of Bottlenose Dolphins when we have them riding at our bow. They are wonderfully well coordinated, rising in turns to blow, never jostling for position, rolling over on their sides to watch us watching them, and finally diving deeply in formation, twisting back and reappearing on the surface a long way astern. When ships are not available, we have seen Bottlenose Dolphins surfriding in shore breakers or on storm waves in mid-ocean.

When undisturbed they seldom leap like the hyperactive Common Dolphin (*Delphinus delphis 75*), but we have seen individual animals suddenly breach, hurling themselves 5 m (16 ft) or more into the air in a way which presages the kind of performance they can be persuaded to put on in captivity.

In the field the most likely source of confusion is with other species which are predominantly blue or grey, with tall curved

dorsal fins, i.e. the Roughtooth Dolphin (*Steno bredanensis 39*) and the spotted dolphins (*Stenella* spp. *73* and *74*). The most useful characteristics by which each can be distinguished are:

Tursiops average size 3 m (10 ft), often more; bulky; short beak, clearly marked off from melon; no spots.
Steno seldom more than 2.4 m (8 ft); slender, long thin beak, not clearly demarcated from the forehead; irregular blotches on belly.
Stenella usually around 2.4 m (8 ft); slender; longish beak, well demarcated from melon; many regular spots.

Bottlenose Dolphins often school with a number of other species, including Shortfin Pilot Whales (*Globicephala macrorhynchus 50*), and can be seen in the company of Great Right Whales (*Balaena glacialis 1*) and Humpback Whales (*Megaptera novaeangliae 10*) on their migrations.

Stranding Bottlenose Dolphins are often stranded, singly and in small groups. A beached individual is usually easy to identify by its robust body and its stubby beak. Inside the mouth are 18–26 relatively large teeth (usually 24 or 25) on each side of both jaws. There are 65 vertebrae; and 5 of the 14 pairs of ribs are double headed.

Natural History One of the secrets of the widespread success of this species is its catholic appetite. Bottlenoses eat 8–15 kg (15–33 lb) a day, feeding largely on inshore bottom-dwelling fish, but they will take eels, catfish, sharks, rays, hermit crabs, shrimps, mullet, and even pelagic fish as large as yellowtails (*Seriola dorsalis*). They have been seen in captivity to deal with large species by rubbing the fish on the bottom or against a rock until the backbone cracks and the head can be removed for easier swallowing.

In many areas, Bottlenoses have taken to following trawlers and shrimp boats, feeding on fish stirred up or discarded by the nets; but they can easily hunt co-operatively for themselves. There is one record of a group in the Black Sea chasing a school of bluefish into a shallow bay and holding it there by deploying two of their number to act as sentinels while the rest hung back outside the bay, taking turns to come in and feed.

Most feeding takes place in relatively shallow water, but dolphins off the west coast of Africa are said to dive to 600 m (2,000 ft) over the steep edge of that narrow continental shelf, and to have specially large and strong middle-ear bones to deal with pressure at this depth.

This species lives for 25–30 years, maturing usually at the age of 6. Courtship is involved, beginning with an elaborate male pre-copulatory posture, in which he throws his body into a striking S-shape. This is followed by head stroking in which each animal may caress the other gently for an hour or more, using the beak or flippers or stroking the genital area with sweeps of the soft fluke tips. Finally, when mouthing and nuzzling reach a certain fever pitch, the female hangs motionless at the surface with only her blowhole exposed as the male twists his tailstock around her. Intromission lasts 10–30 seconds, and gestation for 12 months. Calves are born in

Two Bottlenose Dolphins supporting a third which is stunned and carrying it to the surface to breathe

Colour variations in Bottlenose Dolphin

spring and summer, usually in a social group with several dolphins gathered around whistling while 2 adult female 'midwives' wait for the baby to emerge tail first. They may sometimes tug on its tail to help it along and they always move in together to guide the calf up to the surface for its first breath. Lactation is under the voluntary control of the mother, squeezing milk under pressure into the waiting mouth of a nursing calf, who continues to be fed for about a year. The calving interval is at least 2 years and each female Bottlenose can expect to have about 8 calves in her lifetime.

The usual social unit amongst Bottlenose Dolphins is a group of less than 15, but there are records of as many as 1,000. Cohesion is tight and mutual assistance and support are common. Apart from co-operating in feeding and child care, Bottlenoses seem also to join in exploratory and defensive manoeuvres. There is one well-documented account of 5 travelling up a lagoon in Baja California. They detected a barrier of hollow aluminium poles thrown across a narrow part of the channel by a research vessel and stopped 400 m (1,320 ft) away, well beyond visual range, and huddled close to the bank. One dolphin then went forward slowly on its own, explored the barrier, apparently decided that it posed no threat, returned to the group and, after much excited vocalization (all of which was recorded) the group passed together between the poles without hesitation.

In an example of co-operative defence, 2 males, both born in captivity in Florida, dealt similarly with a 1.5 m (5 ft) lemon shark (*Triakis semifasciata*) in a tank, hitting it hard with their beaks in mid-body. In at least one other instance, wild Bottlenose Dolphins have been seem ramming a large shark with their heads, hard enough to lift it clear of the water.

In many areas Bottlenose Dolphins enjoy a close relationship with local fishermen, co-operating with them in netting activities in return for a share of the spoils, or perhaps simply performing out of interest and curiosity. In one recent case on the west coasts of England and Wales, a solitary male Bottlenose called Beaky took to towing boats around harbours, moving anchors, disputing the ownership of buoys, playing with and imitating swimmers and water skiers, and eventually abducting 2 women and a child.

A group of untrained Bottlenose Dolphins in captivity in South Africa regularly mimic furseals, skate and loggerhead turtles; in one case, using a seagull feather held in its beak as a scraper, one dolphin copied the actions of a human diver cleaning the inside of the glass on underwater viewing ports, complete with a vivid imitation of the sound of the demand valve on his aqualung and blowing a stream of bubbles out its blowhole to copy the pattern of exhaled air. The Bottlenose actually performed this task so effectively that, after just one demonstration, it was never necessary for a diver to do that job again.

The most devastating example of mimicry we have encountered in any animal also took place in that same tank. A human observer on the outside of one of the viewing ports, in an idle and offhand gesture, blew a cloud of cigarette smoke

Above: group of Bottlenose Dolphins corner shoal of fish and hang back taking turns to feed two at a time, while another two act as sentinels, keeping the fish school in position

Top left: group of Bottlenose Dolphins waiting while one goes ahead alone to scout a barrier set up by a research vessel

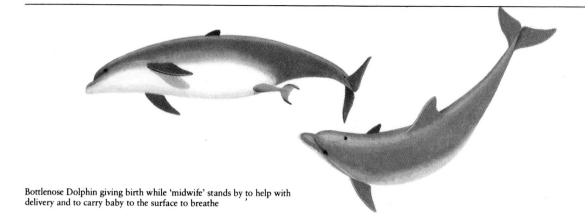

Bottlenose Dolphin giving birth while 'midwife' stands by to help with delivery and to carry baby to the surface to breathe

toward a young dolphin peering through from the other side. The dolphin immediately sought out its mother, returned with a mouthful of milk, waited until the smoker was at the window again and then blew the milk out in a cloud against the glass, producing precisely the same effect underwater that the smoke had had in the air.

Besides whistling, clapping, grunting, chuckling, squeaking, rasping, popping and belching, Bottlenose Dolphins produce a rapid train of clicks, emitting 1,000 or more discrete sounds per second. These are unquestionably used for echolocation and seem to be focused and moderated by the shape and size of the melon. Dolphins can change the frequency in a click sequence, moving the band up and down and varying the energy peak. They can give off broad blankets of sound and narrow focused clicks at the same time, perhaps by using each nasal passage separately. They can flatten, shorten or shape the beams of sound they transmit and can even direct the main beam forwards while simultaneously sending out a smaller feeler beam in another direction. With this complex apparatus Bottlenose Dolphins can make the most detailed analysis of any object at a distance, discriminating even between different types of metal by analysing their precise frequency composition, something we have only just learned to do with sophisticated engineering instruments. It is even possible that dolphins may, by means of echoes, be able to penetrate each other's bodies, checking on mood and emotional state in the same way that we watch each other's faces for telltale clues.

Each individual dolphin has a stereotyped and distinctive 'personal signature' whistle which is partly the result of its unique anatomy, but which seems at least in part to be learned from those around it.

Status Bottlenose Dolphins are generally still common, although pollution and the great reduction in many stocks of fish, have led to markedly diminished numbers in some areas. Bottlenose Dolphins are too strong to be captured in nets as easily as some of the smaller species, but in many cases they have been, and still are, hunted with guns and harpoons. In Ireland, West Africa, the Caribbean and Japan small numbers are taken each year in coastal operations. In some places this hunt is prompted more by fear of competition for dwindling fish stocks than it is by the usual whaling motives. In many areas, a direct and recent threat to the species is posed by the numbers being captured and taken alive for display.

Distribution Known from all warm and temperate waters, worldwide. It is most often seen close inshore, even entering rivers and estuaries and is seldom found in the open ocean, but it is obviously capable of making long crossings of open areas of deep sea. We have seen groups well over 800 km (500 miles) from the nearest land or shallow water.

There is some evidence for co-ordinated migration in several populations of Bottlenoses, particularly those found in temperate areas. This movement takes place toward the equator in autumn and back to richer feeding grounds in the spring.

Sources ANDREW (1962) intelligence, ANDREWS (1911) taxonomy, BEACH & HERMAN (1972) memory, BLYTH (1848) taxonomy, BROWN & NORRIS (1956) tool-using, CALDWELL & CALDWELL (1972) sounds, DALL (1873) taxonomy, EHRENBERG (1832) taxonomy, EVANS & DREHER (1962) exploration, GRAY (1862) taxonomy, GRAY (1866) taxonomy, GRAY (1964) live capture, HERMAN & ARBEIT (1973) learning, HUBBS (1953) epimeletic behaviour, KELLOGG (1961) sounds, KELLOGG & RICE (1964) discrimination, LAHILLE (1908) taxonomy, LANTZ & GUNASEKERA (1951) in Sri Lanka, LILLY (1962) sounds, LILLY et al (1968) mimicry, LYDEKKER (1903) taxonomy, LYDEKKER (1908) taxonomy, McBRIDE & HEBB (1948) intelligence, MONTAGU (1821) original description, MOROZOV (1970) co-operation in feeding, NORRIS (1965) open-ocean release, NORRIS & PRESCOTT (1961) exploratory behaviour, OHSUMI (1972) in Japan, PILLERI & GIHR (1972) taxonomy, ROSS (1977) in South Africa, RUPPELL (1842) taxonomy, SIEBENALER & CALDWELL (1956) epimeletic behaviour, TAVOLGA & ESSAPIAN (1957) behaviour, TAYLER & SAAYMAN (1973) mimicry, WOOD (1973) use by US Navy, WIEGMANN (1841) taxonomy.

Bottlenose Dolphin male showing precopulatory posture

Synonyms

As our knowledge of cetaceans improves, their relationships become more clear and it is often necessary to change their names. This can become confusing, even for professional taxonomists, but it is especially difficult for amateurs, who may not have access to the latest specialist literature.

This is a list of important changes made in recent years. Old names (many of which still crop up in books and papers) are given first in alphabetic order. Beside them are the new names agreed by most contemporary authorities.

This synonymy deals with all the cetacean names used in this book, and with all the names in current or recent use in the literature. It also includes some archaic names where these have played an important role in the taxonomic history of a species. It is not, however, an exhaustive list.

For a more complete survey of all the known names in use since 1758, see PHILIP HERSHKOVITZ in his 'Catalog of Living Whales' – Bulletin of the United States Museum, Smithsonian Institution, Volume *246*: 1–259 (1966).

Balaena albicans	*Delphinapterus leucas*	*Delphinus densirostris*	*Mesoplodon densirostris*
Balaena ampullata	*Hyperoodon ampullatus*	*Delphinus desmaresti*	*Ziphius cavirostris*
Balaena australis	*Balaena glacialis*	*Delphinus dussumieri*	*Delphinus delphis*
Balaena gibbosa	*Eschrichtius robustus*	*Delphinus eschrichtius*	*Lagenorhynchus acutus*
Balaena japonica	*Balaena glacialis*	*Delphinus eutropia*	*Cephalorhynchus eutropia*
Balaena marginata	*Caperea marginata*	*Delphinus fitzroyi*	*Lagenorhynchus obscurus*
Balaena maximus	*Balaenoptera musculus*	*Delphinus fluviatilis*	*Sotalia fluviatilis*
Balaena musculus	*Balaenoptera musculus*	*Delphinus frontatus*	*Steno bredanensis*
Balaena novaeangliae	*Megaptera novaeangliae*	*Delphinus gangetica*	*Platanista gangetica*
Balaena physalus	*Balaenoptera physalus*	*Delphinus geoffrensis*	*Inia geoffrensis*
Balaena rostrata	*Balaenoptera acutorostrata*	*Delphinus griseus*	*Grampus griseus*
Balaena sieboldii	*Balaena glacialis*	*Delphinus guianensis*	*Sotalia fluviatilis*
Balaenoptera australis	*Balaenoptera physalus*	*Delphinus heavisidii*	*Cephalorhynchus heavisidii*
Balaenoptera bonaerensis	*Balaenoptera acutorostrata*	*Delphinus intermedius*	*Feresa attenuata*
Balaenoptera brydei	*Balaenoptera edeni*	*Delphinus kingi*	*Delphinapterus kingi (?)*
Balaenoptera davidsoni	*Balaenoptera acutorostrata*	*Delphinus longirostris*	*Stenella longirostris*
Balaenoptera huttoni	*Balaenoptera acutorostrata*	*Delphinus melas*	*Globicephala melaena*
Balaenoptera patachonicus	*Balaenoptera physalus*	*Delphinus nesarnack*	*Tursiops truncatus*
Balaenoptera robusta	*Eschrichtius robustus*	*Delphinus obscurus*	*Lagenorhynchus obscurus*
Balaenoptera rorqual	*Balaenoptera physalus*	*Delphinus orca*	*Orcinus orca*
Berardius arnouxi	*Berardius arnuxii*	*Delphinus pallidus*	*Sotalia fluviatilis*
Berardius arnouxii	*Berardius arnuxii*	*Delphinus pernettensis*	*Stenella plagiodon*
Berardius arnuxi	*Berardius arnuxii*	*Delphinus peronii*	*Lissodelphis peronii*
Berardius hectori	*Mesoplodon hectori*	*Delphinus phocaenoides*	*Neophocaena phocaenoides*
Catodon candicans	*Delphinapterus leucas*	*Delphinus phocoena*	*Phocoena phocoena*
Cephalorhynchus albifrons	*Cephalorhynchus hectori*	*Delphinus plagiodon*	*Stenella plagiodon*
Cephalorhynchus albiventris	*Cephalorhynchus eutropia*	*Delphinus plumbeus*	*Sousa chinensis*
Delphinorhynchus australis	*Ziphius cavirostris*	*Delphinus ponticus*	*Delphinus delphis*
Delphinapterus borealis	*Lissodelphis borealis*	*Delphinus rissoanus*	*Grampus griseus*
Delphinapterus dorofeevi	*Delphinapterus leucas*	*Delphinus rostratus*	*Inia geoffrensis*
Delphinapterus friemani	*Delphinapterus leucas*	*Delphinus sowerbensis*	*Mesoplodon bidens*
Delphinapterus peronii	*Lissodelphis peronii*	*Delphinus tropicalis*	*Delphinus delphis*
Delphinus acutus	*Lagenorhynchus acutus*	*Dioplodon europaeus*	*Mesoplodon europaeus*
Delphinus albirostris	*Lagenorhynchus albirostris*	*Diolpodon gervaisi*	*Mesoplodon europaeus*
Delphinus amazonicus	*Inia geoffrensis*	*Dolichodon layardii*	*Mesoplodon layardii*
Delphinus aries	*Grampus griseus*	*Electra clancula*	*Cephalorhynchus hectori*
Delphinus attenuatus	*Stenella attenuata*	*Electra hectori*	*Cephalorhynchus hectori*
Delphinus bairdii	*Delphinus delphis*	*Epiodon chathamensis*	*Ziphius cavirostris*
Delphinus blainvillei	*Pontoporia blainvillei*	*Eschrichtius gibbosus*	*Eschrichtius robustus*
Delphinus bredanensis	*Steno bredanensis*	*Eschrichtius glaucus*	*Eschrichtius robustus*
Delphinus capensis	*Delphinus delphis*	*Eubalaena glacialis*	*Balaena glacialis*
Delphinus cephalorhynchus	*Cephalorhynchus commersonii*	*Feresa intermedia*	*Feresa attenuata*
Delphinus chinensis	*Sousa chinensis*	*Feresa occulta*	*Feresa attenuata*
Delphinus clymene	*Stenella clymene*	*Globicephala brachyptera*	*Globicephala macrorhynchus*
Delphinus coeruleoalbus	*Stenella coeruleoalba*	*Globicephala edwardi*	*Globicephala melaena*
Delphinus commersonii	*Cephalorhynchus commersonii*	*Globicephala leucosagmaphora*	*Globicephala melaena*
Delphinus cruciger	*Lagenorhynchus cruciger*	*Globicephala macrorhyncha*	*Globicephala macrorhynchus*

Globicephala scammoni	Globicephala macrorhynchus	Physeter breviceps	Kogia breviceps
Globicephala sieboldii	Globicephala macrorhynchus	Physeter microps	Physeter macrocephalus
Globicephalus edwardsii	Globicephala melaena	Physeter simus	Kogia simus
Globicephalus macrorhynchus	Globicephala macrorhynchus	Physeter tursio	Physeter macrocephalus
Globicephalus melas	Globicephala melaena	Platanista indi	Platanista minor
Globicephalus rissii	Grampus griseus	Prodelphinus attenuatus	Stenella attenuata
Globicephalus scammonii	Globicephala macrorhynchus	Rhachianectes glaucus	Eschrichtius robustus
Grampidelphis griseus	Grampus griseus	Rorqualis borealis	Balaenoptera musculus
Grampus orca	Orcinus orca	Sagmatius amblodon	Lagenorhynchus australis
Grampus rectipinna	Orcinus orca	Sibbaldus borealis	Balaenoptera musculus
Hyperoodon butskopf	Hyperoodon ampullatus	Sotalia borneensis	Sousa chinensis
Hyperoodon desmaresti	Ziphius cavirostris	Sotalia brasiliensis	Sotalia fluviatilis
Hyperoodon rostratus	Hyperoodon ampullatus	Sotalia chinensis	Sousa chinensis
Inia boliviensis	Inia geoffrensis	Sotalia gadamu	Tursiops truncatus
Lagenorhynchus coeruleoalbus	Stenella coeruleoalba	Sotalia guianensis	Sotalia fluviatilis
Lagenorhynchus electra	Peponocephala electra	Sotalia lentiginosa	Sousa chinensis
Lagenorhynchus fitzroyi	Lagenorhynchus obscurus	Sotalia pallida	Sotalia fluviatilis
Lagenorhynchus ogneri	Lagenorhynchus obliquidens	Sotalia plumbea	Sousa chinensis
Lagenorhynchus superciliosus	Lagenorhynchus obscurus	Sotalia sinensis	Sousa chinensis
Lagenorhynchus thicolea	Lissodelphis borealis	Sotalia teuszii	Sousa teuszii
Lagenorhynchus wilsoni	Lagenorhynchus cruciger	Sotalia tucuxi	Sotalia fluviatilis
Megaptera boops	Megaptera novaeangliae	Sousa borneensis	Sousa chinensis
Megaptera longipinna	Megaptera novaeangliae	Sousa lentiginosa	Sousa chinensis
Megaptera nodosa	Megaptera novaeangliae	Sousa plumbea	Sousa chinensis
Megaptera osphyia	Megaptera novaeangliae	Sousa queenslandensis	Sousa chinensis
Megaptera poeskop	Megaptera novaeangliae	Stenella alope	Stenella longirostris
Meomeris phocaenoides	Neophocaena phocaenoides	Stenella dubia	Stenella attenuata
Mesoplodon australis	Mesoplodon grayi	Stenella euphrosyne	Stenella coeruleoalba
Mesoplodon floweri	Mesoplodon layardii	Stenella frontalis	Stenella attenuata
Mesoplodon gervaisi	Mesoplodon europaeus	Stenella graffmani	Stenella attenuata
Mesoplodon guntheri	Mesoplodon layardii	Stenella lateralis	Stenella coeruleoalba
Mesoplodon haasti	Mesoplodon grayi	Stenella malayana	Sousa chinensis
Mesoplodon hotaula	Mesoplodon ginkgodens	Stenella marginata	Stenella coeruleoalba
Mesoplodon knoxi	Mesoplodon hectori	Stenella microps	Stenella longirostris
Mesoplodon mirum	Mesoplodon mirus	Stenella pernettensis	Stenella plagiodon
Mesoplodon pacificus	Indopacetus pacificus	Stenella roseiventris	Stenella longirostris
Mesoplodon sowerbensis	Mesoplodon bidens	Stenella styx	Stenella coeruleoalba
Mesoplodon thomsoni	Mesoplodon layardii	Steno attenuatus	Stenella attenuata
Mesoplodon traversi	Mesoplodon layardii	Steno compressus	Steno bredanensis
Neobalaena marginata	Caperea marginata	Steno perniger	Steno bredanensis
Neomeris phocaenoides	Neophocaena phocaenoides	Steno rostratus	Steno bredanensis
Neophocaena asiaeorientalis	Neophocaena phocaenoides	Steno tucuxi	Sotalia fluviatilis
Neophocaena sunameri	Neophocaena phocaenoides	Stenodelphis blainvillei	Pontoporia blainvillei
Neophocaena phocoenoides	Neophocaena phocaenoides	Stenopontistes zambezicus	Steno bredanensis
Nodus densirostris	Mesoplodon densirostris	Susu gangetica	Platanista gangetica
Orca intermedia	Feresa attenuata	Susu platanista	Platanista gangetica
Orcaella fluminalis	Orcaella brevirostris	Tursiops abusalem	Tursiops truncatus
Orcella fluminalis	Orcaella brevirostris	Tursiops aduncus	Tursiops truncatus
Orcinus rectipinna	Orcinus orca	Tursiops catalania	Tursiops truncatus
Petrorhynchus capensis	Ziphius cavirostris	Tursiops dawsoni	Tursiops truncatus
Phocaena albiventris	Cephalorhynchus eutropia	Tursiops fergusoni	Tursiops truncatus
Phocaena australis	Lagenorhynchus australis	Tursiops gadamu	Tursiops truncatus
Phocaena brevirostris	Orcaella brevirostris	Tursiops gephyreus	Tursiops truncatus
Phocaena crassidens	Pseudorca crassidens	Tursiops gillii	Tursiops truncatus
Phocaena dalli	Phocoenoides dalli	Tursiops hamatus	Tursiops truncatus
Phocaena dioptrica	Phocoena dioptrica	Tursiops nesarnack	Tursiops truncatus
Phocaena obtusata	Cephalorhynchus eutropia	Tursiops nuuanu	Tursiops truncatus
Phocaena rissonus	Grampus griseus	Tursiops parvimanus	Tursiops truncatus
Phocaena spinipinnis	Phocoena spinipinnis	Tursiops perniger	Tursiops truncatus
Phocaena albus	Delphinapterus leucas	Ziphius grebnitzkii	Ziphius cavirostris
Phocaena vomerina	Phocoena phocoena	Ziphius layardii	Mesoplodon layardii
Phocoenoides truei	Phocoenoides dalli	Ziphius novaezealandiae	Ziphius cavirostris
Physeter bidens	Mesplodon bidens	Ziphius savii	Ziphius cavirostris
Physeter catodon	Physeter macrocephalus	Ziphius sechellensis	Mesoplodon densirostris

Records and First Aid

More than most other disciplines, cetology depends on contributions from enthusiasts. A large part of the body of information on abundance, distribution and behaviour has been and will continue to be supplied by sailors, whalers, fishermen, coast guards, beachcombers and divers. This guide has been designed with these people in mind and arranged in a way that makes it possible for anyone to make a reasonably accurate diagnosis in the field.

This on its own is not enough. Even an accurate identification is of little use unless it is supported by relevant background information. We urge everyone seeing cetaceans in the water, or finding them stranded on the shore, to keep accurate records and to supply these without delay to the nearest relevant authority.

A. Sightings at sea

Provide as much as possible of the following information:

 1 Date of sighting.
 2 Local time.
 3 Observer's name. (And name of ship or plane if relevant.)
 4 Observer's eye-level height above or below water.
 5 Weather conditions: wind speed and visibility most important.
 6 Sea conditions: size of waves, etc.
 7 Conditions of observation: number of observers, how long was watch kept?
 8 Duration of sighting: including estimate of diving time.
 9 Distance of sighting from observer.
10 Movement relative to observer: speed and heading, including ship or plane speed, etc., if relevant. Details of ship's course.
11 Identity of sighting: species diagnosis, supported by estimates of:
   a) size;
   b) number, including age and sex if possible;
   c) size and shape of dorsal fin;
   d) size and shape of blow;
   e) colour and marking;
   f) were flukes visible?
   g) presence of tags or markers.
12 Presence of other species: birds or fish.
13 Details of behaviour: breaching, spinning, feeding, etc.
14 Reaction to observer or vessel: did they bowride, avoid, etc.
15 Address of observer.

If photographs or sketches were made during the sighting, copies of these should be included, or mention made of them, in the report.

If the sighting is made as part of a regular watch kept on a coast or from a vessel at sea, it may be equally interesting to a cetologist to know where and when no cetaceans of any kind were seen.

B. Records of stranded cetaceans

It is worth bearing in mind that all marine mammals in many countries are now protected under laws which make it an offence to take all or any part of them away or to damage or deface the specimen. The first priority is to inform the nearest authority (addresses are given below), but if this is impossible or likely to take too long, then there is a great deal a careful observer can do to make sure that the animal is preserved and recorded.

If it is dead and is likely to be washed away by the tide, pull it further up the beach. Remember that even a specimen in an advanced state of decomposition can be useful. Discard nothing.

a) Take photographs or make sketches from as many angles as possible; ensuring that features such as teeth, baleen plates, ventral grooves, flippers, flukes, fins and unusual scars or markings are all recorded.

b) Examine the animal for external parasites, particularly in grooves, around eyes, mouth and blowhole. Draw or photograph these and, if possible, preserve at least one of each kind by freezing or by placing in 40–70 per cent isopropyl alcohol. Ordinary rubbing alcohol or, in an emergency, pure spirit such as gin or vodka will do.

c) Make all the basic measurements indicated in the diagram, or, if time permits, take the full series of measurements in the list (which might be of interest to a cetologist). Most scientific data are expressed in metric units, but use whatever units are available. All the measurements are made in a straight line, not around the curve of the body or organ. Beak measurements are taken from the tip of the upper jaw even where the lower one protrudes further. The tiny external ear aperture is located just below and behind the eye, but it might be necessary to scrape away some of the skin to expose it. Ventral grooves are always counted along a line between the flippers.

 1 Tip of upper jaw to deepest part of tail notch.
 2 Tip of upper jaw to centre of anus.
 3 Tip of upper jaw to centre of genital slit.
 4 Tip of lower jaw to end of ventral grooves.
 5 Tip of upper jaw to centre of navel.
 6 Tip of upper jaw to top of dorsal fin.
 7 Tip of upper jaw to leading edge of dorsal fin.
 8 Tip of upper jaw to anterior insertion of flipper.
 9 Tip of upper jaw to centre of blowhole.
10 Tip of upper jaw to external ear opening.
11 Tip of upper jaw to centre of eye.
12 Tip of upper jaw to angle of mouth.
13 Tip of upper jaw to apex of melon.
14 Maximum width of beak.
15 Length of throat grooves.

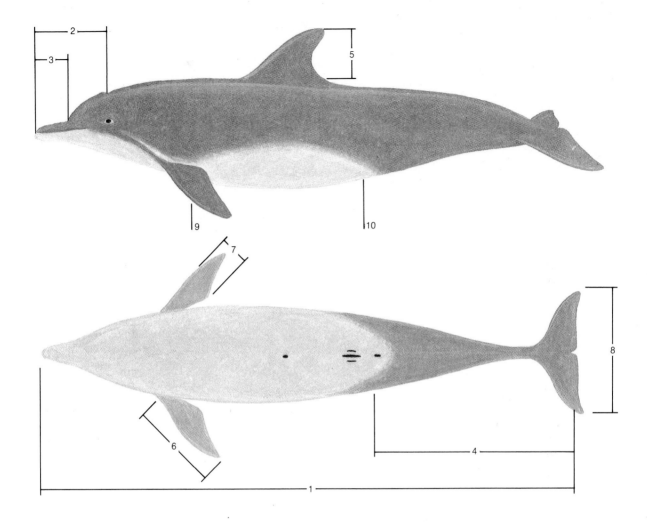

Basic measurements necessary for record purposes

16 Number of throat grooves.
17 Projection of lower jaw beyond upper, if any.
18 Centre of one eye to centre of other eye.
19 Length and height of eye.
20 Centre of eye to angle of mouth.
21 Centre of eye to external ear opening.
22 Centre of eye to centre of blowhole.
23 Blowhole width and length.
24 Flipper width at widest point.
25 Flipper length at longest point.
26 Height of dorsal fin.
27 Length of base of dorsal fin.
28 Total span of extended flippers.
29 Fluke span.
30 Fluke width at widest point.
31 Depth of fluke notch.

32 Notch of flukes to centre of anus.
33 Notch of flukes to centre of genital slit.
34 Notch of flukes to navel.
35 Girth at anus.
36 Girth at armpit of flipper.
37 Girth at eye.
38 Length of mammary slit.
39 Length of genital slit.
40 Length of anal slit.

Teeth are counted in 4 series (right upper, right lower, left upper and left lower). Baleen plates are counted at the base in 2 series (right and left), and it is usual also to record the length of the longest plate and the average number of bristles per centimetre (measured over any 5 cm).

d) Once the necessary permission has been obtained from the relevant authority, or when it is clear that they will not be coming or cannot be contacted, it is appropriate to preserve all or part of the specimen. If possible, freeze a small cetacean intact. Otherwise, as a minimum, preserve the head, flipper, fin, flukes and if possible the reproductive tract. This should be done in 10 per cent neutral formalin. Stomach contents are often of interest and should be preserved in 40 per cent alcohol. The rest of the body should be buried in sand well above the high tide line and carefully marked so that it can be recovered later. This is a good way of cleaning the flesh off the bones, but it is a rather crude procedure involving the loss of some vital parts such as the hyoid and ear ossicles and should be done only as a last resort with a valuable specimen.

C. Addresses

1 United States of America:
a) Scientific Event Alert Network (SEAN), National Museum of Natural History, Smithsonian Institution, Washington DC. Telephone (800) 325 6000 – charge to ID 1776.
b) National Marine Fisheries Service, Northeast region – (617) 281 3600, Southeast region – (813) 893 3145, Northwest region – (206) 442 7676, Southwest region – (213) 548 2517.
c) Coast Guard or Local Police.

2 United Kingdom:
a) Marine Mammal Department, British Museum of Natural History, Cromwell Road, London, SW7. Telephone 01-589 6323.
b) Dolphin Survey Project, Department of Anatomy, University of Cambridge, Downing Street, Cambridge CB2 3DY. Telephone (0223) 68665 or 68398.
c) Coastguard, Receivers of Wreck or Local Police.

3 Canada:
a) Fisheries Research Board of Canada, Department of the Environment, Ottawa, Ontario K1A 0H3.
b) Arctic Biological Station, Box 400, Ste Anne de Bellevue, Quebec H9X 3L6.

4 Australia:
a) Australian National Parks and Wildlife Service, Box 636, ACT 2601. Canberra. Telephone (062) 497355.
b) CSIRO, Box 21, Cronulla, New South Wales 2230.

5 South Africa:
a) Marine Mammal Laboratory, Sea Fisheries Branch, Box 251, Cape Town.
b) Port Elizabeth Museum, Box 13147, Humewood 6013, Port Elizabeth, Cape.

6 Mexico:
a) Instituto Nacionale de Investigaciones Biologia Pesquera, Division de Vertebrados Marinos, Mexico 7, D.F.
b) Instituto de Biologia, Universidad Nacional Autonoma de Mexico, Apartado Postale 70–153, Mexico 20, D.F.

7 Norway:
Institute of Marine Research, Nordnesparken 2, Bergen-Nordnes.

8 Netherlands:
a) Research Institute of Nature Management, Kemperbergerweg 11, Arnhem.
b) Dolfinarium Hardewijk, Strandboulevarde, Hardewijk.

9 Belgium:
Koninklijk Belgisch Institut voor Natuurwetenschappen, Vautierstraat 31, Brussels 4.

10 France:
a) Museum National d'Histoire Naturelle, 57 Rue Cuvier, Paris V^e
b) Musée d'Histoire Naturelle, 28 rue Albert Ier, 17000 La Rochelle.

11 Iceland:
Hafrannsoknastofnunin, Marine Research Institute, Skulagata 4, Reykjavik.

12 Japan:
a) The Whales Research Institute, 1–31 Etchujima, Koto-ku, Tokyo.
b) Far Seas Fisheries Research Laboratory, 1000 Orido, Shimizu, Shizuoka-ken 424.

13 New Zealand:
a) National Museum of New Zealand, Private Bag, Wellington.
b) New Zealand Ministry of Agriculture and Fisheries, Private Bag, Dunedin, Otago.

14 Spain:
Comisio de Cetalogia, Institucio Catalana d'Historia Natural, Apartado de Correos 593, Barcelona.

15 Sweden:
Naturhistoriska Riksmuseet, Forskningsavdelningen, S 10405 Stockholm.

16 Soviet Union:
a) Insitute of Oceans, Academy of Sciences of the USSR, Moscow 109387.
b) Ministry of Fisheries, 121 Rozhdestvensky Boulevard, Moscow K-45.

17 Uruguay:
Museo Nacional de Historia Natural de Montevideo, Casilla de Correo 399, Montevideo.

FIRST AID

The stranding of individual whales, dolphins and porpoises usually involves animals that are already ill or injured. Many of these are due to die anyway, but some can recover and, with a little help, make their own way back to the ocean. Mass strandings are another matter altogether, because the majority of the animals involved are healthy and much can be done to help them survive.

The first point to bear in mind is that cetaceans are now protected in most countries by comprehensive marine mammal legislation which makes it an offence to harass, harm, capture or kill any of them, or to remove them or any part of them from the sea or shore. But there are a number of actions which can and should be taken in the name of first aid, to care for stranded animals which are still alive.

Single Strandings

i. Find out if the animal is still alive.
This is not as simple as it sounds. All whales are voluntary breathers; their respiration is under conscious control and 15 minutes or more may elapse between blows. It seems to be a common reaction in many species to become immobile under stress and so it is necessary to examine an animal very closely and for a long period before it finally is declared dead and beyond further aid.

None of the usual methods of detecting life in man works very well with whales. It is almost impossible, for instance, to detect a heart beat through the thick layers of blubber. The most sensitive areas in a whale tend to be the eyes and the area around the blowhole and a gentle touch on either of these spots may elicit some visible response.

ii. If the animal is alive, make sure that it is stable.
If it is still in the water, make sure that it remains upright, otherwise it is likely to drown. Small dolphins and porpoises can be supported by hand, but it may be necessary to prop up large whales mechanically. Beach mattresses, inflatable surfboards, wads of foam rubber, boat fenders or even canvas deckchairs all make suitable wedges, but great care must be taken not to damage the animal's skin, which is surprisingly delicate. If it becomes necessary to attach any ropes, webbing or straps, make sure that these are padded with rubber or cloth to prevent rope burns or friction.

If the animal is high and dry, try to remove any rocks, pilings or other hard objects beneath or near it which may damage the skin. Cetaceans rest most comfortably on their bellies. Beach sand piled up against the flanks forms an effective prop to prevent the animal toppling over while waiting for the returning tide, but take care not to cover the flippers or flukes, because it is through these that the animal regulates its temperature. It is important that the flippers remain completely free, so scoop sand out beneath them and let them hang loose, preferably into a hole filled with water. Make certain that the animal never lies on its own flippers as this can restrict circulation and result in permanent damage.

iii. Keep the animal cool.
The greatest problem facing a stranded cetacean is overheating. If possible, build a make-shift shelter to provide shade. Otherwise, cover the animal's body, or as much of it as possible, with light-coloured cloths, sheets or towels and keep these moist by pouring water over them. In the case of large whales, keep at least the flippers and flukes cool in this way and arrange to have the rest of the body sprayed with water as often as possible. Take care *never* to cover the blowhole or to pour water into it. On very hot days, it might be effective to pack plastic bags filled with crushed ice around the flippers and flukes.

If it is impossible to provide shade or cover, or if the animal has been or is likely to be exposed for a long time, it is important to prevent the skin from cracking. Apply a thin film of lanolin, petroleum jelly or zinc oxide to all exposed areas. Do *not* use suntan lotions or other perfumed preparations which might contain ingredients harmful to delicate cetacean skin.

iv. Keep the animal quiet.
Set up careful crowd- and noise-control. Try to ensure a minimum of handling or disturbance for the animal since it is already, by the very nature of its situation, under considerable stress. At night, make certain that no lights or flash bulbs are shone directly into its eyes.

There is some evidence to show that many cetaceans, particularly young ones, may benefit from the presence and proximity of someone who, with gentle touch or soft sound, offers companionship and consolation; but be careful not to overdo this concern or crowd the animal in any way and never touch the eyes or blowhole.

As a rule a single stranded cetacean is there on the shore because it is not well enough to swim. So do *not* attempt to return it to the sea. Contact the nearest relevant authority and wait for the arrival of someone with the experience necessary to make a proper diagnosis.

If this is not possible, or there seems likely to be an inordinate delay, it may be necessary to take further action. If the tide is about to rise, or there seems to be a reasonable chance of the animal's recovery, it can be assisted to return to the ocean.

v. Move the animal very carefully.
Use the utmost care in this. *Never* push or pull on the flippers; these are very easily injured and dislocated. Try not to touch the head or the tail flukes. If the animal is in the water or partly afloat, push on its sides or at the base of the dorsal fin. Spread the effort as evenly as possible by applying the flat of many hands to a wide area of the animal's flank or back. Never roll it over on to its side underwater or use any hooks or crowbars.

The most effective way of moving a small cetacean is with a sling which can be improvised from towels, blankets or tarpaulin. Lift the animal gently on to the fabric or work this carefully under the body until the bulk of it is supported. It is best if the head and tail hang slightly over the edges of the sling. Then carry the animal into water deep enough to support its own weight and release the sling once it is clear that the animal can keep itself upright and swim.

In the case of large cetaceans, and where it is possible to arrange for a mechanical hoist or crane, the animal can be lifted on to a more rigid structure like a cradle or a cargo flat, but care must be taken to cover this with protective pads. To assist with loading calculations, the following approximations will give some idea of the weights involved in handling toothed whales:

Length	Weight
2 m (6.5 ft)	about 100 kg (225 lb).
3 m (10 ft)	about 500 kg (1100 lb).
4 m (13 ft)	about 900 kg (2000 lb).
5 m (16.5 ft)	about 2000 kg (4500 lb).

Where baleen whales are concerned, weights range from 1500 to 3500 kg per m (1100–2400 lb per ft), depending on the species.

In most solitary strandings the animal winds up right back on the beach again. If this seems to be the result of disequilibrium, with the animal obviously unable to maintain an even keel and staggering around in circles like a drunk, then it may be worth persisting for a while until it regains its sense of balance. But if it returns directly and deliberately to the beach, then there is no further point in going on trying to push it out to sea. Just make it as comfortable as possible on the shore.

Before returning any animal to the sea, try to make a positive identification. Take photographs and go through as much of the process of measurement and description as time will allow. The full list of information required by cetology is given above.

vi. As a last resort for any animal which is certain to die and is in obvious distress, it may be necessary to kill it humanely.
This is not only difficult but may also be illegal. Wait, if you can, until the proper authority is present to make such a decision. But if this is impossible, then use a large bore rifle or handgun to put a shot directly into the animal's brain. For a non-biologist, this might be hard to find, but remember that the brain of all cetaceans is displaced to the very back of the head. The skull drawings in this book will help to locate it precisely, but, as a general rule, it is effective to aim the shot from above, a short distance behind the line joining the eyes.

Frank Robson of New Zealand has perfected a technique of killing stranded whales by a single thrust of a sharp lance into the jugular vein, but this takes skill and experience.

Mass Strandings

These require a totally different response. They are apparently encouraged by the existence of an ill or injured individual which is usually the first to beach. If a potential mass strand-ing is discovered at this early stage, it can sometimes be averted by killing the first animal ashore and preventing it from summoning the others to its aid.

Identification of such an animal and such a situation requires some knowledge of cetaceans and their behaviour and the killing of the beached individual may be against local law, so great care should be taken to do so only with the proper authority, or when a mass stranding seems certain and otherwise inevitable.

In most circumstances, the mass stranding is only discovered when it is already well under way and it is no longer possible to identify or isolate the trigger individual. Then the following priorities prevail:

i. Deal with the animals in the water first.
Keep them from coming out on to the beach. This is usually very difficult, but with some small cetaceans it may be possible to hold the animals bunched together in shallow, sheltered water. This is best achieved by a large and well-organized group of people, who can keep the animals quiet and upright while avoiding the risk of injury to themselves or to the whales. Do not try to push the animals back out to sea at this stage. They will not go, and any uncoordinated attempt to make them could break up the group and result in a large number of single strandings scattered over many miles of beach.

ii. Get all the beached animals back into the water.
Again, this is easier said than done, but with some small cetaceans it is possible with a well coordinated effort by a number of people. The object is to get the entire school together in one place in the shallows at the same time and then to move them gently out to sea. The greatest care must obviously be taken not to injure any of the animals in this process.

iii. Guide the entire group out to sea.
If they still refuse to go, it is sometimes possible to persuade them to do so by forcibly restraining a leader (if such can be identified), securing it to a boat, and luring the group out after it.

iv. Care for those that are too large or too ill to be moved.
First aid should be given in the same way as that prescribed for solitary strandings, while preventing if possible any communication between them and those still in the water. If this can only be achieved by killing them, then this might be the proper and humane thing to do. As soon as possible, call the nearest relevant authority.

See Appendix Two for addresses.

Biography

A number of names crop up repeatedly in the history of cetology. From the long list of these, we have selected just 100 for inclusion here. These are not the only ones involved, nor are they necessarily the most important; they are simply those who occur in the text of our guide and about whom a little more may wish to be known:

ABEL, Clarke (1780–1826). English botanist and physician. On Lord Macartney's Expedition of 1816–17. Wrote *Narrative of a Journey to the Interior of China.* Shipwrecked with all his collection.

AGASSIZ, Jean Louis Rodolphe (1807–1873). Swiss-American naturalist. Worked on collections made in South America by SPIX and VON MARTIUS. *Nomenclator Zoologicus.* Pioneer palaeontologist. Professor at Neuchâtel and later at Harvard. Great teacher. Founded Museum of Comparative Zoology at Harvard.

ALLEN, Glover Morrill (1879–1942). American mammalogist. On Central-Asiatic Expedition with ANDREWS.

ANDERSON, John (1833–1900). Scottish naturalist. Superintendent of Indian Museum in Calcutta. On Expedition to Yunnan and Burma with Major A. G. Duff which discovered *Balaenoptera edeni.*

ANDREWS, Roy Chapman (1884–1960). American naturalist and explorer. On cruise of *Albatross* to Far East in 1909–10, Korea 1911–12 Alaska 1913 with BORDEN. Director of American Museum of Natural History.

BAIRD, Spencer Fullerton (1823–1887). American zoologist and collector. Organized expeditions of *Albatross.* Founder of Woods Hole Oceanographic Institute. Secretary of Smithsonian Institution.

BAUDIN, Nicolas (1750–1803). French explorer. Expedition to Australia on *Geographe* in 1800–04 with naturalist PERON.

BERARD, August (1796–1852). French Vice Admiral. Served on *l'Uranie* 1817–21, *Coquille* 1822–25. Commanded corvette *Rhin* to New Zealand in 1846.

BLAINVILLE, Henri Marie Ducrotay de (1777–1850). French naturalist and physician. Student of CUVIER, later enmity between them. First to use external characteristics in taxonomy. Professor at Musée Nationale D'Histoire Naturelle.

BLANFORD, William Thomas (1832–1905). English naturalist. On geological survey of India. Naturalist to Persian Boundary Commission. Collected for British and Indian museums.

BLYTH, Edward (1810–1873). English naturalist. Compiled illustrated edition of CUVIER. Forerunner of DARWIN – anticipated natural selection with his 'localizing principle'. Curator of the Museum of Asiatic Society of Bengal in Calcutta.

BOROWSKI, Georg Heinrich (1746–1801). German zoologist and collector.

BOUGAINVILLE, Baron Louis Antoine de (1729–1811). French navigator. First French Expedition around world 1766–69. *Voyage autour du Monde.* Expedition to Malouines (Falklands) and Straits of Magellan 1763/64.

BOWDOIN, James (1726–1790). American amateur zoologist. Colonial Governor of Massachusetts. First President of American Academy of Arts and Sciences.

BRAVARD, Auguste. French palaeontologist. Collected porpoises in Argentina. Collection purchased by the British Museum in 1854.

BUFFON, Comte George Louis Leclerc de (1707–1788). French naturalist. Keeper of Jardin du Roi. Catalogued King's Museum, assisted by DAUBENTON. First to present isolated facts in comprehensive form in *Histoire Naturelle, generale et particulière.*

BURMEISTER, Herman Karl Conrad (1807–1892). German entomologist. Professor at Cologne and Halle. Director of Zoological Museum at Halle. Director of Buenos Aires Museum. Great naturalist, expert on Brazilian fauna. Made meticulous notes and drawings.

BURNES, Sir Alexander (1805–1841). British explorer. Political envoy. On mission to Maharajah of Lahore up Indus in 1831. Travelled in disguise to Caspian Sea. Assassinated in Kabul.

CLIFT, William (1775–1849). English anatomist. Curator of Hunterian Museum at Royal College of Surgeons. OWEN's father-in-law.

COMMERSON, Philibert (1727–1773). French botanist. On first French voyage round the world with BOUGAINVILLE.

COPE, Edward Drinker (1840–1897). American palaeontologist. Collected amongst hostile Indians, discovered dinosaurs. Created 'Law of Trituberculy' to explain origin of mammalian teeth. Editor of *American Naturalist.*

CUVIER, Baron Georges Leopold Chrétien Frederic Dagobert (1769–1832). French anatomist. Succeeded DAUBENTON at Collège de France. Professor of Anatomy at Musée Nationale d'Histoire Naturelle in Paris. Founded both sciences of comparative anatomy and palaeontology. *La Regne Animal.* President of Council of State for Napoleon and Minister of Interior to King Louis Philippe.

DALL, William Healey (1845–1927). American conchologist. Studied under AGASSIZ. Quartermaster to SCAMMON. Surveys of Alaska. On *Humboldt* to Bering Sea. Pioneer on Arctic zoology.

DAUBENTON, Louis Jean Marie (1716–1800). French naturalist and physician. Illustrated BUFFON. First Director of Jardin du Roi.

DELALANDE, Antoine (1787–1823). French collector. Expedition to Cape in 1818 with VERREAUX. Collected first complete specimens of great whales.

DESMOULINS, Antoine (1796–1828). French physiologist. Anatomy of the nervous system of cetaceans.

DUSSUMIER, Jean Jacques. French master mariner and collector. Travelled to Far East and South East Asia between 1818 and 1837. Sent several thousand specimens back to Paris Museum.

DUVERNOY, Georges-Louis (1777–1855). French anatomist. Worked with CUVIER.

EDEN, Sir Ashley (1831–1887). English diplomat. Chief Commissioner of British Burma in 1871. Lt. Governor of Bengal in 1877.

EHRENBERG, Christian Gottfried (1795–1876). German naturalist. On HEMPRICH Expedition to Red Sea in 1820–26. With HUMBOLDT in Russia.

ELLIOT, Sir Walter (1803–1887). English civil servant. Member of Council of Governor of Madras. Archaeologist and keen amateur naturalist and collector.

ERXLEBEN, Johann Christian Polycarp (1744–1777). German veterinarian.

ESCHRICHT, Daniel Frederick (1798–1863). Danish zoologist. Professor at University of Copenhagen.

FERREIRA, Alexandre Rodrigues (1756–1815). Portuguese explorer.

FITZINGER, Leopoldo Josef Franz Johann (1802–1884). German-American taxonomist.

FITZROY, Robert (1805–1865). English Vice Admiral. Hydrographer and meteorologist. Commander of *Beagle* 1831–36.

FLOWER, Sir William Henry (1831–1899). English physician. Conservator of Museum of Royal College of Surgeons. Director of British Museum (Natural History).

FORSTER, Johann Reinhold (1729–1794). German naturalist. On COOK's second world voyage with his son Johann Georg Adam.

FORSTER, Johann Georg Adam (1754–1794). German explorer. On COOK's second world voyage – wrote his own account.

FRASER, Francis Charles (1903–1978). English cetologist. On *Discovery* Expedition 1926–33. Marine Mammal Section of British Museum. *Giant Fishes, Whales and Dolphins.*

FREMINVILLE, Comte Christophe Paulin de la Poix (1787–1848). French archaeologist and sailor. Mounted private expeditions to Spitzbergen, Caribbean, Brazil and Senegal.

GAIMARD, Joseph Paul (1790–1858). French naturalist. With QUOY on *l'Astrolabe* in New Zealand and Pacific 1826–29. On *La Recherche* to Arctic 1835–36. Also on *L'Uranie* and *La Physicienne.*

GEOFFROY, Etienne Saint Hilaire (1772–1844). French naturalist. Collaborated with CUVIER on

285

taxonomy. Professor at Paris Museum. Instructed by Napoleon to plunder Portuguese museums.

GERVAIS, Paul François-Louis (1816–1879). French zoologist and physician. Professor at Faculty of Sciences in Paris. Pioneer in study of fossil vertebrates. Succeeded CUVIER and BLAINVILLE.

GESNER, Konrad von (1516–1565). German-Swiss naturalist. Botanist known as the 'German Pliny'. Founder of modern zoology.

GILL, Theodore Nicholas (1837–1914). American taxonomist. Librarian of the Smithsonian Institution.

GLOGER, Constantine Wilhelm Lambert (1803–1863). German ornithologist. Gloger's Rule (northern forms are lighter coloured). Zoogeography.

GRAY, John Edward (1800–1875). English zoologist. Keeper of Zoology at British Museum. Created largest collection in Europe. Pioneer of cetacean taxonomy.

HAAST, Sir Julius Johann Frank von (1822–1887). German-New Zealander. Founder and Director of Canterbury Museum in Christchurch. Geologist.

HARMER, Sir Sidney Frederic (1862–1950). English palaeontologist. Director of British Museum (Natural History). First to keep cetacean stranding records.

HECTOR, Sir James (1834–1907). New Zealand zoologist, Curator of Wellington Colonial Museum.

HOSE, Charles (1863–1929). English physician. Resident in Sarawak between 1884 and 1907.

HUBBS, Carl Leavitt (1894–1973). American zoologist. At Scripps Institute of Oceanography. Taxonomy of cetaceans.

HUMBOLDT, Baron Friedrich Heinrich Alexander von (1769–1859). German explorer. Friend of FORSTER. In South America from 1799 to 1804. In Russia from 1829 with EHRENBERG. Naturalist and geographer, Kosmos.

HUNTER, John (1728–1793). Scottish naturalist. At St George's Hospital in London. Anatomy of cetaceans. His collection formed the nucleus of that in the Royal College of Surgeons.

KELLOGG, Remington (1892–1968). American zoologist. Pioneer of cetacean taxonomy at Smithsonian Institution.

KÜKENTHAL, Willy Georg (1861–1922). German zoologist. Worked in West Indies, Japan, Malay Archipelago and Arctic.

LACÉPÈDE, Bernard Germain Etienne, Comte de la Ville sur Illon (1756–1825). French naturalist and musician. Student of BUFFON – completed his Histoire Naturelle.

LAYARD, Edgar Leopold. South African zoologist. Curator of South African Museum in Cape Town.

LEBECK, Heinrich Julius. Dutch traveller. Mont Master in Batavia.

LESSON, René Primavère (1794–1849). French zoologist. On DUPERRY Expedition to Pacific 1822–1825 on La Coquille.

LINNAEUS, Carolus (Carl von Linné) (1707–1778). Swedish botanist. Pioneer of

taxonomy. Species Plantarum in 1753. Systema Naturae tenth edition in 1758 marks beginning of modern system of classification.

LÖNNBERG, Axel Johan Einar. Swedish naturalist. Director of Natural History Museum in Stockholm. Expeditions in Antarctic and all over the world.

LYDEKKER, Richard (1849–1915). English naturalist and geologist. Geological Survey of India 1874–82. Catalogued fossil vertebrates in British Museum.

MILLER, Gerrit Smith (1869–1950). American zoologist. Curator of Mammals at Smithsonian Institution.

MONTAGU, George (1751–1815). English amateur naturalist. Lt. Colonel of militia in Wiltshire. The Sportsmans Directory.

OLIVER, Walter Reginald Brook. New Zealand zoologist. At Colonial Museum in Wellington.

ORBIGNY, Alcide Dessalines d' (1802–1857). French palaeontologist. Travelling naturalist for Paris museum. In South America.

OSBECK, Per (1723–1805). Swedish explorer. Travelled in China and East Indies.

OWEN, Sir Richard (1804–1892). English palaeontologist. Hunterian Professor and Conservator of Museum at Royal College of Surgeons. Superintendent of British Museum (Natural History). Comparative anatomist, last of the natural philosophers.

PALLAS, Peter Simon (1741–1811). German naturalist. Travelled in Asia 1768–74, Russia, Siberia and China. Founded museum at St Petersburg. Published STELLER's Journals. Geologist.

PALMER, Theodore Sherman (1868–1955). American naturalist. Responsible for Whaling Treaty of 1936.

PEALE, Titian. American painter. Son of portraitist Charles Willson Peale. Illustrated natural history.

PERNETTY, Dom Antoine Joseph (1716–1802). French cleric. On BOUGAINVILLE's expedition to South America 1763–64.

PERON, François (1775–1810). French naturalist. On BAUDIN's Expedition to Antarctic on Le Geographe 1800–04.

PHILIPPI, Rudolph Amandus (1808–1904). German-Chilean zoologist.

PLINY, Gajus Secundus Plinius (24–79). Writer and anthologist. Uncle of Pliny the Younger. Travelled to Africa, France, Syria. Published 37 volumes on natural history.

QUOY, Jean René Constant (1790–1869). French zoologist. On Astrolabe with GAIMARD.

RACOVITZA, Emile (1868–1947). Belgian naturalist. Naturalist to Belgian Antarctic Expedition on Belgica 1897–99.

REINHARDT, Johannes Theodor (1816–1882). Danish zoologist. Travelled in Greenland and Brazil.

ROXBURGH, William (1757–1815). English physician and botanist. Superintendent of Botanical Gardens in Calcutta. Studied Bengali flora.

RUDOLPHI, Carl Asmund (1771–1832). German anatomist. Founder of Berlin Zoological Museum. Comparative anatomy and physiology.

SCHLEGEL, Hermann (1804–1884). Dutch naturalist. Director of Rijksmuseum in Amsterdam.

SIEBOLD, Karl Theodor Ernst von (1804–1885). German zoologist. Professor at University of Munich. Comparative anatomy. Founded 'Zeitschrift für Wissenschaftliche Zoologie'.

SLIJPER, Everhard (1907–1968). Dutch zoologist. Professor at University of Indonesia at Bogor and University of Amsterdam. On whaler Willem Barendsz.

SOWERBY, James (1757–1822). English artist and naturalist. Drew fossils and flowers. Member of extraordinary dynasty of explorers and naturalists, including Arthur de Carle, George and John Edward.

STEJNEGER, Leonhard Hess (1851–1943). Norwegian naturalist. Curator of United States National Museum. Pioneer of Alaskan zoology.

STELLER, Georg Wilhelm (1709–1746). German explorer. First naturalist to explore North Pacific and Alaska. With BERING on his last voyage in 1741.

SWINHOE, Robert (1836–1877). English naturalist. Travelled and collected in China and India. British Consul in China.

TEMMINCK, Coenraad Jacob (1770–1858). Dutch naturalist. Travelled and studied ornithology in Japan.

TRAILL, Thomas Steward (1781–1862). Scottish physician. Professor of medical jurisprudence in Edinburgh. Editor of eighth edition of Encyclopaedia Britannica. Co-founder of Royal Institution.

TRUE, Frederick William (1858–1914). American mammalogist. At American Museum of Natural History in New York.

TURNER, Sir William (1508–1568). English naturalist. First to bring natural history to scientific level in modern times.

VAN BÉNÉDEN, Pierre Joseph (1809–1894). Belgian palaeontologist. Curator of natural history museum at Louvain.

VAN BREDA, Jacques Gisbert Samuel (1788–1867). Dutch palaeontologist.

VERREAUX, Jules (1807–1873). French collector and taxidermist. Travelled to Cape with DELALANDE and brothers Alexis and Edouard.

WAGLER, Johann Georg (1800–1832). German ornithologist.

WAGNER, Johann Andreas (1797–1861). German zoologist.

WAGNER, Johann (1833–1892). German palaeontologist.

WATERHOUSE, George Robert (1810–1888). English zoologist. Curator of Zoological Society of London. Keeper at British Museum. Worked on Darwin's collections.

WEBER, Max Carl Wilhelm (1852–1937). German zoologist. On Siboga Expedition. The 'Weber Line' between Asian and Australian fauna.

WIEGMANN, Arend Friedrich August (1802–1841). German herpetologist in MEYEN's Expedition.

WIEGMANN, Carl Arend Friedrich (1836–1901). German naturalist. With WEBER in East Indies. Son of Arend Friedrich August.

BIBLIOGRAPHY

ABEL, R. S. (1971) 'Cephalorhynchus hectori – sightings, capture, captivity.' *Inv. on Cetacea 3*: 171–179.

AGUAYO, A. L. (1974) 'Baleen whales off continental Chile'. In SCHEVILL.

AGUAYO, A. L. (1975) 'Progress report on small cetacean research in Chile'. *J. Fish. Res. Board Can. 32*: 1123–1143.

ALDRICH, H. L. (1889) *Arctic, Alaska, and Siberia*. Rand McNally: Chicago.

ALLEN, J. A. (1908) 'The North Atlantic right whale and its near allies'. *Bull. Am. Mus. Nat. Hist. 24*: 277–329.

ALLEN, G. M. (1923) 'The black finless porpoise'. *Bull. Mus. Comp. Zool. 65*: 233–257.

ALLEN, G. M. (1925) 'Burmeister's porpoise'. *Bull. Mus. Comp. Zool. 67*: 251–261.

ALLEN, G. M. (1941) 'Pygmy sperm whale in the Atlantic'. *Field. Mus. Nat. Hist. Zool. Series. 27*: 17–36.

ALLEN, R & NEILL, W. T. (1957) 'White whales of the Amazon'. *Natural History* (June): 324–329.

ALPERS, A. (1961) *Dolphins: The Myth and the Mammal*. Houghton-Mifflin: London.

ALPERS, A. (1963) *Dolphins*. Butler & Tanner: London.

AL-ROBAAE, K. (1965) 'Bryde's whale in the south east Pacific'. *Norsk. Hvalfangst Tidende 54*: 141–148.

AL-ROBAAE, K. (1970) 'First record of the speckled dolphin in the Arabian Gulf'. *Saugetierk. Mitt. 18*: 227–228.

AMUNDIN, M. & AMUNDIN, B. (1974) 'On the behaviour and study of the harbour porpoise in the wild'. *Inv. on Cetacea 5*: 317–328.

ANDERSEN, S. (1969) 'Epimeletic behaviour in the captive harbour porpoise'. *Inv. on Cetacea 1*: 203–205.

ANDERSON, H. T. (ed.) (1969) *The Biology of Marine Mammals*. Academic Press: NY.

ANDERSON, J. (1871) 'Description of a new cetacean from the Irrawaddy River, Burmah'. *Proc. Zool. Soc. Lond.*: 142.

ANDERSON, J. (1878) *Anatomical and zoological research: two expeditions to Western Yunnan in 1868 and 1875*. Quaritch: London.

ANDERSON, S. & KNOX-JONES, J. (eds.) (1967) *Recent Mammals of the World*. Ronald Press: New York.

ANDREW, R. J. (1962) 'Evolution of intelligence and vocal mimicking'. *Science 137*: 585–589.

ANDREWS, R. C. (1908) 'Description of a new species of *Mesoplodon* from Canterbury Province, New Zealand'. *Bull. Amer. Mus. Nat. Hist. 24*: 203–215.

ANDREWS, R. C. (1911) 'A new porpoise from Japan'. *Bull. Amer. Mus. Nat. Hist. 30*: 31–51.

ANDREWS, R. C. (1911) 'Description of an apparently new porpoise of the genus *Tursiops*'. *Bull. Amer. Mus. Nat. Hist. 30*: 233–237.

ANDREWS, R. C. (1914) 'Monographs of the Pacific Cetacea, 1: The California Gray Whale'. *Mem. Amer. Mus. Nat. Hist. 1*: 231–285.

ANDREWS, R. C. (1916) 'Monographs of the Pacific Cetacea, 2: The sei whale'. *Mem. Amer. Mus. Nat. Hist. 1*: 291–388.

ANGOT, M. (1954) 'Observations sur les mammifères marins de l'Arcipiel de Kerguelen

…' *Mammalia 18*: 1–111.

ANON. (1929–) *International Whaling Statistics*. Published annually by the Bureau IWS at Sandjefjord, Norway.

ANON. (1975) 'Oil industry worries about narwhals'. *Marine Mammal News 1*: 5.

ANON. (1978) 'The northern bottlenose whale'. Review by Endangered Species Productions of Ayer: Massachusetts.

ARISTOTLE (335 BC) *Historia Animalium*. Loeb Classical Library. Heinemann: London (1964).

ARSEN'EV, V. A. (1961) 'Lesser rorquals of the Antarctic'. *Rep. Conf. Ichthy. Comm. USSR. Acad. Sci. 12*: 125–132 (Russian).

ARVY, L. (1973) 'Mammary glands, milk, and lactation in cetaceans'. *Inv. on Cetacea 5*: 157–200.

ARVY, L. (1977) 'Asymmetry in cetaceans'. *Inv. on Cetacea 8*: 161–201.

ARVY, L. & PILLERI, G. (1972) 'Comparison of the tongues of some odontocetes'. *Inv. on Cetacea 4*: 191–200.

AZZAROLI, M. L. (1968) 'Second specimen of the rarest living beaked whale'. *Monitore Zool. Ital. 2*: 67–79.

BACKUS, R. H. (1966) 'A large shark in the stomach of a sperm whale'. *J. Mammal. 47*: 142.

BACKUS, R. H. & SCHEVILL, W. E. (1966) '*Physeter* clicks'. In NORRIS.

BAKER, A. N. (1972) 'New Zealand Whales and Dolphins'. *Tuatara 20*: 1–49.

BALDRCDGE, A. (1972) 'Killer whales attack and eat a gray whale'. *J. Mammal. 53*: 898–900.

BANKS, R. C. & BROWNELL, R. (1969) 'Taxonomy of the common dolphins of the Eastern Pacific'. *J. Mammal. 50*: 262–271.

BARABASH-NIKIFOROV, I. I. (1935) *Bull. Soc. Nat.* (Moscow) *44*: 249.

BARNARD, K. H. (1954) 'A Guide to South African Whales and Dolphins'. No. 4. South African Museum.

BASTIAN, J. (1966) 'The transmission of arbitrary environmental information between bottlenose dolphins'. In BUSNEL.

BATESON, G. (1966) 'Problems in cetacean and other mammalian communication'. In NORRIS.

BATESON, G. (1974) 'Observations of a cetacean community'. In McINTYRE.

BATTEAU, D. F. & MARKEY, P. R. (1967) *Man-dolphin Communication*. Listening Inc: Arlington, Massachusetts.

BEACH, F. A. & HERMAN, L. M. (1972) 'Preliminary studues of auditory problem solving …' *The Psychological Record 22*: 49–62.

BEALE, T. (1839) *The Natural History of the Sperm Whale*. Van Hoorst: London.

BEAMISH, P. & MITCHELL, E. (1971) 'Ultrasonic sounds recorded in the presence of a blue whale'. *Deep Sea Research 18*: 803–889.

BEAMISH, P. & MITCHELL, E. (1973) 'Short pulse length audio frequency sounds recorded in the presence of a minke whale'. *Deep Sea Research 20*: 375–386.

BEDDARD, F. E. (1900) *A Book of Whales*. John Murray: London.

BEDDARD, F. E. (1902) *Mammalia*. Macmillan: London.

BEE, J. W. & HALL, E. R. (1956) *Mammals of Northern Alaska*. University of Kansas: Lawrence.

BELKOVICH, V. M. (1960) 'Some biological observations on white dolphin from the airplane'. *Russ. Acad. Sci.; Zool. Rec. 39*: 1414–1419.

BENJAMINSEN, T. (1972) 'On the biology of the bottlenose whale'. *Norwegian J. Zool. 20*: 233–241.

BENJAMINSEN, T. & CHRISTENSEN, I. (1979) 'The natural history of the bottlenose whale'. In WINN & OLLA.

BENSON, S. B. & GROODY, T. C. (1942) 'Notes on the Dall porpoise'. *J. Mammal. 23*: 41–51.

BERZIN, A. A. (1971) 'The Sperm Whale'. N.O.A.A. (from Russian).

BEST, P. B. (1960) 'Further information on Bryde's whale from Saldanha Bay, South Africa'. *Norsk Hvalfangt Tidende 49*: 201–215.

BEST, P. B. (1967) 'Distribution and feeding habits of baleen whales off the Cape Province'. *Investl. Rep. Div. Sea Fish. S. Afr. 57*: 1–44.

BEST, P. B. (1967–1970) 'The sperm whale off the west coast of South Africa'. *Investl. Rep. Div. Sea. Fish. S. Afr. 61*: 1–27; *66*: 1–32; *72*: 1–20; *78*: 1–12; *79*: 1–27.

BEST, P. B. (1969) 'A dolphin from Durban'. *Ann. S. Afr. Mus. 52*: 121–135.

BEST, P. B. (1970) 'Exploitation and recovery of right whales off the Cape Province'. *Rep. Div. Sea. Fish. S. Afr. 80*: 1–20.

BEST, P. B. (1970) 'Records of the pygmy killer whale from southern Africa, with notes on behaviour in captivity'. *Ann. S. Afr. Mus. 57*: 1–14.

BEST, P. B. (1974) 'Status of the whale populations off the west coast of South Africa'. In SCHEVILL.

BEST, P. B. (1975) 'Status of Bryde's whale'. FAO ACMRR.

BEST, P. B. (1979) 'Social organization in sperm whale'. In WINN & OLLA.

BIERMAN, W. H. & SLIJPER, E. J. (1947) 'Remarks upon the species of the genus *Lagenorhynchus*'. *Kon. Ned. Akad. Wetenschap. 50*: 1353–1364; *51*: 127–133.

BIRD, J. E. (1977) 'Whales, whaling, dolphins and porpoises: an annotated bibliography'. *American Cetacean Soc.* ACSSD-1.

BLANFORD, W. T. (1891) 'The Fauna of British India'. *2*: Mammalia. London.

BLAINVILLE, M. de (1817) *Nouveau Dictionaire d'Histoire Naturelle*. Paris.

BLYTH, E. (1859) 'On the rorqual of the Indian Ocean …' *J. Asiat. Soc., Calcutta 28*: 481–498.

BOROWSKI, G. H. (1781) *Gemeinnüzzige Naturgeschichte des Thierreiches*. Berlin.

BOSCHMA, H. (1938) 'On the teeth and some other particulars of the sperm whale'. *Temminckia 3*: 151–278.

BOSCHMA, H. (1950) 'Maxillary teeth in specimens stranded on the Dutch coasts'. *Proc. Kongl. Neder. Akad. Wet. 53*: 775–786.

BOWERS, C. A. & HENDERSON, R. S. (1972) 'Project Deep Ops'. *Naval Undersea Tech. Pub. No. 306*.

BOYER, W. D. (1946) (Letter to Editor) *Nat. Hist. 55*: 96.

BRAHAM, H. et al (1979) 'Preliminary report of the 1978 spring bowhead whale research program results'. *Rep. Int. Whal. Commn. 29*: 291–305.

BRIGHTWELL, T. (1846) 'Observation on a specimen of the bottlenosed dolphin'. *Ann. Mag. Nat. Hist. 17*: 21.

BRITISH COLOUR COUNCIL (1938) *Dictionary of Colour Standards*. London.

BROWN, D. H. (1960) 'Behaviour of a captive Pacific pilot whale'. *J. Mammal. 41*: 342–349.

BROWN, D. H. (1962) 'Further observations on the pilot whale in captivity'. *Zoologica 47*: 59–64.

BROWN, D. H. et al (1966) 'Observations on the behavior of wild and captive false killer whales ...' *Contr. Sci.* No 95: 1–32.

BROWN, D. H. & NORRIS, K. S. (1956) 'Observations on captive and wild cetaceans'. *J. Mammal. 37*: 311–326.

BROWN, R. (1979) *The Lure of the Dolphin*. Avon: New York.

BROWN, R. J. (1976) 'Whales: a bibliography with abstracts'. *Nat. Tech. Inf. Serv.* PS 76/0111.

BROWN, S. G. (1954) 'Dispersal in blue and fin whales'. *Discovery Reports 26*: 355–384.

BROWN, S. G. (1957) 'Whales observed in the Indian Ocean'. *Marine Observer 27*: 157–165.

BROWN, S. G. (1958) 'Whales observed in the Atlantic Ocean'. *Marine Observer 28*: 142–146; 209–216.

BROWN, S. G. (1960) 'Swordfish and whales'. *Norsk Hvalfangst Tidende 8*: 345–351.

BROWN, S. G. (1961) 'Observations on pilot whales in the North Atlantic Ocean'. *Norsk Hvalfangst Tidende 6*: 225–254.

BROWNELL, R. L. (1964) 'Observations of odontocetes in central California waters'. *Norsk Hvalfangst Tidende 3*: 60–66.

BROWNELL, R. L. (1965) 'A record of the dusky dolphin from New Zealand'. *Norsk Hvalfangst Tidende 8*: 169–171.

BROWNELL, R. L. (1965) 'An anomolous colour pattern on a Pacific striped dolphin'. *Bull. S. Cal. Acad. Sci. 64*: 242–243.

BROWNELL, R. L. (1974) 'Small odontocetes of the Antarctic'. Antarctic Map Folio Series. Folio 18: 13–19.

BROWNELL, R. L. (1975) '*Phocoena dioptrica*'. Mammalian Species No. 66. American Society of Mammalogists.

BROWNELL, R. L. (1975) 'Progress report on the biology of the Franciscana dolphin in Uruguayan waters'. *J. Fish. Res. Board Can. 32*: 1073–1078.

BROWNELL, R. L. (1976) 'Status of the cochito in the Gulf of California'. FAO ACMRR.

BROWNELL, R. L. & BOICE, R. C. (1965) 'North Atlantic pilot whale with a triangular fin'. *Bull. S. Cal. Acad. Sci. 64*: 120–121.

BROWNELL, R. L. & HERALD, E. S. (1972) '*Lipotes vexillifer*'. Mammalian Species No. 10. American Society of Mammalogists.

BROWNELL, R. L. & NESS, R. (1970) 'Preliminary notes on the biology of the Franciscana'. *Proc. 6th Ann. Conf. Biol. Sonar and Diving Mamm.* 23–28.

BROWNELL, R. L. & PRADERI, R. (1976) 'Status of the Burmeister's porpoise ...' FAO ACMRR.

BROWNELL, R. L. & PRADERI, R. (1979) 'Taxonomy and distribution of Commerson's dolphin'. *Rep. Sci. Com. Int. Whaling Commn. 31*: SM23.

BRYDEN, M. M. et al (1977) 'Some aspects of the biology of *Peponocephala electra*'. *Aust. J. Mar. Freshwater Res. 28*: 703–715.

BUDKER, P. (1958) *Whales and Whaling*. Harrap: London.

BULLEN, F. T. (1899) *The Cruise of the Cachalot*. Appleton: New York.

BULLIS, H. R. & MOORE, J. C. (1956) 'Two occurrences of false killer whales ...' *Amer. Mus. Novitates* No. 1756.

BURMEISTER, H. (1865) 'Description of a new species of porpoise ...' *Proc. Zool. Soc. Lond.* 228–231.

BURT, W. H. (1952) *A Field Guide to the Mammals*. Houghton Mifflin Co.: Boston.

BURTON, R. (1973) *The Life and Death of Whales*. Deutsch: London.

BUSNEL, R-G. (ed.) (1966) *Animal Sonar Systems*. Lab. Phys. Acoustique. Juoy-en-Josas.

BUSNEL, R-G. (1966) 'Information on the human whistle language and sea mammal whistling'. In NORRIS.

BUSNEL, R-G. (1973) 'Symbiotic relationship between man and dolphins' *N.Y. Acad. Sci. 35*: 112–131.

BUSNEL, R-G. & DZIEDZIC, A. (1966) 'Acoustic signals of the pilot whale ...' In NORRIS.

CABRERA, A. (1960) 'Catalogo de los mamiferos de America del Sur'. *Rev. Mus. Arg. Cien. Nat. 4*: 309–731.

CABRERA, A. & YEPES, J. (1940) *Mamiferos Sud-Americanos*. Compania Argentina de Editores: Buenos Aires.

CADENAT, J. (1956) 'Un delphinid encore mal connu de la côte occidentale d'Afrique'. *Bull. IFAN 18*: 555–566.

CADENAT, J. (1959) 'Rapport sur les petits cetacés ouest-africains'. *Bull. IFAN 21*: 1367–1409.

CADENAT, J. & PARAISO, F. (1957) 'Nouvelle observation de *Sotalia* sur les côtes de Senegal'. *Bull. IFAN 19*: 324–332.

CALDWELL, D. K. & CALDWELL, M. C. (1966) 'Observations on the distribution, coloration, behavior and audible sound production of the spotted dolphin'. *Los Angeles County Mus. Contr. Sci. 104*: 1–28.

CALDWELL, D. K. & CALDWELL, M. C. (1971) 'Sounds produced by two rare cetaceans stranded in Florida'. *Cetology 4*: 1–6.

CALDWELL, D. K. & CALDWELL, M. C. (1972) *The World of the Bottlenose Dolphin*. Lippincott: Philadelphia.

CALDWELL, D. K. & CALDWELL, M. C. (1975) 'Dolphin and small whale fisheries of the Caribbean ...' *J. Fish. Res. Board Can. 32*: 1105–1110.

CALDWELL, D. K. & CALDWELL, M. C. (1973) 'Marine Mammals of the Eastern Gulf of Mexico'. In JONES et al.

CALDWELL, D. K. et al 'Production of pulsed sounds by the pygmy sperm whale'. *Bull. S. Cal. Acad. Sci. 65*: 245–248.

CALDWELL, D. K. et al (1971) 'Cetaceans from the Lesser Antillean Island of St. Vincent'. *Fish. Bull. 69*: 303–312.

CALDWELL, D. K. et al (1966) 'Behaviour of the sperm whale'. In NORRIS.

CALDWELL, D. K. et al (1976) 'First records for Fraser's dolphin in the Atlantic ...' *Cetology 25*: 1–4.

CALDWELL, D. K. et al (1971) 'Recent records of marine mammals from the coasts of Georgia and South Carolina'. *Cetology 5*: 1–12.

CALDWELL, M. C. & CALDWELL, D. K. (1964) 'Experimental studies on factors involved in care-giving behaviour ...' *Bull. S. Cal. Acad. Sci. 63*: 1–21.

CALDWELL, M. C. & CALDWELL, D. K. (1966) 'Epimeletic behaviour in cetacea'. In NORRIS.

CALDWELL, M. C. & CALDWELL, D. K. (1970) 'Statistical evidence for individual signature whistles in Pacific whiteside dolphin'. *Cetology 3*: 1–9.

CALDWELL, M. C. & CALDWELL, D. K. (1979) 'The whistle of the Atlantic bottlenose dolphin – ontogeny'. In WINN & OLLA.

CALDWELL, M. C. et al (1966) 'Sounds and behaviour of the Amazon freshwater dolphin'. *Contr. Sci. Los Angeles County Mus. 108*: 1–24.

CALDWELL, M. C. et al (1973) 'Statistical evidence for individual signature whistles in the spotted dolphin'. *Cetology 16*: 1–21.

CALDWELL, M. C. et al (1965) 'Observations on captive and wild Atlantic bottlenose dolphin ...' *Contr. Sci. Los Angeles County Mus. 91*: 4–9.

CARRIGHAR, S. (1978) *Blue Whale*. Gollancz: London.

CASPERS, H. (1957) 'Black Sea and Sea of Azov'. In HEDGPETH.

CHANDLER, R. et al (1977) 'Who is that killer whale?' *Pacific Search 11*: 25–35.

CHAPMAN, D. G. (1974) 'Estimation of population parameters of Antarctic baleen whales'. In SCHEVILL.

CHITTLEBOROUGH, R. G. (1953) 'Aerial observations on the humpback whale'. *Aust. J. Mar. Freshwater Res. 4*: 219–226.

CHITTLEBOROUGH, R. G. (1965) 'Dynamics of two populations of the humpback whale'. *Aust. J. Mar. Freshwater Res. 16*: 33–128.

CHRISTENSEN, I. (1976) 'The history of exploitation and the initial status of the North East Atlantic bottlenose whale'. FAO ACMRR.

CLARKE, M. R. (1976) 'Buoyancy control as a function of the spermaceti organ in the sperm whale'. *J. Mar. Biol. Ass.* (UK) *58*: 19–26.

CLARKE, M. R. (1979) 'The head of the sperm whale'. *Scientific American 240*: 106–117.

CLARKE, R. (1954) 'Open boat whaling in the Azores'. *Discovery Reports 26*.

CLARKE, R. (1962) 'Whale observations and whale marking off the coast of Chile ...' *Norsk Hvalfangst Tidende 51*: 265–287.

CLARKE, R. (1965) 'Southern right whales on the coast of Chile'. *Norsk Hvalfangst Tidende 54*: 121–128.

CLARKE, R. & AGUAYO, A. (1965) 'Bryde's whale in the south east Pacific'. *Norsk Hvalfangst Tidende 54*: 141–148.

CLARKE, R., MACLOED, N. & PALIZA, O. (1976) 'Cephalopod remains from the stomachs of sperm whales ...' *J. Zool. Lond. 180*: 477.

COPE, E. D. (1866) 'Third contribution to the history of the Balaenidae and Delphinidae'. *Proc. Acad. Nat. Sci. Phil. 18*: 293–300.

COUSTEAU, J. Y. (1963) *The Living Sea*. Harper & Row: New York.

COUSTEAU, J. Y. & DIOLE, P. (1972) *The Whale*. Doubleday: New York.

CUMMINGS, W. C. et al (1972) 'Sound production and other behaviour of southern right whales'. *San Diego. Soc. Nat. Hist. Trans. 17*: 1–14.

CUMMINGS, W. C. & THOMPSON, P. O. (1971) 'Underwater sounds from the blue whale'. *J.*

Acoust. Soc. An. 50: 1193–1198.
CURTIS, L. (1963) 'The Amazon dolphin at the Fort Worth Zoological Park'. *Inter. Zoo Yearbook 4*: 7–10.
CUVIER, G. (1812) 'Rapport fait a la classe des Sciences mathematiques et physiques ...' *Ann. Mus. d'Hist. Nat. Paris.* 19: 1–16.
CUVIER, G. (1823) *Recherches sur les ossements fossiles.* Casmir: Paris.
CUVIER, G. (1817–1829) *La Régne Animal.* Déterville & Crochard: Paris.
DALE (1732) *History and antiquities of Harwich and Dovercourt.* London.
DALL, W. H. (1873) 'Preliminary descriptions of three new species of cetacea from the coast of California'. *Proc. Calif. Acad. Sci. 5*: 12–13.
DALL, W. H. (1874) 'Catalogue of the cetacea of the North Pacific ...' In SCAMMONS.
DART, J. O. (1969) 'The whale with the spiralled tooth'. *Los Angeles Co. Mus. Nat. Hist. Quart.* 7: 22–27.
DAUGHERTY, A. E. (1965) *Marine Mammals of California.* Calif. Dept. of Fish & Game: Sacramento.
DAVIES, J. L. (1960) 'The southern form of the pilot whale'. *J. Mammal. 41*: 29–34.
DAVIES, J. L. (1963) *The Whales and Seals of Tasmania.* Tasmanian Museum and Art Gallery.
DAVIES, J. L. (1963) 'The antitropical factor in cetacean speciation'. *Evolution 17*: 107–116.
DAVIES, J. L. & GUILER, E. R. (1957) 'A note on the pygmy right whale'. *Proc. Zool. Soc. Lond. 129*: 579–589.
DAVIS, R. A. & FINLEY, K. J. (1979) 'Distribution, migrations, abundance and stock identity of eastern Arctic white whales'. *Sci. Comm. Rep. Intl. Whaling Commn. 31*: SM10.
DAWBIN, W. H. (1966) 'The seasonal migratory cycle of humpback whales'. In NORRIS.
DAWBIN, W. H. (1966) 'Porpoises and porpoise hunting in Malaita'. *Aust. Nat. Hist. 15*: 207–211.
DAWBIN, W. H. et al (1970) 'Observations on the electra dolphin'. *Bull. Brit. Mus. Nat. Hist. Zool. 20*: 173–201.
DAWSON, E. (1960) 'On a large catch of the finless black porpoise'. *J. Mar. Biol. Ass. India* 1: 259–260.
DERANIYAGALA, P. (1960) 'Some southern temperate zone snakes, birds and whales that enter the Ceylon area'. *Spolia Zeylanica 29*: 79–85.
DERANIYAGALA, P. (1963) 'Mass mortality of the new subspecies of little piked whale and a new beaked whale from Ceylon'. *Spolia Zeylanica 30*: 79–84.
DESMAREST, A. G. (1817) *Nouveau dictionaire d'Histoire Naturelle.* Deterville: Paris.
DESMOULINS, A. (1822) *Dictionaire Classique d'Histoire Naturelle.* Paris.
DEVINE, E. & CLARK, M. (ed.) (1967) *The Dolphin's Smile.* Macmillan: New York.
DEWHURST, H. W. (1834) *The Natural History of the Order Cetacea.* London.
DOBBS, H. E. (1977) *Follow a Wild Dolphin.* Souvenir: London.
DONNELLY, B. G. (1967) 'Observations on the mating behaviour of the southern right whale'. *S. Afr. J. Sci. 63*: 176–181.
DONNELLY, B. G. (1969) 'Further observations on the southern right whale'. *J. Reprod. Fert.*: 176–181

D'ORBIGNY, A. & GERVAIS, P. (1847) *Voyage Amerique Meridionale 4*: 32.
DREHER, J. J. (1961) 'Acoustics in dolphins'. *J. Acoustic. Soc. Amer. 33*: 1799–1800.
DREHER, J. J. (1966) 'Cetacean communication: small group experiment'. In NORRIS.
DUDLEY, P. (1725) 'An essay upon the natural history of whales'. *Phlios. Trans. Roy. Soc. Lond. 33*: 256–269.
DUGUY, R. (1968) 'Note sur *Globicephala macrorhyncha*'. *Mammalia 32*: 113–117.
DUGUY, R. (1974) 'Contribution a l'étude des mammiferes marins de la côte nord-ouest Afrique'. *Rev. Trav. Inst. Peches marit. 39*: 321–332.
DUGUY, R. & ROBINEAU, D. (1973) 'Cetacés et phoques des côtes de France'. *Ann. de la Societe des Sciences Naturelles de la Charente-Maritime. 9.*
DUGUY, R. & VAN BREE, P. J. H. (1968) 'Catalogue des Cetacés ...' *Ann. de la Societe des Sciences Naturelles de la Charente-Maritime. 4*: 1–27.
DULLES, F. R. (1933) *Lowered Boats.* Harcourt, Brace: New York.
DUNN, D. J. (ed.) (1978) 'The Humpback Whale'. *Waters 3*: 1–33.
DUVERNOY, G. L. (1851) 'Memoire sur les caracteres osteologiques ...' *Ann. Sci. Nat. Paris Zool. 3*: 1–72.
EARLE, S. A. (1979) 'Humpbacks: the gentle whales'. *Nat. Geographic 155*: 2–25.
EGEDE, H. (1742) *Des alten Grönlandes Naturell-historie.* Kopenhagen.
ELLERMAN, J. R. & MORRISON-SCOTT, T. C. S. (1951) 'Checklist of Palaearctic and Indian Mammals'. British Museum (Nat. Hist.): London.
ELLERMAN, J. R. et al (1953) 'Southern African Mammals'. British Museum (Nat. Hist.): London.
ERDMAN, D. S. (1962) 'Stranding of a beaked whale on the south coast of Puerto Rico'. *J. Mammal. 43*: 276–277.
ERICKSON, A. W. (1978) 'Population studies of killer whales in the Pacific Northwest ...' *Nat. Tech. Inf. Srv.* PB-285 615.
ERXLEBEN, J. (1777) *Systema Regnum Animale.*
ESCHRICHT, D. G. (1862) 'On the species of the genus *Orca*'. In FLOWER (1866).
ESSAPIAN, F. S. (1955) 'Speed-induced skin folds in the bottlenosed porpoise'. *Breviora 43*.
EVANS, P. G. H. *Guide to the Identification of Cetaceans in British Waters.* Mammal Society Publication.
EVANS, W. E. (1967) 'Vocalization among marine mammals'. In TAVOLGA.
EVANS, W. E. (1973) 'Echolocation by marine delphids and one species of freshwater dolphin'. *J. Acoust. Soc. Am. 54*: 191–199.
EVANS, W. E. (1974) 'Radio-telemetric studies of two species of small odontocete cetaceans'. In SCHEVILL.
EVANS, W. E. (ed.) (1974) 'The California Gray Whale'. *Marine Fisheries Review 36*: 1–64.
EVANS, W. E. & BASTIAN, J. (1969) 'Marine mammal communication: Social and ecological factors'. In ANDERSON.
EVANS, W. E. (1962) 'Observations on scouting behaviour ...' *Bull. S. Calif. Acad. Sci. 61*: 217–226.
EVANS, W. E. & POWELL, B. A. (1966)

'Discrimination of different metallic plates by an echolocating delphinid'. In BUSNEL.
EVANS, W. E. & PRESCOTT, J. H. (1962) 'Observations of the sound production capabilities of the bottlenosed porpoise ...' *Zoologica 47*: 121–128.
FABRICIUS (1780) *Fauna Groenlandica.*
FEHRING, W. K. & WELLS, R. S. (1976) 'A series of strandings by a single herd of pilot whales ...' *J. Mammal 57*: 191.
FEJER, A. A. & BACKUS, R. H. (1960) 'Porpoises and the bowriding of ships under way'. *Nature 188*: 700–703.
FERREIRA, A. R. (1791) *Viagem Filosofica.*
FISHER, H. D. & HARRISON, R. J. (1970) 'Reproduction in the common porpoise ...' *J. Zool. 161*: 471–486.
FISH, J. F. & VANIA, J. S. (1971) 'Killer whale sounds repel white whales'. *Fishery Bull. 69*: 531–535.
FISH, M. P. & MOWBRAY, W. H. (1962) 'Production of underwater sound by the white whale'. *Sears Found. J. Mar. Res. 20*: 149–162.
FITCH, J. E. & BROWNELL, R. L. (1968) 'Fish otoliths in cetacean stomachs and their importance in interpreting feeding habits'. *J. Fish. Res. Board Can. 25*: 2561–2574.
FITCH, J. E. & BROWNELL, R. L. (1971) 'Food habits of the Franciscana'. *Bull. Mar. Sci. 21*: 626–636.
FLOWER, W. H. (1866) *Recent memoirs on the cetacea by Professors Eschricht, Reinhardt and Lilljeborg.* Ray Society: London.
FLOWER, W. H. (1878) 'A further contribution to the knowledge of the existing ziphioid whales'. *Trans. Zool. Soc. Lond. 10*: 415–437.
FLOWER, W. H. (1882) 'On the cranium of a new species of *Hyperoodon* ...' *Proc. Zool. Soc. Lond.*: 392–396.
FLOWER, W. H. (1885) *List of the specimens of cetacea in the zoological department of the British Museum.* Taylor & Francis: London.
FODOR, B. (1971) 'The sperm whale: a bibliography'. *U.S. Dept. Int. Bibliog. Ser. No. 25.*
FORD, J. K. B. & FISHER, H. D. (1978) 'Underwater acoustic signals of the narwhal'. *Canad. J. Zool. 56*: 552–560.
FORSTER, J. G. A. (1779) *Observations made during a voyage around the world.* Robinson: London.
FORSTER, J. R. F. (trans) (1770) *KALM's Travels into North America.* Eyres: Warrington.
FRASER, F. C. (1934) *Report on Cetacea Stranded on the British Coasts ...* (1946); (1953); and (1974). British Museum (Nat. Hist.) Lond. Nos. 11–14.
FRASER, F. C. (1945) 'On a specimen of the southern bottlenose whale'. *Discovery Reports 23*: 19–36.
FRASER, F. C. (1949) 'A specimen of *Sotalia teuszii* from the coast of Senegal'. *J. Mammal. 30*: 274–276.
FRASER, F. C. (1950) 'Two skulls of *Globicephala macrorhyncha* from Dakar'. *Atlantide Report No. 1 Sci. Res. Danish Exped. Coasts Trop. W. Afr.* 49–60.
FRASER, F. C. (1950) 'Note on a skull of Hector's beaked whale'. *Proc. Linn. Soc. Lond. 162*: 50–52.
FRASER, F. C. (1955) 'A skull of *Mesoplodon gervaisi* from Trinidad, West Indies'. *Ann. Mag.*

Nat. Hist. 8: 624–630.

FRASER, F. C. (1955) 'The southern rightwhale dolphin'. *Bull. Brit. Mus. (Nat. Hist.) Zool. 2*: 750–758.

FRASER, F. C. (1956) 'A new Sarawak dolphin'. *Sarawak Mus. J. 7*: 478–503.

FRASER, F. C. (1958) 'Common or harbour porpoises from French West Africa'. *Bull. Inst. Français Afr. Noir* (Ser A) *20*: 276–285.

FRASER, F.C. (1966) 'Comments on the Delphinidea'. In NORRIS.

FRASER, F. C. (1966) 'Guide for the Identification and Reporting of Stranded Whales, Dolphins and Porpoises on the British Coasts'. *Brit. Mus. Nat. Hist. Lond.*

FRASER, F. C. (1968) 'Notes on a specimen of *Phocoena dioptrica* from South Georgia'. *Brit. Ant. Survey Bull. 16*: 51–56.

FRASER, F. C. (1976) *British Whales, Dolphins and Porpoises.* British Museum (Nat. Hist.) London.

FRASER, F. C. & NOBLE, B. A. (1970) 'Variation of pigmentation pattern in Meyen's dolphin'. Inv. on Cetacea *2*: 147–163.

FRASER, F. C. & PURVES, P. E. (1960) 'Hearing in cetaceans' *Bull. Brit. Mus. (Nat. Hist.) Zool. 7*: 1.

FRAZER, J. F. D. (1976) 'Herd structure and behaviour in cetaceans'. Mammal. Rev. *6*: 55–59.

FREMINVILLE, C. P. de (1830) 'Observations zoologiques faites pendant un voyage sur les côtes d'Afrique et du Bresil'. *Ann. Sci. Nat. 21*: 101–104.

FROST, P. G. H. & BEST, P. B. (1976) 'Design and application of a coded format for recording observations of cetaceans at sea'. *S. Afr. J. Ant. Res. 6*: 9–14.

FROSCH, R. A. (1964) 'Underwater sound: deep ocean propagation'. *Science 146*: 889–894.

GALBREATH, E. C. (1963) 'Three beaked whales stranded on the Midway Islands'. *J. Mammal. 44*: 422–423.

GAMBELL, R. (1976) 'World Whale stocks'. *Mammal. Rev. 6*: 41–53.

GASKIN, D. E. (1967) 'Luminescence in a squid and a possible feeding mechanism in the sperm whale'. *Tuatara 15*: 86–88.

GASKIN, D. E. (1968) 'Distribution of Delphinidae in relation to sea surface temperature ...' *New Zealand J. Mar. Freshwater Res. 2*: 52–534.

GASKIN, D. E. (1968) 'The New Zealand Cetacea'. *Fish. Res. Bull.* No. 1.

GASKIN, D. E. (1971) 'Distribution of beaked whales off southern New Zealand'. *New Zealand J. Marine Freshwater Res. 5*: 318–325.

GASKIN, D. E. (1972) *Whales Dolphins and Seals.* Heinemann: Auckland.

GASKIN, D. E. (1976) 'The evolution, zoogeography and ecology of cetacea'. *Oceanogr. Mar. Biol. Ann. Rev. 14*: 247–346.

GASKIN, D. E. et al (1974) '*Phocoena phocoena*'. *Mammalian Species* No. 42. American Society of Mammalogists.

GERVAIS, P. (1850) 'Memoire sur le famille des cetacés ziphioides'. *Ann. Sci. Nat. Paris. Zool. 14*: 5–17.

GERVAIS, P. (1853) 'Remarques sur les mammiferes marins qui frequentent les côtes de la France'. *Bull. Soc. Centrale d'Agric. Hérault 40*: 140–156.

GERVAIS, P. (1855) *Histoire Naturelle des Mammiferes.* Paris.

GERVAIS, P. (1855) *Zoologie et Palaentologie Françaises.* Paris.

GERVAIS, P. & D'ORBIGNY, M. A. (1844) 'Seance du 27 Avril'. *Bull. Soc. Philom.* 38–39.

GESNER, C. (1604) *Historiae Animalium,* Cambieri: Frankfurt.

GEWALT, W. (1976) *Der Weisswal.* Ziemsen Verlag: Wittenberg.

GIBSON-HILL, C. A. (1949) 'The whales, porpoises and dolphins known in Malayan waters'. *Malay. Nat. J. 4*: 44–61.

GIBSON-HILL, C. A. (1949–1951) 'The whales, porpoises and dolphins known in Sarawak waters'. *Sarawak Mus. J. 5*: 288–296.

GIHR, M. et al (1972) 'Meteorological influences on the daily feeding rate of the Indus dolphin in captivity'. *Inv. on Cetacea 4*: 33–43.

GIHR, M. & PILLERI, G. (1969) 'Hirn-Korpergewichts-Beziehungen bei Cetacean'. *Inv. on Cetacea 1*: 109–126.

GILL, T. N. (1865) 'On two species of Delphinidae from California in the Smithsonian Institution'. *Proc. Acad. Nat. Sci. Philadelphia 17*: 177–178.

GILMORE, R. M. (1959) 'On the mass strandings of sperm whales'. *Pacific Nat. 1*: 9–16.

GILMORE, R. M. (1961) *The Story of the Gray Whale.* Privately printed.

GOLLEY, F. B. (1966) *South Carolina Mammals.* Charleston Museum.

GOODALL, R. N. P. (1978) 'Report on the small cetaceans stranded on the coasts of Tierra del Fuego'. *Sci. Rep. Whales Res. Inst. 30*: 197–230.

GOODALL, R. N. P. (1979) 'Exploitation of small cetaceans off southern South America'. *Rep. Sci. Comm. Int. Whaling Comm. 31*: SM3.

GOODALL, R. N. P. & POLKINGHORN, J. T. (1979) 'Preliminary report on sightings of small cetaceans off Southern America ...' *Rep. Sci. Comm. Int. Whaling Comm. 31*: SM3.

GOODWIN, G. G. (1945) 'Record of a porpoise new to the Atlantic'. *J. Mammal. 26*: 195.

GOODWIN, G. G. (1953) 'Catalogue of the type specimens of recent mammals in the American Museum of Natural History'. *Bull. Am. Mus. Nat. Hist. 102*: 207–412.

GRAY, J. (1936) 'Studies in animal locomotion ...' *J. Exptl. Biol. 13*: 192–199.

GRAY, J. (1948) 'Aspects of the locomotion of whales'. *Nature 161*: 199–200.

GRAY, J. E. (1827) 'Description of the skulls of two apparently undiscovered species of dolphins ...' *Phil. Mag. Annals 2*: 376.

GRAY, J. E. (1828) *Spicilegia Zoologica.* Treutel: London.

GRAY, J. E. (1846) 'The zoology of the voyage of H. M. S. Erebus and Terror' ... In RICHARDSON & GRAY.

GRAY, J. E. (1849) 'Descriptions of three new species of Delphinidae'. *Proc. Zool. Soc. Lond.*: 1–3.

GRAY, J. E. (1856) 'Description of a new species of dolphin from the upper parts of the River Amazon'. *Ann. Mag. Nat. Hist. 18*: 157–159.

GRAY, J. E. (1864) 'On the cetacea which have been observed in the seas surrounding the British Islands'. *Proc. Zool. Soc. Lond.*: 195–248.

GRAY, J. E. (1865) 'Notes on the whales of the Cape, with descriptions of two new species'. *Proc. Zool. Soc. Lond.*: 357–359.

GRAY, J. E. (1866) *Catalogue of seals and whales in the British Museum.* London.

GRAY, J. E. (1870) 'The geographical distribution of the cetacea'. *Ann. Mag. Nat. Hist. 35*: 387–394.

GRAY, J. E. (1871) 'Notes on the *Berardius* of New Zealand'. *Ann. Mag. Nat. Hist. 8*: 117.

GRAY, J. E. (1871) *Supplement to the catalogue of whales and seals in the British Museum.* London.

GRAY, J. E. (1874) 'Description of the skull of a new species of dolphin'. *Ann. Mag. Nat. Hist. 14*: 238–239.

GRAY, J. E. (1875) '*Feresa attenuata*' *J. Mus. Godeffroy* (Hamburg) *8*: 184.

GRAY, W. B. (1964) *Porpoise Tales.* Barnes: NY.

GRAYCE, R. L. (1957) 'Key to the marine mammals of New England'. *Mass. Audobon Soc. Bull. 41*: 417–419.

GREENDALE, R. G. & BROUSSEAU-GREENDALE, C. (1976) 'Observations of marine mammal migrations ...' *Fish. Mar. Serv. Res. Dev. Tech. Rep. 680*: 25.

GUILER, E. R. (1978) 'Whale strandings in Tasmania since 1945'. *Pap. Proc. Roy. Soc. Tasmania 112*: 189–213.

GULLAND, J. (1972) 'Future of the blue whale'. *New Scientist 54*: 198–199.

GULLAND, J. A. (1974) 'Distribution and abundance of whales in relation to basic productivity'. In SCHEVILL.

GUNTHER, A. E. *A Century of Zoology at the British Museum.* Privately published.

GUREVICH, V. S. (1979) 'Worldwide distribution and migration patterns of the white whale'. *Rep. Sci. Comt. Intl. Whaling Comm. 31*: SM14.

HAAN, F. W. R. de (1966) 'Listening underwater ...' In NORRIS.

HALE, H. M. (1962) 'Occurrence of the whale *Berardius arnuxii* in southern Australia'. *Rec. So. Aust. Mus. 14*: 231–243.

HALE, H. M. (1964) 'The pygmy right whale in Australia'. *Rec. So. Aust. Mus. 14*: 679.

HALEY, D. (ed.) (1978) *Marine Mammals.* Pacific Search Press: Seattle.

HALL, J. (1970) 'Conditioning Pacific white-striped dolphins for open-ocean release'. *NUC Tech. Pub.* No. 200.

HAMILTON, J. E. (1941) 'A rare porpoise of the South Atlantic'. *Discovery Reports 21*: 227–234.

HAMILTON, J. E. (1952) 'Cetacea of the Falkland Islands'. *Comm. Zool. Mus. de Hist. Nat. de Montevideo 4*: 1–6.

HAMILTON, R. (1843) *The Naturalists Library — Volume Six.* Lizars: Edinburgh.

HANCOCK, J. (1965) 'Killer whales kill and eat a minke whale'. *J. Mammal. 46*: 341.

HANDLEY, C. O. (1966) 'A synopsis of the genus *Kogia*'. In NORRIS.

HAQUE, A. K. M. A. et al (1977) 'Observations on the behaviour and other biological aspects of the Ganges susu'. *Sci. Rep. Whales Res. Inst. 29*: 87–94.

HARMER, S. F. (1922) 'On Commerson's dolphin and other species of *Cephalorhynchus*'. *Proc. Zool. Soc. Lond.*: 627–638.

HARMER, S. F. (1927) *Report on cetacea stranded on the British Coasts* ... British Museum (Nat. Hist.) No. 10.

HARRISON, R. J. (1972) *Functional anatomy of Marine Mammals.* Academic Press: London.

HARRISSON, T. (1960) 'South China Sea dolphins'. *Malay. Nat. J. 14*: 87–89.

HART, T. J. (1935) 'On the diatoms of the skin film of whales ...' *Discovery Reports 10*: 247–282.

HAWLEY, F. (1958–1960). *Whales and Whaling in Japan*. Kawakita: Kyoto.

HAYES, W. D. (1953) 'Wave riding of dolphins'. *Nature 172*: 1060

HAYES, W. D. (1959) 'Wave-riding dolphins'. *Science 130*: 1657–1658.

HECTOR, J. (1873) 'On the waves and dolphins of the New Zealand seas'. *Trans. New Zealand Inst. 5*: 153–170.

HECTOR, J. (1878) 'Notes on the whales of the New Zealand seas'. *Trans. Proc. New Zealand Inst. 10*: 331–343.

HEDGPETH, J. W. (1957) 'Treatise on Marine Ecology and Palaeocology'.

HEEZEN, B. C. (1957) 'Whales entangled in deep sea cables'. *Deep Sea Research 4*: 105–115.

HENDERSON, D. A. (1972) *Men and Whales at Scammon's Lagoon*. Dawsons: Los Angeles.

HERALD, E. S. (1967) 'Bouto and Tokashee – Amazon dolphins'. *Pacific Discovery 20*: 2–9.

HERALD, E. S. (1969) *Field and aquarium study of the blind river dolphin*. Steinhart Aquarium: San Francisco.

HERMAN, L. M. & ANTINOJA, R. C. (1977) 'Humpback whales in the Hawaiian breeding waters'. *Sci. Rep. Whales Res. Inst. 29*: 59–85.

HERMAN, L. M. & ARBEIT, W. R. (1973) 'Stimulus control and auditory discrimination learning sets in the bottlenose dolphin'. *J. Expt. Anal. Behav. 19*: 379–394.

HERSHKOVITZ, P. (1966) 'Catalog of Living Whales'. *Bull. U.S. Mus. Smithsonian Inst. 246*: 1–259.

HERTEL, H. (1969) 'Hydrodynamics of swimming and wave-riding dolphins'. In ANDERSON.

HESTER, F. J. et al (1963) 'Jumping and spinning behaviour in the spinner porpoise'. *J. Mammal. 44*: 586–588.

HINTON, M. A. C. (1925) *Report on the papers left by the late Major Barrett-Hamilton ...* Crown Agents: London.

HINTON, M. A. C. & PYCRAFT, W. P. (1922) 'Preliminary note on the affinities of the genus *Lipotes*.' *Amer. Mag. Nat. Hist. 10*: 232–234.

HOESE, H. D. (1971) 'Dolphin feeding out of water in a salt marsh'. *J. Mammal. 52*: 222–223.

HOLLOWAY, C. W. (1974) *A note on the current status of the Indus River dolphin*. Management of Wildlife in Sind: IUCN.

HOLM, J. L. & JONSGARD, A. (1959) 'Occurrence of the sperm whale in the Antarctic and the possible influence of the moon'. *Norsk Hvalfangst Tidende 4*: 161–182.

HOUCK, W. J. (1976) 'The taxonomic status of the species of the genus *Phocoenoides*'. FAO ACMRR No. 114.

HOUSBY, T. (1971) *The Hand of God*. Abelard-Schuman: London.

HOY, C. M. (1923) 'The white flag dolphin of the Tung Ting lake'. *China J. Arts. Sci. Shanghai 1*: 154–157.

HUBBS, C. L. (1946) 'First records of two beaked whales from the Pacific Coast of the United States'. *J. Mammal. 27*: 242–255.

HUBBS, C. L. (1953) 'Dolphin protecting dead young'. *J. Mammal. 34*: 498.

HUBBS, C. L. (1954) 'Natural history of the gray whale'. *Proc. 15th Int. Congr. Zool.* (Sect 3): 313–316.

HUNTER, J. (1787) 'Observations on the structure and oeconomy of whales'. *Phil. Trans. Roy. Soc. 77*: 371–450.

HUSSON, A. M. & HOLTHUIS, L. B. (1974) 'The valid name for the sperm whale'. *Zool. Med. 48*: 205–217.

ICHIHARA, T. (1963) 'Identification of pygmy blue whale in the Antarctic'. *Norsk Hvalfangst Tidende 5*: 128–130.

ICHIHARA, T. (1966) 'The pygmy blue whale, a new species from the Antarctic'. In NORRIS.

INTERNATIONAL CODE OF ZOOLOGICAL NOMENCLATURE – adopted by the XV International Congress of Zoology, London July 1958. Revised, London 1964.

IREDALE, T. & TROUGHTON, E. le G. (1933) 'The correct generic name for the grampus or killer whale ...' *Rec. Aust. Mus. 19*: 28–36.

IREDALE, T. & TROUGHTON, E. le G. (1934) 'A checklist of the mammals recorded from Australia'. *Mem. Aust. Mus. 6*: 1–122.

IVASHIN, M. V. (1972) 'Kalikovyi gladkii kit'. *Zool. Zh. 51*: 1715–1723.

JAMES, P. et al (1970) 'First western Atlantic occurrence of the pygmy killer whale'. *Fieldiana: Zool. Field. Mus. Nat. Hist. 58*: 1–3.

JOENSEN, J. P (1976) 'Pilot whaling in the Faeroe Islands'. *Ethnol. Scandinavica*: 1–42.

JOHNSON, D. H. (1964) 'Mammals of the Arnhem Land Expedition'. *Rec. American-Australian Sci. Exped. Arnhem Land 4*: 426–515.

JONES, J. I. et al (1973) 'A summary of knowledge of the eastern Gulf of Mexico'. *State Univ. Syst. Fla. Inst. Oceanogr.*

JONSGARD, A. (1961) 'Studies on the little piked whale or minke whale'. *Norsk Hvalfangst Tidende 5*: 1.

JONSGARD, A. (1966) 'Biology of the North Atlantic fin whale'. *Hvalradets Skrifter 49*: 5–62.

JONSGARD, A. (1966) 'The distribution of Balaenopteridae in the North Atlantic Ocean'. In NORRIS.

JONSGARD, A. (1968) 'A review of Norwegian biological research on whales in the northern North Atlantic. *Hvalfangst Tidende 37*: 164–167.

JONSGARD, A. & NORDLI, O. (1952) 'Concerning a catch of white-sided dolphins on the west coast of Norway'. *Hvalfangst Tidende 41*: 229–232.

KALM, P. (1770) 'Travels into North America'. In FORSTER.

KASUYA, T. (1972) 'Some informations on the growth of the Ganges Dolphin ...' *Sci. Rep. Whales. Res. Inst. 24*: 57–108.

KASUYA, T. (1973) 'Systematic consideration of recent toothed whales based on the morphology of tympano-periotic bone'. *Sci. Rep. Whales Res. Inst. 25*: 1–103.

KASUYA, T. (1977) 'Age determination and growth of Baird's beaked whale'. *Sci. Rep. Whales Res. Inst. 29*: 1–20.

KASUYA, T. (1978) 'The life history of Dall's porpoise ...' *Sci. Rep. Whales Res. Inst. 30*: 1–63.

KASUYA, T. & ICHIHARA, T. (1965) 'Some informations on minke whales ...' *Sci. Rep. Whales Res. Inst. 19*: 37–43.

KASUYA, T. & MIYAZAKI, N. (1976) 'An observation of epimeletic behaviour of *Lagenorhynchus obliquidens*'. *Sci. Rep. Whales Res. Inst. 28*: 141–143.

KASUYA, T. et al (1974) 'Growth and reproduction of *Stenella attenuata* ...' *Sci. Rep. Whales Res. Inst. 26*: 157–226.

KASUYA, T. & NISHIWAKI, M. (1971) 'First record of *Mesoplodon densirostris* ...' *Sci. Rep. Whales Res. Inst. 23*: 129–137.

KASUYA, T. & NISHIWAKI, M. (1975) 'Recent status of the population of the Indus dolphin'. *Sci. Rep. Whales Res. Inst. 27*: 81–94.

KASUYA, T. & RICE, D. W. (1970) 'Notes on baleen plates and on arrangement of parasitic barnacles of gray whale'. *Sci. Rep. Whales Res. Inst. 22*: 39.

KATONA, S. et al (1975) *A Field Guide to the Whales and Seals of the Gulf of Maine*. Privately published.

KATONA, S. et al (1979) *Identification of humpback whales by fluke photographs*. Privately published.

KAWAMURA, A. (1974) 'Food and feeding ecology in the southern sei whale'. *Sci. Rep. Whales. Res. Inst. 26*: 25.

KELLOGG, R. (1928) 'The history of whales ...' *Quart Rev. Biol. 3*: 29–76 and 174–208.

KELLOGG, R. (1932) 'New names for mammals proposed by Borowski in 1780–1781'. *Proc. Biol. Soc. Washington 45*: 148.

KELLOGG, R. (1940) 'Whales: Giants of the sea'. *Nat. Geographic 77*: 35–90.

KELLOGG, R. (1941) 'On the identity of the porpoise *Sagmatius amblodon*'. *Field. Mus. Nat. Hist. 27*: 293–311.

KELLOGG, W. (1961) *Porpoises and Sonar*. Univ. of Chicago Press: Chicago.

KELLOGG, W. & RICE, C. (1964) 'Visual problem-solving in a bottlenose dolphin'. *Science 143*: 1052–1055.

KELLOGG, W. & RICE, C. (1966) 'Visual discrimination and problem solving in a bottlenose dolphin'. In NORRIS.

KEMPER, B. (1979) 'History of use of narwhal and beluga ...' *Rep. Sci. Comm. Int. Whaling. Comm.* SC 31 SM 16.

KENYON, K. (ed.) (1971) *Reports of Standing Committee on Marine Mammals*. American Society of Mammalogists.

KIMURA, M. & PERRIN, W. F. (1976) 'Progress report on studies of the biology of the striped dolphin ...' *Southwest Fish. Centre Ad. Rep.* LJ-76-11

KLEINENBERG, S. E. (1978) 'Mammals of the Black Sea and the Sea of Azov'. *Dept. Env. Fish. Mar. Serv. Div. Trans. Series* No. 4319.

KLEINENBERG, S. E. (1969) *Beluga: investigation of the species*. Israel Program for Sci. Tran.

KORNERUP, A. & WANSCHER, J. H. (1978) *Methuen Handbook of Colour*. Eyre Methuen: London.

KRAMER, M. (1961) 'The dolphin's secret'. *J. Amer. Soc. Nav. Eng. 73*: 103–107.

KRITZLER, H. (1952) 'Observations on the pilot whale in captivity'. *J. Mammal. 33*: 321–324.

KRUGER, L. (1966) 'Specialized features of the cetacean brain'. In NORRIS.

KÜKENTHAL, W. (1892) '*Sotalia teuszii* – ein pflanzenfressenden delphin aus Kamerun'. *Zool. Jahrb. Syst. 6*: 442–446.

LACÉPÈDE, B. G. (1804) *Histoire Naturelle des Cetacés*. Paris.

LAHILLE, F. (1903) *Las ballenas de nuestros mares*. Escula Naval Militar: Buenos Aires.
LAHILLE, F. (1908) 'Nota sobre un delfin'. *Ann. Mus. Nac. Buenos Aires 16*: 348–365.
LAHILLE, F. (1912) 'Nota preliminar sobre una nueva especie de Marsopa del Rio dela Plata'. *Anal. Mus. Nac. Hist. Buenos Aires 23*: 269.
LAMB, F. B. (1954) 'The fisherman's porpoise'. *Nat. Hist. 53*: 231–232.
LANG, T. G. (1966) 'Hydrodynamic analysis of cetacean performance'. In NORRIS.
LANG, T. (1966) 'Hydrodynamic analysis of dolphin fin profiles'. *Nature 209*: 1110–1111.
LANG, T. G. & NORRIS, K. S. (1966) 'Swimming speed of a Pacific bottlenose porpoise'. *Science 151*: 588–590.
LANG, T. G. & PRYOR, K. (1966) 'Hydrodynamic performance of porpoises'. *Science 152*: 531–533.
LANG, T. G. & SMITH, H. A. P. (1965) 'Communication between dolphins in separate tanks by an acoustic link'. *Science 150*: 1839–1843.
LANTZ, A. W. & GUNASEKERA, C. (1955) 'Commercial utilization of dolphins in Ceylon'. *Dept. Fish. Ceylon Bull. 3*: 1–14.
LATTIN, G. de (1967) *Grundriss der Zoogeographie*. Fischer: Jena.
LAWS, R. (1961) 'Reproduction, growth and age of southern fin whales'. *Discovery Reports 31*: 327–486.
LAYNE, J. N. (1958) 'Observations on freshwater dolphins in the upper Amazon'. *J. Mammal. 39*: 1–22.
LAYNE, J. N. (1965) 'Observations on marine mammals in Florida waters'. *Bull. Fla. State Mus. Biol. Sci. 9*: 131–181.
LAYNE, J. N. & CALDWELL, M. C. (1964) 'Behaviour of the Amazon dolphin in captivity'. *Zoologica 49*: 81–108.
LEATHERWOOD, S. et al (1976) 'Whales, dolphins and porpoises of the western North Atlantic'. *NOAA Technical Rep.* NMFS CIRC-396.
LEATHERWOOD, S. & EVANS, W. E. (1979) 'Some recent uses of potentials of radiotelemetry in field studies of cetaceans'. In WINN & OLLA.
LEATHERWOOD, S. et al (1972) 'The whales, dolphins and porpoises of the eastern North Pacific'. *Nav. Underseas Cent. Tech. Pub.* 282.
LEATHERWOOD, S. & WALKER, W. A. (1976) 'The northern rightwhale dolphin'. FAO ACMRR.
LEATHERWOOD, S. & WALKER, W. A. (1979) 'The northern rightwhale dolphin in the eastern north Pacific'. In WINN & OLLA.
LEBECK, H. J. (1801) *Delphinus gangeticus beschrieben ...' Neue Schr. Ges. Naturf. Freunde* (Berlin) 3: 280–282.
LESSON, R. P. (1826) 'Indications de quelques Cetacés nouveau ...' *Ferussacs Bull. Sci. Nat. Geol. 7*: 373–374.
LESSON, R. P. (1828) *Complements des oeuvres de Buffon ou histoire naturelle des animaux rares*. Paris.
LEUNG, Y. M. (1965) 'A collection of whale lice'. *Bull. So. Calif. Acad. Sci. 64*: 132–143.
LEUNG, Y. M. (1967) 'An illustrated key to the species of whale lice'. *Crustaceana 12*: 279–291.
LEUNG, Y. M. (1970) '*Syncyamus* from the western Mediterranean'. *Inv. on Cetacea 2*: 243–247.
LIEN, J. & MERDSOY, B. (1979) 'The humpback is not over the hump'. *Nat. Hist.*: 46–49.

LILLJEBORG, W. (1861) In FLOWER (1866).
LILLY, J. C. (1961) *Man and Dolphin*. Doubleday: New York.
LILLY, J. C. (1962) 'Vocal behaviour of the bottlenose dolphin'. *Proc. Amer. Phil. Soc. 106*: 520–529.
LILLY, J. C. (1962) 'Interspecies Communication'. McGraw Hill Yearbook.
LILLY, J. C. (1963) 'Productive and creative research with man and dolphin'. *Arch. of Gen. Psychiatry 8*: 111–116.
LILLY, J. C. (1963) 'Distress call of the bottlenose dolphin ...' *Science 139*: 116–118.
LILLY, J. C. (1963) 'Modern whales, dolphins and porpoises as challenges to our intelligence'. In MONTAGU & LILLY.
LILLY, J. (1963) 'Critical brain size and language'. *Persp. Biol. and Med. 6*: 246–253.
LILLY, J. C. (1964) 'Animals in aquatic environments: adaptation of mammals to the ocean'. Handbook of Physiology and Environment.
LILLY, J. C. (1965) 'Vocal mimicry in *Tursiops*: ability to match numbers and durations of human vocal bursts'. *Science 147*: 300–301.
LILLY, J. C. (1966) 'Sonic-ultrasonic emissions of the bottlenose dolphin'. In NORRIS.
LILLY, J. C. (1967) *The Mind of the Dolphin*. Doubleday, New York.
LILLY, J. C. et al (1968) 'Reprogramming of the sonic output of the dolphin: sonic burst count matching'. *J. Acoust. Soc. Amer. 43*: 1412–1424.
LILLY, J. C. & MILLER, A. (1961) 'Sounds emitted by the bottlenose dolphin'. *Science 133*: 1689–1693.
LILLY, J. C. & MILLER, A. (1961) 'Vocal exchanges between dolphins'. *Science 134*: 1873–1876.
LINDEN, E. (1975) *Apes, Men, and Language*. Dutton: New York.
LINNAEUS, C. (1758) *Systema Naturae*. (Tenth edition) Stockholm.
LLOZE, R. (1973) 'Contributions a l'étude anatomique, histologique et biologique del' *Orcaella brevirostris* du Mekong'. Thesis: Univ. Toulouse.
LOCKLEY, R. M. (1979) *Whales, Dolphins and Porpoises*. David & Charles: London.
LOCKYER, C. (1977) *A voyage of discovery*. Pergamon Press: Oxford.
LOCKYER, C. (1978) 'The history and behaviour of a solitary wild, but sociable, bottlenose dolphin ...' *J. Nat. Hist.*
LOCKYER, C. et al (1978) 'Some field observations and experiments on a bottlenosed dolphin'. *Progress in Underwater Science 3*: 177–190.
LONGMAN, H. A. (1926) 'New records of cetacea'. *Mem. Queensland Mus. 8*: 266–278.
LONNBERG, E. (1934) 'A new dolphin from the Pacific coast of Mexico'. *Arkiv. für Zool. 26*: 1–11.
LOWERY, G. H. (1974) *The Mammals of Louisiana ...* Louisiana State Univ. Press.
LYDEKKER, R. (1901) 'Notice of an apparently new estuarine dolphin from Borneo'. *Proc. Zool. Soc. Lond.*: 88–91.
LYDEKKER, R. (1903) 'Notes on the Trivandrum cetaceans'. *J. Bombay Nat. Hist. Soc. 15*: 40–41.
LYDEKKER, R. (1909) 'On an Indian dolphin and porpoise'. *Proc. Zool. Soc. Lond.*: 802–808.
McBRIDE, A. & HEBB, D. O. (1948) 'Behavior of the

captive bottlenose dolphin' *J. Comp. & Physiol. Psychol. 41*: 111–123.
McBRIDE, A. F. & KRITZLER, H. (1951) 'Observations on pregnancy, parturition, and post natal behaviour in the bottlenose dolphin'. *J. Mammal. 32*: 251–266.
McCANN, C. (1962) 'The occurrence of the southern bottlenose whale in New Zealand waters'. *Rec. Dom. Mus. Wellington 4*: 25–27.
McCANN, C. (1962) 'The taxonomic status of the beaked whale *Mesoplodon hectori*'. *Rec. Dom. Mus. Wellington 4*: 83–94.
McCANN, C. (1962) 'The taxonomic status of the beaked whale *Mesoplodon pacificus*'. *Rec. Dom. Mus. Wellington 4*: 95–100.
McCANN, C. (1963) 'Occurrence of Blainville's beaked whale in the Indian Ocean'. *J. Bombay Nat. Hist. Soc. 60*: 727–730.
McCANN, C. (1964) 'A coincidental distributional pattern of some of the larger marine mammals'. *Tuatara 12*: 119–124.
McCANN, C. (1964) 'A further record of Blainvilles beaked whale from the Indian Ocean'. *J. Bombay Nat. Hist. Soc. 61*: 179–180.
McCANN, C. (1964) 'The female reproductive organs of Layards beaked whale'. *Rec. Dom. Mus. Wellington 4*: 311–316.
McCANN, C. (1974) 'Body scarring on cetacea'. *Sci. Rep. Whales Res. Inst. 26*: 145–155.
McCANN, C. (1975) 'A study of the genus *Berardius*'. *Sci. Rep. Whales Res. Inst. 27*: 111–137.
McCANN, C. & TALBOT, P. H. (1963) 'The occurrence of Trues beaked whale in South African waters ...' *Proc. Linn. Soc. Lond. 175*: 137–144.
MACKINTOSH, N. A. (1965) *The Stocks of Whales*. Fishing News: London.
MACKINTOSH, N. A. (1966) 'The distribution of southern blue and fin whales'. In NORRIS.
MACKINTOSH, N. A. (1966) 'Observations on whales from ships'. *Marine Observer 22*: 87–90.
MACKINTOSH, N. A. & WHEELER, J. F. G. (1929) 'Southern blue and fin whales'. *Discovery Report 1*: 257–540.
McINTYRE, J. (1974) *Mind in the Waters*. Scribners: New York.
McLACHLAN, G. R. et al (1966) 'A record of *Berardius arnouxi* from the south east coast of South Africa'. *Ann. Cape Prov. Mus. 5*: 91–109.
McNALLY, R. (1977) 'Echolocation: cetaceans sixth sense'. *Oceans 10*: 27–33.
McNULTY, F. (1973) *The Great Whales*. Doubleday: New York.
McNULTY, F. (1975) *Whales: their life in the sea*. Harper & Row: New York.
MAGNOLIA, L. R. (1977) 'Whales, whaling and whale research: a selected bibliography'. *Spec. Lit. Surv.* 52 TRW Systems California.
MAIGRET, J. et al (1976) 'Observations de cetacés sur les côtes de Mauritanie'. *IFAN* No. 4.
MANSFIELD, A. W. (1971) 'Occurrence of the bowhead in Canadian Arctic waters'. *J. Fish. Res. Board. Can. 28*: 1873–1875.
MANSFIELD, A. W. et al (1975) 'The narwhal in eastern Canadian waters'. *J. Fish. Res. Board Can. 32*: 1041–1046.
MARINE MAMMAL COMMISSION (1976) 'Marine Mammal Names'. Washington DC.
MARTENS, F. (1675) *Spitzbergische oder Grönlandische Reise Beschreibung gethan im Jahr 1671*. Hamburg.

MARTIN, H. B. et al (1971) 'Methods for radio tracking marine mammals in the open sea'. *Proc. IEEE Conf. Eng. Ocean Env.*: 44–49.

MARTIN, R. M. (1977) *Mammals of the Seas*. Batsford: London.

MATTHEWS, L. H. (1937) 'The humpback whale'. *Discovery Reports 17*: 7–92.

MATTHEWS, L. H. (1938) 'The sei whale'. *Discovery Reports 17*: 183–290.

MATTHEWS, L. H. (1938) 'The sperm whale'. *Discovery Reports 17*: 113–168.

MATTHEWS, L. H. (1978) *The Natural History of the Whale*. Weidenfeld: London.

MAURY, M. F. (1852) 'Explanations and sailing directions to accompany the wind and current charts . . .' Secretary of US Navy: Washington.

MAYR, E. (1969) *Principles of Systematic Zoology*. McGraw Hill: New York.

MEAD, J. (1962) *Killers of Eden*. Angus & Robertson: London.

MEAD, J. & PAYNE, R. (1975) 'A specimen of the Tasman beaked whale from Argentina'. *J. Mammal. 56*: 213–218.

MEYEN, F. J. F. (1833) 'Beitrage zur Zoologie . . .' *Nova Acta Acad. Cesareae Nat. Curios. 16*: 549–610.

MILLER, G. S. (1918) 'A new river dolphin from China'. *Smithsonian Misc. Coll. 68*: 1–12.

MILLER, G. S. & KELLOGG, R. (1955) 'List of North American Recent Mammals'. *Bull. U.S. Nat. Mus. 205*: 1–954.

MILLER, T. (1975) 'The World of the California Gray Whale' Baja Trail.

MITCHELL, E. D. (1968) 'Northeast Pacific stranding, distribution and seasonality of Cuviers beaked whale'. *Can. J. Zool. 46*: 265–279.

MITCHELL, E. D. (1970) 'Pigmentation pattern evolution in delphinid cetaceans: an essay in adaptive coloration'. *Can. J. Zool. 48*: 717–740.

MITCHELL, E. D. (1972) 'Whale pigmentation and feeding behaviour'. *Amer. Zool. 12*: 60.

MITCHELL, E. D. (1973) 'The status of the world's whales'. *Nat. Can. 2*: 9–25.

MITCHELL, E. D. (1974) 'Trophic relationships and competition for food in northwest Atlantic waters'. *Proc. Can. Soc. Zool. Ann. Meeting*.

MITCHELL, E. D. (1974) 'Present status of northwest Atlantic fin and other whale stocks'. IN SCHEVILL.

MITCHELL, E. (1975) 'Porpoise, dolphin and small whale fisheries of the world'. *IUCN Monograph* No. 3.

MITCHELL, E. D. & KOZICKI, V. M. (1975) 'Autumn stranding of a northern bottlenose whale . . .' *J. Fish. Res. Board Can. 32*: 1019–1040.

MIYAZAKI, N. (1976) 'School structure of *Stenella coeruleoalba*'. FAO ACMRR.

MIYAZAKI, N. & WADA, S. (1978) 'Frasers dolphin in the western north Pacific'. *Sci. Rep. Whales Res. Inst. 30*: 231–244.

MIZUE, K. et al (1971) 'The underwater sound of the Ganges river dolphin'. *Sci. Rep. Whales Res. Inst. 23*: 123–128.

MIZUE, K. et al (1968) 'Underwater sound of the Chinese finless porpoise . . .' *Bull. Fac. Fish. Nagasaki Univ. 25*: 26–32.

MIZUE, K. & YOSHIDA, K. (1961) 'Studies on the little toothed whales in the west sea area of Kyushu'. *Bull. Fac. Fish. Nagasaki Univ. 11*: 33–48.

MIZUE, K. et al (1966) 'On the ecology of the Dalls porpoise . . .' *Bull. Fac. Fish. Nagasaki Univ. 19*: 1–36.

MOHL, B. et al (1976) 'Sperm whale size determination'. FAO ACMRR.

MONTAGU, A. & LILLY, J. C. (1963) *The Dolphin in History*. Univ. of Calif.

MONTAGU, G. (1821) 'Description of a species of *Delphinus* which appears to be new'. *Mem. Wernerian Nat. Hist. Soc. 3*: 75–82.

MOORE, J. C. (1953) 'Distribution of marine mammals in Florida waters'. *Am. Midl. Nat. 49*: 117–158.

MOORE, J. C. (1958) 'A beaked whale from the Bahama Islands . . .' *Am. Mus. Novitates* No. 1897: 1–12.

MOORE, J. C. (1960) 'New records of the Gulfstream beaked whale'. *Am. Mus. Novitates* No. 1993: 1–35.

MOORE, J. C. (1963) 'Recognizing certain species of beaked whales of the Pacific Ocean'. *Am. Midl. Nat. 70*: 396–428.

MOORE, J. C. (1966) 'Diagnoses and distributions of beaked whales of the genus *Mesoplodon* . . .' In NORRIS.

MOORE, J. C. (1968) 'Relationships among the living genera of beaked whales'. *Fieldiana*: Zool. 53: 209–298.

MOORE, J.C. (1972) 'More skull characters of the beaked whale'. *Fieldiana*: Zool. 62: 1–19.

MOORE, J. C. & GILMORE, R. M. (1965) 'A beaked whale new to the western hemisphere'. *Nature 205*: 1239–1240.

MOORE, J. C. & PALMER, R. S. (1955) 'More piked whales from the southern north Atlantic'. *J. Mammal. 36*: 262–433.

MOORE, J. C. & WOOD, F. G. (1957) 'Differences between the beaked whales – *Mesoplodon mirus* and *Mesoplodon gervaisi*'. *Am. Mus. Novitates* No. 1831: 1–25.

MOREJOHN, G. V. (1979) 'The natural history of Dall's porpoise in the North Pacific Ocean'. In WINN & OLLA.

MORGAN, D. W. (1979) 'The vocal and behavioral reactions of the beluga to playback of its sounds'. In WINN & OLLA.

MOROZOV, D. A. (1970) 'Dolphins hunting'. NOAA translation.

MÖRZER BRUYNS, W. F. J. (1960) 'The ridge-backed dolphin of the Indian Ocean'. *Malay. Nat. J. 14*: 159–165.

MÖRZER BRUYNS, W. F. J. (1966) 'Some notes on the Irrawaddi Dolphin'. *Zeit. Saugetierk. 31*: 267–320 and 33: 106–107.

MÖRZER BRUYNS, W. F. J. (1969) 'Sight records and notes on false killer whales'. *Saug. Mitt. 17*: 351–356.

MÖRZER BRUYNS, W. F. J. (1971) *Field Guide of Whales and Dolphins*. Mees: Amsterdam.

MÖRZER BRUYNS, W. F. J. & BAKER, A. N. (1973) 'Notes on Hector's dolphin from New Zealand'. *Rec. Dom. Mus. 8*: 125–137.

MROZEK, C. (1978) 'Giant nightingales of the deep'. Oceans (March).

MULLER, J. (1954) 'Observations on the orbital region of the skull of Mystacoceti'. *Zool. Meded. 32*: 279–290.

MULLER, O. F. (1776) 'Zoologiae Danicae'. (Handwritten).

NAKAJIMA, M. & NISHIWAKI, M. (1965) 'First occurrence of a porpoise *Electra electra* in Japan'. *Sci. Rep. Whales Res. Inst. 19*: 91–104.

NAYMAN, J. (1973) *Whales, Dolphins and Man*. Hamlyn: London.

NEMOTO, T. (1955) 'White scars on whales: lamprey marks'. *Sci. Rep. Whales Res. Inst. 10*: 69–77.

NEMOTO, T. (1959) 'Food of the baleen whales with reference to whale movements'. *Sci. Rep. Whales Res. Inst. 14*: 149–290.

NEMOTO, T. (1970) 'Feeding patterns of baleen whales in the ocean'. In STEEL.

NEWMAN, M. (1970) 'Narwhals captured'. *Vancouver Aquarium Newsletter 14*: 1–3.

NICKERSON, R. (1977) 'Brother Whale'. Chronicle: San Francisco.

NISHIMURA, S. & NISHIWAKI, M. (1964) 'Records of the beaked whale *Mesoplodon* from the Japan Sea'. *Bull. Seto Mar. Biol. Lab. 12*: 323–334.

NISHIWAKI, M. (1962) '*Mesplodon bowdoini* stranded at Akita Beach . . .' *Sci. Rep. Whales Res. Inst. 16*: 61–77.

NISHIWAKI, M. (1962) 'Aerial photographs show sperm whales' interesting habits'. *Norsk Hvalfangst Tidende 10*: 395–398.

NISHIWAKI, M. (1963) 'Taxonomical consideration on genera of Delphinidae'. *Sci. Rep. Whales Res. Inst. 17*: 93–103.

NISHIWAKI, M. (1965) '*Feresa attenuata* captured at the Pacific coast of Japan'. *Sci. Rep. Whales Res. Inst. 19*: 65–90.

NISHIWAKI, M. (1966) 'A discussion of rarities among the smaller cetaceans caught in Japanese waters'. In NORRIS.

NISHIWAKI, M. (1966) 'Distribution and migration of marine mammals in the North Pacific area'. *Proc. 11th Pacific Sci. Congr. Symp.* No. 4: 1–49.

NISHIWAKI, M. (1967) 'Distribution and migration of marine mammals in the North Pacific area'. *Bull. Ocean Res. Inst. 1*: 1–64.

NISHIWAKI, M. (1970) 'A Greenland right whale caught at Osaka Bay'. *Sci. Rep. Whales Res. Inst. 22*: 45–62.

NISHIWAKI, M. (1975) 'Ecological aspects of smaller cetaceans, with emphasis on the striped dolphin'. *J. Fish. Res. Board Can. 32*: 1069–1072.

NISHIWAKI, M. & HAYASHI, K, (1950) 'Copulation of humpback whales'. *Sci. Rep. Whales. Res. Inst. 3*: 183.

NISHIWAKI, M. & KAMIYA, T. (1958) 'A beaked whale strands at Oiso Beach'. *Sci. Rep. Whales Res. Inst. 13*: 53–84.

NISHIWAKI, M. & KAMIYA, T. (1959) '*Mesoplodon stejnegeri* from the coast of Japan'. *Sci. Rep. Whales Res. Inst. 14*: 35–48.

NISHIWAKI, M. et al (1965) '*Feresa attenuata* captured at the Pacific coast of Japan in 1963'. *Sci. Rep. Whales Res. Inst. 19*: 65–90.

NISHIWAKI, M. et al (1965) 'A rare species of dolphin from Arari'. *Sci. Rep. Whales Res. Inst. 19*: 53–64.

NISHIWAKI, M. & NORRIS, K. S. (1966) 'A new genus *Peponocephala* for the odontocete cetacean species *Electra electra*'. *Sci. Rep. Whales Res. Inst. 20*: 95–100.

NOBLE, B. A. & FRASER, F. C. (1971) 'Description of a skeleton and supplementary notes on the skull of a rare porpoise'. *J. Nat. Hist. 5*: 447–464.

NORMAN, J. R. & FRASER, F. C. (1948) *Giant Fishes, Whales and Dolphins*. Putnam: London.

NORRIS, K. S. (ed) (1961) 'Standardized methods

for measuring and recording data on the smaller cetaceans'. *J. Mammal. 42*: 471–476.

NORRIS, K. S. (1965) 'Trained porpoise released in the open sea'. *Science 147*: 1048–1050.

NORRIS, K. S. (ed.) (1966) *Whales, Dolphins and Porpoises*. Univ. Calif. Press: Berkeley.

NORRIS, K. S. (1969) 'The echolocation of marine mammals'. In ANDERSON.

NORRIS, K. S. (1976) *The Porpoise Watcher*. John Murray: London.

NORRIS, K. S. et al (1965) 'Open ocean diving test with a trained porpoise'. *Deep Sea Research 12*: 505–509

NORRIS, K. S. & EVANS, W. E. (1967) 'Directionality of echolocation clicks in the roughtooth porpoise'. *Marine Bio-acoustics 2*: 305–306.

NORRIS, K. S. et al (1974) 'New tagging and tracking methods ...' In SCHEVILL.

NORRIS, K. S. et al (1972) 'Sound production in the freshwater porpoises *Sotalia fluviatilis* and *Inia geoffrensis*'. *Inv. on Cetacea 4*: 251–259.

NORRIS, K. S. & McFARLAND, W. N. (1958) 'A new harbour porpoise of the genus *Phocoena* from the Gulf of California'. *J. Mammal. 39*: 22–39.

NORRIS, K. S. & PRESCOTT, J. H. (1961) 'Observation on Pacific cetaceans ...' *Univ. Calif. Publ. Zool. 63*: 291–370.

NORRIS, K. S. et al (1978) 'The behaviour of porpoises and tuna ...' *US Dept. Comm.* PB 283 970.

OBERTHUR, R. & DAUTHENAY, H. (1905) *Repertoire de Couleurs*. Paris.

ODELL, D. K. (1979) 'A preliminary study of the ecology and population biology of the bottlenose dolphin in south east Florida'. *US Dept. Comm.* PB 294 336.

OGAWA, T. (1936) 'Studien uber die Zahwale in Japan'. *Botany & Zool. 4*: 2017–2024.

OHSUMI, S. (1958) 'A descendant of Moby Dick, or a white sperm whale'. *Sci. Rep. Whales Res. Inst. 13*: 207–209.

OHSUMI, S. (1966) 'Sexual segregation of the sperm whale in the North Pacific'. *Sci. Rep. Whales Res. Inst. 11*: 39–46.

OHSUMI, S. (1971) 'Some investigations on the school structure of the sperm whale'. *Sci. Rep. Whales Res. Inst. 23*: 1–25.

OHSUMI, S. (1972) 'catch of marine mammals ... along the coast of Japan'. *Bull. Fish. Res. Lab. Shimizu 7*: 137–166.

OHSUMI, S. (1979) 'Provisional report of the Brydes whale caught under special permit in the southern hemisphere'. *Rep. Int. Whal. Commn. 29*: 267–273.

OLIVER, W. R. B. (1922) 'The whales and dolphins of New Zealand'. *N.Z. J. Sci. Tech. 5*: 129–141.

OLIVER, W. R. B. (1937) '*Tasmacetus shepherdi* a new genus and species of beaked whale from New Zealand'. *Proc. Zool. Soc. Lond. 3*: 371–381.

OLIVER, W. R. B. (1946) 'A pied variety of the coastal porpoise'. *Dom. Mus. Rec. Zool. 1*: 1–4.

OLSEN, O. (1913) 'On the external characters and biology of Brydes Whale ...' *Proc. Zool. Soc. Lond.*: 1073–1090.

OMMANNEY, J. D. (1971) *Lost Leviathan*. Dodds & Mead: New York.

OMURA, H. (1958) 'North Pacific right whale'. *Sci. Rep. Whales Res. Inst. 13*: 1–52.

OMURA, H. (1959) 'Brydes whale from the coast of Japan'. *Sci. Rep. Whales Res. Inst. 14*: 1–33.

OMURA, H. (1966) 'Brydes whale in the Northwest Pacific'. In NORRIS.

OMURA, H. (1972) 'An osteological study of the Cuviers beaked whale ...' *Sci. Rep. Whales Res. Inst. 24*: 1–34.

OMURA, H. et al (1955) 'Beaked whale *Berardius bairdi* of Japan'. *Sci. Rep. Whales Res. Inst. 10*: 89–132.

OMURA, H. et al (1969) 'Black right whale in the North Pacific'. *Sci. Rep. Whales Res. Inst. 21*: 1–78.

OMURA, H. & SAKIURA, H. (1956) 'Studies on the little piked whale from the coast of Japan'. *Sci. Rep. Whales Res. Inst. 11*: 1–37.

OMURA, H. et al (1970) 'Osteology of pygmy blue whale'. *Sci. Rep. Whales Res. Inst. 22*: 1–27.

ORR, R. T. (1948) 'A second record of Cuviers whale from the Pacific Coast ...' *J. Mammal. 29*: 420–421.

ORR, R. T. (1950) 'Rarity of the deep'. *Pacific Discovery 3*: 13–15.

ORR, R. T. (1953) 'Beaked whales from California with comments on taxonomy'. *J. Mammal. 34*: 239–249.

OSBECK, P. (1757) *Reise nach Ostindien und China*. Koppe: Rostock.

OSGOOD, W. H. (1943) 'The mammals of Chile'. *Zool. Series Field Mus. Nat. Hist. 30*: 1–268.

OWEN, R. (1846) *A History of British Fossil Mammals and Birds*. London.

OWEN, R. (1853) *Descriptive Catalogue of the Osteological Collection in the Museum of the Royal College of Surgeons*. London.

OWEN, R. (1861) *Essays and observations on natural history, anatomy, physiology, psychology and geology by John Hunter FRS*. London.

OWEN, R. (1865) 'On some Indian cetacea collected by Walter Elliot Esq.' *Trans. Zool. Soc. Lond. 6*: 17–47.

OWEN, R. (1866) *The Comparative Anatomy and Physiology of Vertebrates*. London.

PALLAS, P. S. (1776) *Reise durch Verschiedene Provinzen der Russichen Reichs*. Berlin.

PALMER, J. F. (1837) *The works of John Hunter FRS*. London.

PALMER, R. S. (1954) *The Mammal Guide*. Doubleday: New York.

PALMER, T. P. (1899) 'Notes on three genera of dolphins'. *Proc. Biol. Soc. Washington 13*: 23–24.

PALMER, R. S. & REILLY, E. M. (1956) 'A precise colour standard'. In Volume 1 of *Handbook of American Birds*. Yale University Press.

PARKER, W. R. (1933) 'Pelorus Jack'. *Proc. Linn. Soc. Lond. 146*: 2.

PARRY, D. A. (1949) 'The anatomical basis of swimming in whales'. *Proc. Zool. Soc. Lond. 119*: 49.

PARRY, D. A. (1949) 'The swimming of whales and a discussion of Gray's paradox'. *J. Exp. Biol. 26*: 24.

PAULI, D. C. & CLAPPER, G. P. (ed) (1967) 'An experimental 45 day undersea saturation dive at 205 feet'. ONR Report ACR 124.

PAYNE, R. (1976) 'At home with right whales'. *Nat. Geog. 149*: 322–339.

PAYNE, R. & McVAY, S. (1971) 'Songs of humpback whales'. *Science 173*: 587–597.

PAYNE, R. & PAYNE, K. (1971) 'Underwater sounds of southern right whales'. *Zoologica 56*: 159–165.

PAYNE, R. & WEBB, D. (1971) 'Orientation by means of long range acoustic signalling in baleen whales'. *Ann. New York Acad. Sci. 188*: 110–142.

PEALE, T. R. (1848) 'United States exploring expedition during the years 1838 to 1842 ...' Philadelphia.

PEDERSON, T. & RUUD, J. T. (1946) 'Bibliography of whales and whaling'. *Hvalradets Skrifter* No. 30.

PENNER, R. H. & MURCHISON, A. E. (1970) 'Experimentally demonstrated echolocation in the Amazon river dolphin'. *Naval Undersea Center Tech. Pub.* No. 187.

PERNETTY, A. J. (1769) *Journal historique d'un voyage fait aux iles Malouines en 1763 et 1764*. Etienne de Bourdeaux.

PERNETTY, A. J. (1773) Pernetty's voyage (translation). Goldsmith: London.

PERON, F. (1807) *Voyage de découverte aux terres australes*. Imperiale: Paris.

PERRIN, W. F. (1968) 'The porpoise and the tuna'. *Sea Frontiers 14*: 166–174.

PERRIN, W. F. (1969) 'The barnacle *Conchoderma auritum* on a porpoise'. *J. Mammal. 50*: 149–151.

PERRIN, W. F. (1970) 'Color pattern of the eastern Pacific spotted porpoise'. *Zoologica 54*: 135–142.

PERRIN, W. F. (1972) 'Variation and taxonomy of spotted and spinner porpoise'. Ph. D. thesis. Univ. of California in Los Angeles.

PERRIN, W. F. (1972) 'Color patterns of spinner porpoises of the eastern Pacific and Hawaii ...' *Fish. Bull. 70*: 983–1003.

PERRIN, W. F. (1973) *Annotated bibliography of the genus Stenella*. Marine Mammal Investigations: La Jolla.

PERRIN, W. F. (1975) 'Variation of spotted and spinner porpoise in the eastern tropical Pacific and Hawaii.' *Bull. Scripps Inst. of Oceanog, 21*: 1–206.

PERRIN, W. F. (1975) 'Distribution and differentiation of populations of dolphins of the genus Stenella in the eastern tropical Pacific'. *J. Fish. Res. Board Can. 32*: 1059–1067.

PERRIN, W. F. (1976) 'First record of the melonhead whale in the eastern Pacific ...' *Fish. Bull. 74*: 457–558.

PERRIN, W. F. et al (1976) 'Growth and reproduction of the spotted porpoise ...' Fish. Bull. 74: 229–269.

PERRIN, W. F. et al (1977) 'Growth and reproduction of the eastern spinner dolphin'. *Fish. Bull. 75*: 725–750.

PERRIN, W. F. & HUBBS, C. L. (1969) 'Observations on a young pygmy killer whale ...' *Trans. San Diego Soc. Nat. Hist 15*: 297–308.

PERRIN, W. F. & HUNTER, J. R. (1972) 'Escape behaviour of the Hawaiian spinner porpoise'. *Fish. Bull. 70*: 49–60.

PERRIN, W. F. et al (1979) 'Progress in reducing incidental kill of dolphins in the US tuna purse seine fishery ...' *NOAA Admin. Rep.* LJ 79 19.

PERRIN, W. F. et al (1977) 'Spinner dolphins in Atlantitic'. *Scond Conf. Biol. Mar. Mammals*: San Diego.

PERRIN W. F. & WATKIN, W. A. (1975) 'The rough-toothed porpoise in the eastern tropical Pacific'. *J. Mammal. 56*: 905.

PERRIN, W. F. et al (1973) 'Rediscovery of Frasers dolphin'. *Nature 241*: 345–350.

PHILIPPI, R. A. (1893) 'Die delphini aus der Sudsjutze Sudamerika'. *Anal. Mus. Nac. Chile.* 6: 12.

PHILIPPI, R. A. (1896) 'Los craneos de los delfines Chilenos'. *Anal. Mus. Nac. Chile 12:* 1–19.

PIGG, J. & CUMMINS, W. C. 'Cetaceans of Bay of Bengal and Indian Ocean'. Unpublished manuscript.

PIKE, G. C. (1951) 'Lamprey marks on whales'. *J. Fish. Res. Board Can. 8:* 275–280.

PIKE, G. C. (1956) 'Guide to the whales, porpoises and dolphins of the northeast Pacific and Arctic waters of Canada and Alaska'. *Fish. Res. Board Can. Circ. 32:* 1–14.

PIKE, G. C. & MACASKIE, I. B. (1969) 'Marine Mammals of British Columbia'. *Fish. Res. Board Can. Bull.* 171.

PIKE, G. C. & GIOVANDO, L. (1963) 'Whales and dolphins of the West Coast of Canada'. *Fish. Res. Board Can. 68:* 1–31.

PILLERI, G. (1967) 'Behaviour of *Pseudorca crassidens* off the Mediterranean Spanish coasts'. *Rev. Suisse Zool. 74:* 679–683.

PILLERI, G. (1969) 'On the behaviour of the Amazon dolphin'. *Rev. Suisse Zool. 76:* 57–91.

PILLERI, G. (1970) 'Observations on the behaviour of *Platanista gengetica* ...' *Inv. on Cetacea 2:* 27–60.

PILLERI, G. (1971) 'Observations on the copulatory behaviour of the gangetic dolphin'. *Inv. on Cetacea 3:* 31–33.

PILLERI, G. (1971) 'On the La Plata dolphin off the Uruguayan coasts'. *Inv. on Cetacea 3:* 59–67.

PILLERI, G. (1971) 'Epimeletic (nurturant) behaviour by the La Plata dolphin'. *Inv. on Cetacea 3:* 74–76.

PILLERI, G. (1971) 'Intelligence under water'. *Documenta Geigy Nautilus 9:* 2–4.

PILLERI, G. (1971) 'Original description of the Gangetic dolphin'. *Bull. Brit. Mus (Nat. Hist.) Zoo. 21:* 345–348.

PILLERI, G. (1972) 'Cerebral anatomy of the Platanistidae'. *Inv. on Cetacea 4:* 44–70.

PILLERI, G. (1972) 'Field observations carried out on the Indus dolphin ...' *Inv. on Cetacea. 4:* 22–29.

PILLERI, G. (1972) *Zoologisch-cetologische Expedition nack West Pakistan.* Verlag Hirnanatomisches Inst.: Bern.

PILLERI, G. (1978) 'William Roxburgh, Heinrich Julius Lebeck and the discovery of the Ganges dolphin'. *Inv. on Cetacea 9:* 11–21.

PILLERI, G. & GIHR, M. (1969) 'On the anatomy and behaviour of Risso's dolphin'. *Inv. on Cetacea 1:* 74–93.

PILLERI, G. & GIHR, M. (1971) 'Differences observed in the skulls of *Platanista gangetica* and *indi*'. *Inv. on Cetacea 3:* 13–21.

PILLERI, G. & GIHR, M. (1972) 'Contribution to the knowledge of the cetaceans of Pakistan'. *Inv. on Cetacea 4:* 107–162.

PILLERI, G. & GIHR, M. (1972) 'Burmeisters porpoise off the Punta del Diablo'. *Inv. on Cetacea 4:* 163–172.

PILLERI, G. & GIHR, M. (1973–1974) 'Contribution to the knowledge of the cetaceans of southwest and monsoon Asia'. *Inv. on Cetacea 5:* 95–149.

PILLERI, G & GIHR, M. (1975) 'On the taxonomy and ecology of the finless black porpoise'. *Mammalia 39:* 657–673.

PILLERI, G. & GIHR, M. (1976) 'The current state of research on the Chinese river dolphin'. *Inv. on Cetacea 7:* 149–157.

PILLERI, G. & GIHR, M. (1977) 'Observations on the Bolivian and the Amazonian bufeo ...' *Inv. on Cetacea 8:* 11–76.

PILLERI, G. & GIHR, M. (1977) 'Neotype for *Platanista indi*.' *Inv. on Cetacea 8:* 77–81.

PILLERI, G. et al (1971) 'Further observations on the behaviour of *Platanista indi* in captivity'. *Inv. on Cetacea 3:* 34–42.

PILLERI, G. & KNUCKEY, J. (1969) 'Behaviour patterns of some Delphinidae observed in the western Mediterranean'. *Zeit. f. Tierpsych. 26:* 48–72.

PILLERI, G. et al (1971) 'Physical analysis of the sounds emitted by *Platanista indi*.' *Inv. on Cetacea 3:* 22–30.

PILLERI, G. et al (1976) 'Sonar clicks, directionality ... of the Indus dolphin'. *Inv. on Cetacea 7:* 13–43.

PILLERI, G. et al (1976) 'The black finless porpoise is not black'. *Inv. on Cetacea 7:* 161–164.

PLINIUS, G. S. (77) *Historiae Naturalis.* Loeb Classical Library: London (1967).

POPE, C. H. (1940) *China's Animal Frontier.* Viking Press: New York.

PORTER, J. W. (1977) '*Pseudorca* stranding'. *Oceans 10:* 8–15.

POULTER, T. C. (1968) 'Marine Mammals'. In SEBEOK.

POULTER, T. C. (1970) 'Ultrasonic frequencies recorded from three captive blind dolphins'. *Proc. 7th Ann. Conf. Biol. Sonar and Diving Mamm.*

PRADERI, R. (1971) 'Contribucion al conocimiento del genero *Phocoena*'. *Rev. Mus. Arg. Cien. Nat. Buenos Aires. Zool. 7:* 251–266.

PRADERI, R. (1979) 'Considerations on the population of Franciscana ...' *Rep. Sci. Comm. Intl. Whaling Commn. 31:* SM4.

PRINGLE, J. A. (1952) 'Two specimens of the beaked whale *Mesoplodon densirostris* ...' *Ann. Cape Prov. Mus. 3:* 61–63.

PRYOR, K. (1969) 'The creative porpoise'. *J. Exp. Anal. Behav. 12:* 653–661.

PRYOR, T. et al (1965) 'Observations on a pygmy killer whale from Hawaii'. *J. Mammal. 46:* 450–461.

PURVES, P. E. (1963) 'Locomotion in whales'. *Nature 197:* 334–337.

PURVES, P. E. & MOUNTFORD, M. O. (1959) 'Ear plug laminations in relation to the age composition of a population of fin whales'. *Bull. Brit. Mus. (Nat. Hist.) Zool. 5:* 125–154.

PURVES, P. E. & PILLERI, G. (1978) 'The functional anatomy and general biology of *Pseudorca crassidens* ...' *Inv. on Cetacea 9:* 67–227.

QUOY, J. R. C. & GAIMARD, J. P. (1824) *Voyage autour du monde exécuté sur les corvettes de S. M. l'Uranie et la Physicienne.* Paris.

QUOY, J. R. C. & GAIMARD, J. P. (1830) *Voyage de découverte de l'Astrolabe exécuté par ordre du Roi pendant les années 1826 et 1829.* Paris.

RACK, R. S. (1952) 'Blackfish hunting off St. Vincent'. In *Fisheries in the Caribbean* Caribbean Commission: Trinidad.

RACOVITZA, E. G. (1903) 'Expedition Antarctique Belgique 1897–1899'. Brussels.

RANKIN, J. J. (1953) 'First record of the rare beaked whale *Mesoplodon europaeus* from the West Indies'. *Nature 172:* 873.

RAVEN, H. C. (1942) 'On the structure of Mesoplodon densirostris ...' *Bull. Am. Mus. Nat. Hist. 80:* 23–50.

RAY, C. (1961) 'A question in whale behaviour'. *Nat. Hist. 70:* 46.

RAY, G. C. & SCHEVILL, W. (1974) 'Feeding of a captive gray whale'. *Marine Fisheries Rev. 36:* 31.

RAY, G. C. & WARTZOK, D. (1976) 'Radio tagging of fin and blue whales'. In LEATHERWOOD & EVANS (1979).

REEVES, R. R. (1977) 'Hunt for the narwhal'. *Oceans 10:* 50–57.

REINHARDT, J. (1862) '*Pseudorca crassidens* et for den Danske fauna nyt hvaldyr'. *Ovzgy. Danske Vidensk. Selsk. Forh.*

RICE, D. W. (1961) 'Sei whales with rudimentary baleen'. *Norsk Hvalfangst Tidende 5:* 189–193.

RICE, D. W. (1967) 'Cetaceans'. In ANDERSON & KNOX JONES.

RICE, D. W. (1977) 'The humpback whale in the North Pacific'. Rep. Workshop on Problems Related to Humpback Whales: Hawaii.

RICE, D. W. (1977) 'A list of the marine mammals of the world'. (3rd ed.) *NOAA Tech. Rep. NMFS SSRF* 711.

RICE, D. W. & SCHEFFER, V. B. (1968) 'A list of the marine mammals of the world' (1st ed.) *US Dept. Int. Fish Wildl. Serv. Spec. Sci. Rep.* No. 579.

RICE, D. W. & WOLMAN, A. A. (1971) 'The life history and ecology of the gray whale'. *Spec. Publ. No. 3 Am. Soc. of Mammal.*

RICHARDSON, J. & GRAY, J. E. (ed.) (1846) *The zoology of the voyage of H.M.S. Erebus and Terror ...* London.

RIDGWAY, S. (ed.) (1972) *Mammals of the Sea.* Thomas: Springfield.

RIDGWAY, R. (1886) *A nomenclature of colours for naturalists.* Little, Brown: Boston.

RIDGWAY, R. (1912) *Colour standards and Colour nomenclature.* Washington.

ROBBINS, C. H. (1899) *The Gam.* Ochs: Boston.

ROBERTSON, R. B. (1954) *Of Whales and Men.* Knopf: New York.

ROBSON, F. (1976) *Thinking Dolphins, Talking Whales.* Reed: Wellington.

ROBSON, F. D. & VAN BREE, P. J. H. (1971) 'Some remarks on a mass stranding of sperm whales ...' *Zeit. f. Saugetierk. 36:* 55–60.

ROE, H. S. J. (1967) 'Seasonal formation of laminae in the ear plug of the fin whale'. *Discovery Reports 35:* 1–30.

ROEST, A. I. (1964) '*Physeter* and *Mesoplodon* strandings on the central California coast'. *J. Mammal. 45:* 129–136.

RONDELETTI, G. (1554) *Libri de Piscibus Marinas.* Bonhomme: Ludguni.

ROSS, G. J. B. (1969) 'Evidence for a southern breeding population of Trues beaked whale'. *Nature 222:* 585.

ROSS, G. J. B. (1970) 'The occurrence of Hectors beaked whale in South African waters'. *Ann. Cape Prov. Mus. 8:* 195–201.

ROSS, G. J. B. (1977) 'The taxonomy of bottlenosed dolphins in South African waters ...' *Ann. Cape Prov. Mus. 11:* 135–194.

ROSS, G. J. B. (1979) 'Records of pygmy and dwarf sperm whales from Southern Africa ...' *Ann. Cape Prov. Mus. 11:* 259–327.

ROSS, G. J. B. et al (1975) 'New records of the pygmy right whale from South Africa ...' *J. Fish. Res. Board Can. 32:* 1005–1017.

ROSS, J.C. (1847) *A voyage of discovery and research in the southern and Antarctic regions*. John Murray: London.

ROXBURGH, W. (1801) 'An account of a new species of *Delphinus*, an inhabitant of the Ganges'. *Asiat. Res.* (Calcutta) 7: 170–174.

SAAYMAN, G. S. et al (1972) 'Observations on inshore and pelagic dolphins ...' *Koedoe* 15: 1–24.

SAAYMAN, G. S. & TAYLER, C. K. (1973) 'Social organization of inshore dolphins in the Indian Ocean'. *J. Mammal.* 54: 993.

SAAYMAN, G. S. & TAYLER, C. K. (1973) 'Some behaviour patterns of the southern right whale'. *Z. f. Saugetierk.* 38: 172–183.

SAAYMAN, G. S. & TAYLER, C. K. (1979) 'The socioecology of humpback dolphins'. In WINN & OLLA.

SAEMUNDSSON, B. (1939) *Zoology of Iceland*. Munksgaard: Copenhagen.

SAMARAS, W. F. (1974) 'Reproductive behaviour of the gray whale in Baja California'. *Bull. S. Calif. Acad. Sci.* 73: 57–64.

SANDERSON, I. T. (1958) *Follow the Whale*. Cassell: London.

SAUER, E. G. F. (1963) 'Courtship and copulation of the gray whale in the Bering Sea ...' *Psych. Forschung* 27: 157–174.

SAWTELL, C. C. (1962) 'The ship Ann Alexander of New Bedford'. Mystic. Conn. Mar. Hist. Assoc.

SCAMMON, C. M. (1874) *The Marine Mammals of the North Western Coast of North America*. Carmany: New York (Reissued by Dover: New York in 1968).

SCHEFFER, V. B. (1950) 'The striped dolphin on the coast of North America'. *Am. Midl. Nat.* 44: 750–758.

SCHEFFER, V. B. (1970) *The Year of the Whale*. Souvenir Press: London.

SCHEFFER, V. B. & RICE, D. W. (1963) 'A list of the marine mammals of the world'. (2nd ed.) *U.S. Fish. Wildl. Serv. Spec. Sci. Rep.* 431

SCHEFFER, V. B. & SLIPP, J. W. (1948) 'The whales and dolphins of Washington State ...' *Am. Midl. Nat.* 39: 257–337.

SCHENKKAN, E. J. & PURVES, P. E. (1973) 'The comparative anatomy of the nasal tract and the function of the spermaceti organ in Physeteridae'. *Bijdr. Dierk.* 43: 93–112.

SCHEVILL, W. E. (1964) 'Underwater sounds of cetaceans'. In TAVOLGA.

SCHEVILL, W. E. (ed.) (1974) *The Whale Problem*. Harvard Univ. Press.

SCHEVILL, W. E. & LAWRENCE, B. (1956) 'Food finding by a captive porpoise'. *Breviora* 53: 1–15.

SCHEVILL, W. E. et al (1972) *Biology of Whales*. Harvard Univ. Press.

SCHEVILL, W. E. & WATKINS, W. A. (1966) 'Radio tagging of whales'. *Woods Hole Oceanogr. Inst.* 66: 1–15.

SCHEVILL, W. E. & WATKINS, W. A. (1971) 'Pulsed sounds of the porpoise *Lagenorhynchus australis*'. *Breviora* 366.

SCHEVILL, W. E. et al (1967) 'The 20 cycle signals and *Balaenoptera*'. In TAVOLGA.

SCHLEGEL, H. (1841) *Abhandlungen auf dem Gebiete der Zoologie und vergleichende Anatomie*. Arnz: Leiden.

SCHMIDLY, D. J. & SHANE, S. H. (1976) 'A biological assessment of the cetacean fauna of the Texas coast'. Mar. Mamm. Comm. Washington.

SCHOLANDER, P. F. (1959) 'Wave riding dolphins:

how do they do it?' *Science 129*: 1085.

SCHOLANDER, P. J. (1959) 'Wave riding dolphins'. *Science 130*: 1658.

SCHULTZ, J. & PYLE, C. (1965) 'Cat bites whale'. *Yachting 118*.

SCORESBY, W. (1820) *An account of the Arctic Regions; with a history and description of the northern whale fishery*. Constable: Edinburgh.

SEBEOK, T. A. (ed.) *Animal Communication*. Indiana University Press.

SEED, A. (1971) *Toothed whales in eastern North Pacific and Arctic waters*. Pacific Search: Seattle.

SERGEANT, D. E. (1962) 'On the external characters of the blackfish or pilot whales'. *J. Mammal.* 43: 395–413.

SERGEANT, D. E. (1962) 'The biology of the pilot or pothead whale in Newfoundland waters'. *Bull. Fish. Res. Board Can.* 132: 1–84.

SERGEANT, D. E. (1973) 'Biology of white whales in western Hudson Bay'. *J. Fish. Res. Board Can.* 30: 1065–1090.

SERGEANT, D. E. (1979) 'Summary of knowledge on populations of white whales and narwhals in Canadian waters'. *Rep. Sci. Comm. Intl. Whaling Comm.* 31: SM5.

SERGEANT, D. E. & BRODIE, P. F. (1975) 'Identity, abundance and present status of populations of white whales in North America'. *J. Fish. Res. Board. Can.* 32: 1047.

SERGEANT, D. E. & FISHER, H. D. (1957) 'The smaller cetacea of eastern Canadian waters'. *J. Fish. Res. Board Can.* 14: 83–115.

SERGEANT, D. E. et al (1970) 'Inshore records of cetacea of eastern Canada'. *J. Fish. Res. Board. Can.* 27: 1903–1915.

SERVICE, R. (1896) 'Mammalia of Solway'. *Ann. Scot. Nat. Hist.* 20: 201–210.

SHOU CHEN-HUANG (1962) *Economic Mammals of China*. Sci. Pub. House: Peking.

SIBBALD, R. (1684) *Scotia Illustrata*. Edinburgh.

SIEBENALER, J. B. & CALDWELL, D. K. (1956) 'Cooperation among adult dolphins'. *J. Mammal.* 37: 126–128.

SIMPSON, G. G. (1961) *Principles of Animal Taxonomy*. Columbia Univ. Press.

SIVASUBRAMANIAN, K. (1964) 'Predation of tuna longline catches in the Indian Ocean by killer whales ...' *Bull. Fish. Res. Stn. Ceylon* 17: 221–236.

SLIJPER, E. J. (1962) *Whales*. Hutchinson (revised): London (1979).

SLIJPER, E. J. (1976) *Whales and Dolphins*. Univ. of Michigan Press.

SLIJPER et al (1964) 'Remarks on the distribution and migration of whales based on observations from Netherlands ships'. *Bijdr. tot de Dierk.* 34: 1–93.

SMALL, G. L. (1971) *The Blue Whale*. Columbia Univ. Press.

SOUTHWELL, T. (1884) 'The bottlenose whale fishery in the North Atlantic Ocean'. *U.S. Comm. Fish and Fisheries* 1882: 221–227.

SOWERBY, J. (1804) *The British Miscellany*. London.

SOWERBY, A. de C. (1936) 'China's Natural History'. *Roy. Asiat. Soc.*; Shanghai.

SPONG, P. (1974) 'The whale show'. In McINTYRE.

SPRINGER, S. (1967) 'Porpoises vs. sharks'. *Amer. Inst. Biol. Sci. Conf. on the shark porpoise relationship*: Washington.

STARBUCK, A. (1878) 'History of the American whale fishery ...' *U.S. Comm. Fish and Fisheries Rep.* 1875: 76.

STEEL, J. H. (ed.) *Marine Food Chains*. Univ. Cal. Press: Berkeley.

STEJNEGER, L. (1883) 'Contributions to the history of the Commander Islands'. *Proc. U.S. Nat. Mus.* 6: 58–89.

STENUIT, R. (1969) *The Dolphin – cousin to man*. Dent: London.

STEPHENSON, A. B. (1975) 'Sperm whales stranded at Muriwai Beach ...' *N.Z. J. Mar. Freshwater Res.* 9: 299–304.

STIRLING, A. C. (1934) 'Ambergris'. *Chemist & Druggist* (March 17).

TALBOT, F. H. (1960) 'True's beaked whale from the southeast coast of South Africa'. *Nature 186*: 406.

TARUSKI, A. G. (1979) 'The whistle repertoire of the North Atlantic pilot whale ...' In WINN & OLLA.

TAVOLGA, M. C. (1966) 'Behaviour of the bottlenose dolphin ...' In NORRIS.

TAVOLGA, W. M. (ed.) (1964) *Marine Bioacoustics*. Pergamon: Oxford.

TAVOLGA, M. C. & ESSAPIAN, F. S. (1957) 'The behaviour of the bottlenose dolphin ...' *Zoologica 42*: 11–31.

TAYLER, C. K. & SAAYMAN, G. S. (1973) 'Imitative behaviour by Indian Ocean bottlenose dolphins in captivity'. *Behaviour 44*: 286–298.

TAYLOR, R. J. F. (1957) 'An unusual record of three species of whale being restricted to pools in Antarctic sea ice'. *Proc. Zool. Soc. Lond.* 129: 325–331.

TEMMINCK, C. J. (1847) *Fauna Japonica*. Lugundi Batavorum.

THOMAS, O. (1898) 'The technical names of the British mammals'. *The Zoologist* 2: 99–103.

THOMAS, O. (1911) 'The mammals of the tenth edition of Linnaeus'. *Proc. Zool. Soc. Lond.*: 120–158.

THOMPSON, P. O. & CUMMINGS, W. C. (1969) 'Sound production of the finback whale ...' *Proc. 6th Ann. Conf. Biol. Sonar Diving Mamm.*: 109.

THOMPSON, T. J. et al (1979) 'Mysticete sounds'. In WINN & OLLA.

TIETZ, R. M. (1963) 'A record of the speckled dolphin from the south east coast of South Africa'. *Ann. Cape Prov. Mus.* 3: 68–74.

TOBAYAMA, T. et al (1973) 'Records of Frasers Sarawak dolphin in the western North Pacific'. *Sci. Rep. Whales Res. Inst.* 25: 251–263.

TOMILIN, A. G. (1937) 'Ecological classification of cetacea'. Fish. Res. Board. Can. 95: 1–9.

TOMILIN, A. G. (1946) 'Thermoregulation and the geographical races of cetacea'. *Compt. Rend. Acad. Sci. URSS* 54: 465–468.

TOMILIN, A. G. (1951) *A field guide to cetaceans*. Moscow. (Russian)

TOMILIN, A. G. (1957) *Mammals of eastern Europe and northern Asia*. Moscow.

TOWNSEND, C. H. (1935) 'The distribution of certain whales as shown by logbook records of American whaleships'. *Zoologica 19*: 3–93.

TRUE, F. W. (1884) 'Suggestions to the keepers of US life-saving stations ... means of collecting and preserving specimens of whales and porpoises'.

TRUE, F. W. (1885) 'On a new species of porpoise from Alaska'. *Proc. U.S. Nat. Mus.* 8: 95–98.

TRUE, F. W. (1885) 'Contributions to the history of the Commander Islands ...' *Proc. U.S. Nat. Mus.* 8: 584–585.

TRUE, F. W. (1889) 'Contributions to the natural

history of the cetaceans ...' *U.S. Nat. Mus. 36*: 1–192.

TRUE, F. W. (1904) 'The Whalebone Whales of the Western North Atlantic'. *Smithsonian Contribution to Knowledge 33.*

TRUE, F. W. (1913) 'Diagnosis of a new beaked whale of the genus *Mesoplodon* from the coast of North Carolina'. *Smithsonian Misc. Coll. 60*:1–2.

TRUITT, D. (1974) *Dolphins and porpoises: a comprehensive annotated bibliography of the smaller cetacea.* Gale Research: Detroit.

TURNER, W. (1872) 'On the occurrence of *Ziphius cavirostris* in the Shetland Seas'. *Trans. Roy. Soc. Edinburgh 26*: 759–778.

TURNER, W. (1912) *The marine mammals of the anatomical museum of the University of Edinburgh.* London.

VAN BÉNÉDEN, P. J. (1881) 'Notice sur un nouveau dauphin de la Nouvelle Zelande'. *Bull. Acad. Roy. Belge 1*: 877–888.

VAN BÉNÉDEN, P. J. (1889) *Histoire naturelle des cétacés des mers d'Europe.* Brussels.

VAN BÉNÉDEN, P. J. & GERVAIS, M. P. (1880). *Osteographie des cétacés vivants et fossiles.* Bertrand: Paris.

VAN BREE, P. J. H. (1966) 'On skull of *Tursiops aduncus* found at Mossel Bay, South Africa'. *Ann. Natal Mus. 18*: 425–427.

VAN BREE, P. J. H. (1971) 'On two skulls of *Delphinus dussumieri'. Beaufortia 18*: 169–172.

VAN BREE, P. J. H. (1971) 'On *Globicephala sieboldii* and other species of pilot whales'. *Beaufortia 19*: 79–87.

VAN BREE, P. J. H. (1972) 'On the validity of the subspecies *Cephalorhynchus hectori bicolor'. Inv. on Cetacea 4*: 182–186.

VAN BREE, P. J. H. (1973) '*Neophocaena phocaenoides asiaeorientalis* – a synonym of the preoccupied name *Delphinus melas'. Beaufortia 21*: 17–24.

VAN BREE, P. J. H. (1975) 'Preliminary list of the cetaceans of the southern Caribbean'. *Stud. Fauna Curacao 48*: 79–87.

VAN BREE, P. J. H. (1976) 'On the correct Latin name of the Indus susu'. *Bull. Zool. Mus. Univ. Amsterdam 5*: 139–140.

VAN BREE P. J. H. (1968) 'On a skull of *Peponocephala electra* from Senegal'. *Beaufortia 14*: 193–202.

VAN BREE, P. J. H. & DUGUY, R. (1964) 'Sur un crane de *Sotalia teuszii'. Zeit. f. Saugetierk. 30*: 311–314.

VAN BREE, P. J. H. & GALLAGHER, M. D. (1978) 'On the taxonomic status of *Delphinus tropicalis'. Beaufortia 28*: 1–8.

VAN BREE, P. J. H. & NIJSSEN, H. (1964) 'On three specimens of *Lagenorhynchus albirostris'. Beaufortia 11*: 85–93.

VAN BREE, P. J. H. & PURVES, P. E. (1972) 'Remarks on the validity of *Delphinus bairdii'. J. Mammal. 53*: 372–374.

VAN BREE, P. J. H. & PURVES, P. E. (1975) 'On the dimensions of three skulls of the species of dolphin *Lipotes vexillifer'. Beaufortia 24*: 1–5.

VAN DER BRINK, F. H. (1967) *A Field Guide to the Mammals of Britain and Europe.* Collins:London.

VAN ERP, I. (1969) 'In quest of the La Plata dolphin'. *Pacific Discovery 22*: 18–24.

VAN GELDER, R. G. (1960) 'Results of the Puritan-American Museum of Natural History Expedition to Western Mexico'. *Am. Mus. Novitates* No. 1992.

VAN HEEL, W. H. D. (1962) 'Sound and cetacea'. *Neth. J. Sea Res. 1*: 407–507.

VAN HEEL, W. H. D. (1963) 'Catching *Phocoena phocoena* for scientific purposes'. *Bull. Inst. Oceanogr. Monaco 1*: 23–27.

VAN HEEL, W. H. D. (1966) 'Navigation in cetacea'. In NORRIS.

VAN UTRECHT, W. L. & VAN DER SPOEL, S. (1962) 'Observations on a minke whale from the Antarctic'. *Zeit. Saugertierk. 27*: 217–221.

VENABLES, B. *Baleia! Baleia!*. Knopf: New York.

VILLALOBOS, D. C. & VILLALOBOS, J. (1947) *Atlas de los Colores.* El Ateneo: Buenos Aires.

VON HAAST, J. (1876) 'On a new Ziphioid whale'. *Proc. Zool. Soc. Lond*: 7–13.

VON HAAST, J. (1876) 'Further notes on a new genus of ziphioid whale from the New Zealand seas'. *Proc. Zool. Soc. Lond.*: 457–458.

WALKER, E. P. (1964) *Mammals of the World.* Johns Hopkins Press: Baltimore.

WALKER, R. A. (1963) 'Some intense, low-frequency, underwater sounds of wide geographic distribution, apparently of biological origin'. *J. Acoust. Soc. Amer. 35*: 1816–1824.

WALKER, T. J. (1975) *Whale Primer.* Cabrillo:California.

WARSHALL, P. (1974) 'The ways of whales'. In McINTYRE.

WATERHOUSE, G. R. (1838) 'On a new species of the genus *Delphinus'. Proc. Zool. Soc. Lond.*: 23.

WATKINS, W. A. (1966) 'Listening to cetaceans'. In NORRIS.

WATKINS, W. A. (1976) 'A probable sighting of a live *Tasmacetus shepherdi* in New Zealand waters'. *J. Mammal. 57*: 415.

WATKINS, W. A. (1977) 'Acoustic behaviour of sperm whales'. *Oceanus 20*: 50–58.

WATKINS, W. A. et al (1971) 'Underwater sounds of *Monodon'. J. Acoust. Soc. Amer. 49*:595–599.

WATKINS, W. A. & SCHEVILL, W. E. (1974) 'Listening to Hawaiian spinner porpoises ...' *J. Mammal. 55*: 319–328.

WATKINS, W. A. & SCHEVILL, W. E. (1977) 'The development and testing of a radio whale tag'. In LEATHERWOOD & EVANS (1979).

WATKINS, W. A. & SCHEVILL, W. E. (1977) 'Sperm whale codas'. *J. Acoust. Soc. Am. 62*:1485–1490.

WATKINS, W. A. & SCHEVILL, W. E. (1977) 'Spatial distribution of sperm whale underwater'. *Deep Sea Research 24*: 693–699.

WATKINS, W. A. & SCHEVILL, W. E. (1979) 'Aerial observation of feeding behaviour in four baleen whales'. *J. Mammal. 60*: 155–163.

WATKINS, W. A. et al (1977) 'Underwater sounds of *Cephalorhynchus heavisidii'. J. Mammal. 58*: 316–320.

WEBB, N. G. (1977) 'Symbolic thinking in dolphins'. *Search 1*: 38–44.

WEBB, N. G. (1978) 'Women and children abducted by a wild but sociable adult male bottlenose dolphin'. *Carnivore 1*: 89–94.

WEBB, N. G. (1978) 'Boat towing by a bottlenose dolphin'. *Carnivore 1*: 122–130.

WEBB, J. E. et al. (1977) *Guide to Living Mammals.* Macmillan: London.

WEBER, M. (1923) 'Die Cetaceen der Siboga Expedition'. *Siboga Expeditie Monogr. 58*: 1–38.

WELLINGS, C. E. (1944) 'The killer whales of Twofold Bay, NSW, Australia'. *Aust. Zool. 10*: 281–293.

WELLINGS, H. P. (1964) *Shore whaling at Twofold Bay, assisted by the renowned killer whales.* Wellings: Eden.

WENZ, G. M. (1964) 'Curious noises and the sonic environment in the ocean'. In TAVOLGA.

WHEELER, J. F. G. (1946) 'Observations on whales in the South Atlantic Ocean in 1943'. *Proc. Zool. Soc. Lond. 116*: 221–224.

WHITEHEAD, H. & PAYNE, R. (1976) 'New techniques for assessing a population of right whales without killing them'. UN FAO ACMRR.

WHITFIELD, W. K. (1971) 'An annotated bibliography of dolphin and porpoise families Delphinidae and Platanistidae'. *Spec. Sci. Rep. Mar. Res. Lab. St. Petersburg* No. 27.

WILLIAMSON, C. J. (1977) 'Pilot Whales'. *New Scientist 73*: 481.

WILLIAMSON, G. R. (1973) 'Counting and measuring baleen and ventral grooves of whales'. *Sci. Rep. Whales Res. Inst. 25*: 279–292.

WILLIAMSON, K. (1945) 'The economic and ethnological importance of the caaing whale in the Faeroe Islands'. *Northwest Nat. 20*:118–136.

WILLUGHBY, F. (1685) *Ichthyographia.* London.

WILSON, E. O. (1975) *Sociobiology.* Harvard Univ. Press.

WINN, H. E. & OLLA, B. L. (1979) 'Behaviour of Marine Mammals'. *Current Perspectives in Research 3.* Plenum Press: New York.

WINN, H. E. & PERKINS, P. J. (1976) 'Distribution and sounds of the minke whale ...' *Cetology 19*: 1–12.

WINN, H. E. et al (1970) 'Sounds of the humpback whale'. *Proc. 7th Ann. Conf. Biol. Sonar Diving Mamm.*

WINN, H. E. et al (1970) 'Sounds and behaviour of the northern bottlenose whale'. *Proc. 7th Ann. Conf. Biol. Sonar Diving Mamm.*

WOLMAN, A. A. & JURASZ, C. M. (1977) 'Humpback whales in Hawaii ...' *Mar. Fish Rev. 39*: 1–5.

WOOD, F. G. (1973) *Marine Mammals and Man.* Luce: Washington D.C.

WOOD, F. G. et al. (1970) 'Behavioural interactions between porpoises and sharks'. *Inv. on Cetacea 2*: 264–277.

WOOD, F. G. & RIDGWAY, S. H. (1967) 'Utilization of porpoises in the Man-In-The-Sea Program'. In PAULI & CLAPPER.

WOODCOCK, A. H. (1948) 'The swimming of dolphins'. *Nature 161*: 602.

WOODCOCK, A. H. & McBRIDE, A. F. (1951) 'Wave riding dolphins'. *J. Exp. Biol. 28*:215–217.

WRAY, P. *The northern bottlenose whale.* ESP: Ayer.

WUERSIG, B. (1976) 'Radio tracking of dusky porpoise in South Atlantic'. FAO ACMRR.

WUERSIG, B. (1978) 'Occurrence and group organization of *Tursiops truncatus'. Biol. Bull. 154*: 348–359.

WYMAN, J. (1863) 'Description of a white whale'. *Boston J. Nat. Hist. 7*: 603–612.

YABLOKOV, A. V. & KLEVEZAL, G. A. (1969) 'Whiskers of whales and seals and their distribution, structure and significance'. *Fish. Res. Board Can. Trans. Series* 1335.

YAMADA, M. (1954) 'Some remarks on the pygmy sperm whale'. *Sci. Rep. Whales Res. Inst. 9*:37–58.

YAMADA, M. (1954) 'An account of a rare porpoise *Feresa* from Japan'. *Sci. Rep. Whales Res. Inst. 9*: 59–88.

ZENKOVICH, B. A. (1937) 'Weighing of whales'. *C.R. Acad. Sci. USSR. 16*: 177–182.

ZORGDRAGER, C. G. (1720) *Bloeyende opkomst der aloude en hedendaagsche Groenlansche visschery.* Amsterdam.

INDEX

ACKNOWLEDGEMENTS

The author and publishers wish to thank the following for permission to reproduce photographs:

Pages 12–13 Humpback Whale and Calf *(Megaptera novaeangliae 10)* photo by James Hudnall (Seaphot)
44–45 Young Great Right Whale breaching *(Balaena glacialis 1)* photo by Jen and Des Bartlett (Survival Anglia)
52–53 Tail flukes of Humpback Whale *(Megaptera novaeangliae 10)* photo by Bora Merdsoy (Seaphot)
66–67 Two Great Right Whales one a rare 'white' whale *(Balaena glacialis 1)* photo by Jen and Des Bartlett (Survival Anglia)
76 Grey Whale *(Eschrichtius robustus 4)* photo by Flip Schulke (Seaphot)

81 Blue Whale *(Balaenoptera musculus 6)* photo by Ken Balcomb (World Wildlife Fund)
101 Bottlenose Dolphin *(Tursiops truncatus 76)* photo by Horace Dobbs
106–107 Harem school of Great Sperm Whales *(Physeter macrocephalus 36)* photo by Institute of Oceanographic Sciences (Seaphot)
205 Adult male Great Killer Whale *(Orcinus orca 51)* photo by Ken Balcomb (World Wildlife Fund)
222–223 Pacific Whiteside Dolphin *(Lagenorhynchus obliquidens 57)* photo by Ken Balcomb (World Wildlife Fund)

All diagrams and maps are by Diagram Visual Information